THE ENCYCLOPEDIA OF
MOTORCYCLES

THE ENCYCLOPEDIA OF
MOTORCYCLES
FROM 1884 TO THE PRESENT DAY

GENERAL EDITOR: ALAN DOWDS

THUNDER BAY
P·R·E·S·S

San Diego, California

Thunder Bay Press
An imprint of the Advantage Publishers Group
5880 Oberlin Drive, San Diego, CA 92121-4794
www.thunderbaybooks.com

Library of Congress Cataloging-in-Publication Data

Dowds, Alan.
  The encyclopedia of motorcycles : from 1884 to the present / Alan Dowds.
      p. cm.
  Includes bibliographical references and index.
  ISBN 978-1-59223-782-1 (alk. paper)
  1. Motorcycles--Encyclopedias. I. Title.
  TL439.D69 2007
  629.227'5--dc22
                          2007011575

Project Editor: Michael Spilling
Picture Research: Terry Forshaw
Design: Joe Conneally

Printed in China

1 2 3 4 5 11 10 09 08 07

CONTENTS

INTRODUCTION

The dictionary definition of an Encyclopedia is a book covering all branches of knowledge, or all aspects of one subject. So according to this strict, stiff definition, we would have to reconsider the title of this book. Because within these pages, rather than covering all aspects of motorcycling, we've instead confined ourselves to the bikes themselves. All types of motorcycles, from the primitive pioneer machines that first appeared in the latter years of the nineteenth century, right up to the incredible two-wheeled missiles that represent the pinnacle of motorcycle design and engineering in the first decade of the twenty-first century.

You can only imagine what motorcycling's earliest pioneers would have thought of the 2006 Suzuki GSX-R1000, as they toiled away at their crudely-made, but

The EA Superb 250cc (15.25ci) SOS model was a ground-breaking bike for its time, combining a powerful engine with excellent handling.

brilliantly-conceived contraptions. Sure, they would have been stunned by the performance, the materials used and the radical appearance of the Japanese supersports bike. But I like to think they would approve wholeheartedly of it – as something clearly born from the same concepts and passions that drove their own inventions: a desire for the freedom, excitement and plain good fun that riding a motorcycle has provided for over 125 years.

The story of the motorcycle is, in some ways, a rather secondary niche within that of the internal combustion engine. Daimler Benz is often credited with producing the

A Triumph Bonneville T120 is taken through its paces. The Bonneville was crucial to Triumph's sales in the 1960s and 1970s, and was upgraded with a new engine in 1973.

first vehicle powered by such a device, and it was a bicycle, rather than a car which holds this accolade, according to most reliable authorities. Although it was underpowered, unreliable, and pushing at the boundaries of available materials, this new engine was clearly the future, and quickly began to sweep aside various experimental steam-powered vehicles.

Enthusiast's Pastime

But in the years before World War I, motorcycling was essentially still a niche, eccentric pastime for wild-eyed enthusiasts, rather than an established activity or practical mode of transport. However, the impetus of industrial progress engendered by the large-scale destruction of the the Great War also boosted the motorcycle industry – only for it to be knocked down again in the 1930s with the Depression and a worldwide downturn in economic activity.

In the first sixty years of the twentieth century, a motorcycle was pretty much the only personal motorised transport available to a common working man in Europe, even if in the United States the motorcar had already become accessible to the masses. Industrial production methods were well-established, and a more-affluent working class began to demand affordable motorised transport. Cheap automobiles for everyone were still a way off, so it was on a motorbike – often British, often with a huge three-seat sidecar attached – that those workers made their way to the factories during the week, and to the seaside on their holidays.

By the late 1960s though, cheap family cars were available throughout Europe, and this began the long, slow transformation of the motorcycle from an essentially utilitarian device to a largely leisure-oriented consumer product. This was also the period

First launched in 1996, the M2 Cyclone provided the base model for Buell's range of racing machines. With an enormous 1200cc (73ci) engine, the Buell M2 Cyclone has power to spare.

when the European motorbike-building industry began to be replaced by the Japanese. The big four firms – Honda, Kawasaki, Suzuki and Yamaha had been building bikes ever since Japan emerged from the destruction of World War II. Their early efforts were seen as something of a joke in the rather complacent head offices of the British bike industry. They were extremely primitive, utilitarian devices, aimed solely at getting a ravaged Japanese society moving again at the most basic level. But these were proud, effective companies, and they soon began to set their sights much higher. Soichiro Honda in particular was a passionate engineer, who dreamed of producing high-performance sporting machinery to compete at the famous TT races on the Isle of Man. And throughout the 1960s, Japanese machines began to lose their comic reputation as they improved in reliability, performance and design.

Japanese Dominance

It was 1969 that the future shape of motorcycling became clear. That was the year that Honda released its CB750 – a four-cylinder, 750cc (46ci) superbike, with cutting-edge engine and chassis technology. It swept the lacklustre British opposition aside, cruelly exposing the lack of investment and absence of vision that would finally kill off the British bike industry in the early 1980s.

The rest of the 1970s brought ever more radical leaps forward in technology and design from all four Japanese manufacturers, with classic machines such as Kawasaki's Z1 and Yamaha's RD250. Engineers experimented with two-stroke engines, turbochargers and even Wankel rotary designs. Various engine layouts were tried, from singles, to parallel twins, tandem twins, and V-twins. Inline- and V- triples, fours and even straight sixes were also built, as the industry searched for the best powerplant package. Disc brakes replaced drums, cast aluminium wheels replaced wire-spoked designs and every year brought new innovations in chassis and engine designs. By the 1980s though, a pattern had been set for the typical Japanese bike – a four-cylinder four-stroke engine in a sporting chassis. Plastic bodywork began to appear, improving wind protection and aerodynamic performance, and engines increased in power output.

The rest of the motorcycling world was moving forward too, although at a slightly slower pace. The Italian bike industry had suffered almost as badly as the British firms through the 1970s, but Ducati bounced back in the 1980s, and its 916 superbike of 1993 resurrected the Italian reputation for fine design and high-performance machinery. BMW in Germany continued to turn out solid, dependable touring machines, and Triumph in the UK was reborn in the early 1990s with a range of Japanese-influenced sports machines. The US market was still dominated by the sole home manufacturer, Harley-Davidson, but even there, the Japanese were gaining market share every year.

So, as the first decade of the twenty-first century moves on, the motorcycle world has changed radically. The biggest headache for motorcycle manufacturers is ever-tightening emissions regulations that mean all new bikes need advanced catalysts, fuel injection and other pollution-reducing measures.

In Europe, fans of sportsbikes ride them on racetracks purely for fun. Commuters beat the congestion in big cities on convenient, practical scooters. Touring fans ride large-capacity, super-luxurious continent crossers, and stylish city workers ride their fashionable roadsters to high-rise glass and steel office towers. But for all the fun, practicality and thrills provided by their steeds, they still owe a debt to those early pioneers.

The 1994 Gilera RC600 was a superb racing machine capable of competing with the best in its class on the race track.

CHAPTER ONE

THE FIRST MACHINES

1884–1909

Like most new industries, the motorcycle business did not just appear in one clearly-defined step. In fact, it was as much a product of two other new technologies – the bicycle and the internal combustion engine – as anything else. The later end of the industrial revolution was providing the materials science and production methods necessary to build new, improved versions of these useful machines. This in turn transformed them from unusual conversation pieces to practical, usable commodities, and it was inevitable that someone would marry up one of the new 'safety bicycles' with the emerging petrol-fuelled internal combustion engine. There had been steam-powered bikes and trikes before, notably the 1869 French Michaux

'boneshaker' powered by a Perreaux steam engine, the American L.D. Copeland's 1884 machines and the Dalifol, another French design. But it was Gottlieb Daimler in Germany and Edward Butler in England who built the first petrol-powered machines. Butler's 'Petrol-Cycle' trike was patented in 1884 and built in 1887, Daimler's patent was later by a year, but his 'Reitwagen' bike appeared first, in 1885. In terms of commercially-successful machine, the 1894 Hildebrand and Wolfmüller was the first serially-produced machine. Several hundred of the water-cooled twin-cylinder, 1,488cc (91ci) four stroke were built, and its performance of 2.5bhp@240rpm, allowed a heady 40km/h (25mph) top speed. Motorcycling was up and running!

Left: This James 500cc (31ci) was hand-built during the 1920s. The James marque always built its own engines, although it was more economical to fit Villiers engines in the larger capacity models.

BUTLER

Edward Butler patented the first petrol-powered vehicle in 1884. This rather curious device was a tricycle design with the single wheel at the rear. The front wheels were steered by levers and the rear one was driven by a two-stroke engine with two cylinders, one on each side of the wheel. Butler's engine was relatively advanced, featuring water-cooling and electric ignition. Butler also designed a vertical-cylinder engine, but never constructed one.

A second machine, powered with a four-stroke engine, was patented in 1888 and featured an epicyclic gearing system. However, although Butler successfully demonstrated his machines and bought patents, his venture found no backers.

Butler received a second chance with the withdrawal of legislation that tended to discourage investors, and in 1896 he carried out another set of demonstrations. This, too, came to nothing and the project fell by the wayside. Butler's ideas were good and his designs sound, but in the end these innovative machines were killed off by economic rather than engineering considerations.

Despite its strange appearance, Butler's prototype was quite advanced in most ways. It featured direct drive, however, while others were already exploring better methods.

TRIUMPH

Triumph was established in 1885 and is still in business. The company has gone through several incarnations in its long history – a history that is, to some extent, a history of motorcycles in general.

From 1885 to 1936, Triumph was guided by the company's founder, Siegfried Bettmann. Initially, it made bicycles, but in 1902 Triumph mounted a Belgian 239cc (15ci) Minerva engine on a strengthened cycle frame, and its first motorcycle was born. It was capable of a respectable 40km/h (25mph). Triumph's early motorcycles were all based on bicycle frames.

Triumph's first major success came in 1907, when it took second place in the first Isle of Man TT. A year later, Triumphs took first, third, fourth and fifth, and the 1911 catalogue featured a TT Racer model. In 1914, the British Army took delivery of 100 Triumphs for use by dispatch riders, and these established the Triumph's reputation for reliability.

In the interwar years, Triumph kept pace with, even led, motorcycle development. Pedals disappeared and kick-starters were fitted, and the company introduced impressive new models, including the 1922 Fast Roadster. The firm shed its bicycle manufacturing business in 1923 and began producing cars alongside its burgeoning motorcycle business, which was producing 1000 vehicles a week at this point.

During the 1930s, Edward Turner took over the reins.

Triumph survived the Depression, though the firm suffered like everyone else. As sales fell, a new range was marketed, winning races and awards and helping Triumph to weather the difficult times. Turner knew how to use the image of Triumph's bikes to best advantage, and despite the economic situation Triumph remained a world leader, selling to police forces as well as private buyers. Turner's stint as general manager ran through World War II, during which Triumph made military equipment, and on into the post-war years until 1976.

For a short time, Triumph was part of the NVT (Norton Villiers Triumph) group, which collapsed in 1977. Triumph survived this too, as well as serious labour disputes and the formation of a Workers' Collective. After several years of getting by, Triumph resurged under the leadership of John Bloor, who bought the firm after the Workers' Collective went bankrupt.

Triumph's renaissance began in 1990 with the launch of new models, and its success was such that the existing plant could not keep pace with demand. A new factory had to be built, construction beginning in 1999. Britain's oldest motorcycle manufacturer is still going strong.

The classic lines of a 1970s Triumph scrambler, with bash plate and excitingly high exhausts to complement its very robust appearance.

HILDEBRAND & WOLFMÜLLER

In 1894, the Hildebrand & Wolfmüller was the first motorcycle that was available for purchase. Between one thousand and two thousand examples of the first series production motorcycle were sold. This was the first vehicle to be termed a 'Motorrad' (motorcycle).

The engine used hot tube rather than electric ignition and was a two-cylinder design. The cylinders were located on opposite sides of the frame and lay in a horizontal position. At about 2.5hp, the machine could run at up to 40km/h (25mph). Like some other designs of the period, the engine was water-cooled, the rear mudguard containing the radiator. The firm did not develop more advanced engines and was left behind by other manufacturers. It closed down in 1897.

DALIFOL

FRANCE c.1895–1900

Although the internal combustion engine became available in the 1880s, steam-powered motorcycles were able to compete with their petrol-powered rivals for a few years. The Dalifol was one such example. Based on a bicycle frame and powered by a single-cylinder steam engine, the Dalifol might have been capable of up to 40km/h (25mph). The main problems with steam power were the need to carry a lot of water and to wait while the boiler came up to temperature. As internal combustion engines became more than a novelty, steam passed away and vehicles like the Dalifol faded into history.

Though the idea seems odd today, the Dalifol was a workable, if rather clumsy, attempt at a powered two-wheeler using steam power.

DE DION-BOUTON

FRANCE 1895–1910, 1926–30 AND 1955–66

De Dion-Bouton began by making steam engines. A steam-engined quadricycle was built in 1883 and the firm's first petrol engine appeared in 1889. Experiments led to the invention in 1894 of the De Dion axle, separating driving components from suspension. This design is still used today.

In 1884, De Dion-Bouton marketed a powered tricycle that was copied by other manufacturers, sometimes without permission. The engine was mounted vertically behind the rear axle. The trike used conventional bicycle pedals and a chain.

Count De Dion founded the Automobile Club de France, and in 1901 tricycles were phased out as the company concentrated on producing four-wheeled vehicles. Steam-powered vehicles also began to be phased out at this time as internal combustion became more reliable. De Dion-Bouton experimented with electric power, but nothing came of this.

After a period of manufacturing bicycles, De Dion-Bouton faded from the scene for a while. The name re-emerged for a while (1926–30) for the manufacture of motorcycles, but the original firm was long gone by this time. A second resurgence of the De Dion-Bouton name (1955–66) was simply as a brand identity on a range of scooters and mopeds.

With its engine mounted low between the rear wheels, this De Dion-Bouton tricycle represents a clever and entirely useable design.

BEESTON

The businessman Harry Lawson attempted to gain control of the infant motor-vehicle industry by buying patents and firms, and by setting up businesses.

Beeston, founded in 1896, was one of his firms.

Beeston entered the market with a tricycle copied from a De Dion-Bouton design, followed

quickly by a quadricycle. Both featured a rear-mounted engine delivering 1.25hp. A true motorcycle followed: also using a De Dion engine, it was derived

from a bicycle design and made 43km/h (27mph) in tests. However, the trike was considered more viable, a mistake that led to Beeston closing down in 1901.

HUMBER

Another bicycle firm that moved into powered vehicles, Humber produced an electrically powered tandem in 1898. Along with a range of other rather curious vehicles, the tandem was discontinued in 1899 and Humber began producing true motorcycles in 1902. Both 1902 models were successful, but by 1905 Humber was more interested in cars.

No motorcycles were produced until 1909, when Humber returned to the market with a 3.5hp model, and the following year entered the Isle of Man TT. More models followed and in 1911 Humber won the TT.

New models were added to the range in 1912 and 1913, including sidecar variants and another unusual design featuring

a three-cylinder engine configuration driving a car gearbox. Only a few of these were made, but the design seems to have been workable.

Development continued throughout World War II, though only one model remained in production for a time. The range was gradually expanded into the 1920s and then remained static

until 1930, by which time Humber was again concentrating on cars. No motorcycles were constructed after 1930.

Humber's range was at its largest in the early 1920s, and was composed mainly of machines like this workhorse 349cc (21ci) side-valve single.

SAROLEA

Sarolea, like fellow Belgians FN, started out in the arms trade, making precision weaponry. After a move into the field of bicycles, Sarolea began to produce motorcycles. Sales outside of Belgium were good, especially after the end of World War I, when a major marketing push was begun.

Sarolea entered the competition scene to promote its vehicles, and

began winning major races from 1923 onwards. By 1925, Sarolea was the dominant manufacturer in Belgium and a major force on the competition scene. In 1925 alone, Sarolea machines won 23 races in Italy. The machine that delivered this spectacular success was the 23M Racer.

Sarolea retired from competition in 1926, after a season that included controversial events

during the Tour of Italy. The race started well, but Sarolea's entries were crippled by locals throwing nails on the road ahead of them.

The Wall Street Crash and the subsequent Depression made life difficult for all manufacturers. Sarolea survived these difficult times by making good decisions. One such decision was to cut right back on high-end machines and concentrate on cheap utilitarian

models. Sarolea then won a contract to produce motorcycles for the Belgian military.

In the late 1940s and 1950s, the firm introduced new models but ran into difficulties in the mid-1950s. Deals with FN and Gillet-Herstal followed but failed to save Sarolea, which merged with Gillet-Herstal in 1960. Three years later, production of Sarolea models ceased.

BIANCHI

Businesslike yet elegant, this 1950s-vintage 250cc (15ci) overhead-valve single is a classic creation of Edoardo Bianchi's genius. In their day, Bianchi machines were world-beaters, setting records and winning races. The bicycles in the backdrop are a reminder of the past and the shape of things to come – Bianchi started out and ended up as a manufacturer of pedal cycles.

Edoardo Bianchi was an innovator who created Italy's first pneumatic-tyred vehicle, a bicycle, in his small workshop. He moved to larger premises and rode the boom of bicycle manufacture throughout the 1890s. Bianchi also experimented with motorized vehicles. His first attempt, a tricycle with a De Dion engine, caught fire. Undeterred, he produced a motorcycle in 1901 and began selling it in 1902. The engine was licensed from De Dion, but the motorcycle itself was built entirely in the Milan factory.

Bianchi went from strength to strength, opening a huge new factory and moving into the field of cars and, later, aero engines.

Bianchi began entering races in the 1920s and set a couple of records. By now, the firm was facing competition from rival firms and was able to use its competition success to maintain its market position.

After World War II, the firm specialized in low-end commuter machines during the period of recovery from the war, and did not return to Grand Prix racing until the late 1950s. Despite some success, Bianchi gradually faded away and ceased producing motorcycles in 1967. Today – perhaps fittingly, given its origins – Bianchi produces bicycles as part of the Piaggio group.

EXCELSIOR

Excelsior started out as a bicycle firm called Bayliss, Thomas and Company. It is probable that this firm became the first British motorcycle manufacturer around 1896, when they began buying in engines to power their vehicles.

Excelsior was always competitive on the track and in the marketplace. The firm offered free trials to potential customers and notched up a series of records, including the first mile-a-minute in 1903.

The Excelsior name was adopted in 1910, though British Excelsiors sold in Europe retained the Bayliss Thomas name into the 1930s. The first major competition victory was in 1929, when Leslie Crabtree won the Lightweight TT. A road-going 'replica' of Crabtree's machine, the B14, met with considerable demand and became Excelsior's flagship model.

Excelsior's 'golden age' unfortunately coincided with the Depression, and though its machines won acclaim for their competition success, this, unfortunately, was not matched by the sort of sales figures that might have been achieved in less difficult times.

Just before and after World War II, Excelsior proceeded in somewhat less dramatic fashion, marketing among other things a 98cc (6ci) Autobyke, which was a forerunner of the modern commuter moped. The firm's fortunes went gradually downhill until it went out of business in 1965, despite an attempt to cash in on the popularity of scooters in the early to mid-1960s.

HOLDEN

Colonel Holden built Britain's first four-cylinder motorcycle in 1897. The original engine was air-cooled and the front wheel, which was larger than the rear one, had pedals to assist with starting. This machine could reach 39km/h (24mph) and was the basis for a similar motorcycle with a water-cooled engine. This engine could deliver 3hp and was considered to be very good.

However, the overall design of the Holden, with its small rear wheel, was not viable and the firm ceased production in 1902.

WERNER

The Russian-born Werner brothers were journalists who liked to experiment with vehicles. Their first attempt was a bicycle fitted with a Labitte engine, and was followed by a 0.75hp version with the engine mounted above the front wheel. This 'Motorcyclette' attracted some sales upon its release onto the market in 1897.

The Werners came up with some good ideas, including a system of surface carburetion, but their vehicle was top-heavy and tended to catch fire if it fell over. It was also underpowered and required constant pedal assistance.

Despite improvements to the engine and the selling of a licence to a British concern, it was obvious that a redesign was overdue. This appeared in 1901. The 'New Werner' layout became the industry standard for decades, the engine being moved to a position low down and with juts in front of the bottom frame bracket. The Werners recognized the need for a more securely braced frame and incorporated the crankcase as a structural member.

Werner's new design began to win races in 1902, and the range was continually improved over the next few years. However, the Werners were soon overtaken by their rivals and ceased to innovate. They did market an interesting tricar in 1906, but this was not enough. By the time Werner went out of business in 1914, the firm was making cars only.

BROUGH

The quality on all Brough motorbikes was superb, as demonstrated by the immaculate finish on the saddle tank of this 1920s model.

William Brough built a car in 1898 and, four years later, a motorcycle. Experimentation eventually led to an improved design and in 1908 Brough was marketing 2.5hp and 3.5hp models.

In 1910, Brough built an advanced experimental engine with a rotary valve above the cylinder and a sleeve-valve that shielded the sparking plug when it was not firing. A year later,

Brough moved on to build a flat-twin engine. His continuing experimentation eventually culminated in an 8hp V-twin engine, which was used in the Brough Monocar. Production of motorcycles based on these designs continued until 1925.

CLÉMENT & CLÉMENT-GLADIATOR

After making a fortune in the bicycle boom of the late 19th century, Adolphe Clément set up Clément-Gladiator-Humber in 1896. The firm initially produced both cars and motorcycles. The 'Humber' was soon dropped, but Clément-Gladiator continued.

The firm's first vehicle was a De Dion-powered tricycle in 1898, and this was soon followed by a motor bicycle powered by a Clément-built engine. This vehicle was designated the Autocyclette. Its modest 1hp engine could drive it at 48km/h (30mph).

Clément inevitably was drawn into competition. The trend at the time was towards increasing engine size to get more power, and Clément decided to outdo everyone else. In 1903, he produced a machine powered by a V-four engine of around

1200cc (72ci). It was possibly the world's first racing four and required a specially designed frame. Clément's road machines were somewhat more conventional.

As if there was not enough confusion over the firm's name, the Louis Clement marque appeared in 1919. Meanwhile, Clément itself continued to produce a range of models powered by engines from different manufacturers as well as their own. By the 1930s, JAP engines were being used more or less exclusively.

The Depression hit Clément as hard as anyone. For a while, it was possible to maintain sales by making cosmetic changes to existing models, but eventually the firm ceased trading in 1935.

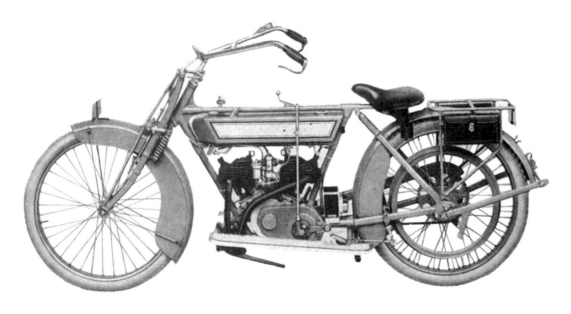

A curious hybrid of pedal and motorcycle features, Clement machines were dated in many ways, but in terms of huge engines some models were way ahead of the pack.

EADIE

Albert Eadie manufactured bicycles, sewing machines and rifle parts under a variety of brand names, including Royal Enfield. His 1898 tricycle was more or less a copy of the De Dion design and

used a De Dion engine. The engine was located behind the rear axle, creating weight distribution problems. This vehicle was followed by a motor bicycle, which used a range of engines from

different manufacturers. Eadie motorcycles faded away as the Royal Enfield brand dominated. However, Eadie was foremost a parts supplier, and kept a close eye on engineering trends. He

knew enough to be able to merge his firm with BSA. He joined the board of BSA in 1907 and helped design their first motorcycle, which went to market three years later.

FIGINI

Using the engine as part of the frame was a fairly advanced idea, but the rest of the Figini machine was unimpressive, suffering from a high centre of gravity. It was not a great success.

Figini was part of a curious setup whereby Lazzati and Figini operated as a single firm sharing premises but producing entirely separate lines. Lazzati built bicycles fitted with De Dion engines while Luigi Figini did things his own way.

The Figini design incorporated the engine as the lower part of the seat tube, set lower than the Werner or Indian models of the same period.

The pedal shaft ran across the top of the crankcase. Neither Lazzati nor Figini was much of a success; Lazzati folded in 1904 and Figini a few years later.

PRINETTI & STUCCHI

Another firm that started out making bicycles, Prinetti & Stucchi began looking into powered vehicles in 1898, producing a tricycle fitted with a De Dion engine behind the rear axle. An apprentice at the works – one Ettore Bugatti (who would later become a legend in the world of cars) – added a second engine to the tricycle and began entering races with it.

Meanwhile, Prinetti & Stucchi began building a version of the tricycle with a new front fork that carried two wheels and a forecar mounted between them. Bugatti used one of these quadricycles as the basis of his first car, fitting four De Dion engines to power it.

Prinetti & Stucchi moved into motorcycles, producing fairly conventional designs. In 1902, the name changed to Stucchi. Stucchi continually improved the technical aspects of its machines, but in the mid-1920s the firm closed down.

RENÉ-GILLET

René-Gillet first produced bicycles with a motor attached to the front forks. This unwieldy arrangement fell out of favour, so the firm began producing 500cc (31ci) V-twin motorcycles from 1903 onwards. Engine size increased steadily, and René-Gillet designs became known for their power. Sidecar combinations were common, and were popular with the French military.

Although René-Gillet at one point was marketing 996cc (61ci) motorcycles, it was also producing smaller machines, and after World War II production consisted of 98cc (6ci) and 250cc (15ci) designs. The firm ceased trading in 1957.

COVENTRY EAGLE

Coventry was a great centre of the British bicycle manufacturing industry, and Coventry Eagle was just one of many firms based there. It built bicycles and tricycles, mainly by assembling parts bought from other firms. The Coventry Eagle's designs were well made and popular, and it trundled unobtrusively along for several years.

A range of small motorcycles and sidecar combinations was brought to market, and in the mid-1920s the firm produced its best known model, the Flying Eight. This sporting twin used a JAP engine and was the second most expensive motorcycle on the market.

Until 1928, Coventry Eagle did not favour two-strokes, but in 1928 the firm began to use Villiers two-stroke engines in a range of bikes built with pressed-steel components. Coventry Eagle was one of the first to adopt the technique and was very successful with it for the next decade.

Coventry Eagle continued to produce a range of motorcycles through the 1930s and attempted to ride out the war years with a reduced line. These were not successful and production ceased in 1940.

The most famous Coventry Eagle design, the Flying Eight. It was anything but cheap, but with a 976cc (58ci) JAP overhead-cam V-twin aboard, it was certainly powerful.

EYSINK

Eysink traded for around 75 years despite achieving little. It began working on automobiles and motorcycles by the turn of the century. The Dutch Army used Eysink motorcycles in Word War I, and between the wars a new range appeared, mostly powered by bought-in engines.

Eysink was the only Dutch motorcycle marque to compete in road racing before and after World War II, and to compete in a pre-war Isle of Man TT race in 1934.

In 1948, an Eysink won the new 125cc (8ci) class in the Dutch TT, but Eysink bikes were not competitive in the official world series, introduced in 1949. Involvement in racing ended in 1955.

After World War II, the firm was mainly interested in small capacity two-strokes. They produced 98cc (6ci) and 250cc (15ci) scooters and, until the late 1970s, offered tandem bicycles and sports mopeds.

LAURIN & KLEMENT

Founded in the 1890s as a bicycle manufacturer, Laurin & Klement moved to larger premises in 1989 and produced their first motorcycle a year later. Early designs made use of Werner engines, which were mounted over the front wheel. However, by 1903 the firm was using an engine of its own design, mounted within the frame. Products were sold as the Slavias at home, Germanias in Germany (where they were built under licence) and as Republics everywhere else.

In 1905, Laurin & Klement marketed their first four-cylinder machine and also moved into car manufacture. The firm widened its base further and began making commercial vehicles and aero engines, ceasing to build motorcycles in 1909. It was bought by Skoda in 1925 and its badge was used for two years on some Skoda products.

MOTOSACOCHE

The earliest Motosacoche machines were simply powered bicycles, as with this 211cc (13ci) model. Later machines were purpose designed as motorcycles, while the firm was very successful selling engines to other manufacturers.

The best known and most successful of Switzerland's motorcycle firms, Motosacoche also supplied engines to many others under their MAG label. In their early years, they also used the HADC name, an abbreviation of their company name. The name Motosacoche was introduced later for what was essentially a clip-on unit for a bicycle. 'Motosacoche' means 'motor-in-a-saddle-bag'.

The firm's first true motorcycle soon followed, and by 1909 it was also supplying engines for use aboard Royal Enfield machines. A close association developed between the two firms.

An enlarged version of the clip-on engine was marketed in 1911, and the same year saw the start of Motosacoche Acacias Geneva, or MAG, a firm that supplied engines to other motorcycle manufacturers. MAG engines were used by many marques and in most major European countries.

Throughout the 1920s, Motosacoche continued with its clip-on unit and MAG engines. Their own range of motorcycles was adapted to suit the market as trends changed, and by the start of the 1930s their machines had drum brakes, saddle tanks and all the other fixtures and fittings of that period.

In the interwar period, Motosacoche built a handful of overhead-camshaft racing engines for selected customers and had some successes, but in the main they stuck to producing their range up to 1939. A very radical design was trialled just after World War II, but it never achieved market success.

In the 1950s, Motosacoche seemed to be doing well and keeping pace with the times and changing fashions. Their road range was joined by a motocross model, but this was their last model and the firm ceased trading in 1956.

OK (OK-SUPREME)

OK started out as a bicycle-making firm called Humphreys and Dawes in 1882. Motorcycle manufacture began in 1899, using engines obtained from other firms. Ernie Humphreys rode an OK-Precision to third place in the Lightweight TT in 1912. OK achieved more racing success with the fastest laps in the 1922 and 1923 Lightweight TT and a win in the Ulster GP.

OK became OK-Supreme in 1927, when Humphreys bought out partner Charles Dawes. Dawes went on to great success making bicycles while OK-Supreme won the Lightweight TT in 1928 and, two years later, produced its finest machine, the TT30 Lighthouse. Though the Lighthouse was excellent, it was difficult to manufacture, so cheaper and simpler models were marketed. The firm produced a utilitarian 250cc (15ci) design just before World War II, then faded away.

PEUGEOT

Peugeot is best known today as a car manufacturer, but the firm began in 1885 making bicycls899, and in 1903 Peugeot began making engines for sale to other firms as well as for use in its own designs.

The firm began producing cars in 1907 and developed a range of advanced race bikes from 1913 onwards. By the mid-1920s, Peugeot was mainly building utilitarian designs. These were soundly designed and well put together, but were also inexpensive and thus popular in the marketplace.

Production was interrupted by World War II and resumed in 1940 with a range of mopeds, scooters and small motorcycles. However, the motorcycle lines were curtailed in 1959 and it was not until 1980

Despite some less than flattering colour schemes, Peugeot's range of small workhorse machines like this post-war 125 single were popular and sold well.

that Peugeot began to construct them once again. These were small machines, however, and did not achieve much success in a marketplace dominated by Honda.

Peugeot did rather better with scooters and mopeds, and it continues to have a strong marketplace presence in this field.

VICTORIA

Founded in Nurnberg as a bicycle factory, Victoria began trading in 1886 and produced its first motorcycles in 1899. The company's first internal-combustion machines featured either Fafnir or Zedel single-cylinder engines. They continued to sell these until 1918, with only minimal changes.

After World War I, a new range appeared, powered by a 493cc (30ci) horizontally opposed, twin-cylinder engine built by BMW. In 1923, when BMW began building complete motorcycles, Victoria quickly engaged BMW's former designer, Martin Stolle.

Stolle developed a family of new overhead-valve engines for Victoria. These were built at the Sedlbauer factory in Munich, which was bought by Victoria in the late 1920s. Bigger engines followed, though Stolle left and was replaced by Gustav Steinlen, who designed the first supercharged German racing machine in 1925.

In the 1920s and 1930s, Victoria built a range of two-strokes, ranging from 98cc (6ci) to 198cc (12ci), a 497cc (30ci) inlet-over-exhaust single and some overhead-valve twins

designed by Stolle. These featured triangular pressed-steel frames and completely enclosed unit-construction engines. During World War II, production mainly focused on the four-stroke single,

which was extensively used by the German Army.

After the war, Victoria recovered quickly, initially concentrating on small, utilitarian two-stroke designs. By the 1950s, the firm was fully re-established and was producing new models, including powerful bikes and scooters. However, the mid-1950s downturn in the German motorcycle industry, attributable among other factors to the availability of cars, forced Victoria to re-evaluate its range. The firm managed to stay afloat, merging with DKW and Express in 1958, but the slide continued and Victoria disappeared in 1966.

Advertising from an age before mandatory helmets and reinforced leathers, showing Victoria's intended market niche – popular transport for trendy young people. The youth market has always been critical to motorcycle manufacturers.

BUCHET

Buchet was mainly involved in engine design and manufacture, constructing engines for cars, motorcycles and aircraft. The firm also built a small number of complete machines with two or three

wheels. Buchet machines were involved in racing from 1900 onwards, and took first place in the motorcycle class of the Circuit du Sud Ouest.

Buchet also took part in events held on banked cycle tracks,

where they were also used to pace the pedal cyclists. Monster engines were built to power these machines, but as early as 1903 it was becoming obvious that greater efficiency was the key. Smaller and much more efficient

engines followed. Buchet continued to build motorcycles in a small way for some years, but then moved on to the more lucrative car market in 1910. Motorcycle production ceased the following year.

CHATER-LEA

ENGLAND 1900–36

Founded in London by William Chater-Lea in 1890, Chater-Lea began as a component supplier. The first motorcycles appeared in 1900. These were essentially built to order using a variety of engines, but within a few years Chater-Lea had one main model that was intended for sidecar use.

By 1909, Chater-Lea was using a three-speed gearbox and crankshaft-mounted clutch on the sidecar outfit, then added alternative V-twin engines and further solos. For 1913, it reverted to one model, the 8hp twin sidecar, but added a 269cc (16ci) two-stroke with two-speed gearbox and belt final drive, both of these continuing for 1916.

After World War I, the firm re-emerged in 1920 with a small two-stroke design, and added a 976cc (60ci) JAP V-twin for 1921 and a 488cc (30ci) side-valve single of its own design for 1922.

More models were added for the next two years. During this period, the firm achieved considerable success, at Brooklands, where Dougal Marchant was the first to exceed 160km/h (100mph) on a 350cc (21ci).

New models appeared and did well, and in 1928 the firm moved to Letchworth Garden City, Hertfordshire. A handful of new models appeared, including a dirt track machine, but by 1930 only

Long and low, Chater-Lea's racing machines made an impression in the 1920s racing scene. There were also customized record-breaking machines, some of which were very successful.

the road bikes were in production. These were slowly phased out and the firm then returned to general engineering.

HINDE

NETHERLANDS c.1900 AND 1936–38

Hinde, a bicycle manufacturer in Amsterdam, briefly flirted with powered transport at the beginning of the 1900s.

Their motorcycle was conventional for the time, being a heavy-duty bicycle frame powered by a 2hp De Dion engine. However, it became apparent that Hinde was doing better out of bicycles than motorcycles, and the powered line was dropped.

The Hinde name was revived in 1936 by another firm located in Amsterdam, who built a small range of simple and well put together machines using German Ilo engines.

These were produced for only three years and were in many ways typical machines of the era.

Indeed, there were many similar motorcycles on the market. Production was cut short by rationalization within German industry in 1938, which may have cut off the supply of the Ilo engines.

LAMAUDIERE

FRANCE 1900–03

Sometimes also known as Lamaudiere et Labrem, this obscure firm did some pioneering work in its short life.

At that time, the internal combustion engine was still in its infancy, and although manufacturers understood that more power meant more speed, records, racing success and good business, they were less clear about how best to get that power. It was obvious that a bigger engine made for greater power, and many manufacturers built ever-bigger engines without regard to the real key factor – efficiency. The Lamaudiere took size to an extreme. It had a large, crude engine mounted in a modified bicycle frame with rigid forks.

It also had direct belt drive, a saddle perched on a sub-frame to be directly over the rear wheel, and a pedalling gear with a massive front sprocket to give it the high gearing it needed for speed.

This was an obsolete design even in 1903, and all such monstrous devices disappeared from the marketplace soon after.

LIBERATOR

FRANCE c.1900–LATE 1920s

Liberal laws in France (and also Belgium and Germany) encouraged early development of the transportation industry, and firms in these nations often ended up supplying parts to others. They also tended to set the trend for future development.

Liberator followed the lead of Werner, another French company, in their first motorcycle design.

They also produced rear-engined tricycles, which were popular for a time. However, the uneven balance of these machines saw them fall from favour. The motorcycle, later attached to a sidecar after some early efforts with tricars and quads, proved more successful.

Liberator did well in the early years of the century, but by the late 1920s, it was struggling. Once the Depression began to bite, the firm had to close down.

MINERVA

Founded by Sylvain de Jong to produce bicycles, Minerva was involved with De Dion-Bouton in the early days. The firm's first product, in 1900, was powered by a Zürcher & Lüthi engine, and a licence was obtained to manufacture these engines. From 1901, Minerva had its own motorcycle, which was propelled by an engine hung from the downtube of a standard bicycle with belt drive to the rear wheel.

Minerva was soon selling engines to other firms as well as making its own machines. The 1903 model featured a vertically mounted engine and by 1904 Minerva was offering 2hp, 2.75hp and 3.5hp singles.

There was also a 7hp V-twin for racing and a road 4.5hp V-twin in 1906. Production continued until 1909 and numbered about 25,000 machines. Minerva continued to manufacture cars until 1939.

In 1953, Minerva returned with a 150cc (9ci) scooter, which was in fact a licence-built MV Agusta, and a tricar, built from two scooters. The firm then quietly vanished from the scene.

An early Minerva machine, clearly showing the belt drive mechanism to the back wheel. Placing the engine under the downtube made for a low centre of gravity and improved stability. Minerva built complete bikes for only a few years, though its car manufacturing division lasted a lot longer.

QUADRANT

This is a 1903 Quadrant of the type used by Tom Silver to set a new Land's End to John O'Groats record and in other long-distance trials. The Quardant had great endurance – it could run all day, every day.

Birmingham-based Quadrant fitted a Minerva engine to the downtube of a heavy-duty bicycle. A forecar was soon added, and by 1903 the company had mounted an engine of its own design in a loop frame.

In 1904, Quadrant added a forecar with twin 2.5hp engines, mounted side by side with a clutch between them so that one or both could be used. After a move to Coventry in 1908, Quadrant introduced a new 550cc (34ci)

engine. A 2hp lightweight was added for 1911, and a 4hp model for sidecar work during the year. In 1913, a more suitable V-twin appeared: its 7hp engine featured overhead inlet valves, a two-speed gear, all-chain drive and a new, centre-spring fork. A handful of new models appeared during World War I, and afterwards Quadrant limited its output to singles. It made a couple of sports bikes in the 1920s, but ran into difficulties and closed down in 1927.

REX (REX-ACME)

Birmingham-based Rex started out as car manufacturers in 1899. Moving to Coventry at the turn of the century, the firm produced its first motorcycles using engines of its own design. Rex also produced the first telescopic forks in 1906.

From 1911, and under new ownership, Rex continued to make its own engines, also producing a separate range of Rex-JAP machines for nearby Premier motorcycles. In 1919, the firm took over neighbours Coventry-Acme, adopting the name Rex-Acme two years later. By 1926, its range included at least 15 models, varying in capacity from a 172cc (10ci)

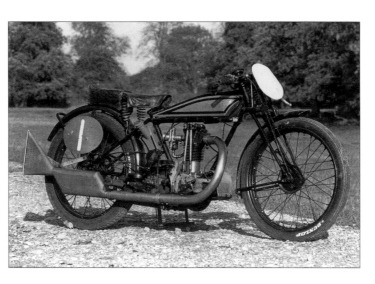

Villiers to a 746cc (46ci) JAP V-twin.

Rex–Acme achieved considerable success in the racing scene but was unable to turn this into profit, and the Depression of the 1930s hit the firm hard. In 1932, the bankrupt company was taken over by a sidecar manufacturer, Mills-Fulford, which stopped motorcycle production the following year.

A 498cc V-Twin similar to that ridden by Wal Hadley to second place in the 1926 Isle of Man TT. Rex (and Rex-Acme) was mainly competitive in the smaller classes; this machine was an exception.

ALLRIGHT

Cologne-based Köln-Lindenthaler Motorenwerke AG built motorcycles under various names, including Allright. Other marque names used up to 1907 were Roland and Tiger, but these were the same machine. Engines came from FN, Kelecom or Minerva and, by 1905, from Fafnir.

First imported to Britain by the South British Trading Co. of London, Allright bikes were badged as the Vindec Special from 1903. This was changed to VS in 1909 to avoid confusion with the native Vindec produced by Brown Bros. Naturally, import ceased in 1914.

After the war, Allright took over the Cito firm (in 1923), adding the KG machine to its range. Motorcycle production ceased in 1927, although parts were manufactured for others.

AUTOMOTO

Automoto started out producing a car, the Chavanet, in 1898 but moved on to motorcycle production in 1901 under the Automoto name. Initially using a copy of a De Dion engine, Automoto began buying in engines from many sources. Early designs were typical for the time – in other words, they were rather primitive – but soon developed into a sound product line.

After World War I, Automoto built a series of models that, although heavy, fulfilled a demand for sturdy, long-lasting machines. The firm continued manufacturing throughout the 1920s, adapting to new developments, but in 1931 it was taken over by Peugeot. Automoto continued producing utilitarian models, some of which were fitted with Peugeot engines.

Post-war, the company used French AMC and British Villiers engines along with some from other European countries. Few exceeded designs of 250cc (15ci) as a result of the French tax system, which gave preference to the smaller capacities.

BAT

Founded by Samuel Batson, a keen cyclist, BAT benefited from careful preliminary work. Batson developed and patented a range of improvements and, in 1901, built a motorcycle to demonstrate them.

No existing firms were interested, so in 1902 Batson set up his own manufacturing business in South London. The new machine, powered by a De Dion engine, set a number of records, giving rise to the slogan 'Best After Test'.

From 1903, Minerva engines were used and BAT machines continued to break records. TH Tessier, who had made many of these rides, bought out the company in 1905 and began using JAP, Stevens and Soncin engines. Soon the firm was exclusively using JAP engines.

BAT designs became well known for their comfort and speed, and the range expanded but was then slimmed down to make production easier. The year 1913 brought the release of more models, all V-twins with various forms of transmission, and BAT continued to enjoy sporting success.

During World War II, some machines were sold to Russia, but motorcycle production eventually gave way to shell-case manufacture. BAT resurged in 1919, new models being built from pre-war spares. A 4hp V-twin was added and in 1922, Tessier's sons took over. BAT bought Martinsyde in 1925, whose two V-twins were added to the BAT range in its final year.

The first BAT motorbike was built as a 'technology demonstrator' to show what could be done. Other manufacturers were unconvinced but the public wanted these bikes – and so was launched a quarter-century career in the industry.

DURKOPP

Founded in Bielefeld in 1867, Durkopp was one of the pioneers of German motorcycling. Like so many other early motorcycle firms, the company originally made bicycles (from 1889) and began constructing motorcycles as early as 1901. By 1905, it made not only singles and V-twins, but also an air-cooled, in-line, four-cylinder model.

Durkopp ceased motorcycle production just prior to the outbreak of World War I, but resumed in the 1930s with bicycles powered by auxiliary 'clip-on' engines of 60cc (4ci), 75cc (5ci) and 98cc (6ci) capacities. True motorcycles were not offered again until 1949, when models powered by 98cc (6ci) Sachs and 123cc (8ci) Ardie and Ilo engines appeared.

From 1951, only Durkopp-made engines were used, such as in the 1954 Diana scooter. The Diana was fast and stylish, with good handling, and its popularity helped Durkopp to achieve success during the boom of the mid-1950s and to weather the depression that followed.

Durkopp was a diversified company with a solid general engineering presence, and gradually moved out of the motorcycle business. Production of the various Diana models ceased in 1960, by which time 24,963 had been manufactured.

Durkopp's 1954 Diana scooter. A classic scooter design, the Diana was good enough (and sold well enough) to help carry Durkopp through the difficult times of the late 1950s.

FN

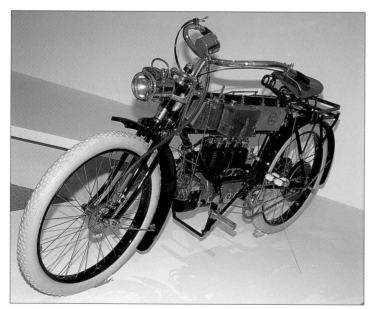

FN (La Fabrique Nationale d'Armes de Guerre) started out in 1889 as an arms company in competition with Sarolea. After the obligatory bicycle-making stint, the firm began making motorized cycles in 1901. The initial rather crude model was replaced in 1904 by a much better and more popular model designed by Paul Kelecom.

Kelecom designed a number of four-cylinder motorcycles in the next few years, leaving the

FN's 498cc (30ci) in-line four-cylinder 1908 model delivered 9hp and was capable of 45km/h (28mph). Like many machines of the time, it retained pedals, but using them would have been very hard work for the rider.

company in 1926. After this, only singles and twins were built. Singles were FN's main product line for most of the company's existence, and were often characterized by being ugly but robust.

Before the outbreak of World War II, FN returned to its roots. Along with rivals Gillet-Herstal and Sarolea, it designed and built a number of specialized military motorcycles and other vehicles. Some were modified after the war for other roles, such as delivery trucks. FN began to decline after the war, despite some motocross success with four-stroke singles; production was increasingly limited to lightweight two-strokes and a moped design. FN ceased production in the mid-1960s.

GRIFFON

Griffon's first design was a heavy-duty bicycle powered by a Clément engine. From this humble beginning, Griffon moved on to produce a range of vehicles

powered by single or V-twin Swiss Zedel engines. The twins did respectably well in racing events while the singles were intended for road use.

Griffon continued to use Zedel engines, as well as some from Anzani, after World War I. The firm did well enough in the early '20s, but was taken over by Peugeot

near the end of the decade. Grifons of the 1930s and the post-war years were simply Peugeots wearing a different badge.

HOBART

Coventry-based Hobart built a primitive machine in 1901 and refined it into a good design. By 1903, it had developed a strong contender and was built for several years, despite a lapse in production between 1906 and 1910.

After World War II, Hobart offered a range of small-engined designs, using Blackburne and JAP engines as well as one of its own design. Production of full machines was phased out, but Hobart went on supplying engines to other firms for some years.

INDIAN

George Hendee and Oscar Hedstrom founded the Hendee Manufacturing Company in 1900 as a partnership to sell motorcycles under the Indian trademark. In 1901, they built about six motorcycles and sold three. Despite this inauspicious beginning, Indian was the biggest motorcycle manufacturer in the world by 1915, constructing 31,950 motorcycles that year.

The earliest Indians were well-made, if unremarkable, 215cc (13ci) singles. Their success was due to good marketing rather than any outstanding virtues of their own. Publicity campaigns, mostly at bicycle shows and competitions, resulted in more orders than the firm could fill. This was assisted by a good showing in the TT in 1911 – coming in first, second and third.

Indian kept up with the latest technical innovations, fitting

twist-grip controls and incorporating new ideas into their designs.

A long association with the police began in 1907 with a sale to the New York police force. It is possible that the left-hand throttle control was a result of police influence.

Government contracts were not without their problems. The first 20,000 machines sold to the US

A 1916 vintage 8-valve 1000cc (60ci) V-twin, without Indian's trademark large front mudguard. The heavy engine would make pedalling something to be dreaded. Five examples of this machine still exist.

government were produced at an increasing loss due to poor cost control and estimating errors. Nor was this the only such incident in the company's history.

Indian is chiefly famous for its long rivalry with Harley-Davidson, and for three models: the Scout, the Chief and the Four. Its rivalry with Harley largely drove the early development of the motorcycle industry in the US.

Indian ceased production in the mid-1950s. The modern company, Indian, is treated as a separate entity in a later section of this book.

NSU

NSU (Neckarsulm Stickmachen Union) began in 1873 as a knitting-machine maintenance and manufacturing concern. In time, it became one of Germany's most famous motorcycle manufacturers, alongside BMW and DKW. With its design, innovation and production methods, to say nothing of its sporting successes, before and after World War II, NSU was a world leader

NSU began experimenting with motorcycles and by 1900 had constructed a crude, if sturdy, prototype powered by a Zedal clip-on engine. Soon afterwards, NSU began using its own engines and produced a range of V-twins.

The firm was aware of the publicity that racing success could bring, and of the role of racing machines in proving new concepts. In 1905, NSU produced its first purpose-built racing machine and opened a sales office in London. Sales in Britain were very good indeed, though the outbreak of World War I brought this to an end.

NSU spent the war making munitions, but was producing motorcycles again by 1922. It recruited ex-Norton designer Walter Moore and did very well until World War II broke out.

NSU continued to make transport during the war, including pedal and motorcycles plus aircraft components and other vehicles. The firm was able to restart production almost immediately after the war, and grew rapidly.

After the war, the company's successes included the Quickly moped, a licence-built Lambretta scooter, and the Prima, a scooter of NSU's own design. The firm returned to racing and record-breaking attempts and achieved some impressive results. Meanwhile, the directors made the decision to enter into partnership with Dr Felix Wankel.

NSU's involvement with the Wankel engine enabled it to produce the award-winning RO80 car, but at the cost of allowing the motorcycle business to die off. The firm stopped making motorcycles in 1963, and financial troubles caused by problems with the RO80 drove NSU under in 1969. It was absorbed into the Volkswagen corporation and vanished.

The first all-in-house motorcycle built by NSU was this 1906 single-cylinder model. Before this, Swiss ZL engines were bought in. NSU machines were extremely popular in Britain for a time.

OEC

A 1930s OEC with the unusual duplex steering system clearly evident. Surviving examples might command a price of £25,000 or so today.

The Portsmouth-based Osborne Engineering Company was a motorcycle firm that began with imported Minerva engines. For years, it produced a range of workmanlike but unexceptional machines. In 1920, John Osborne took over from his more conservative father, Frederick.

In 1921, OEC began making Blackburne motorcycles and engines, under the name OEC-Blackburne. The smallest model was a 147cc (9ci) Villiers, whilst the largest, up to 998cc (61ci), used large, V-twin JAP engines.

OEC was best known for its 'duplex' steering system of 1927, designed by Fred Wood. This curious mechanism was one of the factors that caused the company to be dubbed the 'Odd Engineering Co'. The duplex system was heavy, but stiffer than girder forks, giving unparalleled stability at speed and some of the advantages of more complex hub-centre designs. Other OEC oddities included a 998cc (61ci) sidecar outfit, the 'Taxi', with a steering wheel.

OEC machines were popular for speed record attempts due to their stability at high speed, and OEC continued to innovate into the 1930s and 1940s. However, after World War II, things took a downturn and the firm's string of advanced concepts came to an end. After a few more workmanlike designs, OEC faded away in 1954.

RALEIGH

Nottingham-based Raleigh was famous for bicycles long before building a motorcycle, and afterwards too. Raleigh's first motorcycle was built in 1901, with an imported Schwann engine driving the front wheel. This model was soon replaced by one in which the 3hp engine was set vertically ahead of the pedals; the new bike also incorporated a frame stronger than most then available. Raleigh took over the Sturmey-Archer firm, which made engines and gearboxes.

This motorcycle set a new time of under 51 hours for the journey from Land's End to John O'Groats, despite many stops. The engine gave no trouble at all and the ride was a remarkable feat on the roads of the time. However, the downturn in trade led to Raleigh abandoning motorcycles after 1906 to concentrate on bicycles.

Raleigh returned in 1920 with an interesting and totally new flat-twin model. In 1922, this was joined by conventional singles, and in 1924 the flat-twin was replaced by 798cc (49ci) V-twin models. In that year and the next, Raleigh demonstrated their reliability with long solo rides.

By 1929, the firm was selling Sturmey-Archer engines to several other makers, a practice that continued up to 1933. Raleigh's motorcycle range was then rationalized, with the smallest models being dropped and others receiving new engines. However, Raleigh stopped motorcycle production at the end of 1933. The firm continued with bicycles and a three-wheeled car and van introduced in 1930. These were dropped in 1935, restricting the company to bicycles for many years after that.

The Raleigh marque returned late in 1958 for a 49cc (3ci) moped using a Sturmey-Archer two-stroke engine with V-belt drive to a countershaft. The engine was made by BSA and a version with a clutch was added

After abandoning the motorcycle trade for a few years, Raleigh returned in the 1920s with machines like this one. Production lasted only a few years, though it was revived yet again into the 1960s, without great success.

for the next year. At the end of 1960, this design was replaced by one built under licence from Motobécane, and a copy of the French Mobylette was added to the range. A scooter was marketed in 1961, but was withdrawn three years later.

During the next decade, Raleigh produced a number of variations on the moped theme, most using the same basic engine and transmission. Only one variant survived into the 1970s, and Raleigh went back to what it did best – building bicycles.

ROYAL ENFIELD

ENGLAND 1901–70

The Enfield Cycle Company, located near Birmingham, produced motorized tricycles and quadricycles from 1899 onwards, using the customary De Dion, Minerva and MMC engines. From 1901, Enfield was making motorized bicycles with a front-mounted engine.

Production ceased from 1905–10, then resumed with a 2.25hp MAG-powered V-twin, and this was followed by other machines, including a sidecar combination with a JAP 770cc (47ci) engine.

Royal Enfield incorporated a number of innovations in its machines, including the rubber cushion hub, (a rubber shock absorber in the rear hub). The 1913 model had a Royal Enfield engine with an automatic oil pump.

Royal Enfield retained its interest in bicycle manufacturing. During World War II, the firm supplied bicycles to the Allied forces, delivering a smaller volume of JAP-engined sidecar combinations that saw action as machine-gun carriers and field ambulances.

Post-war production centred on the 976cc (60ci) Royal Enfield-engined V-twin as well as the 225cc (14ci) two-stroke. In 1924, the JAP engine in use on some models was replaced by an engine of Royal Enfield's own design. A range of good models and careful administration got the firm through the Depression years. One range of this time was the Bullet, launched in 1930 and available in various engine sizes.

During World War II, Royal Enfield sold thousands of motorcycles to the British forces. One notable model was the Flying Flea, which could be folded and placed in a canister to be airdropped with paratroops. During the war, the firm operated from an underground factory known as The Cave, which remained in service afterwards.

Royal Enfield bought much of its wartime production back from the War Office and sold the refurbished machines on the private market.

Royal Enfield had always had an interest in trials and offroad riding, and its swinging-arm rear suspension proved to be excellent for trials bikes. Enfield designs enjoyed considerable success in competition, adding to the firm's reputation. Production was diverse in the post-war years, with many different models coming off the line. The biggest was the Meteor, the largest production bike in Britain after the disappearance of rival manufacturer Vincent. It was popular for sidecar use. The Meteor gradually evolved into the Interceptor.

However, the motorcycle market in Britain was in a downturn in the 1960s. Royal Enfield was taken over by the Smith group in 1962, which spelled the end of the Bullet line. Other designs were implemented but gradually Enfield Precision, as the firm was now known, slimmed down its lines and concentrated on fulfilling military contracts. Tools and equipment for making Bullets were sold off in 1967 and production moved to Madras, India. Indian-made Bullets are available in Britain and seem to cope well with the rugged motoring conditions in India. By 1970, Royal Enfield was gone.

Opinions are divided about the huge mudguard and fairing on the 1958 Crusader 250: clumsy or stylish? The Crusader was available without it for those who preferred it that way.

WERNER

1901

In the early days of motorcycle design, opinion was divided on where to position the engine. Three solutions were found.

One method was to hang the engine unit from, or above, the frame downtube using a clip-on, with the drive to the rear wheel either direct or over one or more jockey pulleys.

A second, less typical, arrangement was to hang the engine out behind the rear wheel or to tuck it in behind the seat tube, either low down towards the rear of the bottom bracket or high up under the saddle.

A third, even more unusual solution was to build it into either the front or rear wheel. Although all of these options were explored, the original Werner layout, with minor variations, proved to be the best solution for most machines and it remains so today.

An early belt-drive, Werner-powered bicycle. Despite its obviously primitive nature, the layout of this machine has remained the standard for motorcycles ever since.

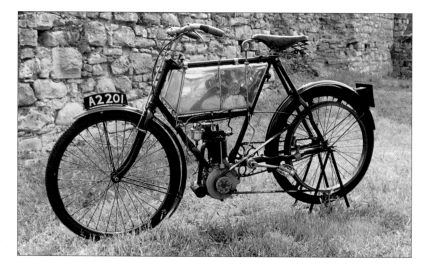

AIGLON

Aiglon manufactured bicycles, cars and motorcycles, and adopted the Werner layout. The firm also did a lot of work in developing early internal combustion engines. The first Aiglon machine was a typical motorized bicycle with rather inadequate brakes, and development continued up to the outbreak of World War I. After the war, Aiglon was bought by Peugeot. Production was moved, but the Aiglon brand was retained and a range of models was produced.

The early French lead in development of motor transport was eroded in the 1920s, forcing French firms to consolidate their efforts and concentrate on their home market. Aiglon continued producing motorcycles as part of the Peugeot group until 1954.

ALCYON

Founded by Edmond Gentil, Alcyon was named after a mythical bird of lightness. Its founder bought out a number of small firms, including Amor, Labor, La Française, Lapize, Olympique and Thomann, merging them under the banner of Gentil et Cie.

The first Alcyon model was a Werner-type machine powered by an engine manufactured by Zurcher et Lothi. Development led to a range of V-twin machines and, by the 1920s, Alcyon was producing British-style bikes featuring its own innovations. Alcyon designed its own frames and forks, which were continually updated with new ideas, and powered them with engines bought in from other suppliers.

Alcyon continued manufacturing until 1957, by which time the range included mopeds and scooters as well as motorcycles.

Alcyon was a long-lived manufacturer that constantly updated its ideas and designs. This 1940s two-stroke single is a typically neat and tidy design.

ARIEL

Ariel started out as a bicycle company and has the distinction of being the first to use the tensioned wire-spoked wheel. This was invented in 1870 by the company's founders, James Starley and William Hillman. This new device was named Ariel: the spirit of the air.

In 1896, the company merged with the Westwood Manufacturing Company to produce cycle components and moved to the Selly Oak site in Birmingham, which would eventually house Ariel's huge industrial complex. The company's first powered vehicle, a quadricycle with a

This 1958 Ariel Huntmaster is essentially a rebadged 650cc BSA Golden Flash. By this period in the firm's history all of its twins were basically BSA machines thinly disguised.

De Dion engine, was produced in 1898. It was more than a little unstable, and a better tricycle version followed.

In 1902, the Starley and Westwood Company was taken over by Components Ltd, which vastly increased the resources available to the designers.

The first motorcycle built at Selly Oak used a Kerry engine and did well in competition. Ariel was soon using White and Poppe engines and began building similar units themselves under licence. Designs in this period were workmanlike rather than exceptional, though this trend might have been broken had the Arielette design not been sidelined by World War I.

After the war, Ariel went on producing a range of motorcycles using bought-in engines, but was beginning to lag behind the field leaders in terms of quality. Ariel responded by hiring some of the best designers available, and new machines were more impressive in terms of styling and quality.

Perhaps the most important development of this period was the Square Four engine, designed for Ariel by Edward Turner. Mounted in a 'Sloper' frame, the prototype caused a sensation in 1930. Ariel's fortunes improved and the Red Hunter singles became very popular.

After World War II, Ariel became part of the BSA Group. Predictably, it endured for a time but eventually disappeared into the larger BSA identity. The last generation of Ariel's designs began in fairly mediocre fashion, but at the end Ariel was still producing good ideas and impressing everyone in the field of trials riding.

CURTISS

USA 1902–12

The name Curtiss is more normally associated with aviation, and its founder, Glen Curtiss, later became famous in that field. Hammonsport-based Curtiss produced an early range that rivalled Indian on the racing scene of the time, and which featured twist-grip controls before they were fitted to Indians.

Curtiss liked to experiment with engines, and he did create some record-breaking machines. He built a V8 that set an unofficial record of 219km/h (136mph). However, a later attempt failed when a universal joint broke and the engine's power twisted the machine's frame.

From 1910, Curtiss' road models were also sold as the Marvel, and advertising materials of the time made much of the Curtiss engine. In 1912, the Curtiss marque dropped from the motorcycle market as Glen turned his attention to the field of aviation.

JAMES

ENGLAND 1902–66

Founded as the James Cycle Company in Birmingham, James constructed its first motorcycle in 1902, when a motor was added to a bicycle design. At first, clip-on FN and Minerva engines were used.

In 1908, James began to produce an innovative design by P.L. Renouf, which may well have been the pioneering design for internally expanding brakes. New models followed, some of them quite advanced. Designs included solos and sidecar combinations, and featured a foot-operated all-metal clutch, a device popular with speedway riders into the 1950s.

After World War I, the James line included a small autocycle and overhead-valve 250cc (15ci), 500cc (31ci) and 750cc (46ci) V-twins. In the 1930s, as times became harder, it proved more economical to buy in engines from Villiers than to build them in-house. The product line was slimmed down in the mid-1930s and again in 1938.

James supplied vehicles to the military during World War II and returned to the civilian market in 1946. The 98cc (6ci) Autocycle proved a good seller in the post-war market because it was economical to run, and new models were slowly added to the range as the economic situation improved.

James was taken over by Associated Motor Cycles in 1951, and made an unsuccessful foray into the scooter market. Through the 1950s, the James and Francis-Barnett lines (both owned by Associated Motor Cycles) gradually merged.

Despite some success in the offroad market, the rising dominance of Japanese makers spelled doom for many British firms, including Associated Motor Cycles. Its collapse in 1966 took James out of the picture.

A 500cc (30ci) overhead-valve James of 1925 vintage. Within a few years James had ceased to build engines in-house and was buying in proprietary units from Villiers.

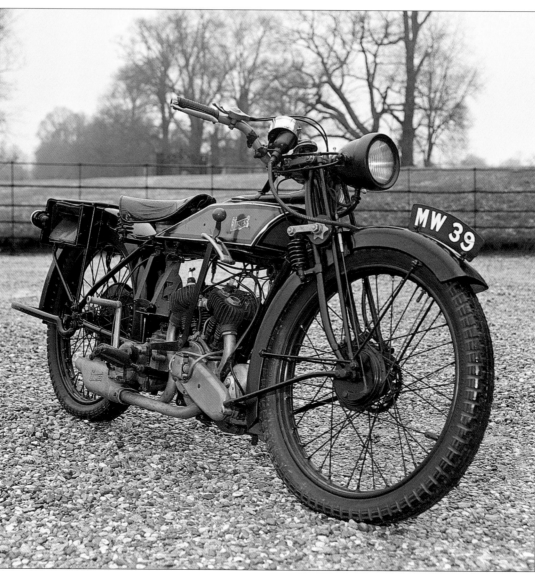

MAGNAT-DEBON

Based out of Grenoble, Magnat-Debon was named after its founders, Joseph Magnat and Louis Debon, and was founded in 1893 to make bicycles. Its first motorcycle, constructed in 1902, was powered by a De Dion engine. Magnat-Debon became De Dion agents, but also used engines from other manufacturers as well as their own designs.

Magnat-Debon models achieved some competition success, partly as a result of experimentation and willingness to try out new ideas. However, by 1923 the firm was struggling and was bought out by Terrot.

For a time, Terrot built Magnat-Debon models with Blackburne engines and used JAP engines in its own designs. Gradually, however, the lines merged and the Terrot design style became dominant.

This was especially true after World War II. The Magnat-Debon badge lived on for a while on some models, but no traces were left by 1958 and Magnat-Debon faded into the pages of history.

A 350cc Magnat-Debon from the 1930s. At this time the marque was moving away from its original styling and its machines were increasingly following the design practices of new owners Terrot.

MERKEL

The Merkel was built in Milwaukee, Wisconsin. Like so many other early designs, the first model was based on a standard bicycle with the frame braced above the bottom bracket by an added tube. A small engine was mounted above this tube, and inclined to lie along the downtube. Its exhaust connected to the downtube, with an outlet at the top of the seat tube via small holes – a method also used by other firms with some variations.

Gradual evolution took place from 1903 onwards, and production moved to Pottstown, Pennsylvania in 1908, when the firm was taken over by the Light Manufacturing & Foundry Company. Some machines went to marked under the Merkel-Light identity.

In 1909, the firm started using the Flying Merkel name in advertising, and considerable resources were put into racing for the publicity it garnered. Heavy investment in the field enabled Merkel to hire skilled riders and, before long, it was competing with the dominant Indian machines on the board tracks, even setting records.

Racing involvement ended in 1911, when Merkel was bought by the Miami Cycle & Manufacturing Company of Middletown, Ohio, which used the Flying Merkel badge on its machines. The market shrank, largely as a result of the war, and Merkel disappeared.

Well put together and advanced for the time, Merkel machines were also aggressively marketed. The V-twin engine sat in a loop of the frame and used an all-chain drive.

NORTON

ENGLAND 1902–PRESENT

Norton was founded in 1898 and supplied parts to other manufacturers, including most of the components for the Clement-Garrard, for some years before producing its first machine.

The first Clement-powered Norton appeared in 1902. Later machines used Peugeot engines with considerable success, winning the first Manx TT at an average of 58.3km/h (36.2mph) for 270km (168 miles). This was a pretty decent average in a race that lasted over four and half hours and included two falls, a burst tyre at 97kpm (60mph) and several plug changes among other delays. It was not long before Norton built its first in-house engines.

The most notable of these was a new 475cc (28ci) single that grew to 660cc (40ci) for 1909 and became known as the 'Big Four' for its rated power output. The firm got into financial difficulties in 1911–12 but still managed to break a number of records in this period, and produced the ancestor of the classic 16H.

Norton took nine out of the first 14 places in the 1920 TT, with standard sports models rather than custom racers. More racing success followed, with wins at Brooklands and elsewhere that year and the next. In 1924, a Norton won the Senior TT outright.

Times were hard in the late 1920s, but Norton got through the Depression with the help of the CS1 super-sports machine. Then, with the outbreak of World War II, both the Big Four and the 16H donned military colours and went off to do their bit.

The 498cc Manx Norton of 1950 was one of the great classic motorcycles. It was winning races into the 1960 even though by rights it should have been outclassed by the twins, fours and even V-8s that were ranged against it. However, it had a rival.

In 1949, Norton had fielded the 500cc Dominator twin, and its 29bhp was not enough to make it a lively ride in its original heavy frame. In 1952, however, it received a 'featherbed' frame, creating the Dominator 88, whose excellent handling compensated for its moderate power.

It was around this time that Norton hit yet another rough patch and was absorbed into AMC. Norton machines continued to appear under the AMC marque, including the 1962 650SS, the best of all the Dominators. This led to the 750cc Atlas and the Commando. When AMC collapsed in 1966 it was bought out and Norton became part of Norton-Villiers-Triumph, in which guise the Commando lived on for a time.

NVT went under in 1978, but Norton survived, building rotary-engine machines, including the Interpol 2 police bike and the F1 race replica. These were not sufficient, however, to keep Norton afloat.

Despite bursting tyres, falling off on corners and having to stop and change plugs several times, Normal Fowler rode this machine to victory in the very first Isle of Man TT.

PEERLESS

ENGLAND 1902–08

The short-lived Peerless marque was a Bradbury under another name, manufactured at the same factory in Oldham, Lancashire. Like the Bradbury, the Peerless was built to a Birch design with the crankcase cast around the lower end of the downtube and the bottom bracket. A door on the left side enabled the crankshaft to be installed with the one-piece head and cylinder fixed vertically to the casting. The engine was installed in the frame, and the overall concept was rather basic. However, the Peerless performed well for its size; indeed, it was better than most of its contemporaries. The Peerless thus remained on the market for some years.

ROVER

ENGLAND 1902–25

The Rover name is more commonly associated with cars than motorcycles. Like virtually everyone else, Rover's founder John Kemp Starley began by building bicycles, in Coventry.

Starley opened his business in 1877 and began using the name Rover in 1884. The first powered cycle came in 1888 and was an electric powered tricycle. In 1896, the Rover Cycle Company was born.

Rover Cycles imported Peugeot motorized cycles for a feasibility study. Seeing the potential, Rover produced a 2.75hp motorcycle, which came out in 1902. However, production ceased in 1905 after 1250 or so machines were made.

Rover motorcycles returned in 1910 with JAP-engined models and others using an engine designed by John Greenwood. From 1915 an Ariel three-speed transmission was used, and after 1918 a number of JAP-powered V-twins were produced. In 1923, Rover began launched a new line of single-cylinder bikes, but these do not seem to have been a huge success; the firm produced only cars after 1925.

TERROT

FRANCE 1902–61

Charles Terrot's first motorcycle, powered by a Zedel engine, was produced in 1902. Prior to this, Terrot built tricycles and quads powered by De Dion engines. Terrot's designs were successful enough for the firm to grow, and by the end of World War I the firm was building two- and four-stroke machines using JAP and Blackburne engines. Terrot models of the 1920s had a British character, though influenced by French styling.

In the 1930s, Terrot began using its own engines and produced a broad range, including a velomoteur and motorcycles of various sizes. The smaller models continued after World War II and were joined by a scooter in 1951. However, the firm joined the Peugeot group in 1954 and the Terrot name disappeared in 1961.

VINDEC

The Vindec name had been around for a while but was first advertised when it appeared on a 225cc (14ci) two-stroke motorcycle built in 1914 by Brown Brothers of London. Before that, the firm was a very low-key operation known for supplying parts and the Brown motorcycle. More powerful machines were produced soon after and development continued throughout World War I.

Afterwards, Vindec marketed a 225cc (14ci) two-stroke single, and then added a 976cc (60ci) side-valve JAP V-twin for 1920. These were followed by new models. Since Brown Brothers was a trade wholesaler, most Vindec machines were probably bought-in badged designs from

established firms. Models from this era bore a strong resemblance to those of the Rex-Acme factory.

In and after 1924, production of new models slowed down. A handful of new designs did,

however, make their way onto the market before 1929, the firm's final year.

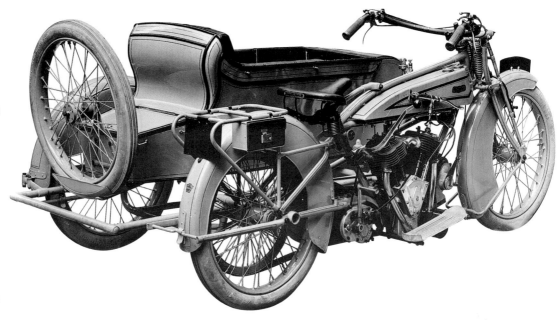

A 1915-vintage Brown motorcycle with sidecar. Note the extensive mudguarding and large footrests, which provided a measure of weather protection to the rider and passenger.

WANDERER

Early Wanderer machines were constructed by Winkelhofer & Jaenicke in Saxony. These were fairly primitive, rear-wheel-driven designs with a single-cylinder engine mounted vertically in a loop frame, on what was essentially a heavy-duty bicycle.

Wanderer's range was quickly expanded to include more singles as well as V-twins in several

different capacities, which became increasingly advanced as time went on. The cycle parts became heavier to take the increased loads, and over time the models assumed a typical pre-World War I form.

After World War I, Wanderer's most important product was a range of V-twins. These were of unit construction with either side-

or overhead-valves, and some of the latter type had eight valves. In 1928, the range was replaced by a unit-construction single. Unfortunately, this innovative model came at just the wrong time and overextended the firm financially. It did not have sufficient capital to remain afloat until sales began to match investment.

Wanderer was taken over by German rival NSU, for which it produced a Sachs-engined lightweight for a time. Some designs, drawings and production equipment were sold to F. Janacek of Prague, who began building the Janacek-Wanderer. The name of this model was soon abbreviated to Jawa, spawning a whole new marque.

WHITE & POPPE

White & Poppe, based out of Coventry, was better known for its motorcycle engines than whole machines. From 1902, White & Poppe found a ready market for its engines in the

emergent car and motorcycle industries. The firm also produced its own complete bikes, including 498cc (30ci) vertical twins and 347cc (21ci) two-strokes.

White & Poppe is best known for the work of Erling Poppe, who began designing motorcycles in 1922. He made a number of significant advances in areas such as silencing, comfort and

cleanliness, before going on to design cars and heavy vehicles. His most renowned creation, however, was the Sunbeam S7, which was a BSA machine.

BSA

BSA started out in 1954 as an association of 14 gunsmiths who joined forces to supply arms to British forces for the Crimean War. The firm's logo of three stacked rifles is still in use by its successor, BSA Regal.

In 1861, BSA was a publicly listed company (Birmingham Small Arms), now located in the Small Heath factory, where it remained for 110 years. It began making bicycle components in the 1880s and the first powered model came

along in 1903. This machine was powered by a Minerva engine.

In 1910, BSA marketed its first all-BSA machine and added another to the range in 1913. The firm became well known f or its V-twins and made a range of sidecars to go with its motorcycles. During World War I, BSA built Daimler cars and supplied 1.5 million rifles to the military, among other diversified activities. Motorcycle production also continued apace.

V-twins were the order of the day for the 1920s, but in the 1930s BSA was mainly producing single-cylinder machines. Military sales were good during the war years, and at one point the firm owned 67 factories, which were involved in a wide range of industrial activities. By the mid-1950s, BSA was the largest motorcycle manufacturer in the world. It owned Triumph, Ariel, Sunbeam and several other marques.

However, with the rise of advanced Japanese imports, BSA faced strong competition and was very slow to respond. Various models went to market and performed poorly as BSA struggled to create a competitive design. Losses mounted through the 1970s, and in 1972 BSA was acquired by Manganese Bronze.

Manganese Bronze owned Norton and was mostly interested in BSA's car body division. A plan was proposed to rescue the

motorcycle division, but this was scuppered by a workers' sit-in at the Meridien plant. From the sit-in emerged a Workers' Cooperative, which operated the plant for a time.

Norton Villiers Triumph took over what remained of BSA's motorcycle production. From this emerged Norton Motors (the rotary-engined project), which passed through a succession of owners, eventually falling under the control of the Canadian Aquilini family, the holders of the UK rights to the BSA motorcycle name.

Two other parts of the original Norton Villiers Triumph group – BSA Co and Andover Norton – were later disposed of in management buy-outs. These merged in 1991 to become a new BSA Group, which was then taken over by Southampton-based interests to become BSA Regal in 1994,

BSA Regal has diverse light engineering interests, and in 1996 unveiled a new BSA model, the Gold SR. Although the original BSA is gone, its legacy lives on.

Bert Hopwood redesigned the A7 Star Twin into the 646cc A10 Golden Flash, which was outwardly quite similar but was altogether more impressive thanks to lightweight and advanced construction.

DIAMANT
GERMANY 1903–08 AND 1926–40

In the mid-1900s, Diamant produced a small range of machines, originally based around Fafnir engines and later using their own designs. These soon faded from the scene, but the firm re-emerged in 1926 with a range powered mainly by Kühne engines.

In 1927, Diamant merged with the Elite car firm and became associated with Opel during the following year, which led in time to the EO motorcycle.

From 1928, the Diamant factory produced Opel machines, but only for two or three years. After that, the EO was built for two years before production again ceased due to lack of demand.

In 1937, Diamant began manufacturing again, marketing a range of fairly conventional lightweight motorcycles that used Sachs engines. Production was curtailed by World War II, and this time it did not restart.

EXPRESS
GERMANY 1903–58

Founded in Nurnberg as a bicycle manufacturer in 1882, Express-Werke AG entered the motorcycle industry in 1903. Its first offering was typical: a Fafnir engine mounted on a heavy bicycle frame. The first racing model, boasting an impressive (for the time) 8hp, went to market the following year.

Although Express built good motorcycles and did reasonably well, it never really became a household name like some of its competitors. After World War I, the firm left the motorcycle industry, reverting to making pedal cycles.

In 1933, Express had another try at the motorcycle industry with a range of two-stroke lightweights. At the outbreak of World War II, however, it again returned to bicycles and was the major supplier of these to the German armed forces throughout the war.

Express made another comeback after the war and by 1950 was manufacturing a new range of lightweight motorcycles powered by Fichtel and Sachs engines, as well as large numbers of pedal cycles. The German population was desperate for transportation and Express worked flat-out to meet the need. Utilitarian models were supplemented by more sophisticated machines, and Express continued to do well – even through the recession of 1956–57.

In 1958, everything seemed to be well with Express after 75 years in business, but late in the year it merged with DKW and Victoria to form Zweirad Union.

FAFNIR
GERMANY 1903–06

Prior to World War I, Fafnir was a major engine supplier whose clients included many different firms. The firm's products were typical of the times; indeed, Fafnir held a licence to build Werner style engines and was thus channelled down the same route as everyone else. Fafnir also produced a range of motorcycles under its own name for a short time. For 1903, two models were available, with 289cc (18ci) and 353cc (22ci), engines. By 1905, Fafnir motorcycles featured a countershaft gearbox, but these were discontinued a year later and Fafnir concentrated on engines, which were exported all over Europe.

HARLEY-DAVIDSON

The first proto-Harley was a one-off. It was designed in 1903 by Bill Harley, Arthur Harley made the patterns and Walter Davidson built it. Production was modest – two more were built and sold in 1904 and eight in 1905.

After this, demand exploded and production with it: 50 were sold in 1906; 100 in 1907; and 450 in 1908. In 1909, Harley-Davidson produced the first of the V-twins for which it is legendary.

Harley-Davidson sold a lot of machines, though at first these were inferior in quality and speed to rival Indian models. Competition between the two led to commercial and engineering innovation, and to a great extent drove the development of the US motorcycle industry.

Harley-Davidson sold large numbers of machines to the US government during World War I and better financial controls meant that this brought more benefits to it than to Indian.

During this period, Harley made sure that much of their production (almost half) was reserved for the civilian market, allowing it to steal much of Indian's market share while its rival was distracted by government contracts. Harley was also dominant in the racing world, and gradually Indian was squeezed out of the market until it went under.

In the early 1920s, however, the main threat to Harley-Davidson was the low-cost automobile, which was eating up much of the personal transport market. The firm tightened its belt, curtailed its heavy racing involvement and weathered the decline.

Harley-Davidson continued to do reasonably well overseas, especially in places like Australia, where there were vast expanses of long, open roads like those in much of America. It was becoming obvious that Harley-Davidson was being left behind by the march of progress, however.

Harley-Davidson responded by introducing new models with more advanced features. These were introduced slowly, and with a great many teething troubles. However, once a model worked out its faults and proved itself, it stayed in production for a very long time by motorcycle standards. For example, the 737cc (45ci) Flathead, introduced in 1929, was used in road bikes until 1951 and in the three-wheeler Servi-Car until 1974.

Not all of Harley-Davidson's efforts during this period were good. The flat twin of 1919–22 was horribly underpowered and even the so-called Superpowered Twin was distinctly unimpressive when it was compared with a contemporary Brough Superior. That said, the company's successes outweighed its failures.

One advantage for Harley-Davidson, which has helped even their mediocre designs to do well in the marketplace, is that 'Harley

Mystique' – 'Of course it's a good bike, it's a Harley!' A machine that looks great as well as being reliable is what the average Harley-Davidson buyer wants, especially if it feeds their fantasy of being a biker. As long as it starts first time, makes that wonderful V-twin noise, and has a Harley badge on the side, speed and handling are secondary considerations.

At times when the company has forgotten this basic fact about its fans, market share has fallen, even threatening the existence of the firm. When it has played to the audience, it has done very well indeed. Harley-Davidson's big successes came not from increased performance but by improving reliability (in particular, preventing oil leaks), and by paying ever more attention to looks.

Harley's successful designs have tended to retain a basic form, making cosmetic changes. Different tanks, forks and handlebars create the illusion of a wide range of models and target different niche markets, but underneath them all is essentially the same machine.

Harley-Davidson was incorporated in 1907 but was a family-dominated business until it went public 1965. This culminated three years later in a takeover by American Machine and Foundry (AMF), which was willing to invest large sums in the company. Unfortunately, AMF did not understand the motorcycle business, and market share fell. This trend, coupled with rising losses, continued until a management buyout in 1981–82, which turned things around and set the stage for the firm's continued success.

Huge, unsophisticated and making a sound like a tractor, this 1990s Electra Glide is ideal for long-distance cruising and also appeals to users to whom riding a Harley is more important than any amount of horsepower or handling.

HUSQVARNA

Husqvarna started out as a bicycles and armament firm. The first powered machines were fitted with Moto-Rêve, NSU and FN engines, and in 1920 Husqvarna produced its own engine, a 550cc (34ci) side-valve V-twin. Engines were imported from Sturmey-Archer and JAP and used in other models.

Husqvarna's most famous model was a 1932 racing bike powered by the new 498cc (30ci) overhead-valve V-twin engine, designed by Folke Mannerstedt and Calle Heimdahl. It performed well in competition, winning the Swedish Grand Prix on three successive occasions and breaking the

Manx lap record in the 1934 TT.

In 1935, the company built its first two-stroke, a 98cc (6ci) two-speed machine, which set a precedent for its post-war production. The focus of its attention was on off-road competition, and by 1960 Husqvarna had become a world-

class contender, winning 10 World Motocross titles in the next decade.

In 1986, the Cagiva group acquired Husqvarna's motorcycle division. A year later, production was transferred to Italy and a new range emerged, which is still in production today.

JAP

Founded in London by J.A. Prestwich, JAP was a manufacturer of engines from the outset. The firm dabbled for a while in complete motorcycles but quickly returned to its core business. The first JAP engine was a single-cylinder four-stroke in 1901, and other designs quickly followed.

In 1903, JAP offered a motorcycle built on a BSA frame, followed by a second, lightweight, design. Production of these models, and a three-wheel design, continued until 1905. After this, a new set of designs was marketed, but by 1908 JAP was concentrating on the engine business and ceased production of complete machines.

LLOYD

The Birmingham-based Lloyd Motor Engineering Company built its first machine in 1903. It was powered by a Stevens engine and constructed from stock parts. Design and building was carried out by the firm's owner, W.J. Lloyd, who had been involved with Quadrant. By 1908, Lloyd's machines were being sold as the LMC, two models being offered for sale. These were developed as new technical innovations came along, gaining two-speed gears in 1914 and the option of a countershaft gearbox in 1916.

After a hiatus due mainly to the war, Lloyd returned in 1919 with a 597cc (36ci) single and a 842cc (51ci) V-twin, though only the twin was available in 1920. In 1921, a larger V-twin was added to the range, but the firm ceased production in 1922.

MAFFEIS

Founded in Milan by brothers Bernardo and Carlo Maffeis, who had been involved with Sarolea up to that time, Maffeis built its first machine in 1903. This was a typical primitive proto-motorcycle powered by a Sarolea engine.

Carlo was heavily involved in competition before World War I, and his machines replaced their Sarolea engines with Maffeis-designed ones in a sturdy but basic machine. Road versions were a little more sophisticated, and in the 1920s the firm started to use Blackburne engines.

After 1931, Maffeis machines were built and sold by Cesare Galimberti to an uprated specification, using both Blackburne and JAP engines. Production continued until 1935.

MARS

Nurnberg-based Mars used both Swiss Zedel and German Fafnir engines on its machines in the early years, but switched to a custom-made Maybach engine for its 1920 Der Weisse Mars model. 'The White Mars' did well, but hard times in Germany brought production to a close in 1924.

Karl and Johann Muller, two leading engineers at the Mars factory, re-opened it in 1926 with new financial backing. They were not able to use the Mars title for a long time, so their machines were marketed under the MA brand name. In the late 1920s and throughout the 1930s, a variety of imported engines were used, including Sturmey-Archer, JAP, Villers and Sachs. After World War II, the firm was able to use the Mars name once again and resumed production in 1950 with a range of lightweights. By 1957, however, Mars was in financial difficulties, and it closed in 1958. Its model range was absorbed by Gritsner-Kayser.

A 1920 'White Mars' in rather unusual sidecar configuration. Note the box-section frame, manufactured for Mars by Maybach from riveted, pressed-sheet steel.

NEW HUDSON

Based in Birmingham, New Hudson started out as a bicycle manufacturer and, like many others, built a primitive vehicle powered by a De Dion engine. This experiment was not a success and no further models followed until 1910.

New Hudson's 1910 range consisted of two JAP-powered models and the following year brought a new model with an engine developed in-house. Production was slimmed down during the war years and only a single model was available immediately afterwards. By 1922, the range was expanding again and the firm enjoyed both commercial and racing success in the late 1920s.

New Hudson struggled on into the Depression years, staying afloat for a while by selling cut-price machines. However, due to a combination of hard times and technical problems New Hudson was forced to cease production in 1933.

The New Hudson name re-emerged on a 1940 autocycle powered by a 98cc (6ci) Villiers engine. This machine remained on offer for the remaining history of the firm. Taken over by BSA in 1945, New Hudson continued to produce machines until 1958, at which point it disappeared into BSA's larger identity.

The 1914 New Hudson V-twin had a 6hpn engine designed in house, replacing the previous JAP unit. It also featured a three-speed rear hub.

NEW IMPERIAL

New Imperial started out in Birmingham when its founder, Norman Downs, bought out Hearl and Tonks' bicycle business. A powered machine was constructed in 1903, initially using Precision and JAP engines.

Later, New Imperial became known for its own engine designs.

At first, New Imperial did not do well in competition. Its JAP-engined entry did badly in the Isle of Man TT in 1913, and it was not until 1922 that a JAP-engined machine enjoyed success, setting the fastest lap in the Junior TT at 90.86km/h (56.46mph). More successes followed and 'New Imp', as the firm became known, became a solid competition presence. The firm also began constructing its own engines.

In 1932, just as the Depression was biting, New Imperial updated almost its entire range with advanced unit-construction engines, in which the engine and gearbox were fabricated as a unit and linked by gears. This layout is used by most modern motorcycles, but it was novel at the time.

Meanwhile, the New Imp race team were setting records and impressing everyone in competition. Some of their machines were fast, but frightening to ride. It was aboard one such machine in 1934 that 'Ginger' Wood became the first rider of a British multi-cylinder machine to cover more than 160.9km (100 miles) in a single hour, averaging 164.5km/h (102.2mph). In 1936, a New Imp became the last British four-stroke to win the event, by a record-breaking margin of two minutes.

Although New Imperial's competition successes were impressive, they were not accompanied by the hoped-for commercial success. Founder Norman Downs died in 1937 and the firm suffered from lack of leadership. It was bought out by Ariel/Triumph in 1939.

1937 was the beginning of the end for New Imperial, with the death of founder Norman Downs. However, that did not stop it putting out some great-looking machines.

OLYMPIC

The Olympic was a fairly typical 'proto-motorcycle' designed in 1903 by a Wolverhampton-based bicycle maker, F.H. Parkyn. Very few of these MMC-engined vehicles were produced, and the design disappeared in 1905.

Another Olympic appeared in 1919. This was a quality lightweight from the same stable, though the firm had moved premises by this time. Originally powered by a Verus engine, the model used a 261cc (16ci) Orbit for a year, then a 269cc (16.4ci) Villiers in 1921. Four-stroke Blackburne engines were also used. Different engine suppliers were used in 1923 – this time, Villiers and JAP. These frequent changes of supplier may be connected with budget difficulties. Whatever the truth of that, production ceased in 1923.

PUCH

Puch was founded in 1891 as a bicycle manufacturer. It was sold to a German business group in 1897 and opened a new plant in 1899, where it built its first motorcycle in 1903 and an automobile in 1910.

Puch motorcycles did quite well in early competitions, but after 1910 its presence diminished rapidly. Nonetheless, the firm itself was well established as a leading manufacturer by 1914, when founder Johann Puch died suddenly. The firm expanded rapidly to meet the demand created by war production, but suffered afterwards as a result of politics. The only option was to merge. The first came in 1928, with Austro-Daimler, a car company, the second in 1934, with Steyr, an arms firm that had moved into car and bicycle manufacturer when arms manufacture was forbidden.

Puch produced a famous line of split-single two-strokes, of which the LM (Light Motorcycle), designed by Giovanni Marcelino, was the first. This machine made its debut in 1923 and the design was the basis for Puch motorcycles over the next half century.

During the late 1920s and throughout the 1930s, Puch returned successfully to the racing scene. After World War II, its models achieved considerable export success across Europe and the United States. The motorcycle range was supplemented by mopeds and the Maxi series were the top sellers worldwide in the 1970s.

The motorcycle industry as a whole struggled in the 1980s and Puch suffered, though it managed to stay in business. A merger with Piaggio took place in 1987 and production moved to Italy.

A 1980s-vintage offroader from Friggerio-Puch, powered by a 600cc (40ci) Rotax engine. The partnership with Italians Friggerio foreshadowed the buyout of Puch by Piaggio, another Italian firm.

READING-STANDARD

Reading-Standard's first machine was an Indian copy powered by a Thor engine from Aurora (who had been in the business since 1886). One unusual feature was that the fuel tank also contained oil. It was fitted on the rear mudguard.

In 1905 the tanks were separated, and in 1907 the engine was changed to a side-valve version. Further developments followed, and sales were particularly good from 1917 to 1920.

After this, the firm's fortunes entered a downturn and it was taken over by Cleveland in 1923. Reading-Standard's stocks were sold off during the following year and the name faded out of motorcycle history.

Reading-Standard started out by copying Indian machines, but by 1912 the firm had found its own identity. This model has an upright engine and improved leading-link suspension.

THOR

In 1902, the Aurora Automatic Machinery Company, based in Aurora, Illinois began supplying Indian with engines. Other firms placed orders for engines and many of them began producing what were essentially Indian copies. One such was Aurora's own Thor motorcycle, produced in 1903.

Aurora's contract with Indian ended in 1907, and within a couple more years the other deals had also expired. The Thor remained in production after this, and gradually evolved away from its Indian-clone origins. Changes to the frame came in 1909 and a V-twin version also appeared. These two machines were marketed, in continuously evolving form, until 1915, when the firm made the decision to concentrate on other products.

TWN (TRIUMPH)

Triumph was founded in 1897 in Coventry by two Germans, and produced bicycles for a time. In 1902, the first powered version was marketed and a year later Triumph truly entered the motorcycle business. At this time, the firm founded a factory in Nurnberg.

Early on, most of the German-built Triumphs used engines and other components supplied from Coventry. This arrangement continued until 1929, when the two firms went their separate ways. After this, the German company was known in the export markets as TWN (Triumph Werke Nurnberg), to avoid confusion with the British-based Triumph.

After 1929, the Nurnberg factory built its own 198cc (12ci) and 294cc (18ci) two-stroke engines, together with a range of Swiss MAG engines ranging from 347cc (21ci) to 742cc (45ci). Very soon, TWN secured a licence from MAG to build these engines in Germany, and from 1931 onwards it marketed large numbers of two-strokes in the domestic and export markets.

Politics intervened in the late 1930s, leading to a situation where almost all of the company's production was under the direction of military authorities, and the German armed forces bought large numbers of machines. More than 12,000 of one model, known as

TWN produced a number of split-single two-strokes in the 1950s. The first was a 125, followed by the 250 version (pictured), and later by a similar 350 Boss.

the BD250 W in military service, went to the army. The firm also developed some specialist vehicles, including a scooter that could be dropped by parachute

and a TWN-engined NSU tracked personnel carrier.

TWN was among the first motorcycle manufacturers to resume production after World

War II, albeit with a reduced range. This expanded and received technical updates as the years went on. One such was a custom-designed exhaust system intended

to improve performance and reduce noise.

After a few more good years, TWN was taken over by Grundig and made office equipment

BARRY

Built in Barry, South Wales, this machine made a brief appearance in late 1904 at the Stanley Show in London.
It featured a rotary engine, a flat-twin of about 200cc (12ci), which had a fixed crankshaft while the

rest of the engine rotated around it. This allowed the cylinders and heads to manage without cooling fins at the price of a more complex induction and ignition system.

The rest of the machine was fairly conventional, consisting of a

modified heavy-duty bicycle frame with twin downtubes, between which the engine revolved. Rigid forks, pedals and belt final drive completed the machine.

A new version with a lower engine position was tried in 1905,

and in 1910 a much better engineered version appeared. This was the subject of a patent in the names of W.A. Richards and C.R. Redrup; the latter became known for a radial engine in later years.

FN FOUR CYLINDER

Holden designed the fist four-cylinder motorcycle in 1897, but FN was one of the pioneers of its development. The FN four-cylinder series was the brainchild of the company's chief designer, Paul Kelecom. In 1904, he developed an in-line, air-cooled four-cylinder engine, a design that was advanced for the time and virtually vibration free.

To gain publicity for this new design, FN organised a grand tour of all the major European cities, including London and Paris.

Development work continued and, by 1907, the engine had been enlarged and was mounted in a more advanced machine.

An FN four took third place in the 1908 multi-cylinder category in the Isle of Man TT, covering 255km (158.5 miles) in 4 hours, 11 minutes – an average speed of just over 58km/h (36mph). The FN was the most economical bike in the event, averaging no less than 32km/l (90mpg). The same bike competed in long-distance trials as well as circuit

racing, and did well at whatever was asked of it. Production ceased shortly after Designer Paul Kelecom left FN in 1926.

FN was one of the earliest exponents of the four-cylinder motorcycle. The FN Four was ridden by R.O. Clarke in road races and trials, with impressive results.

ENGINE: 363cc ioe in-line V4, 45x47mm, air-cooled
POWER: n/a
GEARBOX: single–speed
FINAL DRIVE: shaft
WEIGHT: n/a

HERCULES

Founded in 1886 by Carl Marschutz, Hercules produced its first motorcycle in 1904. This was a heavyweight bicycle frame powered by a small engine. Hercules used a range of engine suppliers over the next few years, including Bark, Columbus, Fafnir, JAP, Ilo, Kuchen, Moser, Sachs, Sturmey-Archer and Villiers.

By the 1930s, Hercules was manufacturing a wide range of motorcycles in various engine sizes, and was enjoying considerable competition success. The firm struggled through World War II and overcame economic and physical damage caused by bombing to resume production in 1950. Post-war machines were at first basic, even primitive, in construction. They were cheap and aimed at the commuter market in a Germany that was desperately short of transport. More advanced models followed, and sales were good. Hercules

recovered well and produced more new models into the 1950s. These became more luxurious as the company's fortunes improved, and export success was

considerable. Holland, Belgium and Switzerland were its best export markets.

Although many new models had been introduced in rapid

succession, Hercules kept the range in production more or less unchanged until 1956. This proved a wise decision. Despite the sudden fall in sales that hit

A 200cc (12ci) Hercules twin-port, two-stroke single on display at the company stand at the Berlin Show 1933. Specification included girder forks and rigid frame.

the German market in the mid-1950s, the Nurnberg factory was considerably less vulnerable than others because it was not committed to either an expansion programme or to the costly development of new models during this critical period.

Hercules thus weathered the late 1950s downturn much better than many of its rivals, and even managed to absorb Rabeneick in 1958.

In 1966, Hercules joined the Zweirad Union. This meant that Hercules, along with the rest of the business group, was acquired by the huge Fichtel Sachs industrial empire when the latter acquired Zweirad Union in 1969.

Hercules survived as a marque within the conglomerate, while all around it there were mergers, transfers and selloffs. Fichtel Sachs' backing allowed Hercules to launch the world's first production Wankel-engined motorcycle in 1974.

Sachs itself was taken over by GKN (Guest, Keen and Nettlefold)

in 1976, and yet again Hercules survived the merger. During the late 1970s and early 1980s, Hercules developed a range of roadsters with liquid-cooled Sachs engines, including 50cc (3ci), 80cc (5ci) and a 350cc (21ci) prototype-only twin. Today, it almost exclusively builds 50cc (3ci) machines.

INDIAN SINGLE

USA 1904

In 1904, most motorcycles were still recognizably motorized bicycles, and early Indians were no exception. They did have some more progressive features, however, such as chain rather than belt drive and a carburettor instead of a surface vaporizer or wick. Lubrication was by drip feed with a sight glass, as was common at the time. The very earliest Indian machines were painted deep blue instead of the red that would become synonymous with the name; Indian Red was introduced in 1904, the last year of the bicycle-style frame.

Early Indians were easier to start than to stop. The rider had to pedal to get the machine going, but this was not especially hard. An exhaust valve lifter meant that there was negligible engine compression to overcome.

However, with minimal rear brakes and no front ones at all, and no clutch to disengage the engine, stopping could inevitably still pose serious problems.

ENGINE: 286cc aise vertical single, air-cooled
POWER: n/a
GEARBOX: fixed, via countershaft
FINAL DRIVE: chain
WEIGHT: 45kg (98lb)
TOP SPEED: 50km/h (30mph)

MOTO-RÊVE

SWITZERLAND 1904–25

Moto-Rêve supplied engines to other manufacturers as well as manufacturing its own motorcycles. Its main field of interest was V-twins, and by 1910 Moto-Rêve had a range of them on the market.

The firm entered the 1911 TT races as the M.R., and made experimental alterations to its machines for the race. They went out on the first lap, but the experience gained paid off and was incorporated into the 1912 range. This remained in production until the outbreak of World War I. Afterwards, Moto-Rêve continued to do business until 1925.

An early Moto-Reve V-twin from 1913 or so. The engine used belt drive located on the left side, while the manual pedals employed chain drive to the right side of the rear wheel. This model featured sprung front forks – an advance on earlier versions.

P&M (PANTHER)

ENGLAND 1904–68

Yorkshire-based P&M was founded in 1903 by Joah Carver Phelon and Richard Moore, the name being derived from the founders' initials.

P&M's first motorcycle was typical of the era, using bicycle frames and parts, but it was distinguished by an inclined engine and two-speed gear. The company soon made a name for itself, and with the exception of a lightweight listed for three years from 1910, this single model was to be the mainstay of the firm's output from 1907 into the 1920s.

During World War I, P&M vehicles were used for despatch riding, and immediately after the war only one model was listed. In 1922, a new design appeared. This was a 555cc (34ci) model with an inclined engine and four-speed gearbox and was the only model available in 1923. Around this time, P&M began using the Panther identity in conjunction with its sports models; eventually the firm adopted the name.

Late in 1926, the firm stole the show at Olympia with its 242cc (15ci) transverse V-twin Panthette. This was an impressive machine but was too advanced (and too expensive) for most users, so it failed to sell in any numbers.

Despite the economic conditions of the late 1920s and early 1930s, Panther continued to do well and produced a range of new models, including the Red Panther. This was essentially a remarketed Panther 250 given a distinctive identity by its red-painted fuel tank. This

range served Panther well up to the outbreak of World War II.

During the war, Panther experimented with some new ideas but did not implement them, as it was busy with military contracts. Afterwards, the range was at first very small but was gradually built up. A scooter (the Princess) was added to the range in 1959 but could do little to counter the steady decline of the firm's fortunes. Panther struggled on for a while before ceasing production in 1968.

VELOCETTE

Velocette was founded in Birmingham by a German, Johannes Gutgemann, who took the name John Taylor. He was initially a pill-maker, a business from which he moved (in wonderful nineteenth-century style) into bicycle manufacture in the early 1890s.

Around 1900, Taylor Gue (as the firm was known after William Gue joined it) was making rickshaws and powered forecars in addition to cycles. The firm took over Kelecom Motors in 1904, adopted the trade name Veloce, and promptly went bankrupt.

Veloce returned to bicycle manufacture under Gutgemann and in 1910 had another try at motorcycles. The first machine was perhaps too clever for the general market and did not sell well, but a second model achieved some success. It was marketed as a VMC (Veloce Motor Company).

The first Velocette proper was a 206cc (13ci) two-stroke produced in 1913, and despite the disruption caused by World War I

the firm managed to find solid sales afterwards. Most Velocettes used four-stroke engines, starting in 1925. Competition success came a year later in the TT, when a Velocette won by a whole 10 minutes at an average speed of 107.34km/h (66.70mph).

Also in 1926, Velocette relocated to the former premises of OK Supreme at Hall Green, which was to remain its home until the end. There, the firm turned out some classic motorcycles, including the famous KSS. The KTT, a production racing version of the KSS marketed in 1929, became a staple of the amateur competition scene for many years.

Meanwhile, Velocette also produced more utilitarian machines for the average user, and these also did well. After World War II, it was these simpler, cheaper machines that provided the firm with a steady market share. Attempts to innovate in the field generally were not successful.

The wave of Italian performance bikes coming into Britain made things difficult for Velocette, and though the firm held out for a time, it began to struggle. The final straw proved to be the

development costs associated with the Viceroy scooter.

This clever design was ahead of its time but too expensive to develop and the firm went under in 1971.

A 1954 350cc MAC with classic black paintwork pinstriped in gold. The 'fishtail' silencer was another hallmark of the Velocette marque.

AVRO

Avro is more famous for aircraft than motorcycles, but its founder, A.V. Roe, applied many of the same principles to both. He tried several times to build a motorcycle with excellent weather protection. In hindsight, it seems that what he was trying to do was re-invent the motor car.

In 1905, Roe designed a motorcycle with extra large

mudguards, and by 1913 he designed a vehicle in which the rider sat low, legs either side of a Douglas flat-twin engine. These were followed in 1922 by the Avro Mobile with low seating, full rider enclosure, a 349cc (21ci) Barr & Stroud engine, three-speed Albion gearbox and all-chain drive. The initial full enclosure on the lines of a 'bicar' was later

revised into the form of a 1950s scooter. This machine was road tested in 1926.

In the same year, Roe introduced the Ro-Monocar, which used a 343cc (20.9ci) Villiers engine, a three-speed gearbox, and shaft and worm drive to the rear wheel. He used almost full enclosure and the result was similar to the earlier Avro Mobile.

None of these designs caught on, but in 1957 another attempt saw the arrival of the Avle Bicar with a Velocette 192cc (12ci) LE engine, gearbox and rear axle. Only one was ever made, and Roe finally had to admit that being exposed to the elements was part and parcel of being a motorcyclist.

FÉE

Joseph Barter built his first motorcycle in 1902 and his work brought him into contact with the Douglas firm, which

eventually took over the design. Barter's machine was a 269cc (16ci) flat-twin mounted quite high in a bicycle frame with belt

drive and bicycle brakes. By all accounts, the machine was quiet and had little vibration, and was ideally suited to short trips about

town. It was successful enough that it went into production with Light Motors and was eventually renamed the Fairy.

MONTGOMERY

Montgomery began by making side-cars – its main business interest – though the firm did build motorcycles, enabling it to offer

complete outfits for some years.

The 1905 model had a 5hp V-twin engine and a wicker-work side-car body. The company

claimed that the side-car could be detached in two minutes, while the connections to the machine were flexible on some models, to allow them to bank for corners. In one advertisement, Montgomery showed a motorcycle with a side-car fitted on both sides, supposedly one for the wife, and

the other for the two children.

By 1911, Montgomery had moved to Coventry and was buying suitable machines or constructing them using bought-in parts in the firm's frame. After World War I, Montgomery built a range of models and created a front fork design that was sold to other manufacturers. Production was disrupted for a time due to a major fire in 1925, but went on into the 1930s with much the same models. Production was halted by World War II and did not resume.

When this 1929 model was introduced, the fashion was for inclined engines, so the 346cc (21ci) JAP engine was mounted leaning forward. It also featured a three-speed gearbox.

ZENITH

ENGLAND 1905–50

London-based Zenith launched a curious machine in 1905 – the Bicar. Its frame had a main tube running from the rear-wheel spindle along the machine, round the front wheel and back again. Below this, on each side, ran a second tube to carry the weight of rider and engine, which was hung from joints to eliminate vibration. The engine was a 3hp Fafnir with a free-engine clutch and belt drive to the rear wheel, which had a drum brake. Zenith also offered the Tricar, with a 5hp engine and two speeds, both of which were soon options for the Bicar.

The Bicar and Tricar were somewhat strange, but Zenith's founder, Freddie W. Barnes, also patented a more practical device, the Gradua Gear system, in 1907. This combined a variable engine pulley with movement of the rear wheel to maintain correct belt tension. The system used a series of rods connected to a single handle so that the gear could be altered while on the move. So useful would this prove in hill climbs that some clubs prohibited Zenith machines from their events, and the firm profited from this with its 'barred' trademark.

The Bicar was redesigned in more conventional form. Called the Zenette, it retained the Gradua Gear system. After the firm moved to a location close to Brooklands racing circuit, Barnes used his Zenette to set the first record for the Test Hill early in 1909.

From 1910, the entire vehicle was much more conventional, and also more saleable. The Zenette continued to be offered for that year, and the 1911 range also included the Zenith Gradua with single or V-twin JAP engines. More models appeared for 1913, and these were much revised for 1914. The power units were now all JAP twins.

During 1914, the firm moved to Middlesex, and production resumed after World War I with the JAP twin models. Its involvement in sport did not cease, and in 1928 a JAP-powered Zenith set a motorcycle world speed record at over 200km/h (124mph).

However, Zenith did not do so well in the marketplace. In 1930, the firm was taken over by Writer's, a large London dealer, which listed a reduced range for 1931. All Zenith machines at this time had JAP engines, but as the range expanded once again, Blackburne engines saw use as well for a few years.

Zenith continued producing until the World War II, but afterwards only one model was produced and Zenith quietly faded away.

DEI

ITALY 1906–14 AND 1934–66

Umberto Dei's firm started out making bicycles and moved into the powered market in 1906 with a four-stroke, single-cylinder machine using the conventional heavy bicycle frame.

Production was halted by the outbreak of World War I and resumed in the early 1930s with a range of lightweight motorcycles powered by 100cc (6ci) Sachs engines. The range expanded to include larger models with Villiers and JAP engines.

After World War II, Dei worked with Garelli and used their Mosquito engine as an attachment for bicycles and later to power a moped. Motorcycles up to 150cc (9ci) were powered by Sachs engines.

FRERA

ITALY 1906–36 AND 1949–60

The first Frera machine, marketed in 1906, featured a 500cc (31ci) engine, mounted inclined to the line of the downtube in a simple loop frame. Better models soon followed, including a massive 1144cc (70ci) V-twin, and Frera became involved in competitions around Italy.

During World War II, Frera machines served in solo and sidecar forms, with sidecar combinations often used as ambulances. Afterwards, the firm had a good range in production, all of which sold in large numbers.

Frera did well in competition, which buoyed up sales until around 1930, but after that the firm lost a lot of ground to Moto Guzzi.

Despite a solid 1935 model, production ceased in 1936. It resumed in 1949 with a range of small two-strokes using both bought-in engines and some of Frera's own design.

At this time, however, Frera was a small firm on the fringe of the market and demand declined. Production therefore ceased a second time.

GARABELLO

ITALY 1906–29

Francesco Garabello was an early pioneer in the development of the motorcycle. He never made a great deal of money from his work, but this seems to have been very much a secondary consideration: he was driven more by the desire to make progress.

Garabello's first motorcycles used a bicycle frame and forks. They were driven by single-cylinder engines of various sizes with belt drive to the rear wheel. It was obvious that this was a rather crude arrangement and Garabello worked for some years on ways to improve upon it.

After World War I, Garabello set about incorporating his ideas into new designs. His new model for the 1920s was totally different to his pre-war efforts and was powered by an in-line, four-cylinder, water-cooled engine with a capacity of 1 litre (61ci). This drove back to a gearbox and from there by shaft to the rear wheel, and this substantial assembly went into a suitably sturdy frame with girder forks and fixtures to suit.

This machine was too expensive for the Italian market, so few were sold but nevertheless Garabello produced an even more innovative design later in the decade. This had a 175cc (11ci) single-cylinder engine with a shaft-driven rotary valve in the cylinder head, water-cooling and shaft final drive. This costly exercise did not garner major commercial success and the firm ceased trading in 1929.

This Garabello's water-cooled, single-cylinder 175cc (11ci) engine featured shaft drive to the rotary valve in the cylinder head, and shaft final drive.

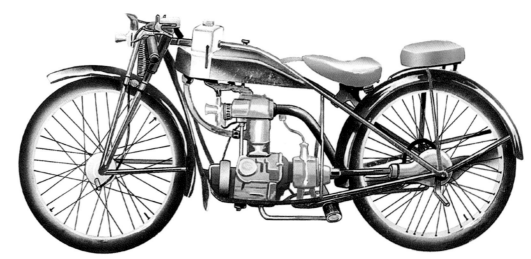

HARLEY-DAVIDSON SILENT GRAY FELLOW

Harley-Davidson's original machines were all finished in black. In 1906, a Renault grey, with carmine pin-striping, was offered as an option. The name Silent Gray Fellow reflected both the paint job and the unusually effective silencer. Engine size started at 405cc (25ci) and increased to 565cc (35ci) in 1906. This engine stayed in production until 1918.

The original machine had a bicycle-type frame but this was soon changed to the loop frame and the final drive was changed from belt to chain. The Silent Gray fellow featured electric ignition and gravity-feed lubrication.

ENGINE: 405cc (24ci) aise vertical single, air-cooled
POWER: n/a
GEARBOX: direct drive
FINAL DRIVE: belt
WEIGHT: n/a
TOP SPEED: 80km/h (50mph)

At its inception, the Silent Gray Fellow was obviously a powered-bicycle type machine. Continual developments turned it into a true motorcycle and the pedals disappeared.

DOT

Dot, whose name has been claimed to mean 'Devoid Of Trouble', was founded in Manchester by Harry Reed. The first machine was powered by a Peugeot engine, though JAP and Precision engines were also used. For several years after 1915, only JAP engines were used.

Dots were successful in early competition, winning the twin-cylinder class of the 1908 TT, and

Harry Reed himself raced for many years. Road machines were fairly typical for the times and developed steadily. The post-World War II range was powered by JAPs, which were joined by Blackburne engines in 1923.

Harry Reed left the firm in the mid-1920s and for a while only a small range was produced, expanding slightly but then contracting as the Depression bit.

Motorcycle production ceased after 1932, though Dot remained in business doing other things.

After World War II, Dot produced a three-wheeled motorcycle truck with a small Villiers engine. This led to a new range of road bikes, followed by trials and scrambling machines. In 1957, the range was expanded by the addition of Dot-Vivi mopeds. However, conditions in the industry in the 1960s led to

a shrinking range. After 1968, machines were supplied in kit form only. When Villiers engines became unavailable, Dot turned to Minarelli for the last few years of construction. Small numbers of bikes were produced until 1977, when a final experiment with a Villiers-type machine was attempted. After that, Dot focused on making shock absorbers for cars and motorcycles.

DOUGLAS

William Douglas was in the foundry business from 1882 and moved into motorcycle production only in 1907. This was

One of Douglas's last machines, the 1953 MkV model. It was not a lack of good products that brought Douglas down but a combination of lack of capital and the occasional poor business decision.

more of an attempt to save his existing business from financial difficulties than the exploitation of a new opportunity, but it

was successful all the same.

Douglas had a difficult career. The firm first ran into financial trouble in 1925 after a massive tax demand, and was then threatened by a fire just two years later. It was sold as a result of family feuds in 1931 to become Douglas Motors Ltd, but went broke in 1933 and was reconstituted as William Douglas Bristol Ltd.

The firm was again in serious financial trouble when it was bought out by the British Aircraft Company in 1936 and became Aero Engines Ltd. After World War

II, it had a new name, Douglas Kingswood Ltd, but it ran out of money and went into receivership, before being rescued by Charterhouse Investment Trust in 1948 as Douglas Sales and Service. This was taken over in 1956 by Westinghouse Brake and Signal, and all motorcycle production ceased in 1957. Douglas then managed to reincarnate itself again, this time as an importer of scooters – but that's another story.

The Douglas motorcycle story starts with a rather primitive little machine called the Fée, or Fairy, designed by John Joseph Barter and built for him by Douglas. The Fairy failed to achieve commercial success and Barter's firm went under. Douglas took Barter on as works manager of a new Douglas motorcycle division, which made an updated version of the Fairy.

Douglas struggled to make many sales in 1907. However, by 1910 marketplace conditions had improved, along with the machine, though it remained very basic. Douglas' sales improved steadily over the next few years and were put to use as despatch bikes during the World War I.

Douglas did better in the early 1920s and produced a string of good machines, of which the 1923 overhead-valve RA was the most popular. Douglases were very popular dirt-track machines, and dirt-track racing was something of a craze in the late 1920s and early 1930s. However, Douglas was struggling against financial and internal problems and did not achieve the success it might have. The firm went broke again despite track success.

There was a resurgence of interest in Douglases with the adoption of transverse engine location in the 1935 Endeavour.

Interest did not equate to sales this time. In 1946, Douglas had yet another attempt with the T35. It was good, but not enough to save the company. Things went steadily downhill and Douglas turned to making Vespas under licence. In 1957, Douglas ran out of lives and faded from the scene.

EXCELSIOR

USA 1907–31

The Excelsior Motor Manufacturing & Supply Company of Chicago, Illinois was not connected in any way with the British firm named Excelsior, or with the much smaller US firm of the same name. The US Excelsior used the American-X badge on machines destined for the UK market until 1921, after which it badged them as Super-X at home and abroad.

The first Excelsior was typical of the time: a bicycle frame and forks fitted with a small engine. Larger engines, some of them V-twins, appeared from 1910 onwards. In 1914, the British Triumph Junior model joined the Excelsior range under licence.

Excelsior' V-twins competed with Indian machines from 1911 onwards. In 1912, an Excelsior was timed at 160km/h (100mph) on a board track near Los Angeles, California. Other successes followed, using machines based on stock ones with tuned engines, open exhausts and stripped of all non-essentials. By 1915, they were listed as 'Big Valve' racers due to the size of both inlet and exhaust valves.

After World War I, the range expanded and new technology was implemented, such as a new trailing-link front fork. Precedence was given to production of bikes intended to compete with Harley-Davidson and Indian models.

Excelsior experimented with V-twins with overhead camshafts for racing purposes. The potential of these was never realized because a team rider was killed in practice at their first outing. After this setback, interest and development flagged.

In 1925, Excelsior introduced the Super-X, featuring unit construction of its V-twin engine and three-speed gearbox. Primary drive was by a train of three helical gears, so the engine continued to turn in its normal direction, which was important for the lubrication of its internals. The whole unit went into a duplex frame and a return was made to leading-link front forks.

The Super-X was a handsome machine and the stock model was soon followed by a factory racing version with an overhead-valve engine for 1926, which had some successes before the firm turned more to hill climbs. The Super-X was restyled in 1929, but in 1931 it sank in that the Depression was going to hurt the motorcycle industry badly, and the firm turned its attention to other endeavours.

The earliest Excelsiors were singles. This is a 1915 V-twin with the cylinders set at 45 degrees. The model also featured all-chain drive through a three-speed gearbox.

TRUMP

ENGLAND 1907–23

Frank A. McNab, the founder of Trump, set a one-hour record of over 77km (48 miles) at Brooklands in 1909. His company used JAP engines, which is why

Trump bikes are sometimes referred to as Trump-JAPs. Better machines appeared in 1910 and were further developed until 1915.

Wartime disruption prevented Trump from doing much until 1921, at which time the firm was known as Trump Motors Ltd, still using JAP engines.

Production lasted only two years, during which several machines were marketed. McNab retired early in 1923 and Trump closed down.

DIAMOND

D.H. & S. Engineering manufactured the Diamond bicycle in Wolverhampton, and entered the motorcycle industry in 1908 with a four-machine range. At this time, the firm became Dorsett, Ford & Mee, or D.F. & M. All of the firm's motorcycles used FN engines. Two were singles, two were V-twins. All were long, low designs of otherwise conventional format for the time.

A more advanced model appeared at the end of 1912, and this was further developed in 1913. After this, the design remained unchanged for a time, and a new model joined it in 1915. A third model, which was powered by a JAP engine, arrived in 1916.

The firm entered the TT several times, but achieved little. New models continued to appear, using Villiers, Blackburne and JAP engines, and later a Barr & Stroud and a Bradshaw. The line shrank in the late 1920s and production ceased temporarily in 1928.

In 1930, a 247cc (15ci) two-stroke design was marketed, and this was joined by others, including two fitted with the ever-popular JAP engines.

However, the range was back to one model by 1933 and afterwards the firm turned to manufacturing trailers and milk-floats.

SCOTT

The first Scott motorcycle was built in 1908 in Bradford. This machine and its successors until 1930 used a patented frame, which changed little in the intervening time. It was powered by a 333cc (20ci) liquid-cooled, two-stroke, parallel-twin-cylinder engine, for which Scott became famous. This engine was patented in 1904, and was not the only innovation to come out of the Scott company.

Alfred Angas Scott was responsible for many important inventions in the motorcycling world. By 1897 he had patented several devices, including a form of calliper brake, a fully triangulated frame, rotary induction valves, unit engine construction, honeycomb radiators and the first motorcycle kick-start.

In events ranging from hill climbs and trials to the 1212 and 1913 Isle of Man Senior TT, Scotts achieved considerable competition success. The TT wins coincided with a move to Shipley in 1912 and continued commercial success.

Alfred Scott died, aged 48, in 1922, and his loss was keenly felt. Scott began to lose ground to firms making more powerful four-stroke machines, and in 1931 the firm went into receivership. It was saved for a time by the Liverpool industrialist Albert Reynolds, but remained underfunded. Some good designs were tabled, but scarce resources meant that production of them was minimal or did not happen at all.

Scott clung on, attracting some interest with a fast 596cc (36ci) Clubman's Special in 1938. However, the outbreak of war prevented this project from achieving success. After the war, the financial situation was impossible and production at Shipley ceased.

The rights to Scott designs were bought by Matt Holder, who also bought up bits and pieces of Royal Enfield, Velocette and Vincent. Holder's firm built small numbers of Scott-designed Flying Squirrels and even produced a revised design. A new model, named the Swift, was announced but never passed the prototype stage. Other designs followed, none of them very successful. Scott engines were still being used when Holder's firm, Aerco, built its last machines. Production ceased in 1979.

WILKINSON

The Wilkinson Sword Company is famous mainly for blades – originally for combat and later for shaving. However, it did experiment in other areas, including motorcycles.

The original design, created in 1908, was a four-cylinder military scouting machine. When military orders did not materialize, the machine was redesigned for the civilian market and named the Wilkinson TAC (Touring Auto Car). Intriguingly, it had a steering wheel instead of handlebars.

Redesigned in 1911, the machine went out as the TMC (Touring Motor Cycle). However, before the TMC could prove itself, World War I broke out and production ceased.

The final incarnation of the TMC's engine was used in the Deemster car.

The world needs more quirky, original projects like the wonderful but rather impractical Wilkinson TAC (Touring Auto Car). Some versions went so far as to use a steering wheel rather than handlebars.

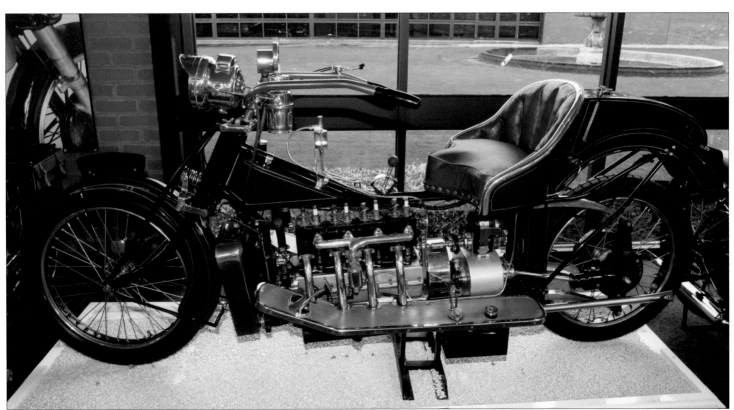

CALTHORPE

Calthorpe was owned by George Hands in Birmingham. The first Calthorpe motorcycle appeared in 1909. It was powered by a White & Poppe engine and was built by the Minstrel & Rea Cycle Co. of Birmingham. It was followed by new models that used Precision engines from 1911 onwards.

The firm produced motorcycles through World War I and added a new model to the range in 1922. This was a 350cc (21ci) two-stroke and, from 1923, was available as a sidecar combination.

Blackburne, Villiers and JAP engines were used from the early 1920s, and in 1925 the Sports model went on sale with Calthorpe's own engine aboard. In 1929, the best-known Calthorpe, the Ivory Calthorpe, appeared; and in 1930 this was the only model available. New and updated versions reached the market throughout the decade, but sales were in decline. The company also made a 'Speedway Special' racer Camden.

In 1937, Calthorpe was marketed exclusively by Pride & Clarke of London, and with a change of colour came a change of name. However, the Red Calthorpe did not achieve a revival in sales figures and the firm went into liquidation.

Calthorpe was bought by Douglas, which was based in Bristol and moved production there. A three-model range powered by Matchless engines was announced for 1939, but the war prevented many from being made.

After the war, when the Douglas factory returned to civilian production, the Calthorpe reappeared as Calthorpe-DMW using a 122cc (7ci) Villiers engine. This led to the DMW range in 1950.

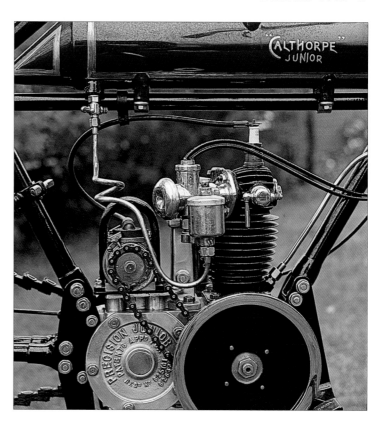

Detail of the Calthorpe Junior's engine. Although it gained a two-speed gearbox from the end of World War II, the machine retained belt drive for a few years longer.

CLYNO

Northamptonshire-based Frank and Ailwyn Smith exhibited their first motorcycles in 1909 and moved to Wolverhampton the following year, taking over the former Stevens works. Clyno marketed an improved version in 1911 and again in 1912, producing a small range of just one or two machines most years.

In 1915, the firm produced a two-stroke sidecar combination for military use as a machine-gun carrier. Some examples were sold to Russia.

After World War II, a two-model range was exhibited in 1919. However, financial issues disrupted production plans and the firm made its last motorcycles in 1923. After this, it concentrated on producing cars.

A Clyno paired up with a rather minimalistic sidecar to create a machine-gun carrier. Combinations of this type were used by various armed forces to make clumsy weapons mobile.

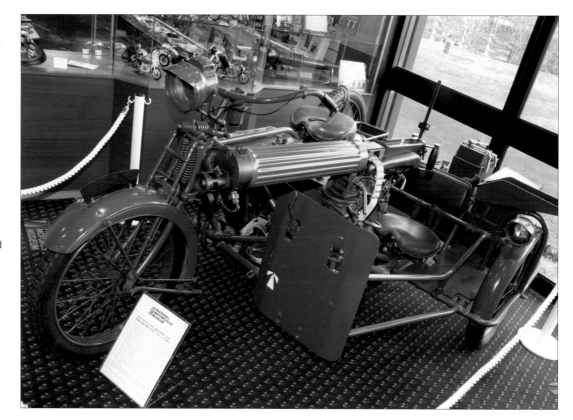

DELLA FERRERA

Founded in 1909 in Turin by Federico Della Ferrera and his brothers, Della Ferrera set out to build high-quality machines. The firm was well organized and achieved good success in the marketplace and on the racetrack.

After World War I, Della Ferrera listed a range of singles and V-twins, which was continually developed using experience gained in competition. In 1921, Federico created a bike for the express purpose of breaking records and wining races. This machine was based on his 494cc (30ci) V-twin, though with several modifications. It was a success, setting records at 140km/h (87mph) and doing well in many 1920s Italian events.

The 1930s were a difficult decade for industry in many countries, and changes in the

Italian taxation system were reflected in the motorcycle trade. Smaller machines were popular early on, but as the tax was removed from larger capacities, these began to make up a larger segment of the market.

At the same time, import duties increased so that sales of other European makes suffered. This was even more obvious in 1935 when, to protect the Italian industry, the tariff rates were considerably increased. Many firms that had used imported engines from Britain for their Italian motorcycles turned to home producers or began to make these items themselves.

By 1939, Della Ferrera had lost much of its market share with only three models in production. The firm turned to war work during World War II, but did not make a return to the motorcycle business afterwards and went bankrupt.

One of the earliest Della Ferrera machines, featuring a flat tank and a side-valve engine.

GILERA

ITALY 1909–PRESENT

Guiseppe Gilera took a job with Milan-based Bianchi in 1902 at the age of 15. He later worked for Moto-Reve and Bucher and Zeda. Along the way, he learned a vast amount about motor vehicles and engineering. Gilera also became a racer, doing especially well in hill-climb events. His dream, however, was to make motorcycles.

In 1909, aged 22, Gilera produced his first model, a 317cc (19ci) four-stroke of unusual design. Next came a V-twin and after that began Gilera's famous line of 500cc (31ci) singles.

After World War I, the demand for motorcycles increased and Gilera opened a new factory close to where the Monza Park was to be constructed. His first model from the new factory, the Turismo, appeared in 1920. A second model appeared in 1935, along with sport versions of both bikes. A new engine design, the Gran Sport, appeared in 1929 and remained in production until 1931.

Gilera was not only one of Italy's largest manufacturers in the late 1920s and 1930s, but was also highly successful in trials and long-distance races. The ultimate goal was the International Grand Prix racing scene and, to that end, the firm acquired the four-cylinder Rondine racing design in 1936. The design was updated and went on to break records and win many races over the next few years.

At the outbreak of World War II, Gilera rivalled Moto Guzzi as Italy's largest motorcycle producer. Its first wartime model, the LTE, was poor but was followed by a sidecar combination, the Marte (Mars), which was significantly better. After the war ended, Gilera continued to dominate the scene. Among its releases were the 1939-designed Nettuno and Saturno machines; the latter is one of the best bikes to come out of Gilera.

A string of impressive bikes was accompanied by race success, though in 1957 Gilera ceased Grand Prix racing for cost reasons. Its return in the mid-1960s did not result in the same glory as previous years, and by now the firm were aiming more at the trials and motocross fields.

The downturn in the motorcycle industry in the late 1960s hit Gilera hard, despite its best efforts. In 1968, the receivers were called in and a few months later Piaggio bought out the firm. This led to a resurgence in the 1970s, with new models and a string of competition successes.

In the 1980s, Gilera was once more at the forefront of Italian motorcycle development, producing some excellent new machines. When Piaggio announced in 1993 that it was curtailing manufacture at the Arcore factory, the home of Gilera for so long, most observers thought the end had come. However, this has proven not to be the case and the Gilera story continues.

The 125cc GFR SP, launched in 1992, was capable of 160km/h (100mph) and could mount a serious challenge against competing designs from Aprilia and Cagiva.

PIERCE

USA 1909–13

Buffalo-based Pierce Arrow, a car-manufacturing firm, produced the first four-cylinder motorcycles to be built in the USA. Pierce machines were distinctive and aimed at the top end of the market; the firm made it quite clear that they were not inclined to compete on price.

Pierce's four-cylinder engine was based on a design used by Belgian firm FN, though Pierce's machines were clearly aimed at the American market and well adapted to it. The basic design was updated in 1910, when it got a 2-speed gearbox, and a new model hit the market the same year.

Few further developments were made and the same two machines remained on sale until 1913. They were expensive, which limited their appeal, though those who could afford them liked them. However, production ceased in 1913 when it became clear that the project was not going to make a profit or even recoup its investment.

CHAPTER TWO

INVENTING DREAMS

1910–1925

By the second decade of the twentieth century, motorcycle design was advancing in leaps and bounds, echoing the improvements in engine design, and moving away from the bicycle design. Early engines used very primitive ignition and carburating technologies – an external burner heating a 'hot tube' that protruded into the cylinder was the first ignition technology, with electric spark ignition following soon after. Getting petrol mixed with air then introducing it into the cylinder was initially achieved by simply drawing the inlet airflow over a small bowl of fuel. Heating the bowl, or using a material wick improved the evaporation process, but the biggest advance here was the 'spray carburettor'.

This used a venturi to reduce pressure in the airflow, and draw fuel through a nozzle to be sprayed into the inlet tract.

Mechanically, most engines were still 'direct drive', that is, the crankshaft was linked to the rear wheel, with no means of disengaging drive to stop or pull away smoothly. There was only one gear too, so speeds were necessarily restricted. World War I brought a host of advances, though – reliable, high-performance machines literally being a matter of life or death, and by the 1920s, gearboxes, magneto ignitions, clutches and kickstarts were all commonplace. Motorcycles began to bear much more relation to the modern motorbike.

Left: The weird-looking Neracar, with its 348cc (21ci) Blackburne side-valve engine, had a conventional three-speed gear box. These curiosities were produced first in the United States and then in England in the 1920s.

AJS & MATCHLESS

The stories of AJS and Matchless, which began as separate entities, are intertwined, and for this reason they are treated as a single marque here. For the midpart of their history, they came together to form AMC, though afterwards they went their separate ways once more.

In 1900, Joe Stevens and his sons became involved in powered transport. In 1910, their first AJS motorcycle appeared. Its name came from the initials of the elder brother, Albert John. This early AJS

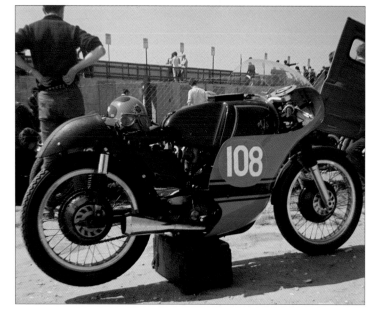

The overhead-cam 349cc 7R was another AJS racer. It won the 1961, 62 and 63 Junior TT and spawned a production version closely based on the original race machine.

was a conventional 292cc (18ci) machine. It was given a bigger engine for 1912 and was joined by a 631cc (39ci) V-twin that became popular for sidecar work.

AJS machines gradually improved, and took both first and second place in the 1914 Junior TT, with two in the first six. AJS rode out the war years with a minimal range and returned in the 1920s with a new range. In the 1920 Junior TT, the six AJS machines were favourites to win, but reliability proved a factor: five

returned before halfway. The sixth, though, was a runaway winner despite being pushed for the last few miles of the race. Improved reliability paid off in the next two years' races, and the AJS marque remained a strong competitor thereafter.

The 'Big Port' sporting range made its debut in 1923, and the firm diversified into wireless production for a few years. A contract to manufacture bodies for the Clyno Nine car was also forthcoming and ran until 1929, when Clyno disappeared. The AJS bike range continually developed during this time.

In 1930, AJS was making commercial vehicle bodies and the AJS Nine car alongside a motorcycle range that won the 1930 TT lightweight class. However, by the following year, the Depression was taking its toll, and the firm moved into other market segments to try to attract a new customer base. This was not a success, and in 1931 the firm closed down. However, this was not the end of the line for the AJS name, which was bought by Matchless.

Matchless was founded in 1899 by Harry and Charlie Collier. They took the familiar route of making bicycles and then adding an engine, which was initially mounted above the front wheel. Early machines used MMC engines in a more sensible position, hanging from the downtube.

The V4 was a water-cooled 495cc (30ci) supercharged machine first produced in 1939. It was capable of 217km/h (135mph) but changes in racing rules after the war prevented it from competing.

Matchless machines were successful in early competition and the range gradually expanded. Power was supplied by Antoine, JAP and White & Poppe engines during this period.

The Matchless range improved steadily, using various engines. Over time, most, and then all, machines became V-twins with JAP or MAG power. This situation persisted through World War I, and immediately afterwards buyers had the choice of the two engine makes, rigid frame or rear suspension, and solos or sidecar forms.

A Blackburne-powered single joined the range in 1923 with a 348cc (21ci) Blackburne engine, and the firm experimented with a light touring car design. The car came to naught, but the motorcycle range continued to increase until the mid-1920s.

The 1930 Silver Arrow was an innovative tourer designed specifically to be quiet and smooth. It was not very exciting, but it was not intended to be. The Silver Hawk, following a year later, had better performance. Production ran on through the Depression years.

After the AJS buyout, it took a couple of years to rationalize the range. The practice of using Matchless engines for most machines began in 1933, and in 1935 real collaboration began with the Matchless G3, which was available with the badges of both marques. The AJS Model 16 also appeared in 1935, and these models were followed a year later by a larger range. Matchless engines were also used by a range of other clients, including Morgan cars. In 1939, the G3 was put into large-scale production for military use and was updated in 1941 to the G3L. It was a success in its wartime role. The immediate post-war range consisted of two machines for each marque, all singles.

After the war, AJS and Matchless machines were built in the same factory and were very similar. However, the firm ran separate racing teams and promoted the idea of competition between the two brands to maintain marque loyalty. Slight differences were maintained between the two marques, such as different seats and silencers.

The range created in the late 1940s remained in production for several years with few real changes. At the time, the combination of AJS and Matchless was using the AMC identity, and took over Norton in 1952, though Norton production remained separate.

The first major change came in 1956, with a revamp of the road range and the addition of new models. These included road and racing machines and took the firm into the 1960s. The range then continued to evolve, and from the early 1960s some Norton parts began to be used, a practice that became increasingly common.

However, in the mid-1960s, AMC was struggling financially, and in 1966 the majority of the range was dropped. The one new 1966 model (the Matchless G85CS scrambler) remained in production until 1969 and some models continued under new ownership.

AMC closed down in 1969 and the factory was demolished, but both the AJS and Matchless names endured.

The AJS badge was used in 1967 by Norton Villiers for a small range. When NVT was created, Fluff Brown created the small FB-AJS range, which ran until 1981 and reappeared in 1987 with a resurrected AJS Stormer design.

Matchless reappeared under Les Harris, who built the Triumph Bonneville. He added a 494cc (30ci) single called the G80, with a British frame, Italian forks and Austrian engine. Sales were not good, and between 1990 and 1993 it was supplied to special order only.

SPRING

Belgium-based Spring (La SA des Ateliers Système Spring) produced unusual multi-cylinder machines in small numbers. The 1910 model had two or four cylinders set across the frame in a 'V' format, with the drive set back and turned to run to the rear wheel. Spring's machines were intended for sidecar work rather than solo use, and further differed from the usual specification of the day in having both front and rear suspension.

Spring continued to demonstrate an interest in suspension at the 1920 Brussels Show, when the firm revealed a new suspension system for its models, using a duplex cradle frame. Spring established a reputation for its type of layout and construction, and, for promotional purposes, then undertook some tests and trials

However, as the market moved towards more traditional motorcycles for sidecar and solo use, Spring ceased to manufacture its unusual machines. It remained in business until 1939 as a general mechanical firm.

ZENITH GRADUA

Most early motorcycles used direct belt drive from the engine to the rear wheel, which meant a fixed ratio and no means of changing this for hills. Adjustable engine pulleys helped, but they required a stop at the foot of each hill to lower the ratio, and another at the top to raise it again. Things improved when Freddie Barnes devised the Gradua Gear, which was fitted to the otherwise conventional Zenith Gradua.

The supposedly infinitely variable gear actually worked from 3:1 to 9:1. This offered such a huge advantage in competition that the marque was banned by some organizers. This turned out to be fine publicity for Zenith and soon led to its 'barred' advertisements and trademark.

ENGINE: 499cc (30ci) sv vertical single, 85x88mm, air-cooled
POWER: n/a
GEARBOX: variable hand change
FINAL DRIVE: belt
WEIGHT: 82kg (180lb)
TOP SPEED: n/a

BENELLI

The Benelli brothers started out in 1911 in the Adriatic town of Pesaro, operating a workshop that repaired automobiles, motorcycles and firearms. Benelli soon began to do a little manufacturing work, starting with aircraft and car components. World War I provided a ready market for their business, and afterwards the deficit of cheap transport created a good market for Benelli's latest product.

The first Benelli foray into the market was a 98cc (6ci) two-stroke auxiliary engine designed to be fitted above the front wheel of a conventional bicycle. It proved too powerful for the frame, so Benelli designed a more robust bicycle

A late 1970s 125cc (8ci) Benelli trail bike, produced during the period after the de Tomaso takeover. It was powered by a single-cylinder, piston-port, two-stroke engine.

frame, which became the first Benelli motorcycle.

The youngest of the Benelli brothers, known as Tonino, became a racing hero. Starting with the 1923 Italian Grand Prix at Monza, Tonino went on to score victory after victory. He then acted as a factory test rider, but was killed during a testing session in 1937.

By the mid-1930s, Benelli was one of the famous big five, or Pentarchia, of the Italian bike industry. The others were Garelli, Moto Guzzi, Gilera and Bianchi, and together they were a powerful force in competition. Joining the supercharger revolution sweeping Europe, they produced some awesome machines, but World War II intervened and afterwards superchargers were banned from major competition.

The war also damaged Benelli directly. The Pesaro factory was

destroyed, delaying Benelli's return to the marketplace. At the same time, one of the brothers, Guiseppe, left after a dispute, to found the Motobi company.

Benelli fought back all the same, entering races with their pre-war models and achieving some good successes. Star rider Dario Ambrosini was killed in 1951, practising for the French GP, and Benelli withdrew from the race scene until 1959.

Meanwhile, production was re-established in the late 1940s, and by 1950 a range of pre-war models was back in production, along with a new 98cc (6ci) two-stroke. A year later, it gained a 125cc (8ci) engine and was then renamed the Leoncino (little lion), Another important Benelli of the early 1950s was the 250cc (15ci) overhead valve Leonessa (Lioness) parallel twin. Together with the

Leoncino, this machine had a long and successful production run throughout the 1950s.

The year 1959 was important for Benelli. First, the firm returned to racing with an updated version of the long-running double overhead-cam single; secondly, production started on a brand new 172cc (10ci) overhead-valve unit single, available in either Turismo or Sport guises.

In 1961, Benelli celebrated its 50th anniversary, and after the death of Guiseppe Benelli, Motobi and Benelli merged their concerns. Motobi models continued to be marketed for many years. Racing success improved throughout the decade, impressive results helped to protect the firm from decline.

Benelli was taken over by the Argentinian industrialist, Alejandro de Tomaso, in late 1971. At that time, the firm had a very mixed

range, and de Tomaso set out to rationalize it. New models during this period showed a distinct Japanese influence.

The recession of the 1980s hurt Benelli like everyone else, and another sell-off occurred. After a period of making 50cc (3ci) machines for the domestic market, the firm was sold yet again.

This time, Benelli began making scooters, but in 1999 it was announced that a four-cylinder superbike was planned to appear early in the new millennium.

Cornering a 231cc Benelli Two-Fifty-Four with the four-into-two exhaust system clearly visible. The engine for this machine came from Moto Guzzi, which was also part of the de Tomaso empire.

DAYTON

One of many firms to set up in the early years of the century, Dayton did not survive World War I. The marque was created when the Davis Sewing Machine Co. of

Dayton, Ohio began to assemble machines from bought-in parts.

It began with a conventional F-head V-twin engine, and then in 1913 began to use the Spacke De

Luxe V-twin built in Indianapolis, Indiana, which went into a loop frame with trailing-link forks.

Improved versions were created for 1914 and 1915, and the later

engines were a built-in unit with a two-speed gearbox. However, this was not enough to make the marque really competitive and production ceased in 1917.

HAZLEWOOD

The JAP-engined Hazlewood appeared in 1911. It featured three-speed gearing and, unusually for the time, a decent set of brakes. A year later, the Colonial model, intended for use in South Africa, appeared.

In 1913, a second model appeared. This was a twin, also powered by a JAP engine and available in two versions. This line continued into 1916, though the single gained a more powerful engine.

After the end of the war, Hazlewood had one model in production for 1920, a 654cc (40ci) V-twin fitted with its own three-speed gearbox. In 1921, a 976cc (60ci) V-twin was added to the range. By 1922, all models

were using chain drive and a pair of JAP-engined singles were added to the range. The following year, only two models were listed, and only one in 1924, the final year of production.

JEFFERSON

The Jefferson name appeared on motorcycles manufactured from 1913 onwards. Prior to this, machines were sold under the name of Waverly, or Kenzler-Waverly. One 1912 model was called the P.E.M. in honour of Percy E. Mack, who designed its engine, spring frame and fork. This multiplicity of names was not uncommon on the American motorcycle scene, particularly before the outbreak of World War I.

The confusion stems from the fact that the machines were built by the Kenzler-Waverly Motorcycle Company of Cambridge and the Waverly Manufacturing Company of Jefferson, while Mack engines were built by the Universal Machinery Company of Milwaukee.

Jeffersons used a well-designed loop frame, with pivoted-fork rear suspension and leading-links at the front. The rear suspension was controlled by a leaf spring fixed to the seat tube and connected to the fork by a short link that ran to the top of the fork sub-frame. In this way, it was not unlike a modern monoshock. Braking was solely on the back wheel, as the dirt roads of the USA of the time made front brakes a bad idea.

Jeffersons were good machines that performed well. However, they were expensive and could not compete with cheaper machines or with the early motor cars then emerging.

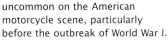

Sold under various names, this machine was available in 1914 under the Jefferson marque. It was quite advanced, with front and rear suspension, chain drive and a gearbox.

LEVIS

Birmingham-based Levis produced their first machine in 1911, a small two-stroke powerful enough to carry a passenger. Designed by Howard Newey, it was marketed first as the Baby, but later as the Popular, which was abbreviated to Levis Pop.

The Pop was very simple and was indeed very popular, especially for new riders. Variants included a ladies' model and a more powerful version marketed for 1914. Indeed, as late as 1920, the Pop was the only Levis model in production.

A 247cc (15ci) TT model appeared in 1921, trading on the fact that Levis had taken the first three places in the 1920 Junior 250cc (15ci) TT. Their machine was second in 1921 and won again in 1922. It also won the French and Belgian TTs that year.

The Pop remained in production until 1924, but more complex variants were added to the range. These had a gearbox and a much larger engine.

By the 1930s, Levis machines were using a four-stroke engine, and production ran on in this format until 1940.

MARTIN

When Harry Martin set up a motorcycle manufacturer in 1910, he was already well known on the competition scene. His first machines were powered by JAP engines. There was a tourer and, predictably, a racing machine.

A bigger racer appeared in 1912, and by 1913 Martin was listing six models. A slimmed-down range was marketed into World War I, when production dropped off. It began again in 1920 with a MAG- and later JAP-powered range. Martin entered the 1921 TT and seemed to be doing well, but production again dropped off and the marque faded from the scene.

MILITAIRE

Militaire started out in 1910 in Cleveland, Ohio, creating a rather strange vehicle based on a car rather than a bicycle. It had a pressed-steel chassis with long, leading-link front suspension. It was steered with a wheel rather than handlebars, and its wooden-spoke wheels were supplemented by small side wheels to support the vehicle while it was stationary.

It was marketed in 1911 with a fairly standard F-head engine. This was updated in 1912 and again in 1913, achieving its classic format with an in-line, four-cylinder engine built-in unit with clutch, and a three-speed gearbox with a car-type, hand-change lever. The hub steering, wooden wheels and stabilizers remained, but a set of handlebars replaced the steering wheel and the fuel tank was repositioned over the engine.

The design was a commercial failure, mainly because it was marketed as a car with two wheels. Car users saw it as a curious novelty but did not buy it, while motorcycle aficionados were not impressed by its carlike features. The design was sold on and passed through several hands, changing design slightly but remaining essentially a two-wheeled car. After a name change to Miltor, it was given to the US Army for evaluation. A few were taken to Europe for trials but performed poorly. A final version (with sidecar) appeared in 1920. It, too, failed and the Militaire passed quietly away.

A later version of the curious Militaire, with handlebars rather than a steering wheel. With its outrigger wheels and hub-centre steering, the Militaire was never sure whether it was a car or a motorcycle, and was not a success in the marketplace.

NUT

Named for the initials of its home town, Newcastle-upon-Tyne, NUT had backing from the Angus Sanderson firm. From the outset, the firm was active in

competition, with manager Hugh Mason and Robert Ellis representing the firm. Ellis finished sixth in the 1912 Junior TT, using a 344cc (21ci) Moto-Rêve V-twin engine. The 1913 range used only JAP engines, and these machines had a good showing at the Junior TT. Mason had a serious accident in practice but still managed to win, and Ellis came in eighth.

After World War I, the firm moved to new premises and continued building a range of V-twins powered by its own engines, with three-speed Sturmey-Archer gearboxes. However, the firm also suffered the all-but-obligatory financial troubles.

A name change to Hugh Mason & Co. Ltd did not help, but things stabilized by 1923, when it gained

A NUT V-twin dating from 1914, the year after the firm won the Junior TT with a 345cc (21ci) machine. NUT concentrated on V-twin models and built its unusual motorcycles until 1933.

a new identity as the NUT Engine & Cycle Company. Production was reduced to one machine, a side-valve V-twin of 700cc (43ci), which was available in several specifications to meet most requirements.

In 1924, the firm benefited from heavy promotion by Maudes Motor Mart, at the time the exclusive dealer, and a range of new models was added in the late 1920s. These used JAP engines specially prepared for NUT and were equipped to a high standard, with a corresponding price tag.

Another move of premises disrupted production for 1930, but the range was back in production the year after. Some new designs were created, but these were too expensive to implement, and production of the existing range dropped steadily off until it ceased entirely in 1933.

POPE

The Pope car company built its first motorcycle under the Pope name in 1911. Before that, its motorcycle division operated as the American Cycle Manufacturing Company, which sold identical bicycles under a range of brand names. This was a common practice at the time, permitting the same manufacturer to have several outlets in the same town.

These cycle outlets provided a good route into the motorcycle sales arena since their customers were already used to the idea of two wheels and were receptive to the idea of a bicycle that did the work of pedalling for its rider. Some experience and knowledge also carried over from pedal cycles to motorbikes.

The Pope marque began with a simple F-head single with belt drive, which was joined by a V-twin in 1912. The single was basic and typical of the times, but the twin was both complex and innovative. In 1914, it was updated further with a two-speed transmission option; and a three-speed gearbox was available for 1916.

The single-speed version remained in production alongside the more complex version until 1918, when production of all models ceased.

The first Pope machine was this 1911-vintage F-head single featuring a magneto mounted in front of the engine and trailing-link forks. Drive was by belt, with pedal backup.

RUDGE

Rudge was founded in 1868, in Wolverhampton, and had been making bicycles for more than 40 years by the time its first motorcycle was produced at Coventry in 1910. Its machines were conservative in design but well made and fast.

In 1911, the firm demonstrated that it was a force to be reckoned with: a Rudge lapped Brooklands at around 107km/h (66.47mph) and covered 97.5km (60.45 miles) in one hour, the first 500cc (31ci) motorcycle ever to do so. A modest showing in the Isle of Man Senior TT that year was the beginning of a prominent race presence and led to the Multi,

which was named for its infinitely variable gears.

After the introduction of the Multi, there were few changes for well over a decade. This was partly due to World War I, but the firm's financial troubles meant that there was also little development money available. However, in the 1920s, the Multi's belt drive was looking very dated, so the Four was implemented in 1924. The name referred to both its four-valve head and its four-speed gearbox.

The Four was successful and developed over the next few years, winning the 1928 Ulster Grand Prix at a record speed of

128.87km/h (80.078mph). This gave rise to the most famous of all Rudges, the Ulster. Further racing success followed, including a notable incident when Rudges took first, second and fourth place in the Isle of Man Lightweight TT in 1931. The fourth-placed rider was Ernie Nott, who was leading by more than four minutes when a tappet lock-nut come loose on the last lap. Holding it in place with his finger, he brought the bike in to fourth place.

This was the golden age of the Rudge marque, as the firm also exported engines under the Python badge. Racing was very expensive, however, and more financial

difficulties led to Rudge being bought out by – of all people – His Master's Voice (HMV), the gramophone and radio company. HMV continued to make fine motorcycles, but there was no official involvement in racing after 1932. A private team, the Graham Walker, continued to race Rudges for a couple of years, but the glory days were passing.

In the latter days, a few new designs appeared, including a potentially useful military motorcycle, but during World War II the firm turned to war work, making wireless sets, and afterwards it did not return to making motorcycles.

RUDGE MULTI

The Rudge Multi was named for its gearing system, which worked in a simple but ingenious way. The engine and rear-wheel pulleys were each made of two flanges, intersecting as a V-form that drove the belt. If the two flanges were moved closer together, the effective diameter of the pulley increased; if they were moved further apart, the effective diameter decreased.

By a clever system of linkages, the effective diameter of the two pulleys could be varied in a way that kept the belt tension constant as one expanded and the other contracted, thereby providing the different gear ratios.

ENGINE: 499cc (30ci) ioe single, 85x88mm, air-cooled
POWER: n/a
GEARBOX: infinitely variable
FINAL DRIVE: belt
WEIGHT: n/a
TOP SPEED: n/a

Changing gear was by means of a hand lever with a very long throw. Although, theoretically, the gear ratios were infinitely variable between the limits set by the maximum and minimum diameters of the two pulleys, a set of notches in the gear-lever 'gate' meant that certain ratios could be set and held without the rider keeping his hand on the lever.

The Multi was in production from 1911 to 1922, by which time it was very dated. Its 'infinitely variable' gears did not, in fact, have a particularly immense range of ratios.

SUN

Sun started out as a bicycle manufacturer in Birmingham, and produced its first motorcycles in 1911. These were 270cc (16ci) and 590cc (36ci) Precision-engined machines. A Villiers-powered 346cc (21ci) model followed in 1913.

After World War I, Sun entered the Isle of Man TT with models powered by the 269cc (16ci) Vitesse VTS (Valveless Two-Stroke, or rotary disc-valve). Its road machines were powered by Villiers, Blackburne, JAP and Vitesse engines, ranging in capacity from 98 (6ci) to 650cc (40ci).

Motorcycle production ceased in 1932, but the Sun kept making bicycles and in 1948 introduced a 98cc (6ci) Villiers-powered Autocycle and the Sunwasp scooter. More powered machines followed for the 1950s, including motorcycles, scooters and off-roaders. All had small engines (less than 250cc/15ci) and at this time Villiers engines were used exclusively. Sun was acquired by Raleigh in 1961, and after this, bicycles only were manufactured.

Sun produced a range of workhorse two-stroke designs using engines bought in from Blackburne, JAP, Villiers and Vitesse. Early models, like this one, had pedals – fitting, for a firm that started and ended its career as a bicycle manufacturer.

VULCAAN

Cycling has always been very popular in the Netherlands, probably because the land is very flat. Vulcaan (or Vulkaan, is it is sometimes spelled) got its start making bicycles. In 1911, it produced a range of models powered by single and V-twin, side-valve Zedal engines supplied by the Swiss firm Zürcher & Lüthi.

The machines were conventional for the time, using heavy-duty bicycle parts. They featured a tubular frame, girder forks, wire wheels and belt drive, with some form of gear and minimal brakes.

Later on, Vulcaan built some engines itself using a combination of its own components and its stocks of Zedal parts. This became more of a problem as World War I continued, and the firm reverted to bicycle manufacture. After the war, Vulcaan imported motorcycles from Britain.

WOOLER

John Wooler spent his entire career creating unique motorcycle designs. The first was a two-stroke with double-ended pistons in order to avoid crankcase compression. Mounted horizontally, the engine made use of a variable-ratio belt-drive system. A form of plunger suspension was fitted both front and rear.

Next was a 1911 fore-and-aft flat-twin with a 348cc (21ci) engine mounted in-line with the frame. By 1923, this design had been updated to an overhead-valve layout. These machines, painted bright yellow and dubbed 'flying bananas', were entered in the Isle of Man TT.

In 1926, Wooler purchased the London-based P & P marque, formed in 1920 by Erling Poppe and Gilmour Packman. Where this might have led is open to speculation; in the event, the Depression forced P & P to close in 1930.

Wooler then re-emerged in 1945, this time with an unusual flat-four design. Its cylinders were stacked like a pair of bunk beds on either side of the crankcase. This was itself distinctly unconventional, but the really unique feature was the way in which the pistons were connected to the crankshaft; this featured rods, a T-beam, a master-rod and gudgeon pins. The valves were mounted in parallel to each other.

John Wooler continued experimenting, and died in 1956, an innovator to the end.

ABC

Originally founded in Surrey, near the famous Brooklands race track, to build aero engines, the All British (Engine) Co. began producing motorcycles in 1912. Head designer Granville Bradshaw agreed to produce some special parts for Les Bailey to fit to his 350cc (21ci) Douglas. These included cylinders, overhead-valve

gears, pistons and connecting rods. The resulting machine set a new kilometre record for its class, at more than 116km/h (72mph).

Also in 1912, ABC announced a new 494cc (30ci), flat-twin, overhead-valve engine, mounted in line with the frame. It was of unusual design, with the cylinders in line with one another. The following year, two ABC bikes entered the Senior TT (along with others using the ABC engine), but were forced to retire.

Things went a bit better in 1914, and ABC set new 500cc (31ci) records at Brooklands. This was followed by the

announcement of a two-model range, the TT and the Touring. The flat-twin engine was used in both bikes, but the TT version used an overhead valve while the Touring had an overhead exhaust and side inlet. Both featured chain drive and a three-speed Armstrong gearbox, all fitted in a conventional frame with leaf-sprung wheels.

During World War I, though ABC mainly produced engines for military use, it did bring a few motorcycles to market. Between 1915 and 1916, these were fitted with the ABC four-speed gate-change gearbox and spring frame – a sophisticated setup at the time.

In 1919, just after the war, the definitive ABC bike appeared. It was actually built by Sopwith Aviation, and used an overhead-valve 398cc (24ci) flat-twin engine set transversely across the frame and a built-in unit with the four-speed, gate-change gearbox. The light short-stroke engine was very advanced for the time and was mounted in an equally sophisticated, even revolutionary, machine. Orders came in thick and fast, but the bike was difficult and expensive to make, which slowed its market entry down.

In the meantime, ABC also produced the Skootamota, one of

A 1919 ABC 398cc flat-twin. Despite the machine's dated appearance, with footboards, the engine was quite advanced and was constructed in unit with the four-speed gearbox.

the best scooters of its time. Built on a simple tubular frame with no suspension, it had wire wheels with external-contracting band brakes on both. The engine sat above the rear wheel and was derived from a wartime flat-twin. The design was updated in 1920 and remained in production until ABC went under in 1923.

ABC's demise owed much to the fact that Sopwith had gone into liquidation in 1921. They had made only about 3000 motorcycles and their financial troubles dragged ABC down with them. The name survived for a time; the French Gnome & Rhone firm produced licensed ABC engines until 1925.

HENDERSON

Founded in 1912 in Detroit by Tom and William Henderson, Henderson was sold in 1917 to Ignaz Schwinn, who added the marque to his Excelsior line. The brothers remained with the group until 1919, when they left to create the Ace.

Hendersons were well suited to long-distance work. In 1913, a Henderson was ridden right around the world, the first time this had been done on two wheels. All Henderson models had an in-line four-cylinder engine set along the frame, and chain final drive. The original machine was of unusual design, with a long wheelbase and a frame that extended ahead of the engine.

This was not repeated in later models.

Even after the sale to Excelsior, Henderson motorcycles kept their basic design, with some small changes, for many years. They got a new engine in 1920 and were gradually improved with new features as dictated by trends in the marketplace.

In 1929, some more major changes were made to the engine, exhausts and general styling, creating a machine that was several years ahead of most of its competition. However, it became obvious that the Depression was going to last for many years. Production ceased in 1931 and the firm went back to making bicycles.

REGAL

Regal machines were made by Ernest Smith & Woodhouse of Birmingham and were sometimes called Regal-Precision due to their Precision engines. In 1912, the firm marketed two tourers and a larger machine for sidecar use. These were typical period designs.

After entering the 1912 Senior TT and setting records at Brooklands that year, the firm continued to buy in engines from other manufacturers and to name their machines accordingly. Thus in 1913 there were two Regal-Green models and three Regal-Precisions. In 1914, the two-stroke Regal-Peco was added, and more Peco models the following year. However, 1915 was the final year for Regal.

SEARS

Sears Roebuck, the Chicago-based international department store, marketed a range of motorcycles for a few years, though it did not manufacture them. Instead, the firm used engines from Spacke Machine Company of Indianapolis, Indiana. Assembly was carried out by the Excelsior Cycle Company of Chicago, Illinois, which also provided the parts. The 1913 Sears twin was manufactured by Spacke, who put the Sears logo on them at the time of manufacture. Sears Roebuck sold them nationwide through their retail outlets as well as mail order.

That Excelsior company was not the motorcycle manufacturer of the same name (also based in Chicago) but a small bicycle-making firm. Sears then took the finished machines to market.

The Sears motorcycles included singles and V-twins in a loop frame with girder front forks for the singles and a trailing-link with leaf spring for the twins. They had a chain drive and rear brake only, which was standard practice in the United States at the time. In most other ways, these machines were typical for the time. They remained available until 1916, then disappeared.

The V-twin version of the Sears motorcycle, which was sold under several names. Although it had a big (1147cc/69ci) engine, pedals were also fitted.

SUNBEAM

Marston Ltd was founded in 1790, and by 1887 had created a division called Sunbeamland Cycles. Under the direction of John Marston, Sunbeam moved into motorcycle manufacture in 1912, a little later than many of its rivals. Meanwhile, Charles Marston had started Villiers Engineering in 1898 to build bicycle components, which eventually became a major producer of engines.

Sunbeam began building the Sunbeam-Mabley car in 1901, and by 1905 had decided to separate car and bicycle manufacture.

In 1912, the first Sunbeam motorcycle appeared in a similar black livery to the firm's motorcycles. It was powered by a 347cc (21ci) side-valve single-cylinder engine of the firm's own design.

A V-twin model appeared next, using 770cc (47ci) JAP, MAG and AKD engines, and a single-cylinder 499cc (30ci) machine followed late in 1913. The latter was ridden to joint second place in the 1914 Isle of Man TT and was supplied to the Allied forces during World War I.

Soon after John Marston died, the motorcycle business was sold off. It was taken over by Imperial Chemical Industries (ICI) in 1922. Sunbeams continued to do well in competition, winning the Senior TT in 1920 and 1922. After 1924, the marque also moved more into the European competition scene.

Sunbeam was slow to follow trends in the marketplace, and this, ironically, helped it get through the Depression. With little innovation and a slimmed-down range, Sunbeam was still in fairly good shape in 1937, when it was sold off to Matchless, becoming part of Associated Motor Cycles. The existing Sunbeam range was then slowly phased out and replaced with new models.

In 1938, Sunbeam bicycles were sold to BSA; and in 1943, BSA also acquired Sunbeam motorcycles. It went on to market the Erling Poppe-designed S7 in 1946 and a revised (S8) version in 1949.

The Sunbeam identity was then used for BSA's scooter projects, with little success. Sunbeam scooters were as good as anyone else's, but failed to become popular and, with their demise, Sunbeam motorcycles faded from the scene. No trace remained by 1964.

BAILEY FLYER

The Bailey Flyer was too innovative for most buyers. The flat-twin engine was acceptable but the shaft final drive put many people off.

The Bailey Flyer was one of a number of rather unusual machines that emerged in the early days of the industry. Like many others of the same stamp, it was not available for long, its fate decided by external events.

Production was begun by McLeod Manufacturing of Portland, Oregon, but this was taken over by the Bailey-Flyer Autocycle Company of Chicago, Illinois. The machine was powered by an F-head, flat-twin 1000cc (61ci) engine set along the frame. The flat-twin layout was popular because it caused little vibration.

What made the Bailey Flyer unusual was its final drive, which used shaft drive to the rear wheel, requiring two sets of bevel gears to turn the transmission line. The machine was fitted with a two-speed gearbox; the clutch was installed in the rear hub. The rest of the machine was fairly conventional, but its unusual layout hampered sales. Production was curtailed by World War I and did not resume.

BLACKBURNE

Burney & Blackburne of Hertfordshire produced the Blackburn motorcycle, which gained an 'e' in 1913 when the firm moved to new premises in Surrey. The Blackburn(e) was powered by a 499cc (30ci) side-valve engine with a one-piece crankshaft. The latter, along with a large flywheel, made it a very smooth-running engine.

The Blackburne was updated with new forks, and a single-speed TT model also appeared. Both were produced until 1916. After World War I, OEC of Hampshire manufactured the marque.

OEC produced three models for 1919: a three-speed single, a 2.75hp, two-speed single and an 8hp V-twin combination. Two of these were in production through to 1921, but only the twin was in production in 1922.

From 1923 to 1925, the firm traded as OEC Blackburne, building engines for other manufacturers. It finally closed down in the 1930s.

CYCLONE

The Cyclone was a very advanced machine for its time, but was in production for only three years. Cyclones were built on a loop frame, always finished in yellow, and had trailing-link forks. The engine was a V-twin with overhead camshafts driven by shaft and bevels that also drove the magneto. In an era of F-head motors, this was unusual, and engines were built to high standards.

Board or track racing machines had no suspension and direct drive to the rear wheel. They were very fast, clocking up 177km/h (110mph) laps of steeply banked board circuits and topping 144km/h (90mph) on dirt ovals.

Although the Cyclone had a few problems due to its advanced design, it performed well overall. However, production ceased after 1915 and attempts to begin again in a new site after World War I came to naught.

A 996cc Cyclone. These machines were successful in racing for a few years but were gradually shouldered out by larger firms with more money to spend.

JAMES 600 PERFECT

The James motorcycle company was building its own engines by 1913. These were both two- and four-strokes.

The main products were the 500cc (31ci) side-valve V-twin and a big 599cc (37ci) side-valve single. The single featured a distinctive pineapple-finned vertical cylinder.

The James machine was based on a cycle frame with fuel tank beneath the top tube and engine cradled in the bottom bracket.

In some ways, it was quite advanced, with chain drive, stirrup brakes at the front, and a foot-operated, all-metal clutch. The 599cc (37ci) machine was also available as a sidecar combination.

ENGINE: 599cc (36ci) sv single
POWER: 7hp
GEARBOX: 3–speed, hand change
FINAL DRIVE: chain
WEIGHT: 164kg (360lb)
TOP SPEED: 72km/h (45mph)

DOUGLAS DESPATCH RIDER BIKE

ENGINE: 348cc sv longtidunally mounted flat twin, 60.8x80mm, air–cooled
POWER: n/a
GEARBOX: 2–speed, hand change
FINAL DRIVE: belt
WEIGHT: n/a
TOP SPEED: 80km/h (50mph) approx

Douglas stubbornly clung to the idea of having pedals on their motorcycles until 1914, when they finally abandoned the concept. The 1914 Despatch Rider bike was a 350cc (21ci) model built in large numbers for the armed forces in World War I. More than 25,000 were delivered.

The machine was not without problems. It was not as good at slogging through the mud as the 550cc (34ci) Triumph singles that were also in wide use, and the low-mounted sparking plugs would sometimes short out in deep puddles.

However, on reasonably solid ground, the Douglas was well regarded by its users. A sidecar variant with a bigger engine was introduced in 1916.

Douglas machines made a name for themselves as despatch bikes in World War I. They offered good reliability and were easy to ride, being light and nimble, though they were less effective in mud than their Triumph competitors.

CLEVELAND

The Cleveland Motorcycle Manufacturing Company (which was in no way connected with a British company of similar name) produced its first motorcycles in 1915. These were 222cc (14ci), two-stroke, single-cylinder machines with in-line crankshafts and chain drive. They were popular and gained an enlarged engine soon after release.

The Cleveland Lightweight was on the market from 1915 to 1927. It clearly showed its heritage as a powered bicycle, but nevertheless went on to become arguably the most successful two-stroke machine ever produced in the USA.

In 1922, Cleveland bought the Reading Standard Company, and in 1924 marketed a 350cc (21ci) side-valve single-cylinder machine. Although it had a similar frame design to its predecessor, it did not sell as well. Cleveland's first four-cylinder model followed a year later. This, too, was not a commercial success and was replaced in 1926 by a bigger-engined model.

In 1929, Cleveland brought out the Tornado, with its 1000cc (61ci) engine and three-speed gearbox. However, by now machines in the same class, but with better performance, were already on the market. Coupled with the Depression, the competition was too much for Cleveland and the firm shut down in 1929.

The 600cc (40ci) four-cylinder Cleveland model of 1925. It did not sell well enough to keep the company afloat during the Depression years – the firm closed down four years after releasing this machine.

INDIAN POWERPLUS

The Powerplus was a lot more powerful than its predecessor in the Indian range, even though it went back to side-mounted valves. It was also much easier to maintain. The Powerplus therefore became the basis for most of Indian's subsequent successful engines.

The Powerplus showed its worth in the hands of 'Cannonball' Baker in 1915. He rode from Vancouver to Tijuana – 2669km (1655 miles) – in 3 days, 9 hours and 15 minutes, though he did stop for a three-hour nap in Fresno.

The Powerplus helped Indian regain a lot of ground against Harley-Davidson and Excelsior, who were both getting ahead in the power stakes.

Unfortunately, this came a little too late. As the Powerplus appeared, Harley-Davidson was beginning a winning streak in competition, which rather eclipsed Indian's efforts.

ENGINE: 998cc (60ci) sv inline V–twin, air-cooled
POWER: 17bhp
GEARBOX: 3–speed hand change
FINAL DRIVE: chain
WEIGHT: n/a
TOP SPEED: 100km/h (60mph) approx

MONET-GOYON

Monet-Goyon started out by fitting the Wall Auto Wheel to bicycles. This curious device was designed to be fitted to the side of a standard bicycle's rear wheel. Although the firm moved on to using more conventional Villiers and MAG engines, it did create a tricycle just after the end of World War I. This was powered by a four-stroke engine mounted inboard of the right rear disc wheel; the left rear wheel was connected to the pedals. Intended for use by war invalids, it later gained a 147cc (9ci) Villiers two-stroke engine.

Monet-Goyon also built a scooter-like vehicle called the Vélauto, and a lightweight motorcycle. The latter was followed by others of similar design using Villiers engines.

From 1926 onwards, Monet-Goyon added four-strokes to its range, using MAG engines, and in the early 1930s it began constructing its own 350cc (21ci) side-valve engine. This remained in production for more than 20 years. The firm bought out Khler-Escoffier in 1929 and used their engines in some designs from then on.

In the early 1930s, the range was quite large and expanded further in 1932 with the addition of a velomoteur with a 100cc (6ci) engine. A range of motorcycles using the same engine followed. Interest on light vehicles continued through the 1940s and into the 1950s. The Starlette scooter, with a 99cc (6ci) Villiers engine, was followed by the Pullman 125 in 1956. This was a stylish and popular machine, but it was not enough to keep Monet-Goyon in business, and the marque faded away at the end of the 1950s.

ARDIE

Ardie was named after its founder, Arno Dietrich, who was killed in a racing accident in 1922. The first machines came out of the Nurnberg factory in 1919. These were 305cc (19ci) and 348cc (21ci) two-stroke singles, but after Dietrich's death and the transfer of the firm to the Bendit factory, a range of machines were put into production. The most popular of these used a 490cc (30ci) overhead-valve engine; the others ranged from 246cc (15ci) to 996cc (61ci). After 1925, the firm used JAP engines.

Ardie designs were forward-looking rather than traditional, making use of advanced alloys and adding touches of luxury to their machines. However, in the hard times of the 1930s, the firm began using simpler tubular steel frames to cut costs. This was accompanied by a move from JAP engines to others made by Bark, Kuchen, Sachs and Sturmey Archer.

Attempts to implement new designs were interrupted by World War II, and the firm was taken over by Durkopp just after the war. Ardie began to manufacture its own engines at this time. These were small two-strokes ranging from 122cc (7ci) to 344cc (21ci). They went into a range of well put together commuter motorcycles, which were exactly what post-war Germany needed. This saw the firm through into the 1950s.

Ardie began making mopeds in 1953 and achieved record sales in 1955. However, the late 1950s were not a good time to be a motorcycle manufacturer in Germany, and just three years later Ardie went out of business.

A 500cc (30ci) side-valve single-cylinder Ardie 1931 model. Early versions used engines from JAP but later on Ardie turned to other manufacturers to supply its power units.

BLACK PRINCE

The Black Prince was designed by E.W. Cameron of Doncaster, Yorkshire. Almost everything about it was unconventional, though the prototype engine was successfully demonstrated. The machine never made it into production and Cameron committed suicide in 1920, which ended any chance of the machine being made.

The Black Prince design was advanced for its time, with a pressed-steel frame and an unusual suspension system. The machine could be powered by either a 292cc (18ci) Union engine or a 396cc (24ci) flat-twin two-stroke with a single spark plug. The plug was installed in a tube that connected the two combustion chambers. This tube also contained an automatic poppet valve, which controlled the passage of the mixture from the common crankcase to the pistons.

Cameron's unfortunate death also sank the Black Prince Runabout, a three-wheeler. The latter was actually about to go into production and might have been a success.

BROUGH SUPERIOR

George Brough was born in 1890 and, as best he could remember, first rode a motorcycle in about 1900. It was one of the original Werners; hardly a performance machine, but it caught young George's imagination. Just a few years later, before his 20th birthday, he was racing flat-twins built by his father.

George went into partnership with his father to build motorcycles. However, he wanted something faster and more luxurious, so he founded his own firm in 1919. Two years later, his first machine was built and named Brough-Superior to distinguish it from the previous Broughs.

From the outset, George Brough wanted to build the very best machines he could, in small numbers, for the top end of the market. He bought in engines from the same manufacturers (mainly JAP, MAG and Matchless) as other marques, but paid extra for improved finishing and quality control, and took only the top-of-the-line models.

Brough also knew how to create a reputation and to present his products. They were beautifully finished – well enough that Rolls-Royce did not protest when Brough promoted his machines with the slogan 'the Rolls-Royce of motorcycles'. As well as the attention to detail and the sheer quality of the machines, competition results were an important factor in establishing their reputation.

Broughs were successful in competition and were ridden by several big names. Alongside George Brough himself were Eric Fernihough, Freddie Dixon, E.C.E. Baragwanath and Bert Le Vack – to name just a few. The Brough-Superior marque also benefited from celebrity connections: T.E. Lawrence (Lawrence of Arabia) owned seven at various times and had an eighth on order when he was killed – riding a Brough.

The V-twins were the backbone of Brough-Superior's reputation, but George Brough never stopped experimenting and creating unusual – sometimes one-off – machines. How much of this was in the cause of progress and how much was intended to simply get attention is hard to say. The policy worked well.

Early Brough-Superior machines were powered by 986cc (60ci) JAP engines, but a range of options were available as standard options or on special order. These included side-valves, push-rod and overhead-cams (including four-cams), and eight-valves. Different engine sizes were also available at times: 680cc (41ci), 750cc (46ci), a big side-valve 1096cc (67ci) for touring, probably with a sidecar, and (briefly) a 500c (31ci). Other than a few experimental machines like the prototype air-cooled four design, the only four produced by Brough-Superior was the 800cc (49ci) Austin Four.

Many components were modified or built to order, though many firms bought in modified components, so George Brough's requirements may not always have been unique. He did have his name cast into some components, however, which would have required setting up specially.

In 1923, the SS80 was launched. It came with a written guarantee that it had been timed at 129km/h (80mph) over 400m

(the quarter-mile). A year later, the guarantee for the SS100 claimed a speed of 161km/h (100mph). This, according to the literature, was on 'a Private Road, one-and-three-quarter miles [2.8km] long'. Nonetheless, the claim passed into popular folklore as having been achieved at Brooklands.

The SS100 was Brough-Superior's flagship model until the outbreak of World War II. It gained increasingly powerful engines over this time and other improvements to its already magnificent looks and performance.

Brough-Superior did not resume production after the war. It has been suggested that George Brough was not confident about being able to source suitable engines, which makes a nice story but is probably not true. It is more likely that he realized that the market had changed and that the successful firms of the future would be builders rather than assemblers. Integrated designs were the way forward, and Brough was not inclined to compete but fail. This theory is borne out by

the performance of the Vincent-HRD Series A Rapide. In 1939, one was independently timed at 177km/h (110mph), a figure that the SS100 would struggle to match.

It has also been suggested that World War II killed the Brough-Superior Dream, or Golden Dream. This resembled two BMW flat twins stacked one atop the other, with geared crankshafts like a Square Four. In all probability, however, the war was not responsible. A handful were built and were very unreliable. It is more likely that the project was

The Brough Superior engine had 35bhp. Although this may not seem like very much today, this was four times greater than the contemporary BMW and more powerful than most small cars of the period.

another of George Brough's attention-grabbing one-offs.

Whatever the truth, Brough-Superior passed into the pages of legend during World War II. Only about 4000 machines were ever built, and of them about 10 per cent were SS100s. Their very scarcity is part of their mystique.

BSA SIDEVALVE V-TWINS
ENGLAND 1919–39

In 1919, BSA began producing a range of V-twins that remained in production, more or less unchanged, for the next two decades.

The first was the Model E, a 770cc (47ci) side-valve machine with the cylinders splayed at 50°. The resulting engine was compact but ran hot with a lot of vibration.

These machines used total-loss lubrication, in which oil

undertook a journey through the bike's moving parts and ended up on the road. First, it was hand-pumped from the 2.3l (0.6 gallon) tank to lubricate the cylinders and crankshaft. Unburned oil would collect in the crankcase and escape through a valve onto the primary chain. From there, it would eventually find its way onto the road surface.

These machines had a very

unimpressive performance in terms of acceleration, but provided good pulling power for sidecar work. They were expensive, especially when a sidecar was factored into the price, but very solidly built with a forged steel backbone.

The last model, the G14, went to market in 1938 and was not greatly different to the first. For a design to remain in production

more or less unchanged for 20 years suggests that BSA got it right with this one.

ENGINE: 986cc (59ci) V-twin, air-cooled
POWER: 25bhp at 3800rpm
GEARBOX: 4–speed hand change
FINAL DRIVE: chain
WEIGHT: 191kg (420lb)
TOP SPEED: 121km/h (70mph)

COCKERELL
GERMANY 1919–24

Fritz Cockerell created a rather unusual machine in the Megola, which featured a five-cylinder rotary engine built into the front wheel. However, when he began producing machines under his own name, he used much more

Fritz Cockerell's machines look somewhat strange but they were well designed, with the engine set horizontally so that it could be concealed in the manner of a scooter.

conventional designs.

Based initially in Munich, Cockerell built small two-stroke, singles with a horizontal cylinder. His lightweight bikes were simple but well designed, with a low-mounted engine and belt drive. They were well put together and did well in national competition.

In 1924, Cockerell sold his firm to Abako, but continued to design two-stroke motorcycle engines in various sizes as well as diesel and automobile engines.

COTTON

ENGLAND 1919–PRESENT

Francis Willoughby Cotton built his first prototype motorcycle around 1913. He was a lawyer, and used his legal skills to prevent his design from being copied. It was indeed worth copying, as its layout created a machine that handled very well. Cotton's frame consisted of four straight tubes running from headstock to rear wheel, and could accommodate almost any engine.

Cotton's early bikes used Villiers engines and a range of transmissions. In 1923, the range was expanded with new machines.

Racing success also came that year when Stanley Woods won his first TT on a Cotton. Cotton's bikes did well in competition over the next two years and took the first three places in the 1926 Lightweight TT.

Now well established in the marketplace, Cotton produced a wide range of machines using mainly JAP and Blackburne engines, and some from Villiers, Sturmey-Archer and Rudge. The range expanded in 1932, despite the difficult economic times.

Cotton's diversity served the firm well, and it got through the

Depression and then World War II intact. By the end of the 1930s, the firm was making a Villiers-powered lightweight. Everything else used JAP engines.

Relatively few machines were in production in the early 1950s, however, and in 1954 Pat Onions and Monty Denley took over and began favouring two-stroke engines. Most came from Villiers in this period. Through the late 1950s and the 1960s, Cotton was mainly concerned with sports and competition machines, but sales steadily declined.

Villiers ceased making engines in 1968 and Cotton began obtaining engines from elsewhere. Minarelli and DMW powered some models, and Cotton became involved with CCM and Armstrong, which led to the 1979 Cotton-EMC road racer. Eventually, the Cotton identity became part of Armstrong and the marque faded away.

However, in 1991 Fluff Brown revived the marque, and replica 1960s Cottons became very popular. They were built by AJS Motorcycles of Andover, Hampshire.

DKW

GERMANY 1919–66

Exactly what DKW stands for is a matter of some debate. The company's founder, J.S. Rasmussen, offered an explanation in 1963, when he was 85. The most popular idea is that DKW stands for Das Kleine Wunder, the little miracle, referring to a small car introduced in 1928. Perhaps the most charming suggestion is that it stands for Der Knabishe Wunsche, the schoolboy's dream, a term coined in the inter-war years, when DKW cars were winning every race in sight. Alternatively, it may mean Dampf Kraft Wagen, a reference to

Rasmussen's first engine, a steam powerplant for cars.

In many ways, they are all true; DKW has at different times and to different people stood for all three phrases. It has always represented great motorcycles, which is all that matters to most people.

DKW was founded in 1919 as J.S. Ramussen and spent its early days in experimentation. In 1921, it introduced a two-stroke auxiliary engine for a bicycle. This 122cc (7ci) unit was designed by Hugo Ruppe, and by 1922 about 25,000 had been sold. This was the

beginning of the firm's long involvement in two-stroke engine manufacture and development.

Things did not go too well in 1921–22, with the release of the 122cc (7ci) Golem and 142cc (9ci) Lamos. These were very comfortable little machines, but were not good sellers. However, Rasmussen and Ruppe went on to produce a much more successful range, starting with the SM (Steel Model).

The SM was a 173cc (11ci) single cylinder machine with a pressed-steel frame. Other

manufacturers copied the idea, but DKW was ahead of the curve. Its success was such that it was able to absorb some 16 other companies by 1927 and employed 15,000 people in that year.

By 1930, DKW was the world's largest motorcycle manufacturer

A 1957 RT175 single. The RT range was extremely successful and several engine sizes were available, including singles and twins. They were all excellent road bikes.

and was growing at an enormous rate. However, it was making losses and running up huge debts. Rasmussen countered the problem by creating Auto Union AG in 1932. Auto Union was a merger of DKW, Horch, Audi and Wanderer. Its symbol of four interlinked circles is still displayed on Audi cars.

Within Auto Union, Horch, Audi and Wanderer built cars, while DKW concentrated on motorcycles. The group weathered the tough years of the Depression and emerged in a good position to dominate the domestic and export markets.

Further pioneering work in the field of two-stroke engines was undertaken, resulting in engines with greater power and more even firing, and this was instrumental in the firm's unassailable Grand Prix presence in the late 1930s. Its 250cc (15ci) and 350cc (21ci) machines won races and set records and, in 1938, sales were at an all-time high.

During World War II, the firm produced a range of military machines, such as the NZ250 and NZ350. During this period, one of the world's all-time greatest motorcycles was designed by Hermann Webber. This was the RT125, and after the war it was copied by virtually everyone.

DKW lost its factory at the end of the war, as it was in the eastern part of the country and fell under Communist control. A new works was set up at Ingolstadt and production resumed, starting with the RT125. It went on sale in 1949, two years after a version was taken out on the racing scene. In 1952, a three-cylinder 350cc (21ci) appeared and was impressive in competition until the firm ceased competing in 1956.

In the early 1950s, things looked good. A range of two-stroke singles (and one twin) was selling well, and in 1954 the new Ingolstadt plant produced its 250,000th motorcycle. It had also turned out 122,000 cars since its creation a decade before. However, 1956 was a very bad year for German motorcycle manufacturing and DKW ran into trouble.

The RT125 was a truly world-class machine: light, rugged and possessing good performance. Small wonder that it became the most-copied motorcycle design in history.

The Hummel (bumblebee) moped was not successful enough to turn things around, and the firm was increasingly relying on car sales to support the motorcycle side of the business.

As the crisis deepened, DKW merged with Express and Victoria to create Zweirad Union. The DKW marque faded into the larger identity and the 'schoolboy's dream' came to an end.

DUNELT
ENGLAND 1919–35 AND 1957

Birmingham-based Dunelt was spun out of the Sheffield steel firm Dunford & Elliott. Its first machine was exhibited in 1919 and went into production the following year. It was powered by a 499cc (30ci) two-stroke single with a double-diameter piston and cylinder, which was difficult to assemble due to its unusual configuration.

The Dunelt was excellent for use with a sidecar due to a large external flywheel, which gave it good pulling power even at low speeds. However, the trade-off was rather modest acceleration. As a result, it was mainly offered as a sidecar combination.

The Dunelt was sufficiently successful that three new versions appeared in 1923 and eight more in 1924. The range was updated in 1925 – at which point, milk-truck and fire-engine versions also emerged.

Up to 1926, Dunelt used 499cc (30ci) engines, but that year a 249cc (15ci) machine arrived, followed by a sports variant.

In 1929, the range was slimmed down, but a four-stroke 348cc (21ci) machine was introduced. This machine won the Maudes Trophy that year, and a new Dunelt model won it again in 1930.

Dunelt began the 1930s with a good range of machines in production. It experimented with an overhead camshaft in 1930, but decided that this was too noisy, and produced side and overhead-valve machines for 1931. Bird names were given to new models that year rather than the numbers that had been usual until that point.

Near the end of 1931, the firm moved to Sheffield, and model numbers again became standard practice. Sheffield-built machines were known as Sheffield-Dunelts for the next couple of years.

Although a couple of new models appeared after this period, Dunelt's day was passing, and the company went out of business in 1935.

In 1957, a 50cc (3ci) moped bearing the Dunelt name appeared for a short while, but after that Dunelt was truly gone from the motorcycle scene.

FRANCIS-BARNETT
ENGLAND 1919–64

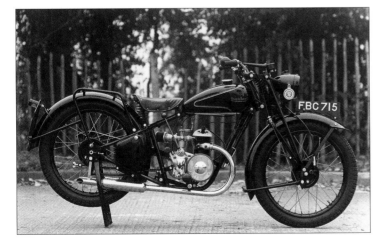

The 122c Francis-Barnett Merlin was a sound and well-made workhorse commuter machine, but it was not able to cope with competition from BSA's Bantam.

In 1919, Gordon Francis and father-in-law Arthur Barnett founded Francis and Barnett Ltd. Gordon's father, Graham Francis, put up some of the initial capital and had a seat on the board, and when Excelsior moved to Birmingham, Francis and Barnett Ltd (which had become known as 'Fanny-B' by that time) moved into the vacated Coventry factory.

The first model to come out of the Coventry factory was a 292cc (18ci) JAP-engined side-valve machine with two speeds and belt final drive, which made its appearance in 1920. A similar 346cc (21.1ci) machine came soon after, followed by a range of four-stroke singles of up to 350cc (21.3ci).

Francis-Barnett is commonly associated with two-strokes. The first of these were produced in the early 1920s. All used Villiers engines and most were singles. The Pullman, a 344cc (20.9ci) parallel twin introduced in 1927, deviated from this and, although initially promising, suffered from overheating problems.

In 1923, Francis-Barnett introduced a novel cost-cutting method with its bolted-together frames. The marque achieved some impressive publicity in 1926 and 1927, when these machines were ridden to the summits of Snowdon and Ben Nevis. The firm made excellent use of one machine's impressive fuel economy, referring to its

69km/litre (196mpg) capability as 'cheaper than shoe leather'.

Another famous two-stroke was the Cruiser, which used a conventional welded frame instead of the bolted version. It appeared in 1933 and was in production until 1940. One reason for its popularity was the practical nature of its layout, which looked a lot like a scooter. The four-stroke Stag also used a welded frame, and

these two machines were joined in 1938 by the unit construction 125cc (8ci) Snipe and a pedal-assisted 98cc (6ci) moped, the Powerbike.

Early in World War II, Francis-Barnett attempted to create a military version of the Snipe. Work was well underway when the factory was destroyed by the same air raid that claimed Triumph's nearby premises. Through the war

the firm struggled on but did not resume production until 1945.

Post-war machines were all two-strokes, initially using Villiers engines of 98cc (6ci) to 248cc (15ci). Francis-Barnet became part of AMC in 1947, and a decade later it began building its own engines. These were a failure, and Francis-Barnett went back to using Villiers units. By now, however, the marque was losing its unique

identity. Its machines were red and those made by James, another AMC firm, were green. There were few other differences.

Francis-Barnett's final machine was the impressive-looking 150cc (9ci) Sports Fulmer 90. For all its looks and features, it was not enough to save motorcycle manufacturing in Coventry, and 1964 was the last year for 'Fanny-B'.

GARELLI

The RGS50 was just one of Garelli's popular family of offroad bikes. While 50ccs (3cis) does not represent much engine, Garelli knew how to wring the maximum performance out of such a small powerplant.

Turin-born Adalberto Garelli was another young, gifted Italian who did so much for the motorcycle industry, thanks to a combination of genius and enthusiasm. In 1908, aged 22, Garelli gained a degree in engineering, and in 1909 began working for Fiat on its two-stroke engine. In 1911, when Fiat decided it was not so keen on two-strokes,

Garelli left to build a prototype motorcycle.

Garelli joined Bianchi in 1914, then moved on to Stucci, for whom he won an Army competition for a military motorcycle design. In 1919, he set up his own motorcycle factory near Milan.

The first Garelli model was a 350cc (21ci) split-single,

which was a success both in the marketplace and in racing. It remained in production until 1926, but from 1927 Garelli became more involved in military manufacturing and his interest in motorcycles waned. By 1936, the Garelli marque effectively had ceased to exist.

However, after World War II, Garelli returned. The first product was an engine called the Mosquito, which was designed to be fitted to pedal cycles. It was a big success and paved the way for a return to the production of motorcycles in the mid-1950s.

In 1961, Agrati and Garelli merged to form the Agrati-Garelli group. The alliance was mutually beneficial and Garelli returned to

making sports machines. Some were developed specifically to break records, and they did. In 1963 at Monza, in appalling weather, Garelli set several records. The 50cc (3ci) 24-hour record set that day still stands.

In the 1970s, Garelli was heavily involved in developing mopeds and was a market leader. Through the mid-1980s, the firm's racing team had a very high profile. This was accompanied by the launch of new racing and trials machines.

By 1985, however, Garelli was not doing so well. New models and even a reincarnation of the Mosquito auxiliary cycle engine did not manage to turn this around. Agrati was increasingly dependent on bicycle sales and its British arm had closed down. A final attempt was made in 1987 to save the firm with a management reshuffle, but this came too late. The Garelli brand name was saved from oblivion by a takeover, becoming part of the much smaller firm Fantic in 1991.

GARELLI 350 SPLIT-SINGLE

This machine was Adalberto Garelli's first machine to be marketed by his own firm. It had been developed and improved from his original 1913 machine and was a mature and well-tried design at its appearance.

The split-single engine was first conceived in 1912. It consisted of two parallel cylinders cast in a single block with a common combustion chamber, each with a capacity of 174.6cc (10.7ci), making a total of 349cc (21ci). Adalberto Garelli demonstrated its capabilities in 1914 when he ascended the Moncenisio Pass in northern Italy on the prototype machine, becoming the first person to do so under power.

Adalberto Garelli on the machine that established his company in the marketplace. The 350cc (21ci) two-stroke, split-single engine was his own invention.

Further proof of the worth of the split-single came from its race performance. On its first outing, the machine won the Milano–Napoli road race, and this was only the first of many victories. The machine won the 1921 Circuit of Lario and the 1922 Grand Prix at Monza, and in 1922 it also became the first Italian motorcycle to win abroad, at Strasbourg. Italy's first national racing champion, Ernesto Gnesa, won his

title at Monza in 1922 on a Garelli.

The split-single was also used in many record attempts. On 7 September 1922, it chalked up no less than eight world records, and in the following year it set a staggering 76 world records. Distance, time and endurance meant nothing to the Garelli; it was unstoppable.

The split-single's final record attempt was made in 1926, when three machines ridden by 14 riders

in an alternating sequence kept going for 138 hours, clocking up speeds of 131km/h (81.5mph).

As if this was not enough, the Garelli 350 also chalked up some mechanical records; it was the first motorcycle to mount an oil tank for separate lubrication, and used an expansion chamber-type exhaust. The final 1926 model produced 30hp at 4500rpm and had a top speed of 141km/h (87.5mph).

ENGINE: 349cc (21ci) sv vertical split–single, (2x174.6cc), air-cooled
POWER: 20bhp at 4500 rpm
GEARBOX: 2–speed hand change
FINAL DRIVE: belt or chain
WEIGHT: 97kg (213lb)
TOP SPEED: 141km/h (87.5mph)

GILLET-HERSTAL

BELGIUM 1919–60

Gillet-Herstal marketed its first motorcycle, designed by Fernand Laguesse, in 1920. This was a 301cc (18ci) two-stroke with a two-speed gearbox on a loop frame with girder forks. A sidecar variant with a 750cc (46ci) MAG V-twin engine was added later in the year.

In 1922, Gillet-Herstal added a 996cc (61ci) machine and uprated the two-stroke to 347cc (21ci). Competition involvement led to some new ideas. Laguesse developed a new water-cooled engine with opposed pistons and a 347cc (21ci) two-stroke with a rotary valve built into one mainshaft and three primary gears on the other for the gearbox ratios. The latter powered Français Andrieux and Robert Sexé on their round-the-world ride in 1926.

For 1926, Gillet-Herstal introduced a 499cc (30ci) overhead-valve engine, following the firm's normal practice of unit construction. This engine was installed vertically in a conventional frame. As time passed, the machine was updated with better brakes, a foot-operated gear change and improved forks.

A desire for race success led to the recruitment in 1928 of Van Oirbeek. The former FN designer was put to work on racing engines, and came up with three overhead-camshaft, unit-construction singles of 348cc (21ci), 499cc (30ci) and 582cc (36ci). These, and the existing overhead-valve machines, won trophies and set records in solo and sidecar configuration.

The year 1930 brought new models with 398cc (24ci) and 499cc (30ci) side-valve plus 346cc (21ci) overhead-valve engines, all of which were of unit construction. In 1932, a 547cc (33ci) side-valve engine appeared, and this was increased to 600cc (37ci) the following year. Another 600cc (37ci), this time an overhead-valve model, followed soon after.

Gillet-Herstal reacted to the Depression by bringing out a 166cc (10ci) lightweight two-stroke, and followed this with a 100cc (6ci) vélomoteur and another lightweight, of 123cc (8ci). These cheap machines, along with the single-cylinder four-strokes, formed the basis of the range up to 1939.

Military contracts came in the mid-1930s, and one design, the

720cc (44ci) model, was produced specifically for military sidecar work. It was powered by a 708cc (43ci) twin-cylinder, two-stroke engine built-in unit with a four-speed and reverse gearbox.

After the war, Gillet-Herstal gave some of its four-strokes telescopic front forks and discontinued other models, effectively creating a new range. This was joined in 1946 by the Superconfort model, a 239cc (14ci) two-stroke with rear suspension. Similar models followed and soon the whole range had gained rear suspension. As times got harder, a licence-built scooter was marketed, and a moped design came in 1956, a year after Gillet merged with FN and Saroléa. This was not enough to save the marque and production ceased in 1960.

GNOME & RHÔNE

FRANCE 1919–59

After making a name as an aircraft firm and producing a British design under licence from 1919, Gnome & Rhône began producing its own designs from 1923. These were high-quality singles ranging from 300cc (18ci) to 500cc (31ci). From 1931, the firm produced flat-twins as well as a 250cc (15ci) single, and in 1935 began building an overhead-valve 724cc (44ci) machine, the Type X. This was one of the largest French motorcycles and was considered both prestigious and excellent for sidecar work.

The last offering before World War II was an 800cc (49ci) machine for the French Army. After the war, the firm returned to smaller, high-quality 125cc (8ci) and 200cc (12ci) two-strokes. However, it fell victim to the tough market conditions of the late 1950s and ceased production in 1959.

After its big 800cc (50ci) machine for the French Army, Gnome & Rhone turned to smaller designs such as this 1942 100cc R1. This trend continued for the remainder of the firm's existence.

MARTINSYDE

At the end of World War I, the aircraft firm Martin & Handasyde was seeking a new outlet for its facilities. Motorcycles, particularly the sidecar sector, seemed ideal and the firm began producing designs accordingly.

Rather than buy in engines, the firm produced one of its own, using a design bought from Howard Newman. This used a three-speed gearbox built under licence from AJS, driving a machine that was built from conventional cycle components. This eventually let Martinsyde down. The engine and drive were good, but the rest of the machine was not really up to the standards required by high-end users.

A second machine was added to the range for 1920. In 1921, production was reduced, although a sports machine was added to the range. This was followed by the V-twin Quick Six in 1922, and the year after that a 347cc (21ci) single appeared in Sports and Touring variants.

Production was not great, and Martinsyde went under in 1923. The remaining stocks were bought up by BAT and the resulting machines were sold as BAT-Martinsydes until 1925.

NIMBUS

The 1919 Nimbus was a curious candidate for a success story, but it managed to remain in production for almost 40 years virtually unchanged. It was produced by Fisker & Nielsen in Copenhagen to a design that was prototyped in 1917.

The design was functional rather than stylish and managed to cram a four-cylinder engine based on an FN design into its very robust frame, along with swing-arm rear suspension. The latter was unusual at the time. The machines were very well made and, although they were not fast, they did well in endurance events due to their ability to keep going steadily when more impressive performers began to struggle.

Until the very last incarnation of the original, or 'Stovepipe', Nimbus, its basic setup did not change. The Nimbus's designer, Fisker, saw no need to change a design that did its job well, and the longevity of the machine suggests that he had a point.

About 1300 of the original 'Stovepipe' Nimbus were built until 1928, at which point a plan was hatched to increase production to 1000 per year. This came to naught. The Nimbus Mk II, marketed in 1934, was cheaper to make and more basic than the original, perhaps in keeping with the times. It did feature telescopic forks, however, which may well have been the first on any machine.

The 1934 model received a new engine, an advanced 750cc (46ci) overhead-cam four. It delivered decent but unimpressive power through a three-speed gearbox to a shaft drive. Cooling was not good and though the 1934 Nimbus could deliver 22hp and make up to 96km/h (60mph), it was not sensible to maintain such a speed, because this caused damage to the cylinder head.

The Mk II remained in production until 1958 with the same basic design. Parts were interchangeable between machines built 20 years apart. Near the end of its life, the Nimbus design was substantially changed, with a new rotary-valved four-cylinder engine, but this never went into production.

The strip-steel frame of the Nimbus looks rather primitive, and in many ways it is. The machine was hardly advanced when it was first produced in 1919, and yet it remained in production for almost 40 years.

ABC TWIN

After World War I, ABC decided to build an advanced machine using the tried-and-tested, flat-twin configuration it had used before the war. The flat-twin was prized for its good balance and lack of vibration.

The new machine gained overhead-valves on a short-stroke

The 1920 version of the ABC Twin gained chain drive but was otherwise little different from previous models, with a flat-twin engine in unit with the four-speed gearbox and leaf-spring front and rear suspension.

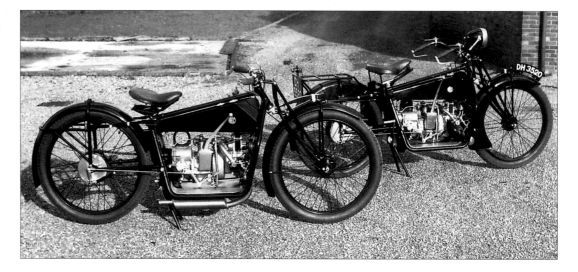

engine built-in unit with the four-speed gearbox, and other advanced features.

It had rear suspension and the frame tubes were spread apart to act as crash bars and carry leg shields under the footboards. In some significant ways, it was a two-wheeled car rather than a motorcycle.

The resulting machine was expensive and could be tricky to handle. Its main problem, however, was that its smooth running made it too easy for it to run too fast, often shedding the pushrods.

The ABC Twin worked well if properly maintained, but it was perhaps more trouble than it was worth.

ENGINE: 398cc (24ci) ohv flat-twin, air-cooled
POWER: n/a
GEARBOX: unit 4-speed hand change
FINAL DRIVE: chain
WEIGHT: 110kg (243lb)
TOP SPEED: 100km/h (60mph)

ACE

USA 1920–28

Philadelphia-based Ace was founded by William Henderson, who started out in 1912 making motorcycles under his own name. Ace began building motorcycles in 1919. All of Ace's machines used an in-line four and were based on the original Henderson design. The main difference, though, was that Henderson wanted to build machines that were lighter and more agile than his original ones.

Ace bikes used a 1220cc (74ci) F-head engine built-in unit with a three-speed gearbox. The crankcase was split horizontally with three main bearings for the crankshaft, while lubrication was by both splash and pump. A multi-plate clutch took the power to the hand-change gearbox. The blue-painted frame was tubular with leading-link forks, as was normal in the USA at that time. Also conventional was the fitting of a rear-wheel brake only; on the dirt roads of the time, a front brake was dangerous to use.

The Ace bike was successful in the marketplace and set a new Los Angeles to New York record in 1922. However, William Henderson was killed the same year while involved in road tests. Arthur Lemon, his successor, continued to develop the Ace, which was popular for its smooth running, power and stable handling.

1923 brought a new speed record using a lightweight version of the production machine, which was timed at over 208km/h (129mph) and managed 171km/h (106mph) pulling a sidecar. However, due to financial difficulties Ace ceased production at the end of 1924, twice lurching back into life before being bought out by Indian in 1927. Indian produced the Ace for one year before creating its own replacement design.

BEARDMORE PRECISION

ENGLAND 1920–25

F.E. Baker Ltd. of Birmingham was renowned as the maker of Precision engines. During World War I, the firm designed and developed an advanced model powered by a 349cc (21ci), two-stroke, built-in unit with a two-speed gearbox. This machine was launched immediately after the war, in 1919. The following year, as a result of association with the William Beardmore engineering group, it became known as the Beardmore.

The engine was a conventional two-stroke with a novel lubrication system – the magneto drive chain doubled as an oil conveyor. The gearing system was also unusual; sprockets at either end of the crankshaft connected through-chains to differing-sized sprockets mounted on a countershaft.

Gear selection was via expanding clutches. The engine and gear were contained in aluminium casings as a complete unit.

Like many other machines of the era, the Beardmore Precision used cycle parts for much of its construction. Some components were tubular and others were of pressed steel. The fuel tank served as the top tube of the frame and the deep-section mudguards doubled as stressed supports for both wheels. The machine also featured large footboards swept upwards at their front ends to become leg shields.

The machine also featured suspension on both wheels, with a rocking-action fork at the front and cantilevered arms at the rear. It was, however, underpowered and for this reason (as well as its generally unusual setup) it did not achieve much success in the marketplace. A sports version was tried in 1921 before the power issue was solved by fitting a 598cc (36ci) side-valve engine with a three-speed gearbox in unit.

More versions followed. One used a sleeve-valve 348cc (21ci) engine from Barr & Stroud with three-speed gearbox, and another used a new 496cc (30ci) sleeve-valve engine. The latter was entered in the 1922 Senior Isle of Man TT, but all three machines retired, which did nothing for the Beardmore Precision's image.

A replica of the race machine, available with either sprung or rigid frame and a revised link-action girder fork, was exhibited at the 1922 motorcycle show along with a two-speed 348cc (21ci) sleeve-valve. A sports version appeared in 1923 and was followed by a 246cc (15ci) sleeve-valve in a tubular frame. These models were built until 1924.

In 1924, Frank Baker left the firm. He eventually set up a marque under his own name. Meanwhile, a range of experimental racing bikes were being entered in the TT. These included a 250cc (15ci) overhead-valve with leaf-spring controlled valves and an overhead-cam 350cc (21ci) single with four valves, two carburettors and shaft-driven camshaft. Neither was very successful, but the 250cc was added to the range for 1925.

No more new models followed, and the marque faded from sight, though Beardmore worked with cars for some years.

CHAISE

FRANCE 1920–39

In some ways, this firm was a French equivalent of the British JAP or Villiers, supplying engines to many different makers. Chaise offered a broad range, of which the centrepiece was a set of four-stroke singles of 250cc (15ci), 350 (21ci) and 500cc (31ci). At times, Chaise also made two-strokes of 175cc (11ci) and 250cc (15ci), and a small 100cc (6ci) two-stroke single for velomoteur use.

The 350cc (21ci) and 500cc (31ci) engines were built with overhead-valves as well as a single overhead-camshaft. The magneto, dynamo and speedometer were all gear-driven and the engine was a built-in unit with a three-speed gearbox and gear primary drive. The oil was carried in a wet sump, so the unit was fully self-contained, which made it easier for users to mount on whatever machine was desired.

In 1930, Chaise exhibited a four at the Paris Show, just before Ariel and Matchless unveiled theirs at the London Show.

The Chaise Four was a very narrow-angle 750cc (46ci) V-four, with its built-up crankshaft having the throws offset against the cylinder angle to improve even running. It had a camshaft on each side for the overhead-valves and a line of pushrods running up the sides of the engine to the rockers, all the valve gear being exposed.

Chaise was an innovative firm that provided good, easy-to-integrate engines to French manufacturers up until 1939.

First presented at the 1930 Paris show, the Chaise Four featured a narrow-angle V-four engine and shaft final drive. Most Chaise machines were singles.

FEW PARAMOUNT

ENGLAND 1920 AND 1926–28

The F.E. Waller company did not enter the motorcycle market until 1920. Prior to this, it had made valve spring covers under the FEW identity, and used this brand name for their 6hp JAP engined V-twin machine, which had a low sports frame and Saxon forks. A prototype was built, but the machine was not taken up by any manufacturer.

Six years later, FEW tried again, this time with something that was more two-wheeled car than motorcycle. This machine, the Paramount, was again powered by a JAP engine, either a 976cc (60ci) V-twin or a 600cc (37ci) single.

The Paramount Special carried only the rider, who sat in a low-mounted bucket seat.

The Paramount Duo had a second seat and was available with either engine; the Special was available only with the V-twin. All three versions had very similar configuration: a low frame with the headstock supported by tubes that ran up to it and its girder forks. The panels extended down to cast-alloy footboards, forward to act as leg shields and back over the rear wheel for luggage.

The three models remained in production until 1928. In 1927, the 600cc (37ci) single was renamed the Paramount Popular and its engine changed to a Blackburne 499cc (30ci) single. Only small numbers of these unusual vehicles were ever made, and not all of those were actually sold.

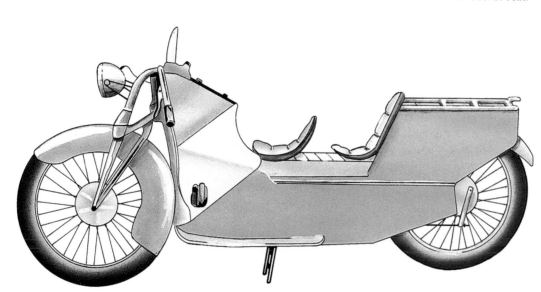

The Paramount Duo's peculiar, fully enclosed appearance failed to win it much popularity. Many other machines that used this concept were likewise unsuccessful.

GALLONI

ITALY 1920–31

Alberto Galloni's firm, based in Borgomanero, entered the motorcycle industry in 1920 with a line of 494cc (30ci) and 744cc (45ci) V-twins. These had side valves and magneto ignition, and both models were available in Turismo and Sport forms, with a three-speed gearbox and all-chain drive in a conventional format with girder forks. Overall, Gallonis machines were similar to many on the market already. The main difference was a patented rear suspension method.

Soon afterwards, the firm marketed a range of 250cc (15ci), 350cc (21ci) and 500cc (31ci) singles with side- or overhead-valves. These used similar cycle parts to the twins, with the separate three-speed gearbox and all-chain drive, but used a rigid frame rather than Galloni's rear suspension system.

With good coverage of the market spectrum, Galloni was one of the leading firms for a few years, and through the 1920s its machines followed industry trends. However, Galloni lost ground to other firms late in the decade, and as the Depression deepened the firm was unable to carry on. The company closed down in 1931.

HAGG TANDEM

ENGLAND 1920–24

Every now and then, someone would attempt to build a motorcycle with good weather protection for the rider and the machinery. This machine, built by Arthur Hagg, was one such.

Powered by a 349cc (21ci) Precision two-stroke engine driving through a two-speed Burman gearbox, the Hagg Tandem was first displayed at the Olympia Show in 1921. Its frame had a large diameter sloping top tube with angle steel members to carry the works and the front and rear suspension.

The engine and gearbox were protected by hinged side panels that could be opened to provide access for servicing. Above that was the cylindrical saddle tank and saddle, while below were footboards that ran forward to deep leg shields. Behind the access panels, the machine was enclosed far enough back to partially enclose the rear wheel. This section supported the pillion rider's bucket seat, which had sides.

Although an improved and less noisy version was created and a more conventional variant was marketed, Hagg's machine never achieved in the marketplace and went out of production after 1924.

The Hagg Tandem offered a sleeve-valve engine, Biflex forks and good weather protection but ultimately failed to find many buyers.

MAS

ITALY 1920–56

Milan-based Mas (Motoscafo Anti Sommergibile) provided motorcycles to the civilian and military markets, and did well in competition with its range of 123cc (8ci) overhead-valve models. It put out a large range of models during the 1930s, ranging from a 248cc (15ci) side-valve to a large, 568cc (35ci) side-valve single.

In 1938, the firm's founder, Alberi Seilig, left to found a new business (the short-lived Altea factory). Mas then began to supply a number of 348cc (30ci) overhead-valve singles to the Italian Army, and the firm went on producing civilian and military motorcycles after the war. The first of its post-war models was a 122cc (7ci) overhead-valve Stella Alpine.

The Stella Alpine incorporated an innovative idea formulated by the machine's designer, Guidetti. The cylinder was cast in the form of two concentric cylinders. The inner one was joined to the outer by a number of vertical fins in a single-casting operation. This was intended to provide efficient cooling at low speeds in much the same way as a stationary engine is kept cool; in other words, the engine itself could provide its own cooling.

Despite its clever cooling system, the Stella Alpine was not a commercial success. After it came a prototype 492cc (30ci) parallel twin with single overhead-camshaft, but this never made it to production. A range of overhead-valve and overhead-cam, single-cylinder 175cc (11ci) appeared in the 1950s, but these too failed to sell in any real numbers. After staving off the end for a time by producing humble 125cc (8ci) two-strokes and a 49cc (3ci) scooter, all with bought-in German Sachs engines, Mas went under in 1956.

PULLIN-GROOM

Cyril Pullin won the Senior TT in 1914 and embarked on a 40-year career of creating unusual motorcycles. His very first offering was a collaboration with S.L. Groom, gaining it the name Pullin-Groom.

The Pullin-Groom had an unusual frame constructed from a pair of steel pressings welded together. The fuel, oil tanks and the engine were inside. Servicing was by means of access panels. More steel pressings were used to build up the rocking fork at the front. Suspension at the rear was by pivoted forks. The wire wheels were interchangeable and could be quickly swapped over, but the only braking was by a drum brake on the rear wheel. This could be applied by hand or foot.

The Pullin-groom was powered by a 200cc (12ci) two-stroke of the company's own design, driving through a two-speed epicyclic gearbox with all-chain drive.

Overall, the design impressed observers, but it was too advanced for the general public and did not succeed in the marketplace. The machine was withdrawn from sale in 1923, but reappeared later with a 310cc (19ci) engine in 1924. It vanished again after 1925, and this time it did not resurface.

BARR & STROUD

Although Barr & Stroud is best known as an engine supplier, the firm did build a complete machine for use as a testbed. This was a 350cc (21ci) AJS frame with Brampton Biflex forks, three-speed gearbox and all-chain drive. The 348cc (21ci) engine fitted to this model was unusual in that it used a sleeve valve, which combined reciprocating and partial rotating movements to align the ports that controlled the gas flow in and out of the cylinder.

This engine also deviated from convention in that the cylinder and the upper crankcase half were cast as one, with a separate cylinder head with front exhaust and rear inlet ports. An oil pump went on the outside of the timing cover. The general appearance, however, was basically similar to contemporary engines.

The testbed machine was workable, so it was put it into production at the end of 1921. A 499cc (30ci) single and a 999cc (61ci) V-twin were added to the range, but the sleeve-valve engine had some inherent problems and was not a commercial success.

BROUGH SUPERIOR

The Brough Superior may well have been the first production machine to use a saddle tank arrangement. Its tank is one of the most outstanding features of the machine in terms of both design and decoration. The Superior used a JAP engine with a single-cam and single-valve springs. Pistons were light-alloy with two compression rings and a scraper ring, and lubrication was a total-loss system via both hand-pump and foot-pump.

From this original model came the SS80 with twin cams and double valve springs, and by 1927 the SS80 was delivering 25hp in its standard form or 30hp in more expensive 'special' form. There was also a 988cc (60ci) side-valve JAP version, the so-called Mark II with a MAG inlet-over-exhaust engine, and a variant with a 999cc (61ci) Barr and Stroud sleeve-valve engine.

With the world's first saddle tank and incredible power by the standards of the time, the Brough Superior was destined to be one of the world's best and fastest machines.

ENGINE: 498cc (30ci) overhead-valve, in-line V–twin, air-cooled
POWER: 19–311bhp
GEARBOX: 4–speed hand change
FINAL DRIVE: chain
WEIGHT: n/a
TOP SPEED: 145km/h (90mph)

DELLA FERRERA RECORD MODEL

This very fast machine was based on a road model and was mostly conventional, though it did have some interesting features. Its V-twin engine had its cylinders set at an angle of 45°, and the bore and stroke were equal at 68mm (2.7in), which was rather unusual in an era when longer strokes were more common. These dimensions gave a 94cc (6ci) capacity.

The crankcase was split vertically, with a main bearing in each half. To suit the big ends, the cylinders were offset side by side on the crankpin and mounted to the crankcase on four studs. Four further studs were used to locate the cylinder heads and fitted with long nuts to hold them down, which extended up to carry the rocker spindle plates and camshaft bearings. The inclined valves had

springs while each head had stubs for both inlet and exhaust ports.

It was Della Ferrera himself who used the machine in its record attempt. The result was a very impressive (for the time) figure of 145km/h (90mph). This was the current best for any Italian bike, but an Indian had been timed at over 165km/h (103mph) in 1920, and this was accepted as the world record.

ENGINE: 494cc (30ci) ohv V–twin, 68x68mm, air-cooled
POWER: 20bhp at 5300rpm
GEARBOX: 3–speed hand change
FINAL DRIVE: chain
WEIGHT: n/a
TOP SPEED: 140km/h (85mph)

GARANZINI

Garanzini was founded by Oreste Garanzini, the 1921 Italian 350cc (21ci) champion. He imported a British machine, the Verus, and renamed it Veros for the Italian market. After a while, he began producing machines of his own design.

Garanzini's first was a 349cc (21ci) side-valve single, which was sold both as a two-speed Sport and as a three-speed Luxus with bigger wheels and an oil-bath for the chain final drive. In 1922, the firm began using 350cc (21ci) JAP engines and used the name Garanzini-JAP or sometimes JAP-Garanzini. A little later, the range widened and began to include machines powered by Blackburne four-strokes of varying sizes and Villiers two-strokes of 147cc (9ci) to 248cc (15ci).

Garanzini himself was heavily involved in racing and entered a 350cc (21ci) JAP-engined machine with a four-valve head and three-speed gearbox at Monza in 1923. His track experience fed back into, and inspired, new bike designs.

In 1925, the range included a 250cc (15ci) overhead-valve single, a 350cc (21ci) side-valve single,

three 350cc (21ci) singles (two side-valve, one overhead-valve), and 500cc (31ci) and 615cc twins. All of these models used Garanzini's patented fork design.

The following year, Garanzini fielded new Standard, Sport and Super-Sport models, ranging from 250cc (15ci) to 680cc (41ci). The 250 CTO had a shaft-driven

overhead-cam in an oil-cooled cylinder head, delivering 12hp at 7000rpm, and a new 175cc (11ci) overhead-cam lightweight was introduced at Monza.

In 1927, the firm introduced several new models, including two revised 250s, a side-valve 350 with a modified JAP side-valve engine and a JAP-engined 680. The range further expanded in 1929 with Villiers-powered two-strokes and JAP four-strokes, but production ceased in 1931.

Italian designs are normally known for their flair and style, but there are always exceptions. The clunky, dated appearance of this 1927 Garanzini is one of them. It retained a flat tank several years after the style had moved in the direction of saddle tanks.

LUTECE

Lutece was one of a number of firms that appeared in the wake of World War I but did not survive the difficult times of the mid-1920s. Based out of Colombes, Seine, Lutece produced heavyweight machines. This was unusual for a French company; lightweights were more common

and, generally, more popular.

The other unusual feature of Lutece designs is that they built twins, but not in the usual V-twin configuration. Instead, a vertical-twin layout was used. Lutece's first design was a top-end luxury machine with a big engine. This 1000cc (61ci) vertical-twin

machine mounted its engine along the frame and drive straight back to the clutch and gearbox. Final drive was by a shaft to the rear wheel.

The frame was robust and had both front and rear suspension, with a generally American appearance to it. The Lutece was a

big machine and was useful for sidecar work, but it was also expensive. It failed to achieve commercial success and the firm's fortunes declined. The last Lutece machine was rather different – a 100cc (6ci) velomoteur – but nothing could save the firm by then, and it vanished in 1926.

MEGOLA

The rather implausible Megola was produced by Megola Motoren Aktiengesellschaft of Munich. This grew out of the firm Mego, founded in 1920 by Teilhaber Meixer and Fritz Cockerell (who was spelling his name with a G, rather than a C, at the time). Joined by a Herr Landgraf in 1921, Mego became Megola.

Power came from a 637cc (39ci) five-cylinder radial engine, which produced a modest 6–8hp. Later versions more or less doubled this output. There was no gearbox;

drive was constant-ratio, though it was possible to change performance by altering the size of the front wheel. Starting was either by pushing the machine or by putting it on its stand and spinning the front wheel manually to start the engine. By dropping

The Megola's five-cylinder radial engine, mounted in the front wheel, is clearly evident in this picture. The only way to keep the engine running when the machine is stationary is to put it up on its stand.

off the stand, the rider could then lurch into powered motion.

Between 1921 and 1925, Megola built about 2000 of these machines, which were designed to be easy to maintain. This was just as well as they sometimes needed decarbonizing after just 2000–3000km (1000–2000 miles). The cylinders could be removed with the spokes of the front wheel in place.

Amazingly, these odd machines did rather well in competition for a few years.

MERAY

HUNGARY 1921–44

Based out of Budapest, Meray manufactured a broad range of machines from 175cc (11ci) to 1000cc (61ci). Their chosen method was to buy in a lot of the necessary parts, particularly engines and gearboxes but also smaller components.

Engines came from a number of different sources: Villiers, Blackburne, JAP, Puch and Moto-Rêve. The Villiers were two-stroke units with flywheel magnetos, but the others had side- or overhead-valves, both with magneto ignition.

Meray's completed machines were fairly conventional, built on a tubular or occasionally cradle frame with girder forks, wire wheels and, by the end of the 1920s, drum brakes. By the mid-1930s, the firm was producing an engine in house for its machines.

This was a single-cylinder, four-stroke engine available in 346cc (21ci) and 496cc (30ci) capacities.

Meray did well up until World War II, but afterwards the Hungarian motorcycle industry was nationalized and the firm's separate identity faded away.

MILLER-BALSAMO

ITALY 1921–59

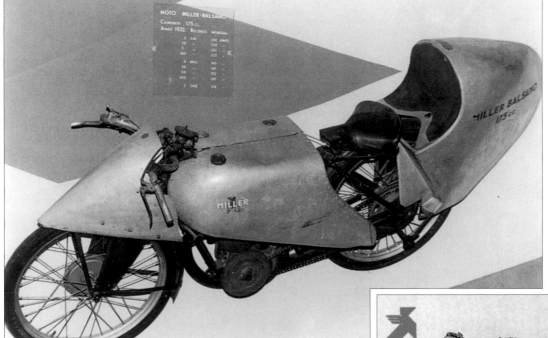

This Milan-based firm was founded by the three Balsamo brothers: Ernesto, Edgardo and Mario. They produced their first machine in 1921: a 123cc (8ci) two-stroke, which was followed by a popular 174cc (11ci) overhead-valve model using a Swiss Moser engine. The Balsamo brothers were keen on the idea of enclosing the working parts of their motorcycles.

The firm did well enough, and achieved success in races and record attempts. In the 1930s, Miller-Balsamo began using British engines in its machines. The commonest of these was the Rudge (Python), available in capacities from 174cc (11ci) to 498cc (30ci). A new 246cc (15ci) overhead-valve single appeared just before World War II, and a 200cc (12ci) machine featuring full enclosure.

After the war, Miller-Balsamo got back into production quickly and marketed the Jupiter, a fully enclosed 246cc (15ci) overhead-valve machine, which featured hydraulically controlled rear suspension and compressed air forks. Another of its interesting features was a gear indicator. The Jupiter got around the usual problem of enclosed designs – difficulty of maintenance – by using large hinged panels.

The new range also included a non-enclosed version of the Jupiter and an updated variant of the pre-war 200cc (12ci) machine. These were followed by a 169cc (10ci) overhead-valve single, but the decline of the industry in the 1950s caused Miller-Balsamo to close down just before the new decade.

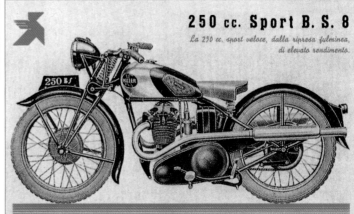

Miller-Balsamo machines were highly successful record breakers and racing bikes in the 1930s. This 174cc (10ci) Rudge-powered machine is a speed record breaker.

MOLARONI

ITALY 1921–27

As seems to be the way with Italian motorcycle firms, Pesaro-based Molaroni was founded by brothers just after World War I. Two products initially appeared: a 300cc (18ci) single mounted vertically and the other a 600cc (37ci) flat twin set along the frame. Both were two-strokes and were fairly typical of the period.

An updated version of the 300cc (18ci) single was soon brought out, and another version that was essentially the 300cc (18ci) bored out but retaining the existing stroke to make a 345cc (21ci) machine. In addition, the firm began buying in four-stroke Blackburne engines to build a new set of models. The most popular of these was a 350cc (21ci).

These machines were decent enough, but were thoroughly unexciting. Electric lights, a feature implemented more quickly by other manufacturers, were slow to appear and came in as an extra rather than a standard component. Molaroni could not compete effectively and so faded from the marketplace after a relatively short six years.

MOTO GUZZI

A more 'busy' design in terms of appearance than most Moto Guzzis, this 1929 racer is still clean and elegant. Moto Guzzi fans have always favoured the flat-single engine and been a little sceptical of others.

Moto Guzzi machines have always tended to cause almost as much aggravation as pleasure. Somehow, despite their faults, Moto Guzzis have remained popular. Perhaps it is because they are built with passion rather than cold efficiency, or perhaps because a certain segment of the motorcycle fraternity is every bit as quirky as the machines they ride.

In the past, Moto Guzzis have suffered from a range of faults: rattling; changing colour if left out in the sun too long; and having a multiplicity of wires, all of them yellow, to track when performing maintenance. This sort of thing is less common in recent times, but to some extent it was all accepted as part of the experience of owning a Moto Guzzi, in the way that some classic car fans rave about the 'driving experience' when describing a car that others might consider too much like hard work to drive.

Moto Guzzi was founded by Carlo Guzzi and Giorgio Parodi, who built their first prototype as the GP (Guzzi & Parodi) in 1920. There should have been a third man in the team, a mutual friend from their days in the Italian Air Force named Giovanni Ravelli, but he was killed in a flying accident just after the war ended. The firm's logo, an open-winged eagle, was adopted in his memory.

By the time the first production bike appeared, the Moto Guzzi

name had been adopted, and this machine, the Normale, was the first of what became a classically Moto Guzzi design: a 500cc (31ci) over-square single, with the cylinder parallel with the ground. The 'flat single' would, with variations, be a Moto Guzzi hallmark until 1976.

The other classic Moto Guzzi design was conceived as the powerplant for a decidedly odd military vehicle. This was a tricycle affair with vestigial tracks on the rear wheels, steered from the front wheel. It was nicknamed 'mulo meccanico', or 'mechanical mule'. From this peculiar project came a classic engine design, the transverse, 90-degree V-twin.

The Mechanical Mule project ran from 1960 to 1963 and then faded away, but the engine went into the V7 motorcycle that came out in 1967. The transverse V-twin was used in a range of machines thereafter, in capacities

ranging from 350cc (21ci) to 1100cc (67ci).

Moto Guzzi also produced a range of smaller singles over the years. The 1932 P175 was the first road-going, overhead-valve engine that was to benefit from advances in engine design. Indeed, it delivered only 1hp less than the Normale, which had a much larger engine. The PE250, in production from 1934 to 1939, was actually more powerful than the original 500cc (31ci).

The other classic small single, appearing in 1956, was the Lodola. This was originally a 175cc (11ci) overhead-cam, but later was given a 235cc (14ci) pushrod engine. This was the last design by Carlo Guzzi himself. It was unusual in that the cylinder was inclined at 45 degrees rather than being flat, which did cause some head-scratching among Guzzi purists.

Two other singles are worthy of special mention. The Galetto first appeared as a 150cc (9ci) show model in 1950 and entered production as a 160cc (10ci) machine. The engine was enlarged to 175cc (11ci) in 1952, and again increased in capacity in 1954 via a 5mm (0.2in) increase in stroke. In 1961, the Galetto was substantially redesigned and given electric starting, finally going out of production.

The other unusual single, the Stornello, was introduced as a 125cc (8ci), but later grew to 160cc (10ci) before disappearing in 1975. While never a particularly exciting machine, it did offer the Guzzi magic at a very modest price.

After World War II, Italy desperately needed transport, and Moto Guzzi produced a range of machines to meet this need. The first was the 64cc (4ci) Guzzino, which was later supplemented and then replaced by the Zigolo, initially 98cc (6ci) and later 110cc (7ci). The Guzzino was not the smallest Moto Guzzi ever; that distinction is shared by the 49cc (3ci) Dingo lightweights and Trotter mopeds.

After the De Tomaso takeover in 1970, a number of Benellis were produced under the Moto Guzzi badge. While some of these were very fine machines, some Moto Guzzi fans dispute that they are the 'real thing'. Whatever the truth of that, the firm was taken over again in 1993, this time by Finprogetti. In 2000, it was sold yet again, this time to Aprilia.

A 1975 S3. This 750cc (45ci) machine was produced during the de Tomaso period. Fans might argue whether this is a 'real' Moto Guzzi or a Benelli masquerading as one, whatever the name on the tank might say.

MOTO GUZZI NORMALE

Moto Guzzi's first production machine was the 1921 Normale. The prototype had a chain-driven overhead-cam and four valves, but the production version was a two-valve, inlet-over-exhaust 'flat single', which would bec,ome a classic Moto Guzzi design. The Normale

predates the popularity of saddle tanks and looks rather dated, but it did have the big external 'bacon slicer' flywheel that is one of the most memorable features of the classic big singles.

It was this machine that Moto Guzzi first used for racing. Within a few months, it had won its first race at the Targa Florio. Moto Guzzi would go on winning races for many years (3329 in all) before leaving the race scene in 1957.

This is where it all started, with the 498cc Normale. Delivering 8hp, the Normale could reach 80km/h (50mph), which was enough to start winning races.

ENGINE: 498cc (30ci) ioe single, 88x82mm, air-cooled
POWER: 8bhp at 3000rpm
GEARBOX: 3-speed hand change
FINAL DRIVE: chain
WEIGHT: 130kg (286lb)
TOP SPEED: 80km/h (50mph)

NERACAR

The Neracar was a largely enclosed machine designed in the USA and originally built in Syracuse, New York. It was, however, later built under licence by Sheffield Simplex in Kingston-on-Thames.

The Neracar was built around a pressed-steel, channel-section frame. Its monocoque shell concealed most of the mechanics, with just the cylinder on view, and ran all the way to the front mudguard. The cylindrical fuel

tank went under the low saddle, and braking was via two drum brakes located in the rear hub.

The American model had a 211cc (13ci) two-stroke engine set along the frame, its flywheel placed to drive a friction wheel at right angles and able to move across its face. This varied the ratio between them and was controlled by a lever, while a chain drove the rear wheel. It was an interesting concept, but the market was difficult in the USA

at that time and the Neracar did not catch on.

The idea was exported to Britain, where it found more favour. Early British models mounted the 211cc (13ci) engine, and in 1923 a 285cc (17ci) version appeared.

Performance was on the feeble side of modest, so a 348cc (21ci) side-valve Blackburne engine driving a three-speed gearbox was introduced for 1925, and the following year an overhead-valve.

However, the Neracar still did not sell all that well and Sheffield Simplex was by then suffering financial difficulties. The firm closed down in 1927.

The novel (some would say downright peculiar) Neracar was powered by a 348cc (21ci)side-valve Blackburne engine driving through a three-speed gearbox. Its low riding position and hub-centre steering were just two of its unusual features.

OPEL

Opel started out making bicycles and sewing machines. A range of cars was marketed from 1898, with motorcycles following in 1901. Opel's first bikes were conventional singles, which were in production until 1907.

No more motorcycles appeared until after the war, but in 1921 Opel introduced a 138cc (8ci) side-valve engine designed to be fitted to the left side of the rear wheel of a standard bicycle. Opel was making bicycles at the time, so it

was a small step to begin producing a model with the engine already fitted.

True motorcycles followed, the first a lightweight with a 148cc (9ci) engine and two-speed gearbox. This was followed in 1926

by a 499cc (30ci) side-valve single, designed by Ernst Neumann-Neander and using a frame built up from steel pressings. An overhead-valve version in the same format came in 1928. Opel faded back out of the motorcycle market in 1930.

ZUNDAPP

Where wartime spelled the end for many firms, it spelled the start for Nurnberg-based Zunderund Apparatebau (better known as Zundapp for obvious reasons). Founded in September 1917 as a joint venture between three firms, the company was primarily concerned with the manufacture of artillery fuses. The end of the war left Zundapp with a factory, 1800 workers and no market for its product.

Taken over in 1919 by Fritz Neumeyer, Zundapp moved into motorcycle manufacture in 1921. The firm made more than 3 million bikes over the next six decades. It all started with a model called the Z22, which was powered by a 211cc (13ci) British-made Levis two-stroke. Production was brisk, and more than1000 were made in the first year.

It was obvious to Neumeyer that his firm needed to make a name for its machines in competition. He started early, entering the first-ever Zundapp machine to come off the lines in North Bavarian reliability trials in September 1921. It was ridden by the German champion Metsch, who would long be associated with the Zundapp marque.

The Z22 sufficed for a while, but by the time the firm had been making motorcycles for three years, new models were appearing. These used in-house engine designs, including a 249cc (15ci) version of the original Levis.

Zundapp was a forward-looking firm and embraced modern assembly-line techniques in 1924, coinciding with the beginning of a motorcycle-buying boom in Germany. By the end of the year, 10,000 machines had come off the lines, and they sold well. Success in the national 17-day touring race helped raise the profile of the firm at just the right time.

From 1926 onwards, Zundapp established branches in all of Germany's major commercial centres, starting with Berlin. In the process, he set up a nationwide dealer and service network. Within two years, a new plant was needed since the four existing factories could not cope with demand, and after its opening Zundapp was producing more than 4200 machines a month. However, sales fell off quickly, down to just 300 machines a month at the end of 1929.

The Depression was a difficult time for Zundapp, but it got through thanks to good management. By 1933, it was on the road to recovery with a new range of 398ccc (24ci) and 348cc (30ci) twins and a 598cc (36ci) flat four, all of them designed by Richard Kuchen.

Next came a small two-stroke in 1934, named the Derby. It was a 174cc (11ci) lightweight delivering 5.5hp, and incorporated some new engine design ideas that were later used in other Zundapp two-strokes.

Once again, Zundapp found itself in the position of being so popular that the factories could not meet demand. On top of this, there were demands for military machines as Hitler's regime re-armed Germany. New models during this period included the KS600 flat twin with a 597cc (36ci) engine and the DS350, the first Zundapp to use a foot pedal gear change.

From March 1940, Zundapp was again committed to war work and was not supplying the civilian market. However, it was able to keep making motorcycles and produced its 250,000th machine in March 1942.

This historic machine was a KS750, which had been designed as a military motorcycle. It had an integral sidecar with the wheel

driven via a lockable differential. It had two sets of four forward and reverse gears and a flat-twin engine. Like the BMW R75, this was one of the definitive German motorcycles of World War II.

Zundapp lost a lot of its production facilities at the end of the war, and had just 170 workers in 1945, compared to 4000 in 1944. It was not until the summer of 1947 that motorcycle manufacture recommenced with a range of updated pre-war models. The first new design was the DB201, a two-stroke single.

Next came the KS600. It had a pressed-steel frame, and looked very dated, so it was quickly replaced by the KS601. Nicknamed the 'Green Elephant', it had a 597cc (36ci) overhead valve engine and could drive at nearly 141km/h (88mph), making it the fastest German street bike of the time. These machines were excellent for sidecar work and so they also sold well in that market.

Zundapp moved its factory to Munich in early 1950 and continued to do very well. Development concentrated on small two-strokes, and the KS601 twins were phased out. Zundapp also found success in the scooter

Emerging from the hard times of the late 1960s, Zundapp was approaching its peak sales when the single-cylinder, two-stroke GS125 Enduro first went to market in 1972. Ten years later the bubble burst, but for the moment Zundapp was riding high with machines like this one.

market with the Bella, which sold more than 130,000 units.

In 1955, Zundapp launched the 200S, which was the first of a new family of machines that ran on until the 250 Trophy S was made in the late 1960s. During this period, Zundapp also achieved excellent sporting success and provided the winning machines for the German national squad.

The late 1960s were hard times for the whole German motorcycle industry, but the firm fared far better than most. Indeed, in 1965, sales of mopeds, lightweights and scooters were at near record levels. However, the firm hit its peak in 1977, when it sold 115,000 machines, but declined surprisingly quickly after that. In 1981, sales dropped by almost 50 per cent and again, by more than 40 per cent, the following year. In 1984, the firm went bankrupt.

BEKAMO

Bekamo was a short-lived firm based in Berlin. Its machines were designed by Hugo Ruppe, who had earlier worked for DKW. They used an advanced 129cc (8ci) two-stroke engine with a pumping piston in a second cylinder in the base of the crankcase. In some versions, this piston controlled the

inlet phase as well as increasing crankcase compression, while two transfer ports passed the mixture to the combustion chamber above the main piston with its deflector top. Early models had a wooden frame, but a more conventional tubular metal construction with light girder forks was soon adopted.

Bekamo engines were produced under licence by other firms, including Böhme, Eichler, MFZ, TX and Windhoff, and were sold to other manufacturers for use in a range of machines. By 1925, the firm was in trouble and the Berlin plant closed. This was not quite the end, though. For some time, the

German plant had been supplying engines and, for a while, complete machines to a second plant at Rumburk in Czechoslovakia. After the Berlin closure in 1925, the remaining facilities were transferred there and assembly continued for five years before Bekamo was wound up.

BMW

BMW (Bayerische Motoren Werke) was formed in 1918 by the amalgamation of the Bayerische Flugzeugwerke (Aeroplane Works)

and the Gustav Otto Flugmaschinesfabrik (Flying Machine Factory). This was the end of World War I, and demand for

combat aircraft in Germany fell rather rapidly after this. The firm therefore moved into the motorcycle marketplace.

BMW managed to succeed despite two failed projects. These were the two-stroke single Flink and the M2B15 flat-twin.

The breakthrough came when Max Friz, one of the founders of the Flugzeugwerke, designed the transverse flat-twin R32. This machine sold fairly well and was the basis for further development. It gained overhead valves and a lot more power in 1925 to become the R37, but this model and the R32 were replaced in 1926 by the more advanced R42 and R47.

Ever-more-powerful machines followed, and as the 1930s dawned BMW was setting records and winning races. It pushed the world motorcycle speed record up to 244.4km/h (151.9mph) in 1932, and by the end of he decade the firm was producing blown 500cc (31ci) racers that delivered about 70hp.

BMW made engines for the Luftwaffe and motorcycles for the army during World War II. Afterwards, it was restricted in what it could do, and it relied on a range of singles. At one point, it seemed that BMW might even leave the motorcycle industry, but instead it came storming back with the R90S and R100RS.

Next came the 'Brick', an in-line, longitudinally mounted, liquid-cooled straight-four, which BMW

imagined would replace the seemingly immortal 'boxer'. There was also a K75, or three-quarter-brick, which was really the 1000cc (61ci) engine with one cylinder removed to give 750cc (46ci). The year 1992 brought a new generation of overhead-valve, four-valve-per-cylinder boxers, which soon diversified more

interestingly than the brick series, even though the bricks rose to 1200cc (73ci) to preserve their power advantage.

BMW fans sometimes like to pretend that the C1 scooter never existed, but it was merely one facet of a broad range that brought the firm up to the present. BMW has been through some

The R90S, introduced in 1973, was BMW's first real 'superbike'. With an 898cc (55ci) engine, it was both powerful and stylish, with a real airbrushed paintjob.

tough times and has never been fashionable so much as solid. It has always done its own thing – and well enough to survive.

HECKER

In the years between the two world wars, Hecker grew to become a major manufacturer. Early machines used engines of founder Hans Hecker's own design and included 245cc (15ci) two-strokes and 346cc (21ci) overhead-valve singles. Next was a range powered

by JAP and MAG engines, including a 746cc (46ci) V-twin with inlet-over-exhaust valve operation, then a couple of lightweights with square-tube frames and either 73cc (4ci) or 98cc (6ci) Sachs two-stroke power units. Production began again in 1948 with a 123cc (8ci)

machine, the K125. For a time, this constituted the entire range, but in 1950 it was joined by the V200, which had a 197cc (12ci) Villiers engine. More 'K' models followed in 175cc (11ci), 200cc (12ci) and 250cc (15ci) capacities. Single-cylinder Ilo engines were used for

all these machines. Hecker won a number of sporting events in the 1950s, most notably the 1954 ISDT. However, the mid-1950s were a terrible time for German motorcycle manufacturing and Hecker was caught unprepared. The firm struggled and succumbed in 1957.

MOTOBÉCANE (MOTOCONFORT)

Founded in 1922 by Abel Bardin and Charles Benoît, Motobécane is primarily famous for its long-running range of practical and reliable machines, which included the Mobylette moped. The firm sometimes used the Motoconfort brand for some of its products.

The first Motobécane machine was prototyped in 1922 but did not go into production until 1924. Motobécane's business model favoured mass production of a single model. In 1924, that model was a 175cc (11ci) two-stroke available in two versions – one for men and one for ladies.

An updated version appeared in 1928, and some 150,000 had been sold by the end of the following year. At that time, a slightly enlarged range included four-stroke machines with 348cc (21ci) and 495cc (30ci) Blackburne side- and overhead-valve engines, and a year later a more complex machine was

marketed. This was powered by a 500cc (31ci), in-line, four-cylinder, side-valve engine built-in unit with the gearbox. This model, too, received an update in 1931 and was enlarged to 750cc (46ci). It was never produced in very large numbers, however; Motobécane still favoured mass-marketing smaller machines.

Motobécane got through the 1930s with a range of singles that also included a velomoteur. After the inevitable halt due to the war, it resumed production with a range of four-strokes with telescopic forks and plunger rear suspension.

The 1949 Mobylette moped was an important release for Motobécane. The first model had the most basic specification but other versions followed. These

retained the 50cc (3ci) engine but gained features such as automatic clutch, automatic variable gear ratio, telescopic front forks, plunger rear suspension, pivoted-fork rear suspension and better brakes.

The basic version of the Mobylette remained a good seller, proving that Motobécane had chosen a good business model from the outset. It was accompanied by other models

including a vertical twin, a scooter and a 350cc (21ci) two-stroke triple.

In the 1970s, Motobécane developed a 125cc (8ci) twin that took second in the world championship. However, times were hard in the 1980s and even with the guaranteed income generated by the eternal Mobylette, Motobécane could not continue. It was sold to Yamaha, which continued to build machines in the factory.

This 500cc (30ci) model dates from 1937, and was amongst Motobécane's finest bikes.

SERTUM

Sertum started out making precision instruments, but from 1922 it began manufacturing motorcycles. The first machine was a 174cc (11ci) side-valve model, closely followed by a cheaper 119cc (7ci) two-stroke. The range grew, and through the 1920s and 1930s Sertum constructed a range of singles and twins with side-valve and overhead-cam engines available.

Sertum machines acquired a reputation for reliability and also did well in competition, particularly the International Six Days' Trial (ISDT) and long-distance road races such as the Milano–Taranto event.

Production was interrupted by World War II, but Sertum was soon back in production and was again competing in the IDST in 1947. The range at this point was basic: a girder-fork, rear-sprung 250cc (15ci) overhead-valve single and a similar 500cc (31ci). A 500cc (31ci)

A factory machine entered by Sertum in the 1939 ISDT, held near Salzburg in Austria. Sertum had a strong presence in long-distance events like the ISDT and the Milano-Taranto race.

vertical twin was on the cards, but the decision about whether to implement production had not yet been made. The firm also displayed a new sports 250cc (15ci) with a pressed-steel frame.

The year 1948 was good for Sertum. Together with the others of the 'big five' Italian manufacturers (Gilera, Bianchi, Parilla and Moto Guzzi), it accounted for almost 98 per cent of motorcycle registrations in Italy that year. There were 33 other manufacturers, who between them divided up just over 2 per cent of the sales that year. However, things began to go downhill, and by 1951 Sertum had become the first of the big post-war Italian manufacturers to go under.

TORNAX

During the 1920s and 1930s, Tornax built quality motorcycles powered by JAP and Columbus (Horex) engines and a small sports car that used a three-cylinder DKW two-stroke engine. World War II caused major disruption, and it was not until 1948 that the firm returned to production under the leadership of new owner Ernst Wewer.

The post-war line was entirely new, using 125cc (8ci) and 175cc (11ci) Ilo single-cylinder, two-stroke engines. Unusually for the times, Tornax machines were quality bikes rather than utilitarian transport, and both models sold well in Germany and northern Europe. It was clear though that the market was becoming harder. Tornax responded with a major development programme that resulted in new 200cc (12ci) and 250cc (15ci) machines.

Although the programme got some results, sales did not recoup investment. Tornax got into financial difficulties just as the mid-1950s recession really began to bite. It closed down in 1955. The name reappeared between 1982 and 1984 on a range of 50cc (3ci) and 80cc (5ci) machines powered by Minarelli engines, before disappearing for good.

TRIUMPH FAST ROADSTER

Triumph's 1922 Type IR 'Fast Roadster' was a 499cc (30ci) machine designed by piston and combustion chamber specialists Ricardo & Co. It featured pushrod-actuated overhead-valves with centrally positioned spark plugs, with both sets of valves arranged at 90 degrees to one another. The piston was aluminium, running in a bore machined from steel billet, and there was a single inlet manifold from the carburettor, while exhaust emissions passed away down two separate pipes.

The rest of the IR was more conventional. In some ways, it was even dated. Its frame and most other components came from the Model H, though it had druid-pattern girder forks. With a top speed of 121km/h (75mph), the Type IR was known as the 'Riccy' after the engineer Harry Ricardo.

In 1927, the Type IR was replaced by the Type TT. This machine also had a new engine, designed by Brooklands racer Victor Horsman. It featured a twin-port overhead-valve head, enclosed lubricated valvegear and roller-bearing rockers, driving through a three-speed gearbox with traditional crossover drive. The hub brakes were the expanding internal type front and rear, while new front forks incorporated large fabric-friction discs and a steering damper.

ENGINE: (Type R) 499cc (30ci) single–cyclinder, 4–ohv four–stroke, air-cooled
POWER: 20bhp
GEARBOX: 3–speed
FINAL DRIVE: chain
WEIGHT: 109kg (240lb)
TOP SPEED: 121km/h (75mph)

UT

UT started out by building its own 246cc (15ci) two-stroke engine, with a horizontal cylinder. It soon proved more cost effective to buy in engines from Bekamo, Blackburne and JAP. While this transition was going on, UT was gaining notice for its participation in road races around Germany.

After managing to survive the Depression and World War II, UT returned to the market in 1951 with a range of two-stroke singles using 123cc (8ci) and 174cc (11ci) Ilo engines. Sold under the model designation KTN, these machines made their debut in 1951. They sold very well indeed, and production was increased in 1953, with new models were introduced. These included the KTV 175, TS 200, TS 250 and TS 252.

More models arrived in 1955 and 1956, but by this time UT was racing towards a crash. As the German motorcycle market went into free fall in the late 1950s, UT's sales dropped off fast and the firm closed its doors in 1959. Its last two years were spent selling off the remaining stocks; in reality, the firm had died in 1957.

AJS BIG PORT

The name 'Big Port' was applied, by fans rather than the makers, to Tom Sheard's TT-winning machine. It referred to the large exhaust fitted to the racing machine and was applied to the road model too. The Big Port was a light machine that, despite moderate power, possessed good acceleration and handled well enough to maintain a high average speed. With the ignition retarded, it could trundle along happily in town; on open road, it was fast and fun.

Although the Big Port was built for only a few years, it established an enviable reputation for itself and for its makers.

ENGINE: 348cc (21ci) ohv vertical single, 74x81mm, air-cooled
GEARBOX: 3–speed hand change
FINAL DRIVE: chain
WEIGHT: 95kg (210lb)
TOP SPEED: 135km/h (80mph)

ARISTOS

Designed by Johannes Passler, the Aristos was introduced in 1923 and was on sale for only about a year. Its design was based somewhat on that of the Mars, which was a more successful machine all round.

The Aristos had a pressed-steel frame. There was absolutely

nothing wrong with this concept, but at the time it was something of a radical idea, which meant that this method of construction was used mainly by firms willing to explore other avenues of experimentation. In the case of the Aristos, this led to its curious and rather ineffective cooling system.

The twin radiators designed to cool the 614cc (37ci) longitudinally mounted, side-valve flat-twin were, for some reason, located on each side of the rear wheel. This did promote good airflow and thus good cooling, meaning that they worked poorly even before they had been covered

in mud and general filth from the road surface.

On top of this, the Aristos had a very low seat position, giving a low centre of gravity and therefore good stability but at the price of a feeling of insecurity on the part of the rider. The design quickly faded from the marketplace.

BMW R32

The 1923-vintage R32, designed by Max Fritz. It boasted a 494cc (30ci) flat-twin engine and was successful enough in the marketplace to merit further development, leading to a long line of machines.

ENGINE: 494cc (30ci) sv transverse flat twin, air-cooled
POWER: 8.5bhp at 3300rpm
GEARBOX: 3–speed hand change
FINAL DRIVE: kardan shaft
WEIGHT: 120kg (264lb)
TOP SPEED: 90km/h (56mph)

BMW's 1923 offering was the handsome R32. It retained a flat-tank design where others were

already moving to saddle tanks, but the design was clean and elegant and, of course, beautifully

made. It was soon updated, creating the R37 model. The next versions were R42 and R47; this

numbering system probably made sense to someone at the time.

Other variations on the theme established with the R32 included a range of twins derived from the R39 single in 1925. In 1927 came the R52, the R57 and a side-valve version of the R52. In 1928 came the side-valve R62 and overhead-valve R63. By this time, the top-end model was three times as powerful as the R32.

DELTA-GNOM

After World War I, there was a need for powered transport right across Europe. Delta-Gnom met that demand by producing a two-stroke auxiliary engine for a bicycle, and quickly moved into true motorcycles. The first used an enlarged form of the original engine, but within two years Delta-Gnom was producing a 250cc (15ci) two-stroke engine of its own design for motorcycle use. Bought-in engines were also used, including JAP side- and overhead-valve single and V-twin four-strokes.

Production was interrupted between 1928 and 1932, at which point Delta-Gnom put its previous line back into production, with a few modifications. JAP engines were still in use, but the machines showed gradual evolution with saddle tanks, larger brakes and improved electrics.

The German takeover of Austrian industry in the run-up to

World War II interrupted production for a second time in 1938. After the war, Delta-Gnom produced a range of small two-strokes using bought-in engines from Ilo, Puch

or Rotax for a time. It then disappeared, another victim of the general troubles that beset the motorcycle industry in the mid-1950s.

This 1929 Delta-Gnom was produced during a transition period for the firm and used an in-house designed 498cc (30ci) engine.

DOUGLAS RA

Developed by Les Bayley, the overhead-valve RA was an attempt to update earlier twins. The main improvement was increased stability gained by positioning the engine lower in the frame and thus lowering the centre of gravity of the whole machine.

The RA also made use of light alloys for a lower overall weight. The 500cc (31ci) version of the RA weighed in at only 116kg (257lb).

The machine's name was probably derived from the British Research Association, which developed the braking system

used in the machine. This included an early version of disc brakes and was very effective in stopping such a light machine – at least by the standards of an era in which brakes were not considered very important and were, in general, alarmingly poor.

ENGINE: 348cc (21ci) sv longitudinally mounted flat twin, 60.8x60mm, air-cooled
POWER: n/a
GEARBOX: 3–speed hand change
FINAL DRIVE: chain
WEIGHT: n/a
TOP SPEED: n/a

DRESCH

Dresch produced a broad range of machines, including a 100cc (6ci) velomoteur and a 750cc (46ci) machine. The firm built its own engines, but also bought them in from Chaise, JAP and MAG. Early machines were fairly

conventional, but in 1930 the firm introduced something a little different. This model boasted a 500cc (31ci), in-line, tandem-twin, four-stroke engine with side-valves. The engine drove through a three-speed, hand-change

gearbox with shaft drive to the rear wheel, and was mounted in a pressed-steel frame with girder forks.

Other, more conventional machines were also produced, including 250cc (15ci), 350cc

(21ci) and 500cc (31ci) singles. While of a fairly standard design, these benefited from the firm's flair for design and styling. However, production stopped in 1939 and did not resume after the war.

GD

Named (or, perhaps, initialled) after its founder Guido Dall'Oglio, GD was later known as GD-Ghirardi due to an association with Ghirardi. To confuse matters further, Dall'Oglio also built a machine under his surname in 1926.

GD made its name with a 125cc (8ci) horizontal single two-stroke machine, which won at Monza despite its two-speed gearbox. This machine was associated with the racing heroes Alfonso Drusiani, Frederico Castellani, Gugliemo Sandri and Amilcare Rosetti.

In 1928, the line was expanded by the addition of a four-speed 250cc (15ci) two-stroke parallel twin, which was followed by 175cc (11ci) and 350cc (21ci) overhead-cam four-strokes. In 1929, a 100cc (6ci) two-stroke was also marketed, but by then GD

was past its peak. The firm's fortunes declined steadily through the 1930s until it finally faded away, probably disappearing in 1939. There are some indications that GD machines were still available in 1943, but this is not certain.

GRINDLAY-PEERLESS

Coventry-based Grindlay-Peerless was a sidecar manufacturer of repute before entering the motorcycle marketplace with a range of machines designed to provide impressive motive power to sidecar combinations. The first model was powered by a 999cc (61ci) sleeve-valve Barr & Stroud

V-twin engine driving a three-speed Sturmey-Archer gearbox. It was a good-looking machine that mated up well (unsurprisingly, really) with Grindlay-Peerless sidecars.

More machines followed, mainly with smaller engines. The first, in 1924, was a 488cc (30ci) machine powered by a overhead-valve JAP

single. In 1925, this model was replaced by a 499cc (30ci) sleeve-valve Barr & Stroud. Then came three smaller machines, one with a 348cc (21ci) sleeve-valve engine and the other two with 344cc (21ci) and 346cc (21ci) overhead-valve JAP engines.

The 488cc (30ci) JAP returned to the range in 1926, and in the

same year Bill Lacey won at Brooklands on a 344cc (21ci) JAP-powered Grindlay-Peerless. In 1928, he set the 500cc (31ci) one-hour record at 166km (103.3 miles). A year later, he increased this to 169km (105.25 miles) in 1929.

In 1927, the sleeve-valve engines were dropped, leaving the 344cc (21ci), 346cc (21ci) and 488cc (30ci) JAP machines. The following year, two more models appeared. These were a 677cc (41ci) side-valve JAP V-twin and a 172cc (10ci) Villiers two-stroke. The range grew again in 1929, but in 1931 the range was slimmed down, losing the Villiers and JAP V-twin engines. The rest of the JAPs went the following year and Grindlay-Peerless began using the Rudge Python engine in 348 and 499cc (30ci) capacities.

In 1932, there were three models with Python engines. More variants were added for the next year, but in 1935 the firm left the motorcycle industry to pursue other areas of interest.

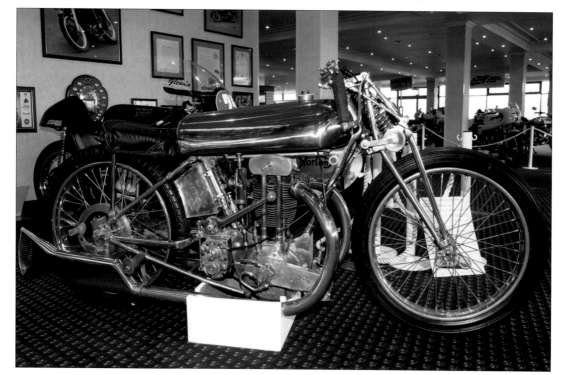

A 1927 JAP-powered Grindley-Peerless. Although the firm was well known for its sidecar combinations, its machines were also very successful in setting speed records.

HOREX

GERMANY 1923–58 AND 1980S

Along with his son Fritz, Friedrich Kleeman was involved in several business ventures in the early 1920s. One was Columbus Motorenwerke of Oberusel, which built auxiliary engines for bicycles and larger units for motorcycles. In 1923, the Kleemans founded a new firm to build complete motorcycles.

This venture was named Horex, from a combination of the brand name Rex and the town where the company was founded, Bad Homburg. It produced its first machine in 1924. This initial model was powered by a 248cc (15ci) overhead-valve Columbus engine, but larger capacities soon followed.

Competition success fuelled demand, and the firm grew quickly. Columbus engines were sold to other manufacturers, including AWD, Tornax and Victoria. Eventually, Columbus and Horex merged their engine production, bringing it to Bad Homburg.

In addition to achieving market success with the Ghom, a 63cc (4ci) engine with 'clip-on' attachments for any ordinary bicycle, Horex began producing a stream of innovative machines designed by Hermann Reeb. Beginning with 498cc (30ci) and 596cc (36ci) side-valve and

overhead-valve singles, the firm then produced a range of 198cc (12ci), 298cc (18ci) and 346cc models, all with overhead-valve.

In 1932, Reeb designed a pair of large-capacity vertical twins of 598cc (36ci) and 796cc (49ci) with chain-driven overhead-cam. Other vertical twins designs had appeared, but Reeb's was a vast improvement.

All this innovation brought success in the marketplace and at race meetings, and through the mid-1930s Horex did very well. The range included four-valve singles in 500cc (31ci) and 600cc (37ci), and Reeb's overhead-cam parallel twin in 980cc (60ci). Their top seller was the S35, which was powered by a 348cc (21ci) Sturmey-Archer engine.

After the war, Horex got back to business as quickly as possible – well ahead of most. The machine that led the company back to its place in the market was the 350 Regina. In 1950, a racing version of this machine appeared, with a modified engine. The racing variant produced 25hp and was capable of around 161km/h (100mph). It was impressive, but the overhead-cam Norton and AJS machines were faster.

A series of racing twins was implemented, under the name Imperator – not to be confused

with other machines of that name. The first of these appeared in 1951, but suffered from a lack of power and needed redesigning. The result was a much more impressive machine, which took victory at Hockenheim in 1952. However, there were reliability issues that prevented much in the way of further success.

Horex singles did well in competition from 1952 to 1954 and a new racing twin was

Factory rider Freidl Schon tries out the new double overhead-cam 497cc (30ci) race machine at Dieburger a month before its impressive competition debut at Hockenheim in May 1952.

developed in 1954. However, sales fell off rapidly in 1955 putting the firm in difficulties. It closed down in 1958. The Horex name resurfaced for a short time in the 1980s, but seems now to be gone forever.

LA MONDIALE

BELGIUM 1923–34

Based in Brussels, La Mondiale produced its first machine in 1923. This was a 308cc (19ci) two-stroke with a pressed-steel frame and rocking fork. The engine was inverted and enclosed by the sides of the frame, with a bucket seat for the rider atop the fuel tank.

Although it was unusual in terms of concept and engineering, the machine was taken up by Fondu of Vilvorde at the end of 1925 and was produced in various forms, including a Sport version in 1926. All had 350cc (21ci) Blackburne engines. The Tourisme model of 1927 was built on the same frame, and was powered by a 344cc (21ci) Villiers in-line, two-stroke, twin-cylinder engine.

The year 1928 saw another new engine, this time a 500cc (31ci) Chaise engine, and Jules Fondu achieved some competition success with the machine. Despite a continued racing presence, however, there were no big wins. Nonetheless, the firm continued to introduce innovative new variants, including one with a nickel-plated frame and five-speed gearbox, and to experiment with different engines and machinery. The year

1932 saw the introduction of a range of four-stroke models with 350cc (21ci), 500cc (31ci) and 600cc (37ci) side-valve engines, plus 350cc (21ci) and 500cc (31ci) overhead-valve engines.

These were hard times, however, and La Mondiale's policy of tying up capital in experimentation made

it vulnerable. Unconventional machines were not selling as well as previously, and although the firm attracted interest and even admiration, it could not overcome the financial challenges of the time. After culling its range for a couple of years, it went out of business in 1934.

A 1929 overhead-valve single model, featuring shaft drive and La Mondiale's distinctive, stylized frame. It was La Mondiale's habit of undertaking expensive (although admittedly attractive) innovation that ultimately killed off the company.

OLLEARO

ITALY 1923–52

This Turin-based firm was named for its founder, Neftali Ollearo. The first model was a simple, small two-stroke, but this was just a beginning. Ollearo was willing to experiment and innovate, and quickly began building unconventional overhead-valve, single-cylinder engines built in unit with the gearbox. These were available from 175cc (11ci) to 500cc (31ci) and went into fairly conventional frames, which had a rigid frame and sprung forks.

As the years passed, styling and components changed gradually. Ollearo machines gained a saddle tank when these became fashionable and bigger drum brakes when customers decided they wanted motorcycles that would not only go fast but also stop on demand. In 1932, the first four-speed gearbox had been introduced, and most models gained one soon afterwards. Another experiment was a curious three-wheeled vehicle, in which the driver more or less rode a motorcycle within the car body.

After World War II, the firm carried on for a while. A bicycle attachment engine proved very popular, but by 1952 the Ollearo name was no longer listed among motorcycle manufacturers.

MAUSER

GERMANY 1924–27

The Mauser name is most commonly associated with weaponry, but there was little need in a demilitarized Germany, so the firm turned to motor vehicles. It made an inauspicious start with the Einspurauto, or single-track car. This strange machine was powered by a 510cc (31ci) side-valve single engine mounted horizontally in front of the rear wheel.

The Einspurauto worked well enough despite being underpowered and also unmanoeuvrable at low speeds. Its main problem was that it looked like a monstrosity, and this put people off before they had even given it a try. Mauser cancelled the production run after three years, though Einspurautos were built elsewhere for a time.

MM

ITALY 1924–57

This 125cc (8ci) MM racer had little in the way of streamlining, so the rider had to do the best he could. Minimizing wind resistance could be an uncomfortable business for the racer of the 1920s, but with limited power available, it made a real difference.

from 174cc (11ci) to 344cc (21ci), which were also successful. The chain drive was used in many MM designs right up to the 1950s.

In 1936, a 344cc (21ci) MM broke a number of world records on the Florence–Pisa autostrada, while the race team achieved considerable success. Alfonso Morini departed a year later to set up his own business (Moto Morini), and it was without him that Mazzetti struggled to get production going again after the damage done to the works by World War II.

Mazzetti succeeded despite the odds, and was producing 350cc (21ci) and 500cc (31ci) bikes from 1947, though these were updated pre-war designs. Although they were updated, MM never really recovered from the war despite a valiant effort, and in 1957 the firm closed down.

Founded by Mario Mazzetti and Alfonso Morini and named after their initials, MM launched its first machine in 1924. This was a 125cc (8ci) two-stroke racer with a two-speed gearbox. It was slow to achieve competition success, but won its class in the 1927 Monza Grand Prix.

From 1930, MM changed tack and began producing four-strokes. The first was a 175cc (11ci) overhead-valve model, which was followed by a race variant with a chain-driven overhead-cam. Despite the Depression, this machine was followed by others with similar engines, ranging

RUDGE FOUR

ENGLAND 1924

Introduced as both a 350cc (21ci) and a 500cc (31ci), the Rudge Four was a significant step forward from the Multi, which had been in production from 1911 to 1923. Early Fours had many dated features: flat tanks, which even then created an old-fashioned look; non-unit gearboxes; a dummy-rim brake on the back wheel; a rigid rear end; total-loss lubrication; and exposed valve gear.

However, the Four was a more modern machine despite these hallmarks of an earlier era. Its most striking feature was the twin big-bore exhausts running back from the upright cylinder. The cast-aluminium silencer bearing the legend 'RUDGE-FOUR' was also highly noticeable. The 350cc (21ci) version broke several records, but was dropped from the line in 1925, leaving just the 500cc (31ci) in production.

ENGINE: 499cc (30.5ci) ohv single, 85x88mm, air-cooled
POWER: 25bhp
GEARBOX: 4-speed hand change
FINAL DRIVE: chain
WEIGHT: n/a
TOP SPEED: 150km/h (90mph)

SUNBEAM MODEL 90

Designed by John Greenwood as racing machines, the Model 80 (347cc) and Model 90 (493cc) were not what might today be termed 'user-friendly'. That said, they evolved into comfortable road machines over the next four years. They were not the first Sunbeams to be powered by the firm's own overhead-valve engines; that distinction goes to a group of 1923 racing machines.

In 1926, the Model 90 gained twin-port cylinder heads as an option, which became standard in 1927. Druid-pattern girder forks and a three-speed crossover hand-shift gear change was standard on both on road and racing machines. The racers were impressive, winning the 1928 and 1929 Senior TTs.

In 1929, the Model 90 gained a saddle tank, in accordance with emerging trends. All vintage Sunbeams were finished in elegant black enamel with gold coachlines.

ENGINE: 493cc (30ci) single–cylinder, air-cooled
POWER: 5hp
GEARBOX: 3–speed hand change
FINAL DRIVE: chain
WEIGHT: 136kg (300lb)
TOP SPEED: 121km/h (75mph)

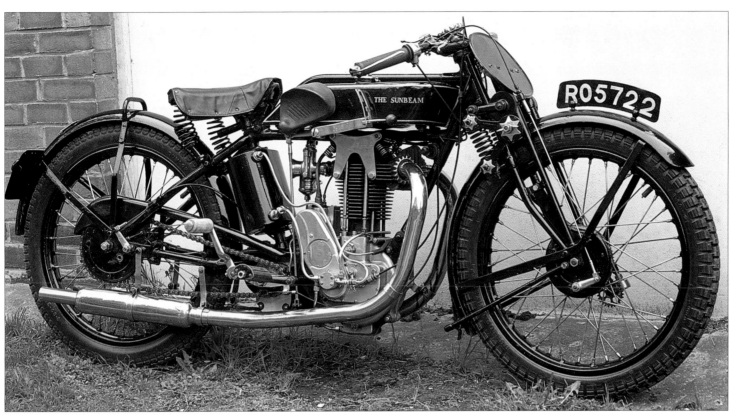

First introduced as a competition machine in 1923, the 493cc Model 90 won the 1928 and 1929 Senior TT. It gained a saddle tank in 1929.

BIANCHI FRECCIA CELESTE RACER

ENGINE: 348cc (21ci) dohc vertical single– cylinder
POWER: n/a
GEARBOX: 3 or 4–speed
FINAL DRIVE: chain
WEIGHT: n/a
TOP SPEED: 150km/h (93mph)

Designed by Mario Baldi, this machine was dominant on the Italian racing scene for five years, from 1925 onwards.

The Bianchi Freccia Celeste (Blue Arrow) single was powered by a 348cc (21ci) engine with double overhead-cams. The camshafts and coil-valve springs were completely enclosed in an oil-tight compartment, which was unusual at the time.

The Bianchi Freccia Celeste was not only fast, but also reliable and tough. In the hands of the works team, it won all three of Italy's premier speed events: the long-distance Milano–Taranto, the TT-like Lario race and the Italian GP.

Bianchi's race stars of 1928, pictured at Monza: Nuvolari (seated), Zanchetta (centre), Moretti (right) and the incredible 350cc (21ci) machine that dominated its class for several years.

The exploits of Tazoi Nuvolari at the 1925 Italian Grand Prix say a lot about both the team and the machine.

He was wearing a plaster cast as the result of a car crash on the same circuit a week previously, and he started from the back of the grid, but nonetheless won the race and set a record speed into the bargain.

The Bianchi machine was utterly unassailable in the Italian 350 class for the next five years. Nuvolari won the Italian Grand Prix in 1926, 1927 and 1928.

In 1929, he became the first man to lap Monza at over 145km/h (90mph).

BOHMERLAND

CZECHOSLOVAKIA 1925–39

Bohmerland, which uses the name Cechie in German-speaking areas, built some very odd machines during its 14 years of production. Some examples are preserved in the National Technical Museum in Prague.

Most Bohmerland models were four-stroke singles. The 598cc (36ci) model had good performance but a very odd setup.

With the saddle lower than the tops of the wheels and the top of the overhead-valve engine higher than that, the open pushrods and valve gear were just in front of the rider's crotch, which could be unsettling.

Another oddity was the double pillion seat on the extremely long touring version and its twin auxiliary torpedo-shaped fuel

tanks on the sides of the rear wheel. Although these machines had strange frames and a dated engine, they used cast-alloy wheels, which have a very modern appearance.

A new 350cc (21ci) Bohmerland was announced in 1938, but production had only just begun when the outbreak of World War II intervened.

This photograph shows the 1925 Bohmerland with sidecar. The bike itself could carry three people on the seat, plus one in the sidecar. Everything about the Bohmerland, including its rather garish paint job, was unusual. Although few models were made, a large proportion have survived in various collections.

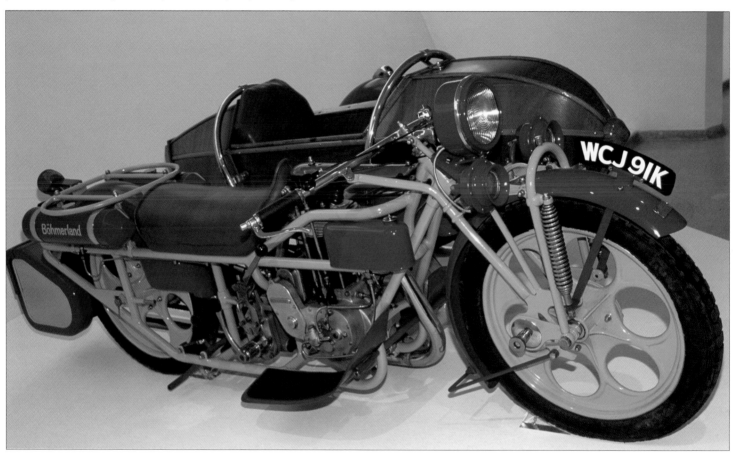

EXCELSIOR SUPER-X

USA 1925

ENGINE: 746cc (45ci) ioe V–twin, 76.2x81.75mm, air-cooled
POWER: n/a
GEARBOX: unit 3–speed hand change
FINAL DRIVE: chain
WEIGHT: 150kg (330lb)
TOP SPEED: n/a

To avoid confusion with the British firm of the same name, the first Excelsiors were sold in the UK as American-X. They entered the British market in 1921, and in 1925 they gained the Super-X name.

The Super-X was a 750cc (46ci) F-head design with a single exhaust. The engine was constructed in unit with the gearbox, and primary drive was by a train of gears enclosed by the engine unit castings. These were sturdy and topped by twin tanks for petrol and oil on the left

and just petrol on the right. The final drive was chain. The Super-X was also available as a Super Sport

version, which did well on the board and dirt tracks, and later in hill climbs.

The 1931 model, featuring built-in gear primary drive and leading-link forks.

MAMMUT

The name Mammut has been used by two companies and one motorcycle model, none of which are related. This earliest incarnation of the name was established to manufacture machine tools and made the move into motorcycle production in the mid-1920s.

Mammut's entry was typical of the times. Powered by a 198cc (12ci) Baumi two-stroke engine driving a separate gearbox and with a chain final drive, the machine had a basic tubular frame featuring girder forks, wire wheels and minimal brakes.

Mammut used 197cc (12ci) and 246cc (15ci) engines of their own design in some models, and bought in 200cc (12ci) to 500cc (31ci) four-strokes from JAP and Blackburne of Britain and MAG in Switzerland. Villiers engines were used later on. From 1929, Mammut machines were built on pressed-steel frames made under licence from the British firm Coventry Eagle. This went on, with a variety of engines and frames used, until 1933. It may be that links with Britain were becoming unpopular at that time; whatever the reason, production ceased in 1933.

An early Mammut, with 346cc (21ci) side-valve JAP engine and separate gearbox. Later machines gained a pressed-steel frame but by 1933 the name had vanished.

VELOCETTE KSS

With the KTT racer dominating the TT scene, it made sense to derive road machines from it. The KSS was the 'super sports' sister model and offered a most impressive performance for its time. Variants remained in production for several years, including the 1936 Mk2 version,

which was accompanied by the KTS tourer.

The Mk2 had an improved engine, which was less prone to leaking oil. However, the bevel-drive overhead-cam engine was very expensive to produce, and it was not really practical to keep it in production. It did resurface in

1946, but disappeared again not long after.

The 348cc (21ci) overhead-cam KSS was much admired among fans of sports road machines, but it was expensive to produce and was withdrawn after a few years.

ENGINE: (Mk 1) 348cc (21ci) ohc single, 74x81mm, air-cooled
POWER: n/a
GEARBOX: 4–speed foot change
FINAL DRIVE: chain
WEIGHT: 191kg (420lb)
TOP SPEED: 129km/h (80mph)

WINDHOFF

Windhoff's first machines were 122cc (7ci) and 173cc (11ci) water-cooled two-strokes with a horizontal cylinder. Their engines were built under licence from Bekamo. The rest was conventional with a separate gearbox, all-chain drive, a rigid frame, girder forks and drum brakes.

In 1927, Windhoff cast off convention and launched a new design with a 746cc (46ci) overhead-camshaft, in-line four-cylinder, oil-cooled engine. The headstock was bolted to the front end of the engine, with the gearbox and rear frame to the back. The machine also featured

a three-speed, hand-change gearbox with shaft drive to the rear wheel. The machine had trailing-link forks and drum brakes on both wheels.

While it seems like a good machine, this bike did not sell well, which doomed a 996cc (61ci) version never to get past the

prototype stage. The Four was replaced in 1929 by a flat with a 996cc (61ci) side-valve engine built in unit with the gearbox. This, too, sank without trace in the tough marketplace of the time. Windhoff was able to struggle on for a while by licence-building Villiers-powered lightweights.

CHAPTER THREE

THE WAR YEARS

1926–1944

Strangely, the terrible years of the 1930s Depression did not have such a drastic effect on motorcycling as may be imagined. Motorcycling was a pioneer, enthusiast's pastime, already restricted to the wealthy, and it was the upper classes who had the time and cash to experiment with the ever-improving machines of the time. Multi-cylinder bikes began to appear, supplementing the basic single cylinder engines which powered most machines. V-twins like the Brough Superior set new power and speed benchmarks while names like BMW began to appear on the scene. BMW's 1923 flat-twins were the first in a range of bikes that still has a huge influence on motorcycling today. The majority of bikes were mundane runarounds though, and early two-stroke machines began to appear, their cheap, easy-to-manufacture powerplants attracting interest in Germany and the UK.

As World War II approached, the luxury-end machinery of racetracks and wealthy enthusiasts was approaching what might be seen as modern levels of performance. Famously, the 1939 Norton 500 single was capable of putting out 48bhp – nigh-on 100bhp/litre, which was a very decent level of tune for a four-cylinder engine in the 1980s. Chassis technology was still along way behind though. Most bikes had solid rear ends, although basic sprung suspension was being developed. Front suspension was common, though of the most basic type, while brakes and tyres hadn't improved so much over those on bicycles.

Left: A pair lovingly-restored Rudge Ulster's race along a highway. First produced in 1928, the single-cylinder Ulster is generally considered the greatest of Rudge's many motorbikes.

AJW

Founded by and named after Arthur John Wheaton, a publisher, AJW entered the motorcycling world in the mid-1920s. Early products were mainly lightweights, but by 1930 the factory was producing 11 different models, ranging from the 172cc (10ci) Villiers-engined BF through to the massive overhead-valve Anzani powered 994cc (61ci) V-twin.

AJW bought in engines and components, and assembled these on frames of its own make. The best known models were the 172cc (10ci) and 196cc (12ci) Black Foxes and the 347cc (21.1ci) and 343cc (20.9ci) Silver Foxes. Bigger models included the 500 Double Port, powered by a 498cc (30ci) JAP engine. Sales were quite good, though AJW never in fact achieved the production volumes of the bigger companies.

While others were struggling to survive the Depression of the 1930s, AJW was producing new models each year. These included the Foxes, Vixenette, Vixen and Flying Vixen. However, the firm

One of AJW's final models, the Wolfhound of 1976 was built with Italian components, including a two-stroke engine from Minarelli. Most of the company's revenue at the time came from imported mopeds.

began to struggle in the late 1930s, and the range was cut down, leaving only the 488cc (30ci) overhead-valve, JAP-engined Flying Fox in 1938. A couple of 249cc (15ci) Villiers-powered models reappeared for 1939 and 1940, but too late to save the firm.

After the war, J.O. Ball bought the firm, and production began again in 1948. There were two models, including a JAP-engined speedway bike, and JAP engines powered the early 1950s range of roadsters. In the 1970s, the firm imported Giuletta mopeds with AJW tanks and decals. It closed in 1980.

BSA SLOPER

Named for its forward slanted engine, the Sloper was good looking, dependable, quiet and reasonably quick. Its 493cc (30ci) long-stroke engine offered enclosed pushrods and rockers (although the valve springs were exposed), sited above large, sturdy crankcases containing a gear-type oil pump. The long stroke motor developed easy, long-legged power, while massive flywheels smoothed the single's power

pulses. The duplex frame carried girder front forks, while the rear end was unsprung. From 1932, the original three-speed gearbox was replaced by four-speed transmission. From its launch in August 1926 (as the Model S), the Sloper eventually appeared in six different models with capacities ranging from 349cc (21ci) to 595cc (36ci). These included two side-valve and four overhead-valve versions. In standard trim, the

overhead-valve 500cc (31ci) was good for speeds of more than 112km/h (70mph). A 'race kit' was available from BSA, which comprised of a high-compression piston and special spark plug, valves and springs, although the bike's stolid image was scarcely in keeping with such tuning.

ENGINE: 493cc (30ci) ohv single, 80x98mm, air-cooled
POWER: up to 25bhp at 4800rpm
GEARBOX: 3-, later 4-speed hand change
FINAL DRIVE: chain
WEIGHT: n/a
TOP SPEED: 116km/h (72mph)

The well-loved Sloper was in production for nine years, during which time it gained a four-speed gearbox. The hand-change mechanism on the left side remained the same.

DARDO

In the mid-1920s, unit construction was becoming popular in Italy, some time before it became common in other countries. Italian manufacturers were competing for a relatively small customer base and had to keep innovating to stay ahead. Dardo chose to use unit construction from the outset. They produced machines powered by small two-stroke engines that had the cylinder in a horizontal position.

Dardo's first machines were a 125cc (8ci) and 175cc (11ci), allowing the firm to enter two of the main classes of the Italian market. Both had two-speed gearboxes and were well put together along conventional lines.

Once they got established, Dardo added a four-stroke model to the range, a 175cc (11ci) overhead-valve machine with a horizontal cylinder like the two-strokes. This was a route taken earlier by the much better-known Moto Guzzi.

Like many small firms, Dardo found the motorcycle market a difficult place for reasons both technical and commercial. They timed their departure well, leaving the industry just before the Depression hit.

MCEVOY

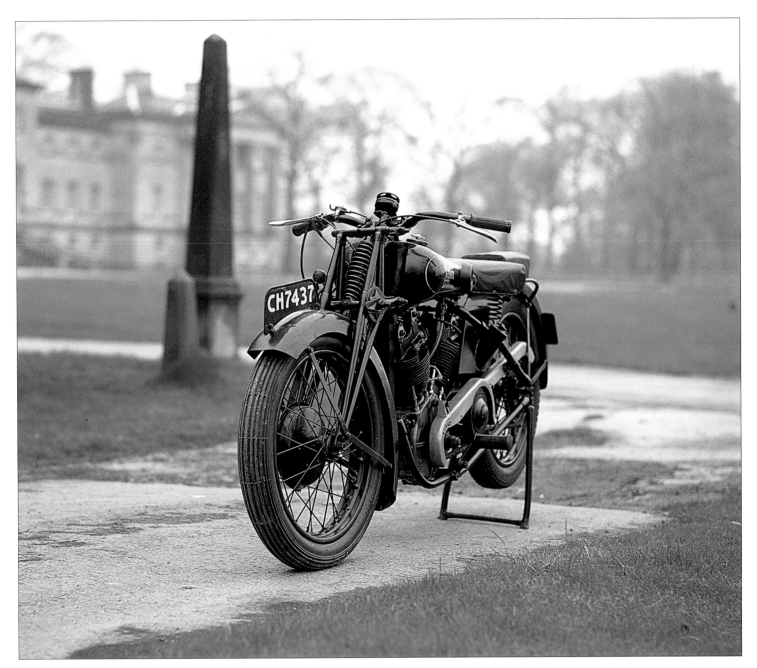

Based in Derby, McEvoy built some very impressive machines in its short period of operation. Founder Michael McEvoy had worked for Rolls-Royce and was an expert on superchargers and a keen competitor. So too were financier Cecil Allerhead Birkin, whose brother was the famous Bentley racing driver 'Tim' Birkin, and chief engineer George Patchett, who had previously worked for Brough Superior.

Sadly, it was competition that destroyed McEvoy before the firm really got going. George Patchett rode a supercharged 996cc (61ci) McEvoy-JAP in the 1926–27 season, with very impressive results, but in 1927 Birkin was killed in an accident while practising for the TT. This deprived the firm of their funding and forced its closure a little later.

The prototypes that were constructed before the firm went under give an inkling of what might have been. These include a 346cc (21ci) three-valve, overhead-cam single and an air-cooled, overhead-cam straight four of only 500cc (31ci). The production bikes included some very big, fast machines: supercharged and eight-valve big twins and normally aspirated four-valve big twins. More modest, but still capable of more than decent performance, were the 498cc

McEvoy was primarily interested in performance. Although the firm's bikes were well finished, it was the immense (for the time) power of the top-end machines that really defined the company's identity.

(30ci), 348cc (21ci) and 248cc (15ci) side-valve singles using Blackburne and JAP engines and a 172cc (10ci) two-stroke with a Villiers engine.

MONARK

The Monark story really begins with a motorcycle built in 1913. The firm that built it made lightweights under the Esse banner from 1920 to 1925, and adopted the name Monark in 1927. The first true Monarks were Blackburne-powered 250cc (15ci) and 600cc (37ci) side-valve and overhead-valve singles.

By the mid-1930s, Monark was more interested in mopeds and was manufacturing motorized bicycles powered by 98cc (6ci) Ilo two-stroke engines. Sweden was neutral and therefore relatively unaffected by World War II, and Monark supplied motorcycles to the Swedish military during this period. These were based on a design by Husqvarna, and powered by 500cc (31ci) Albin overhead-valve, four-stroke engines.

After the war, the firm returned to making Ilo-powered 50cc (3ci) and 250cc (15ci) machines, rapidly growing to become the country's biggest producer. A 500cc (31ci) Albin-powered Monark machine won the 1959 World Motocross Championship. This was the only Monark four-stroke after 1945, though the same Albin engine and Monark frame provided the inspiration for the short-lived Lito motocross bikes of the early 1960s.

In 1960, Monark took over the old Nymans Verkstäder firm, which assembled the Royal Enfield Bullet in Sweden under the name NV. The takeover also gained Monark Crescent and Apollo firms in the NV takeover. After a reshuffle, they became Monark Crescent Bolagen, or MCB.

Monark's production bikes of the 1960s and 1970s were 50cc (3ci) to 175cc (11ci) two-stroke lightweights with Sachs and Morini engines. As well as off-road models, it produced its own works road-racing machines in the early 1970s. Sales were not good and the firm went under in 1975.

The Monark 125 ISDT at rest and in action. This machine came out in the last years of the company's existence, during a foray into the off-road and road-racing markets.

SOS

SOS was founded by Leonard Vale-Onslow, who was born in 1899 and was still riding motorcycles a century later. The initials stood originally for 'Super Onslow Special' and later for 'So Obviously Superior'. As the name suggests, the range was aimed at the upper end of the market. The main SOS sports model was the 172cc (10ci) AA, later known as the Brooklands. It was available in track, road-racing or trials specification to special order.

SOS started out using JAP four-stroke and Villiers two-stroke power units. However, from 1931 onwards, only Villiers units (in sizes from 172cc/10ci to 346cc/21ci) were used in addition to the firm's own 148cc (9ci) and 172cc (10ci) water-cooled engines. This change coincided with a move from Hallow, near Worcester, to Birmingham.

In October 1933, Tommy Meeten, a Villiers specialist from Redhill, Surrey, gained control of SOS. In 1936, he opened a dealership in London, named Meeten's Motor Mecca. It became the centre for Villiers parts in southern England for the next 50 years.

Vale-Onslow remained in the industry as a motorcycle dealer in Birmingham, and SOS manufacturing also stayed in that city until Meteen closed the factory at the beginning of World War II.

SOS bikes were prestige machines, and it shows. They were built in small numbers to exacting standards of construction and finish – only fitting for machines conceived by a man who would still be riding on his 100th birthday.

ASCOT PULLIN

Ascot Pullin was founded by Cyril Pullin, an ex-racer who won the Senior Isle of Man TT in 1914. His 'New Wonder Motor Cycle', was introduced to great fanfare but ended up beset with problems.

The Ascot Pullin was an innovative machine featuring a 496cc (30ci) overhead-valve unit construction engine set horizontally. This drove through a three-speed gearbox placed above the crankcase. Ignition was by gear-driven magneto and lubrication was dry sump.

The engine was fitted into a frame built from steel pressings, with similar forks, and the mechanics were hidden under pressed covers.

The machine was also nicely fitted out, even featuring a windscreen and wiper. However, it was sluggish and slow, and handled clumsily. Sales were not good, so Pullin decided to introduce a sidecar to go with his motorcycle. It was built using pressed-steel sides, ends and floor, all welded together to create a rigid monocoque. Sales were still very poor and Ascot Pullin closed down in 1930.

The Ascot Pullin was just a little too innovative for its own good. Trying to implement a new pressed-steel frame design, unit-construction engine/gearbox and other features all at the same time caused serious problems in development, and the end result did not sell well.

INDIAN SCOUT

USA 1928

Of all the Indian models, the Scout is probably the best known. The very first Scout came out in 1921 with a 606cc (37ci) engine that produced 12hp. It could manage 90km/h (55mph). In 1928, a more powerful version appeared, which more or less killed off sales of the smaller cousin. The 1928 Scout had a 750cc (46ci) engine, with bigger bore and stroke, and from 1931 only this version was listed.

The best of all the Scout models was the 1928 101, which was introduced to compete with the then-new Excelsior of the same capacity. This was a light and responsive machine – at least, by American standards. It was quickly updated with the addition of slightly modified Chief flywheels, increasing stroke length and therefore upping capacity to 935cc (57ci). Everyone was impressed by these more powerful Scouts,

particularly Harley-Davidson, which began to feel the pressure.

The 1932 Motoplane was a variant of the 101 Scout, built on a Prince single frame. It boasted dry-sump lubrication, better cooling via bigger fins and better breathing with a bigger carburettor for more power. To help cope with the Depression, a smaller and cheaper Scout, the Junior (or Pony) Scout was marketed with a 500cc (31ci) engine.

ENGINE: 745cc (45ci) sv in-lineV-twin, 73x88.9mm, air-cooled
POWER: 21 bhp
GEARBOX: 3-speed hand change
FINAL DRIVE: chain
WEIGHT: n/a
TOP SPEED: 121km/h (75mph)

The V-twin scout was introduced in 1928 and various models appeared thereafter. This is a 741cc (44ci) military version, dating from the 1930s.

RUDGE ULSTER

ENGLAND 1928

The Ulster gained its name from the 1928 Ulster Grand Prix – which it won. The machine existed before that as a Rudge Four with a saddle tank and quite large drum brakes by the standards of the time. It continued to win races: in 1930, it won the Ulster TT, the Dutch TT, the German Grand Prix, the Czechoslovak Grand Prix and the Brooklands 200-mile (322km) solo with various riders. The latter victory was the only time that the Brooklands 200-mile (322km) solo race was won at over 160km/h (100mph). The Ulster averaged 161.05km/h (100.07mph), setting the record by the skin of its teeth.

In addition, Rudge was coming in the top three in races all over Europe. The team benefited from

the expertise of some of the top riders of the era, but the bike's performance was also quite extraordinary. The firm did well selling ready-to-race Ulster replicas, but also produced a road model called the 500 Special. This was effectively a downrated version of the Ulster. It was still very quick by the standards of other road machines in the period. The Ulster remained in production until 1933.

ENGINE: ohv single, 85x88mm, air-cooled
POWER: 33bhp approx
GEARBOX: 4-speed hand change
FINAL DRIVE: chain
WEIGHT: n/a
TOP SPEED: 170km/h (105mph) approx

The Ulster is the best-known of all Rudge machines, mainly as a result of its spectacular racing performance in the late 1920s.

UNIVERSAL

Universal started out with a 190cc (12ci) two-stroke machine, built under the name Helvetia and fitted with an engine from PA. Soon afterwards, the firm began using its own name and building fairly conventional machines with two- and four-stroke engines from Anzani, Ilo and JAP as well as the Python from Rudge.

Universal also built a range of race bikes using 248cc (15ci) Python and 996cc (61ci) V-twin JAP units. Contracts to the Swiss Army came in by the mid-1930s, and Universal began building its own design of 680cc (41ci) and 990cc (60ci) side-valve, V-twin engines in order to fulfil these orders.

After the end of World War II, Universal introduced a new design with an overhead-valve, flat-twin engine built in unit with the gearbox. It was an extremely tidy setup, with the single carburettor, electrical equipment and air cleaner all enclosed. Final drive was by shaft drive, and all this went into a duplex frame with telescopic front forks and plunger rear suspension.

This machine first appeared in 1946, and while the 500cc (31ci) model was also offered in side-valve form, the twin soon grew to 580cc (35ci). A 250cc (15ci) version of the same basic design also followed. The military contracts suited Universal, and over time the firm began to concentrate more and more on the flat-twins, building them primarily for army and police use.

Universal's 580cc (35ci) flat-twin in the late 1940s. These well-built and tidy machines were the shape of things to come from Universal, which increasingly built flat-twins for government contracts.

VINCENT

In 1928, Conrad Vincent, father of Philip Vincent, bought out HRD and began work on a new motorcycle. The first Vincent-HRD had a sprung frame and a JAP 500cc (31ci) single. Later versions used Rudge Python and Sport Python engines. Sales were poor, but the model was followed by Vincent's own 500cc (31ci) single in 1934.

Further development resulted in the Series A Rapide, which was exhibited at the Olympia Motor Show in 1936. The A model was produced until 1939, and was followed after the war by the far superior Series B, C and D machines. These looked and performed much better than their predecessor, and so a legend was born.

The Vincent's looks were part styling and part components. The massive engine was put there to drive the machine, and the fact that it looked just right was simply fortunate. The styling – which was a combination of black gloss, light-alloy, chrome and stainless steel – was inspired. The ride on the hinge-in-the-middle frame, with its constantly varying saddle angle, seemed strange at first, but it soon became natural.

As to performance, the Series B Shadow delivered a modest (by today's standards) 55hp, but it was a light machine capable of reaching 193km/h (120mph) or more on a long enough straight. Vincents have at times been modified to break records, such as the flying-mile records for motorcycles and for sidecars. Reliability was also very good, and maintenance, when it was required, needed few tools.

This was a deliberate policy on the part of the designer – and one that anyone who has ever encountered an unusual fastener halfway through dismantling an engine will greatly appreciate.

Despite producing these wonderful motorcycles, Vincent's other ventures were not so successful. These included a three-wheeler car, the Picador engine for a target drone, the Firefly auxiliary cycle motor and an industrial two-stroke, which was also fitted to what would now be called a jet-ski, in 1956–58. In addition, Vincent acted as a distributor for the NSU Quickly. None of them was a success.

While not spectacular in performance, the Comet was highly reliable and capable of covering a lot of ground at a very respectable pace.

CWS

Another Polish machine, the CWS was conceived as a motorcycle for use solo or with a sidecar by the Polish Army, and became a casualty of World War II. The Army offered a prize for a suitable design, and after some experimentation the MIII was accepted. Early versions used some imported components, but later on the machine was entirely Polish.

The engine was a 45? V-twin with 1000cc (actually 995.4cc/61ci) capacity. With a compression ratio of just 5:1, it could tolerate very bad fuel. It would also start in temperatures of –39˚C (–39˚F), a necessity in the Polish winter. The engine's power output was modest at the top end, but with a flat power curve it could at least deliver reasonable horsepower across a range of throttle settings.

Controls were probably a throttle on left and a manual ignition advance/retard on the right, after the practice followed by Indian. Both wheels (and the sidecar wheel) had mechanical drum brakes and there was also a parking brake. Machines left the factory finished in black with gold and cream, or khaki with gold trim

lines. The army, which bought most of the bikes, probably used camouflage patterns in service.

The primary drive was geared and very strong. The multiple-plate clutch had five steel plates and six copper/asbestos ones. It was operated by a foot pedal on the left. Gear change for the three-speed transmission was on the right. Final drive was by chain.

The overall machine weighed in at 270kg (594lb), while the sidecar

combination weighed 375kg (825lb). It was a little lighter and faster than the BMW R75 sidecar outfit, though less powerful. Experimentation started in 1938 with a powered sidecar wheel, but the war prevented any results from reaching the production stage.

About 3400 machines were built from 1933 to 1939, and the Polish army felt that its home-grown combination was better than the American ones it had been using

One of the prototype CWS V-twins that became the MIII. This was a tough and rugged machine capable of handling the appalling conditions of the Polish winter, and was well received by its users.

up to then. Unfortunately, the disasters that overcame Poland in World War II destroyed this promising marque along with a great deal else.

HARLEY-DAVIDSON FLATHEAD 45

Three versions of the Flathead 45 were made: the low-compression D, standard-compression DL and high-compression DLD, giving a range of performances. The first models had twin headlights and cast-iron pistons; the latter were replaced with alloy ones in 1930. The pre-1936 R model had a greater rake to

their steering, which improved stability but was less necessary as roads improved. The post-1936 W model benefited from a recirc-ulating oil system developed for the Knucklehead. This and the piston change were the only changes to the engine during its long career, though the high-compression variant disappeared early on.

These were big, heavy and slow machines that, nevertheless, did well in competition, because they benefited from rules that favoured similar designs. The Flathead 45 engine was not installed in motorcycles after 1951, but it remained in production until 1974 and was used in the Servi-Car.

ENGINE: 743cc (44ci) sv in-line V-twin, 70x97mm, air-cooled
POWER: 23bhp at 4600rpm
GEARBOX: 3-speed hand change
FINAL DRIVE: chain
WEIGHT: n/a
TOP SPEED: 105–120km/h (65–75mph)

JAWA

Jawa got its start in 1929, when Frantisek Janecek of the National Arms Factory in Prague decided that he would like his company to begin making motorcycles. He was not the first arms manufacturer to take this route.

Rather than begin trying to produce a design from scratch, Janecek began making Wanderers under licence from their German manufacturer. They became known as Jawas, a name derived from Janacek and Wanderer.

In 1930, George Patchett joined the firm and began to produce some impressive designs, including a 500cc (31ci) racing machine with a pushrod engine. Over the next few years, Jawa ceased to be a minor licence-

builder and became a major player on the scene, though licence-building continued with a line of Villiers and Wanderer engines.

In 1932, the first two-stroke Jawa appeared. It used a 173cc (11ci) Villiers engine and was of fairly advanced design. It was followed by several road machines with two-stroke or side-valve engines, all designed by George Patchett. However, at the outbreak of World War II, he returned to Britain.

Undeterred, Jawa continued to develop motorcycle designs (in great secrecy) throughout the war. Despite the loss of Patchett, these were very good designs, including a modern 248cc (15ci) two-stroke single featuring unit construction,

telescopic front forks and plunger rear suspension. This machine established the automatic clutch design that would be used on Jawa's production roadsters for several years.

Just after the war and despite nationalization, Jawa was well placed to dominate the Czech motorcycle industry and was able to take over the rival Ogar factory in 1947. In 1949, the Communist regime in Czechoslovakia decided that Jawa and another of its rivals, CZ, should work together on some projects. More significantly, it authorized Jawa to become involved in motorsport.

During this time, Jawa produced a 346cc (21ci) two-stroke twin that used many of the components of

the previous single. The first of the racing machines designed by Vaclav Sklenar then made their debut. These were 348cc (21ci) and 498cc (30ci) double-overhead-cam vertical twins in supercharged and unsupercharged forms. More race machines followed and a new set of parallel-twins was entered in track events. Jawas competed in off-road events as well, and did very well indeed.

Jawa rose to dominate the six-day trials for many years, with 250cc (15ci), 350cc (21ci) and 360cc (22ci) single-cylinder, two-stroke Jawas winning the Trophy contest in 1958, 1959 and 1962. Further success came in the 1970s with victory in 1970, 1971, 1972, 1973, 1974, 1977 and 1978. Jawa

mod II

also did well in tarmac racing, taking many high placings from the early 1950s to the mid-1970s, mainly with double-overhead-cam parallel-twin four-strokes in the 500cc (31ci), and 250cc (15ci) and 350cc (21ci) classes.

In the 1960s, Jawa developed a new 350cc (21ci) from earlier, smaller models. It was an updated design – a double-overhead-cam, parallel-twin with the vertical shaft relocated between the cylinders at the rear and driving the inlet camshaft by means of bevels. A horizontal shaft, lying along the top of the engine, took the drive forward to the exhaust camshaft. Each cylinder barrel and head was a separate casting in light alloy, while steel liners were employed for the cylinder bores. Lubrication was by means of a wet sump rather than the previous dry sump and separate oil tank. Later, a four-valves-per-cylinder engine was used, but did not prove as reliable as the original two-valve unit.

Jawa's 500cc (30ci) double overhead-cam race machine pictured in 1954. This machine was a huge success in competition, winning first time out at Zandvoort in the capable hands of Jan Koster.

In the mid-1960s, Jawa made another takeover, this time of the Eso concern, and thereby gained Eso's speedway engine. This was a hugely successful design and has been raced worldwide; the latest four-valve version is still in use.

Although Jawa did build a 350cc (21ci) single-overhead-cam twin street bike in the 1950s and a Rotax-powered 500cc (31ci) in the mid-1980s, all the rest of its post-war roadster production used single and twin two-stroke engines. Today, Jawa still concentrates on two-strokes for its main range, a formula that has served the firm well for many years.

A 250 Springer of the immediate post-war period. Jawa was going from strength to strength at this time and had come to dominate the Czech motorcycle industry. Entry into motorsport soon after brought excellent competition results.

LECH

The short-lived Lech motorcycle was Poland's first. It was designed by Waclaw Sawicki and Wladyslaw Zalewski. The former was a Polish industrialist, the latter an engineer who had returned to Poland after emigrating to the USA.

The Lech's engine was an up-to-date design with a 5hp, 500cc (31ci) V-twin engine boasting light-alloy pistons, detachable cylinder heads and positive lubrication. The bottom end was built up and ran in roller bearings in more traditional style. The engine was designed in house; and although some parts were imported, the great majority of the machine was Polish.

The remainder of the bike was more traditional, featuring a dated-looking flat tank and no brakes on the front wheel. There were two independent braking systems on the rear wheel, an internal expanding drum brake and a band brake. In 1930, the machine gained a drum brake on the front wheel and a saddle tank.

The gearbox was a standard three-speed with hand-change and there was no rear suspension. Racing versions and a single are reported to have been developed, but there is little evidence of them.

Although the Lech was a creditable first attempt, it was never built in numbers, and production stopped in 1932. This was partly due to the Depression, but there may have been other factors involved. The very low production numbers suggest that demand was not high, or perhaps that the firm was simply not able to produce enough machines to become viable.

SCOTT FLYING SQUIRREL

Scott experimented with three-speed transmissions from 1923 onwards, but it took until 1926 to develop one that could be used on a TT racer. After being proven in racing, it appeared on the following year's road models.

Scott produced a range of 'TT Replica' models, and the 1929 Flying Squirrel is the most highly regarded of them all. It was a street copy of the long-stroke twin that took third in the 1928 TT and was available as RZ and RY models, in 498cc (30ci) and 596cc (36ci) respectively. It was a very stiff machine with a robustly built frame, solidly mounted engine and rigid rear end. The forks looked like girders but were actually of a braced telescopic design.

A revised version appeared in 1930 with revised porting and crankshaft design, and with a 'Powerplus' PZ (500cc/31ci) or PY (600cc/37ci) engine. Although Scott stopped making TT Replica versions in 1934 and the engines gained detachable cylinder heads (DPZ and DPY motors) around the same time, much the same engines were still in production in the 1970s.

Perhaps the best of all Scott roadsters, the Flying Squirrel was a fine race-replica machine. The smaller version originally delivered 24bhp but this was soon upgraded for even better performance.

ENGINE: 498/596cc (30/36ci) two-stroke parallel-twin, 66.6/73x71.4mm, liquid-cooled
POWER: up to 24bhp at 5000rpm (498cc)
GEARBOX: 3-speed hand change
FINAL DRIVE: chain
WEIGHT: 165kg (364lb)
TOP SPEED: 137km/h (85mph)

BERNADET

Bernadet, a family firm run by three brothers, began making a range of motorcycles from 100 cc (6ci) to 500cc (31ci) during the Depression.

Engines came from Chaise and Train and were mated to a conventional frame and parts. Unsurprisingly, given the period, production numbers and thus sales were not great. After 1934, the firm ceased motorcycle production for a time.

The Bernadet boys returned in 1947, entering a 125cc (8ci) scooter into a marketplace that was desperate for motorized transport. The Ydral engine was fully enclosed and drove through a four-speed gearbox. There was no rear suspension.

In 1950, a new model appeared with rear suspension. It also

boasted a 250cc (15ci) Violet split-single, two-stroke engine and carried a spare wheel. In 1951, this changed to a fixed front mudguard with the headlamp on the apron.

For 1953, Bernadet brought out a Texas version of the 250cc (15ci) with American-style saddlebags and fringed seats. The offering for 1954 was the 50cc/3ci (later 85cc/5ci) Cabri, which was followed by the Guépar. However, by 1959 the company was out of business.

A 'Texas' version of the Bernadet scooter for the Unied States market, with rare decorative fringes and tassels. This version also featured US-style saddlebags.

CM

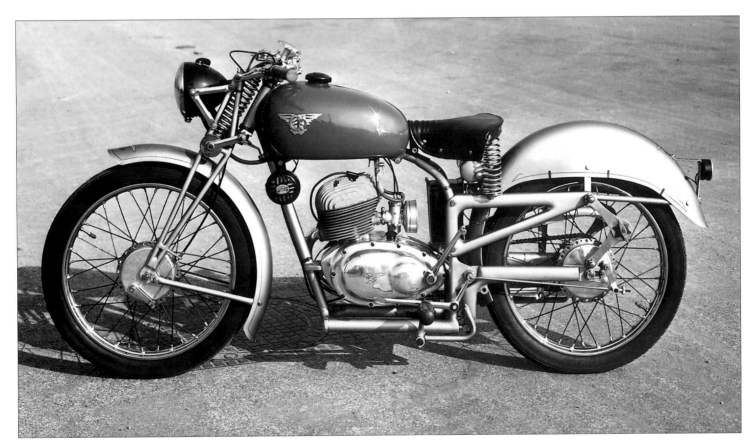

Bologna-based CM was founded by Mario Cavedagna, already a famous rider and engineer. He was assisted by Oreste Drusiani, brother of Alfonso, creator of the 1950s 125cc (8ci) FB Mondial championship-winning Grand Prix racers. However, Cavedagna sold out after a few years and the firm continued under new ownership. To the existing range of 173cc (11ci) to 496cc (30ci) overhead-cam models, they added a brand new 496cc (30ci) overhead-valve

single and a very successful 348cc overhead-camshaft racer.

After World War II, much of the range was discontinued. Only the 500cc (31ci) overhead-valve single and a massive-looking 250cc (15ci) single with chain-driven overhead-cam remained in production. A new range of two-stroke singles of 123cc (8ci) to 173cc (11ci) began to appear, starting in 1944.

This range took CM into the early 1950s, and in 1952 an all-new 248cc (15ci) two-stroke

parallel twin with slightly inclined cylinders was unveiled. In sports form, it was a very capable machine with a maximum speed of more than 128km/h (80mph), which was very fast for a legal road-going 250cc (15ci).
A specially tuned version was fielded for events such as the Milano–Taranto and Giro d'Italia, and also modified to enter short-circuit events.

CM won the 125cc (8ci) and 250cc (15ci) production categories in the 1956 Milano–Taranto, and

A 125 Sport dating from 1950. Whilst retaining features like girder front forks and rather basic rear suspension, this model also looked to the future with an alloy cylinder and head plus unit construction for the engine and gearbox. In appearance, the 125 Sport was very forward looking.

took sixth place overall. However, the firm's days were numbered and it disappeared in 1957.

FRANCIS-BARNETT BLACK HAWK

Despite its ferocious name, the Francis-Barnett Black Hawk offered little in the way of performance. Its frame was both rigid and relatively light by the standards of the day, being fully triangulated from straight tube and jointed by pins.

Francis-Barnetts were advertized as being 'Built like a Bridge'. It was also claimed that the machine could be dismantled and fitted in a golf bag, and that putting it back together again afterwards was not difficult.

The earliest triangulated frames employed leaf-spring front forks, but by the time of the Hawk, conventional coil-spring girders were standard.

The idea for this design had come to Gordon Francis during World War I, when the fragile nature of many conventional frames became all too obvious to him.

The Black Hawk's 196cc (12ci) Villiers single-cylinder engine could be mated to an optional four-speed gearbox. It was a strong machine and economical to run, but this does not make for a predatory reputation.

ENGINE: 196cc (12ci) 2s single, 61x67mm air-cooled
POWER: n/a
GEARBOX: 3-speed hand change
FINAL DRIVE: chain
WEIGHT: n/a
TOP SPEED: 77km/h (48mph)

JONGHI

Established in France, the firm was named after one of its founders, Tito Jonghi. (The other founder was Guiseppe Remondini, a fellow Italian.) It began with quite an advanced model for a first attempt. The 346cc (21ci) side-valve engine was a built-in unit with a three-speed gearbox; it had a rear-mounted magneto, with the one-piece crankcase and gearbox casting sealed by side plates. The external flywheel and primary-drive gears went on the left and the final drive chain on the right. The whole was installed in a rigid frame with girder forks.

Jonghi was able to pull this off, as Remondini had worked for Negas & Ray in Italy, where he designed a similar engine unit. As at Negas & Ray, the first model was quickly joined by an overhead-valve version with exposed hairpin-valve springs and similar cycle parts.

Jonghi established their reputation by winning the 1932 European Grand Prix 350cc race, which was held near Rome. Other successes followed: in 1933, the side-valve model demonstrated its potential by averaging more than 116km/h (72mph) for 24 hours at Montlhéry to secure 10 world records, another fine demonstration of the speed and reliability of the marque. Later came an overhead-camshaft engine, at first for 350cc (21ci) races. This was later reduced in order to enter 250cc (15ci) and 175cc (11ci) events.

The range was extended to add lightweights using small proprietary two-stroke engines. In 1936, Jonghi joined up with the Prester firm and quickly became indistinguishable in all ways other than the tank badge.

After World War II, most models were built under both Prester and Jonghi badges. Most models were small two-strokes with unit construction, three speeds, rigid frame and girder forks; these were later replaced by trailing-links. Both 100cc (6ci) and 125cc (8ci) models were built throughout the company's history and a 250cc (15ci) model was added later.

In 1947, Jonghi brought out a new 125cc (8ci) four-stroke with Italian lines. Intended for road and racing use, it boasted a unit-construction engine with the single overhead-camshaft driven by a train of gears that ran up inside the barrel and head on the right. Camshaft, rockers, valves and hairpin-valve springs were fully enclosed by a single cover. The magneto was driven by chain on the left while the gear primary drive to the four-speed gearbox went on the right with the gears in the timing chest.

The frame had pivoted-fork rear suspension in monoshock form, with the spring unit under the saddle and the trailing-link front forks. This was a fine machine in the best traditions of the firm and remained in production until Jonghi closed its doors in 1956.

A 1955 HS4 twin, one of the last Jonghi machines to appear. The 250c engine, constructed in unit with the gearbox, made use of alloy heads, and light alloys were also used in the full-width hubs.

MALAGUTI

Malaguti came to motorcycles through the familiar route of bicycle manufacture, though starting much later than many who followed that path. Throughout the 1930s, the Bologna-based firm built pedal cycles, and this also continued after World War II. At this time, Italy's industry was in a terrible state. The country had been a battlefield even after the Italian surrender in 1943, and the damage was considerable.

Antonio Malaguti found that there was a high demand for his firm's cycles in the immediate post-war years, many of them to be fitted with an auxiliary engine – originally the Mosquito from Garelli and then the 48c (3ci)

Sachs engine. Later on, Italian-made engines were used. This led to the manufacture of a range of small motorcycles and mopeds in the 1960s, with engines up to 125cc. (8ci).

In the 1970s, it was decided to concentrate on a single market niche: 50cc (3ci) machines. Malaguti also made a push into the export market and began achieving sales in Britain and France. In the mid-1980s, Malaguti was producing about 25,000 machines a year, and this doubled during the 1990s.

With the popularity of scooters at present, Malaguti has found a secure market niche and has become a major player in this arena too.

From the 1970s onwards Malaguti concentrated exclusively on 50cc (3ci) motorcycles, scooters and mopeds. These two ultra-lightweight 50cc (3ci) offroaders are typical of the time, and found a ready market in Britain and the rest of Europe.

VELOCETTE 250 GTP

ENGLAND 1930

Although the firm was always interested in racing, the majority of Velocette's market success was in the realm of everyday road machines like the 1930 GTP roadster. Although rather less impressive than its overhead-cam stablemates, the GTP had the finish and proportions of a genuine motorcycle, and was of higher quality than most British two-stroke machines of the period.

The air-cooled engine relied on deflector pistons rather than the later Schnurle loop technology, breathing through a single carburettor but using twin exhaust pipes. One unusual feature was an oil-metering arrangement, which linked delivery to throttle opening.

The GTP was initially launched with an iron cylinder head and barrel, and a three-speed hand gear change. However, by 1935 it had gained an all-aluminium engine and a Harold Willis four-speed foot change. Production ended in 1940, though a few GTPs were produced for export immediately after the war.

ENGINE: 249cc (15ci) two-stroke single, 63x80mm, air-cooled
POWER: n/a
GEARBOX: 4-speed foot change
FINAL DRIVE: chain
WEIGHT: n/a
TOP SPEED: 97km/h (60mph)

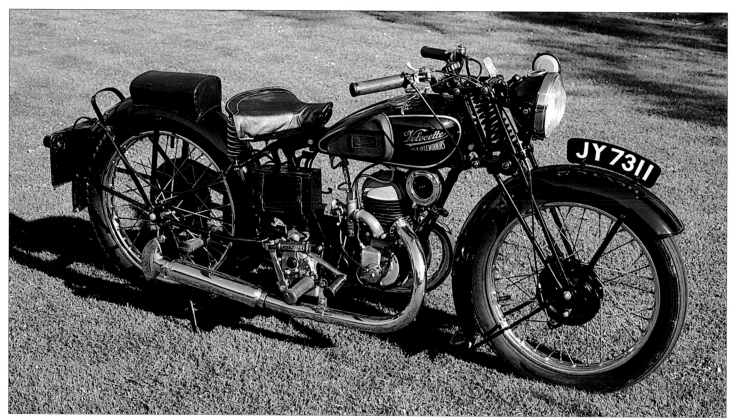

Always very nicely finished, machines like the 250 GTP brought an element of quality to the average user. This model dates from 1936, the year after four-speed hand-change replaced the previous foot-change system.

AJS S3 V-TWIN

ENGLAND 1931

Despite its shiny chrome, solid design, respectable specification and comfortable ride, the S3 was not a success in the marketplace. It was simply not what most motorcycle buyers were looking for.

This machine was a misguided attempt to build a smooth, quiet machine. It was powered by a 498cc (30ci), side-valve, transverse, V-twin engine. For easy access and servicing, the valves were outside the cylinders, so there were two chain-driven camshafts, with the points driven from one of them. The crankshaft drove a shaft running back to the clutch and then to the bevel gears, which drove the three-speed gearbox, final drive being by chain.

The remainder of the machine was broadly conventional, but the cradle-frame twin downtubes splayed out to suit the engine type and meet the lower tubes that supported it. The S3 was fitted out with girder forks, wire wheels, drum brakes and a saddle tank with an instrument panel.

The S3 was a well-designed and comfortable machine, but times were hard. Besides, most potential buyers were less interested in comfort and a smooth ride than performance and an appropriate sound coming from the exhaust. The model was offered for a single year and then quietly dropped.

ENGINE: 498cc(30ci) sv transverse V-twin, 65x75mm, air-cooled
POWER: n/a
GEARBOX: 3-speed, hand change
FINAL DRIVE: chain
WEIGHT: 150kg (330lb)
TOP SPEED: 110km/h (65mph)

Despite its great comfort and excellent performance, the AJS S3 was slow to sell. This, combined with its expensive production costs and the financial difficulties of parent company, meant the motorcycle was only sold for one year before being phased out.

BROUGH SUPERIOR 500

ENGLAND 1931

The Superior 500 was created during the Depression, and it was frequently claimed that it was an attempt to build a more affordable machine to match the hard times everyone was struggling through. It was certainly a good bit smaller than the 1929 Overhead 680, which had previously been Brough's smallest machine. However, it was not really an economy model, as a look at its capabilities and specification will show. In its street-legal guise, the 500 Superior delivered 19hp. Driving through the four-speed gearbox ensured that the 500 would make 137km/h (85mph) with good pulling power for a sidecar. If the lights and the compression plates under the cylinders were removed, the machine became a 31hp racer capable of more than 145km/h (90mph).

This 'smaller and cheaper' machine was the smallest ever made by Brough, but it performed significantly better than the 128km/h (80mph) 1926 Overhead 680 or the Black Alpine 680 that followed it.

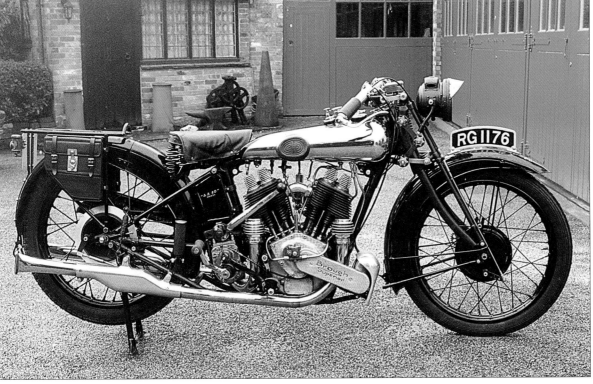

With its big 986cc (59ci) overhead-valve V-twin engine delivering 35 bhp, the Brough Superior had more power available than most small cars of the period, and on a package weighing less than 200kg.

CARNIELLI

Like many other Italian manufacturers, Carnielli started out as a bicycle manufacturer and moved into production of powered machines in the early 1930s. Carnielli machines were also sold under the name of Vittoria, the town where the firm was based.

Carnielli bought its engines in. The smallest was a 100cc (6ci) two-stroke German Sachs, installed in a velomoteur. Virtually all Italian motorcycle firms of the time offered such machines in addition to their more impressive ranges. Larger four-strokes were sourced mainly from JAP and Rudge firms. These ranged from 175cc (11ci) through 250cc (15ci) and 350cc (21ci) models up to a 500cc (31ci) machine.

The machines built around these engines were typical of the times, with a separate gearbox, all-chain drive, rigid frame and girder forks. Rear suspension was added a little later; by 1939, most Italian makes used some form of rear suspension, usually the pivoted-fork type.

After the inevitable disruption of World War II, Carnielli built lightweights and a scooter. Engines for these machines came from Sachs, Ilo, Victoria and NSU. This extensive use of German rather than Italian engines was unusual. Another unconventional trait was the use of the 98cc (6ci) NSU overhead-valve engine; few small engines were four-strokes.

Later in the firm's history, it introduced a folding moped with a 50cc (3ci) Sachs engine, single speed and automatic clutch. It was sold under the Graziella name. The machine rode on 20cm (8in) wheels, and was promoted as the motorcycle in the boot.

DOUGLAS D31

For 1931, Douglas fielded an updated S6 sports-tourer, calling it the D31. As a standard 600cc (37ci), it was designated E31; and as a 500cc (31ci), the C31. There were also A and B31s, which were 350cc (21ci). The chief difference between these was that the A31 was below the 200lb (91kg) tax limit and the B31 weighed in above it.

All models handled well but were fairly basic from a technological standpoint. All had a big external 'bacon slicer' flywheel and therefore gave a smooth ride with plenty of torque. This was more useful to sidecar users than sporting motorcyclists, which was one reason for the E31 model. The only concession to progress was the dry-sump lubrication, which had been added to the specification in 1929.

In 1931, the Douglas range was looking increasingly dated; its TT heritage was fading into the past. William Douglas seems to have understood this. In 1932, the company was sold to a group of investors, who created Douglas Motors Ltd. However, the Douglas Motors project was not a success and some of the company's machine tools were eventually sold to raise funds. In 1934, Douglas bought back the remains of his company and formed William Douglas Bristol Ltd.

ENGINE: 596cc (36ci) sv in-line flat twin, 68x82mm, air cooled
POWER: n/a
GEARBOX: 3-speed hand change
FINAL DRIVE: chain
WEIGHT: n/a
TOP SPEED: n/a

MATCHLESS SILVER HAWK

Launching a sports machine in the middle of the Depression may not have been a great idea, but nevertheless this model was unveiled late in 1930 at the same time as the Ariel Square Four. Its predecessor, the Silver Arrow, was a well-behaved touring machine, but the Silver Hawk was intended to be much more aggressive.

The 592cc (36ci) Hawk engine was essentially a pair of Arrows, but in place of the side-valve twin was a narrow-angle V-four with an overhead camshaft driven by shaft and bevels on the right. The engine itself looked most impressive, but the single carburettor on the left was somewhat less so. Exhaust was via two pipes running down the right-hand side.

The dynamo and coil ignition distributor were skew-gear driven from the camshaft vertical shaft, and the oil tank for the dry-sump lubrication system was bolted to the front of the crankcase.

The Silver Hawk's four-speed gearbox was driven by a duplex chain with Weller tensioner, and the final drive was also by chain. This was all mounted on a Matchless spring frame with girder forks, wire wheels and 20.5cm (8ins) drum brakes.

The Silver Hawk certainly looked good, but it was simply too expensive for its time and did not sell well, though the engine was used by OEC for one of their 1934 models. Silver Hawk production ceased in 1935.

ENGINE: 592cc (35ci) ohc in-line V-four, 50.8x73mm, air-cooled
POWER: n/a
GEARBOX: 4-speed hand change
FINAL DRIVE: chain
WEIGHT: 170kg (375lb)
TOP SPEED: 135km/h (80mph)

The overhead-camshaft V-four engine of the Matchless Silver Hawk and the distinctive tank logo. This impressive machine was released at a bad time and did not survive in the tough marketplace of the Depression.

BATAVUS

The Rijwiel-en-Motorenfabriek Batavus company, based in Heerenveen, joined the pedal cycle market in 1904 as a seller and started building its own machines from 1914. It was not until 1932 that the firm took its first steps into the powered transport marketplace. The first design was powered by a 98cc (6ci) Villiers two-stroke engine. Others followed, using engines from Sachs, Ilo and Villiers. Sizes included 74cc (5ci), 98cc (6ci), 100cc (6ci) and 150cc (9ci).

After the end of World War II, Batavus resumed production of small motorcycles with Ilo and Villiers engines of 148cc (9ci) and 200cc (12ci), and motocross and enduro machines powered by Sachs engines. From 1950, mopeds were also constructed.

While many other firms foundered in the mid to late 1950s, Batavus did well, and this continued throughout the 1960s. By 1970, it had acquired the Dutch moped manufacturer Magneet, and it took over the Phoenix, Fongers

and Germaan moped brands soon after. Magneet had been a bicycle maker, but then made mopeds; Fongers was almost as old as Batavus, and made FN-powered motorcycles; Germaan was founded in 1935 and made lightweight motorcycles that used small-capacity Villiers, Ilo, Csepel and Sachs engine and, in the late 1950s, built the Achilles Capri under licence, marketing it as the Germaan Capri.

In the early 1970s, Batavus was a major player in the moped field,

A Mk 4S moped from Batavus, built in 1975 – just three years before the collapse of the market killed off the firm. The machine is powered by a Sachs engine.

and suffered accordingly when that market largely collapsed in 1976. Production ceased within a few months. However, the Indian firm TVS continued to make Batavus mopeds under licence from 1976.

BROUGH-AUSTIN

The Brough Austin was based around the Austin Seven engine, a water-cooled 750cc (46ci) unit that was stretched to 800cc (49ci), mainly for motorcycle use. It had a very prominent radiator, which was handy for hand-warming, but its most notable feature was the strange double rear wheel with the drive up the middle.

The Brough-Austin was intended for use as a sidecar combination,

though it could allegedly be ridden solo. Only about ten were made and this is perhaps because it is such an odd machine that about half of them are still in existence.

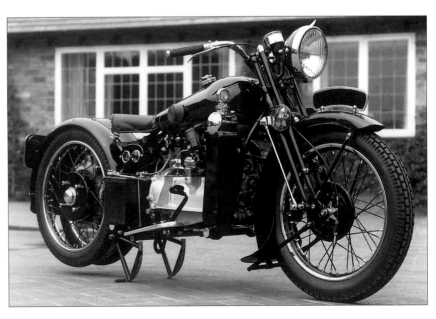

A Brough Austin without sidecar. The distinctive (and peculiar) double rear wheel is clearly evident. Less than a dozen of these machines were made, and they were so remarkable that many survive.

ENGINE: 800cc (48ci) sv in-line straight four, 57.9x76mm, liquid-cooled
POWER: 23bhp at 4600rpm
GEARBOX: 3-speed + reverse
FINAL DRIVE: shaft
WEIGHT: 356kg (783lb) outfit
TOP SPEED: 97km/h (60mph) approx

CZ

Cesk-Zbrojovka, or 'Czech Arms', was founded in 1922 to produce armaments. In 1932, CZ began to build motorcycles. After 1945, when the Czech motorcycle industry was nationalized, CZ and Jawa were merged, but continued to produce models under both badges.

The very first CZ machine was basically an adapted bicycle with a 60cc (4ci) two-stroke engine fitted to the front forks, with direct drive to the wheel. This was replaced by a slightly more advanced model using a 76cc (5ci) engine in a customized frame with chain drive, pedalling gear for starting and a light leading-link front fork. This model was upgraded to 98cc (6ci) and later acquired a three-speed transmission.

In 1934, CZ produced a simple road machine that would be the progenitor of CZ's bread-and-butter range for many years to come. It was a 175cc (11ci) model using a single-cylinder, two-stroke engine driving a three-speed gearbox, with a pressed-steel frame and girder forks. From this beginning came an entire range of machines, starting with a 250cc (15ci) single and then a 175cc (11ci) twin with four speeds and footchange.

A 350cc (21ci) single appeared, and sidecars were added to go with this larger model, providing the CZ range to the end of the 1940s. Despite factory damage during the war, CZ began producing again in 1946, starting with the pre-war 175cc (11ci) and 250cc (15ci) models. These were followed by a new and more modern 125cc (8ci) model with equal bore and stroke, aluminium cylinder head, and unit construction of gearbox and flywheel magneto. Twin exhaust pipes were used and the gear-change pedal and kick-start went on concentric shafts on the left.

CZ machines attracted notice in competition, and in the 1947 IDST a team riding the 125cc (8ci) model came second, behind a team on Jawas. CZ also came second in the 1949 IDST and several times during the 1950s, and then secured victory in several World Championships in both 250cc (15ci) and 500cc (31ci) classes during the 1960s.

In road racing, CZ fielded a series of single-cylinder four-strokes with one or two camshafts, which did respectably well but

Above: From powered bicycles, CZ quickly moved on to workhorse lightweight road machines, which provided the firm's main source of revenue for many years.

Right: A 250 twin dating from 1976. The twin shared much of its design with the 175cc (10ci) single, including unit construction and modern suspension.

never quite made the running for the top slots. These machines followed a design first seen in the late 1930s, though updated for new technology. Race machines included a 125cc (8ci) twin and a 350cc (21ci) single, but their most complex motor was a metric 350cc (21ci) V-four with twin-overhead camshafts and 16 valves. Despite the effort put into this, it was never really on the pace for a factory machine and was retired in 1972.

CZ's main income continued to come from its range of simple road models, all two-strokes of 175cc (11ci) or 250cc (15ci), a 350cc (21ci) twin, and later a 125cc (8ci). These kept to the form of the early post-war machines with unit construction, telescopic forks and, in time, pivoted-fork rear suspension. One quirk was the adoption of a single pedal for both starting and gear changing.

For starting, it was swung up to the usual operating position; once the engine was going, it reverted to the normal horizontal. Operation of the gear lever also lifted the clutch, so the hand lever was not needed when changing gear. This all took some getting used to by riders, and the combined use made the pedal rather heavy for gear change, although it was satisfactory for kick-start.

CZ's first scooter was built in 1946. The early models were joined by the Cezeta in 1958, which used the 175cc (11ci) engine. Mopeds followed in the 1970s, along with trail bikes, motocross and enduro versions of the road machines. These drew on the firm's experience of such events and the ISDT.

The basic line of 125cc (8ci), 175cc (11ci) and 250cc (15ci) singles remained in production, with their lines becoming seen as more traditional because they did not really change over time. With them ran the 350cc (21ci) twin, but eventually much of the range adopted the Jawa badge and were no longer built in the CZ form, although the firm kept its Jawa-CZ title.

CZ road bikes were hardly exciting or inspirational, but they were sound, basic designs that did what was expected of them. The race machines were rather more interesting, and sometimes innovative. They did well in competition over the years. However, success in these two very different arenas was not enough to keep CZ in business forever.

In 1993, the Cagiva group bought a controlling interest. The 125cc (8ci) and a larger 180cc (11ci) single remained in production for a few years, but production finally stopped in 1998.

Above: A post-war 150cc (9ci) dating from 1952. At this point, CZ had recovered from the disruption of World War II and was beginning to make its mark in competition.

DAX

Dax was founded by Pierre de Font-Réaulx and Robert Dahan, who exhibited their first machine at the Paris Show in 1932. This was a stylish but fairly conventional 350cc (21ci).

The engine was a built-in unit with the cross-over gearbox and had overhead-valves closed by hairpin springs, rear-mounted magneto, oil carried in the sump and gear primary drive. The machine had girder forks, drum brakes and a saddle tank.

In 1935, a 500cc (31ci) called the Rafale joined the range, plus an unusual Velomoteur called the Baby. This machine was built to an unusually high standard, with a 100cc (6ci) twin-port, four-stroke, all-alloy, unit-construction engine with overhead-valves closed by hairpin springs and ignition by flywheel magneto. The Baby also featured gear primary drive and a choice of two- or three-speed gearboxes. All this went into a rigid frame with girder forks.

The Baby was a lot faster than most Velomoteurs and the footrests could be locked to become pedals if they were needed.

The overhead valve engine/gearbox unit of a mid-1930s Dax 350cc single. It powered a competent and basically conventional machine.

FUSI

Achille Fusi built motorcycles in Milan for some time under the RAS name before deciding to rename the marque in 1936. He bought up CF and used his own name from then on. This gave access to the 250cc (15ci) face-cam engine built in-house by CF, and production of this continued.

Fusi continued with the same engines he had used when making RAS machines. These were JAP units of 175cc (11ci) to 500cc (31ci), originally imported from Britain but later built under licence. All were singles and most had overhead-valves. These engines were installed in

conventional frames in the style of the period, and gained rear suspension in time.

By 1939, the 175cc (11ci) model was gone and there was a four-model range in production, of which three machines were 247cc (15ci) models, all with the engine inclined in the frame. Two of these

had equal bore and stroke, overhead-valves, four speeds and rear suspension, while the third had a long-stroke, side-valve engine, three speeds and a rigid frame. The fourth was different, with a 499cc (30ci) overhead-valve engine set upright in the frame, four speeds and rear suspension.

After World War II, the firm continued with production of the 250cc (15ci) face-cam engine for a while. It then added a line of small two-strokes, which were fitted with Garelli engine units. These came in various sizes with unit construction of the gearbox and went into frames with front and rear suspension. This line took the firm into the 1950s, but was not enough to get it through that difficult decade.

A Fusi from the late 1940s, with a 250cc (15ci) face-cam engine fitted in a pre-war frame with pivoted-fork rear suspension. The style is typical of Italian machines of the period.

HUSQVARNA V-TWIN RACER

Released in 1932, this machine was involved in competition for only three years, but it was constantly developed in that time. Although it was a fairly simple design, it was capable of beating the racing singles of the time. Indeed, this machine won the Swedish GP three times. It might also have won the 1934 Senior TT, but ran out of fuel after breaking the lap record.

Husqvarna built their machine around a longitudinally mounted 498cc (30ci) V-twin engine, which occupied the whole of the frame. The oil tank thus had to be located at the side of the rear wheel. The long fuel tank occupied the top run of the tubular perimeter frame in a fairly conventional setup.

Other interesting features included hairpin valve springs and tuned exhaust pipes.

ENGINE: 498cc (30ci) longitudinally mounted V-twin
POWER: 44bhp at 6800rpm
GEARS: n/a
FINAL DRIVE: chain
WEIGHT: 127kg (280lb)
TOP SPEED: 190km/h (118mph)

The rearmost of these extended well beyond the rear of the bike. The front girder forks featured a central spring connected to the headstock. At the back was a conical hub with an integral brake drum and sprocket carrier. The V-Twin's performance could have been better than its handling would allow, in spite of the use of alloy materials to minimize the weight.

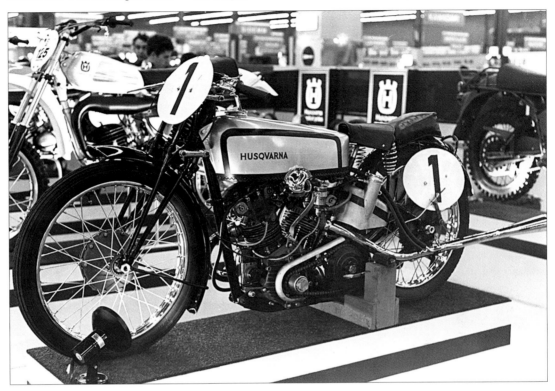

Although 500cc V-twin racer was a fairly simple design, it was able to beat the highly tuned race singles of the competition as well as breaking the Senior TT lap record.

IZH

IZH is named after the first three letters of the company's location, Izhevsk. The firm has been extremely important in Soviet and Russian motorcycle production for more than half a century, and has always been a strong supporter of the two-stroke engine.

In the early days of the firm (the 1930s to 1950s), much of its technology was copied from Western designs. IZH 'borrowed' a lot from German industry in general, and DKW in particular. This started before World War II but was facilitated by the capture of DKW NZ350 motorcycles during the German invasion of Russia.

This featured a long-stroke dimensions of 72 x 85mm (2.8 x 3.3in) for its single-cylinder, twin-port engine. The four-speed transmission featured both hand- and foot-change, whilst the frame was constructed from channel sections of steel pressings with a rigid rear and had blade-type girder front forks.

After the war, the NZ350-inspired IZH continued in production. In the immediate post-war period, racing versions used the same engine and cycle parts. The capture of the DKW's plant at Zschopau by the Communist forces gave access to the actual machinery used to build DKW machines and virtually guaranteed that IZH would continue to follow DKW practice for years to come.

Most of IZH's output was obsolescent or obsolete when it appeared, but in post-war Russia these machines still found a good market. By the 1960s, the firm was supplementing this with specialized machines for competitions such as the IDST. These were no obsolete copies; they were world-class competitors and won many events.

In 1961, the Jupiter was launched, and later the Planeta. The former was a twin-cylinder roadster; the latter a single. Both models sold in massive numbers throughout the Eastern Bloc, and export to the West, including the UK, began in the mid-1970s. Today, these models are still IZH's main production bikes, though new machines are rumoured to be in the pipeline.

IZH gained a lot from the seizure of DKW assets after the Second World War. These 350cc (21ci) two-strokes, pictured at the IZH factory in 1947, were derived from DKW designs.

RABENEICK

As Germany began to recover from the Depression, a new motorcycle firm was setting up in Bielefeld. Founded by and named after August Rabeneick, the firm initially focused on building lightweight machines, most of which were powered by Sachs two-stroke engines.

After World War II, Rabeneick began to construct larger-displacement machines, including a four-stroke horizontally opposed twin in 1951. There was also a wide range of two-strokes with either Ilo or Sachs units, which ranged from 98cc (6ci) to 247cc (15ci), including an interesting 244cc (15ci) Ilo-powered parallel-twin, the F250/2, produced between 1951 and 1957.

Rabeneik's most interesting design was first exhibited in 1953. Powered by a 250cc (15ci) four-stroke overhead-valve single bought in from Universal in Switzerland, the machine had oil-damped telescopic forks, swinging-arm rear suspension and a Denfeld-made dual seat. It was very expensive, however, and never sold in any real numbers.

Rabeneick struggled like everyone else between 1956 and 1957, but managed to get through while other German manufacturers went under. Afterwards, the firm concentrated on smaller machines. In 1962, its largest model was the LM 100/4 lightweight motorcycle, powered by a 98cc (6ci) Sachs engine. The rest of the range were all 50s: the Saxonette moped, the Binetta Super 4 (four-speed) and Super 5 (five-speed), and the R50 scooter.

In 1963 Rabeneick was taken over by Hercules, which had been part of the Zweirand-Union group since 1960. In the 1970s, the Rabeneick plant was used by Fichtel & Sachs.

TAURUS

Founded in 1933, Taurus built a number of different models powered by two-stroke and four-stroke engines over the next three decades. Perhaps its finest hour was the 1938 development of a 499.34cc (30.47ci) double overhead-camshaft single in 1938. This was a pure race machine and was very promising. With more development, it might have posed a real threat to the larger manufacturers such as Bianchi, Gilera and Moto Guzzi. However, Taurus lacked the money for such an expensive undertaking, and the outbreak of war in 1939 killed off the project.

At the end of the war, Taurus found it a struggle to get going again. However, by the late 1940s, full production had been resumed. Operating in a very favourable market, the firm had to contend with a shortage of components as well as competition from new firms such as Aermacchi, Ducati and MV Agusta.

In order to remain competitive, Taurus introduced a new overhead-valve 250cc (15ci) single in the mid-1950s. This featured full unit construction of the engine and transmission and also telescopic front forks and swinging-arm rear suspension with twin shock absorbers. Despite efforts to make this a machine for the future, the new bike was obviously a utilitarian rather than exciting design and failed to achieve the sales figures Taurus needed. Things slid downhill until 1966, when the firm closed down.

Although Taurus mainly produced smaller machines for the commuter market, there were exceptions. One was the 1938 500cc (30ci) racer and another was this, much later, 900cc (54ci) race machine.

VELOCETTE 250 MOV

ENGLAND 1933

Velocette's top-end models in the 1930s were their overhead-cam bikes. However, these were difficult and costly to produce and consequently had very low profit margins. The first attempt by Eugene Goodman to design a more affordable four-stroke was a 350cc (21ci) side-valve machine. This performed very poorly and was scotched, though the chassis was later used for the more successful MOV.

Deriving its name from type M, Overhead-Valve, the MOV was unveiled in 1933. It was a 'high camshaft' design of a broad type, which would last until the company's demise. The cams were driven by gears and were mounted high in the timing chest on the right-hand side of the engine, allowing the use of short, stiff pushrods.

Next came the 349cc (21ci) MAC (known as the MAF when produced for the British forces).

This was essentially an MOV with the stroke enlarged to 96mm (3.8in), while the 495cc (30ci) MSS was a MAC with an 81mm (3.2in) bore. The MOV reappeared briefly after World War II, but was discontinued in 1948. The MAC and MSS continued in production, being redesigned in 1953 and 1954, respectively, with swing-arm rear suspension.

The later Venom and Viper ranges were derived from the MSS. Although less prestigious

than the overhead-cam models, the MOV was perhaps the most commercially successful models in Velocette history.

ENGINE: 248cc (15ci) ohv single, 68x68.25mm, air-cooled
POWER: n/a
GEARBOX: 4-speed foot change
FINAL DRIVE: chain
WEIGHT: n/a
TOP SPEED: 97km/h (60mph)

ASTORIA

ITALY 1934–36 AND 1947–57

Many significant motorcycle design decisions can be traced back to the tax situation in their country of origin. Weights and engine sizes were often chosen to take advantage of or avoid tax brackets. A change in the Italian tax system in the 1930s encouraged the production of more powerful machines (250cc/15ci instead of 175cc/11ci), which in turn stimulated sales of the new, faster designs.

Astoria responded to this demand in 1934, entering the market with a range of 249cc (15ci) and 499cc (30ci) machines powered by overhead-valve Ajax engines imported from AMC. These were basically British AJS units under a different name. Both machines were fairly conventional with magneto ignition and dry-sump lubrication, and the engine was mounted upright in the frame with a separate gearbox. Girder forks,

drum brakes, full electrics and a saddle tank filled out a pretty decent set of specifications. However, another change in financial laws – this time, an increase in import tariffs – made it necessary to use Italian-made engines from 1935. This did not work out, and production ceased in 1936.

In 1947, Astoria returned to the motorcycle marketplace, initially with small numbers of 500cc (31ci) machines, using materials

left over from their pre-war factory. Transport was in great demand in post-war Europe, so even dated designs could find a market. Next, the firm began experimenting with different engines, mainly small 250cc (15ci) two-strokes, although they also used some overhead-valve four-strokes. In true Italian tradition, these engines had unit construction and the machines soon boasted front and rear suspension.

CROCKER

USA 1934–41

Al Crocker was an agent for Indian for many years before deciding to build speedway frames for Indian engines. He began in 1931, and by 1933 there was a complete machine. Although built in Los Angeles, Crocker's machine was very British in style. It was powered by a 500cc (31ci) overhead-valve engine. Later, Crocker experimented with an overhead-cam layout, but this was not suitable for speedway and his racing bikes were built for only two years.

Next, Crocker started producing road machines, beginning in 1936 with a V-twin aimed at the top end of the market. These machines were more or less hand-built to the user's requirements. The basic machine (if anything about it could be called basic) was powered by an overhead-valve engine with gear drive to the three-speed gearbox, a tubular frame, girder forks, wire wheels and drum brakes. The tanks were aluminium and cast in the firm's own foundry, along with many other parts used on the machine.

Many Crockers were manufactured to order: the largest of them was known to have had a 1491cc (91ci) engine, and was the largest-capacity production motorcycle until the Yamaha XV1600A took the title in 1998.

Unfortunately for Crocker, the Harley-Davidson Knucklehead appeared that year and offered much the same but with four speeds and at a much lower price. Crocker's brief market lead was lost, though the machines had a few sales points that Harleys lacked; one was an option on engine capacity by boring and stroking to run from the original 61cid up to 84cid.

Crocker produced very small numbers of bikes, and the firm was losing money. A final attempt, the Scootabout, was also produced in limited numbers. Crocker, ceased motorcycle production in 1942 when the war effort put critical materials in short supply. Indian and Harley received contracts with the US Army for military motorcycle production and Crocker got a contract with Douglas Aircraft to make aircraft parts. That became a more lucrative business than Al Crocker ever enjoyed with motorcycle manufacturing, and in 1942 Crocker Motorcycle became Crocker Manufacturing.

A close-up of the Crocker V-twin engine. Its exposed valve gear was concealed in order to improve appearance. Crocker machines were expensive and often sold at a loss.

DOUGLAS ENDEAVOUR

ENGLAND 1934

Douglas built a wide range of machines during the 1930s, including a number of overhead-valve models and in-line, side-valve twins of 350cc (21ci), 500 (31ci), 600cc (37ci), 750cc (46ci) and 1000cc (61ci). There was also a range of Villiers-engined single-cylinder two-strokes, including a 150cc (9ci) Bantam, a name later used by BSA.

The Endeavour, which was based on a 250cc (15ci) prototype called the Golden Star, joined this range at the beginning of what

might have been a Douglas resurgence. Reliability issues were being dealt with and William Douglas was back at the helm; things were looking up.

The Endeavour was a very good-looking machine in a distinctly BMW style, powered by a transverse twin engine.

However, it lacked the financial backing available to the German company's products and suffered from Douglas' rather poor reputation for reliability. This, along with a high price

tag at a time when nobody had money to spare, meant that sales were not as good as they might have been and the transverse twins did not replace their in-line cousins as Douglas' mainstays.

Douglas was still suffering from under-capitalization, and after the failure of this valiant effort, things went downhill again. Eventually, Gordon England of the British Aircraft Company took the company over. Motorcycle production ceased soon after.

ENGINE: 498cc (30ci) transverse flat twin
POWER: n/a
GEARBOX: 3-speed hand change
FINAL DRIVE: chain
WEIGHT: n/a
TOP SPEED: 97km/h (60mph)

The 500cc Endeavour was the first transverse twin from Douglas. Although cooling was better in this configuration than in-line, the Endeavour was not all that reliable.

RIXE

GERMANY 1934–85

Rixe started out, like so many others, as a manufacturer of pedal cycles, constructing its first powered design in 1934. From then until the outbreak of war in 1939, a range of motorized cycles was marketed with a choice of either 73cc (4ci) or 98cc (6ci) Sachs engines.

After the war ended, Rixe returned with a 98cc (6ci) utility machine, the K98, in 1949. This was followed by a range of machines with a capacity up to 250cc (15ci), which ran throughout the 1950s. In the

next decade, the firm began to concentrate in smaller machines, including various Sachs-engined mopeds. Some of these were specialist designs, such as a moped designed for tradesmen and bearing large front and rear carriers.

Rixe also marketed two 100-class motorcycles, again with Sachs power. The RS100 Tourer featured Earles forks, a low-level exhaust system, comprehensive mud-guarding, 406mm (16in) wheels, full chain enclosure, high handlebars and a rear carrier.

The sporting version was the RS100 Sport; this came with not only a tuned engine, but also a larger tank (with a capacity of 13.5 litres/3.5gallons), a high-level exhaust, flat bars and sprint-type mudguards.

The move towards ever-smaller machines went on into the 1970s, with Rixe producing only mopeds and mokicks (50cc/3ci motorcycles), all with Sachs engines.

However, as the 1980s dawned, slightly larger machines appeared. The first was the 1982 RS80W.

This machine was powered by the new Sachs water-cooled 80SW motor, a 79cc (5ci) unit that provided 8.5hp at 6000rpm, giving a maximum speed of 80km/h (50 mph). The model also boasted five gears, a neat duplex frame, cast-alloy wheels, twin-disc front brake, matching instrumentation and a distinctive silver finish.

However, the 1980s were not a good time to be a motorcycle manufacturer, and Rixe went out of business in the middle of the decade.

GALBUSERA

Galbusera started out using Rudge Python engines built under licence by the Italian Miller firm. The range included 250cc (15ci), 350cc (21ci) and 500cc (31ci) engines, all with four-valve cylinder heads, plus a 175cc (11ci). This was built by Miller especially for the Italian market. The rest were similar to engines used elsewhere in the market.

By 1938, Galbusera had something new to offer, unveiling a pair of machines (a 250cc/15ci and a 500cc/31ci) with unconventional two-stroke engines made by Marama-Toya. Both were multis with the cylinders set in a 90 V. The smaller machine had four cylinders, while the larger engine was a V-eight, with two V-fours coupled in line. Both had a centrifugal supercharger fitted to the front of the crankshaft, where it was fed by a single downdraught carburettor.

The machines were rounded out with a four-speed gearbox built in unit with the engine, which was hung from the frame, and chain final drive. Neither of these machines went into production, but they generated a lot of interest for the firm, whose more conventional designs ran on until the outbreak of war.

After World War II, Galbusera produced lightweights that were mainly powered by Sachs engines,

Galbusera produced a range of machines ranging from the amazing to the very prosaic. Engines were bought in from a range of suppliers.

from 75cc (5ci) to 175cc (11ci), as well as some four-strokes left over from pre-war stocks. This was enough to keep the firm in business until 1955, after which production ceased.

SOKOL

Sokol seems to have aimed its motorcycle designs primarily at military users, although there was a development programme in place that might have led to some interesting machines had the war not happened.

At least four models were built in the period from 1934 to 1939. The smallest was a 200cc (12ci) single (the 200 M411), and there was a much more powerful 1000cc (61ci) V-twin (the 1000 M111), as well as a couple of long-stroke single 'thumpers' (the 500RS M311 and 600RT M211).

The 200 (actually 199.2cc/ 12.1ci) delivered 7hp at 4000rpm. It weighed 100kg (220lb), and was good for about 85km/h (53mph). The 1000cc (61ci) V-twin was also known as a

CWS, but no other details have survived.

The 'thumpers' had tall, inclined cylinders. The 500RS delivered 18hp at 4500rpm or 22bhp at 5000rpm, depending on the variant. It weighed 160kg (353lb) and was good for 125km/h (78mph). This machine may have been a later sporting development of the 600RT, which weighed

146kg (322lb) and had only 15hp for a top speed of 110km/h (68mph).

With a claimed oil consumption of 100ml per 100km (281 miles per pint), it appears also to have had total-loss lubrication, although it may simply have been a prodigious oil-burner.

BMW R17

The R17 was the fastest of the 'star' frame BMWs thanks to the 33bhp engine delivered by its 500cc transverse flat twin engine.

ENGINE: 494cc (30ci) sv transverse flat twin, 83x68mm, air-cooled
POWER: 33bhp at 5000rpm
GEARBOX: 4-speed hand change
FINAL DRIVE: Kardan shaft
WEIGHT: 183kg (403lb)
TOP SPEED: 140km/h (87mph)

BMW's 'star' frame machines began appearing in 1929, starting with the R11 and R16. The R11 was powered by an 18hp 745cc (45ci) side-valve; the R16 had a 25hp overhead-valve 734cc (45ci) engine. These were somewhat strange-looking machines with pressed-steel frames. They were updated in 1935 by the new models – the R17 and the R12, respectively.

The R17 was the most developed of this range, featuring telescopic forks, a four-speed gearbox, and a significantly more powerful engine than the R16. Twin Amal carburettors helped to boost the power output to 33hp. The telescopic forks permitted wheels of the same size front and rear, which were made interchangeable. This remained a BMW feature until 1969. BMW returned to using conventional frames in 1936 with the R5 and also redesigned the engine, giving it twin cams to allow shorter, stiffer and lighter push-rods

for higher engine speeds. Its new tubular frame made the R5 18kg (40lb) lighter than the pressed-steel R17, at 165kg (363lb). Though a little slower, it was lot more precise on the road. Fitting a positive-stop foot change also made it easier to ride at speed. The R6 of 1937 was a side-valve derivative of the R5 with the same power as the R11 and R12, from a smaller engine.

The R51 and R61 of 1938 were essentially similar to the R5 and R6, but featured rear suspension. The

R61 was slightly slower due to a lower compression ratio and slightly greater weight. The R66, also appearing in 1938, was a good bit faster. It delivered 30hp and weighed only 187kg (411lb). The R66's top speed was 145km/h (90mph). Also appearing in 1938 was the R71, using the 745cc (45ci) side-valve engine but now with 22hp at 4600rpm thanks to the twin cams and twin carbs. It was the first 745cc (45ci) side-valve to use these components.

BORDONE

Milan-based Bordone started out in 1935, making three-wheeler delivery vehicles. These used 250cc (15ci) and 350cc (21ci) engines and tubular frames. After 1936, the company improved the engines and

switched to a pressed-steel frame.

Bordone produced only one real motorcycle, the Model NB. It was named after the firm's founder, Nicola Bordone. Designed just before World War II, the Model NB featured a 500cc (31ci)

overhead-valve, four-stroke, single-cylinder engine driving through a four-speed gearbox. The frame had front and rear suspension, using trapezoidal front forks and a conventional swinging-arm.

Production was limited to the first year of the war, though others may have been built afterwards. As late as 1957, Bordone introduced a new three-wheeled delivery wagon with an overhead-valve 650cc (40ci) motor, but no more motorcycles.

FRANCIS-BARNETT STAG

The Stag was built around a Blackburne 250cc (15ci) overhead-valve single designed by Harry Hatch driving through a non-unit Albion gearbox. The standard Francis-Barnett built-up frame was replaced by one with a forged H-section front downtube and a tubular rear. The Stag was well built and robust, with reasonable performance and good economy. As a result, it became quite popular and sold well.

ENGINE: 248cc (15ci) ohv single, 68x68mm air-cooled
POWER: n/a
GEARBOX: 4-speed foot change
FINAL DRIVE: chain
WEIGHT: 113kg (250lb)
TOP SPEED: 97km/h (60mph)

When first unvieled in 1935, the Francis-Barnett Stag surprised everyone by being four-stroke powered – rare in its day.

MATCHLESS G3

The 1935 G3 was the progenitor of the Matchless and AJS single range that ran on to 1966. It established the layout of the rest of the range: vertical engine, separate four-speed gearbox with foot-change, cradle frame and wire wheels with drum brakes.

The first G3 was a 350cc (21ci) built in Clubman form with exposed hairpin valve springs and a high-level exhaust system. This was common at the time, and other details of the machine's construction were equally conventional, such as

the built-up crankshaft, chain drive to the magneto behind the cylinder and dynamo beneath it but rather inaccessible. The electrics were Lucas and the carburettor from Amal, an instrument panel went in the top of the saddle tank and a separate oil tank went on the right beneath the saddle. A cradle frame with duplex downtubes was used up to 1940, when it became a single tube.

During the war years, the G3 was given telescopic front forks (becoming the G3L), and soon

after the war it also gained rear suspension. Alternator electrics were added later, but throughout its development the basic form of the machine remained much the same.

Also produced were 245cc (15ci) and 497cc (30ci) versions, along with competition and sports models badged as Matchless or AJS. All were fine motorcycles and well finished, and the model remained in production for a long time. Perhaps too long: its target market gradually faded away around it.

ENGINE: 499cc (30ci) sv vertical single, 85x88mm, air-cooled
POWER: n/a
GEARBOX: variable hand change
FINAL DRIVE: belt
WEIGHT: 82kg (180lb)
TOP SPEED: n/a

The 1935 G3 was the foundation of the pre-war and post-war single ranges for both Matchless and AJS. They were built in three sizes at first, but only two in its post-war guise.

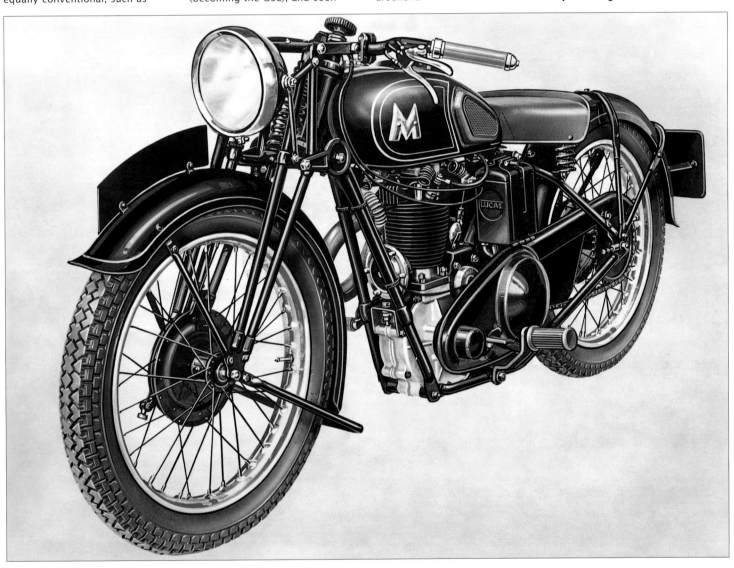

MOTO GUZZI GTW

After the Normale, Moto Guzzi produced the Sport 14, then the Sport 15, both still using inlet-over-exhaust configuration but delivering more than 13hp. This was due to better breathing, a higher compression ratio (although it was still only 4.5:1) and, above all, more revs: maximum power was developed at 3800rpm instead of 3000rpm. Then, in 1935, came the GTW.

This machine was very progressive and incorporated many advances made in the racing world. Rear suspension made its debut with this model, and it also had a foot change for the gears, with a rocking, heel-and-toe movement. Other features included improved engine design with overhead valves for a power output that was impressive for the time. It was certainly enough to drive a light machine like this at

speeds that, just a few years before, had been confined to the racing track.

Other models in the same series were named GTV, GTC and GTCL, and were eventually developed into the legendary Condor, Dondolino and Gambalunga models. The Dondolino was good for well over 160km/h (100mph), and is often quoted at 170km/h (106mph). The racing Gambalunga was even faster.

ENGINE: 498cc (30ci) ioe single, 88x82mm, air-cooled
POWER: 22bhp at 4500rpm
GEARBOX: 4-speed foot change
FINAL DRIVE: chain
WEIGHT: 180kg (396lb)
TOP SPEED: 130km/h (80mph)

RIKUO

JAPAN 1935–45 AND 1953–62

Harley-Davidson achieved very good worldwide sales in the 1920s and moved into many overseas markets, including Japan. The Harley-Davidson Sales Company of Japan developed a large network of dealers, agencies and spares distributors. Harleys were sufficiently well respected to become Japan's official police motorcycle. Meanwhile, the Murata Iron Works was building poor-quality Harley-Davidson copies. The same firm would later build the Meguro, distant ancestor of modern Kawasakis.

After the Wall Street Crash of 1929, the Yen was in deep trouble and it was no longer feasible to import Harleys. Rather than watch

the sales network wither and die, Alfred Childs, the head of Harley's Japanese operation, suggested building machines in Japan. Despite some misgivings on the part of the firm, its first overseas factory was set up at Shinagawa, near Tokyo.

The factory benefited from the loan of tooling, plans, blueprints and expertise from US facilities, and was at the time considered the most modern motorcycle factory in the world. At first, many parts were imported, but the new operation found its feet and was making complete motorcycles by 1935. These were mainly Model VL three-speed 1216cc (74ci) side-valve V-twins. By 1930, this model

had become the official motorcycle of the Japanese Imperial Army.

Later in the 1930s, the military was the de facto ruling power in Japan. It had the chance to convert the Shinagawa plant to build the new overhead-valve Knucklehead, but stayed with the VL, which had proven its durability. The Sankyo corporation took over control of the factory, and began using the Rikuo name for its Japanese 'Harleys'. The 1216cc (74ci) twin was later to become the Rikuo Model 97.

In the late 1930s, as relations between the USA and Japan rapidly deteriorated, Harley-Davidson bowed to the inevitable. The firm cut its losses and sold

out. Military demand increased, especially after the invasion of China in 1937, and Rikuo sub-licensed their designs to Nihon Jidosha (Japan Combustion Equipment Co.). Their machines were 1311cc (80ci) versions of the Rikuo Model 97, and were called Kuro Hagane (Black Iron). That particular enterprise ended as the war drew to a close: the Nihon Jidosha factory was based at Hiroshima.

The Rikuo name also appeared on a range of motorcycles built from 1953 to 1962. The models manufactured were singles of 250cc (15ci) and 350cc (21ci), as well as V-twins of 996cc (61ci) and 1200cc (73ci).

Rikuo started out making what were essentially Harley-Davidsons by any other name, but later on also produced a range of BMW-inspired designs. These included 248cc (15ci) and 348cc (21ci) singles.

BENELLI 250 SUPER SPORT

ITALY 1936

Benelli developed plunger rear suspension during the 1930s. The first model to use it was unveiled in 1936. This was the 250 Super Sport, and soon afterwards the same design appeared on other 250cc (15ci) and 500cc (31ci) models.

Benelli's new 250 single was described as being 'very English

in appearance', which is accurate. The 247cc (15ci) engine had the camshaft drive (by a train of gears) on the offside, with points ignition and dynamo lighting. In typical Italian fashion, there was a rocking gear pedal on the offside for the four-speed gearbox. The 250 usually had hairpin valve springs soft

The 'very English' lines of the 250 Super Sport conceal the first appearance of plunger rear suspension on this new model at its debut in 1936.

enough to be changed by hand. The engine had twin port heads. Lubricating oil was carried in a ribbed forward extension of the crankcase. On some models, a small oil-cooler was mounted on top of this, set between the

duplex front downtubes of the frame.

Some machines had a rather interesting modification to the exhaust system: a lever to put its baffle out of action, allowing relatively quiet operation in town and the opportunity

to make some noise out on the open road. The overhead-cam Benellis were seen as more sporting than Bianchi and Gilera road-going models. Only Moto Guzzi offered machines with similar performance for highway use.

ENGINE: 247cc (15ci) ohc vertical single, 67x70mm, air-cooled
POWER: 16bhp at 6500rpm
GEARBOX: 4-speed foot change
FINAL DRIVE: chain
WEIGHT: 136kg (300lb)
TOP SPEED: 113km/h (70mph)

BSA EMPIRE STAR/GOLD STAR

ENGLAND 1936

BSA was never much concerned with competition, and whenever its machines did compete their performance reinforced this attitude. Six machines were entered in the 1913 TT; the one that made it all the way to the finishing line came in seventh. The next attempt, with another six machines in 1921, was even less impressive.

Despite this less than stellar performance in competition, there were bright spots from time to time. One such was a machine

developed from Herbert Perkins' 1931 500cc (31ci) Blue Star. Parkins' design was further developed by D.W. Munro to become the Empire Star of 1936. In this trim, it covered 805km (500 miles) at Brooklands circuit at an impressive average speed of 118km/h (73.3mph).

Engine development continued under Val Page. The result was a new port design and ignition, plus fully enclosed valve gear in a style typical of BSA's postwar singles. With ultra-high compression, it

produced a very respectable 34hp.

The Empire Star took to the track at Brooklands in June 1937, ridden by Wal Handley. The Empire Star won at an average speed of more than 164km/h (102mph). The reward was a Brooklands gold star medal, so the 148km/h (92mph) road version, called the M24, appeared in catalogues for 1938 under the name Gold Star.

ENGINE: 496cc (30ci) ohv single, 82x94mm, air-cooled
POWER: n/a
GEARBOX: 4-speed foot change
FINAL DRIVE: chain
WEIGHT: 159kg (350lb)
TOP SPEED: 129km/h (80mph)

The Gold Star could top 160km/h (100mph) in racing trim and made a most impressive debut at Brooklands, where it earned a gold star medal and hence its name.

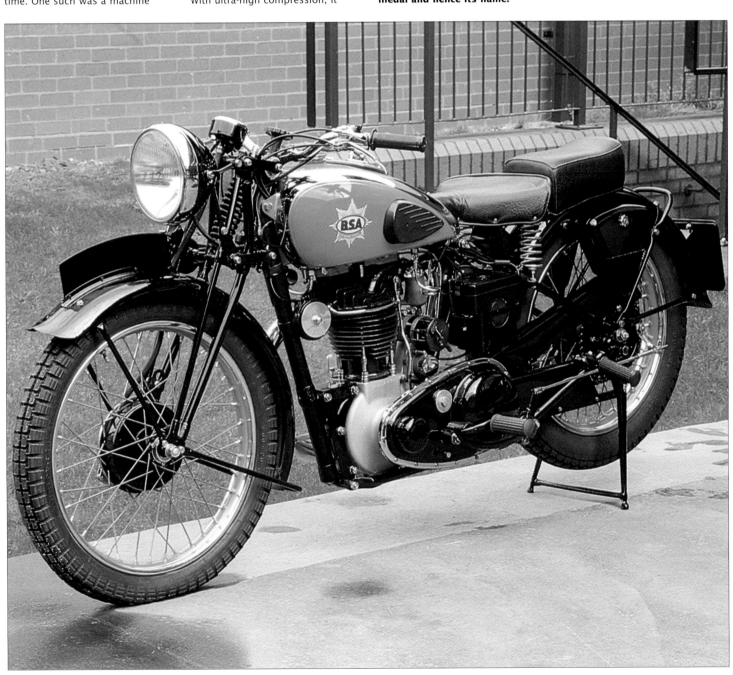

CUSHMAN

USA 1936–65

In the mid to late 1930s, the idea of the scooter was beginning to catch on in the USA. Cushman, based in Lincoln, Nebraska, was already producing a suitable engine for industrial use and decided to see if it could be used to power a scooter. The result was the Auto-Glide range, powered by Husky engines.

Modern scooters, and even those from the 1960s, tend to be quite stylish, but Cushman's offerings were anything but. Not merely basic but rather comical, they went into production in 1937 with a frame made from channel-section steel, no suspension and no gearbox. The engine, as already noted, was an industrial side-valve Husky controlled by a twist-grip throttle. There was no foot brake, and the clutch and rear-wheel brake were foot controlled.

During World War II, Cushman machines were supplied to military users, including US paratroops, but most went to the civilian market. In 1942, the 30 Series went on sale, and the 32 Series followed in 1945. The latter had a sprung front fork and was fitted with Floating Drive, which consisted of an automatic clutch and transmission system.

The 32 Series was still extremely basic, but it now had a luggage compartment, plus front and rear lighting. Its 244cc (15ci) engine was concealed behind a louvered panel, and performance was improved when the engine capacity was increased to 246cc (15ci). In 1946, the 50 series replaced the 30 range.

In the 1960s, it was fashionable amongst Mods in Britain to strip down Italian scooters and get rid of their shiny decoration.

The result closely resembled the original Cushman Highlander. The Highlander developed from the Auto-Glide model supplied to the US military for paratrooper use. After the war, these machines went to the civilian market. They were even more basic than the standard Auto-Glide, with no bodywork and the seat and fuel tank supported on a simple tubular frame. This crude but useable machine became known as the Highlander from 1949. It gained an unusual leading-link front-fork layout a little later.

During the 1950s, a rather peculiar machine became popular in the USA. This was a chopper-like layout but using the small wheels and power unit of a scooter. To compete with the popular Mustang and the Powell A-V-8 models of this type, Cushman produced a predictably crude

device that was rather grandly named the Eagle. It appeared in 1949 and, for reasons that may never be adequately explained, was popular enough to remain in production through to 1965.

Meanwhile, the post-war market was good for scooters, and for a time Cushman did very well with its Auto-Glide and Highlander machines. However, they were gradually displaced by mass-produced Japanese rivals such as the Honda 50 Cub. Once the scooter market began to dry up, Cushman started making golf buggies instead.

The Eagle, marketed by Cushman in 1949 and still in production until 1965, was a rather odd vehicle with motorcycle styling but using tiny scooter wheels. This example dates from 1958.

EXCELSIOR MANXMAN 250 ROADSTER

The designers of this machine (Hatch and Walker) created it because they did not like the idea of the Mechanical Marvel going out to private users. Hatch – Blackburne's chief engine designer – came up with a simpler and more elegant design for an overhead-camshaft single, which used a conventional bevel-driven overhead-cam.

The resulting machine was the Manxman, which was unveiled in 1934 at the Olympia Motorcycle Show in London. This was the original 248cc (15ci) version. A racing four-valve version was built in 1936 and took second in the Lightweight TTs of 1936 and 1937.

ENGINE: 246cc (15ci) ohc single, 63x79mm, air-cooled
POWER: 16bhp at 5000rpm
GEARBOX: 4-speed foot change
FINAL DRIVE: chain
WEIGHT: 135kg (297lb)
TOP SPEED: 121km/h (75mph)

Above: The Manxman first appeared in 248cc (15ci) single configuration but was eventually built in 350cc (21ci) and 500cc (30ci) versions.

Below: This 1936 four-valve version of the Manxman did well in the Lightweight TT in 1936 and 1937.

HARLEY-DAVIDSON KNUCKLEHEAD

USA 1936

The Knucklehead gains its name from the knuckle-like protrusions on the heads. This model was Harley-Davidson's first standard, road-going overhead-valve model. It was introduced in both 999cc (61ci) and 1200cc (73ci) guises with a choice of compression ratios.

It is very easy to see what the Knucklehead was designed to do when it is compared with the lighter and more powerful Vincent Series A Rapide that came out a couple of years later. The Vincent, which was 59kg (130lb) lighter, delivered an increase in power of 10 per cent and a top speed that was 32km/h (20mph) higher – though it was, in fact, designed for much better roads.

The Knucklehead was a powerful machine with a lot of torque, obviously designed to cover long distances on the terrible roads that still covered much of the USA in the 1930s. Apart from early problems with the new four-speed transmission, this was an excellent machine, although it ceased production during the war never to reappear.

ENGINE: 988 cc (59ci) ohv in-line V-twin, 84x90mm, air-cooled
POWER: 40bhp at 4800rpm
GEARBOX: 4-speed hand change
FINAL DRIVE: chain
WEIGHT: 256kg (565lb)
TOP SPEED: 145km/h (90mph) approx.

JONES

ENGLAND 1936

As the motorcycle concept matured and moved away from its powered-bicycle roots, a market niche opened up for a small, cheap machine with pedals and an engine. In later years, a machine of this type would be called a moped. The 1936 version was an Autocycle. The first machine was designed by G.H. Jones in conjunction with Villiers.

The Autocycle was based on the 98cc (6ci) Villiers engine, which was sold as the Villiers Junior.

Pedals were used to start it and to assist when underway. The engine unit included a clutch. Construction was very simple, with the one-piece cast-iron head and barrel laid horizontal, an overhung crankshaft, flywheel magneto and the main castings run back to enclose the chain-driven clutch on its own shaft. An expansion box under the cylinder was part of the unit.

The engine unit was mounted in a simple open frame with sprung forks, saddle, petrol tank and calliper brakes. The pedal shaft ran through the centre of the clutch shaft so that the whole unit could be bolted in place to the special bottom bracket of the frame. However, this feature was deleted before the machine reached the production stage. Jones feared that it might be uncomfortable when pedalling

and Villiers that it could bend in a fall. As a result, the final Villiers Junior engine went to market without it.

The Autocycle design was taken up by Raynal in 1937, and then by others in the next couple of years; most continued after the war ended. Autocycles of one sort and another were in use up until the late-1950s; it was during this decade that the moped took over.

MONDIAL

ITALY 1936–79 AND 1987–PRESENT

In 1929, the four Bosselli brothers – Carlo, Ettore, Guiseppe and Luigi – founded a dealership in Milan. It was named FB, standing for Fratelli Bosselli (the Brothers Bosselli), and at the outset sold mainly GD two-strokes, followed by CM four-strokes a little later. Guiseppe Bosselli rode a CM to victory in the 1935 ISDT.

A 203cc (12ci) double overhead-cam Mondial from 1955. Mondial was a strong exponent of double overhead-cam designs and was a pioneer in using them on small machines.

The brothers acquired a workshop in Bologna, and in 1936 began producing three-wheel delivery trucks, including a model powered by a 600cc (37ci) long-stroke engine. This went on through most of the war years, but ended in 1944 with the destruction of the production facility.

Guiseppe Bosselli inherited his father's title of Count and led his brothers to set up a new production facility in Milan. He correctly predicted that post-war Italy would be desperate for cheap motor transport, but he also knew that racing would bring publicity for his firm's products. Thus the new marque, FB Mondial, produced its first machine as a double overhead-cam, single-cylinder racing bike.

This Drusiani-designed machine won the first 125cc (8ci) world road-racing championship title in 1949, 1950 and 1951. A single-overhead-cam version was built in small numbers for sale to private customers, but it had neither the speed nor the power of the works machines.

Race experience was used in the development of the series production roadster models. A new 200cc (12ci) overhead-valve machine was exhibited at the 1951 Milan Show and became

a vital part of the company's history. It formed the basis for a series of pushrod-engined models that followed. Also unveiled at the same show was an updated version of Mondial's first street bike, a 125cc (8ci) overhead-valve model based on the racer and 125cc (8ci) and 160cc (10ci) utility two-strokes.

The following year's show saw more new Mondial products. These included a new version of the 200 motorcycle and also Mondial's first scooter. The latter used an adaptation of the recently released 160cc (10ci) two-stroke, four-speed, unit-construction engine. On the scooter version of this engine, the symmetrical, pear-shape crankcase covers that enclosed the primary transmission, generator and starter motor for the electric start (not employed in the motorcycle versions) extended to the rear and formed the swinging-arm pivot fork. This meant that the engine, transmission and rear wheel comprised a sub-assembly pivoting under the control of the two rear shock absorbers. A duplex frame was made up of tubes welded at the joints, and steel pressings were employed for the weather shield, floor and partial rear enclosure.

The only real problem with this design was shared with Ducati's Cruiser, which was released at about the same time. Although it was technically advanced, the Mondial scooter was too heavy and expensive to appeal to the general public.

Mondial enjoyed good success in long-distance road events of the 1950s, such as the Milano–Taranto and Giro d'Italia. Drusiani designed several new racing models for Mondial during this period, including a technically advanced 149cc (9ci) double overhead-cam twin, but this was to prove uncompetitive due to its weight. Instead, it was down to a pair of new singles to bring back the glory days.

The high point was 1957. With a seven-speed 125cc (8ci) single and a brand new 249.1cc (15.2ci) double-overhead-cam single (with a choice of five, six or seven gears) and a maximum of 220km/h (137mph), Mondial won both world titles. However, Mondial (along with Gilera and Moto Guzzi) retied from Grand Prix racing towards the end of 1957. The decision to bow out was taken in response to a drop in motorcycle sales throughout Italy and abroad, as the small car began to replace the motorcycle as the

favoured form of family transport.

Mondial got through the difficult times that beset the motorcycle industry in the late 1950s, going on to build a whole series of either overhead-valve or two-stroke models up to 250cc (15ci). There was even a 75cc (5ci) scooter named Lady; with its many chromed fittings and bright colours, it was clearly aimed at the teenage market.

From 1960 onwards, Count Bosselli gradually retired to his seaside retreat, leaving the business in the hands of his nephew. Things gradually went downhill through the 1960s and 1970s, though there were some high points. A renewed interest in racing resulted in the RS125 and 250cc (15ci) two-strokes, designed and ridden by Francesco Villa between 1963 and 1965. Some excellent models appeared in those final years, including the seven-speed V778 enduro with a Sachs engine. However, Mondial closed down in 1979.

There was a flicker of hope in 1987, when the Mondial marque re-emerged with a range of off-road vehicles, a super-sports 125 and a Grand Prix 125 racer. By 1989, this venture had also failed and the once great company was gone, this time forever.

NORTON INTERNATIONAL

Internationals of both 350cc (21ci) and 500cc (30ci) engine sizes were popular with clubman racers, and were continually updated for many years, often receiving new technology soon after it had been race-trialled.

In its new form with a 29bhp 'Carrol' engine, the machine was capable of about 160km/h (100mph). In 1930, the valve gear was enclosed, creating the dry-sump, overhead-cam ('cammy') Norton, which was to dominate racing for decades to come.

The International continued to develop through the 1930s, with race-proven technology adopted as soon as it was appropriate for the road bikes. In 1936, the plunger rear end was tried out on the works racers for the first time, and fitted as standard on Internationals after 1938.

ENGINE: 490cc (29ci) sohc 79x100mm, single, air-cooled
POWER: 40bhp at 6000rpm
GEARBOX: 4-speed foot change
FINAL DRIVE: chain
WEIGHT: n/a
TOP SPEED: 175 km/h (110mph)

The name International, which is usually abbreviated to Inter, actually referred to two models: the Model 30 500cc (31ci) and the

Model 40 350cc (21ci), both of which were introduced in September 1931 for the 1932 season.

An early progenitor of the International was the CS1 of 1927, which was redesigned when Walter Moore left Norton to work for NSU.

ROYAL ENFIELD JF

The multi-valve cylinder head is not as modern as many people think. In fact, the Royal Enfield JF had four valves in its 499cc (30ci) single-cylinder head back in 1936, as did other motorcycles. The multi-valve JF was a popular machine with riders thanks to its smooth power delivery and economical use of fuel. However, the multi-valve head was more expensive to produce than a regular two-valve version. In order to cut costs, Royal Enfield decided to switch to a two-valve model, which was less powerful and also less refined than its predecessor and was not as popular. It retained many of the other JF features such as a rigid frame, fully enclosed pushrods and a chromed exhaust.

ENGINE: 49cc (3ci) air-cooled single-cylinder
POWER: 19bhp
GEARBOX: 3-speed
FINAL DRIVE: chain
WEIGHT: 165kg (364lb)
TOP SPEED: 128km/h (80mph)

SCOTT 3S

Designed by Bill Cull, the 3S was potentially one of the superbikes of its era.
The prototype was an impressive 747cc (46ci) machine, but by the time it was ready to be shown it had grown to 986cc (60ci). Three examples were exhibited at the 1934 Olympia Show, attracting massive interest.

The 3S had a liquid-cooled engine with a 120° crankshaft house in magnesium alloy casing, mated to a car-type clutch and four-speed transmission. This would have made it ideal for shaft final drive, but instead bevel gears drove a conventional sprocket and chain to the rear wheel.

The cycle parts included Webb girder front forks and a DMW swinging-arm rear end. Fuel was carried in pannier-style tanks above the rear wheel on production machines, which became available in 1936. The show bikes had a fuel tank below the main frame rail.

The 3S was extremely expensive for its time and only eight were ever built. In 1959, another batch of 3S triples were adapted for marine use and were demonstrated at the UK Boat Show, but these did not enjoy commercial success either.

ENGINE: 986cc (59ci) two-stroke triple, 75x68.25mm, liquid-cooled
POWER: 40bhp approx
GEARBOX: 4-speed foot change
FINAL DRIVE: chain
WEIGHT: 222kg (490lb)
TOP SPEED: 153km/h (95mph) approx

The 3S, with its 3-cylinder 986cc (59ci) engine, was a new departure for Scott and an attempt to launch a new range. Only a handful were made and the experiment failed. The engine resurfaced later propelling boats, but it was not a success there either.

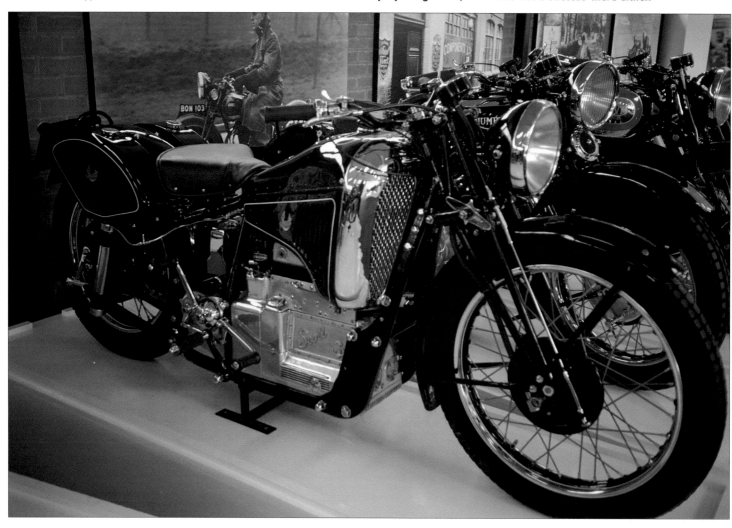

CIMATTI

Cimatti began as a bicycle manufacturer; hardly surprising given that its founder, Marco Cimatti, was an Olympic gold medallist in cycle racing in 1932. The firm began production in 1937, in the small town of Porta Lame. The factory did not survive World War II and the firm was relaunched afterwards.

In 1949, Cimatti built its first motorcycle. At that time, the market was desperate to buy anything that was offered for sale. Cimatti decided to concentrate at the cheaper end of the market, producing mopeds and smaller motorcycles. This policy paid off as the market got tougher, and firms concentrating more on high-value machines found times getting hard. As these firms struggled with financial difficulties, Cimatti was expanding.

In 1960, the factory moved to Pioppe di Salvaro in the Apennines, continuing to build a range of commuter mopeds. The firm won the Italian national 50cc (3ci) trials championship in 1966, 1967 and 1968. There were some larger models too, up to 175cc (11ci). One of these was a new 125cc (8ci) motocross machine that appeared in the early 1970s. A road version of the same machine was also available. These, like all of Cimatti's bikes, used two-stroke engines provided by Minarelli and Franco Morini.

Cimatti made a big push for exports from the early 1970s onwards, driven by the founder's son, Enrico Cimatti. The firm moved into several overseas markets, most notably the USA, France, Norway and Tunisia. Production increased to meet the new demand, and the firm was making 50,000 bikes per year by 1977. At the same time, Cimatti was reducing its workforce and improving efficiency through increased automation.

As the firm entered the 1980s, things seemed to be going well. The range had been cut to concentrate on the 50cc (3ci) sector only, and this seemed to be paying off.

However, the early 1980s were another hard time for the motorcycle industry and Cimatti was one of the casualties. The firm closed down in 1984.

Cimatti made its name with small, lightweight machines and did particularly well with 50cc (3ci) bikes, with engines from Morini and Minarelli.

CRESCENT

SWEDEN 1937–74

For its early history, Crescent was associated with fellow Swedes NV, and many NVs were badged as Crescents. However, Monark bought out NV and Crescent in 1960, creating the MCB Monark Crescent Bolagen group. Like the British Associated Motor Cycles, MCB produced different marques of motorcycle in the same factory. This was located in the west coast of Sweden, in the town of Varberg.

The best-known Crescent was the 500cc (31ci) of 1967, a three-cylinder two-stroke. The 498cc (30ci) engine was Crescent's own design and was built in house. In fact, it had been developed for use as an outboard motor on boats – possibly the first attempt to use a boat engine in a racing motorcycle. Others, including Konig of Berlin, also tried this idea.

As a racing motorcycle powerplant, the Crescent outboard engine had a power output of 64hp at 7500rpm. The pistons were slightly domed and there were three transfer ports per cylinder. The water pump was belt-driven from the crankshaft, outboard of the triple contact breaker assembly. The engine was respectably successful in sidecar competition, taking fourth in the 1973 Finnish Grand Prix. By 1974, however, MCB had moved on to other market areas and was no longer involved with motorcycles.

MEGURO

JAPAN 1937–64

Meguro started out in 1924 making automobile and motorcycle components. The first complete bike, the Z-97, appeared in 1937. This was a British-influenced machine with a 498cc (30ci) overhead-valve engine.

During the war, Meguro provided motorcycles to the military and afterwards went on building British-style machines with either overhead-valve single or overhead-valve parallel-twin engines, ranging from 248cc (15ci) to 651cc (40ci). The largest of these was more or less a straight copy of the BSA A10 design.

In 1960, Meguro became affiliated with Kawasaki Aircraft, part of Kawasaki Heavy Industries.

The firms had been working together for a time, with Kawasaki providing engines to Meguro, among other firms. In 1961, the two merged to create Kawasaki Auto Sales. This pushed Meguro machines and produced the first Kawasaki motorcycle, which drew on Meguro's expertise.

Meguro endured until 1964, then slowly vanished into the larger Kawasaki marque. Kawasaki's first major design was the 624cc (38ci) W1, developed from Meguro designs and therefore owing a lot to the British BSA A10 series. After this, Kawasaki gradually established an identity of its own, but versions of the BSA-derived machine were on sale until the early 1970s.

The neat and tidy powerplant of a 1959 125 Cadet. Soon, Meguro would be taken over by Kawasaki, whose early machines were derived from designs like this one.

MOTO MORINI

Alfonso Morini was born in 1892, in the city of Bologna. He first became involved in motorcycle manufacture in partnership with Mario Mazzetti, forming MM (Morini Mazzetti) in 1924. He left to found his own business in 1937, creating Moto Morini.

The firm's first product was a three-wheel truck rather than a motorcycle. At the outbreak of war, production was switched to military equipment. This included aircraft components, which were mostly made from cast aluminium. As a result, the Moto Morini factory in Bologna was heavily damaged by bombing raids

However, the firm emerged from the destruction better than most, and began producing motorcycles in 1946 with a machine that was heavily influenced by the pre-war German DKW RT125 two-stroke design. Like the German machine, the new Morini had piston-port induction and a unit-construction engine with three speeds. It also boasted girder front forks, plunger rear suspension and 48cm (19in) wheels. A racing version was also constructed for the Grand Prix scene, and was also offered for sale to private customers.

In 1948, work began on the design of a 246cc (15ci) Jawa-like, single-cylinder roadster model with twin exhaust ports. At its release a year later, the machine was intended as a touring bike, although the engine unit was subsequently used to power more of the commercial three-wheel vehicles that Moto Morini continued to produce.

Also in 1949, the first 125cc (8ci) road-racing world championship series was run. It was dominated by FB Mondial, but Morini offered the most serious competition. Mondial's double overhead-cam

four-stroke entry was most impressive, and Morini decided to build a similar machine to take it on. Their version was also a four-stroke, but with a single overhead-cam. It made its race debut in 1950 and won the 125cc (8ci) Italian Senior championship.

However, the new racer was not quite up to the challenge of beating Mondial in the Grand Prix races. It was updated more than once; in 1951, engine upgrades pushed power output from 12hp to 14 hp. In 1952, the engine was converted to double overhead-cam, and the power increased to 16hp. The result of this effort was the company's first Grand Prix win, at Monza. The same rider, Emilio Mendogni, won the last race of the season in Spain.

Meanwhile, Morini had developed a new 175cc (11ci) model with an overhead-valve, unit-construction engine, which was exhibited at the Milan Show in 1952. Within a year, it was joined by a similar model of 160cc (10ci).

In 1954, an enlarged version of the 125 racer was produced for Mendogni to win the 175cc (11ci) class of the Italian Senior Championship. Its success prompted Morini to market a range of 175cc (11ci) overhead-valve roadsters. These reached market in

1955, and there were three models: the Briscola (Trumps), Tressette (Three Sevens) and Settebello (Seven of Diamonds), all named after popular card games in Italy.

All three were popular. The Settebello was the performance model and proved very popular for clubman-style racing and fast road work. From it came an even higher performance model, the Rebello (Rebel). This machine had technical features quite different from a conventional, production-based motorcycle on which it was based. At the time of its introduction (1955), it was one of the most up-to-date designs anywhere in the world.

In 1957, an even more powerful single appeared, the Gran Premio. This was based on the Rebello but was intended for Grand Prix racing rather than production-type events. When the prototype was tested in 1956, it put out 25hp (compared to the 22hp offered by the 175cc/11ci). By the time it hit the track at Monza in 1957, this had increased to 29hp at 10,000rpm from the double overhead-cam engine. The Gran Premio was very successful in the World and Italian Championships right through the rest of the 1950s, and through the 1960s too.

The year 1959 saw the introduction of the 123cc (8ci) overhead-valve Corsaro (Pirate) at Milan in 1959. This machine was derived from the 98cc (6ci) Sbarazzino (Free-and-Easy), which had been successful over the previous three years. The Corsaro was capable of 101km/h (63mph) and would remain in production until the 1970s. It was also built in 150cc (9ci) and 160cc (10ci) engine sizes.

Alfonso Morini died in 1969 and his daughter Gabriella ran the firm until the late 1980s. During this time, Morini was highly successful in the ISDT, winning it several times. The firm also produced its finest motorcycle during this period. Designed in the early 1970s by Dianna Marchesini and Franco Lambertini Jr, the 3˚ was the first of these. It went into production in 1973.

These new machines were built around a 72˚ V-twin with Heron combustion chambers and belt-driven camshaft. The first (the 3˚) was a sports tourer, and it was quickly followed by a higher-performance Sport model, which had a disc front brake and cast-alloy wheels on later models (as did the 3˚). After this came 500cc (31ci) and 250cc (15ci) V-twins plus 125 (8ci) and 250cc (15ci) singles. Costs were kept down by

The highly successful 350cc (21ci) Strada. Light, extremely responsive and comfortable to ride, the '3 1/2' was the first of Moto Morini's new line of V-twins. It appealed to a wide range of users and from street-sports enthusiasts to people just wanting to get around in style.

using modular construction, allowing some components to be interchangeable between models.

A turbo version of the 500cc (31ci) V-twin was exhibited at the Milan Show in 1981, but was never put into production. However, the 500cc (31ci) Camel and 350cc (21ci) Kanguro trial bikes sold well.

The 500cc (31ci) roadster was produced in both five- and six-speed versions, while various custom versions all made use of the V-twin powerplant.

Morini was taken over by the Cagiva group in 1987, and at first things looked hopeful. The first post-takeover model, the Dart, was available as a 350cc (21ci) or a 400cc (24ci) variant, both V-twins in the style of earlier excellent machines. However, Cagiva chose not to develop the Morini marque and allowed it to fade away instead.

ROTAX

Rotax started out in Dresden, as a family business that made rear-wheel assemblies for pedal cycles. It became a public company in 1920 but did not begin making its famous engines until the 1930s, when it was bought out by Fichtel & Sachs. The firm moved to Schweinfurt and manufactured torpedo components for a time.

During World War II, Rotax relocated to Austria to avoid air-raids, and finally moved to Gunskirchen in 1947.

The firm was under government control at first, but was sold to a Vienna-based

private company. It was then purchased by the Canadian-based Bombardier Group, creating Bombardier-Rotax.

Bombardier-Rotax built a broad range of engines for all manner of vehicles, including snowmobiles and agricultural equipment. In 1970, slightly more than 1000 workers at the Rotax factory produced 267,300 engines.

Rotax' interest in racing began in the late 1960s with a 125cc (8ci) built and raced by Heinz Krinwanek. This machine finished fifth in the 1969 world championships. This modest success was followed by more

impressive results in solo and sidecar racing in the early 1970s, using a liquid-cooled 500cc (31ci) twin developed from the Bombardier snowmobile engine.

During the early 1980s, the Rotax Model 256 247cc (15ci) disc-valve in-line twin engine put up a serious challenge to the Japanese monopoly in the 250cc (15ci) racing class. Designed by Hans Holzleitner, this engine was supplied to a wide range of customers, including Armstrong, Aprilia and Kobas.

In the late 1980s, Rotax introduced an air-cooled four-valve single in 500cc (31ci),

600cc (37ci) and eventually 650cc (40ci) versions. A variant of this engine was also used in many street bikes, by makers such as MZ and Jawa.

In recent years, Rotax has been important to the success of the Italian Aprilia concern, supplying both two- and four-stroke engines.

The Rotax 496.7cc twin entered the world Grand Prix racing in 1973 at the Australian GP. The engine was based on the Canadian Bombardier snowmobile unit.

TRIUMPH SPEED TWIN

The 1937 Speed Twin was Edward Turner's masterpiece. It used the same frame as the Tiger 90 Single and cost just a little more. It was, however, 2.3kg (5lb) lighter and, thanks to the

exhaust position, able to lean more when cornering.

The block and head were cast-iron, and the single-throw crank had a central flywheel, split-alloy connecting rods and white-metal

lined big-end caps. Twin camshafts were located ahead of and behind the block, while the valve gear was mounted in separate alloy casings bolted to the head, operated by pushrods housed in

chrome tubes running between the cylinders. The pistons went up and down together, an arrangement that Turner believed provided better torque and more efficient carburation than a twin with a

After being bought by Jack Sangster, Triumph resurged with a line based on the 500cc Speed Twin, which founded a dynasty of bikes that ruled Triumph's range for four decades.

two-throw crank, and better balance than a single-cylinder unit of similar capacity. The inlet camshaft pinion also drove the Lucas Magdyno lighting and double-plunger oil pump. An instrument panel was set in Bakelite plastic and mounted on the tank top. It included a three-position light switch, ammeter and oil-pressure gauge.

The Speed Twin was a very attractive machine with a chromed tank, exhaust pipe, headlight and wheel rims, amaranth paintwork and gold coachlines. It was capable of sustained high speeds, allowing it to win the 1938 Maude's Trophy, a timed run spanning the British mainland. It was so successful that it dominated Triumph's range for over 40 years, being produced in 250, 350 (3T), 500 (5T), 650 (6T) and 750cc (46ci) forms.

The early Speed Twins were known as six-stud models, referring to the bolts securing the cylinder block to the crankcase. These were prone to coming undone at high speeds, a problem that was fixed within two years of launch. Also in 1939, the Speed Twin got telescopic forks to replace its girder forks, and the Tiger 100, a sporting version, was announced. This machine was faster than the standard model due to a higher compression ratio and was able to match the 750cc/46ci-class record at Brooklands, with a time of 189.93km/h (118.02mph).

ENGINE: 498cc (30ci) parallel-twin, 63x80mm, air cooled
POWER: 27bhp at 6300rpm
GEARBOX: 4-speed Triumph, foot change
FINAL DRIVE: chain
WEIGHT: 171kg (378lb)
TOP SPEED: 150km/h (93mph)

INDIAN FOUR

USA 1938

The Four can trace its ancestry back to a 1912 Henderson. That firm had money troubles and was bought out by Schwinn (which made Excelsiors). Then, in 1920, William Henderson produced the Ace. Unfortunately, no matter how good Henderson's bikes were, his business decisions were a lot less successful; Ace machines were sold at a loss and the firm eventually went under in 1924. It was bought up by the Michigan Motors Corporation and finally wound up with Indian in 1927.

Indian essentially rebadged the Ace and marketed it as the Collegiate Four, but it gradually metamorphosed into a more recognizably Indian machine and became known as the Indian Four.

The engine was always a nominal 1261cc (77ci), actually 1265cc (77ci), but other changes occurred along the way.

First, a five-bearing crankshaft replaced the original three-bearing in 1929. The machine got a new frame in 1932, and in 1936 an unusual exhaust-over-inlet valve arrangement replaced the old inlet-over-exhaust layout.

In 1938, the whole engine was re-designed for greater reliability, with better cooling and lubrication, and again with inlet-over-exhaust.

In total, about 12,000 Indian Fours were made; production came to an end in March 1942, after the start of World War II.

ENGINE: 1265cc (77ci) ioe 4s in-line straight-4, 69.8x82.6mm, air-cooled
POWER: n/a
GEARBOX: 3-speed hand-change
FINAL DRIVE: chain
WEIGHT: 200kg (440lb)
TOP SPEED: 160km/h (100mph)

The Four was popular with many police departments, who found its ability to cruise endlessly and deal with bad roads as useful as its good performance. Many civilian users loved it for the same reasons.

SIMSON

GERMANY 1938–PRESENT

Like certain other motorcycle manufacturers, Simson can trace its history back to the arms trade. In 1856, the Ernst Thalmann Hunting Weapon Works began production in the East German town of Suhl, and in 1896 moved into pedal cycles. These were quite advanced and had pneumatic tyres before most other manufacturers adopted them.

Simson went from pedal cycles to cars, producing touring and sporting automobiles under the Simson-Supra name from the mid-1930s onward. Then, in 1938, the first motorcycle appeared. This was a simple machine powered by a Sachs 98cc (6ci) engine.

Simson was out of the motorcycle industry until 1952, largely as a result of the war and subsequent partitioning of Germany. It returned with a humble and basic 49cc (3ci) moped, the SR-1. Next came the SR-2, which became the leading seller of all East German motorcycles in the 1950s and early 1960s. These machines were sold under the AWO brand name, as were all Simsons until the late 1960s.

Encouraged by success so far, Simson then produced its first true motorcycle, the AWO 325, which was powered by a 247cc (15ci) overhead-valve single-cylinder engine. It was in most ways similar to a BMW R26. A series of road models followed, and the AWO 325 was also entered in several races

In 1958, the double overhead-cam Simson RS 250 came out. This was a very impressive machine, which had just about every modern feature available, including a six-speed gearbox. Hans Weinert won the national title riding just such a bike in 1958 and 1959. However, since the end of the 1950s, Simson had concentrated its efforts mopeds, scooters and small motorcycles, all under 100cc (6ci).

By the 1980s, Simson was concentrating entirely on small machines under 100cc (6ci). The S51 was built in several variants, some of which were very basic while others had a higher specification.

ARIEL RED HUNTER

The Red Hunter single appeared in 1932, and a twin appeared later. Powered by a 500cc (31ci) overhead-valve single, it was an elegant machine with its instruments mounted on the fuel tank. The 1939 version had gained Ariel's unique design of rear suspension, which remained in use until swing-arm suspension replaced it in 1954. Roads in the 1930s were not good, so rear suspension was a welcome feature.

The Red Hunter's engine was designed by Val Page, and by 1939 it had gained full valve enclosure, precluding the oily mess experienced with earlier examples.

Its heavy flywheel allowed it to produce easy, usable power, yet the stroke was not so long as to prevent it revving reasonably freely.

The Red Hunter remained in production after the end of the war, changing little other than to gain telescopic front forks. A 350cc (21ci) version, using identical running gear, did appear but was considered to be underpowered.

ENGINE: 497cc (30ci) ohv single, 81.8x95mm, air-cooled
POWER: 26bhp at 5000rpm
GEARBOX: 4-speed foot change
FINAL DRIVE: chain
WEIGHT: 165kg (365lb)
TOP SPEED: 135km/h (84mph)

The 500cc Red Hunter first appeared in 1932 and remained in production for more than 20 years without changing very much. The 350cc (21ci) version was similar but was considered to be underpowered.

DERNY

Beginning in 1939, Derny built some rather unusual machines that were quintessentially French in styling. The earliest were cyclomoteurs in solo and tandem form, with a small engine (supplied by Zürcher) fitted to the downtube and a cylindrical fuel tank mounted on the headstock. The engine inclination varied: the solo model was close to upright, the tandem well angled. The frame tubing was designed and manufactured to run around the motor.

Both models used a complex transmission system starting with a chain that ran to a countershaft fixed above the front bottom-bracket. From there, a second chain ran to the rear wheel of the solo. On the tandem, the second chain ran to a second countershaft above the rear bottom-bracket and thence by chain to the wheel.

A bicycle frame and forks with drum brakes were used for both versions, the frames having extra bracing to suit the added loads. After the war, these two models were listed as the Bordeaux-Paris and the Cyclotandem.

Next came an unorthodox scooter, which was exhibited at the 1952 Paris Show. It had a 125cc (8ci) two-stroke, fan-cooled engine mounted to the left of the front wheel. This drove a three-speed gearbox fixed just behind the wheel by exposed chain, and a further chain drove a roller pressed against the tyre. Steering was affected by the weight of the power unit. The rear of the machine, including the wheel, was enclosed and the seat was mounted on top of the enclosure. It also had stabilizer wheels on each side. Nothing much came of this project, however.

In 1956, Derny introduced the Taon motorcycle, which offered a choice of two engine units: the 70cc (4ci) Lavalette with a three-speed preselector gearbox, or the 125cc (8ci) French AMC two-stroke with horizontal cylinder, built in unit with a three-speed gearbox. In both versions, this hung from a simple rigid frame with twin tubes from the headstock to the rear wheel spindle and loops under the engine. Leading-link forks with rubber band suspension served at the front, and the fuel tank extended forward to enclose the steering head and to carry the headlamp.

For 1957, the Taon came with the AMC engine only, though a Sports model appeared with long leading-link front and pivoted-fork rear suspension. The Sports style changed the saddle for a dual seat that blended well with the tank and rear mudguard. This was Derny's last model; the firm was closed down in 1958.

EMC

Arriving in Britain from Austria in 1937, Josef Erlich was soon involved in motorcycle development, trying out an engine designed and built himself. In 1939, Ehrlich was using an old Francis-Barnett machine at Brooklands for his engine experiments. The result was a split-single two-stroke with a side inlet and rear exhaust.

It was not until 1947 that EMC first machine went into production. It was a 345cc (21ci) version of Ehrlich's split-single design, featuring unusual rectangular fins of alternating depth on the block. The touring version used Petroil lubrication while the sports model had a Pilgrim pump. Both used magneto ignition and a four-speed gearbox. The frame was a rigid duplex design, with Dowty Oleomatic forks. Ehrlich claimed his machine was capable of getting more than 2.75l/100kpg (100mpg), but users found it closer to half that.

The 345s were expensive, but remained in production until 1953.

Various engines were used in the final years of EMC's motorcycle production, creating machines like this 250cc (15ci) JAP-powered model. However, by this time the firm's days were numbered.

Meanwhile, in 1951, Ehrlich built a 125cc (8ci) road-racing model with an Austrian Puch split-single engine, and in 1952 exhibited a road machine powered by a 125cc (8ci) JAP two-stroke engine at Earls Court in London.

EMC closed down in 1953, but Ehrlich continued to be involved in racing for many years. The EMC marque reappeared for a time in the 1980s, when Ehrlich became involved with the Waddon, which became an EMC in 1983. It retained its Rotax tandem-twin, two-stroke engine unit. It won the Junior 250cc (15ci)TT in 1983, 1984 and 1987.

Engine detail of the 1947 350cc (21ci) split-single EMC engine, with two bores in tandem. The oil pump is driven from the chain sprocket for the magneto drive.

NORMAN

Norman, a bicycle manufacturer based in Ashford in Kent, produced its first powered machine in 1939 with an autocycle, the Motobyke, and a true motorcycle, a lightweight 122cc (7ci) machine. The engines for both came from Villiers.

The autocycle started life with rigid forks, but was joined by the De Luxe variant with Webb girders for 1940, plus a lower-geared Carrier model. There was also a 98cc (6ci) version of the Lightweight. That year, Norman also made autocycles for Rudge, but production was interrupted by the war and did not resume until 1946.

After the war, Norman continued to use Villiers engines for its range. The initial models were the 98cc (6ci) Autocycle and the 122cc (7ci) Motorcycle. In 1949, these gained new model names, becoming the model C with a 99cc (6ci) Villiers 2F, and the B1 with a 122cc (7ci) Villiers 10D engine. A new model, the B2, joined the range. It had a 197cc (12ci) Villiers 6E engine, and like the other B model was available in standard or deluxe forms.

Two years later, the model D appeared. This had a 99cc (6ci) Villiers 1F engine and gained rear suspension in 1953, which created the B1S and B2S. The B1 meanwhile was renamed the model E. A 197cc (12ci) competition machine, designated B2C, was added to the range. After 1954, the E and B2 models were discontinued, and the 8E replaced the 6E. The D and B2C were discontinued a year later, and the B1S got a new engine, the 147cc (9ci) Villiers 30C. A twin, named the model TS, was added to the range. It had a 242cc (15ci) British Anzani engine.

The first Norman twins used a 242cc Anzani engine, but from 1958 onwards the 249cc Villiers 2T was fitted instead. This B4 Sports model dates from the early 1960s.

The year 1955 also brought the introduction of Armstrong leading-link front forks, which became standard across the whole range in 1956. The gradual development of the range went on for some years, the most significant developments being the introduction of a moped in 1956 and the adoption of rear enclosure on most models from 1957. In 1961, after being taken over by Raleigh Industries, the firm moved to Smethwick, but 1962 was its final year. The last products were mopeds based on Raleigh models.

WHIZZER

Whizzer's first product was a basic 138cc (8ci) side-valve engine designed to fit into a standard bicycle frame. The carburettor was located behind the unit and the exhaust ran into a finned manifold. The engine had belt drive to a friction roller, which was fitted under the bottom bracket and in contact with the rear tyre, to offer cycling without too much work and at minimal cost.

After World War II, the firm developed a complete motorcycle, building it around the same engine. which was mounted low in the frame. The crankshaft was fitted with a large flywheel on the left-hand end. Outboard of that was a starter pinion, which was rotated by a gear segment formed as part of the kick-starter. Transmission was via a belt running to a jockey pulley positioned up in the corner, between the seat and top frame tubes. A further belt ran to the rear wheel so that the jockey pulley was able to tension both belts, and a clutch was incorporated in this transmission. The frame was rigid, but the forks

were sprung with a rocking action at first. Later on, telescopic forks were used.

Whizzer produced one more model, which had a higher-mounted engine and direct belt

drive in a Schwinn frame with a different telescopic front fork. Whizzers were popular for over 10 years, but were displaced by mopeds and small motorcycles coming out of Europe and Japan.

A Whizzer from 1948, clearly showing the bicycle origins of the design. Machines of this type, with both pedals and motor drive, showed that there was a market for mopeds.

BMW R75

The R75 was designed as a sidecar combination from the outset. It featured a power takeoff with a lockable differential to drive the sidecar wheel and was intended for use as a machine-gun carrier. Given the experiences with dispatch bikes during World War I, it might have made sense to build a machine capable of slogging its way though difficult terrain. After two years of war, a design capable of handling sand in the North African desert or snow on the Russian front would have made sense.

However, BMW decided to build an overhead-valve machine instead of a side-valve, which would have been more practical for the conditions the machine was obviously going to encounter. Lowering the compression ratio to between 5.6:1 and 5.8:1 meant that the R75 only had 26hp available.

However, its gearbox, which had four speeds and reverse, plus a two-ratio transfer box for a total of eight forward and two reverse gears, gave the machine

good adaptability. On the downside, the R75 was a very difficult motorcycle to drive. A skilled rider could handle difficult terrain, but to get the most out of the machine, the sidecar passenger really needed to help the driver with the gear-changing.

At 420kg (924lb), this was a heavy machine. Even with hydraulic brakes, it did not stop well. The Jeep favoured by the Allies was, in practical terms, a vastly superior vehicle, though reputedly, Harley-Davidson's fabled XA flat twin was the result of American admiration for the R75.

The R75 sidecar combination was used in large numbers by the *Wehrmacht* to carry everything from dispatches to machine-guns and also as a reconnaissance asset. While not the ideal vehicle for the role, it got the job done.

ENGINE: 745cc (45ci) ohv transverse flat twin, 78x78mm, air-cooled
POWER: 26bhp at 4000rpm
GEARBOX: variable hand change
FINAL DRIVE: belt
WEIGHT: 82kg (180lb)
TOP SPEED: n/a

HARLEY-DAVIDSON WLA

USA 1941

The WLA was an adaptation of the WL for army use. It was given a heavy-duty luggage rack, a rifle scabbard, blackout lights front and rear and a 'bash plate' below the crankcase. There was also a comprehensive specifications and maintenance plate on the tank. The WLA's actual top speed was higher than the official 105km/h (65mph), but this was the army recommendation.

Some 68,000 WLAs were supplied to the US Army. A further 20,000 WLCs were supplied (the C standing for Canadian), which had a hand clutch and foot change instead of foot clutch and hand change. About 130 of the 44-U Navy version (appropriately finished in battleship grey) were also delivered.

Two factors meant that the WLA's toughness was a considerable asset. Firstly, a motorcyclist coming under fire and having to take cover will part company from the machine in a hurry,

and without much regard to its well-being. Secondly, it is often said that soldiers can break anything at all if they are left alone with it for long enough. This accounts for the insistence

of the military authorities that huge amounts of spares should be available – about 20 sets of spares for every complete machine delivered. For this reason, spares can still be obtained today.

The WL went to war as the WLA and WLC. Big, tough and hard to destroy, it was a good military motorcycle.

ENGINE: 745cc (45ci) sv in-line V-twin, 69.85x96.84mm, air-cooled
POWER: 25bhp at 4000rpm
GEARBOX: 3-speed hand change
FINAL DRIVE: chain
WEIGHT: 245kg (540lb)
TOP SPEED: 105km/h (65mph)

NORTON 16H

ENGLAND 1942

The Norton 16H (standing for Model 16, Home) was named thus to distinguish it from the 17C (Model 17, Colonial). It first reached

the market in 1922, but had an engine designed during World War I. This unit was so primitive that owners had to file the valve stems

in order to set the valve clearance.
In 1929, the 16H gained a saddle tank in place of the old flat one, giving it a slightly more modern

appearance. Three years later, the exhaust swapped sides. Another update in 1935 gave the machine a four-speed box, and in 1938 the 'Cow's Udder' exhaust was fitted, an item widely regarded as the most spectacularly ugly silencer ever fitted to any motorcycle.

The wartime version still had exposed valve gear, which was not covered up until after the war. Even though (or perhaps because) the 16H was extremely primitive, it had a reputation for being not only idiot-proof but at least partially soldier-proof. More than 100 examples were delivered to the armed forces.

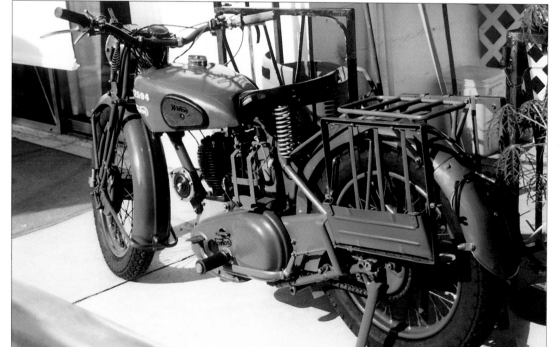

ENGINE: 490cc (29ci) sv single, 79x100mm, air-cooled
POWER: 12.5bhp
GEARBOX: 4-speed foot change
FINAL DRIVE: chain
WEIGHT: 177kg (390lb)
TOP SPEED: 110 km/h (70mph)

The primitive 16H proved to be a good choice for a military motorcycle as it was both simple and tough.

INDIAN MILITARY MODEL 841

Like Harley-Davidson's XA, this machine resulted from a government contract during World War II. However, where the Harley machine copied a pre-war BMW design, the Indian was new and custom-designed for its role. It had state-of-the-art suspension front and rear, and a four-speed, foot-change gearbox instead of the hand change still favoured by Harley-Davidson.

Transverse V-twins were nothing new. Clement Ader built them as early as 1905, and others had followed, including Spring, Stylson, Finzi, Walter and P&M. However, Indian's new take on the concept had excellent cooling, a low centre of gravity and high spark plugs, which was important in wet terrain or fording streams.

Had the funds been available, Indian might have found a good market for a civilian version of the

841. Moto Guzzi certainly did well with a similar design. However, much of Indian's capital was tied up in stockpiles of spares at the end of the war. The firm thought that these were to be paid for under wartime contracts; the US government disagreed. Having already suffered financial embarrassment at the end of World War I, this second blow was more than Indian could take. Though not quite the end for the firm, it made that end more certain.

ENGINE: 745cc (46ci) sv transverse V-twin, 73x88mm, air-cooled
POWER: n/a
GEARBOX: 4-speed foot change
FINAL DRIVE: shaft
WEIGHT: n/a
TOP SPEED: 113km/h (70mph)

ITOM

Itom started out in 1944, making a motor for bicycles, and became well respected for a range of quality 50cc (3ci) and 65cc (4ci) single-cylinder, two-stroke engines, with piston-port induction.

In the 1950s, 50cc (3ci) racing was extremely popular, and Itom became involved. Its early racing models had a three-speed gearbox, geared primary drive and a hand-operated twist-grip gear change. The Mark VII had four gears, and the Mark VIII four gears with foot change.

There was never a factory team, but most 50cc (3ci) competitors were Itom riders for several years from the late 1950s until about 1963. After this, the marque was thoroughly eclipsed by production racing machines from other manufacturers.

However, Itom machines were well respected even then. In 1965, The Motor Cycle reviewed a 50cc (3ci) Itom and commented that: 'It has disadvantages, true enough; but a remarkable, exceptionally smooth engine, allied with exemplary road-holding is compensation enough for any discomfort!' However, despite imports to Britain, sales were falling fast and the factory closed in 1967.

Above: Itom's range of small bikes was popular with privateer racers in the late 1950s and early 1960s. 49cc (3ci) Itoms went all the way to the world championships. This is a 1957 Competizione.

Right: A rather earlier model, complete with pedals and two-stroke single-cylinder engine. The first Itom was a cycle motor, though evolution to true (if small) motorcycles was swift.

CHAPTER FOUR

A NEW DAWN

1945–1954

Post-war, the development of the motorcycle industry rather depended where you looked. The United States had a huge market, industries heavily-expanded for war production and no bombed-out cities. But it was almost too prosperous for motorcycling to flourish: many families could afford to go straight to four wheels for transport, and motorcycles remained a leisure-based pastime.

In Britain, the planned economy of 'war socialism' meant industry was in reasonable shape, but it still took until the early 1950s for bike production to really take off. Continental Europe was ravaged, as was Japan, and here, the emphasis was on basic motorised transport to get people moving again. Britain's

bike builders were turning out powerful single-cylinder machines like the BSA Gold Star, and beginning to see the emergence of the twin-cylinder engine. Meanwhile, in the US, the bike industry was by now essentially one firm, Harley-Davidson, with its air-cooled V-twin range.

In Japan, an engineer called Soichiro Honda was experimenting with small engines that clipped onto pedal cycles, before going on to develop the 98cc Dream in 1949.

Italy and Germany were in a similarly parlous state. Italy's passion for small scooters such as the Vespa and Lambretta was borne from necessity, while BMW in West Germany set about resurrecting itself with its large-capacity flat-twin engine range.

Left: The 1954 Panther Model 100 was a sturdy, tough, reliable machine, ideal for pulling a sidecar.

ALPINO

Alpino started out in 1945, at a period when many manufacturers were closing down due to the effects of the war. Initial production was extremely small but expanded quickly after the war ended.

The first product was the 1945 Alpino, a 48cc (3ci) two-stroke, single-cylinder cycle-motor with chain drive and a two-speed gearbox, which could be installed to drive either the front or rear wheel. This was followed in 1948 by the 48cc (3ci) Model S, which featured a three-speed gearbox and a top speed of 40km/h (25mph). After the appearance of the 60cc Model ST, the same engine was used in a moped, which in turn was the basis for a 98cc (6ci) light motorcycle.

The same engine continued to evolve and grow in capacity, and by 1951 it had become a three-speed 125cc (8ci) with foot-change gears. The same year also saw the introduction of the 48cc (3ci) F48 scooter, which had an unusually advanced frame and suspension for both wheels.

By the end of 1953, Alpino was selling a range of models. At the bottom end were the Alpetta R48, which had friction drive and no gears and the F48 moped. Midrange included the Roma, which had the same 49cc (3ci) engine as the F48, but two speeds and hand-change, and the F48 scooter. The biggest machines were a pair of lightweights with 75cc (5ci) and 125cc (8ci) engines.

Although Alpino made only small lightweight bikes, they were fast. Andrea Bottigelli touched 128km/h (80mph) on a specially prepared 75cc (5ci). Alpino machines also broke records, which included reaching 82km/h (51mph) on a 50cc (3ci) Alpino. This was quite an impressive achievement for a small machine, though such events rarely become the stuff of legend.

Next, a 75cc (5ci) overhead-cam four-stroke racing machine was fielded, though at that point the only four-stroke the company made for road use was the 1955 175cc (11ci). This could top 100km/h (62mph), which was pretty good by the standards of the time. However, a 1956 development of the 75cc (5ci) racer, driving through a four-speed gearbox, could reach almost 120km/h (75mph).

In 1957, even the basic T48 moped acquired a four-stroke engine with unit three-speed gearbox, and in 1959 the company produced a big-wheeled 75cc (5ci) scooter as well as a 50cc (3ci) mini-scooter. Sometime around 1960, however, production ceased.

CEMEC

Cemec – originally named Centre de Montage et de Réparation, or CMR – was founded just after the end of World War II. Its early machines were based on the BMW flat-twin and were built using new and spare parts. There were two models, the R12 and R71, which both used essentially the same 745cc (45ci), flat-twin, side-valve engine built in unit with a four-speed gearbox and shaft drive to the rear wheel.

The main difference between the two models was in the chassis.

The R12 design dated from 1935 and used a pressed-steel frame with no rear suspension. It had telescopic forks, but these retained the pressed-steel style and paint lining of the past. The R71, a design from 1938, used a tubular frame, more modern telescopic forks, plunger rear suspension and a saddle tank.

In 1948, the firm's name changed to Cemec. This was a time when parts were increasingly manufactured in France rather than being bought in, and over the years, the bikes coming out of Cemec's plant began to look more French than German. One reason for this what that BMW was re-establishing itself, and though its first models were small it gradually began producing more and larger bikes, which affected the supply of parts to Cemec.

New models came out of Cemec, including one similar to the R51 with an overhead-valve, metric 494cc (30ci) engine mated to the frame. There was also a similar model based on the 736cc (45ci) overhead-valve engine of the R17 but without its rigid frame. Effectively this bike was a combination of the R51 with the R71 unit fitted with the R75 top halves.

Cemec supplied the French police with many machines, but were not able to obtain military contracts other than to refurbish other makes, including Gnome et Rhone's flat-twin. The firm continued in this manner until 1955, when the name changed to Ratier.

IFA

IFA emerged, more or less literally, from the rubble of World War II. The wreckage of the DKW works in Zschopau, destroyed in the war, lay in the Soviet-occupied eastern zone, putting it out of reach of the firm, which was based in West Germany. DKW itself moved to Ingolstadt and built a new factory, while the wrecked Zschopau works were claimed by a new owner.

This was Industrieverband-Farhzeugebau, which became known as IFA and, later, MZ. The old DKW works were rebuilt, and IFA began turning out copies of the pre-war RT125 and similar DKW models. At that time, transport was in great demand: whatever came out of the factories was eagerly snapped up.

However, this situation could not go on forever – and IFA knew it. The firm began trying out new ideas, often in racing, and by the end of the 1940s was beginning to forge an identity of its own rather than simply turning out copies.

The first of these new machines was a 350cc (21ci) flat-twin two-stroke with shaft final drive. These bikes were sold as MZs from the start of the 1960s.

After starting out with copies of pre-war DKW machines, IFA began forging its own identity with machines like this 350cc (21ci) flat-twin which appeared in 1954.

MONTESA

Montesa was founded in Barcelona in 1945, by Francisco Bulto and Pedro Permanyer. Over the years, it has built up an enviable reputation as a constructor of trials machines. The only really notable Spanish manufacturer that started before Montesa was Sanglas, which had been building heavy police bikes from 1942.

Montesa began with a 98cc (6ci) two-stroke, and in 1946 followed with a 125cc (8ci) machine. Both were used in trials competitions

from the outset. Spain has always had a strong trials scene, perhaps because it has so much countryside that is eminently suited to such activity.

In 1958, Francisco Bulto departed to set up Bultaco, and Montesa carried on making off-road machines powered by its own 123cc (8ci) two-stroke engines. Four years later, it released the Impala, a 175cc (11ci) machine that became something of a legend. This extremely successful bike was followed by a 250cc

(15ci) variant and another intended for road racing. Montesa's range at the time included a number of road-going two-strokes from 49cc (3ci) to 349cc (21ci).

Bultaco was a rival to Montesa, and to compete with that firm's highly successful Sherpa, Montesa fielded the 250cc (15ci) Cota in 1968. Between them, these two machines dominated the trials market. In 1973, the six-speed Cota 172 was released. It was a reasonable but not a great trials machine, as its 158cc (10ci)

engine simply did not deliver the sort of power that was necessary.

By the late 1970s, the market had crumbled, and the reintroduction of the Impala in 1981 coincided with the take-over of the company by Honda. Although this take-over ensured the company's survival, albeit as a Honda assembly plant for small-capacity bikes, the Montesa range itself was limited to just one trials machine, the Cota. This was a formidable-looking bike, and for its time was very much state of the art.

MV AGUSTA

A dramatic photo of the 750S with the optional fairing in place. This machine first went on sale in 1969 and was a real improvement on the ugly tourer that preceded it.

MV was founded by Count Domineco Agusta and built its first motorcycle in 1945. This was a small 98cc (6ci) two-stroke. A racing machine with a four-cylinder engine appeared in 1950, the first of many prestigious machines to come out of the MV stable. It was designed by Piero Remor, who came to the firm from Gilera, along with race mechanic Arturo Magini.

The 1950 MV was powered by a square 494.4cc (30.1ci) double overhead-cam engine, with a 9.5:1 compression ratio and twin

Dell'Orto carburettors. This drove through a four-speed gearbox and produced 50hp. The machine weighed 118kg (260lb), and was capable of 206km/h (129mph), making it faster than either the twin-cylinder AJS Porcupine or the single-cylinder, double-overhead-cam Norton.

It is debatable how much the new machine owed to Remor's previous work for Gilera – it was so very similar. Remor did introduce some features to differentiate his machine from his Gilera designs. These included

shaft- instead of chain-final drive, and torsion-bar suspension, both fore and aft.

More curiously, the MV had gear levers for both sides of the engine. It is likely that this arrangement has never been used since. The rider was required to use both heels, pushing downwards on the nearside to change up, and down on the offside to change down. It was over-complicated and unnecessary, giving added credence to the theory that the system was simply there to distract attention from the fact

that this was in effect a carbon copy of the Gilera engine.

MV's other early racing designs were all 125cc (8ci) machines. Initially they were two-strokes, then later four-strokes. The latter was built as a double overhead-cam and the former as a single overhead-cam. One of the 123.5cc (8ci) double overhead-cam racers won MV its first world title in 1952.

As with the smaller capacity racers, MV's first production motorcycles were predominantly two-strokes. The first was a single-cylinder 98cc (6ci) model, designed during the war and reaching the market in 1945. Intentions to use the Vespa name were dropped following action by Piaggio, who had already registered the name for its range of scooters.

By the end of the 1940s, this 98cc (6ci) model had grown into a 125cc (8ci), available in road and racing versions. MV had also begun production of a whole family of scooters with both two- and four-stroke engines.

At the end of 1952, MV Agusta displayed a new production roadster with a 172.3cc (11ci) single overhead-cam, four-stroke engine. This was to be built in a number of versions, of which the commonest was the Disco Volante (flying saucer), a racing model named Squale (shark).

Another important design making its production debut for the 1953 model year was the Pullman. First seen in public at the Brussels Show in January 1953, it was a distinctive machine powered by the long-serving 123.5cc (7.5ci) piston-port two-stroke engine. It combined, successfully, the best features of both motorcycles and scooters, and went on to sell in considerable numbers.

In 1954, MV produced a 123.6cc (7.5ci) overhead-valve single, their first such design. Others followed. The first of these came in 1956, a 246.6cc (15ci) machine. The year 1958 saw the introduction of an 83.2cc (5ci) machine and another of 172.3cc (10.5ci). There was a 150cc (9ci) and a 300cc (18ci) in 1959, and more models in 1962 and 1964. In 1966, a twin 147cc (9ci) machine appeared and then in 1970 another twin came along, this time a 350cc (21ci).

In the late 1950s, the motorcycle industry took a downturn. In Italy, this was partly due to the production of small, affordable cars as personal transport. This trend endangered MV, but the firm was able to return to aviation and industry, where it had been active in the past, and this provided necessary cash flow. MV did, however, continue to build motorcycles, offering a moped between 1955 and 1959 and a scooter named Chicco, from 1960 to 1964. The Chicco had a specially designed engine, a 155.6cc (9.5ci) single-cylinder two-stroke with a horizontal cylinder.

In the period between the early 1950s and the late 1970s, MV was a force to be reckoned with in racing. It fielded machines in many classes, ranging from 125cc (8ci) singles through to a prototype 500cc (31ci) six-cylinder model, and also including various twins, triples and fours. It was the four-cylinder models that generated the most admiration. MV Agusta won a record number of world championships in all the solo classes, except 50/80cc. Their wins include 75 world championships, 270 Grand Prix victories and 3027 international race wins.

MV did not market a four-cylinder street bike until 1965, though a prototype (designated R19) was shown as early as 1950. The first production model was a 600cc (37ci) tourer of impressively unattractive appearance. It was available for seven years and sold only 135 examples. The next

effort, the 750S, debuted in 1969, and was better. After this came a series of similar but improved machines.

MV Agusta found export markets in no less than 53 countries, including the USA, the UK, Argentina, Australia, France, Germany and Spain. However, the founder, Count Agusta, died in 1971 and after this the firm became increasingly involved in aviation. Motorcycle production ceased in 1978.

In the 1980s, the MV identity was purchased by the Castiglioni brothers. They recruited designer Massimo Tamburini, who produced the Ferrari-inspired F4, launched to public acclaim in 1998.

AMBASSADOR

ENGLAND 1946–64

Ambassador was founded by Kaye Don, who had driven at Brooklands before the war. His first machine was similar to many pre-war designs but was fitted with a 494cc (30ci) side-valve, vertical-twin JAP engine, with the carburettor at the front between the exhaust pipes. A lightweight followed in 1947. This was a simple machine powered by a 197cc (12ci) Villiers 5E engine. It had a three-speed gearbox, rigid loop frame and blade girder forks.

The lightweight did well enough in the market of the time, which craved such machines, and in 1949 it was upgraded with the new Villiers 6E engine. Next came the Embassy, which had telescopic forks. In 1952, another model appeared, the Supreme, this time with plunger rear suspension. Next came the Self Starter, which had a Lucas starter motor. A rather optimistic sidecar model also appeared.

Further upgrades continued, with a new engine throughout the range – initially the Villiers 8E. Later, a more powerful 224cc (14ci) Villiers was fitted to the Supreme. A new pivoted-fork rear suspension and a redesigned frame created the Envoy of 1955. Soon after, the Supreme, which was showing its age, was retired and replaced by the Three Star Special and the Super S, along with an electric-start twin and a 174cc (11ci) scooter in 1961.

A 50cc (3ci) moped was produced in 1962, the year Kaye Don retired. DMW bought out the marque and attempted to move forward with it, but production ceased in 1964.

The Super S replaced the long-serving but dated Supreme, and continued the process of evolution. An electric-start version soon followed, as well as versions with varying degrees of enclosure.

BSA BANTAM D1

ENGLAND 1946

The 123cc (8ci) Bantam D1 reached the market in 1946. Initially, it was for export only, but it was very quickly snapped up in the transport-starved, post-war market. Never a pretentious machine, it did its job very well. The D1 became BSA's best-selling model of the company's entire history and, indeed, was one of the most common machines on British roads. It also did well in trials and scrambling events, and fostered its own class of track racing machines.

Rarely mentioned at the time was the fact that the D1 was more or less a carbon copy of the German DKW RT125. BSA was not the only firm to 'borrow' this design. In many cases, this was quite legal, as the design was included among war reparations to the Allies. The first models were good-looking machines that featured three-speed transmission in unit with the 123cc (8ci) engine, telescopic forks and a rigid rear end. Plunger rear suspension soon followed, giving way to full swing-arm rear in 1955. Other versions appeared as the years passed: a 148cc (9ci) initially and a 172cc (10ci) version from 1960. The last Bantam produced was the 172cc (10ci) Model D14 Super of 1968.

ENGINE: 123cc (7ci) single-cylinder two-stroke, 52x58mm, air-cooled
POWER: 4.5bhp at 5000rpm
GEARBOX: 3-speed foot change
FINAL DRIVE: chain
WEIGHT: 102kg (225lb)
TOP SPEED: 89km/h (55mph)

DUCATI

Ducati started out in the 1920s as a manufacturer of electrical equipment. In 1945, the firm obtained a licence to build the Cucciolo, or 'little puppy dog', an auxiliary 48cc (3ci) four-stroke engine. This sold very well in the difficult post-war transport marketplace, and Ducati made the decision to field a complete motorcycle. It appeared in 1950, powered by a 60cc (4ci) version of the Cucciolo engine.

Ducati recruited Fabio Taglioni as chief designer in 1954. His first product was the 98cc (6ci) overhead-camshaft Gran Sport single, nicknamed Marianna. This was a tough little bike capable of competing in events like the Milano–Taranto and Giro d'Italia (Tour of Italy). It could manage 136km/h (85mph), and it dominated its class on its first outing at the 1955 Giro.

Ducati created a more powerful version by boring the cylinder to 55.5mm (2.2in), increasing displacement to 124.5cc (7.6ci). The engine retained its basic features such as unit construction, an overhead-camshaft driven by shafts and bevels, gear primary drive and wet-sump lubrication. These were kept in place for succeeding models, starting with the 125cc (8ci) GS.

A new 125cc (8ci) double overhead-camshaft engine was constructed for a batch of special Grand Prix machines, which made its debut in spring 1956. However, it was the desmodromic version, with its positive-valve closing and opening mechanism, that established Ducati's reputation. This was developed in early 1956 and won the Swedish Grand Prix in July that year.

Also in 1956, Ducati unveiled its first street machine with a bevel overhead-cam single layout. This was a 175cc (11ci) machine, and it was followed in 1958 by more road machines in the 125cc (8ci) and 200cc (12ci) classes. The same year, a Ducati took second place in the 125cc World Road-racing Championships. The following year, a Ducati took a Grand Prix victory, but the triumph was mixed with financial troubles.

The year 1961 brought a new 250cc (15ci) single. This would be produced in a number of versions, becoming the mainstay of Ducati's production for most of the 1960s. Perhaps the ultimate developments of this machine were the high performance Mach 1 of 1964 and the Mark 3D of 1968.

Mach 1 is generally regarded as the world's first series production 250cc (15ci) capable of 160km/h (100mph), while the Mark 3D was to achieve fame as the world's first

desmodromic roadster. Ducati also produced new models in the 1960s, including the 'widecase' engine in 1968. Racing success followed, including the Barcelona 24 Hours.

Despite all this success, Ducati got into more financial trouble and by 1970 had been baled out by the Italian government at the price of new, government-appointed, management. This new leadership team gave Taglioni permission to design a brand new 750 'L-shape' V-twin. This was broadly similar in concept to the singles, including bevel-driven cams, and the first production version of this new machine, the GT, entered production in 1971.

The year 1972 brought glory when the inaugural Imola 200 was won by Ducati, beating Agostini and MV. A year later, the new 860cc (52ci) brought more succeses, taking the Barcelona 24 Hours and setting a record speed into the bargain. A roadster version of this machine, the 860GT, went on sale in late 1974. However, the mid- to late 1970s were characterized by several failed projects as Ducati tried to broaden its range. A timely refocus in the late 1970s brought victory in the 1978 Isle of Man TT as well as machines such as the Darmah, Super Sport and MHR.

In the 1980s, Ducati took four more world titles with a race version of Taglioni's 500cc (31ci) Pantah. Larger- and smaller-engined

Pantahs went on sale soon after, in sizes from 350cc (21ci) to 650cc (40ci). However, financial difficulties were never far away and Ducati got into trouble again. A 1983 contract to supply engines to rivals Cagiva was followed by a buyout. Cagiva put Massimo Bordi in charge of design and hired Massimo Tamburini as chief stylist. It also provided funding and impetus to develop new machines.

Just before the Cagiva takeover, a new 750cc (46ci) named the F1 appeared. After the change of ownership, this was followed by the 750 Paso sport and Indiana custom models. The Paso got a bigger engine later on, becoming a 900cc (55ci), and the 900 Supersport was launched for 1990. In the meantime, the first four-valves-per-cylinder, double overhead-camshaft, liquid-cooled, fuel-injected superbike had made its appearance. The Paso was still a 90-degree V-twin, the first versions arriving in 1988 as the 851.

Ducati achieved record sales in the 1990s. In part, this was assisted by winning eight of the ten World Super Bike championships in that decade. The most significant models of the period were the SS series, the four-valve models 851cc (52ci), 888cc (54ci), 916cc (56ci) and 996cc (61ci), and the Monster range.

The first SS models were launched in 1991 and eventually there were 350cc (21ci), 400cc (24ci), 600cc (37ci), 750cc (46ci)

Although the Ducati name tends to evoke images of ferocious race and road bikes, Ducati has also produced offroaders during its long and, at times, troubled history.

and 900cc (55ci) versions. These initially had inverted forks, single shock rear suspension and Mikuni carburettors but, from 1998, the larger machine featured fuel injection and new styling.

As well as winning races, Ducati's top-of-the-range, four-valve machines were gaining a reputation for incredible performance even in the hands of non-racing owners. Their great looks and state-of-the-art technical development was a factor in their popularity too.

The Monster series was designed by Migual Angel Galluzi and mounted similar engines to the SS series. These were great-looking bikes that were also practical, and they appealed to a different type of user. Ducati's appeal widened still further with the appearance in 1996 of the ST2 Sport Touring two-valve. A four-valve version was added to the range in 1998.

The American investment house TPG (Texas Pacific Group) bought a 51 per cent share of Ducati in 1996, gaining the rest two years later. In March 1999, Ducati was launched as a public company on the stock market.

GILERA SATURNO

Gilera used astronomical names for many of its machines, for example, Nettuno (Neptune), Marte (Mars) and Saturno (Saturn). The Saturno was originally designed by Guiseppe Salmaggi, who had been working for Sarolea. Gilera benefited greatly from his expertise; the Saturno became its best-known production bike.

The first Saturnos appeared in the early days of World War II, and won two races in the Italian Junior Championship series at Palermo and Modena. However, there was no production machine until 1946, when three Saturno models appeared: Sport, Turismo and Competition. All three were identical but for their engine tuning. A more specialized racing model, named San Remo, appeared in 1947 and produced 35hp at 6000rpm.

The range was then updated and restyled in 1950, gaining telescopic forks along with a full-width alloy front-brake hub. The following year, the rear suspension was changed in favour of vertically mounted twin shock absorbers. These changes went to the track aboard a racing machine built between 1951 and 1956, and named Corsa. Another racing Saturno was designed by Franco Passoni and was a twin cam variant. However, only two machines were ever built.

The Saturno also spawned a motocross machine – in production from 1952 to 1956. Meanwhile, the road bikes were gradually updated. The last two models, Sport roadsters, were produced in 1959 for the 1960 model year. Overall, 6450 Saturnos were manufactured, 170 of them racers.

INDIAN CHIEF

The first Chief appeared in 1921. It was essentially a larger version of the Scout with a 999cc (61ci) engine. It could make over 150km/h (90mph) solo or 110km/h (70mph) with a side-car. Its speed in the latter mode made it popular with bootleggers running booze in the USA during prohibition. However, it was not a very advanced machine, with total-loss lubrication and side-valves.

The Big Chief appeared in 1923 with a 1212cc (74ci) engine, and was updated in both 1925 and 1926. In 1929, the Chiefs received a front brake, though there was little more development until after World War II.

The pre-war Big Chiefs were put back into production as soon as possible after hostilities ceased. One final evolution occurred when the Big Chiefs got an even bigger engine (1340cc/82ci), though they still did not have a foot change or hydraulic forks. This came in just before the end of production in 1953. At this point, Indians were primitive compared to rivals Harley-Davidson, and while a certain segment of the market likes machines that never change, this is not enough to sustain a company.

ENGINE: 1206cc (72ci) sv in-line twin, air-cooled
POWER: 40 bhp
GEARBOX: 3-speed hand-change
FINAL DRIVE: chain
WEIGHT: n/a
TOP SPEED: 140km/h (85mph)

LAMBRETTA

Lambretta was another Italian motorcycle marque that emerged strongly from the chaos of World War II. It was not the first firm owned by founder Ferdinando Innocenti, who had set up his own workshop at the age of 18. At the age of 31, he moved to Rome and developed ways of improving the manufacture of steel tubing. At the age of 40, he relocated to Lambrate, a suburb of Milan, and founded a steel company.

Innocenti's steel plant was largely destroyed during World War II, but he rebuilt it and found a suitable outlet for his wares. This was the cheap transport market. Innocenti realized that other manufacturers were already making inroads into the lightweight motorcycle field, so he decided to make scooters instead, and in 1946 the first Lambretta, the Model A, was launched.

In a bid for publicity, Innocenti built a number of record-breaking machines and a 123cc (8ci) single-cylinder, two-stroke racing motorcycle, named the 2T. This machine appeared in 1949 and included piston-port induction, an offset Dell 'Orto carburettor, a four-speed close ratio gearbox and shaft final drive to the rear wheel.

In 1950, the factory was turning out some 300 scooters a day and also offered two more models, the 125C and LC. More records were set, then broken by Vespa machines. Lambretta rose to the challenge with a streamlined design that reclaimed the lost laurels. It may seem faintly ludicrous that grown men were competing to set speed records on – of all things – scooters. However, they were reaching speeds of 195km/h (121mph) on these machines, and the competition was in deadly earnest.

From 1950 to 1956, Lambretta had an agreement with NSU to permit that firm to licence-build Lambretta scooters. This deal lapsed in 1956, when NSU launched a scooter of its own (the Prima). In the meantime, Lambretta increased its race presence with the 1951 release of a 250cc (15ci) V-twin racing motorcycle.

More mopeds also appeared. The year 1954 brought a 48cc (3ci) model, and in 1958 the Li series was launched. These offered a choice of either 124cc (8ci) or 148cc (9ci) engines. There was also the TV 175, a luxury

model with a 170cc (10ci) power unit and a top speed approaching 97km/h (60mph).

Scooter sales went downhill rapidly from 1962 onwards. Lambretta tried to compensate by launching new models, including the Cento 100, GT200, SX200 and 122cc (7ci) Starstream. However, the decline was industry wide and could not be halted. Innocenti's business empire was not affected as badly as some because it had diversified, having a division making machine tools and another producing formed metal (mainly tubing). Since the other two branches of the firm were mainly selling to the car industry, which was doing well, things were not too bad. Indeed, Innocenti was impressed by the vitality of the car business, and in 1961 his firm began making cars, starting with licence-built British designs, such as the Austin A40.

Innocenti died in 1966, and the firm suffered from a lack of leadership thereafter. By 1975, the firm had serious financial problems and was bought out by the Italian government and then privately by Alejandro de Tomaso. Within a few years, at least one of Innocenti's production facilities in Milan was building Moto Guzzi V35/50 V-twin engines for another section of the de Tomaso empire (see Moto Guzzi). Lambretta scooters are made today, under licence agreements, in Spain and India.

The first Lambretta scooter was the 1947 Model A. Primitive by today's standards, it did the job well enough to be a big success. The rival Vespa featured bodywork enclosing the engine.

MOTO GUZZI GUZZINI

The Guzzini was exactly what the market of the time wanted – cheap, economical and reliable. In the 1950s and early 1960s, it evolved into a more conventional motorcycle.

More than 200,000 Guzzinis were sold, and some users upgraded theirs with a 'big bore' four-stroke conversion kit purchased from an after-market supplier. The success of this conversion prompted the introduction in 1956 of the 73cc (4ci) version of the Cardellino, which had replaced the Guzzino in 1954. This machine featured more conventional 59cm (20in) wheels and a strengthened frame. In 1962, it received an engine upgrade to 83cc (5ci), and remained in production until 1965.

ENGINE: 498cc (30ci) ioe single, 88x82mm, air-cooled
POWER: 23bhp at 5500rpm
GEARBOX: 4-speed foot change
FINAL DRIVE: chain
WEIGHT: 180kg (396lb)
TOP SPEED: 137km/h (85mph)

M oto Guzzi is not a name usually associated with small, cheap two-strokes, but the decision to produce the Guzzini was a good one. In post-war Europe, there was no money for expensive luxury or performance machines, but everyone needed low-cost transport. Moto Guzzi went ahead with a design that suited the market perfectly.

Many manufacturers were producing cheap lightweights, but the Guzzini was a significantly better design than most of its competitors. Weight was kept down by using a light-alloy head and barrel, and the Guzzini had very large wheels for a motorcycle, at 66cm (26in). In this, they were more bicycle than motorcycle.

PARILLA

G iovanni Parrilla founded his first business in Milan, repairing diesel injection pumps and distributing Bosch spark plugs. After World War II, he decided to manufacture motorcycles and thoughtfully modified his name slightly to make his company name more pronounceable.

The first Parilla was a racing machine designed by Guiseppe Salmaggi, who had also created the original Gilera Saturno in 1939. This new machine took to the track in 1946. There were obvious British influences, notably features of the Nortons prominent at the time. The new machine was sold as a track bike (named the Corsa) and also as supersports roadster. Both models boasted a 246.3cc (15ci) single overhead-camshaft engine, with camshaft drive by shaft and bevels.

Commercial release was not until 1947, allowing time for complete testing, and the machine that went out was impressive. It featured very large drum brakes front and rear, and could make 148km/h (92mph). A twin camshaft racing model named the Bialbero was built in both 250cc (15ic) and 350cc (21ci) engine sizes.

In 1950, the Italian motorcycle marketplace was a good place to be, and Parilla proved very successful, bringing out a range of new models. The year 1950 saw single-cylinder two-strokes in 98cc (6ci) and 124cc (8ci), followed by an impressive 348cc (21ci) overhead-valve twin in 1952. Also that year, Parilla debuted the first of its trademark hi-cam models, in which the valves were operated via short splayed pushrods in the nearside of the cylinder.

The first hi-cam model was a 174cc (11ci) machine named the Fox. A hi-cam racing machine, known in Italy as camme rialzata (lifted camshaft), hit the track at Monza. The lessons learned with this prototype machine were incorporated on the production model of the Fox and also on the follow-up racing machine, a new 125cc (8ci) double overhead-camshaft single, which appeared in 1953. This machine was not a great success and for a time Parilla's competition presence was composed of older designs.

Success in off-road trials events was forthcoming in the latter years of the 1950s, and Parilla put a range of machines into production. These included the 49cc (3ci) Parillino moped and the Levriere (Greyhound), which was a 153cc (9ci) two-stroke scooter, and the distinctly unorthodox Slughi (Desert Greyhound).

The late 1950s also saw considerable export success for the company. Indeed, in 1959, Parilla brought out its own magazine *Il Levriere* (*The Greyhound*). However, the firm was, by then, beginning to lose its impetus. A new 125cc (8ci) disc-valve racing model, announced in 1960, was so long in development that it was outdated by the time it hit the track. The firm went downhill from then on, and in 1967 it ceased producing motorcycles. Parilla Kart engines remained in production, however.

The 175 Fox was the first 'high-cam' Parilla machine. It appeared at the Milan show in 1952 and went on the market the following year. Sales were good and the machine remained in production for a decade.

PIAGGIO

ITALY 1946–PRESENT

Piaggio is famous for Vespa scooters, of course, but its origins lie in a general engineering business founded by Rinaldo Piaggio in Genoa in 1884. Piaggio was involved with railways, shipping and, after 1915, aviation. In the 1930s, it received several contracts to build bombers and seaplanes for the Italian Air Force, and also founded Italy's first commercial airline.

After the death of Rinaldo Piaggio in 1938, his work was carried on by his sons Armando and Enrico, and they presided over the rebuilding of the firm after its factory was destroyed in 1945. At a time when the firm was digging itself out of the wreckage, it was obvious that personal transport was the market to pursue, so Piaggio began experimenting with powered two-wheeled vehicles. To this end, it brought in aeronautical engineer Corradino d'Ascanio.

By the end of 1945, d'Ascanio had produced a working prototype for a revolutionary new vehicle.

It had no frame, and consisted instead of a spot-welded steel chassis with mechanicals enclosed by bodywork and the rider protected by legshields. The 98cc (6ci) two-stroke, single-cylinder engine drove the rear wheel through an enclosed gear drive, and the gearchange was by the left-hand handlebar twist grip. Suspension was by single-sided swinging-arm at the rear and stub-axle at the front, which enabled the wheels to be changed easily when required. This design was, of course, the very first Vespa.

The Vespa (Wasp) went into production in early 1946 and can be considered to be something of a success. It sold nearly 2500 units in 1946. More than 10,000 were sold the following year, with a million produced by 1956 and 15 million by 2000. Piaggio scooters were built under licence in Germany from 1950 onwards as well as in the UK and France.

Development was continuous. A 125cc (8ci) four-speed version came out in 1948, along with

rather ungainly three-wheeler commercial derivatives. The G-model appeared in 1953, featuring a neat cable-controlled gear linkage that replaced the original rod-operated shift. The GS150 model, with a 150cc (9ci) engine and slightly enlarged wheels, appeared in 1955. This model and its evolved versions were very popular with Mods in Britain in the early 1960s.

In 1962, Piaggio's range included the 125, 150 Sportique and GS160, which were joined in 1964 by the 90 Standard and in 1965 by the SS180 with a rectangular headlight. The 90cc (5ci) was available in Super Sport trim, with the spare wheel and tool box occupying the step-through platform. In the mid-1960s, Piaggio introduced its Automatic Fuelmix system, which governed the blending of oil and fuel according to throttle position. At the end of the decade, the firm absorbed the Gilera motorcycle marque, which ran for some years but was closed down in 1993.

In the early 1970s, the top of the line Vespa model was the 12hp 200 Rally Electronic. At the other end of the scale, the 50cc (3ci) three-speed VSA offered an affordable entry-level machine. The range was largely restyled in 1978 and gradually evolved into the PK Series, which appeared in 1983. They were subsequently joined by the PK80, which had an electric starter, and the T5, which came out in 1986.

Plastic-bodied scooters were added in 1991, starting with the Sfera, which won the Compasso d'Oro design award. A 125cc (8ci) version of the Sfera was fitted with Piaggio's first four-stroke engine. The 50cc (3ci) Zip and Free models followed, then the Typhoon in 1993. The Zip was available with 50cc (3ci) two-stroke or electric power, while the 125cc (8ci) Skipper of 1995 was the first fully automatic scooter in that capacity bracket.

The biggest Vespa was the Hexagon, which was available in 125cc (8ci) and 180cc (11ci) two-stroke options, or with a Honda 250cc (15ci) four-stroke powerplant.

Piaggio went retro in 1996 with the ET2, which had a distinctly 1960s feel. However, it benefited from 30 years of progress; the 50cc (3ci) engine was fuel injected. A four-stroke version was later marketed.

In 2000, Piaggio's top-end model was the X0 250, a 250cc (15ci) single that required a full motorcycle licence. Ergonomically, this was a most interesting machine. None of its luggage or carrying compartments had an external catch or lock; they were all accessed by inserting the key in the ignition, along with the fuel filler cap and the helmet storage box beneath the seat.

Personal transport at its most basic. There has always been (and most likely always will be) a market for cheap mopeds and scooters. Piaggio has done very well out of this niche market.

SUNBEAM MODEL S7

ENGLAND 1946

Before BSA bought it in 1943, the Sunbeam name was owned by Associated Motor Cycles. The first model to use it after the transfer was the S7, designed by Erling Poppe. This was a high-end machine, which incorporated a range of innovations. It featured a duplex cradle frame supporting the 487cc (30ci) twin-cylinder all-alloy engine, which was mounted

longitudinally with shaft drive from its four-speed gearbox. The overhead-camshaft was chain-driven from the rear of the cylinder block. It also had telescopic front forks, tyre-enveloping mudguards and large drum brakes.

At 116km/h (72mph), the S7 was not especially powerful or fast. In 1949, it was lightened

and redesignated S8, gaining BSA parts, including suspension and wheels. In 1950, the S7 De Luxe came out. This was an S8 with S7 running gear and front forks, plus a new rear-plunger suspension. The S7/S8 remained in production until 1957 and although there were scooters, sadly there were no more Sunbeam motorcycles.

ENGINE: Engine: 487cc (29ci) twin-cylinder, air-cooled
POWER: 25bhp
GEARBOX: 4-speed foot change
FINAL DRIVE: shaft
WEIGHT: 197kg (435lb)
TOP SPEED: 116km/h (72mph)

VELOSOLEX

Velosolex started out producing its rather curious powered bikes in 1946, and little changed throughout the firm's history. Described as resembling 'a very heavy bicycle with a large dead snail on the front mudguard', the Velosolex is not really a motorcycle at all. In fact, in most of Europe, it is not subject to the normal taxes or restrictions that affect motorcycles – such as road fund or insurance.

The Velosolex is started by pedalling. Once it is under way, the friction drive to the engine is engaged by pulling a lever, effectively bump-starting it. The tiny engine is sufficient to power the machine at a modest pace, though some pedal assistance may be in order on hills. A centrifugal automatic clutch takes care of stops and starts along the way. There is a decompressor to stop the engine.

The Velosolex has been in production for more than half a century, and hardly any changes have been made to the basic design. It gained a square-section frame in the 1960s and does not run quite so lean these days, but it is still the same funny-looking contraption it always was. Equipment includes a tiny set of lights powered by a 6-volt system, and not much else.

The Velosolex has a very low fuel consumption. Even today, it gets better than 1.4l/100kmg (200mpg), which is not only economical, but also very environmentally friendly. For this reason, it was relaunched in the late 1990s.

The company was sold after the death of its founder. Yamaha bought the firm and closed it down, but it was resurrected by a Hungarian concern and remains in production today. More than eight

million had been made up to 2000; there is no telling how many of these curious machines will be manufactured in future years.

While hardly the most impressive of machines, the Velosolex has sold in vast numbers for half a century.

AERO CAPRONI

Count Gioni Caproni founded a manufacturing group in 1908. After World War I, this grew into a huge engineering concern that built aircraft, cars and engines for marine, aircraft and industrial applications. Caproni's factories were largely engaged in war work during World War II and needed to return to civilian manufacturing afterwards. The success of other firms entering the motorcycle market showed the way.

Caproni's aircraft plant in Trento was switched to making motorcycles and also a three-wheeled light trucks brand named Capriolo. The first motorcycle was a 73cc (4ci) face-cam design, which had the crankshaft running in line with the frame. The bike also used full unit construction, a four-speed gearbox and a pressed-steel, square-section frame.

This machine was successful enough that the Trento plant

began to produce more models, and another factory owned by the Caproni group, Caproni-Vizzola, was also switched over to motorcycle production. Caproni-Vizzola built motorcycles until 1959, using engines bought in mainly from NSU.

The Trento plant lasted a while longer. Over time, the Capriolo face-cam engine was further developed, and a range of sporting lightweights was built around 98cc

(6ci) and 124cc (8ci) versions of it. There was also a 149cc (9ci) horizontally opposed twin with shaft final drive, which first appeared at the 1953 Milan Show.

Capriolos were successful in off-road events such as the ISDT, and often provided the Italian squad with bikes. However, as sales declined in the mid-1960s and an export bid proved fruitless, the Trento works was closed in 1964.

AJS PORCUPINE

The Porcupine was intended as a race machine, but while successful in its first season, it was soon eclipsed by others.

The Porcupine was designed during World War II as a supercharged flat-twin racing machine. It was never intended for private users. The design had to be altered to use twin carburettors when supercharging was banned

in racing after the war. However, the rest of the design remained intact.

The Porcupine was powered by a 497cc (30ci) engine with twin gear-driven overhead camshafts and gear drives to the magneto

and oil pump. It had a one-piece crankshaft with centre main bearing and many fine internal details, but the most noticeable external feature was the spiky head fins that gave it its name. The four-speed gearbox was gear

driven with chain final drive, and the whole unit went into a tubular cradle frame. The Porcupine won the 500cc World Championship in 1949, but did not quite live up to expectations, being edged out by a Norton design in 1950 and fading away entirely by 1954. The spikes vanished in 1951, and a year later the engine was inclined and the machine known as the E95.

ENGINE: 497.5cc (30ci) dohc horizontal parallel twin, 68x68.5mm, air-cooled
POWER: 54bhp
GEARBOX: 4-speed foot change
FINAL DRIVE: chain
WEIGHT: 140kg (310lb)
TOP SPEED: 210km/h (130mph)

HONDA

The need for cheap personal transport in the wake of World War II was not restricted to Europe. More than 100 firms appeared in post-war Japan to take advantage of the new markets that were opening up. They benefited from high tariffs on imported goods, which effectively restricted the domestic marketplace to local firms.

The firm founded by Soichiro Honda was one of many that appeared in that period. The son of a village blacksmith, Honda served an apprenticeship as a car mechanic and then set up his own repair shop in 1922. He raced cars, and in the 1936 All-Japan Speed Rally he set a record that lasted for 20 years.

Soichiro Honda studied metallurgy at the local technical college and set up a firm making alloy piston rings. His factory was destroyed by an earthquake in 1945, so he sold off what remained, and in 1946 he set up the Honda Technical Research Institute, which eventually became Honda Motor Vehicles. This new firm bought up a large number of army surplus two-stroke engines and began fitting them in bicycle frames to produce a very basic motorcycle.

When the supply of surplus engines ran out, Honda began producing a copy. This was a rather humble 50cc (3ci) engine producing a whole 1hp, but the Honda machines were what the market wanted and they sold well, paving the way for 'proper' motorcycle designs. Evolution was gradual, but by 1949 the firm was producing the D-type, its first true motorcycle. This machine was based on Honda's channel steel frame, powered by a 98cc (6ci)

two-stroke engine driving though a two-speed gearbox. It was a good machine – in fact, one of the best available in Japan at that time.

Honda's accountant, Takeo Fujisawa, now set up a national dealer network. Many of the dealers were small bicycle shops and did not last long, but the network would eventually become vast. Meanwhile, Soichiro Honda concentrated on product design, and by 1950 his company was by far the largest in Japan, dominating the market with a share of almost 50 per cent.

In 1952, Honda unveiled two new models. The more basic of these was the F-model Cub, essentially a powered bicycle. It was light and cheap and sold in massive numbers. For those with a little more money to spend,

Honda offered the E-model Dream. This was based on the frame and cycle parts of the D-model, and powered by Honda's first four-stroke engine. The 146cc (9ci) single-cylinder motor developed 5.5hp. Handling was not great and the machine used a lot of oil.

Honda really understood the concepts behind mass volume production, and manufactured vast numbers of cheap motorcycles, selling them at low prices that made it hard for others to compete. With the firm expanding so well, Soichiro Honda ordered an enormous amount of machine tools from the USA and Europe in 1952. Unfortunately, this move coincided with a downturn in the market and the firm found itself in financial trouble.

Honda was able to weather the financial crisis, and put out its first modern motorcycle the following year. This was the J-model, which featured telescopic forks and torsion-bar rear suspension.

It was powered by an 89cc (5ci) overhead-valve engine and three-speed gearbox with foot-operated change, all mounted in a pressed-steel frame.

Soichiro Honda studied European technology and applied the principles he observed to his own products. One result was Honda's first overhead-camshaft machine, the Dream SA, which was launched in 1955 with a

Somewhat more likely to inspire admiring glances, the CBX1000 of 1968 featured an in-line, six-cylinder engine delivering 105bhp. It was available with or without a fairing.

Very much a bottom-end machine, the Honda Cub was a huge success. Alongside the prestige roadsters and race machines, Honda continues to produce small, affordable machines for a market segment that will never dry up.

246cc (15ci) unit-construction engine. It was quickly followed by the 344cc (21ci) SB version. A process of evolution resulted in the M-series in 1957.

In the late 1950s, Honda began making major inroads into the export market with the Super Cub C100, a step-through machine somewhere between a moped and a scooter. This little 90cc (5ci) machine was not merely an economic success but also had a major social impact by bringing affordable mobility to millions of people. It was economical to run and very usable, and became one of the best-selling motorcycles of all time.

The European influence was very obvious in the C70, which appeared in 1957. A 247cc (15ci) machine, it was obviously influenced by the NSU overhead-cam twins that had impressed Soichiro on his European visits. Next came the C71 with an electric start, making kick-starting redundant. Further developments led to a most impressive range of modestly priced yet very good motorcycles, whose reliability was particularly noteworthy.

By 1960, Honda was using telescopic forks and a tubular frame. The first model to be built in this style was the CB72, but soon the rest of the range followed; this was the beginning of the modern period in terms of the firm's designs. Meanwhile, its

machines were doing well in competition. Its first TT outing was in 1959 and although it achieved little that year, the Hondas came back to take fourth in 1960, dominating the 125cc (8ci) and 250 (15ci) classes the following year. From there, the marque went from strength to strength, fielding exotic machines such as the five-cylinder 125cc (8ci) and the 250cc (15ci) six.

As the firm moved into big-engine racing, so its road bikes also gained larger powerplants. The first large Japanese machine was the CB 450 Dream, released in 1965. It was nicknamed the Black Bomber, and its high performance paved the way for similar performance machines from rivals Suzuki, Yamaha and Kawasaki. As its machines set new standards in the performance marketplace, Honda began to take sales away from traditional marques like BSA and Triumph. The firm was delivering as standard features that had previously been considered a luxury, such as five-speed gearbox, front disc brake and electric start – and at an affordable price.

Honda did not turn its back on the more modest user, however,

and introduced a growing range of small- and medium-capacity machines to match the performance models. By 1970, all models had disc front brakes and new styling, and Honda was producing something for everyone, from extremely basic machines to top-end racers.

In 1975, Honda launched another classic. This was the 1000cc (61ci) shaft-drive Gold Wing. Powered by a flat-four, water-cooled engine fed by four carburettors, it was a heavy machine although the horizontal engine kept the centre of gravity low. The Gold Wing emphasized comfortable high-speed cruising, and evolved steadily. By 1989, it had become the six-cylinder 100hp GL1500.

The year1978 saw the launch of the V-twin CX500. It was dubbed the 'plastic maggot' on its launch and quickly established itself as a low-maintenance machine ideal for despatch riders and other professional users. It grew into the CX650 in 1984, and a turbo version also appeared, though it was not a great success.

Next came a series of more sporting machines powered by V-twin and V-four engines. The latter were particularly

successful, as race-replica machines were extremely popular at the time. This popularity lasted through the late 1980s and into the 1990s, during which time Honda also launched a radical road machine, the NR750. It boasted oval pistons and eight valves per cylinder but, despite producing a lot of horsepower, was no faster than less exotic machines of a similar engine size.

A number of very fine machines emerged in the late 1980s. Of these, the best known is the CBR600, which quickly rose to dominate its class. A good all-round bike with great handling and smooth power delivery, it sold 100,000 examples in eight years of production and was the best-selling motorcycle in the world during that time. It also spawned a sibling sports tourer, the CBR1000.

In 1990, Honda launched the ST100 Pan European, intending it to be the ultimate touring sportster. With an 1100cc (67ci) V-four engine delivering 100hp, it was capable of 210km/h (125mph), and was very successful with professional users such as police, paramedics and motoring assistance firms.

Then, in 1992, came the

CBR900 FireBlade. With a top speed of 266km/h (165mph), the FireBlade brought race handling and immense power to the common man. With 123hp from its 893cc (54ci) in-line four on a light aluminium-beam frame, it was the fastest production motorcycle in the world and has achieved undying fame. However, that did not stop Honda from trying to push the envelope further.

The CBR1100 Blackbird, launched in 1997, was supposed to be in the same vein but did not quite live up to the legend of its predecessor despite being faster.

More recently, Honda has launched the 996cc (61ci) V-twin VTR1000 Firestorm to compete with Ducati. However, it recognizes that the need for affordable, reliable, entry-level personal transport remains as important as ever, offering the 250cc (15ci) Foresight 'super scooter'.

A CBR900 Fireblade on the race track. Combining lightness, tremendous performance and excellent handling, the Fireblade made race performance available to mere mortals.

MOTOM

Motom emerged during the Italian post-war motorcycle boom, and quickly established a reputation for making cheap but good quality machines that were economical to run. The firm did not have much in the way of marketing advantages; there was no race-winning team to generate publicity. What Motom did have, though, was a very advanced manufacturing plant that used the latest machine tools.

Out of Motom's cutting-edge plant came first a 49cc (3ci) overhead-valve auxiliary engine and then, in 1948, a complete machine powered by it. Next, in 1950, came the Delfino (Dolphin), a 163cc (10ci) overhead-valve machine somewhere between a scooter and a motorcycle, which appeared in 1950.

A tweaked version of the 49cc (3ci) machine took the class world record for a standing-start kilometer in 1952, and won its class in the six-day Giro d'Italia. The high point was at Monza in 1958, where more records were broken by a machine that could manage 232km (144 miles) per gallon (4.5 UK litres/4.8 US litres). Meanwhile, 1955 saw the arrival of a new 98cc (6ci) model. With an overhead-cam and horizontal cylinder, this machine was hailed as 'Italy's most advanced lightweight'.

In the mid-1950s, Motom was doing well, with the fifth-largest sales of all Italian manufacturers. However, the downturn of the late 1950s affected the firm badly and despite new models and a bid for exports, Motom closed down in 1966.

Motom built affordable lightweights with very small engines. This engine detail dates from 1961.

WSK

WSK started out as a state-owned concern in 1947, and for some years it produced a single design. This first machine was a 123cc (8ci) single-cylinder two-stroke, whose design borrowed heavily from the DKW RT125, as did many others of the same period.

By the mid-1950s, a 175cc (11ci) machine, which was generally similar, had appeared. Like its stablemate, it was intended mainly for the domestic market and for export among the other Communist-bloc states, although small numbers were sold in the West. WSK's machines were cheap and easy to maintain, and sales were good overall, though not quite on the same level as CZ, Jawa and MZ.

In 1977, Roy Cary of Barron Eurotrade in Hornchurch, Essex, contracted with WSK to supply parts for a 125cc/8ci-class motorcycle to be assembled in the UK, using a five-speed, piston-port, Italian Minerelli two-stroke engine. The project was not a success, and Barron soon stopped production, concentrating upon its various Italian import concessions. No new WSK models appeared after the 1970s, although the firm stopped trading only in 1995.

ARIEL KH TWIN

Edward Turner's 1937 Triumph Speed Twin inspired all the major British manufacturers to introduce their own parallel twin-cylinder models. Ariel's take on the concept was named the KH and was very similar to others of the type.

The KH was an air-cooled, overhead-valve 498cc (30ci) machine featuring a four-speed gearbox. Early examples had cast-iron cylinder barrels and heads, but from 1954 the heads were constructed from light alloy. The machine gained a full double cradle frame with pivoted-fork rear suspension at the same time.

The KH was a workmanlike but unimpressive machine and could not compete with similar but better twins from Triumph, BSA and its rivals. It remained in production until 1957.

ENGINE: 498cc (30ci) ohv parallel twin, 63x60mm, air-cooled
POWER: 25bhp at 5750rpm
GEARBOX: 4-speed foot change
FINAL DRIVE: chain
WEIGHT: 188kg (415lb)
TOP SPEED: 132km/h (82mph)

BETA

Beta moved from cheap urban transport to offroad machines after the hard times of the 1960s, starting with a 125cc (8ci) in the late 1970s.

Beta was founded in 1948 by Guiseppe Bianchi. Like many others, the company did very well in the transport-hungry postwar market. By the early 1950s, Beta had nine models in production, including the Mercurio and Orione. These were overhead-valve machines in 153cc (9ci) and 199.5cc (12ci) respectively. There was also the semi-racing MT (Milano–Taranto) 175, which used a specially tuned 172cc (10ci) version of the touring TV two-stroke model and was capable of 132km/h (82mph).

Beta got through the 1960s, which was a tough time for Italian motorcycle manufacturers. Matters improved in the 1970s, and the general upturn was complemented by a successful move into the off-road sector. Beta built a number of specialized motocross, enduro and trials bikes alongside the road machines. In the late 1970s, there was a new 125cc (8ci) on offer as a touring or sport machine. The sport version had cast-alloy wheels, dual-disc front brake, clip-ons and an expansion-type exhaust.

Beta was successful in the export marketplace and became an important dirt bike manufacturer. Its machines have won several world trials championships.

CORGI

The Corgi was based on the Welbike, a folding machine built by Excelsior for use by air-dropped troops. It was powered by a 98cc (6ci) Villiers single-speed, push-start engine. The Corgi, however, used a 98cc (6ci) Excelsior Spryt engine.

First becoming available for general sale in 1948, the Corgi mounted its engine in a low duplex frame with rigid forks and chain drive. It had a small fuel tank, disc wheels, foldable handlebars, seat and footrests. A kick-start was added soon after

release, along with a dog clutch controlled by hinging the right footrest up to clear the kick-start. A sidecar platform with box also appeared that year.

In 1949, the Corgi gained an optional two-speed gearbox and telescopic forks. These became

standard for 1952, but the marketplace was changing by then and such basic machines were less popular than they had been. It was phased out in 1954, being supplanted by the ranges of moped that were beginning to appear.

FRANCIS-BARNETT MERLIN

The Merlin was a typical Francis-Barnett post-war offering. It was powered by a 122cc (7ci) Villiers '9D' twin port two-stroke engine, employing flat-topped pistons and Schnurle loop cylinder scavenging. The engine was designed in the 1930s but was serviceable enough. Although it looked a little dated, the Merlin was a tidy design and was well put together. It stands comparison with the contemporary BSA D1 Bantam, although it was not by any means a fast machine, with a top speed of well under 80km/h (50mph). One nice feature was the addition of an emergency tank for two-stroke oil.

The Merlin, powered by a 122cc (7ci) Villiers single, was both a sound design and well put together. Despite being a very good machine for its market niche, it was eclipsed by the BSA Bantam, the best-selling UK motorcycle.

ENGINE: 122cc (7ci) 2s single, 50x62mm air-cooled
POWER: 3.2bhp at 4400rpm
GEARBOX: 3-speed foot change
FINAL DRIVE: chain
WEIGHT: 79kg (175lb)
TOP SPEED: 71km/h (44mph)

HARLEY-DAVIDSON PANHEAD

The Panhead got its name from the shape of its valve covers. It was an all-new, overhead-valve engine, with hydraulic valve actuation instead of pushrods, and light-alloy cylinder heads instead of cast-iron. The latter were expected to shed heat faster than cast iron, and the hydraulics were intended to eliminate tappet noise. The Panhead had better lubrication than the preceding Knucklehead,

with 25 per cent greater flow to the overhead-valve gear at one bar pressure.

Panheads were available on 1200cc (73ci) and 988cc (60ci) versions. The latter was nearly as powerful as the original Panhead 1200, though an update to the inlet and exhaust tracts in 1949 provided the 1200 with an additional 10hp. The same year, Panhead machines gained

Hydraglide front forks, though they still had a rigid rear end and hand change.

Foot change and hand clutch became available as options in 1952 – about 15 years later than might have been expected. Also, rear suspension did not appear on the big twins until the Duo-Glide of 1958, which became the electric-start Electra-Glide in 1965.

ENGINE: 1207cc (72ci) ohv in-line V-twin, 87x100mm, air-cooled
POWER: 50bhp approx
GEARBOX: 4-speed hand change
FINAL DRIVE: chain
WEIGHT: 255kg (560lb)
TOP SPEED: 153km/h (95mph) est.

ISO

Isothermos (Iso) was founded in 1939, just in time to be disrupted by World War II. In 1948, the firm was re-formed as Iso Autotiveicoli SpA, and produced a range of autocycles and scooters. These did well enough, so the firm moved into other markets with the Isetta micro car, which had a 236cc (14ci) overhead-valve engine. This was built under licence by several other companies, including BMW, and remained in production until the 1960s

In the two-wheel market, Iso produced a line of motorcycles and scooters, some of which used split-single, two-stroke engines. Iso's small machines developed throughout the 1950s, leading to the 1957 Milano model. Fitted with a 146cc (9ci) single-cylinder,

two-stroke engine, the Milano was a modern-looking machine resembling the offspring of Vespa and Lambretta.

New overhead-valve, four-stroke motorcycles appeared for 1962 – two 125cc (8ci) models and a 175cc (11ci). There was also to have been a 492cc (30ci) overhead-valve flat-twin with BMW influences. Displayed in 1961, it did not, however, enter production. There were no more motorcycles after 1963; the firm sold off remaining stocks and concentrated on cars until finally closing down in 1979.

ISO built cars, motorcycles and scooters. This 1953 machine is powered by a 200cc (12ci), split-single engine.

PARILLA BIALBERO

Guiseppe Salmaggi, developed the Bialbero (double-cam) racer from earlier Parilla overhead-camshaft racing and super-sport models. At its debut in 1948, the Bialbero was capable of a little over 160km/h (100mph). For a racing bike, it was extraordinarily flexible, delivering impressive power even at 3500rpm.

Like its single-camshaft predecessors, the Bialbero used a vertical drive shaft and bevel gears. There was also a series of gears operating the inlet and exhaust camshafts by means of pinions. Each cam was carried by a roller race at the drive end, and a ball race at the other. The camshafts activated the valves through flat-top tappets; valve springs were of the hairpin variety and left exposed. The separate double overhead-camshaft drive

box sat atop the cylinder head in much the same way as the double-camshaft Manx Norton. The machine was lightened by using as many engine castings in electron alloy as possible.

The original 250cc (8ci) model was joined by a 349cc (21ci) version in 1950. The latter was impressive in competition all over Europe while its smaller sibling also continued to be successful.

These two machines were instrumental in promoting Parilla in the Italian and export marketplaces.

ENGINE: 246.3cc (15ci) dohc single, 66x72mm, air-cooled
POWER: 21bhp at 8500rpm
GEARBOX: 4-speed foot change
FINAL DRIVE: chain
WEIGHT: 115kg (250lb)
TOP SPEED: 162km/h (102mph)

VINCENT RAPIDE

The Rapide was reputedly built using an existing frame, which necessitated mounting the engine at a rather unusual angle of 47.5 degrees. The resulting machine became known as the 'plumber's nightmare'. It was fast, at 174km/h (108mph), and had unusually good brakes for the period, but it was not without other faults. The clutch was heavy and could be defeated by full power in the mid gears – as could the gearbox. As its nickname suggests, the Rapide was also very prone to leaking oil.

Only 78 Rapide Series A machines were ever built. After the war, later models used a 50-degree engine mount and leaked a lot less. The Series B ran from 1946 to 1950 and was superseded by models from Series C (1948–54) and finally Series D (1954–55).

ENGINE: 998cc (60ci) ohv in-line V-twin, 84x90mm, air-cooled
POWER: 45bhp at 5300rpm
GEARBOX: 4-speed foot change
FINAL DRIVE: chain
WEIGHT: 206kg (455lb)
TOP SPEED: 190km/h (118mph) approx

Several versions of the big, fast Rapide appeared over 20 years. About two-thirds of the original production run (of just 78 machines) survive today.

VINCENT SERIES C BLACK SHADOW

The Vincent Series C Black Shadow was very similar to the Series C Rapide, which was introduced at the same time. The Black Shadow had a very slightly larger carburettor and a higher compression ratio. This and some other basic modifications, such as polishing connecting rods, resulted in an increase of 10hp.

Most of the other differences were stylistic. The engine cases were enamelled black for identification reasons rather than engineering requirements. The resulting machine was the

fastest off-the-shelf, road-going motorcycle in the world, at a time when Britain's open roads had no speed limits. The Series C Black Shadow remained in production until 1953.

ENGINE: 998cc (60ci) ohv in-line V-twin, 84x90mm, air-cooled
POWER: 55bhp at 5700rpm
GEARBOX: 4-speed foot change
FINAL DRIVE: chain
WEIGHT: 208kg (458lb)
TOP SPEED: 201km/h (125mph) approx

The Shadow featured a black enamelled engine case and a speedometer graduated to 242km/h (150mph). With 55bhp available from the 998cc (60ci) V-twin engine, this was a very fast bike for its time.

VINCENT SERIES C COMET

Vincent's V-twins were more impressive and better known than the singles, but the 500cc (31ci) Series C Comet was still a fast and, overall, very good motorcycle. The Grey Flash of 1949–51 delivered 35hp and was capable of 177km/h (110mph).

In the same period, the 1000cc (61ci) Rapide/Shadow V-twin was also available in super-tuned form, as the Lightning. This machine delivered 70hp, thanks to its fiercer cams, a higher compression ratio, and bigger carburettors.

ENGINE: 499cc (30ci) ohv single, 84x90mm, air-cooled
POWER: 28bhp at 5800rpm
GEARBOX: 4-speed foot change
WEIGHT: 177kg (390lb)
TOP SPEED: 145km/h (90mph) est

Perhaps a little less glamorous than the Shadow, and not so fast, the 500cc (30ci) overhead-valve Comet was nevertheless a very good, and consequently popular, machine capable of 145km/h (90mph).

BMW R24

BMW singles are less famous than the twins, and were never as fast. However, it was limited to 250cc (15ci) as it tried to rebuild after World War II, and a single was the only real option. This machine was the R24, and it was built just as well as every other BMW

machine. Its engine was more or less half a twin turned on its side.

The 12hp R24 carried on from BMW's pre-war range of singles, which had begun with the 198cc (12ci) R39 of 1925 and had gone through a range of engine sizes with model numbers that seemed

to follow no sequence. The successors to this machine actually had model numbers that made some sense: the R25 ran from 1950 to 1955 and the R26 came next (1955–60), finally leading to the 18hp R27, in production from 1960 to 1967.

ENGINE: 247cc (15ci) ohv vertical single, 68mm square, air-cooled
POWER: 12bhp at 5600rpm
GEARBOX: 4-speed foot change
FINAL DRIVE: Kardan shaft
WEIGHT: 130kg (286lb)
TOP SPEED: 95km/h (59mph)

DERBI

Derbi started out in 1922 as a minor manufacturer of bicycles and began building powered machines in 1949, taking the name Nacional Motor, SA. The first

model was the SRS (named for the initials of the firm's founder, Simeón Rabasa Singla), a 49cc (3ci) two-stroke with a two-speed gearbox. This was followed in

1950 with a machine that used the Derbi name for the first time. This new identity came from DERivados de BIcicletas, the Spanish for 'derivative of bicycle'.

This first Derbi was powered by a 250cc (15ci) single-cylinder, twin-port, two-stroke Jawa engine built in unit with a four-speed gearbox. This went into a cradle frame that had telescopic forks and plunger rear suspension in a style that was advanced for its time. It was soon followed by more two-strokes with unit construction, ranging from 90cc (5ci) to 100cc (6ci) and, later, 125cc (8ci). A 98cc (6ci) scooter appeared in 1953 and was joined by a 125cc (8ci) variant in 1955.

The scooters remained in production until 1957, and in that year Derbi introduced its largest machine, a 350cc (21ci) twin with four speeds. It was styled in a manner that became almost a trademark of Derbi's machines.

In the 1960s, Derbi concentrated on smaller models in the range from 50cc (3ci) to 125cc (8ci), and its smallest machines were particularly successful.

Publicity was garnered by involvement in circuit and off-road racing, entering the first 50cc World Championship in 1962. The Derbi machine fought a tooth-and-nail battle with the winning Kreidler, coming home to a close second place. This also put it well ahead of the Honda team.

This and other race activity resulted in a 50cc (3ci) racing machine joining the Derbi range. It was a simple, air-cooled two-stroke with five speeds, which did well in local competitions. Sports road models of 50cc (3ci) and 75cc (5ci) were derived from it, and race kits for these machines were available after market.

By now, Derbi was a major player on the Spanish scene. The firm continued to make

mopeds as well as trials bikes and road-racing machines. Experimentation continued but was sometimes fruitless; a 125cc (8ci) V-twin with geared crankshafts, disc valves and the cylinders one above the other at a narrow angle was not competitive. However, the 50cc (3ci) models did rather better, battling with Suzuki and Kreidler for places in Grand Prix.

Then, in 1969, Angel Nieto took the 50cc (3ci) world title on a Derbi, and did it again in 1970. That year, the firm fielded a new racer, a water-cooled 125cc (8ci) twin. It won first time out, finished second in the title race and went on to take the title in 1971. This victory

was courtesy of Nieto, and he won again in 1972, taking the 50cc (3ci) title for the third time. In 1972, Derbi left the racing scene, though the 1973 range included an Angel Nieto 50cc (3ci) Replica. Although it was stylish, it lacked the performance to do its name justice.

Derbi's mopeds were its main product in the mid-1970s, though there were new motorcycles and a return to the scooter marketplace. A wise move – Derbi has always done best out of its small two-stroke machines.

Derbi is famous for its range of small, lightweight machines with a distinctive styling. This 49cc (3ci) racer dates from the early 1960s. The inset shows its workmanlike single-cylinder engine in close-up.

DOUGLAS 80 PLUS

ENGLAND 1949

After the war, Douglas produced the T35, a transverse twin that was noted both for its advanced design and the tendency of its frame to fracture. The Mark III T35 was the fastest production 350 in 1949, and this incarnation of the machine was designated 80 Plus or 90 Plus. It seems that each engine was tested once it was completed. Those delivering more than 25hp went into machines to

be fitted out as 90 Plus; those with less were built as 80 Pluses.

The name referred to the probable top speed of the machine when completed. Both versions had alloy rims and twin carburettors, as well as the same overhead-cam engine. The 80 Plus was outfitted in maroon and the 90 Plus in metallic gold. For no extra cost, the latter could be supplied in full racing specification.

These machines had very large brakes for their time, relative to the weight of the machine, and this reflected their racing heritage. Under most circumstances, the bikes handled very well indeed, though it was possible for a series of bumps to coincide with the natural frequency of the torsion-bar suspension, causing the bike to bounce around alarmingly.

These were good but expensive machines, costing more than a Triumph 500cc (31ci) twin.

ENGINE: 348cc (21ci) ohv transverse flat twin, 60.8x60mm, air-cooled
POWER: 25bhp approx. at 7500rpm
GEARBOX: 4-speed foot change
FINAL DRIVE: chain
WEIGHT: 179kg (393lb)
TOP SPEED: 137km/h (85mph) approx

ESO

CZECHOSLOVAKIA 1949–64

In 1949, veteran Czech racers Vaclav Stanislav and Jaroslav Simandl, had been in England riding in the ISDT and trying to

source parts for JAP speedway engines. The JAP 500 overhead-valve single was the only option for speedway racers, and spares

could be hard to come by. Stanislav was unable to find all the parts he needed, so Simandl offered to make them.

An argument followed, which prompted Simandl to declare that he would build an entire engine. This he proceeded to do.

Simandl built eight engines, of which half were intended as use for spares. However, there was sufficient interest that the design was further developed, leading to commercial success. The Eso (Ace) engine was used in road and track racing, and the firm grew rapidly, advancing beyond the original copy of a 20-year-old JAP engine design and into new territory. In the early 1950s, Eso produced the short-stroke 497cc (30ci) S-45 (45hp) engine, which was ideal for the long sand tracks of Europe.

In 1954, Jaroslav Cervinka became chief designer for Eso, and not long after that the firm merged with Jawa. Cervinka later designed the famous four-valve Jawa speedway engine, which dominated the sport for many years. Although Eso retained its identity within Jawa until 1964, thereafter it gradually faded into the l arger concern.

The ESO engine was conceived out of necessity and more than a little pride as Vaclav Simandl set out to make good on his boast that he could build an engine suitable for Speedway use. For a time ESO engines and derivatives came to dominate Speedway.

EXCELSIOR TALISMAN

JAPAN 1949

The Talisman was a step forward compared to most contemporary two-stroke machines. The twin-cylinder engine featured a built-up 180-degree crankshaft; in a couple of decades, this layout would be associated with the dominant Japanese designs of the period. Unit construction was not used, however; instead, the four-speed Albion gearbox was bolted to the rear of the engine.

The initial Talisman featured telescopic front suspension with a plunger rear end. The Talisman Sport, which was released in 1953, updated the design with a true swing-arm rear end, twin Amal carburettors and greater cylinder-head finning for improved cooling. Also, the engine size was increased to 328cc (20ci) for the 1959 Special Talisman, with enclosed rear bodywork, which was fashionable at the time. For all their design features, however, the Talismans proved to be poor sellers.

ENGINE: 244cc (15ci) two-stroke parallel twin, 50x62mm, air-cooled
POWER: 12bhp at 4000rpm
GEARBOX: 4-speed foot change
FINAL DRIVE: chain
WEIGHT: 113kg (250lb)
TOP SPEED: 105km/h (65mph)

GUAZZONI

ITALY 1949–79

Another firm that earned its daily bread with small lightweights, Guazzoni also produced sports machines that did well in competition before returning to the economy transport market niche.

After leaving Moto Morini, Aldo Guazzoni set up his own business, in Milan. His firm quickly gained a reputation for innovation and quality. Its bread and butter was a range of small-capacity two-strokes, but there were some more exciting machines too. The first of these, in 1954, was a 191cc (12ci) overhead-camshaft model with telescopic front forks, swinging-arm rear suspension and a full duplex frame. A 13hp tuned version competed in the Milano–Taranto and other long-distance events.

In 1959, Guazzoni began exporting its machines to Britain via the Manchester-based firm DOT. The first was the new Guazzoni 175 horizontal two-stroke, single-cylinder machine. A year later, the 125 Sport, which featured an upright cylinder, also became a DOT import. Guazzoni released more models about the same time, including the 98 Sport, which was simply the 125 with a smaller engine

In the 1960s, Guazzoni built some interesting disc-valve models, notably a 60cc (4ci) racer in 1966, and a 50cc (3ci) version in 1969, which took the Italian Senior Championship that year. Then came a twin-cylinder 125cc (8ci) for GP events. Although powerful, it was outmatched in the big league and was soon withdrawn. In the 1970s, Guazzoni concentrated on a more modest range of mopeds and 50cc (3ci) machines. It closed in 1979.

HOREX REGINA 350

The best-selling of Horex's machines just after World War II was the 350cc (21ci) overhead-valve Regina. A tough and reliable single-cylinder machine offering good fuel economy and easy maintenance, the Regina had a very British character about it. Although power was modest, it was accompanied by impressive torque.

The Regina's engine owed a lot to pre-war designs, but the chassis was all new, with oil-damped telescopic front forks and plunger rear suspension. The engine, gearbox and clutch assembly was used as a stressed member of the frame.

The Regina deservedly achieved considerable success in the motorcycle marketplace. The most popular model was the 350cc (21ci), but there were also 248cc (15ci) and 399cc (24ci) versions. The Regina remained in production until Horex closed its doors in 1958.

ENGINE: 342cc (20ci) ohv vertical single, 69x91.5mm, air-cooled
POWER: 15bhp at 3500rpm
SPORT: 20bhp at 4500rpm
GEARBOX: 4-speed foot change
FINAL DRIVE: chain
WEIGHT: 145.5kg (320lb)
TOP SPEED: 122kph (76mph)
SPORT: 126km/h (78mph)

LAVERDA

In 1873, Pietro Laverda founded a company to build farm machinery. Two generations later, Francesco Laverda decided that he would like a motorbike, so he built one for himself. He put a lot of personal effort into his machine: casting the single piston in his own kitchen, he worked away at his project until, after a whole year, he had created a 74.75cc (5ci) four-stroke overhead-valve engine in unit with a three-speed foot-change gearbox – and then he built a whole motorcycle around it.

Laverda's bike impressed his friends and neighbours, and there were requests for replicas. Thus Laverda entered the world of motorcycle manufacturing, and by 1951 his company had built 500 or so. One was entered in the Milano–Taranto long-distance road race, but retired. Showing the same tenacity as he had in building his prototype, Laverda came back with a team of race-prepared machines, which took the first 14 places in their class.

In 1954, a 98cc (6ci) version became available and Laverda machines dominated the 75cc (5ci) and 100cc (6ci) classes in the Milano-Taranto and made a good showing in the Giro d'Italia (Tour of Italy). Production race-replicas of the Milano-Taranto machines (designated MT) sold well, but the marque lost interest in sport and began to concentrate on road bikes.

The downturn in the Italian motorcycle industry in the 1960s affected Laverda less than most. To carry it through, it was able to rely on its other interests, including foundry work and the manufacture of combine harvesters.

In the meantime, Laverda was ahead of the general move towards bigger engines. In 1966, an overhead-cam 654cc (40ci) twin was displayed at the Earl's Court show. Within a year, this machine had grown to 743.9cc (45.3ci) and the firm decided to get some publicity for the new line of twins by entering long-distance races.

Laverdas won the 1969 and 1970 Oss 24 Hours.

In 1971, the 750 SFC appeared. This machine echoed the very first Laverda in that it was hand built. Its purpose was to win races, and even when it did not come in first, the SFC gained an enviable reputation for tenacity and staying power.

Up until 1969, all Laverdas were singles or twins. A prototype triple was shown in 1969 and attracted a lot of interest, but it was not until 1973 that it was ready for series production (as the 3C, for three cylinder). In the meantime, it underwent extensive development and modification, appearing as a 980.76cc (59.8ci) machine with double overhead-cams driven by a

Laverda's 750 SFC first appeared in 1971 and ran until 1976. This is a post-1974 model, with triple disc brakes in place of the original drums. The final updated version received electronic ignition.

single chain between the second and third cylinders. It had a top speed of 220km/h (137mph), but suffered from a range of issues arising from inadequate testing. The problems were ironed out in the first two years of production, and the 3C gained disc brakes along the way. It was renamed, first as the 3CL and then as the Jota.

Laverda was on top in the late 1970s and early 1980s, winning races and producing well-regarded motorcycles. A two-stroke series appeared, including bikes powered by Husqvarna and Zundapp engines. The latter were a success; most of the others were not.

Then came a new three-cylinder machine, the two-stroke Lesmo. It was a very advanced machine capable of 201km/h (125mph) but never went into production.

Instead, Laverda began lurching from one financial crisis to another, and in 1993 the firm was taken over by Francesco Tognon.

He relaunched the firm with a version of the proven 650 Sport. This was followed by the 750S in 1997.

Work began on a new three-cylinder superbike, but Tognon left in 1998 and there was no money for the project. The firm was taken over by Aprilia in 2000.

LILAC

The Marusho company began building motorcycles under the Lilac name in 1949. The first models were single-cylinder machines powered by a 148cc (9ci) overhead-valve engine with two-speed gearbox and a pressed-steel chassis. More modern designs followed with tubular steel frames and Earles-type front forks. Some featured a form of automatic transmission with a torque converter.

Lilac achieved good commercial success in 1953 with the Baby, a 90cc (5ci) overhead-valve model with shaft final drive. A series of horizontally opposed twins followed, starting with a 339cc (21ci) machine in 1954. All used shaft final drive, a feature that gradually became a Lilac trademark.

In 1959, Lilac fielded a 247cc (15ci) V-twin, which was similar in many ways to the Moto Guzzi V7/V75 of the late 1960s and early 1970s. It featured a tidy duplex cradle frame, telescopic front forks and swinging-arm rear suspension. Later, a larger 188cc (11ci) was introduced. This larger model was sold as part of Lilac's range as the MF-39 Type 300.

In 1964, the R92 appeared and was exported to the USA as the Marusho Magnum. This was a 493cc (30ci) horizontally opposed twin with shaft final drive. However, the machine's reliability was poor, which badly damaged Lilac's reputation. In 1967, the parent firm Marusho closed down, which spelled the end of the Lilac marque.

Lilac's MF39 was powered by a narrow-angle V-twin using shaft final drive. The front-mounted alternator is quite prominent.

LUBE

Lube was founded by Luis Bojarano, and for some years it built machines in the range from 50cc (3ci) to 250cc (15ci), all powered by NSU engines. Frames were of the firm's own design. After NSU ceased making motorcycles, Lube built its own engines, all of which were two-strokes.

One notable two-stroke to come out of Lube was the GP5 racer. At its 1962 debut, it used a 125cc (8ci) engine with piston-port induction and full unit construction. With a compression ratio of 10:1 from its German Mahle piston, this produced 18hp. Designed by Hermann Meier during his stint at Lube before joining Royal Enfield, the GP5 could not compete with new racers from Italy and Japan, so another new engine was created in 1963.

After Meir left, Lube fielded a 246cc (15ci) two-stroke racing twin. This was air-cooled with large areas of finning on both the cylinders and heads, a dry clutch, steeply angled carburettors and five speeds. It competed several times in 1965, including the Spanish GP.

MONDIAL 125 GRAND PRIX

A double overhead-cam 125 GP as ridden by Carlo Ubbiali to win the 1951 world championship. The machine produced 16bhp at 12,000rpm for a top speed of 163km/h (102mph).

This machine first appeared in 1948, and was a revolutionary design. The key to its success was the use of double overhead-camshafts, a practice that was almost unheard of in such a small-capacity engine. The advanced engine design delivered 11hp at a time when most of the opposition could manage only 10hp. The result was a tremendous series of racing successes as the new Mondial demolished all opposition at the 1948 Italian Grand Prix, then set new flying and standing-start kilometre and mile records. Its fastest run was measured at 130km/h (80.8mph) over the flying kilometre, but after streamlining was added a new flying kilometre record was set at over 161km/h (100mph).

After being modified to deliver 13hp, giving a top speed of 145km/h (90mph), the racing Mondial blazed to victory in every race it entered in 1949, taking the world title. Steady development resulted in a machine that could put out 16hp during its last year of competition. After this, the Mondial was eclipsed by new machines from MV and NSU. However, during its glory years of 1949 to 1951, it became not only the first machine to win the new 125cc World Championship, but also the first to win three world championships in a row.

ENGINE: 123.5cc (7ci) dohc 2v single, 53x56mm, air-cooled
POWER: 13bhp at 9500rpm
GEARBOX: 4-speed foot change
FINAL DRIVE: chain
WEIGHT: 98kg (216lb)
TOP SPEED: 163km/h (102mph)

NORTON DOMINATOR

The Dominator was initially built on a rear-suspension frame that owed a lot to pre-war designs. Heavy and more than a little crude, it was not greatly helped by its inadequate brakes. Nor was its performance particularly impressive. The machine was designed to run on poor quality petrol and had a compression ratio of just 6.75:1 as a result. Valve timings were hardly aggressive, suggesting that Norton deliberately left room for improvement in the design.

For all its flaws, the Dominator was a very smooth machine, capable of handling any sort of road without becoming flustered. At a cruising speed of 104–113km/h (65–70mph), the machine was very well behaved, though it was somewhat less well-mannered nearing its top speed of 145km/h (90mph).

ENGINE: 497cc (30ci) ohv parallel twin 66x72.6mm, air-cooled
POWER: 29bhp at 6000rpm
GEARBOX: 4-speed foot change
FINAL DRIVE: chain
WEIGHT: 186kg (410lb)
TOP SPEED: 145km/h (90mph)

The original Dominator was distinctly mild mannered, though its very poor brakes made for a certain amount of excitement at times. Later versions were more aggressive and the improved 'featherbed' frame turned the Dominator into a world-class machine.

OSSA

Manuel Giro was the owner of a very successful company that made cinema equipment. A motorcycle enthusiast, he discovered that after the Spanish Civil War ended in 1939, it was impossible to obtain transport overseas given that the rest of Europe was now fighting. He therefore decided to build his own motorcycles.

Giro's first design was for a 125cc (8ci) machine. This was not a success, though Montesa was able to build on the design to create a production model. Meanwhile, Giro had designed another machine, a 125cc (8ci) single-cylinder two-stroke with a central exhaust port. This first machine, named Ossa, had a three-speed gearbox and could achieve 75km/h (47mph). The original design spawned a range of machines for the commuter market, and race machines were prepared for the ISDT.

In 1954, an improved design was implemented, and this gained a 149cc (9ci) engine in 1958. The same year, a 175cc (11ci) four-stroke roadster also appeared. The firm went back to two-strokes in 1959 with a more sporty version of the 125cc (8ci).

Ossa struggled in the early 1960s, like other Spanish motorcycle manufacturers. However, the firm was joined by Manuel Giro's son Eduardo, a very talented engineer. At the age of 15, he had built an 18,000rpm model aircraft engine, and he was able to draw on this design for his first motorcycle engine, which appeared in 1962. The new engine was a 158.8cc (9.7ci) single cylinder two-stroke, and was the basis of Ossa production for many years.

Eduardo Giro produced a range of engines based on his design. A 175cc (11ci) in 1965 and a 230cc (14ci) in 1966 were followed by a 488.5cc (30ci) twin created from two singles. There was another single in 1975, a 244.3cc (14.9ci) model. Eduardo's engines went into both production machines and competition models. The first of these was the 175 Sport, in 1965. The road version could make 145km/h (90mph), and the race variant took first and second in their class at the Barcelona 24-hour race in the year it was released. More victories followed, along with larger engines, and Ossa won the Barcelona 24-hour outright in 1967, setting a record of 662 laps that stood for some years.

As road-bike market share was lost to a licence-built Fiat machine built by Seat, Ossa moved into dirt machines. Motocross was very popular at the time, and Ossa decided to target this market niche. The result was victory in both the British and European Trials Championships, and consequently good sales of replicas of the race machine.

In 1972, Ossa announced the MAR – Mick Andrews Replica, named for their star rider. Sales were good, though Andrews himself went to work for Yamaha in 1973. Things then went downhill for Ossa, and the firm had to be baled out in 1978 by the Spanish government. Even the return of Mick Andrews could not stop the general decline.

Ossa built its last trials bikes in 1983, and motocross machines disappeared from the range somewhat before that. A new road machine, the Urbe, was the last to be released under Giro family ownership. An attempt was made to relaunch the firm in 1984 as a workers' collective, but the firm went under in 1985.

RUMI

ITALY 1949–62

Bergamo-based Officine Fonderi Rumi was founded just before World War I and built textile machinery until the outbreak of World War II. During the war, the firm desugned and built two-man midget submarines and torpedoes. After the war, it retained an anchor as part of its logo, a reminder of this time.

In peacetime, there was little market for underwater weapons, so Rumi looked for a new market. Like Agusta and Macchi, it decided that motorcycles were the way forward. The first machine appeared in 1949, a 125cc (8ci) two-stroke twin with an 180-degree crankshaft and vertical cylinders. This engine became a Rumi trademark throughout its life as a motorcycle and scooter constructor.

By 1950, Rumi was exhibiting its products outside Italy, and in 1951 its machines appeared at the International Six Day Trial. A year later, the firm launched a sports version, which featured twin carburettors, a tuned engine and patented bottom-link front forks. It delivered 8hp and was capable of 116km/h (72mph).

Rumi gained the services of Guiseppe Salmaggi as designer, and went on to produce a range of new machines, including an experimental 247.36cc (15.09ci)

double overhead-cam racing twin with shaft final drive. Then came the Scoiattolo (Squirrel), which was Rumi's first scooter. Those desiring a little more performance could buy a 125cc (8ci) racer, while the 125cc (8ci) roadster gained 175cc (11ci) and 200cc (12ci) siblings.

The definitive Rumi machine appeared in 1954. This was a

scooter, the Formichino, or Little Ant. This machine went on to become a best-seller and also won the French Bol d'Or endurance race on more than one occasion. Its engine was used in the Junior Gentleman sports/racing bike. The racing version of this machine could attain a little more than 160km/h (100mph).

Rumi mostly produced small workhorse machines, usually powered by their 125cc (8ci) twin-cylinder, two-stroke engine. There were exceptions at times, such as this 250cc (15ci) four-cylinder special build with racing in mind.

TOHATSU

JAPAN 1949–64

The Tohatsu name first appeared in 1939, when the Takata Motor Institute was renamed Tokyo Hatsudoki, abbreviated to Tohatsu. The firm was founded in 1922 to conduct research into internal combustion engines and expanded gradually throughout the inter-war years.

During World War II, Tohatsu supplied generating equipment to the Japanese military, and it emerged from the war with its factories intact. The firm began producing fire pumps as well as motorcycles, and by 1957 the firm boasted a four-model range. All were two-stroke street bikes

with engine sizes of 86cc (5ci), 123cc (8ci) and 199cc (12ci), all of which proved a success. By 1961, Tohatsu had a respectable three per cent share of the Japanese domestic market – which was a lot of bikes.

However, Tohatsu's management realized that the firm needed to enter the competition marketplace if its success was to increase, so in 1961 the first competition machines appeared. These were 125cc (8ci) and 250cc (15ci) motocross bikes and a 50cc (3ci) road racer, the Runpet CR50. The latter was a single-cylinder two-stroke with a close-ratio

four-speed gearbox, a beam-type frame and telescopic front forks. There was also a 124cc (8ci) version capable of 145km/h (90mph).

From these models came the definitive racing Tohatsu models: a 49.8cc (3ci) twin and a completely revamped 125cc (8ci). The latter had an unusual three-piece, split crankcase intended to make maintenance easy. The machine also boasted an innovative chassis design, a twin-duplex affair that provided superb roadholding. This design was so impressive that years after the original engine was phased out,

it was still being used to house other power units. The Tohatsu 50 was the only 50cc (3ci) twin-cylinder machine ever to be offered to private buyers.

Tohatsu racers scored many successes, but plans to field a works team in the 1965 European GP season were scotched by a series of financial troubles. As a result, the motorcycle division of the firm going into liquidation in 1964. The company's stocks of parts and production assets were used to set up Japan Racing Motor Cycles. Most of the engineering staff went to work for Bridgestone, which benefited greatly.

VELOCETTE LE

ENGLAND 1949

As the world recovered from World War II and the desperate shortage for cheap commuter transport receded a little, more upmarket versions began to find favour. The LE was an attempt at such a machine. Powered by an extremely quiet 149cc (9ci) side-valve engine, which was increased to 192cc (12ci) in 1950, the

machine was quite advanced. It had no frame in the conventional sense but was instead built on a chassis formed from a sheet-steel monocoque, with integral mudguards and leg-shields.

The LE was extremely economical to run, giving 2.2l/100km (130mpg), and was both practical and easy to ride.

However, although they found some success as police vehicles, they did not do well in the marketplace. Velocette tried other versions of the same idea, such as the Valiant in 1956 and the Vogue, which used fibreglass for the bodywork. None of them sold very well and eventually the LE and its descendents faded from the scene.

ENGINE: 149cc (3ci) sv flat-twin, 44x49mm, liquid-cooled
POWER: 6bhp at 6500rpm
GEARBOX: 3-speed foot change
FINAL DRIVE: chain
WEIGHT: 120kg (265lb)
TOP SPEED: 89km/h (55mph)

BOND

Lawrence Bond is best known for small three-wheeled cars and some rather peculiar vehicles of other sorts. His first motorcycle appeared in 1950. Its all-alloy frame was made from sheet metal rolled into a large, tapered, oval-section tube, cut away at the rear for a massive mudguard.
The whole frame was then riveted together. The front mudguard was equally large, and both mudguards enclosed most of each wheel.

This odd vehicle had no suspension; optimistically, it was hoped that the big tyres would be adequate for the purpose. It was powered by a 99cc (6ci) Villiers 1F engine hung from the main beam and flanked by large legshields that had built-in footboards.

Soon after the machine's introduction, the tube forks were replaced by telescopic ones. An alternate power unit, comprising a 125cc (8ci) JAP two-stroke engine in unit with a three-speed gearbox, was briefly available in 1951. Also in that year, production was taken over by Leeds based Ellis, but was discontinued in 1953.

In the meantime, Bond designed the more conventional BAC, powered by the 99cc (6ci) Villiers or 125cc (8ci) JAP two-stroke engines, which came out in 1951. The following year there was a scooter, the Gazelle, powered by a 122cc (7ci) Villiers 10D engine. The Gazelle was typical in many ways, but had its engine enclosed in a grille of steel bars. Only the Gazelle was available in 1953, and after that production ceased.

In 1955, Bond designed another scooter, the Sherpa, powered by a 99cc (6ci) Villiers 1F engine under glass-fibre bodywork. Only the prototype was built, but in 1958, after a move to Preston in Lancashire, Bond produced a second. This had a 148cc (9ci) Villiers 31C engine and a three-speed gearbox. A later model used a 197cc (12ci) Villiers 9E engine and four-speed gearbox. Both were restyled for 1960 and remained in production until 1962. After this, Bond concentrated on making cars.

BSA A7 STAR TWIN

Immediately after World War II, BSA brought out a big twin, the Model A7. This 495cc (30ci) machine met a favourable response when it was unveiled in 1946. But, it turned out to be less than successful in terms of performance, tending to 'run-on' through self-ignition when worked hard, partly due to the use of cast iron for the cylinder and head. An improved version was needed.

BSA turned to Bert Hopwood, who redesigned the A7 and turned it into the 646cc (39ci) A10 Golden Flash. The A10 resembled the A7 superficially but was a greatly improved design with extensive use of light alloys and internal improvements. From this came the revised A7, the Star Twin, in 1950.

A more modest version, the A7SS Shooting Star, came out in 1952. While neither model was up to the standard of contemporary Triumph twins, they proved to be worthy machines. If there had been any doubt of that, it was dispelled by the exploits of three Star Twins in 1952. All three were ridden to Austria to compete in the ISDT (International Six Day Trial, now known as the ISDE), a distance of 1609km (1000 miles). These then competed in the event, each machine covering 7885km (4900 miles). The result was a well-deserved Maudes Trophy (awarded for feats of endurance) and a reputation for reliability and toughness that was passed on to subsequent BSA designs.

ENGINE: 495cc (30ci) ohv parallel twin, 62x82mm, air-cooled
POWER: 26bhp at 5750rpm
GEARBOX: 4-speed foot change
FINAL DRIVE: chain
WEIGHT: 170kg (375lb)
TOP SPEED: 137km/h (85mph)

The original A7 was not a great motorcycle and underperformed in the marketplace. After an extensive redevelopment by Bert Hopwood, a much better version, the Star Twin, fulfilled its initial promise.

CECCATO

Bologna-based Ceccato was an engineering firm before and after it entered motorcycle manufacture after World War II.

The company specialized in small-capacity machines, of which its best-known offerings were 75cc and 100cc sport models, powered by a single overhead-cam, unit-construction engine, with the drive to the camshaft by a train of gears up the finned cylinder's offside.

The Ceccato 75 was very successful in the Giro d'Italia (Tour

Ceccato's foray into manufacturing was short lived and resulted in machines powered by versions of the same single-cylinder engine.

of Italy) and similar long-distance road races. It was class winner in the 1956 Milano–Taranto, while the larger-engined 98cc (6ci) version challenged both Ducati and Laverda in the 100cc (6ci) category.

In addition to the excellent range of 4-stroke singles, which also included cheaper models with overhead-valve engines, Ceccato built a 200cc (12ci) two-stroke twin with horizontal cylinders. However, when the motorcycle industry went into decline in the 1960s, Ceccato ceased production to concentrate on its engineering activities.

CYCLEMASTER

The powered two-wheeler concept started out with add-on engines for standard pedal cycles, and this device returned to those roots. A Dutch design built by EMI, it was a replacement for the entire rear wheel of a bicycle, which comprised a 25cc (1.5ci) disc-valve, two-stroke engine, clutch and final drive all within an enlarged hub. Fuel was provided by a petrol tank, mounted above and behind the engine to create a neat, self-contained package.

The Cyclemaster was successful in the marketplace, and in 1952 it gained a larger (32cc/2ci) engine. For 1953, the firm offered a complete machine. Its intended role as a powered delivery bicycle prompted the name Roundsman, and it came with a large carrier over the front wheel.

The firm moved to Chertsey in 1955 and created a new model, the Cyclemate. This was a proto-moped created by mounting the engine in front of the bottom bracket of a Normal bicycle.

Although a dated concept, it proved popular and remained in production until 1960. In this it was more successful than the Piatti scooter, a 124cc (8ci) two-stroke that was introduced in 1956 and phased out just two years later.

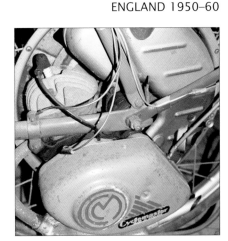

This photograph shows the Cyclemaster wheel used to replace an existing bicycle wheel to provide drive from a 25cc (1.5ci) – later a 32cc (2ci) – two-stroke engine via a clutch and two chains.

GARELLI MOSQUITO

In the transport-starved marketplace of the time, Garelli's first post-war offering was an instant success. This was the Mosquito, a 'clip-on' auxiliary motor for an otherwise conventional bicycle. More than two million were eventually sold.

The original Mosquito was a 38.5cc (2.3ci) two-stroke engine with an external flywheel. Weighing in at 4kg (9lb) and able to run for 64km (40 miles) on 1l (0.26 gal) of fuel, it produced 0.8hp. This allowed speeds of up to 32km/h (20mph). More than 400,000 mosquitos were built in 1952, before the engine was updated. Another version appeared in 1955, this time with a displacement of 49cc (3ci) and a Centrimatic clutch fitted. This clutch assembly was the forerunner of all the centrifugal clutches used on fully automatic mopeds and scooters of today.

In 1955, the success of the Mosquito engine led Garelli to develop a complete machine named the Velomosquito, which was one of the first true mopeds. For 1956, there was a three-speed variant of the Mosquito.

The Mosquito was important to Garelli, helping the firm back into production after the disruption of the war years. It was followed by range of moped scooters and ultra-lightweight motorcycles.

ENGINE: 49cc (3ci) 2s single, 40x39mm, air-cooled
POWER: 1½ bhp at 5000rpm
GEARBOX: single-speed
FINAL DRIVE: chain
WEIGHT: 40kg (90lb)
TOP SPEED: 52km/h (32mph)

IMN

Like many other firms, IMN (Industria Meccanica Neapolitana) realized that there was not much of a market for its main product – in this case, torpedoes – after the end of World War II, and it looked for a suitable market. The result was a range of two-stroke motorcycles from 49cc (3ci) to 248cc (15ci).

After a run of fairly basic machines, IMN unveiled the Rocket in 1956. This was a horizontally opposed, twin-cylinder machine with a displacement of 199cc (12ci). Thanks to a compression ratio of 7:1, the engine developed 11hp at 6000rpm.

The tubular frame was an interesting design, with the engine and gearbox bolted up to form a unit, which was in turn bolted to a substantial light-alloy fork, the nearside arm of which housed the final drive shaft. The entire engine/gearbox assembly pivoted with the rear wheel, and the pivot spindle, which passed through bushes in an extension of the top of the gearbox, was its only point of contact with the frame. This meant that the front and rear wheels were connected only through a single 15mm (0.5in) diameter steel rod.

For all its fascinating features, the Rocket was very unreliable as a result of inadequate testing, and sales were poor. It failed to recoup its high development costs and brought about an untimely end to IMN's motorcycle manufacturing.

In addition to the ill-fated Rocket, IMN brought out the Baio, a radical machine created by former Ducati designer Gian Liugi Capellino, who patented both its engine and frame designs. The Baio was a casualty of IMN's closure in 1958.

JAWA 500 OHC TWIN

Jawa's staple output in the post-war years was its 250cc (8ci) and 350cc (21ci) two-stroke range. Although these supported the firm, it was decided to create a range of four-stroke twins to improve Jawa's image. The first announcement of the new range came in 1948, with prototypes appearing in 1949. These were 488cc (30ci) double overhead-camshaft machines with a four-speed gearbox.

The first production models, designated 15/01, entered series production in 1952 after three years of development. Cycle parts were derived from the 250 Jawa Springer (a twin-port, two-stroke single), featuring a reinforced frame with oil-damped telescopic front forks and plunger rear suspension.

Lubrication was of the dry sump variety, with an oil pump and a separate oil tank with a capacity of 4.5l (1.2 gal). The new machine delivered 26hp and weighed 155kg (344lb). Top speed was given as 140km/h (87mph).

A developed version went into production for 1953 with the designation 15.02. This machine had a more powerful engine (28hp) and a maximum speed of 146km/h (91mph).

In 1954, a dual seat was added, followed by massive full-width brakes. However, despite the prestigious appearance of these machines, they did not sell well. Production ceased in 1958.

ENGINE: 488cc (29ci) dohc 2 parallel twin, 65x73.6mm, air-cooled
POWER: 28bhp at 5500rpm
GEARBOX: 4-speed foot change
FINAL DRIVE: chain
WEIGHT: 156kg (344lb)
TOP SPEED: 146km/h (91mph)

MOTO GUZZI FALCONE

The Falcone was, like many road machines, derived from a race machine. It was essentially a GTW engine installed in an improved, lower frame with a large fuel tank. The first variant was, unusually, a lower performance model with smaller valves and carburettor, a lowered compression ratio. This reduced maximum power to just under 19hp and maximum speed to 120km/h (75mph). Standard fittings did not include a speedometer. This new machine, reaching market in 1954, was named the Falcone Tourismo, the older Falcone having been renamed the Falcone Sport.

The two Falcones then remained in production more or less unchanged for almost 10 years despite being rather outdated when they were first created. The Falcone Turismo was re-launched in 1963, but had not changed much even then. It was finally discontinued in 1967.

However, it did not disappear altogether. People, as a rule, dislike change, and certain segments of the motorcycle marketplace take this attitude to an extreme. Thus, when Moto Guzzi wanted to retire the old warhorse, there remained a substantial number of customers, including the police and military clients, who preferred to stick with what they knew.

The Nuovo Falcone of 1971 was, finally, a step forward, with a wet sump, a steel liner to the light-alloy barrel, fully enclosed valve gear, enclosed flywheel, and more power than its predecessor. It was also a good bit heavier than the earlier version and struggled to reach speeds above 130km/h (80mph), although it did have better brakes and 12-volt electricals. Although the Nuovo Falcone was close to what the uniformed users wanted, it was also unattractive and did not have the same charm as the model it replaced.

In 1974, the Falcone Sahara appeared. This was essentially a civilian variant of the military machine and was an improvement, but commercial success was limited. The Falcone line was discontinued in 1976.

ENGINE: 498cc (30ci) ioe single, 88x82mm, air-cooled
POWER: 23bhp at 5500rpm
GEARBOX: 4-speed foot change
FINAL DRIVE: chain
WEIGHT: 180kg (396lb)
TOP SPEED: 137km/h (85mph)

In production from 1950 to 1976, the Falcone was always a popular machine. All versions retained the original flat-single engine layout.

MZ 125/250 GP RACERS

MZ's 1961 disc-valve, single-cylinder race machine delivered 25bhp at 10,800 RPM, making it the first bike to break the 200bhp/litre barrier. For a time these machines were unbeatable.

MZ was set up by engineer Walter Kaaden, who brilliantly developed the work of tuner Daniel Zimmermann to modify engines for increased race performance. Early on, he was able to wring 20hp out of a 125cc (8ci) engine and get 36hp from a 250cc (15ci) engines, and later, more delicate refinements produced even more power.

MZ Sport competed in road and off-road events, signing international riders and constantly developing engine technology to get ever more power out of small engines. By 1960, MZ could get 23hp from a 123.6cc (7.5ci) engine, and the next year output went beyond 25hp, breaking the 200hp per litre barrier with a top speed of 193km/h (120mph).

The end began in 1961, when star rider Ernst Degner left and went to work for Suzuki. It is possible that Suzuki learned a lot about the techniques of MZ from Degner, and for MZ this was a setback that the firm could not quite overcome. Race results continued to be respectable, but strings of third places were no substitute for the glory of first.

ENGINE: 123.6cc (7ci) disc valve 2s single, 54x54mm, air-cooled
POWER: 25bhp at 10,800rpm
GEARBOX: 6-speed foot change
FINAL DRIVE: chain
WEIGHT: 75kg (165lb)
TOP SPEED: 193km/h (120mph)

NORTON MANX

To many fans, this is the finest Norton of them all. Mating the engine developed in the International with the new 'featherbed' frame created an excellent racing machine that was then used as the basis for innumerable one-off variants.

but the machines continued to compete in classic racing for many years after that. John Tickle bought the rights in 1969 and built a few; Unit Equipe then bought the rights from John Tickle; and Molnar Manx bought production rights in 1994. Although the company mainly sold engines, it also built complete Manxes in frames of its own manufacture.

A well set-up late Manx would exceed 217km/h (135mph), but in truth there is no single definitive Norton Manx. These were racing machines, and over a great many years were the subject of constant experimentation and development, defying all attempts to present a single specification. As they were at the outer edge of the performance envelope, power and weight characteristics of Manxes varied considerably. Some machines were stripped and drilled more than others, while various engine modifications were used at different times.

The Manx engine was a development of the International, with the short stroke adopted in 1938. The frame, however, was the new 'featherbed' design created by the McCandless brothers. The result was that the Manx quickly became the industry standard against which other machines were measures. Norton won both the Junior and Senior TTs in 1953, coming in first, second and third in both events.

The last Grand Prix victory by a Manx was in Yugoslavia in 1969,

ENGINE: 498cc (30ci) ohc single, 82x94.3mm, air-cooled
POWER: 45–50bhp at 6500–7000rpm
GEARBOX: 4-speed foot change
FINAL DRIVE: chain
WEIGHT: n/a
TOP SPEED: 200km/h (125mph) plus

ROYAL ENFIELD TRIALS BULLET

In 1949, Royal Enfield began building its Bullet range, which featured a new frame with swinging-arm rear suspension. This was very successful in off-road trials and scrambling machines. The engine was an all-alloy, overhead-valve single-cylinder design equipped with an integral oil reservoir in the same way as pre-war machines, though it was now relocated to the rear of the engine.

The Trials Bullet had modified suspension and telescopic forks, small-diameter drum brakes, high-rise exhaust, special mudguards, wheels and tyres and a different state of engine tune. It was one of the top trials machines of the 1950s. The Bullet line remained in production with Royal Enfield until 1963. However, even after that, the standard 346cc (91ci) model found a new home in Madras, where it was built under licence.

ENGINE: 346cc (21ci) air-cooled single-cylinder
POWER: 17bhp
GEARBOX: 4-speed
FINAL DRIVE: chain
WEIGHT: 141kg (310lb)
TOP SPEED: 105km/h (65mph)

SCOTT SQUIRREL

The 1950s Squirrel clearly showed its lineage as a descendant of the pre-war Flying Squirrel. Indeed, early post-war models had the same girder forks as their earlier cousins, although these were later replaced by Dowty telescopics. Other than the ignition system, which now used coil ignition rather than the Magdyno, there was little different about the 'new' model.

The last of the Squirrel models continued to rely on the familiar 596cc (36ci) two-stroke twin, and it also still used deflector pistons. Meanwhile, at East Germany's MZ (known formerly as DKW – the firm that, ironically, had once borrowed from Scott's designs), work was beginning that was to revolutionize two-stroke technology. The Squirrel was, quite simply, out of date when it entered production.

ENGINE: 596cc (36ci) two-stroke parallel-twin, 73x71.4mm, liquid-cooled
POWER: 30bhp at 5000rpm
GEARBOX: 3-speed foot change
FINAL DRIVE: chain
WEIGHT: 170kg (375lb)
TOP SPEED: 137km/h (85mph)

The Squirrel belonged to an earlier era even when production began at Scott's works at Shipley in 1950. Even in 1972, Squirrels were still being built at the new plant in Birmingham.

AERMACCHI

The Nieuport-Macchi firm was founded in the Italian town of Varese by Giulio Macchi. From its beginnings in 1912, the firm was important to Italian aviation. Under the name of Aeronautica Macchi, soon shortened to Aermacchi, it built a number of aircraft designs. However, after the end of World War II, the firm needed a new market.

The first ground vehicle to come out of the Aermacchi works was a three-wheeled truck, and the first motorcycle appeared soon afterwards. This was designed by Lino Tonti, who had also worked for Benelli. His creation was very unusual: an open-frame 123cc (8ci) machine with the engine/gearbox unit pivoting with the rear suspension. It sold respectably well and turned in a good performance in long-distance events. More models followed.

In 1955, Tonti created a pair of machines intended specifically for record attempts. They were fully streamlined and powered by 48cc (3ci) and 74cc (5ci) engines respectively. Both were successful in setting a number of records, but Tonti soon left to join FB Mondial. He was replaced by Alfredo Bianchi

Bianchi's first design for Aermacchi was the Chimera, which was unveiled in 1956. It began life as a 175cc (11ci), but a 246.2cc (15ci) version soon appeared. The production machine also lost the full-enclosure styling it had stared out with, and went out 'naked'. It did well and was the basis for a whole generation of Aermacchi motorcycles for more than a decade.

A tuned 175cc (11ci) racing version appeared in 1958, followed by a full racing machine the next year. This was the Ala d'Oro (Golden Wing), and could top 161km/h (100mph). It was joined by a 250cc (12ci) racer for 1960, which made an impressive debut at the Dutch TT. A batch of replicas was made for general sale.

By now, Aermacchi was part owned by Harley-Davidson and had eight road machines in general production. These included four tourers (the Chimeras 175 and 250, the Ala Bianca 175 and the Ala Azzura 250), two sportsters (the Ala Rossa 175 and Ala Verde) and large-wheel scooters (the Zeffiro 125 and 150).

Aermacchi's top-performance production machine at the time was the Ala Verde, capable of 138km/h (86mph). It led the way into the early 1960s as sales increased steadily. Despite some

reliability problems with the race machines, the firm continued to contest Grand Prix events and its racers gradually gained bigger engines before the firm switched to two-stroke racing machines.

The first of the two-stroke bikes appeared in 1967, as well as the M125 Rapido, a road machine whose race variant appeared later that year. This was the basis of Aermacchi's line of racing machines for the late 1960s and onwards. From 1972 onwards, Aermacchi traded under the AMF Harley-Davidson name. The firm closed down in 1978.

Aermacchi produced a family of machines based on the Chimera. Alterations in styling, equipment and engines created touring, roadster and sports versions.

DMW

DMW (Dawson's Motors of Wolverhampton) had been involved in the motorcycle industry before and after World War II, but did not begin manufacturing motorcycles until 1950.

Almost all DMW machines were powered by Villiers engines. The initial range used 99cc (6ci) 1F, 122cc (7ci) 10D or 197cc (12ci) 6E units. These were installed in a frame that, for the largest

machines, offered plunger rear suspension as an option, and in all cases had MP telescopic forks, produced by DMW.

In 1951, DMW produced a pair of De Luxe models with square-section tube frames, and the 99cc (6ci) machine was dropped soon after. A 197cc (12ci) Competition model was added for 1952, and in 1953 the firm surprised observers by bringing out 125cc (8ci) and 170cc

(10ci) machines powered by French overhead-valve engines rather than the usual Villiers units. Two more models followed: one was a 249cc (15ci) overhead-camshaft engine; the other a 125cc (8ci) double overhead-camshaft racing machine, the Hornet.

However, DMW soon returned to the two-strokes, bringing out the Leda with a 147cc (9ci) 29C engine and the Cortina with the 224cc

(14ci) 1H. A number of specialized competition machines also appeared. In 1957, as scooters became more popular, the Bambi was brought out. This machine was powered by a 99cc (6ci) Villiers 4F engine under a monocoque frame that was also the body. The Bambi lasted only until the early 1960s, but it was replaced by the Deemster. This was a 249cc (15ci) machine that was part scooter and part motorcycle.

In 1962, DMW took over Ambassador, and the following year it brought out a new 247cc (15ci) competition model called the Hornet. The range became gradually smaller through the 1960s, and by 1967 there were only two models left in production, the Hornet and the Highland Trials model. Production of motorcycles ended that year, although the firm continued to make parts and Villiers-type engines for a time.

GITAN

San Marino-based Gitan started out with a single-cylinder, two-stroke with piston-port induction, which bore a resemblance to the DKW RT125, and a 160cc (10ci) four-stroke powered by an overhead-valve, unit construction, single-cylinder engine. Of these initial models, the two-stroke was more popular. It began life with blade-type front forks and plunger rear suspension, but eventually received telescopic forks and a swinging-arm frame.

The range was joined in 1955 by a 175cc (11ci) four-stroke single, which was fairly conventional. However, after this, the firm became more adventurous, marketing the Grillo (Cricket), a machine similar in many ways to Honda's C50 Cub model.

Times were hard in the Italian motorcycle industry of the 1960s, but Gitan managed to survive by building mostly utilitarian 50cc (3ci) commuter machines. There were occasional sports bikes too, also ultra-lightweights, which generated publicity and prestige. As things got better and other firms began building bigger machines, Gitan continued to make small bikes. The firm was unable to survive the recession of the 1980s and was closed down in 1985.

Like many other firms, Gitan built a machine based on the incredibly successful DKW 125, and then moved on to its own designs. It survived one recession by making workhorse transport machines but went under in the 1980s.

MIVAL

Mival (Metalimeccanica Italiana Valtrompia SpA) manufactured machine tools but also built motorcycles for a time. The first machine was a 125cc (8ci) two-stroke, and it was joined in 1954 by an Italian version of the Messerschmitt three-wheel car. This was built with a Mival engine rather than the original Sachs.

In 1956, Mival produced the world's first production roadster with an overhead-valve engine and a five-speed gearbox. This was a 125cc (8ci) machine, though Mival did produce larger models, mainly for competition. These included a 175cc (11ci) four-stroke single for the ISDT.

Mival is best known for its motocross machines, and in the 1950s there was a range of unusual 250cc (15ci), 350cc (21ci) and 500cc (31ci) double overhead-cam singles, with five- or six-speed gearboxes. In 1966, the year before motorcycle production ceased, Mival had 10 models in its range, including the Presa Diretta commuter moped and the 200cc (12ci) overhead-valve Principe motorcycle. However, in 1967, the firm left the motorcycle industry.

Mival produced a range of exotic machines with 250cc (15ci), 350cc (21ci) and 500cc (30ci) engines and broke new ground with many models.

MOTOBI

Guiseppe Benelli left the family firm he had helped set up in 1949 to create his own motorcycle company: Moto B Pesaro, quickly shortened to Motobi. The first machine appeared in 1950, a roadster with a horizontal 98cc (6ci), single-cylinder, two-stroke engine. It sold well and spawned a range of similar machines with larger engines.

The first twin, Spring Lasting, came out in 1952, starting life as a 200cc (12ci) machine, but a 250cc (15ci) version soon appeared. Both variants were known for excellent performance and pioneered rotary-valve induction in Italy. The 250cc (15ci) won its class in the 1955 Milano–Taranto race.

After this, the firm decided to go over to four-stroke designs, putting out a pair of singles in 123cc (8ci) and 172cc (10ci) engine sizes. The larger of the two was named Catria and did well on the competition circuit in addition to good sales. However, Guiseppe Benelli died in 1957 and the company passed to his sons Luigi and Marco, who mended fences with the rest of the family. In 1963, Motobi and Benelli merged, though Motobi retained its identity for several years.

Motobi machines were dominant in their class for many years, winning the Italian Junior Championship 10 times between 1959 and 1972. They were successful in other arenas too, with modified versions competing in hill-climbs and other motorcycling events.

FERRARI

There is no connection between the Ferrari company that built motorcycles and the firm that has produced some of the world's most famous cars. Both, though, were based in the same province and had equally high engineering standards.

Ferrari unveiled its first machine in 1952, a parallel twin with an overhead camshaft. This machine boasted a well-designed 199cc (12ci) engine, driving through a four-speed gearbox built in unit. This went into a modern-looking frame with swinging-arm rear suspension and oil-damped telescopic forks. Next, in 1953, came a 175cc (11ci) version. These machines were four-strokes, but it was the two-stroke range that

provided most of Ferrari's income.

Ferrari's two-strokes were built in 98cc (6ci), 124cc (8ci0 and 148cc (9ci) sizes; all were singles. Their famous name and the bright red paintwork could not compensate for the fact that they were overpriced, and sales were never very good. As sales of motorcycles in Italy fell off in the late 1950s, Ferrari Moto was a casualty, closing its doors in 1959.

Ferrari Moto had no connection to the car manufacturer of the same name, but it had a lot in common in terms of quality and liking for red colour schemes. This is a 1955 148cc (3ci) single-cylinder two-stroke.

HEINKEL

Ernst Heinkel was a critical figure in the rise of German air power in the interwar years, and after World War II his firm needed to find a new outlet. Work began in 1951 and resulted in a 149cc (9ci) scooter called the Tourist. This was followed by the 49cc (3ci) Perle (pearl) moped, which

featured a light alloy frame. The Perle was an impressive achievement, being designed and put into production in just six weeks, but it was expensive and did not sell well.

In 1956, after giving the Tourist a new, larger engine, Heinkel released the Kabinen, or 'cabin

scooter'. A distinctly peculiar vehicle, it had car-type steering and an independent suspension powered by either the 174cc (11ci) Tourist engine, or a specially developed 198cc (12ci) version. Then came the Roller 112, a 125cc (8ci) scooter that was not, however, a success.

After Heinkel's death in 1958, the firm began building micro-cars in Ireland and importing them into Britain under the name of Trojan. The Tourist was updated in 1960 and joined in 1962 by a new scooter design, the '150'. Both ceased production in 1965, and the firm returned to aircraft production.

KREIDLER

Kreidler started out as a supplier of semi-finished metal for industrial use across Germany, and got into motorcycle manufacture as a sideline. The firm's expertise with specialized alloys, tubing and forgings stood it in good stead, and the first product, the K50 moped, was a success. The K50 was powered by a very good 49cc (3ci) two-stroke engine; the rest of the machine was conventional.

Having created a machine that sold well, Kreidler concentrated on 50cc (3ci) machines and became known as 'King of the Tiddlers'. A de luxe version of the K50 (named K51) was followed in 1955 by the R50 scooterette. In the same year, the firm introduced a light-alloy cylinder with hard-chrome bore.

The most famous Kreidler machine arrived in 1957 – the Florett (Foil). This was converted into a racing version (the Renn Florett) simply by tuning the engine, changing the handlebars and removing the mudguards. It could reach 121km/h (75mph).

A new model appeared for

1962, with disc-valves and twin carburettors. With a four-speed, foot-change gearbox and three-speed overdrive controlled by a twist-grip, this machine had 12 gear ratios and used chrome-molybdenum in its frame for strength and lightness. Many hours of development in the wind tunnel perfected the machine.

Kreidler machines did well in competition, providing a strong presence in the 50cc (3ci) class. Its riders set new world speed records in the 50cc, 75cc and 100cc categories, and all with the same 49cc (3ci) engine, but it was not until 1973 that the marque finally began winning world titles. In all, it took eight 50cc World

Championships from 1973–1982, along with a 50cc world speed record of 228km/h (141mph).

At the beginning of the 1980s, however, the firm was in financial difficulties despite its racing successes. Sales slumped and despite launching a range of new machines, Kreidler went into liquidation in 1982.

There was nothing 'junior' about the way 50cc (3ci) machines were raced in a bid for the world title – a title taken by Kreidler on eight occasions.

LAMBRETTA 250 V-TWIN RACER

ITALY 1951

Lambretta's 250 V-twin has a peculiar history. In the late 1940s, scooters were big business in Italy and many of the larger motorcycle firms were beginning to expand into the market. Lambretta decided to build a full-sized motorcycle to show that it could – and as a warning to the bigger firms.

Designed by Guiseppe Salmaggi, the excellent Lambretta 250 V-twin was unveiled in 1951. With a top-class engine mated to a 5-speed gearbox, good brakes and telescopic front forks, the machine was built around a novel 'backbone' frame. This comprised a large-diameter single top tube running downwards to pressed-steel lugs, which extended forward to form the main engine mounting. There were no front down members. The design was tested with both torsion bar suspension and hydraulic rear shock absorbers, and was impressively fast. It was never raced, but the testing results alone were enough to make other manufacturers sit up and take notice.

ENGINE: 247cc (15ci) sohc transverse 90-degrees V-twin, 54x54mm, air-cooled
POWER: 30bhp at 8000rpm
GEARBOX: 5-speed foot change
FINAL DRIVE: shaft
WEIGHT: n/a
TOP SPEED: 190km/h (120mph)

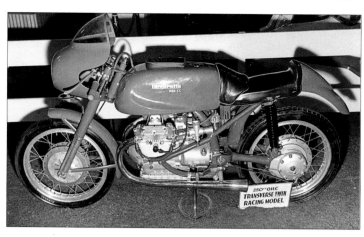

The Lambretta 250cc V-twin racer was designed by Guiseppe Salmaggi and built as a warning to motorcycle manufacturers such as Moto Guzzi that Lambretta could invade their market niche if provoked.

PANNONIA

HUNGARY 1951–75

Pannonia was one of the marques manufactured at the state-owned Csepel factory in Budapest. (The others were Danuvia, Tunde and Panni.) The first Pannonia model, appearing in 1951, was a single-cylinder, two-stroke machine not unlike contemporary Jawas. This was followed by others, including a very good 246cc (15ci) two-stroke twin and a range of off-road competition bikes. These won several Hungarian national motocross titles.

Like many contemporary firms in eastern Europe, Pannonia sold its products under a range of brand names, such as White (for the market in the USA). The main problem with using a range of names was a lack of brand identity. Where other firms had an established reputation as a result of their sporting presence, White had to spend a disproportionate amount on advertising – and the results were still disappointing.

The story was similar in most Western countries, but in Eastern Europe Pannonia did much better. After 1970, however, even this market was beginning to dry up and the firm was forced to close down in 1975.

Pannonia sold its machines under various labels overseas. Bikes such as this 1965 single-cylinder, 250cc (15ci) two-stroke went to the US market under the White label. Sales suffered from a lack of brand identity rather than any deficiency in quality.

TESTI

ITALY 1951–83

Bologna-based Testi used engines bought in from Sachs, Franco Morini and Minerelli to build ultra-lightweight motorcycles and mopeds. Among the most famous models were the Trail King, the Corsa 2000 and the Champion Special P6, a sports moped.

The firm also produced the Militar for military customers. This machine featured an eight-speed gearbox as well as a range of accessories, including a ski attachment, gun-holder, fog lamp, and even a bottle for fast inflation and repair of damaged tyres. The machine found favour with the Italian and Finnish armies.

In 1980, Testi was riding high. The range consisted of 10 machines, all in the 50cc class. In addition to the Militar and Champion Special, there were models aimed at motocross, trials and enduro competition, as well as scooters and mopeds for the commuter market. Testi machines were sold under the Horex name in West Germany by the Roth organization, and in the UK by the Mick Walker Group.

This 1979 Testi is typical of the style. Testi built a range of small machines for on and off road, using engines bought from a range of suppliers.

VICTORIA V35 BERGMEISTER

GERMANY 1951

The Bergmeister (Mountain Master) used an unusual 28 V-twin engine driving through a four-speed box to a shaft final drive. Its claimed top speed of 130km/h (81mph) was impressive, but the ability to deliver power across a wide range of throttle settings was what really caught users' attention.

Actual power output from the 347cc (21ci) engine was modest at 21hp, but the machine was easily capable of pulling a sidecar. It had several other good features, such as excellent brakes and good suspension, but initially suffered from very severe engine vibration problems that took a long time to

eliminate. This meant that the machine could not go out and start recouping its development costs for two years after its debut. This got the company into serious financial difficulty, and when it did finally become available sales were affected by the price tag, which was rather high.

ENGINE: 347cc (21ci) ohv V-twin, 64x54mm, air-cooled
POWER: 21 bhp at 6300rpm
GEARBOX: 4-speed foot change
FINAL DRIVE: shaft
WEIGHT: 176.5kg (389lb)
TOP SPEED: 130km/h (81mph)

ZUNDAPP KS601

GERMANY 1951

Zundapp's KS750 ranked alongside the BMW R75 as one of Germany's classic wartime motorcycles. Returning to civilian production after the war, Zundapp produced the KS600, which was a rather dated design using a

pressed-steel frame, blade girder forks and rigid rear end. However, it was followed by something rather better.

This was the KS601, which became known as the Green Elephant, for its colour scheme

and generally robust character. Powered by a 597cc (36ci) overhead-valve engine with a separate 25mm (1in) Bing carburettor for each cylinder, cast-iron barrels and light-alloy heads, the KS601 delivered 28hp at

4700rpm. Driving through a four-speed gearbox constructed in unit with the engine, this gave a top speed of 145km/h (90mph), making the new Zundapp Germany's fastest production bike. The KS601 was also impressive with a sidecar. It was capable of 120km/h (75mph), and won several International Six Day Trial gold medals during the early 1950s in this configuration.

The Green Elephant was a very good machine, but it was eclipsed by superior sales of BMW's R50/60 series in 1955, and by 1959 it was no longer in production. About 5500 machines were built in total.

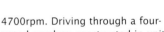

ENGINE: 597cc (36ci) ohv 2v flat twin, 75x67.6mm, air-cooled
POWER: 28bhp at 4700rpm
GEARBOX: 4-speed foot change
FINAL DRIVE: shaft
WEIGHT: 202kg (445lb)
TOP SPEED: 141km/h (87.5mph)

The 'green elephant' (this one is red, as it happens) was capable of making 120km/h (75mph) with a sidecar attached. Solo, it was capable of 141km/h (87.5mph).

ADLER M250

GERMANY 1952

The M250 was based on the 192cc (12ci) M200, which appeared a year earlier. As well as a bigger engine, the M250 had better brakes and a range of minor upgrades. It also boasted plunger rear suspension and leading-link forks with 'clock' springs,

The M250 was successful in competition, winning the Warsage 24-hour race against a field including impressive 350cc (21ic) models, and performed very well in the ISDT. In 1952, Adler entered four machines and took three golds and a bronze; it took five golds the next year. A new version of the M250, and a sports version, were released in 1953. The engine was also used in dirt bikes.

ENGINE: 247.3cc (15ci) 2s parallel twin, 54x54mm, air-cooled
POWER: 16bhp at 5590rpm
GEARBOX: 4-speed foot change
WEIGHT: 140kg (283lb)
TOP SPEED: 114km/h (71mph)

BRIDGESTONE

JAPAN 1952–68

The Bridgestone name is associated today with tyres, and motorcycle production never amounted to more than 10 per cent of the firm's revenue. However, from the early 1950s through to the late 1960s, the firm produced a range of machines, beginning with a simple 49cc (3ci) two-stroke moped. Later models included 98cc (6ci), 175cc (11ci) and 250cc (15ci) singles.

Bridgestone's last machine, the 350GTR twin, was their most noteworthy. It was aimed at the US market and featured the most impressive specification of any two-stroke. It was also extremely fast and could leave many 650cc (40ci) twins standing.

Similar in many ways to the contemporary Suzuki Super Six, the Bridgestone machine was more advanced in several ways, most notably because of its use of disc-valve induction. It also had hard chrome cylinder bores, allowing very tight piston tolerances. Running was smooth and vibration free, and the machine's huge acceleration was matched by good handling and brakes.

Despite claims that the 350GTR could manage more, its top speed was about 150km/h (93mph) – enough to make it the fastest two-stroke road machine ever built. Sales were hampered by the high price tag, however, along with doubts about durability. Bridgestone stopped making motorcycles in 1968, concentrating on its tyre business thereafter.

The Bridgestone 350GTR was a very advanced roadster when it appeared in the late 1960s, featuring six-speed transmission, disc-valve induction, 'Jet-lube' lubrication and coated bores.

COMET

Bologna-based Comet was in business for only five years, but in that time it attracted comment for its interesting and innovative machines. The 175cc (11ci) Moto Comet was designed by Alfonso Drusiani, who had established a reputation with FB Mondial.

The Comet's engine was a vertical twin with light-alloy cylinders and heads, the overhead-camshaft being driven by a chain located between the cylinders. It used overhung cranks, with gear primary and chain camshaft. The four-speed gearbox was built in unit. This was installed in a modern frame with hydraulically damped rear shock absorbers for the swinging-arm and telescopic forks.

Following a 1953 sports version, in 1954 the company demonstrated an experimental variant with a 250cc (15ci) four-stroke engine designed by Drusiani. It used the slide-valve principle. The barrel had three bores in line, a main cylinder between two smaller ones. Three crankshaft assemblies were geared together, with the 'valve cylinder' pistons at half engine speed. There was also a new 250cc (15ci) Comet vertical twin, and a racing 175cc (11ci) single with overhead-cam and outside flywheel.

NSU MAX/SPORTMAX

The NSU 'Max' series of singles included the Max, Supermax, Special Max and the Sportmax, of which the 1952 Max was the first. It was powered by a highly unorthodox 247cc/ 15ci (69x66mm/2.7x2.6in) single overhead-cam engine, which was mounted in a pressed-steel frame with leading-link front forks.

The engine was designed by Albert Roder and featured a type of valve gear unique among motorcycle power units. This used long connecting rods in a tunnel cast integrally on the nearside of the cylinder to drive the overhead-valve gear. At their ends, these rods carried an eye encircling counterbalanced eccentric discs connected to the half-time pinion and the overhead-camshaft. As the engine revolved, so the eccentrics imparted a reciprocating motion, which was transferred to the valve gear. Hairpin valve springs were

used and the entire mechanism was enclosed.

Only a handful of Max models were made in 1952, but the following year about 24,000 were constructed. The model was updated to the Special Max in 1955, getting better brakes and a larger fuel tank. There was also a limited-edition Sportmax racing model, which took the 250cc World Championship.

The NSU Max family comprised the Max, Supermax, Special Max and the Sportsmax (pictured here), a dedicated racer that won the world championship.

The Supermax came along in 1956, with new engine tuning and twin-shock, swinging-arm rear suspension. It was capable of 127km/h (79mph). This model remained in production until 1963, by which time almost 100,000 Maxes of all types had been built.

ENGINE: 247cc (15ci) ohc 2v single, 69x66mm, air-cooled
POWER: 18bhp at 6750rpm
GEARBOX: 4-speed foot change
FINAL DRIVE: chain
WEIGHT: 155kg (342lb)
TOP SPEED: 133km/h (83mph)

NSU RENNMAX

At the same time that NSU was working on the Max series of singles, designer Dr Walter Froede was developing the Rennmax, a 250cc (15ci) double overhead-cam parallel twin. The design was developed over three years and was entirely new.

The initial Rennmax went into production in 1952 with a 247.34cc (15.1ci) engine developing 25hp at 9000rpm. By the end of the year, it was delivering 29hp at 9800rpm, and development continued thereafter. The machine itself was beautifully engineered, with unit-constructed engine and gearbox and considerable use of advanced alloys.

In 1953, the model received a new spine chassis constructed of pressed steel, with the engine supported only at the rear. This, coupled with leading-link front forks, a wrap-around aluminium tank and a miniature fairing, gave the new version a very different look to its predecessor. It could also deliver 32hp and won the World Championship that year.

In 1954, the Rennmax was again updated, with some engine modifications and a lower overall weight. It also gained an extra gear and another 4hp, making for a top speed of 216km/h (135mph). The Rennmax won the World Championship again that year.

This 1953 Rennmax has a 250cc (15ci) double overhead-cam twin and is built on a pressed-steel frame. It features leading-link forks and lightweight aluminium bodywork.

ENGINE: 249.3cc (15ci) dohc 2v parallel twin, 55.9x50.8mm, air-cooled
POWER: 36bhp at 11,200rpm
GEARBOX: 6-speed foot change
FINAL DRIVE: Chain
WEIGHT: Chain
TOP SPEED: 217km/h (135mph)

SUZUKI

Michio Suzuki set up in business in 1909, producing silk-weaving looms in the town of Hamamatsu. His first foray into powered transport, a plan to licence-build Austin 7 cars, fell through in 1937 due to the need to switch to war production. After the war, silk was in short supply, so Suzuki began making agricultural machinery and heaters, and eventually came back to the transport market.

The first Suzuki machine was a 36cc (2ci) powered bicycle called the 'Power Free'. It went on general sale in 1952 and was followed by a 60cc (4ci) model called 'Diamond Free'. This machine won its class in the 1953 Mount Fuji hill climb. Then, in 1954, the first true Suzuki motorcycle appeared. This was the 90cc (5ci) Colleda, a four-stroke with performance good enough to beat 85 other machines up Mount Fuji that year. A 125cc (8ci) two-stroke version followed in 1955.

After building a new factory and exploring the US market, Suzuki produced the 125 Colleda RB race bike. It did respectably well in competition and, with encouragement from Soichiro Honda, Suzuki entered the Isle of Man TT in 1960. Results were uninspiring at first. However, Suzuki managed to lure Ernst Degner away from MZ in 1961, and thus gained insider information about MZ's rotary-valve, two-stroke technology. Suzuki machines won the 50cc (3ci) championship in 1962, and dominated it for several years after that. The firm also won the 1963 and 1965 125cc (7.5ci) titles.

However, the firm's bread and butter was small commuter machines. Typical of these were K and M series two-stroke singles of the early 1960s, which were made in huge numbers: 500,000 of the K10 and K11. The K and M series machines were supplanted in 1964 by the B100P, or 'Bloop'. This remained in production until the mid-1970s, when it was known as the B120 Student. Other machines were similarly long lived.

Although utilitarian, these machines were well made and had many attractive features, including an oil-injection system that negated the need for the rider to mix the fuel and oil himself. Suzukis had separate oil tanks, and these supplied lubricant via the CCI (Controlled Crankshaft Injection) system according to engine revs and throttle opening.

Suzuki road bikes became more sporty in the mid-1960s with the arrival of the T20 Super Six, which was sold in the USA as the X6. It was a 247cc (15ci) two-stroke twin

with a six-speed gearbox, delivering 29hp for a top speed of 145km/h (90mph). Suzuki followed with the T200 and then the T500 Cobra (sold as the Titan in the USA), which could make 177km/h (110mph). This machine remained in production until 1977.

Other additions to the range in the 1970s included the GT380 and GT550, both two-stroke triples, plus the GT125 and GT185 twins. The GT550 was produced until 1977 and the GT380 until 1979. There was also the first of Suzuki's trail bikes, the TS125, which was followed by a range of similar machines in various small engine capacities.

In the mid-1970s, changes were occurring among the mid-range machines, as four-stroke propulsion was replacing two-stroke. One of the new machines was the GS750, an air-cooled, four-cylinder twin-cam design that was similar in many ways to equivalent machines from Honda and Kawasaki, but somewhat quicker. It had a stiffer frame than the Honda and handled better. A year later, Suzuki followed it with the 997cc (61ci) GS1000, which was the largest model to date, and fast at 217km/h (135mph).

Suzuki continued to build basic machines such as the GS400 and its successors, the GS425, 540 and 500. These were inexpensive but reliable, with decent performance and overall good value for money. The trail bikes of the time included the 780cc (48ci) DR800, which was the biggest single on the market. However, the lighter DR350 and DR125 were better off-road machines.

As the 1980s dawned, the GS sports range became the four-valve GSX series, and the tourers were also updated. The 1980 GSX1100 delivered 100hp and was followed in 1981 by the Katana, which was available with various four-cylinder, 16-valve engines ranging from 250cc (15ci) to 1100cc (67ci).

An experiment with turbocharging, the XN85 Turbo, proved unsuccessful. The GSX-R series of race-replica machines did rather better. These were given a marketing boost by the marque's timely win in the 1983 World Endurance Championship, just before the range went on sale. The GSX-750R was very successful in the marketplace and also in clubman racing, and was followed by 250cc (15ci), 400cc (24ci) and 600cc (37ci) versions.

There were steady improvements all across the range, with new sports tourers and a less temperamental GSX-R1100 to accompany the 750 stablemate.

This machine looked great, could manage 249km/h (155mph), and yet coped well with normal riding. In 1990 came the RGV250, a 60hp V-twin capable of 217km/h (135mph). This was about as close as the average customer could get to owning a Grand Prix race bike.

The Bandit 600 of 1995 could have fallen between several stools. It was not a racer, not a tourer, not a typical street machine – but it had characteristics of all three. Many machines of this kind have proven unpopular and vanished without trace, but the Bandit got it right and was bought in large numbers by a wide range of customers. It was followed by a 1200cc (73ci) version and, in 1999, by the SV650 V-twin.

The V-twin TL1000 of 1997 posed a serious threat to Ducati. With a 125hp fuel-injected eight-valve twin-cam V-twin, the TL1000 was not only cheaper but also more user-friendly than a Ducati, and more exciting than Honda's VTR1000 Firestorm. Suzuki followed up with the more powerful TL1000R in 1998, as a basis for the company's V-twin Superbike.

In the late 1990s, the resurgent scooter market offered a new set of possibilities and Suzuki took full advantage. In 1998, it announced

the 250cc (15ci) Burgman superscooter, and followed it with a 400cc (24ci) edition a year later. This was the largest scooter available and could make 161km/h (100mph). Meanwhile, at the other end of the market, the GSX1300R Hayabusa was delivering 173hp. Capable of 0–97km/h (0–60mph) in 2.75 seconds, it could reach 225km/h (140mph) in a further seven seconds.

The T20 Super Six was marketed as the X6 in the USA. Suzuki's first true sports machine, it was capable of 144km/h (90mph) and featured a new 247cc (15ci) engine in its tubular steel frame.

The Suzuki T500 went through several incarnations. Starting in 1968 as the Cobra, it was fast and civilized for a two-stroke but with quirky handling. By the time this 1970 Titan arrived, the T500 had evolved into a very good machine.

TRITON

ENGLAND 1952

Part Triumph, Part Norton – there were as many variants on the concept as there were enthusiastic owners trying to build the very best bike from whatever parts were available.

The name Triton is cobbled together from the names Triumph and Norton – just as the bikes were. Triton was not a 'real' motorcycle marque but the result of countless enthusiasts taking bits of bikes and building themselves a perfect machine – or, at least, trying to do so.

There is no definitive Triton specification. The usual format was to take a Norton 'Featherbed' frame and mate it to a Triumph 500cc (31ci) parallel twin engine, finishing the machine with whatever parts were desired or available. The Norton frame provided a comfortable ride and

good handling while the Triumph engine was affordably powerful.

Backed up by a pretty fair trade in spares from written-off or dismantled bikes, this practice produced a considerable variety of results. Some were monstrosities, most were decent, and some were very good indeed. Anyone willing

to build a bike in this way was bound also to want to fiddle with it. Tritons tended to be drilled for lightness and to have extraneous parts removed, and tended to undergo constant change as the owner scrounged or bought some sought-after part.

Tritons were ridden – usually fast – in all corners of the country, but their most famous haunt was London's North Circular road, and in particular the Ace Café. This was in an age when there were no motorways, and riders did indeed race from one café to another (hence the term 'café racers').

Many bikes were put together from other parts of course, to all manner of home-grown specifications. Norvins (a Norton frame with a Vincent engine) are notable, but were few in number compared to the Triton. Indeed, this unofficial marque is not dead even today. Occasionally, someone will mate up an old Norton frame with a Triumph engine – and another Triton is born.

DEMM

ITALY 1953–82

Milan-based Demm manufactured a wide range of lightweight motorcycles over almost three decades. In the mid-1950s, the firm offered the TL and TV Turismo Lusso, beautifully engineered overhead-cam machines with unit-construction 175cc (11ci) engines and a four-speed gearbox. There was also a pair of 125cc (8ci) machines: the two-stroke Normale Lusso and overhead camshaft Turismo. Both machines used many components in common to reduce costs.

Demm also sold a range of Motocarris three-wheeled trucks, which were almost an obligatory part of any Itlaian marque's range at that time.

These used a different engine, a 175c (11ci) two-stroke with fan cooling. The firm supplied engines to other manufacturers, including Testi, with whom it had a close association.

Despite setting no less than 24 world records in 1956, the Demm range gradually shrank until there was only one model, the Dove, on sale in the 1970s. The recession of the early 1980s finally killed off the marque.

The rather crowded-looking engine space aboard a Demm. The marque primarily made small-engined machines and also sold power units to rivals, including Testi.

DEVIL MOTO

ITALY 1953–57

Devil Moto was another short-lived but briefly impressive Italian marque. The firm started out in 1953, building 125cc (8ci) and 160cc (10ci) lightweights and a 250cc (15ci) three-wheeled delivery vehicle. These modest beginnings

led in 1955 to a 48cc (3ci) moped, the Develino, available in standard and sport configurations. A four-stroke single was launched that year, and the 160cc (10ci) and 175cc (11ci) machines were relaunched in Sport form in 1956.

The 175cc (11ci) delivered 15hp at 7800 rpm, and its top speed of over 135km/h (80mph) would have been considered pretty good for a machine of its size even 20 or 30 years later. The racing version, with 20hp at 11,000 rpm,

a five-speed gearbox and a top speed of more than 180km/h (110mph), was even more impressive. However, Moto Devil could not convert these qualities into market success, and it faded away after 1957.

GEROSA

Brescia-based Gerosa started out with 125cc (8ci) and 175cc (11ci) machines built around their own overhead-valve engines, which were built in unit with the gearbox. This was installed into a tubular frame with telescopic front and pivoted rear forks. The wire wheels had full-width hubs with drum brakes, and alloy rims were fitted to the more sporting versions. It was common practice at the time in Italy to build several variants – tourers, sports and street machines, for example – around a common basic model.

Gerosa discovered that building engines in house was too expensive and began buying from Minarelli, which had cost benefits but eroded the individual style of the machines. For some years, the firm continued to build a range including 50cc (3ci) mopeds and motorcycles, but it was gradually edged out of the market by its larger competitors.

Gerosa originally built its own engines but this proved uneconomical and later machines used bought-in engines, Zundapp in this case.

GREEVES

Greeves was founded in Essex by Bert Greeves and his cousin, Derry Preston-Cobb. The two men went into business as Invacar, building invalid carriages. However, in 1950, Greeves and works manager Frank Byford decided to build a motorcycle as a testbed for a weatherproof rubber suspension then under evaluation. In 1953, the machine went on sale to the general public.

Powered by a 197cc (12ci) Villiers engine, the Greeves was popular with scramblers and trials riders, and the rubber suspension survived for a few years before being replaced with a more conventional setup. The machine's unusual H-section frame also persisted for many years before being joined by a tubular option.

Export sales were good, and a 250cc (15ci) version was produced as a road machine as well as being bought by some police forces. Then came the Hawkstone, a 197cc (12ci) scrambler that was named for the venue and which was very competitive, even against larger machines. Greeves machines won the European 250cc Championship in 1962 and 1963.

Things began to go downhill, however, after excellent Spanish scrambling machines began to be imported into Britain in large numbers. The firm also struggled to find a replacement for its Villiers power units when production stopped. The firm's founders retired in 1977 and production ceased.

The Villiers/Greeves combination proved successful on and off the road, with models like the Anglian.

KTM

KTM (Kraftfahrzeuge Trunkenpolz Mattighofen) built its first motorcycle in 1953. Two years later, the firm's name changed when Ernst Kronreif became Hans Trunkenpolz's partner, though the initials remained the same. The partnership worked out well, with KTM going on to become one of Austria's principal motorcycle producers.

The first machines used 98cc (6ci) Rotax engines. As well as true motorcycles, there were two-stroke mopeds and scoters using Puch, Sachs and Rotax engines. The firm produced competition bikes in the 1950s, but from 1960 to 1965 it concentrated exclusively on building mopeds.

Returning to motorcycle production, KTM began building motocross bikes with its own engines aboard, and these proved to be very successful. In 1977, KTM won the 250cc Motocross Championship. Competition experience fed back into production machines, which were updated accordingly.

Although the firm had some tough times in the early 1990s, it managed to struggle through and brought out a range of off-road machines. These included a 125cc (8ci) two-stroke trail bike as well as 193cc (12ci), 297cc (18ci), and 368cc (22ci) two-stroke and 398cc (24ci), 539cc (33ci) and 625cc (38ci) four-stroke Enduro and Supermoto machines. The latter is a French invention, essentially consisting of scramble and motocross bikes with road tyres.

In 1998, now operating under new management, the firm opened a rider training course at Mallory Park in Leicestershire, England. It also began to experiment with a new V-twin motor soon after.

MASERATI

Maserati is a name more commonly associated with cars than motorcycles, but Carlo Maserati, the eldest of six brothers, was involved with two-wheelers very early on. Carlo built and raced a machine of his own design and won events in 1899 and 1900, before moving into the four-wheel arena where others of his family were already working.

Officine Alfieri Maserati SpA was set up in Bologna in 1914, and spent World War I making spark plugs and working on aero engines. Until World War II, the firm concentrated on racing cars, but was bought out by Adolfo Orsi in 1938 and moved to Modena after the war.

From the Modena works came more Grand Prix cars and also a new range of motorcycles, starting with a 123cc (8ci) two-stroke and a 158cc (10ci) overhead-valve in 1953. The following year, a 175cc (11ci) and a 200cc (12ci) overhead valve single joined the range.

Maserati launched what was probably the world's first production bike with a disc front brake in 1955. The machine was a 246cc (15ci) overhead-valve single with double-helical primary drive gears and twin-plug ignition. In the late 1950s, Maserati produced a 50cc (3ci) race bike, but after 1961 it concentrated on cars.

Maserati's motorcycle line included racing models like this two-stroke 75cc (4.5ci) Competizione dating from 1959. A 49cc (3ci) version was also raced in the mid-1950s.

MONDIAL CONSTELLATION 200

Mondial put out its first 200 in 1951, and unveiled the Constellation in 1952 for the following year's season. This was also a conventional machine; a 12hp, 198cc (12ci) tourer with overhead-valves. The unit-construction engine and gearbox made great use of light alloys (the engine was all alloy) and went into a neat double-cradle frame with enclosed swinging-arm rear suspension and oil-damped telescopic forks.

There were unusual features, such as the forward-operating kick-starter and, on the offside of the engine, a heel-and-toe gear lever of the sort popular among Italian designs, creating a rather cluttered appearance. Overall, however, the machine was built for comfort, economy and style rather than performance.

ENGINE: 198cc (12ci) ohv, 3v single, 62x66mm (2.4x2.6ins), air-cooled
POWER: 12bhp at 6000rpm
GEARBOX: 4-speed foot change
FINAL DRIVE: chain
WEIGHT: 112kg (146lb)
TOP SPEED: 104km/h (65mph)

MZ/MUZ

When the dust began to settle after World War II, the former DKW works at Zschopau were not only badly damaged but were also now located in Communist-held territory. DKW was forced to write them off and operate elsewhere. The factory was rebuilt, and in 1950 it resumed production under the Industrieverwaltung Fahrzenbau (IFA) brand. The first machine to come out of it was a revised DKW RT125.

In 1952, a new design appeared. This was the two-stroke BK350, and bore a resemblance to BMWs of the era. It remained in production until 1959, and during that period IFA machines began going to market under the MZ

(Motorraderwerke Zschopau) banner. The MZ name was first coined in 1953, when engineer Walter Kaaden founded the MZ Sport department to develop competition motorcycles for both road racing and endurance trials.

Early MZ racers were simply adapted road machines, but soon

As IFW moved away from its origins making copies of DKW machines, it gained a new identity in the marketplace as MZ. Early MZs still showed strong West-German influences.

specialist designs were available. By 1955, the 125cc (8ci) racing MZ single-cylinder, disc-valve two-stroke was producing 15hp and could achieve 152km/h (95mph). The 1960 model range included the 125/3, ES 175 and 250, ES 250 with sidecar, and ES 175G/250G, the latter two being complete customer versions of the factory's own International Six Day Trial bikes.

From 1956 to 1961, when he defected and went to work for Suzuki, Ernst Degner was MZ's top rider. After his unexpected departure, several other big names rode MZ machines to victory in Grand Prix racing. The top man in the late 1960s was Heinz Rossner. MZ also did extremely well in events such as the International Six Day Trial, though in the 1970s MZ lost the dominant position to Jawa.

In the 1980s, the ISDT had evolved into the ISDE (International Six Day Enduro) and undergone changes that favoured motocross machines. This let MZ come back strongly with a range of machines featuring air- and water-cooled engines, steeply angled twin rear shocks, leading axle font forks, plastic bodywork and extremely high ground clearance. Later, a brand new 500cc (3ci) with liquid-cooling, monoshock rear suspension, square-section swinging-arm, disc front brake and inverted front forks was fielded.

For many years, MZ roadsters were comfortable to ride but less than exciting. A string of machines intended to dispel this image began in 1969 with the ETS 250 Trophy Sport. One of these machines was the millionth bike to come off the MZ lines in 1970, and overall it was a lighter,

more sporty machine than its predecessors. In the 1970s, it was replaced by the TS250, and this in turn led to the 1983 ETZ model.

The ETZ is often seen as the definitive MZ roadster. An inexpensive machine, it had a couple more horsepower than its predecessor and better brakes. The two-millionth MZ bike was an ETZ 250, and the range included 150cc (9ci) and 125cc (8ci) versions. The 250cc (15ci) could also be converted into a very decent race bike with the addition of a race kit comprising a new cylinder, head, exhaust, piston and gearbox components. MZ racing became very popular in the late 1980s and 1990s.

The disruption caused by the fall of the Iron Curtain in the early 1990s caused MZ to go into a sharp decline, and it became bankrupt in 1991. The company

was reformed as Motorrad und Zweirddwerk (MuZ) in 1992 with a small workforce and new plant, but by 1996 this new firm was also bankrupt. It was bought out by the Malaysian Hong Leong company, which injected a lot of hard cash to develop new machines to revive the marque.

By 2000, MuZ's range included state-of-the-art on-off road bikes that compared with the best.

The MZ identity was first used for development of sport bikes within IFW, and it was these that carried the flag for the new MZ marque, collecting a fair amount of silverware in prestigious events, such as the ISDT, along the way.

NSU QUICKLY

GERMANY 1953

The Quickly N was in production from 1953 to 1962, and sold 540,000 units in that time. Considered by many to be the world's first true moped, it was built around a pressed-steel spine frame, pedalling gear and leading-link front suspension. The 49cc

(3ci) engine delivered 1.4hp and drove through a two-speed gearbox controlled by twist-grip. The machine also had good drum brakes, lights, a luggage rack and an integral stand.

Other variants included the L, TT, TTK, as well as the Quickly-

Cavallino, a lightweight motorcycle with tubular-steel backbone frame, telescopic forks and twin-shock rear suspension. Between all models, more than 1,111,000 Quicklys were sold – the first powered two-wheeler to break the one million sales barrier.

ENGINE: 49cc (3ci) 2s single, 40x39mm, air-cooled
POWER: 1.4bhp at 5200rpm
GEARBOX: 2-speed, twistgrip controlled
FINAL DRIVE: chain
WEIGHT: 36kg (80lb)
TOP SPEED: 51km/h (32mph)

YAMAHA

By 1948, the Nippon Gakki company had been in existence for many years (its founder, Torakusu Yamaha, died in 1916). In that year, having survived both good and bad times, it produced its first motorcycle. This provided the secure backing the firm needed to move confidently into a new marketplace.

The new motorcycle division was named in honour of the company's founder and set about producing a machine that was heavily influenced by the DKW RT125. The new machine was some time in development (and the factory to produce it did also have to be built), and it finally went out as the YA1 in 1955. It was followed by a 175 version in 1956, marking the beginning of the YA series that remained in production until the early 1970s.

Next, Yamaha decided to build a 250cc (15ci) machine. The initial concept was based on the Adler MB250, but by the time the Yamaha 250 appeared as the YD1 it was only vaguely similar. A racing version of the YD1 used a lightweight frame and was a success, taking the first three places at Asama in 1957. Yamahas also took first and second in the 125cc event. This guaranteed

commercial success for the YD1.

Like Suzuki, Yamaha built two-stroke engines for racers and commuters alike. In 1966, it came out with the twin-cylinder YL1, which could do 113km/h (70mph) in standard trim and perhaps twice that when fitted with a factory race kit. There was also a series of 250cc (15ci) twins, which began with the YDS1 in 1959 and evolved steadily into the RD series in 1973. There was also the TD series of production race machines.

Yamaha had been racing in Europe for a while when it finally achieved Grand Prix success. The 45hp 250cc (15ci) RD56 won for the first time at Belgium's high-speed Spa-Francorchamps circuit in 1963. Second places followed at Assen and the Isle of Man. The year after, Yamaha's parallel-twin RD56 took the 250cc World Championship; the first time a two-stroke had won the title. After another win, Yamaha was nudged out by Honda for a couple of seasons, but it came back in 1968.

In the United States, it seemed that everyone wanted a trail bike, so in 1968 Yamaha launched the DT1. This was a custom-designed scrambler rather than a converted road bike. It was a serious

competitor when race kitted and very good even as standard. As competitors began offering similar machines, Yamaha countered with range of machines, including a dedicated motocross machine, the YZ250.

In 1969, Yamaha departed from the usual two-stroke format with its largest bike to date. This was the XS1, a four-stroke vertical-twin. The original 653cc (40ci) machine did not handle well and was replaced with the XS650, which remained in production until the early 1980s.

As well as these big machines, Yamaha also manufactured a range of modest commuter vehicles such as the V50 and V80, which were fitted with two- and three-speed automatic gearboxes with manual selection. These were later replaced by the four-stroke shaft-drive T50 and T80, and in 1972 Yamaha brought out the FS1 sports moped, which was aimed at the teen market. Despite being restricted to 48km/h (30mph) in the UK, the model remained on sale to the end of the century as the FS1 with drum brakes, and the FS1DX with disc brakes.

Technological development continued apace and in 1973 the RD, or 'Race Developed', series

Introduced in 1969, the 653cc (39ci) vertical twin XS-1 was intended to take on market leaders such as the Triumph Bonneville. It struggled with handling issues for a time and along the way evolved into the XS650.

replaced the long-running YDS models. The main improvement was a broader power band. In the case of the new RD250, power came in at 4000rpm instead of 6000rpm. The RD range included 125cc (8ci), 200cc (12ci), 250cc (15ci) and 350cc (21ci) machines, and the two larger models came with a six-speed gearbox. The RD line was restyled in 1975 and the following year, the RD350 became the RD400. However, the series was a casualty of US emissions regulations and went out of production in 1980.

In the late 1970s, a market niche for powerful trail bikes was becoming evident, and Yamaha responded with the 499cc (30ci) four-stroke, single-cylinder, single overhead-cam XT500. Its road-going sibling, the SR500, used the same engine but with larger valves and carburettor internals. This was

The YR range first appeared in 1967, marking the start of a new line of larger two-strokes. The range was the first to have horizontally split engine cases and five-port cylinder barrels.

The YR range first appeared in 1967, marking the start of a new line of larger two-strokes. The range was the first to have horizontally split engine cases and five-port cylinder barrels.

also the beginning of the superbike era, and Yamaha began to explore the concept with the four-stroke XS750. Three years later, this machine received an engine upgrade to 826cc (50ci) and 79hp at 8500rpm. This allowed the machine to make 201km/h (125mph). It also handled well thanks to fully adjustable front and rear suspension, but was superseded by the four-cylinder XJ900.

The RD series made a comeback in the form of the LC, a range of liquid-cooled two-stroke twins. These did well in production racing even before gaining the benefit in 1982 of the Yamaha Power Valve System (YPVS). This consisted of a variable exhaust port whose size and position changed automatically according to engine revs and thereby increased power. Another machine to use this technology was the RD500LC. Introduced in 1984, this 217km/h (135mph) machine was designed to make the most of publicity gained from Grand Prix victories.

The TR1, which appeared in 1980, was a 981cc (60ci) 75-degree V-twin and was in many ways conventional. It was accompanied by the 740cc (45ci) Virago, which in turn spawned a number of versions in sizes from 125cc (8ci) to 1100cc (67ci). Neither machine was groundbreaking, but the 1982 XZ550 was a little more adventurous. A 550cc (34ci) V-twin with liquid-cooling and double overhead-cam, four-

valve cylinder heads (each with twin exhaust port), the ZX550 had a rather odd specification. It was also quite unattractive and lacking in performance.

The XJ series was more conventional and also more successful. The range included machines from 550cc (34ci) to 750cc (46ci), and a turbo machine, aptly named XJ650 Turbo. This was less successful than the 1983 XJ900, which survived in FJ form to the end of the century. Meanwhile, the FZ750, with its liquid-cooled 749cc (46ci), four-cylinder, five-valves-per-cylinder engine, was impressing sports bike fans. It was followed in 1987 by the FZR1000 Genesis, with 135hp and a top speed of 266km/h (165mph).

The FZR1000 used an alloy box-section frame called the Deltabox,

which enabled a lower seat height and promoted better handling. Many of the smaller Yamaha bikes of the late 1980s used the Deltabox, such as the TZR125. The Deltabox frame was not the only new Yamaha concept of the period. There was also the Exhaust Ultimate Power Valve or 'EXUP', which consisted of a valve in the exhaust collector-box to control the gas-pressure wave and thus increase engine output.

By the 1990s, Yamaha was making four-stroke trail bikes such as the XT550, and the smaller XT400. These gave way to the XT600 and the XT600Z Ténéré, which rode a wave of popularity resulting from desert events such as the Paris–Dakar race. These machines had the requisite large fuel tanks and high suspension to go with their image. By 2000,

Yamaha had refined the concept of the dual-purpose model to the extent that the XT600E was probably the best machine available. The lighter XT350 was better for riding off-road, however. The road-going SRX600 used the same four-valve 608cc (37ci) single as the XT, and was popular with elements of the racing fraternity.

Yamaha ended the twentieth century with three notable models. All were top-end supersports machines featuring extremely advanced engine and chassis components, which were developed using technology from Yamaha's Superbike and Grand Prix race machinery.

The 1000cc (61ci) 150hp YZF-R1, introduced in 1998, made an impressive impact in the supersports category, as it was lighter, more compact and more powerful than any of its rivals. Released in the same year, the R7 allowed the private user a chance to experience cutting-edge race technology in a street-legal motorcycle. It was not cheap, however, costing £21,000 in 1999.

The 600cc (37ci) YZF-R6 was launched the following year. With 120hp, and a top speed of 274km/h (170mph), it was incredibly fast and could be cornered at up to 56 degrees from the vertical. With 15,500rpm available, it delivered excellent mid-range power as well.

Yamaha's top-end superbikes are the ones that really capture the imagination. Experience gained on the GP circuit benefits the street user with ever-faster, lighter and simply better bikes.

ZUNDAPP B250 CONCEPT

Zundapp caused a stir at the 1953 Frankfurt show with its Bella Scooter and the 250 Elastic motorcycle, and also with its new overhead-valve horizontally opposed 247cc (15ci) twin, the B250.

Although the new machine was expected to go into production, it was in fact a concept bike created to garner publicity, as it was far too expensive for the general market.

The B250 had an extremely clean engine design, delivering 18.5hp at 7000rpm through a

The B250 Concept was named for its 247cc (15ci) engine. Never intended for production, the bike was developed purely to garner publicity.

four-speed gearbox. The engine featured alloy heads and barrels with reborable cast-iron liners and needle-roller, big-end bearings of a

similar type to the KS601 Green Elephant. Unusually for such a small machine, final drive was by shaft.

The frame was also novel, with the transverse flat twin engine slung below two widely spaced, large-diameter tubes, which ran downward and rearward from the steering head. The tubes terminated above and slightly in front of the rear-wheel spindle to form upper supports for the rear shock absorbers. According to Zundapp, this setup largely counteracted the effects of torque reaction.

ENGINE: 247cc (15ci) ohv 2v flat twin, 54x54mm, air-cooled
POWER: 18.5bhp at 7000rpm
GEARBOX: 4-speed foot change
FINAL DRIVE: shaft
WEIGHT: n/a
TOP SPEED: n/a

ZUNDAPP BELLA

The Bella scooter was one of Zundapp's best sellers, remaining in production from 1953 to 1964, with more than 130,000 models sold in that time. The initial version was the Bella 150, or R150, with a 147cc (9ci) engine driving through a four-speed gearbox built in unit with it to give a top speed of 80km/h

(50mph). In 1954, Zundapp reacted to a customer requirement for greater performance by bringing out the R200.

The Bella used an unusual frame, consisting of a large diameter downtube and two backbone members arching over the engine and rear wheel. Over this frame was fitted pressed-steel

The 198cc R200 Bella was developed from a 147cc (9ci) version and, along with the enlarged engine, also offered better all round performance.

bodywork. The suspension used open coil springs, controlled by a single hydraulic damper fitted on the nearside of the fork.

ENGINE: 147cc (9ci) 2s single, 57 x 58mm, air-cooled
POWER: 7.3bhp at 6000rpm
GEARBOX: 4-speed foot change
FINAL DRIVE: chain, fully enclosed
WEIGHT: 158kg (350lb)
TOP SPEED: 80km/h (50mph)

ADLER RS250

In addition to its road bikes, Adler built small numbers of competition bikes, including track and dirt racers. The Adler 247.3cc (15ci) engine was used by private racers before the firm fielded its own race machine.

Then, in 1953, a race-kitted Adler impressed everyone with its performance in speed trials Hannover, even though it did not win the event.

Adler responded by building a batch of over-the-counter racing models for private sale, based on the standard M250 roadster. These machines had a number of interesting features, including a lightweight frame, altered suspension and a tuned engine, which benefited from considerable experimentation with gas flow.

The result was a machine capable of 193km/h (120mph), which was very impressive for a production-based engine.

ENGINE: 247.3cc (15ci) 2s parallel twin, 54x54mm, air-cooled (some later engines water-cooled)
POWER: 24bhp at 7800rpm
GEARBOX: 4-speed foot change
FINAL DRIVE: chain
WEIGHT: 102kg (115lb)
TOP SPEED: 103km/h (120mph)

ARIEL SQUARE FOUR

Designed by Edward Turner, the Square Four was a most imposing motorcycle. The engine effectively comprised two vertical twins on a common crankcase, with paired transverse crankshafts, geared together at their centres. A single chain-driven overhead camshaft controlled the valves and the wet-sump crankcases split horizontally. The original 497cc (30ci) version was a light and compact powerplant, but as is the way of things, it grew to 596cc (36ci) and ultimately 996cc (61ci), and as it did so its character completely changed.

The 'Squariel', as it became known, had one major weakness.

The cylinder head was prone to distortion, since the rear cylinders sat in the heat shadow of the front ones, and early attempts to race a supercharged four tended to result in 'head warping'. A normally aspirated version won the Maudes Trophy by covering 1126km (700 miles) in 668 minutes, but still suffered from serious overheating, which limited the engine's performance.

A revised range of fours appeared, starting in 1937. Available in both 597cc/36ci (the 4F) and 997cc/61ci (4G) form, these bikes featured pushrod valve actuation in place of overhead-cam, vertically split crankcases and had much heavier flywheels. The range gained plunger rear suspension in 1939. The 4F disappeared after the war, and by 1948 the 4G had gained telescopic forks. It was also considerably lighter, mainly due to a light alloy cylinder head and block.

The last Square Four appeared in 1954. It could deliver 45hp, but only at the price of an over-stressed engine. The plunger rear suspension was looking very dated by this time, and production ended in 1958. A revised version

ENGINE: 997cc (60ci) ohv square four, 65x75mm, air-cooled
POWER: 45bhp at 5500rpm
GEARBOX: 4-speed foot change
FINAL DRIVE: chain
WEIGHT: 220kg (485lb)
TOP SPEED: 166km/h (103mph)

appeared in the mid-1970s; there had been a hint of a replacement in 1962, in the form of a prototype designed by BSA, but this did not go into production.

The original Turner design used a light alloy, overhead-cam 500cc (30ci) powerplant, which somehow grew to 996cc (60ci) by 1954. The final version was designed by Val Page and appeared in 1954.

BIANCHI TONALE

The first Tonale (Tone), designed by Sandro Columbo, appeared in 1954. The main production model was a 175cc (11ci) sports roadster with a maximum speed around 112km/h (70mph). It was a fairly basic and unpretentious machine, but a good seller; the standard 175 Tonale was one of Bianchi's staples until it was taken out of production in 1967. It also served as the basis for several more specialized versions.

The racing variant was available in two engine sizes: the standard 175cc (11ci) and a larger 220cc (13ci), which was built from 1954 to 1956 and was capable of 160km/h (100mph). The Cross 175 and 200 models were purpose-built motocross bikes developed from the Tonale.

There were also special bikes for record-breaking, and in 1957, Bianchi set a series of speed records at Monza with a streamlined 175 Tonale. Although based on the standard production bike, this borrowed a number of components from the racers. Running on alcohol, with a compression ratio of around 10:1, it reached 193km/h (120mph).

ENGINE: 174cc (10ci), sohc single, 60x61.8mm, air-cooled
POWER: 8bhp at 7000rpm
GEARBOX: 4-speed foot change
FINAL DRIVE: chain
WEIGHT: 116kg (256lb)
TOP SPEED: 111km/h (69mph).

The Tonale, designed by Sadro Columbo, appeared in 1954. Several variants used the 175cc (10.5ci) powerplant as their basic setup.

GILERA 500 GP FOUR

Between 1949 and 1963, Gilera won six world championships plus 38 solo and eight sidecar Grand Prix victories with its four-cylinder 500cc (31ci) machines. When Geoff Duke arrived at Gilera in 1953, a new bout of development began. The immediately resulting model retained its engine unchanged but gained a frame that looked a lot like a Norton Featherbed. In 1954, the focus was shifted to the powerplant, and under the guidance of Franco Passoni, Gilera made a number of adjustments to the engine design and mounting.

As well as changing stroke length and valve dimensions, Passoni implemented modifications to the crankshafts and had a five-speed gearbox installed. By the time he was finished, the 500cc (31ci) four-cylinder Grand Prix Gilera had reached its definitive form. A 350cc (21ci) version joined the range in 1956.

During the mid 1950s, the GP Four was raced by Gilera's factory team, including world champion Geoff Duke. As late as 1963, it was still winning races in world-class competitions.

ENGINE: 499.49cc (30ci) dohc 2v straight 4, 52x58.8mm, air-cooled
POWER: 70bhp at 10,500rpm
GEARBOX: 5-speed foot change
FINAL DRIVE: chain
WEIGHT: 150kg (330lb)
TOP SPEED: 260km/h (161.5mph)

GILERA B300 TWIN

Gilera's B300 twin attracted a lot of attention at the 1953 Milan show. Its choice of engine size, 305.3cc (19ci), was a result of a decision not to be directed by category limits but instead to simply build an engine that would do the job at hand as well as possible.

The B300 took many features from the 150cc (9ci) machine introduced the previous year, borrowing such engine and cycle parts as parallel valves, coil valve springs, wet multi-plate clutch, built-up crankshaft, four-ring piston and dynamo lighting. It also featured telescopic forks, twin shocks, swinging-arm rear suspension and full-width polished-alloy brake hubs. The wheel rims and silencers were of light alloy.

The machine was not especially powerful, with a modest top speed of 113km/h (70mph). It did offer a very nice, smooth ride though, and it was built for touring, not performance. An evolved version, the 300 Extra, came out in 1955 along with a smaller 250 Export. The model achieved some overseas sales success (notably to the USA) and remained in production until 1966.

ENGINE: 305.3cc (18ci) ohv 2v parallel twin, 30x54mm, air-cooled
POWER: 15bhp at 6800rpm
GEARBOX: four-speed foot change
FINAL DRIVE: chain
WEIGHT: 150kg (330lb)
TOP SPEED: 125km/h (77.5mph)

The B300 overhead-valve twin first appeared at the 1953 Milan show and remained in production until 1969. This Series 2 model dates from the early 1960s.

HOREX IMPERATOR 400

The Imperator had little in common with the 497cc (30ci) racing machine of the same name fielded by Horex in 1952–53, which was probably just as well. The new Imperator was given a 392cc (24ci) engine to take advantage of a road fund and insurance threshold; prices went up about 25 per cent at 400cc (24ci).

The Imperator was a very competent roadster, with a chain-driven, single overhead-cam, unit-construction engine. In terms of both appearance and engineering, it was the most modern German machine in series production at the time. It was comfortable to ride yet capable of 135km/h (84mph), which was pretty good for a sports tourer of the day, and the specification was of a high standard overall. Unfortunately, the Imperator's release coincided with a drastic downturn in the German motorcycle industry, and it failed to turn its obvious quality into success in the marketplace.

ENGINE: 392cc (23.5ci) sohc parallel twin, 61.5x66mm, air-cooled
POWER: 26bhp at 6500rpm
GEARBOX: 4-speed foot change
FINAL DRIVE: chain
WEIGHT: 180kg (396lb)
TOP SPEED: 135km/h (84mph)

„Imperator"

The 392cc overhead-cam Imperator twin first appeared in 1954. It was, in many ways, the forerunner of the Japanese middleweight machines that became available two decades later.

JUNAK

POLAND 1954–64

Junak built only one model, the M10. It started life as a heavy 500cc (31ci) design with military applications, but somewhere along the line it became a 350cc (21ci) overhead-valve machine. Unveiled in 1954, it did not enter production for two years due to labour and tool shortages. In the first year of production, 1956, around 30 machines were more or less hand built, but the following year the number increased to 253. There were big plans to make 20,000 a year, but these never came to fruition.

By the time production really got underway, in 1958, the machine's faults (such as very poor lights) were well known, and this affected sales. It was also relatively expensive compared to many imported machines, which did not help. Despite this, the M10 sold in many countries, including: Bulgaria, Cuba, Hungary, Libya, Mongolia, Syria, Turkey, Uruguay, the USA and Venezuela.

Some changes were made during the M10's production life span, and many private users also made their own modifications. Production ceased in 1964, and a planned replacement design never went beyond the prototype stage.

PANTHER MODEL 100

ENGLAND 1954

For the entire history of the company, P&M always had at least one model in production that used the engine in place of the frame downtube. The engine itself grew in size over the years. In the Model 100, it was an overhead-valve 594cc (36ci) model, and like all P&M engines, this was tough, sturdy, reliable and long lasting. It also delivered good torque at low revs, which was useful for sidecar work.

The Model 100 was conventional for its time, starting out as a rigid frame with girder forks; these were replaced by telescopic forks in 1947. Pivoted-fork rear suspension was available as an option from 1954, but the rigid version ran on to 1957. The Model 100 lasted until 1959, when it was supplanted by the Model 120.

ENGINE: 594cc (35.5ci) ohv inclined single, 87x100mm, air-cooled
POWER: 23bhp at 5000rpm
GEARBOX: 4-speed foot change
WEIGHT: 185kg (406lb)
TOP SPEED: 120km/h (70mph)

The Model 100 first went on sale in 1932 and was developed from earlier machines. This is the form it took in the mid-1950s, when rear suspension became available. It was replaced by the Model 120, with a larger engine.

TOMOS

Tomos began by licence-building Puch motorcycles and Citroen cars. In 1961, the firm achieved international notice in the Coupe d'Europe (European Cup) 50cc (3ci) championship series.

There were eight rounds in the 1961 Coupe d'Europe. Three were held in Belgium, two in Germany and one each in the Netherlands, Spain and Yugoslavia. Kreidler and Tomos were favourites for the title.

Kreidler won, but the Tomos team fought them tooth and nail all the way, even winning on the Germans' home ground at Hockenheim.

In 1962, the Coupe d'Europe became a full world

championship, and Tomos produced a new machine especially to challenge for the title. Named D7-62 (seven-speed, 1962), the Tomos entry had an entirely new engine with a vertical cylinder and a piston with no rings. The new racer was a disappointment, but Tomos was still able to compete successfully in the 50cc (3ci) racing class until the category was replaced with an 80cc class in the early 1980s.

For many years, Tomos had a division in the Netherlands, where it also found its best export market. From there, the firm sold mopeds all across Europe, including the UK. In the mid-1990s, however, Tomos became a casualty of the political upheavals in the former Yugoslavia.

Tomos specialized in building small machines, and built them well. They were very competitive in the 50cc class until it was abolished. These machines (an ATX50 and an AT50) date from the last years of the company.

VINCENT BLACK PRINCE

The Black Prince was created by enclosing the mechanicals of a Vincent Shadow, and weighed only 1kg (2lb) more than a Series C Shadow.

The Black Knight was a Black Prince with a Rapide engine rather than the Shadow unit.

Unfortunately, Vincent was struggling at the time. The firm had been heavily reliant on a contract with the Argentine police, which fell through in 1948, and it went bankrupt a year later.

Although there was a comeback and a valiant attempt to turn things around, Vincent was losing money on every machine despite the high price tag, and so the series D was the last of the line.

Big, powerful and impressive, the Black Prince is considered one of the most magnificent machines ever built. Unfortunately, the end of the road was just ahead for Vincent.

ENGINE: 998cc (60ci) ohv in-line V-twin, 84x90mm, air-cooled
POWER: 55bhp at 5700rpm
GEARBOX: 4-speed foot change
FINAL DRIVE: chain
WEIGHT: 209kg (460lb)
TOP SPEED: 185km/h (115mph) approx

CHAPTER FIVE

CHANGING TIMES

1955–1964

By the mid-1950s, the immediate effects of the war had faded, and the weaknesses of the British bike industry were laid bare. Lack of investment in new models, old working practices, and dated technology, left companies like Norton and Triumph wide open to up-and-coming competition from overseas.

However, British firms had some success in road racing – over the years, Norton won 94 Isle of Man TT races – but real race success had become the preserve of the Italians, and MV Agusta in particular. Between 1955 and 1964, it won eight 500cc Grands Prix titles (Gilera won the other two), five 250cc and five 125cc titles. Together with Moto Guzzi and a host of smaller firms, these Italian companies were establishing the passion and competitiveness that would sustain that country's biking culture right up to the present day.

But it was in East Asia that the modern motorcycle culture was really developing. Amidst post-war reconstruction, quality-based working practices and heroic efforts in technology, the Japanese companies were rapidly developing.

Honda was well established, and winning GP titles as early as 1961. Kawasaki began building bikes in 1949, Suzuki in 1952 and Yamaha in 1955. They began with small commuters, then started making what were essentially copies of bigger competitor's machines. But now their era was about to begin in earnest.

Left: The Royal Enfield Continental had a 250cc (15.25ci) engine – small for the period. But it was a practical motorcycle capable of good speeds, as well as having additional features such as clip-on handlebars designed for race competitions.

350 THREE-CYLINDER RACER

GERMANY 1955

DKW two-strokes showed their worth in the 1930s, becoming world leaders on the race circuit. World War II brought this to a stop and caused immeasurable disruption to the firm. Afterwards, when it relocated to Ingolstadt in West Germany, DKW tried to repeat its past glories.

The first 'new' race machines were not new at all, but were specially tuned versions of the 125cc (8ci) roadster. These were followed in the early 1950s by brand new two- and three-cylinder models. It was with the triple that the re-born DKW marque achieved its greatest success.

The 250cc (15ci) twin first appeared at Hockenheim in April 1952, and the 350cc (21ci) triple

arrived a month later. At that time, the DKW racing effort was in the hands of the young engineer Erich Wolf, who had previously tuned Austrian Puch and earlier types of DKW engines. He was not particularly successful, and after a couple of seasons his design work was passed on to another engineer, Hellmut Georg. At the same time, Robert Eberan von Eberhorst, a former assistant to the legendary Ferdinand Porsche, was placed in overall control of DKW's racing division.

The efforts of Georg and von Eberhorst, resulted in the 350cc (21ci) triple, evolving into a world-class machine. This was not a painless process. Initially, the new designers kept Wolf's basic design

for the machine more or less unchanged, retaining the layout of two vertical cylinders and one horizontal one. However, Wolf's version had been optimized for lightness, and the result of tinkering was to create an unreliable machine.

Fixing this problem necessitated an upgrade of not only the engine components but also the chassis, brakes and suspension. The bike was also given a revised exhaust system, which, for the first time, made use of expansion chambers. The final result was a machine with more power and far greater durability.

The new 350cc (21ci) made a serious challenge for the 1955 and 1956 World Championships. In the

end, after a hard-fought competition, it was beaten by the single-cylinder Moto Guzzi. DKW's management decided to withdraw from Grand Prix racing at the end of 1956, though the firm went out on a high when their top rider, August Hobl, took the runner-up position in the 350cc World Championship series.

ENGINE: 348.48cc (21ci) 2s triple 53x52.8mm, air-cooled
POWER: 46bhp at 9700rpm
GEARBOX: 5-speed foot change
FINAL DRIVE: chain
WEIGHT: 145kg (320lb) with streamlining
TOP SPEED: 225km/h (140mph)

BERNEG

ITALY 1955–61

Berneg was another short-lived Italian marque that had good ideas and designed interesting bikes, but which ultimately failed. The firm was set up in Bologna in the early 1950s by Paride Bernardi and Corrado Negrini, and took its name from its founders.

The first Berneg machine was the Iridea, which is thought to have been designed by Alfonso Drusiani. This was an unusual machine, being a parallel twin at a time when most other manufacturers were concentrating

on singles. Berneg was willing to innovate, making use of developments such as overhead-cams, light alloys and well-chosen gear ratios to build machines that were small and light, but powerful.

The Iridea was a 158cc (10ci) four-stroke parallel twin with an overhead-cam driven by duplex chain in a light-alloy head. Primary drive was by chain and went to a four-speed foot-change gearbox. Final drive was also by chain. The tubular frame featured telescopic forks and rear suspension, and the

Berneg's machines were conventional in layout and appearance, but they benefited from a willingness to pursue new concepts and innovations. They deserved better than to just fade away.

bike had a top speed in excess of 100km/h (62mph).

The Iridea remained in production for two years and was followed in 1957 by the Fario, which is variously recorded as a 174cc (10.6ci) or 185cc (11.2ci) machine. Mechanically very much like the Iridea, the Fario came in two versions. The basic model was capable of 105km/h (65mph), and

the Gran Turismo could reach 120km/h (75mph). Berneg then produced a Sport model that was even faster. However, just two years after its 1959 debut, the company went bankrupt. The company's failure was not for lack of good ideas or because its bikes were poor – indeed, the reverse was true. In the end, Berneg went under for financial reasons.

DOUGLAS DRAGONFLY

The Dragonfly was the production version of a prototype machine named the Dart. Considerable interest in the forthcoming Dragonfly was generated by displays at the 1955 Earl's Court Show, but this had largely dissipated by the time the Dragonfly went on sale nine months later. Douglas was not too concerned with motorcycles at the time, as it was concentrating mainly on building and marketing Vespa scooters under licence. In the event, the Dragonfly turned out to be the last Douglas motorcycle.

The Dragonfly used an engine and transmission designed and built in house, and was then built up using bought-in parts. Whether by accident or design, the resulting machine was well integrated – better in that respect than the Plus machines built in-house. With only a single carburettor, the Dragonfly was underpowered, but it was a pleasant and agile machine to ride. Like other Douglas designs, it was also somewhat overpriced.

ENGINE: 348cc (21ci) ohv transverse flat twin 60.8x68mm, air-cooled
POWER: 17bhp at 6000rpm
GEARBOX: 4-speed foot change
FINAL DRIVE: chain
WEIGHT: 178kg (392lb)
TOP SPEED: 116km/h (72mph)

The Dragonfly (left) was put together from bought-in parts around an in-house engine and transmission. Unusually, for a transverse flat twin, the Dragonfly used chain drive. It was a better machine than the 80 Plus it is pictured with, but it was the last production Douglas.

MOTO MORINI SETTEBELLO

ITALY 1955

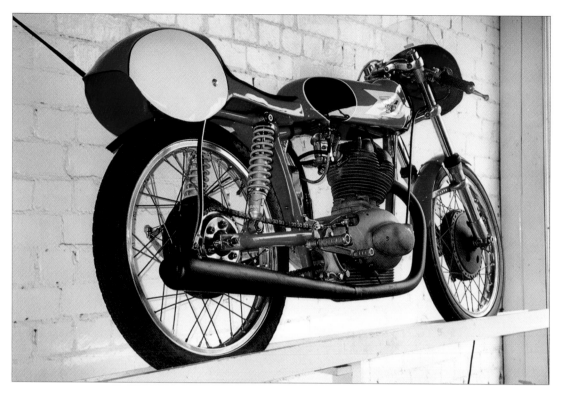

The Settebello was unusually fast for a 175cc (11ci) single in the 1950s. Even without modification or tuning it would make 145kph (90mph).

The Settebello was one of three machines that appeared in 1955. These were the Briscola (Trumps), Tressette (Three Sevens) and Settebello (Seven of Diamonds). All were revised versions of the first overhead-valve Morini, which made its public debut at the Milan Show in November 1952. The basic version featured a unit-construction engine; four-speed, fast-change gearbox; telescopic front forks; and swinging-arm, twin-shock rear suspension.

Predictably, of the three variants, it was the Settebello that won the most public acclaim. It was the sports model, and testers raved about it, while enthusiasts dreamed of owning it. This was an excellent fast road machine or clubman racer.

The standard Settebello came with clip-on handlebars, a tuned engine (featuring a high-compression piston and special camshaft), a large Dell 'Orto carburettor, conical brake hubs cast in aluminium, alloy wheel rims, a bulbous 18l (4.75 gallon) fuel tank, sprint saddle and lightweight, pressed-steel mudguards.

The cylinder barrel of the 172.4cc (11ci) engine was of cast iron, with an aluminium cylinder head, whilst the crankcase formed a stressed member for the frame. The engine casing was left in a matt finish to promote cooling. In standard form, the Settebello could achieve 145km/h (90mph), which was impressive for the period. It was very competitive in sports machine races, notably in Italy and France.

Many novice racers began their careers aboard an overhead-valve Morini single. Among them was the great Giacomo Agostini, who was World Champion 15 times. The Settebello was more than just a fast bike; it also possessed superb road-holding and handling characteristics, so it was at its best on a light, bumpy circuit, where its lightness and handling gave it an advantage over more powerful machinery. It was competitive under such conditions well into the 1960s.

ENGINE: 172.4cc (10ci) ohv 2v single, 60x61mm, air-cooled
POWER: 17bhp at 8000rpm
GEARBOX: 4-speed foot change
FINAL DRIVE: chain
WEIGHT: 129kg (285lb)
TOP SPEED: 145km/h (90mph)

RATIER

FRANCE 1955–62

Ratier started its existence in 1945 as CMR, became Cemec in 1948, and was renamed Ratier in 1955. Its designs were derived from the BMW flat-twin, but as time passed they acquired a more French character. This was especially true once the Ratier name was adopted. BMW machines gained leading-link front and pivoted rear forks in 1955, but Ratier decided on the more modern concept of telescopics; BMW did not follow suit until 1969. However, in most other ways, BMW and Ratier machines remained very similar.

In 1955, there were two models on offer, a 494cc (30ci) and a 594cc (36ci). Both were overhead-valve designs with coil ignition and twin carburettors. The four-speed gearbox was in unit with the engine, and the shaft drive to the rear wheel ran in-board of the right fork leg. The frame featured the modern suspension system, while large drum brakes were fitted into full-width hubs front and rear. A separate headlamp appeared at the top of the forks or was blended into them.

Ratier sold its bikes mainly to the French police, outfitted with a single seat and wireless equipment. Civilian machines for the domestic and export market had a dual seat. In the USA, Ratier machines were promoted as the official motorcycle escort of French President Charles de Gaulle.

Ratier rebadged some remaining Cemec machines as Ratiers, but after a time only the 594cc (36ci) machine remained in production. That, too, ceased production in 1962 – and, with it, Ratier's business.

Ratier's sales were mainly on police contracts or to users who liked the idea of riding the bike of the French President's escort.

ROYAL ENFIELD

Since 1955, the Enfield Bullet has been built under licence by the Madras Motor Company. The process began with imports of complete machines, but over time, more of the parts were manufactured in India. Eventually the company was making entire bikes, and continued to do so even after 1971, when Royal Enfield stopped making motorcycles in Britain.

It is not hard to see why the Bullet became so popular in the Indian market. It is extremely robust and easy to repair, and handles well even on poor roads. It also looks great and gives very good fuel mileage at 3.8l/100km (over 70mpg).

Of course, the Bullet is showing its age somewhat, and there have been some attempts to update it. A new-build Indian Bullet now has 12V electrics, but it is still basically the same model that was exported to India more than 50 years ago. It retains all the virtues, and all the vices, of a classic British single of the 1950s.

The Bullet is very slow by modern standards. The 346cc (21ci) variant, the only version available until the 1980s, was a long-stroke, two-valve single with a compression ratio of just 7.25:1, giving 18hp at 5625rpm. With a weight of 163kg (359lb), this did not make for impressive acceleration. Maintenance was also annoyingly frequent: the tappets

had to be set and the contact-breaker assembly cleaned every 800km (500 miles); and a general lubrication was required each month or every 2000km (1200 miles) – whichever came first.

The Bullet also had a number of peculiarities, notably in the gearbox. While the US market had standardized gear change on the left side, the Bullet had it on the right. Its operation was odd too: it operated up-for-down; one up, three down. Most users would expect one down, three (or four)

up, but the Bullet just had to be different. There was also a heel-operated neutral selector – just in case the rider could not find neutral anywhere else.

The Bullet was slowly updated over the years. As well as the introduction of 12V electrics, the machine was given better brakes, eventually using a twin leading-shoe. A 500cc (31ci) version was introduced in 1984, largely as a response to requests from overseas dealers. The new engine had a compression ratio of only 5.5:1, and the resulting increase in power was less impressive than might have been expected – a mere 22 per cent to 22hp. Peak power now came in at 5400rpm. However, torque was increased by more than 27 per cent, giving very smooth power delivery. Top speed increased to more than 125km/h (almost 80mph) from a previous 120km/h (75mph). There was also an overhead-cam prototype in 1990, although this was sleeved down to 250cc (15ci).

Until the 1990s, the Bullet's drawbacks were irrelevant. The market was such that consumers had to buy what they could get, and they sometimes waited months for their machine. With the liberalization of the market, everything changed. Japanese imports were increasingly available, and the Bullet needed to compete.

To retain its place in the market, the company began looking to build better and faster versions of the Bullet. Various designers were contacted, including the legendary

The 1964 Continental GT was the end result of a process of evolution that began in 1956 with the Crusader Sports. A unit-construction 250cc (15ci) single with a five-speed gearbox, it was good looking and fun to ride.

Fritz Egli in Switzerland. The result was an improved engine. Versions became available with swept volumes of 535cc (33ci) and 624cc (38ci).

Improvements were also made to the gearbox, which was made more conventional in operation by moving it to the left and reconfiguring it to go 'backwards': up-for-up; one down and three up. A five-speed transmission from Criterion Engineers in the UK was considered, and the company even consulted styling experts to decide if the machine's appearance should be altered.

The Bullet is an incredible success story, and seems set to go on for a while yet. Its long-term viability probably rests upon the question of whether the classic appeal of the machine can be retained while updating its performance to suit modern buyers. In particular, a reduction of maintenance requirements is necessary.

In the meantime, however, the Bullet has been going strong for half a century. So its current makers can be forgiven for the slight inaccuracy of their statement that 'today it is the only British bike still being manufactured anywhere in the world'.

Royal Enfield started out buying in engines from various other British manufacturers, but in the 1920s the firm switched to using its own designs. These contributed to the good looks of their machines.

VESPA GS150

Piaggio introduced the Vespa GS150 in 1955, just a decade after the company's first scooter went to market. It quickly became the industry-standard machine. The GS150 evolved through five phases of updates to the electrical system and auxiliary components, to become the VS5 of 1962, the year when it was superseded by the GS160.

The original GS150 had faired-in handlebars, but the brake and clutch cables were still exposed, as they had been on earlier Vespas.

Like all Vespas, the GS150 featured leg shields, a front mudguard that turned with the wheel, and bubbles or blisters either side of the central section.

The 150cc (9ci) single-cylinder two-stroke motor was housed in the right-hand bubble, while the left-hand one was for storage and battery housing.

Scooters were always perceived as the transport of the young and trendy, and the GS150 achieved cult status among early 1960s British Mods, as shown in the film *Quadrophenia*.

The Vespa's bubbles were frequently chromium-plated and some Mods liked to adorn the bikes with similarly festive paraphernalia. Others, though, objected to the shiny bits, and tore them off. Then, on holiday weekends, the bikes were driven in slow-moving convoys to British coastal resorts.

ENGINE: single cylinder air-cooled 2-stroke
POWER: 5.5bhp
GEARBOX: 4-speed constant mesh
FINAL DRIVE: n/a
WEIGHT: n/a
TOP SPEED: n/a

VICTORIA SWING

The Victoria Swing was a somewhat unusual design that appeared in Germany and went on display at various shows all over Europe in 1955. Its advanced unit-construction engine was influenced not by existing motorcycle practice but by scooter practice.

The 197cc (12ci) engine was mounted almost horizontally in a duplex cradle frame, fixed rigidly to an internally ribbed, cast-iron strut that carried the rear wheel. This wheel was linked to the spindle of the four-speed gearbox by an enclosed final-drive chain tensioned by an eccentric jockey sprocket. To provide rear suspension, the engine unit pivoted from the frame below the crankcase.

The upper rear portion of the frame and the rear mudguard were integral welded-up pressings, reinforced to take the upper mountings of the twin, adjustable, rear shock absorbers. The rear of the engine was enclosed, under detachable panels fitted to the frame. The silencer did its job well, whilst also impressively huge.

Front suspension was provided by leading links connected by covered links to a bridge piece that bore on a coil spring, with a co-axial damper placed in front of the steering head. A small fairing was built into the top of the forks, and this carried the headlamp and speedometer. Both rider and passenger had a large seat, in two sections, and in 1956 the machine was updated with an electrically operated fuel gauge and brake warning lights.

The interesting feature of the Swing was its gear-change mechanism. It was not possible to fit a conventional foot-controlled gear change to the engine setup, so gears were changed by using buttons mounted on the left handlebar. The system was remarkably simple, consisting solely of a powerful electromagnet that operated the gear selector pushrod. There was even an emergency circuit for use when the battery was flat.

Unfortunately, this clever design went on sale during hard times for the motorcycle industry. Sales were poor across the board, and untried new designs tend to suffer most in such circumstances. At another time, the Swing might well have achieved greater success – but this was not to be, and production ceased in 1962.

ENGINE: 197cc (12ci) two-stroke horizontal single, 65x60mm, air-cooled
POWER: 11.3 bhp at 5300 rpm
GEARBOX: 4-speed press-button change
FINAL DRIVE: enclosed chain
WEIGHT: 131kg (289lb)
TOP SPEED: 97km/h (60mph)

AERMACCHI CHIMERA

Replacing Lino Tonti as chief designer at Aermacchi in early 1956, Alfredo Bianchi was given the task of producing a factory machine. This became the Chimera (Dream), and it stole the show at Milan in 1956. Unfortunately, despite its ultra-modern appearance and early promise, the Chimera failed to deliver and flopped badly in the marketplace.

Bianchi went back to work on the Chimera and removed some of the ostentation. By the time he was finished, he had created some of Italy's best known sports and racing machines, such as the Ala Verde and Ala d'Oro. Neither could have happened without the Chimera, making it a pivotal model in Aermacchi's history.

The use of both steel and aluminium enclosure panelling was a distinctive feature of the Chimera. The panels could be very easily removed, which was welcome. Underneath, despite the outward appearance of the machine, it was fairly conventional. The 172.4cc (11ci) overhead-valve engine featured a horizontal cylinder, roller bearing big-end, coil ignition, wet sump

The Chimera looked great and attracted a lot of interest at the 1956 Milan show, but sales were poor. A stripped-down version did much better and founded a dynasty of excellent race bikes.

lubrication, multi-plate clutch, gear primary drive and a four-speed gearbox. Running on a 7:1 compression ratio, maximum power was 13hp, giving a top speed of more than 105km/h (65mph).

Some features were innovative, such as the near-horizontal single rear shock absorber, although this was not used on the subsequent sports and racing models. In other ways, however, the Chimera was actually quite conservative. Many Italian designers thought overhead camshafts to be absolutely imperative, but Bianchi decided on pushrod-operated valves, for simpler maintenance and because he believed that overhead-valve layout was not needed for his machines. Nor would it appear that he was wrong: over the next 15 years, his overhead-valve horizontal Aermacchi single was as fast as the more complex and expensive machines.

ENGINE: 172cc (10ci) ohv horizontal flat single, 60x61mm, air-cooled
POWER: 13bhp at 7000rpm
GEARBOX: 4-speed foot change
FINAL DRIVE: chain
WEIGHT: 122kg (269lb)
TOP SPEED: 110km/h (68mph)

APRILIA

ITALY 1956–PRESENT

Aprilia started out in 1956 as a bicycle manufacturer, producing its first powered machine in 1960. This was, unsurprisingly, a moped, and production of powered two-wheelers was a sideline for some time, as Aprilia's main income came from pedal cycles.

However, the bicycle market was declining in the mid-1970s and a plan was hatched to create a series of motocross bikes. This plan was backed by a faction of workers at the Naole factory near Venice, and resulted in a range of bikes available with different engine sizes. The power units came from various sources, including Minerelli, Sachs, Hiro and ultimately Rotax, with whom Aprilia remains associated.

The machines were a success, and works-supported Aprilia motocross bikes won the 125cc and 500cc Italian Championship titles in both 1976 and 1977. This encouraged Aprilia to enter the enduro market and, later on, the trials market. The latter was approached with care and deliberation, the world-renowned rider Sammy Miller advising on the development of the prototype.

By 1981, the company was producing 4500 motorcycles per annum, which seemed pretty good. However, a year later, things really took off, with the launch of the ST 125 roadster. Powered by a liquid-cooled Rotax two-stroke engine and featuring monoshock rear suspension and modern styling, the ST125 became a massive success virtually overnight. This convinced the company's president, Ivano Beggio, that Aprilia should be selling more street motorcycles. Until then, besides the dirt bikes, Aprilia had sold only 50cc (3ci) ultra-lightweight machines and a range of mopeds.

Aprilia deliberately targeted the youth market. The management researched it thoroughly, examining what young people wore, what colours were in fashion, what music they listened to, and even what films and television programmes they watched. The effort paid off handsomely.

For example, while other Italian manufacturers were complaining about legislation that made wearing a helmet compulsory, Aprilia turned it to a commercial advantage, marketing its own helmets in fashionable designs and colours. The firm also had the advantage of a relatively young workforce. During the 1980s, the average age of its employees was under 30 and even the president was only in his early forties. The net result of this was that Aprilia became an icon to the Italian youth.

Aprilia also practised strong niche marketing. The roadster models were split into three distinct marketing categories: replica racer, Paris-Dakar-style rally bike, or custom cruiser. There was no middle ground, no workaday designs. The commuter moped was long gone from the range. Its involvement in motocross ceased in the early 1980s, but Aprilia's sporting traditions continued with participation in trials, rallies and, from the mid-1980s, road-racing. It even offered replicas of its successful works machines for sale to the public.

By 1986, production was up to 40,000 units, of which almost half were in the all-important 125cc (8ci) sector. This made Aprilia the third-biggest seller in the Italian market – an incredible achievement for a company that had barely been heard of a decade before.

The next challenge was to break into foreign markets, and here again Aprilia demonstrated the good business sense that a successful marque needs. It embarked on a five-year plan, which cost 60 billion lire ($38 million) and was aimed at expanding the model range to include 25 machines, up to an engine capacity of 1000cc (61ci).

This was ambitious stuff, but there was more. Not only did Aprilia plan to build the existing twin-cylinder, 250cc Grand Prix racer (built from 1989 with V, rather than in-line, engine configuration); it also intended to enter the 125cc and 500cc World Championship categories. In 1988, the 276cc (17ci) Climber rotary valve, single-cylinder trials bike arrived. This machine set an industry first in its sector by using liquid-cooling.

In 1985, Loris Reggiari was Aprilia's first works Grand Prix rider. He also helped the company develop title-winning bikes nine years later, when Max Biaggi took the 250cc crown. Biaggi and fellow Italian Valentino Rossi became multiple World Champions riding Aprilias.

Aprilia produced its first modern scooter, the 50cc (3ci) Amico, in 1990. It was an instant success, and gave the company a headstart in the scooter boom of the late 1990s. Other important Aprilia models at this time included the Extrema, a race replica; the Red Rose, a custom machine available with 50cc (3ci) or 125cc (8ci) engines; and the Pegaso, which featured 652cc (40ci) and five valves.

Also in the early 1990s came a joint venture with Rotax and BMW to build BMW F650 Funduro four-valve singles. The project was a success: between 1992 and 1999, 60,000 were sold worldwide. Meanwhile, the Dutch two-stroke expert Jan Wittereen was recruited to develop the existing 125cc (8ci) and 250cc (15ci) racing models. He was also involved with a larger V-twin, the RS400V GP racer, which appeared in 1994.

In the mid-1990s, new additions to the range included the Suzuki RGV-powered RS 250 and the Leonardo scooter with a range of four-valve engines with 124cc (8ci), 150cc (9ci) and 250cc (15ci). Annual production figures in 1996 exceeded 100,000 units; Aprilia had become one of the biggest European manufacturers.

In 1997, after launching the RSV Mille superbike, Aprilia had a complete range of bikes from 50cc (3ci) to 1000cc (61ci). With the purchase of the Moto Guzzi marque in 2000, the firm became Europe's largest motorcycle manufacturer.

An early (1992) Aprilia Pegaso. Ostensibly a dirt bike, the Pegaso was also an excellent road machine with a five-valve, double overhead-cam, single-cylinder engine.

MALANCA

The Malanca marque was named after its founder, Mario Malanca, who set up his firm in Pontecchio Marconi, Bologna, in 1956. The marque is best known for its long-running line of parallel twin-cylinder two-strokes for both road and racing use.

The marque achieved impressive race success from 1973 and 1976, when Otello Buscherini gained several victories and leader-board placings in the 125cc World Championship series.

Buscherini's machine was fitted with a 123.5cc (7.5ci) liquid-cooled, disc-valve, twin-cylinder engine, producing 36hp at 14,000rpm. This gave it a fighting chance against the dominant Yamaha and Morbidelli machines at a time when little else could compare. However, Buscherini's death in an accident during the 1976 Italian Grand Prix more or less ended Malanca's challenge for the top slot.

During the late 1970s and early 1980s, Malanca's road-going 124.9cc (7.6ci), piston-ported twins were well known for their high performance, particularly in liquid-cooled form. However, the marque's success was destined to come to a close in the mid-1980s. The emergence of a new generation of ultra-high performance 125cc (8ci) machines from Aprilia, Cagiva and Gilera eclipsed the twin-cylinder Malanca. As its performance was outdone, so its sales position declined.

In 1985, Malanca made an attempt to turn things around, sponsoring the up-and-coming Marco Lucchi on a special 250cc (15ci) twin-cylinder racer.

The resulting performance was very impressive and garnered considerable publicity for the firm, but in the end this was not enough. The financial situation continued to deteriorate, and in 1986 the Malanca factory was closed.

One of the very first 1950s-vintage Malancas. Race technology filtered quickly into the road bikes, which for a time were very popular in the high-performance end of the market.

MOTO GUZZI LODOLA 175

The Lodola, the last of Carlo Guzzi's own designs, was something of an oddity. It was light and handled beautifully, but the original 175cc (11ci) version lacked power. Nor was the finish all that good, and the electricals left something to be desired. In 1959, the model was upgraded to 235cc (14ci) and the expensive-to-build, chain-driven overhead-cam was replaced with more pedestrian, pushrod valve gear. The resulting increase in power (more than 20 per cent, to 11hp at 6000rpm) compensated for an increase in weight of just over 6kg (13lb).

It is probably not coincidental that the year after the Lodola appeared, Moto Guzzi gave up racing – despite 25 years of success. The Lodola was definitely a tourer, not a sports machine.

ENGINE: 175cc (11ci) ohc single, 62x57.8mm, air-cooled
POWER: 9bhp at 6000rpm
GEARBOX: 4-speed foot change
FINAL DRIVE: chain
WEIGHT: 109kg (240lb)
TOP SPEED: 115km/h (70mph)

The original 175cc (11ci) overhead-cam Lodola. The later 235cc (14ci) push-rod version was more practical but less interesting. The Lodola marked a change for Moto Guzzi as it's a tourer rather than a racer.

MV AGUSTA 500 FOUR

MV put out its first 500cc (31ci), four-cylinder race machine in 1950, but it was not until 1956 that the design matured and began to achieve success.

In the interim, the machine had received a number of technical improvements and the firm benefited from the expertise of Englishman John Surtees, who was as proficient in the workshop as he was on the track. His arrival marked a turning point in MV's history.

Although 1955 had not produced much in the way of race results, MV engineers had made considerable technical progress. Streamlining was given prominence and the frame was re-designed to provide a lower centre of gravity.

The Earles front fork was abandoned in favour of a new MV-built telescopic assembly. Various

rear shock absorbers were tried (MV and British Girling types); the double-sided front brake was equipped with massive air-scoops; and the fuel tank was also reshaped to provide a longer, lower style.

Along the way, many avenues were explored. In 1951, MV tried out the 500 racer with four carburettors, and in 1952 the engine was largely revised. This included a change from shaft- to chain-final drive. The double-side gear change had already been axed in favour of a conventional lever on the offside. The result of all this work was that in 1955 the machine was delivering 65hp at 11,000rpm, which was upped to 67hp in 1957.

Meanwhile, Surtees won the first race of the 1956 500cc World Championship series on a 1955 machine. He had intended to

The MV Agusta 500 Four won its first 500cc World Championship for MV Agusta as early as 1956. In 1965, it passed the torch to a newer model – but by then, this mechanical hero had nine world titles to its name.

compete on the newer model, but had collided with a cow on a mountain road during practice. Although Surtees himself avoided serious injury, the bike did not; the fate of the cow is unrecorded.

Surtees won the next two rounds as well before crashing – on a different bike, a 350 MV Four – and breaking his arm. Since the championship was run over six races and the remaining three all had different winners, Surtees still won the 500cc championship for MV Agusta.

He won again in 1958, 1959 and 1960. Gary Hocking won in 1961, and then Mike Hailwood took over, winning four times in a row from 1962 to 1965.

The Four was eventually retired in favour of the new three-cylinder model, which Giacomo Agustini used to continue MV's winning streak, taking the 1966 championship, and, later, many more titles. The new triple was a fabulous machine, but it was the 500 Four that led MV's march to racing glory.

ENGINE: 497.5cc (30ci) dohc 2v straight four, 53x56.4mm
POWER: 67bhp at 11,000rpm
GEARBOX: 5-speed foot change
FINAL DRIVE: chain
WEIGHT: 118kg (260lb)
TOP SPEED: 233km/h (145mph)

PARILLA 175 SPORT

A well-restored 1957 Parilla MSDS 175 single. This machine was a race-tuned version of the Sport and was capable of more than 160km/h (100mph). It was a commercial success right to the end of Parilla's production career.

Parilla's first high-cam machine was the Fox, which appeared in 1952. It was then developed into the 175 Sport, an unconventional but successful machine that remained in production for a decade.

Perhaps the main deviation from the norm was that the 175 Sport employed valves operated through short splayed pushrods on the nearside of the engine. These ultra-short inclined pushrods were driven from a single chain-driven camshaft, mounted at the top of the timing case, and this was kept in adjustment by a Weller-type tensioner.

The valve angle was 90 degrees, while the pressed-up crankshaft featured a caged-roller big-end and phosphor-bronze small-end; tappet adjustment was by a simple screw and locknut method, and the valve springs were of the coil variety. The gear-change and kick-start levers were both situated on the offside of the bike and there was a four-speed gearbox and helical-cut, primary-drive gears.

Parilla introduced the Gran Sport and later the MSDS Formula 3 versions, both with even more performance, for use in racing events. Both were very successful; in 1957, Parilla won the 175cc class of the famous Giro d'Italia. The instrument of victory was a Gran Sport ridden by Giuseppe Rottigni. Rottigni's machine averaged 97.25km/h (60.78 mph) for the entire nine-stage, 2043km (1277 mile) event. Out of the original 240 starters, only 100 finished at all.

In race tune (Gran Sport or MSDS configuration), the hi-cam Parilla could achieve 160km/h (100 mph), putting it on a par with other Formula 3 models from Ducati, Moto Morini and Motobi. However, there was an upward tendency in engine size. The 175cc (11ci) engine became a 199cc (12ci) and then a 247cc (15ci) in the 1960s; in the latter form, it achieved considerable success in the USA.

Ron Grant rode a 250 Parilla to finish as runner-up in the 1964 US Grand Prix, and Norris Rancourt chalked up a string of victories from 1962 until 1965. Rancourt's machine was not a factory entry, but a privately tuned bike owned by enthusiast Orrin Hall.

By this time, the Yamaha twin cylinder TDI was eclipsing even the fastest four-stroke singles. However, the Parilla continued to be a success in the marketplace. Besides the larger engined versions, the 175 Sport remained on sale in Europe right up to the point when Parilla ceased trading in 1967.

ENGINE: 174cc (10ci) ohv 2v single, 59.8x62mm, air-cooled
POWER: 14bhp at 7800rpm
GEARBOX: 4-speed foot change
FINAL DRIVE: chain
WEIGHT: 129kg (284lb)
TOP SPEED: 125km/h (78mph)

BSA GOLD STAR DBD34

Known almost universally as the 'Goldie', the Gold Star was the best-loved machine to come out of the BSA stable. It was both the ultimate clubman's production racer and the hottest single-cylinder street racer of the 1950s. Its name was inherited from the pre-war M24 Gold Star, and although post-war versions were effectively little more than improved overhead-valve B31/32 and B33/34 roadsters, the results were most impressive.

When it first appeared in 1947, the 350 Gold Star was designated the B32GS and was available in varying states of tune to suit different sporting activities, whether scrambles (motocross),

trials or road racing. Two years later, a 500cc (31ci) version with a plunger frame was added. Model designations progressed from B to ZB (1949–52), BB (1953), CB (1953–55), DB (1955–56), and DBD (1957–63). In all cases, Gold Star engine numbers ended with the letters GS.

In 1949, the 500cc (31ci) Gold Star made its name in fine style, winning no less than 11 gold medals at the ISDT. The following year, it acquired swing-arm rear suspension, and very quickly dominated the Clubman's TT races to such an extent that there was little point in entering anything else. For example, 63 out of 68 entries in 1955 were Gold Stars.

The Gold Star was built with a range of specifications, of which the most popular DBD34 model had a huge Amal GP carburettor, no tickover, no air-cleaner and a tendency to foul spark plugs. In road trim, it produced around 38hp at 7000rpm, and could deliver about 5hp more when race tuned. By comparison, the 350 Gold Star could manage 25hp.

In 1963, BSA decided that the Gold Star was too expensive to produce, and closed the line down. It was followed by the C15, a 250cc (15ci) single intended for

trials and scrambles. The C15 gradually received bigger engines, including 250cc (15ci), 440cc (27ci) and 500cc (31ci). Jeff Smith won two world motocross titles aboard this machine.

ENGINE: 499cc ohv single, 85x88mm, air-cooled
POWER: 38bhp at 7000rpm
GEARBOX: 4-speed foot change
FINAL DRIVE: chain
WEIGHT: 191kg (420lb)
TOP SPEED: 177kph (110mph)

Right: Power and prestige in motion; the 'Goldie' blew everything else away in clubman racing in the mid-1950s. It was the fastest street machine available, but was too expensive to build.

DUCATI 175

ITALY 1957

The Ducati 175 first appeared at the 1956 Milan Show. It attracted some interest as the first Ducati production model to be offered with the single overhead-camshaft, bevel-driven engine. This engine was directly developed from Fabio Taglioni's original Ducati design, the racing-only 98cc (6ci) Gran Sport Marianna of 1955.

Ultimately, the 175 was offered in a wide variety of guises. These included: S (Sport), T (Turismo), Americano (Custom), Formula 3 (Racer) and Motocross (Dirt Bike).

However, the Sport model was by far the most popular in the series. With its top speed of 135km/h (84mph), it was faster than many contemporary 500cc (31ci) bikes, and yet it was economical to run. With careful throttle use (admittedly something that is rare in sport-bike enthusiasts), the 175 could manage almost 2.78l/100km (100mpg).

With a dry weight of only 103kg (200lb), a whip-free chassis that provided superb handling and large, full-width aluminium brake hubs, the Ducati 175 accelerated, handled and stopped better than anything in its class.

The 175 was the first series-production Ducati with a bevel engine. Along with the popular Sport, variants included touring, race and dirt-bike versions of the basic 175.

ENGINE: 174.5cc (11ci) sohc 2v single 62x 57.8mm, air-cooled
POWER:
T – 11bhp at 7500rpm
S – 14bhp at 8000rpm
F – 316bhp at 9000rpm
GEARBOX: 4-speed foot change
FINAL DRIVE: chain
WEIGHT: n/a
TOP SPEED:
T – 121km/h (75mph),
S – 135km/h (84mph),
F – 161km/h (100mph)

HARLEY-DAVIDSON XL

USA 1957

When the XL was introduced in 1957, 40hp was quite respectable when delivered reliably by a machine of under 900cc (55ci). The XL was also well behaved on the road, which did its reputation no harm. In 1958, power was increased by higher compression (thanks to domed pistons), bigger valves and a lighter valve train.

In 1959, the cams were made a little more aggressive, and by 1962, the XL Sportster was one of the best and fastest Harley-Davidsons of any era. It was also one of the few road-going bikes that genuinely echoed the early sporting days of the Harley-Davidson company.

By 1968, the company was claiming 58hp at 6800rpm for its machine, and in 1972 both the bore and stroke were increased to give a 1000cc (61ci) variant. This engine was used to excellent effect in the XLCR.

ENGINE: 883cc (53ci) ohv in-line V-twin, 76.2x96.8mm, air-cooled
POWER: 40bhp at 5500rpm
GEARBOX: 4-speed foot change
FINAL DRIVE: chain
WEIGHT: 230kg (500lb) approx
TOP SPEED: 170km/h (105mph) approx

Harleys are not renowned as sports machines, but the XL represented a move in that direction. Despite its weight, the powerful XL delivered 170km/h (105mph) along with good reliability and a smooth ride.

KREIDLER FLORETT

The Florett (Foil) was something of a departure from the norm, in that it used a flat-single engine. Imme had done so in the early 1950s, but no German marque had tried it since. The Florett's power unit was entirely new: a horizontal-cylinder, 49cc (3ci) piston-ported engine driving through a three-speed gearbox to power a super-lightweight machine that was available with and without pedals. It could thus be sold both as a moped and as a motorcycle.

Whether or not it was sold as a moped, the Florett had a full motorcycle-type suspension with Earles-pattern front forks and a swinging-arm at the rear, full-width alloy brake hubs and fan-cooling for the engine. In its guise as a true motorcycle, the Florett could achieve 80km/h (50mph). In common with other Kreidler models, the bore was hard chrome plated directly onto the aluminium cylinder, while the gearbox was still operated by twist-grip control. The pressed-steel frame, together

Kreidler was famous for ultra-lightweights, and this is the definitive one. The Florett was available as a moped or a true motorcycle.

with the deeply valanced mudguards, fully enclosed chain and partly covered engine.

The Florett had a very different look from the other moped-cum-motorcycles of the era – and a very modern look at that. Although the frame remained an open 'U' shape, the fuel tank and saddle (either in single or dual form) had only a small gap between them. It was sufficiently popular and long lasting that the factory presented owners who had completed 100,000km (62,137 miles) with a solid gold tiepin bearing the Kreidler emblem.

With the Florett, Kreidler found and exploited a virtually untapped market for a cheap and reliable 50cc (3ci) machine that looked like a full-blown motorcycle but came at a fraction of the usual cost. The Florett was also successful in

racing events and long-distance trials such as the International Six Days' Trial (ISDT).

The Florett was immensely popular in its home market and also in the Netherlands, where 100,000 machines had been sold by 1971. Right up to the closure of the Kreidler factory in the early 1980s, a machine named Florett was still in production, though by

this time it was a 79.8cc (4.9ci) ultra-lightweight motorcycle.

ENGINE: 49cc (3ci) two-stroke single, 40x39.5mm, air-cooled
POWER: 3.5bhp at 6500rpm
GEARBOX: 3-speed foot change
FINAL DRIVE: chain
WEIGHT: 84kg (185lb)
TOP SPEED: 80.5km/h (50mph)

MINERELLI

The Minarelli story began in 1951, when Franco Morini and Vittorio Minerelli built their first machine, the 125cc (8ci) Gabbiano (Seagull), which was powered by a single-cylinder, two-stroke engine. This was quickly followed by the Vampire, with an overhead-valve 200cc (12ci) unit. Vampires were sold under the FBM brand name and, from 1956, FBM supplied other motorcycle companies with both two- and four-stroke engines ranging from 48cc (3ci) to 174cc (11ci).

Morini left FBM in 1957 to form the Franco Morini engine-manufacturing firm, and the company's name was adjusted to FB Minerelli (although the FB was later dropped).

Meanwhile, in the 1960s, Minerelli developed a 175cc (11ci) record breaker and, by the early 1970s, was supplying a vast range of engines, including 49cc (3ci), single-speed automatic units for the Italian moped industry, through to 125cc (8ci) and 175cc (11ci), multi-speed assemblies for dirt-bike manufacturers. These engines were supplied

Minarelli is famous for its engines. Its bikes are there mainly to carry the engine to racing victory and thus guarantee new sales.

to firms both at home and abroad.

Spanish rider Angel Nieto brought the firm some well-deserved publicity when he won the 1979 and 1981 125cc World Road-racing Championships. His machine was a liquid-cooled, disc-valve, parallel-twin designed by the German two-stroke specialist Jorg Moller. Minerelli also constructed a 50cc (3ci) single,

again with disc-valve induction and liquid-cooling. It was entered in a number of events but never achieved the success of its twin-cylinder, larger-engined brother.

Minerelli eventually sold these machines to Garelli, which developed them further and won several 125cc world titles until the late 1980s, when the firm switched to single cylinders for the class.

Minerelli has never built standard production machines, concentrating instead on constructing engines to supply to other manufacturers. However, its highly successful sporting machines have shown that, should it ever become necessary, the firm will be capable of building complete motorcycles to go on sale to the general public.

MOTOTRANS

Mototrans started out licence-building Ducatis in the late 1950s, at a time when Spain was under strict import restrictions imposed by the Franco regime. These were intended to protect Spanish jobs by banning imports of certain foreign goods, notably motorcycles. As a result, Ducati and other marques, such as Moto Guzzi and MV Agusta, were made locally.

Like many other manufacturers, the firm was set up in Barcelona, where it quickly established itself as a major force in Spanish motorcycling, a position it maintained for 25 years. The first production models appeared in 1957 and were, at first, straightforward copies of existing

Italian versions, the initial batch being 175cc (11ci) Sport overhead-cam singles.

The first in-house Mototrans designs appeared in the 1960s. Two of these were racers, the '285' single, which was shared by Bruno Spaggiari and Giuseppe Mandolini when they won the 1964 Barcelona 24 hours endurance race at record speed, and the MT250 248cc (15ci) four-cylinder. The latter was designed by the former Benelli engineer, Renato Armaroli.

In the early 1970s, Mototrans built a five-speed version of the Italian 125/160cc (8/10ci) overhead-cam Ducatis and a version of the 250cc (15ci) bevel single, the 24 Horas (24 Hours).

There was also a series of two-strokes, including the Mini, Pronto and Senda.

A new variation on the familiar overhead-cam single theme arrived in 1976 with the new 300cc (18ci) Electronica. It was followed by the 250cc (15ci) Strada, 350cc (21ci) Forza (touring) and Vento (sport). While the Italian influence was obvious, Spanish features were creeping into the design. For example, the Mototrans take on Ducati designs often included features not seen on Itlaian machines, such as cast-alloy wheels, electric start and 12V electrics.

In 1978, Mototrans unveiled its first completely in-house production model, the MTV

406.61cc (24.8ci) Yak 410. The Italian influence had finally been left behind and the new machine looked more Japanese than European. Its styling was similar to Suzuki's recently released SP 370.

However, Mototrans got into financial trouble near the end of 1981. The firm rallied and was able to resume production in 1982, but just a year later, the firm succumbed.

A 1979 Mototrans 350 Forza. It was powered by an overhead-cam bevel Ducati, single-cylinder engine and featured electric start, disc front brake and 12-volt electrics.

ZANELLA

Zanella has the distinction of being the only South American marque that is both wholly owned by South Americans and which has built and raced its own machines in track events. Others have had their stockholders overseas or have made only roadsters and dirt bikes.

Like many other motorcycle firms, Zanella was founded by Italians. The Zanella brothers left their home just north of Venice to move to Argentina in 1948, and there set up a firm that initially specialized in metallurgy. In 1955,

Zanella began manufacturing components for the Argentinian motor car industry.

Zanella built its first motorcycles in 1957. Most components (about 80 per cent) came from Italy, with the remainder fabricated in house. In 1958, the firm acquired a licence from Ceccato to manufacture its 100cc (6ci) two-stroke.

A new factory was built in 1959–60, and from it came the first motorcycle Zanella built entirely in Argentina. The firm also

followed Italian practice and began making three-wheeled trucks, and these began to be exported, along with motorcycles, in 1961. Starting with Paraguay, Zanella was soon selling its machines all across South America and in the USA. A racing programme was also implemented.

The firm continued to expand in the mid-1960s, with a full range that included the popular SS125 roadster and a larger version with a 168cc (10ci) engine. The firm's racing machines developments

dominated domestic competition for the next 20 years.

After many good years of exports across the Americas, Zanella entered the European market in the early 1980s with a successful 80cc (5ci) Grand Prix racer. A presence at the biennial Milan Show resulted in an agreement with Cagiva to market the Zanella commuter moped. Italian bikes had been imported to South America for a long time but now, at last, came movement in the opposite direction.

ARIEL LEADER AND ARROW

ENGLAND 1958

Designed by Val Page, the Ariel Leader was something entirely new when it appeared in 1958. Featuring a pressed-steel beam frame and unit construction, twin-cylinde,r two-stroke engine, the machine's fully enclosed bodywork looked great and was easy to keep clean.

The Leader was fairly light and agile, and powerful enough to give enjoyable performance, but at the same time it was tidy, quiet and functional. The engine design was inspired by the German Adler twin and built in unit with four-speed transmission driving a chain to the rear wheel. Power delivery was smooth and responsive, although petrol lubrication remained a necessary chore.

In standard configuration, the Leader was pretty good, but a range of options was also offered. In 1959, it was joined by a faster, more conventional-looking sports version, the Arrow. It had the same frame, with the fuel tank under the seat in the same manner as Honda's Gold Wing.

The Arrow weighed 27kg (60lb) less than the Leader and the later 'super sports' Golden Arrow developed 4hp more for a top speed close to 126km/h (80mph).

There was also a 197cc (12ci) variant. Racing versions of the Arrow did not set the world on fire, but were able to achieve respectable success in competition.

ENGINE: 249cc (15ci) parallel twin two-stroke, 54x54mm, air-cooled
POWER: 16bhp at 6400rpm
GEARBOX: 4-speed foot change
FINAL DRIVE: chain
WEIGHT: 163kg (360lb)
TOP SPEED: 113km/h (70mph)

The Leader was something of an unusual design and shared many innovative features with its racing derivative, the Arrow.

HONDA C50 SUPER CUB

JAPAN 1958

Honda's humble C50 was one of those vehicles that changed the face of transportation. Other examples include the Model T-Ford and the Mini, and the Super Cub's influence was no less profound.

The most basic of Honda's step-through machines was the Honda 50, powered by a 49cc (3ci) four-stroke single. It could manage 64km/h (40mph), sufficient to cope with urban traffic.

The 50cc (3ci) Super Cub first appeared in August 1958, bringing mobility to the masses, not just in the industrialized nations but in the developing world, where good roads were few and far between.

The step-through configuration of these machines meant they were practical and easy to mount, while weather protection was afforded by the enclosed chain, the fairings and leg shields.

As was typical with Honda products, no matter how basic, these machines were well made and very reliable, making them particularly popular in the developing world. In just the first five months of production, through to the end of 1958, more than 24,000 were sold.

The CS90, introduced in 1964, was the first new model to receive the chain-drive overhead-cam engine. Its all-alloy single-cylinder motor was built with the barrel horizontal and the cam running directly into the head. It delivered 8hp. Variants included the overhead-cam C50 (1967); the C70 and C90 gave slightly better performance.

The C110 motorcycle-style version used the C100's engine, but mounted suspended from a pressed-steel frame. The tiny CZ100 Monkey Bike, in production from 1960, also used the C100 engine and transmission with 128mm (5in) wheels in a rigid frame and forks.

From 1960 onwards, Honda sold half a million step-through bikes a year. By 1983 some 15 million had been built and sales continued to be good, showing no signs of stopping. This humble little machine is the most successful powered two-wheeler of all time.

ENGINE: 50cc (3ci) four-stroke single cylinder, overhead cam
POWER: 8bhp
GEARBOX: n/a
FINAL DRIVE: chain
WEIGHT: n/a
TOP SPEED: n/a

Unexciting in appearance, the Honda C50 Super Cub nevertheless caused a revolution by bringing convenient, reliable and, above all, cheap transport to the general public.

BULTACO

Bultaco is named for its founder, Francisco Bulto. He left Montesa, a firm he had helped found, because of its reluctance to become involved in racing. Setting up on his own near Barcelona, he began producing a range of small-capacity, two-stroke race machines.

Bultaco racers were soon appearing in Grand Prix events – and doing very well. Meanwhile, the firm was marketing a range of very quick road machines,

including the 250cc (15ci) Metralla, which boasted a top speed in excess of 160km/h (100mph). The firm was also gaining a reputation for excellent trials machines. Sammy Miller's victory in the 1965 Scottish Six Days Trial showed that the Bultaco two-stroke was well on its way to taking a dominant position in off-road trialling.

The Bultaco two-stroke edged out the Swedish Husqvarna for the place of 250cc (15ci) class leader,

Although Bultaco is primarily famous for its off-road machines, the firm also made some very competitive road-racing machines. Like all Bultacos, this TSS 350 is an air-cooled, two-stroke single.

and by the time the inaugural Trials World Championship was established in 1975, Bultaco was reigning supreme. Bultacos won the event for five straight years, prompting Bulto's old company, Montesa, to build competition machines such as the 172 Cota and 250 Cota.

On the road-racing front, Angel Nieto and Ricardo Tormo won no less than a total of four 50cc world titles, all on Bultacos, up to 1981. However, even while these victories were being won, troubles in the workplace and a series of strikes began to cripple the company, and soon after it went under.

MATCHLESS G50

Ever since the appearance of the 7R, customers had been clamouring for a 500cc (31ci) version, but it was not until 1958 that they got it. Matchless had built 500s before World War II, but the first post-war offering was the G45, which was simply a tuned G9 engine in 7R cycle parts. This was never really satisfactory, and the change from the G45 to the G50 single was better received.

The G50 retained the stroke of the 7R and gained its capacity

The G50 appeared in 1958, but potential buyers had been clamouring for it since the R7's launch 10 years previously. The 500cc (30ci) single remained in production for only five years before AJS ceased making bikes.

from an increased bore. It also used the same layout, with the single camshaft driven by chain from a half-time pinion in the gear train to the magneto. An alloy casting enclosed both drives, and since the valve gear was fully enclosed, this made for an oil-tight engine.

The G50 was easy to maintain because it used the same four-speed gearbox and cycle parts as the 7R – an advantage for private owners running in both classes. It also meant that any chassis changes were easily applied to both models. In 1963, AMC produced the G50CSR, combining the old engine with the CSR cycle parts and lights in order to run in the Daytona 200 race. Dick Mann rode his G50CSR to a very close second place, just 3m (10ft) behind the winner.

The G50 was built until AMC ceased production in the early part of 1963.

ENGINE: 496cc (30ci) ohc vertical single, 90x78mm, air-cooled
POWER: 51bhp at 7200rpm
GEARBOX: 4-speed foot change
FINAL DRIVE: chain
WEIGHT: 130kg (285lb)
TOP SPEED: n/a

PATON

Paton got its start from a decision in 1957 by FB Mondial, Guzzi and Gilera to cease Grand Prix competition. This left a number of engineers lacking a job, among them Giuseppe Pattoni, who had been chief mechanic for the FB Mondial squad. He teamed up with designer Lino Tonti, another former Mondial employee, and created a 124cc (8ci) double overhead-cam racer for sale to top-line privateers for the 1958 season. The Paton name was derived from the names of its two founders. Although Tonti left to work for Bianchi, Pattoni

(and the Paton name) stayed, creating a series of race machines during the next four decades.

One of the firm's first customers was Stan Hailwood, whose son Mike was starting out on the road to racing glory. Mike Hailwood rode his Paton to seventh place in the 1958 125cc TT. Next came the first machine solely created by Pattoni. This was a twin-cylinder model that achieved third place in the 1964 250cc TT, ridden by Alberto Pagani.

Backing was forthcoming from a Liverpool-based Scot, Bill Hannah,

allowing the model to be further developed into a 350cc (21ci) and later a 500cc (31ci). The later 500s produced 65hp in two-valve form, with the final version gaining four valves per cylinder in a double overhead-cam configuration. This delivered 70hp, good enough for Paton rider Angelo Bergamonti to beat world champion Giacomo Agostini and win the 1967 500cc Italian Senior Championship.

The twin remained in production into the 1970s, but in 1976 Pattoni designed a 492cc (30ci) cross-port, liquid-cooled,

two-stroke, four-cylinder model. In 1984, a new twin-crankshaft, close-coupled four, consisting of two 250cc (15ci) twins mounted one above the other, with the cylinders spaced at 115 degrees, aroused considerable interest.

For some 20 years, Peppino Pattoni – as he was to become known in racing circles – carried on with the help of Gianemillo Marchesani. However, Marchesani was killed in a car crash in the early 1980s, and his place was taken by Pattoni's son, Roberto.

In 1967, a Paton machine was used by Angelo Bergamont to win the 500cc Italian Championship, beating Giacomo Agostini to do so. Paton engines benefited from design by the world's top race engineers.

AJS MODEL 18

The G3 series of singles were badged as Matchless and AJS, but both versions were very similar. AJS machines mounted the magneto in front of the engine in post-war years, with Matchless copying this for 1952; and both switched to alternator electrics for 1958, also gaining a cast-alloy primary chaincase at the same time. This replaced the old pressed-steel type with its sealing problems, while the points went into the timing chest.

After 1958, the engine of the 18 received only one more major change, an alteration to the bore and stroke for 1964. However, the cycle components were updated in 1960 with a new frame that had duplex downtubes. By 1964, all the road singles were fitted with Norton Roadholder forks and Norton hubs, which were used until production ceased.

The model 18 was accompanied by the 348cc (21ci) model 16. Both were dependable and economical machines with good brakes, and were considered to be excellent for daily transport and weekend trips. However, they were not very exciting and their ancestry was too obvious. Time had moved on, and while these were worthy bikes, they were outdated. In time, they disappeared, to be superseded by a new generation with different qualities.

ENGINE: 497cc (30ci) ohv vertical single, 82.5x93mm, air-cooled
POWER: n/a
GEARBOX: 4-speed foot change
FINAL DRIVE: chain
WEIGHT: 179kg (394lb)
TOP SPEED: 140km/h (85mph)

By 1960, most of the AJS model range had dispensed with the magneto, but off-road versions such as this 18CS retained it, along with a different carburettor.

MATCHLESS G12CSR

Towards the end of the 1940s, there was a trend towards vertical twins. AMC's first move in that direction was the 498cc (30ci) AJS model 20 and Matchless G9, with megaphone silencers and dual seat. Both had overhead-valve engines, four speeds, telescopic forks and rear suspension.

A larger, 593cc (36ci), version appeared in 1956, and from 1958 was available in CS and CSR forms. The CS was built as a street-scrambler machine for off-road work, with the lights optional and easily detachable.

The CSR was a high-speed sports machine that combined the tuned CS engine and other parts for fast road use. The suffix letters officially stood for Competition Sprung Roadster, but the rest of the world disagreed, dubbing the CSR the 'Coffee Shop Racer'.

The 593cc (36ci) twin was replaced in 1959 by a 646cc (39ci) version in standard, CS and CSR forms plus sports 498cc (30ci) models for just one year. The larger twins proved fast and popular, and were soon offered in a variety of colour finishes.

All models were available with a range of options, which created something of a production headache despite the fact that all versions used common parts.

However, G12CSR ran on to 1966, having been joined a year earlier by the G15 series, which used the 745cc (45ci) Norton Atlas twin engine. AMC also produced essentially identical machines under the AJS badge.

ENGINE: 646cc (39ci) ohv vertical twin, 72x79.3mm, air-cooled
POWER: n/a
GEARBOX: 4-speed foot change
FINAL DRIVE: chain
WEIGHT: 173kg (381lb)
TOP SPEED: 180km/h (108mph)

The 180km/h (108mph)-capable performance (or 'Coffee Shop Racer') variant of the G12 was fast and powerful, and was available with all kinds of options and extras.

PARILLA SLUGHI/OLIMPIA

ITALY 1959

The Slughi, or Desert Greyhound, was designed by Piero Bossaglia and was unveiled at the Milan Show in 1957. It was built with both two-stroke and four-stroke engines and also sold in a revised form as the Olimpia.

The design was built around a fabricated pressed-steel backbone extending to form the base for the seat and rear mudguard. The horizontal engine was suspended from the backbone, with detachable panels covering the sides of the power unit (left naked on the Olimpia) and continued rearwards beyond the hub. Movement of the tubular rear fork was controlled by a rubber block concealed inside the frame backbone.

In concept and appearance, the Slughi bore a striking resemblance to the Aermacchi Chimera, which had caused quite a stir at the previous year's Milan Show without achieving much in the marketplace. However, even though the Slughi was similar, even to the extent of having a horizontal, unit-construction, four-speed, overhead-valve engine, it was much smaller and cheaper and sold well in the commuter market.

The major disadvantage of the Chimera was its lack of decent weather protection, and the Slughi dealt with this by having an optional set of elegant and efficient leg shields and a large windshield, all of which could be fitted quickly.

The first Slughi models went on sale for the 1959 model year and

The 1959 Parilla Olimpia used a 97.7cc (6ci) air-cooled, overhead-valve engine with a horizontal single cylinder engine. The legshields and enclosure were optional and could be quickly removed.

featured a 97.7cc (6ci) pushrod engine. The same pushrod engine was also used on the Olimpia. Later Slughi/Olimpia models came with a choice of either a 125cc/8ci (actually 114cc/7ci) two-stroke, or the original '98' overhead-valve four-stroke engines. At least twice the number of the smaller engined models were sold compared to the larger two-stroke version.

The engine layout of both versions was tidy, with the two basic motors sharing many components, including the gearbox, the clutch and electrical items. This helped

keep production costs down and allowed for an affordable market price. The four-stroke engine's fuel consumption was very good indeed, at better than 2.3l/100km (125mpg).

ENGINE: 97.7cc (6ci) ohv horizontal single, 52x46mm, air-cooled
POWER: 6.5rpm at 7200rpm
GEARBOX: 4-speed foot change
FINAL DRIVE: chain
WEIGHT: 78kg (172lb)
TOP SPEED: 85km/h (53mph)

PUCH SGS 175/250

ITALY 1959

The Puch SGS 175 and 250 models could trace their ancestry all the way back to the Harlette split-single, created in 1923. This machine was the first Puch to depart from the then conventional crossflow system of scavenge. This was not the first to be used on a motorcycle, but it was certainly one of the most successful, staying in production for 50 years and culminating with the SGS machines.

The Puch layout differed from the earlier Garelli and the later German Triumph (TWN) split-singles in that

its pistons did not rise and fall side by side in unison. The essence of split-single scavenge is two cylinders sharing a cylinder head, the two pistons taking part in both induction and power strokes. The exhaust port is in one cylinder, the transfer port in the other.

The SGS range ran through the 1950s and 1960s with 175cc (11ci) and 250cc (15ci) engines, but the engine design was developed from concepts proven in much earlier machines. This is a 1961 model.

A 1960 SGS. The highly successful split-single design offered good fuel consumption and smooth running without any loss of performance, and achieved strong sales in Europe and the USA.

The Puch employed a 'Y'-shaped connecting rod shared by both the pistons, and as the rod began its stroke, the angle meant that one of the pistons – except at the top and bottom centres – was 'ahead' of the other. This piston was used to control the exhaust port. Thus the exhaust port could open and close early, which gave plenty of time for the exhaust gases to escape before the transfer port was opened.

The split-single had other advantages: there was no need for a deflector on the piston crown because the shared cylinder wall acted as a deflector. This allowed for lighter pistons, which were free from the distortion that can result from uneven heating.

The most important advantage of the split-single was that it allowed the engine to run smoothly at all times and with superior fuel consumption, like that of a good four-stroke.

The 248cc (15ci) unit-construction power pack of the type used in the SGS first appeared in 1948. The design was updated in 1953 with telescopic forks, swinging-arm rear suspension and a pressed-steel chassis. Delivering 16.5hp, the Puch split-single line was sold in the USA as the Allstate from 1954, through the Sears Chain Store Company.

ENGINE: 248cc (15ci) 2s split-single, 78x45x2, air-cooled
POWER: 16.5bhp at 5500rpm
GEARBOX: 4-speed foot change
FINAL DRIVE: chain
WEIGHT: 163kg (360lb)
TOP SPEED: 115km/h (72mph)

RICKMAN

ENGLAND 1959–75

Rickman was founded by two brothers of that name, Derek and Don. The firm was chiefly known for its off-road machines, but later earned a solid reputation for high-quality roadster and racing frames. The Rickman brothers believed that there were 'plenty of good engines and good frames about in the '60s, but it wasn't often that you got the two together', so they set out to build a chassis that was both strong and light, and able to carry a range of engines.

The result was their 'Metisse' chassis, originally sold as chassis 'kits'. From 1970 to 1974, however, the firm produced some 12,000 complete off-road machines using Bultaco and Zundapp 125cc (8ci) and 250cc (15ci) two-stroke engines. During this period, Rickman was Britain's largest motorcycle manufacturer.

Although the firm was initially uninterested in roadsters, the demise of Royal Enfield in 1969 left stocks of about 200 Series II 736cc (45ci) Constellation engines lacking a home. These were bought up by Rickman and built up into a road machine that was named the Interceptor. It was given an excellent frame, as might be expected from Rickman, and wound up being both light and very affordable.

The Interceptor was built using only high quality components, including Rickman's own forks and some of the first modern disc brakes. Indeed, it was described by a French magazine as 'the Rolls-Royce of motorcycles'. Although only 205 were built, the Interceptor did lead to a new project.

In the early 1970s, Japanese four-cylinder machines such as the Honda CB750 were known for their impressive power, but their handling left something to be desired. Rickman adapted the Interceptor chassis to mount the excellent Japanese engines in a machine that had handling to match their capabilities.

However, from 1975 onwards, the company increasingly concerned itself with the production of accessories rather than chassis parts.

Rickman's most famous creation was the Metisse frame, made available to fit a variety of engines. These frames are still made today, allowing enthusiasts to build up replica classics or their own ideal machine.

ROKON

New Hampshire-based Rokon produced its first machine in 1959, and it was a most curious machine. The Trailbreaker was originally powered by a 131cc (8ci) Chrysler marine two-stroke engine with pull-cord start, driving a three-speed gearbox with an automatic clutch. From there, both of the enormous wheels were driven.

From the gearbox came separate power feeds to each

wheel. A chain took the power up to the rear end of the frame top tube, where a cross-shaft split the drive between a chain to the rear-wheel sprocket and a shaft that ran up the top tube. At the steering head, a universal joint took care of the steering movement of the fork and connected to a second cross-shaft that carried the chain into the front-wheel sprocket. Both cross-shaft assemblies had gear pairs

within them to turn the drive.

The frame was tubular with the engine installed horizontally and the gearbox behind it, giving excellent ground clearance. The only suspension was provided by the large-diameter, low-pressure balloon tyres. These had tractor treads and were fitted to light-alloy wheels formed as drums so that they could carry petrol or water. When empty, the wheels

acted as buoyancy chambers. Braking was achieved by a single mechanical disc on the front cross-shaft, which effectively retarded both wheels.

This very unusual machine could climb extremely steep slopes and was built in various plants, with occasional breaks in production. A later version had a 340cc (21ci) Sachs two-stroke engine and automatic transmission.

TRIUMPH BONNEVILLE

The T120 Bonneville was introduced at the 1959 Earls Court Show, and quickly came to dominate production racing with its powerful twin-carburettor 650cc (40ci) two-cylinder engine. The original Bonneville featured the familiar headlamp nacelle, but Triumph quickly reverted to the traditional unfaired headlight

arrangement so that it could be detached when the bike was ridden in competition.

From 1963 onwards, the Bonneville had unit-constructed engines and gearboxes, most of the engine internals remaining unchanged. One notable difference was the rearward extension of the crankcase to incorporate the

gearbox, like the smaller-capacity machines.

The T120 gained upgraded (12V) electrics and a revised tank badge in 1966. The brakes were improved twice – first in 1968 with twin leading-shoe front brakes;

then in 1973, when the machine was given a front disc brake.

The Bonneville spawned a number of variants. The T120TT model was intended purely for scrambling; it was never intended for road use. A small batch of

Right: The T120 Bonneville was vital to Triumph's market success. The bike gained a new frame in 1971 and a different engine in 1973.

Charles to Lady Diana Spencer, was marked with a special edition model. The T140 Royal had alloy wheels and Bing carburettors. Meanwhile, the rubberized anti-vibration engine mountings tried on police-use Bonnevilles entered general production in 1982, in conjunction with an all-alloy, eight-valve engine fed by twin Amals. The resulting model was named the T140 TSS Bonneville. A custom version called the T140 TSX was also available, sporting brighter colours, a two-level seat and high-rise bars.

The year 1983 saw the arrival of a new version, the Phoenix 900. It featured an all-new, water-cooled eight-valve twin with chain-driven overhead-cams. The engine was code-named 'Diana' and acted as a stressed member of the frame, which had monoshock rear suspension, alloy wheels, disc brakes and telescopic front forks.

The final incarnation of the Bonneville was produced by the

Above: The original Bonneville appeared in 1959 with twin carburettors and a 650cc (40ci), twin-cylinder engine. It quickly established itself as a force to be reckoned with on the circuit and the showroom.

Right: The Bonneville was eventually edged out by the new powerful, sophisticated Japanese imports.

T120RT production racers was constructed to contest the US-based AMA series in 1970 using bored-out 744cc (45ci) engines. These were very successful in the hands of Gene Romero, who won in 1970, and came second on another in 1971.

Also in 1971, the Bonneville was relaunched as the TR120R unit twin. It was built on a wholly new frame, which featured enlarged top and seat tubes acting as the oil tank. This had the undesirable effect of raising the height of the seat and thus the centre of gravity. The machine received new slender forks and conical hubs, as well as flashing indicators, and cosmetic changes were made too. These included new side panels and megaphone-style silencers.

The Bonneville got a new engine in 1973, along with a re-designation as the T140. The new engine was initially 725cc (44ci) and was later enlarged to 744cc (45ci) like the US T120RT racer. There were also major revisions to the cylinder head. All Triumph models now had the option of a five-speed gearbox, which was indicated by a Roman 'V' for '5' in the designation, as in T140V. However, the cycle parts and running gear of the old T120 were not changed.

However, the Bonneville was losing ground to the new wave of big four-cylinder Japanese machines, such as the Honda CB750 and Suzuki GT750, which were stealing the limelight by offering affordable, reliable performance. Matters were not helped by industrial disputes. Indeed, during the Triumph workers' 18-month sit-in, which began in September 1973, only a handful of machines left the factory.

The bikes that did make it out of the factory gates were mostly T140Vs, and most Bonnevilles produced during the protest were delivered during the final months of the dispute, between March and May 1975.

The new 1976 T140V Bonneville used the familiar 744cc (45ci) engine in twin-carburettor format, but the gearshift was swapped

over to the left-hand side and a rear disc brake fitted. The following year, 1977, was the Queen's Silver Jubilee, and Triumph marked the occasion with a special edition machine in red, white and blue livery: 2400 were built.

In 1978, another upgraded model appeared on the US market. This was the T140E, which featured a new cylinder head and carburetion that was better suited to US emissions requirements. It replaced the T140V on the UK market in 1979, at which time it gained electronic ignition. The T140ES was equipped with an electric starter from 1981, and an Executive model appeared in 1980, complete with a Sabre faring, Sigma panniers and a top-box.

Another Royal occasion, this time the marriage of Prince

Newton Abbot-based Racing Spares concern of Les Harris, which was granted a five-year licence to make Bonnevilles. Although the frame and cycle parts were much as before, the engine components were made on new CNC lathes for greater precision. Kick-starters and Amal carburettors were used once more, but there were parts from new sources; forks from Paioli, instruments from Veglia and Italian Brembo brakes. The last of the Devon Bonnevilles was produced in 1988.

ENGINE: (T120) 650cc (39ci) parallel-twin, 71x82mm, air-cooled
POWER: 46bhp
GEARBOX: 4-speed foot change
FINAL DRIVE: chain
WEIGHT: 183kg (404lb)
TOP SPEED: 177km/h (110mph)

BIANCHI RASPATERRA MOTOCROSS

The Raspaterra (ground-scraper) series of motocross machines was designed by Lino Tonti and was closely related to the 318cc (19ci) MT61 military motorcycle of the same period. There were three variants available in 1960: 250cc (15ci), 350cc (21ci) and 400cc (24ci) bevel-driven, twin-cam single-cylinder machines, all of which were outwardly similar.

Engine features included elektron crankcases and twin-plug ignition, and all three offered a good range of power across various throttle settings, though high revs were common. Indeed, the 250cc (15ci) was safe to 10,000rpm, a most impressive figure for a four-stroke dirt bike of the period.

The 400cc (24ci) machine was a larger-bore version of the 350cc (21ci); these two were more popular than the 250cc (15ci), which was the first to appear. The 250cc (15ci) was ridden by factory tester and motocross rider Vincenzo Soletti, who turned in a number of excellent performances, including a win in the 1959 250cc Italian Motocross Championship.

The Raspaterra enjoyed a number of victories in Europe. In March 1960, a sole example of the Raspaterra, a 400cc (24ci), was exported to Terry Hill (a leading race sponsor of the era) in Belfast, Northern Ireland. There it was used for both motocross and grass track events at various meetings.

ENGINE: 400cc (24ci) dohc single, air-cooled
POWER: 22bhp at 6000rpm
GEARBOX: 4-speed foot change
FINAL DRIVE: chain
WEIGHT: 180kg (398lb)
TOP SPEED: 129kph (80mph)

Bianchi factory rider Carlo Caroli aboard a single-cylinder Raspaterra during the 1960 Swiss Motocross Grand Prix.

BMW R69S

The R69S is the last BMW bike accepted by purists as the 'real thing'; later models are not true BMWs – or so we are told. In addition to this claim to fame, it was also the fastest production road-going BMW of the pre-'stroke' era. The bikes were nicely put together, although they were not built to a very good design.

In some ways, the R69S was the precursor to BMW's new machines, but in others it was a throwback to the days of fast tourers.

It was the ultimate development of a lineage that began in 1951, the year that BMW

resumed production of twins with the R51/2. The R51/2 was followed by the very similar R51/3 and the R67, which was a 590cc (36ci) machine with slightly more power. Then, in 1955, BMW adopted the distinctive Earles forks. Other than this, the 494cc (30ci) R50 was essentially an R51/2 with another couple of horsepower. It remained in production until 1969.

The R60, a member of the same family of machines, produced 28hp from the 590cc (36ci) engine. This led to the R69, a version of the sporty R67/3 with Earles forks and delivering 35hp. This in turn led to the R69S, with a 68 x 68mm (2.7 x 2.7in) 'square' engine. At the same time, the S version of the R50 appeared, though the original outlived the R50S in production.

ENGINE: 590cc (35ci) ohv transverse flat twin, 72x73mm, air-cooled
POWER: 42bhp at 7000rpm
GEARBOX: 4-speed foot change
FINAL DRIVE: Kardan shaft
WEIGHT: 202kg (444lb)
TOP SPEED: 175km/h (109mph)

According to purists, the R69S was the last true BMW motorcycle, paving the way for the R90 and R100 series to come.

BULTACO METRALLA

The Metralla was a high-quality sports roadster. It differed from equivalent Japanese models by being essentially a motocross engine attached to a race-designed chassis and cycle parts.

The concept was a huge success: Bultaco Metrallas took the first three places in the 250cc

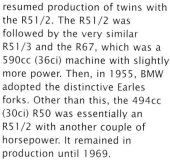

production class at the 1967 Isle of Man TT races.

The piston-port, oil-and-petrol-fuelled, two-stroke engine was a simple design that did not use performance aids like reed- or rotary-valves. The specification also included a six-speed gearbox, expansion-chamber exhaust, enclosed final-drive chain, and a twin leading-shoe front drum brake complete with an air scoop. The Metralla was in production for more than a decade.

ENGINE: 244cc (15ci) single-cylinder two-stroke
POWER: 25bhp
GEARBOX: 5-speed, foot change
FINAL DRIVE: chain
WEIGHT: 123kg (271lb)
TOP SPEED: 137km/h (85mph)

Although the Metralla was based on a road-going frame and cycle parts, and powered by a motocross engine, the resulting combination was very competitive on the tarmac.

ELMECA-GILERA

Gilera withdrew from Grand Prix racing at the end of the 1950s, and instead turned to trials riding as an arena in which to generate publicity. After Piaggio took over Gilera in 1969, interest in trials continued unabated, and much of the company's development work was done in conjunction with Elmeca, based near Turin. Elmeca was an established name in the off-road field and had a history of working with Gilera. The Elmeca-Gilera brand name was used for trials bikes intended for the general market.

Gilera withdrew at the end of 1974, and for several years (until Gilera returned in 1980) Elmeca built a number of Gilera-inspired designs under licence. These made a big impression in off-road sport in Italy and across Europe. Part of their success was due to the excellent rotary-valve two-stroke engine introduced by Gilera in 1968. Various versions were eventually built, including 100cc (6ci), 125cc (8ci) and 175cc (11ci) models.

An updated 123.5cc (7.5ci) engine was introduced for the 1973 season, and it achieved victory in that year's European two-day enduro championship series. Elmeca-Gilera machines were also used that year by the Italian national squad in the Silver Vase Trophy at the International Six-Days Trial (ISDT). For 1974,

there was a new 175cc (11ci), which, like its smaller brother, had rotary-valve induction and a six-speed gearbox.

Production versions of these machines were very competitive until around 1977, at which point a new breed of enduro bike, such as SWM and KTM, began to eclipse them.

An Elmeca-Gilera 125cc (8ci) motocross bike using a tuned version of the Elmeca-Gilera enduro engine was built from 1976 until 1979. It differed from the original works Gilera models in that it had a shorter stroke of 53.6mm (2.11in), instead of 54mm (2.12in), giving an engine size of 122.7cc (7.5ci) and

For two decades the Elmeca concern had close connections with Gilera, producing specialized dirt bikes like this 1976 125 Regolarita model.

producing 24hp. This machine was ridden by Dario Nani to win the 1978 Italian Motocross title.

MZ WANKEL

During the early 1960s, MZ were several years ahead of their rivals in building a Wankel-engined street bike. However, the resulting 174cc (11ci) machine never went into series production.

MZ's first Wankel prototype featured shaft drive and water-cooling. The engine remained oil-cooled, while the cycle parts were based around the production ES 250 of the same era. In 1965, a more advanced, air-cooled version was produced, but this too was destined never to go into production.

The MZ design incorporated rotating pistons lying crossways to the direction of the travel, cleverly integrated into a conventional-looking engine casing and housing four foot-operated gear ratios. The machine had a strangely shaped silencer due to the unorthodox positioning of the outlet at the top of the engine. The KKM 175L produced 24hp at 5750rpm and could achieve a very respectable 129km/h (80mph).

The project was a technical success but was not commercially

viable. The main problem was that the firm would have been obliged not only to retool its production lines to build these radically different machines but also to obtain a licence from NSU to make use of Wankel's concepts.

Wankel-engined machines did finally go into production a decade later, but both designs (the Hercules W2000 and Suzuki RE5) were financially embarrassing for their respective manufacturers. MZ seems to have made the right decision in not pursuing their unorthodox design.

ENGINE: 174cc (10ci) rotary single, air-cooled
POWER: 24bhp at 5750rpm
GEARBOX: 4-speed foot change
FINAL DRIVE: chain
WEIGHT: n/a
TOP SPEED: 130kph (81mph)

The MZ Wankel did not make it into production, though the project is still of significant historical and technical interest. A series of prototypes powered by Wankel engines was created by MZ, culminating in the liquid-cooled KKM 175W (1963) and air-cooled KKM 175L (1965). Both designs were the work of chief development engineer Herbert Friedrich, and owed a lot to the work of Felix Wankel, the father of the rotary piston engine, at NSU.

BIANCHI 350 DOHC TWIN RACER

ITALY 1961

In 1960, Lino Tonti designed a 250cc (15ci) double overhead-cam, parallel-twin machine intended for racing, and a year later it was upgraded to 350cc (21ci). Both versions had engine and six-speed gearbox in unit, mounted in a lightweight frame with a series of small-diameter tubes and an oval-section brace from the top of the steering head to the centre section of the frame.

The engine featured a built-up crankshaft, while a train of gears ran up between the cylinders to drive the camshafts. Electron alloy

was employed for the cam boxes, clutch housing and integral oil sump; the crankcase, cylinder barrels and heads were aluminium alloy. Each head featured dual spark plugs, firing simultaneously due to a pair of Bosch 6V double-ended coils aft of the steering head.

The 350 had its first outing at Monza in 1960, ridden by Brambilla in the Italian Grand Prix. Brambilla was joined the following year by Scottish riders Bob McIntyre and Alastair King. In the early part of the season, the new

Bianchi struggled with poor reliability, but it performed well in the Dutch TT; McIntyre was beaten by MV's Hocking, though only by a narrow margin.

McIntyre left to ride for Honda in 1962. A few months later, Bianchi signed up ex-MV rider Remo Venturi. He rode a 500cc (31ci) version of the twin in a successful bid to beat MV Agusta for the 1964 Senior Italian

Championship title. The next year, however, Bianchi ceased producing motorcycles.

ENGINE: 350cc (21ci) dohc parallel twin, 64x52.5mm, air-cooled
POWER: 51bhp at 11,000rpm
GEARBOX: 6-speed foot change
FINAL DRIVE: chain
WEIGHT: 127kg (280lb)
TOP SPEED: 210km/h (135mph)

Lino Tonti's twin-cylinder, 350cc (21ci,) double overhead-cam racer was fast but unreliable. It managed to turn in a credible race performance but it was the 500cc (31ci) version that finally took the Italian title.

KAWASAKI

JAPAN 1961–PRESENT

Kawasaki Heavy Industries is a huge business group (one of the largest in the world) and has interests in a variety of fields, including shipping, aircraft, railways and, of course, motorcycles. Where most of the dominant Japanese motorcycle firms set out to build bikes, Kawasaki Motorcycles arrived by a very different route.

The motorcycle arm of Kawasaki is small compared to some of the firm's other interests – but everything is relative. Kawasaki motorcycles is a major manufacturer responsible for some of the best bikes on the market.

Coming late to the motorcycle industry, Kawasaki missed most of the turbulent events of the 1950s. This was the time when the

Japanese industry expanded massively, spawning large numbers of firms until a rash of takeovers and mergers reduced the numbers again. The 1950s also saw the build-up of a massive home market protected by very high import tariffs and the start of expansion overseas to North America and Europe.

Most of the Japanese firms of the early post-war era came into the transport business to provide cheap mobility at a time when the average buyer was desperate for anything that would move under its own power. The early results were often crude, but lessons were soon learned and progress made. Such was the story of Honda, Suzuki, Yamaha and many smaller firms.

The Kawasaki story was altogether different. The firm traces its origins to a shipyard founded by Shozo Kawasaki in 1878, a period of rapid industrial and maritime growth in Japan. The firm had grown large and prosperous by 1901, when it diversified into railways and then civil engineering. By 1911, Kawasaki was involved in marine transportation, then sheet steel and, later, aircraft – and thus engines.

World War II caused massive destruction and disruption, and afterwards all but one division of Kawasaki was involved in the work of reconstruction. The aircraft factory was at a loose end, however, with nowhere to apply its skills and machinery. As had

happened elsewhere, particularly in Italy, producing motorcycles seemed just a short step from producing aircraft, and so the Kawasaki aircraft division turned to making motorcycle parts for other firms.

Kawasaki quickly became involved in supplying complete engine units, which kept the division productively employed until 1959. However, by then the firm's products were falling behind those of other manufacturers, and there were other options available. Hard questions had to be asked, including the most notable: Was it worth continuing in the motorcycle industry?

In the end, the decision to carry on was made on the basis of consumer image. Kawasaki was well known in the shipping, railways and aircraft industries, but was not a familiar name with the general public. Motorcycles might raise its profile, and since the firm was already involved, continuing seemed a good idea.

Kawasaki had links with the Meguro firm dating back to pre-war days, and it had been building complete machines under the Meihatsu label. However, if Kawasaki wanted publicity from their machines, it needed something more impressive. The obvious answer was to compete.

The firm was at that time active only in the home market, so there was no need to worry about expensive Grand Prix bikes for overseas competition. Instead, Kawasaki decided to contest the Japanese Motocross championships. The firm's engineers created a race machine by tuning up a stock bike and painting the fuel tank red, and Kawasaki went to the races.

The Red Tank Kawasakis were a storming success, taking the first six places in the 125cc class. As well as winning races, the firm learned lessons about both engineering and marketing – in particular, that distinctive colour schemes were good marketing tools. In later years, competition Kawasakis were lime green, and became known as Green Meanies.

A trend towards larger, four-stroke trail bikes led to this dual-purpose 1991 KLE. It had a twin-cylinder engine in a trail chassis, which was modified for urban use.

This was a good start, but Kawasaki needed to build up a reputation. It lacked the experience that other firms had gained over the hard years, and as the home market became saturated, it was obvious that the firm needed to move on to the world stage.

Early products were a small range of simple two-stroke singles using the same basic engines in a variety of guises. This enabled Kawasaki to offer road and trial models, some in touring and others in sports form. In time, this was extended to mini machines and motocross models.

The technical details of these machines were all similar, with the air-cooled engine having its cylinder inclined forward a little from the vertical. Induction was usually by a rotary disc on the side of the crankshaft, but sometimes by the piston. Lubrication was by a pump with throttle-controlled output in nearly all cases, and ignition by a crankshaft-mounted flywheel magneto that also charged the battery.

The immensely successful Red Tank Kawasakis were simply tuned versions of the stock machine, showing just how good the production model was by taking the first six places in the Japanese 125cc (8ci) championships.

The engine drove a four- or five-speed gearbox built in unit with it by gear primary drive to a multi-plate clutch. The gearbox was of the cross-over type and the rear chain was either guarded or fully enclosed. This engine and gearbox unit was mounted

in either a conventional tubular frame constructed of steel tubes welded together, or a spine frame built up from steel pressings. Virtually all models had telescopic front forks and pivoted-fork rear suspension, while wheels were wire-spoked and had drum brakes. The fixtures and fittings were suited to the intended purpose of the model; the road machines had a dual seat, lights, turn signals, a silencer and a horn. The trial machines differed little but had off-road tyres and more ground and mudguard to wheel clearance.

Kawasaki was able to build up a good range of models, all of which used the same basic parts, keeping costs down. The same 90cc (5ci) engine with its five-speed gearbox served no less than 14 essentially similar models before it was bored out to 100cc (6ci). It continued in this form into modern times.

These small machines represented bread-and-butter for Kawasaki, but more was needed. The basic machines formed a good base for the firm's motorcycle business and allowed it to gather some experience of off-road

requirements along with stock road needs. However, all the major firms offered similar models with equally long production lives, so the aim of raising the firm's profile was not going to be achieved in this manner.

On top of that, Kawasaki's tentative forays into the US market in 1964 had shown that it lacked a product able to compete against the many Japanese and European machines asvailable. Something else was needed to grab public attention.

Kawasaki went back to Meguro for an answer. The first attempt

was a 250cc (15ci) four-stroke single, but this had little impact in a market where performance was all-important. Next, Kawasaki turned to the larger Meguro K2 500cc (31ci) twin. This machine looked a lot like the BSA twin, although its internals were very different.

By 1966, the 500cc (31ci) K2 had been expanded into the 624cc (38ci) W1. It proved popular in Japan, becoming the best-selling machine of its size, the largest model on sale in Japan, and also a favourite with the police. Kawasaki confidently launched it in the USA, but things did not go according to plan. The W1 failed to match up against the competition. Once word got around that the W1 could not stay with the big English twins, sales nosedived. The Kawasaki twins remained in production for some years, being built in touring and sports forms right up to 1975, but essentially as a home-market model.

Kawasaki considered the lessons offered by its experience in the US market and came to one conclusion: speed was essential, but acceleration was key. Many potential customers had only a passing interest in long-distance cruising, economy or handling. What counted on the street was the stop-light race.

The existing large but heavy twins were never going to do this job. Their top speed was impressive, but they were slow to reach it. Something quicker and more exciting was needed if Kawasaki was to become known for performance.

The firm decided to approach this goal from two different directions. As an interim measure, it brought in a series of two-stroke twins, at first of 247cc (15ci) and later of 338cc (21ci). First seen in 1966, the smaller had an air-cooled engine with disc valves on each side, a five-speed gearbox built in unit with it, a conventional frame and forks, drum brakes and all the expected features of the period.

Most of all, it had acceleration: it could cover a standing 400m (0.25 miles) in 15 seconds and reach around 161km/h (100mph). Plenty of big four-stroke twins could exceed this new top speed; what they could not do was to keep up with it off the line.

The W1, introduced in 1966, clearly shows the influences of classic British BSA twins. The series was popular in Japan but was unable to achieve anything much in the American market, prompting a rethink in design policy.

Within a few months, there was a racing version and a street scrambler with its twin exhaust systems mounted high on the left. These were listed as the Samurai, and early in 1967 were joined by a larger version. This was named the Avenger and was built in both the street scrambler and road forms. Produced up to 1971, the new twins established Kawasaki as the class leader for performance, but the firm was determined to go even further.

In 1968, Kawasaki introduced the 499cc (30ci) H1. Also known as the Mach III, the H1 was a three-cylinder two-stroke with the barrels in-line across the machine and fed by three carburettors mounted behind them, so piston-controlled induction replaced the discs of the twins. One stylish exhaust system ran along the left side of the machine, and two went on the right.

This made the H1 easily recognizable on the road. At that time, Agostini was winning Grand Prix races on an MV Agusta three with a similar exhaust arrangement, so the stylistic decision was a good one.

The rest of the H1 was typical of the time, with pump lubrication, an early form of electronic ignition and a five-speed gearbox built in

unit with the engine. The frame was tubular with telescopic front forks, rear suspension and drum brakes, and it was this, as much as the power from the engine, that made for the excitement the model could generate.

The Mach III was very fast for a 500cc (31ci), with a claimed top speed close to 193km/h (120mph) and capable of covering a standing 400m 0.25 miles) in under 13 seconds. This acceleration plus a short wheelbase meant that it was hard to avoid either a wheelie or smoking rear tyre away from the lights. That was nothing, however, compared to what could happen when cornering.

The H1's engine had an abrupt kink in its power band on a machine that really needed smooth power delivery. With its light weight and short wheelbase, the machine was not really up to handling 60hp anyway, and when power delivery sharply increased midway round a corner, the results could be...interesting. For those seeking an exciting ride, though, this was the machine to have.

The machine's performance was matched by its fuel consumption, which was equally prodigious. Few users cared much, except when looking for a petrol station with a nearly dry tank. Anything

over 48km (30 miles) to a UK gallon (1.2 US gallons) indicated that the rider was not fully using the machine's performance.

Few machines have ever offered such ferociously fast acceleration, high speed and wild handling as the H1, and it was soon joined by other triples, including a racing version, the H1R. In 1971 came the 748cc (46ci) H2 with even more performance but an improved chassis, plus the 249cc (15ci) S1 and 346cc (21ci) S2, which offered more respectable behaviour.

In 1973, the latter became the 400cc (24ci) S3, and in time the triples lost some of their raw edges and became more civilized, while the escalation of fuel prices took the edge off the fun. After 1976, only the 250cc (15ci) and 400cc (24ci) were left to run to the end of the decade, both lacking the glamour and wild fever of the first Mach III.

Part of the reason for the taming of the triples was the alternative approach taken by Kawasaki in its quest to be the street performance leader. In contrast to the two-strokes, this was to be achieved through a sophisticated route, and a four-stroke, four-cylinder machine of more than ample power was chosen to reach this

The ZX-6R was a strong entry in the performance 600cc (37cc) class for 2000. With plenty of power, a six-speed gearbox and excellent handling, it was a highly competitive machine.

aim. Work began in 1967 before the triples were launched, but an unexpected setback came in 1968, just a month after the Mach III was released.

As Kawasaki watched the reactions of the public to the outrageous Mach III, Honda launched its fabled CB750 four at the Tokyo show. It seemed that Kawasaki had been beaten to it. However, Kawasaki decided that it could take on and beat the CB750. It would let Honda test the market for a big four with its single-camshaft engine, electric start and disc brakes – and then build on those lessons to create something even better.

The result was the Z1, launched in September 1972 at the Cologne Show. This machine was even more impressive than its Honda competitor, boasting a 903cc (55ci) capacity, not just one but two overhead-camshafts, the expected electric start, four exhaust systems, disc front brake as well as the usual fixtures and fittings. It ran to 209km/h

(130mph), was able to cover a standing 400m (0.25 miles) in just over 12 seconds, and handled as well as any large and heavy machine at that time. This meant it was fine for fast touring, but less so for sports work.

The Z1 was quickly adapted for production racing. There was also a 750cc (46ci) version known as the Z2 for the Japanese home market (which was restricted to that capacity), and in 1976 the Z1 became the Z900, when it was joined by a custom version known as the Z900 LTD.

In the mid-1970s, Kawasaki began to expand its range, especially the four-strokes, and to use a revised system for coding them in two forms. The first was the marketing code used to identify the machine and year for its specification and maintenance data. It comprised two or three letters followed by the basic capacity and a suffix letter and number, this last usually altered each year to reflect changes. The second code for the model was often the first code minus the suffix number, but in time it became the code by which the machine was known and advertised.

Two-stroke codes began with the letter K and four-strokes with Z, except for some off-road models coded KL, much like the two-strokes whose style they copied. There were a few exceptions beginning with A in the two-strokes and B, E or V in the four-strokes, but the real difference for

The GPZ 900R, better known as the Ninja. Introduced in 1984, the Ninja was in production for a decade before being withdrawn. Such was the demand that it went back into production for 1996–97.

the latter was the use of series codes and names such as GPX, ZZ-R, LTD, Tengai, Eliminator or Ninja. There was a logic behind the system, but it became more complex over the years as the range grew and new styles made their appearance on the market.

The expansion of the four-stroke range resulted in a long string of custom models, beginning in 1976 with the Z900LTD. The changes were fairly minor: cast-alloy wheels, twin front discs, twin megaphone-style silencers and a two-level seat.

Later models became more radical over the years.

Also new for 1976 was the Z750B, powered by a 745cc (45ci) twin-cylinder double overhead-cam engine fitted with the balancer shafts. This system was already in use in the Z400 twin series, which was first seen in 1974 with a 399cc (24ci) overhead-cam engine. Both twins had five speeds and electrics on a machine that was well put together in the Japanese style of the period.

Meanwhile, Kawasaki's two-stroke line was moving in the direction of off-road models: trail, enduro and motocross, plus mini machines for the younger rider and sometimes trials models. The basic road bikes, mainly in 90cc (5ci), 100cc (6ci) and 125cc (8ci) sizes, remained in production. Indeed, the 125cc (8ci) is still around today and has changed little since its introduction. Kawasaki's participation in

Left: One of the best sports bikes of the 21st century, the Kawasaki ZX-12R has a massive 1199cc (73ci) engine. It is now one of the most popular bikes in the supersport class.

motocross racing provided a wealth of experience that benefited the entire two-stroke range, and an image that assisted sales of the entire line.

In 1977, the big four grew to 1016cc (62ci), creating the Z1000 and Z1000LTD custom models. These were joined by a new four-cylinder model, the Z650B in the style of the Z1 and with the same specification. With it came the Z650C. This machine boasted cast-alloy wheels, but was hardly a custom model, as it retained the same 652cc (40ci) double overhead-cam engine.

At the other end of the scale was the Z200, a 198cc (12ci) overhead-cam single produced for the commuter market. From it came the KL250 in 1978, a 246cc (15ci) overhead-cam single introduced for the trail market. The engine unit was based on the Z200, but the cycle components were selected and configured to suit off-road use.

One version of the Z400 was given a six-speed gearbox for 1978 while another true custom model appeared as the Z650SR or Z650D with the expected features plus a cross-over pattern for the exhaust pipes. Another version of the big four was added as the Z1-R. This machine had a distinctive style with a cockpit fairing plus new tank, seat base, side panels and cast-alloy wheels.

The majority of Kawasaki's two-stroke range continued in the established capacities with models coded KH for the road; KE for trail; KD for mini motocross and, later, for enduro; KDX for enduro; and KX for motocross, which ran up to a 400cc/24ci. There was also a KV mini, KC economy, KM mini trail, KT trials and KR for a road model based on a racer. One interesting model in the KV series was the Agi. This machine was intended for farm work and came with rack, protection bars and a large spade.

The motocross models were at the forefront of technical innovation with a disc-valve engine for the KX125, but not the KX250 or KX400. The smaller machines had reed-valve induction for 1978; the largest had been dropped from the range by then.

Right: The Kawasaki Z1-R has an added turbo chager. Most of the big Japanese motorcycle nanufacturers have tried this on their big sports bikes, often with little obvious benefit in improved power or performance.

In 1979 came a lot of new releases. Among them was a new batch of four-strokes. The trail single was joined by the KLX250, which then evolved into a street-legal enduro machine. In the 250cc (15ci) road class, the Z250A appeared with a 249cc (15ci) overhead-cam, twin-cylinder engine rather than the expected single: it was listed as the Scorpion. Two 400cc (24ci) twins were added, one with a mild custom style, the other far more radical. Another four-stroke appeared: the 498cc double overhead-cam Z500B, a fine motorcycle in the Kawasaki style. There was also a Z750D four, sold in South Africa only. The Z1000 had changes and improvements made to it, and was joined by a shaft-drive version that proved equally fast at 217km/h (135mph).

Perhaps the main event for 1979, and certainly as far as the four-stroke market was concerned, was the introduction of the Z1300. This was a very large machine with a 1286cc (78ci) six-cylinder double overhead-cam, water-cooled engine driving a five-speed gearbox with shaft final drive. It was large and heavy, essentially a fast tourer rather than a sports model, as were the Honda CBX and Benelli Sei sixes.

A junior motocross KX80 was added to the two-strokes with the choice of 79cc (4.8ci) or 83cc (5ci) capacity, and later also of a large or small front wheel. The KDX arrived in 1980 to introduce a true enduro type based on a combination of the existing trail KD175 and motocross technology. At the same time, the rear suspension of the main KX models changed to a rising-rate type

called Uni-Trak, which had been developed on the works Grand Prix machines that won the firm several titles in the 250cc and 350cc classes.

Thus in 1980 Kawasaki had a huge range of bikes on the market. There were six 250cc (15ci) road models: three singles, two twins and one triple two-stroke. All these models in the same class created some confusion, and this was also true of the next size class. Three Z400 twins were joined by four 444cc (27ci) Z440 models in various forms, one with an important alteration – the use of a toothed-belt final drive.

To further extend the range, the Z400J four and two 554cc (34ci) Z550 models were added, and the Z750 four went onto general sale with a custom version, and was joined by a Z750 custom twin. Electronic fuel injection appeared on a Z1000, although with limited success, and a version of the Z1300 with fairing and full luggage equipment joined the stock model.

For 1981, Kawasaki introduced a pair of 50cc (3ci) two-strokes: a road and a trail machine. These were partnered by 80cc (5ci) versions and there were yet more four-strokes, including Z305 twins. A more important introduction was the Z550H, which became better known as the GPZ and introduced Uni-Trak to the road range. This was soon joined by a GPZ750.

The other real change in 1981 was made to the KX125; it turned to liquid-cooling for the engine, something that soon was adopted by the KX line and then the enduro line. An offshoot was the AR125 of

1983 with liquid-cooling and many features derived from road racing, including Uni-Trak. There was also a new family of big machines; the Z1100 series in various forms, from sports to touring.

In 1984, Kawasaki introduced an important new model, the ZX900, better known as the GPZ900R and sold in the USA as the Ninja. There was also a 750cc (46ci) and both had liquid-cooled, 16-valve engines to set new performance standards. Equally new, and moving into a new area, was the KL600 single with liquid-cooling, four valves and a package with enduro styling to emphasize its dual-purpose nature. The firm also offered the Z750 Turbo – but, like other Japanese firms, Kawasaki found turbo machines to be a dead end.

The two-stroke KR250 tandem twin of the same year was a race replica based on the disc-valve machines that had won eight world titles. It was later replaced by the KR-1, a parallel twin, but the day of the hot two-stroke was past, and Kawasaki instead concentrated on its motocross, enduro and trail models to leave just one road model: the KH125, for basic, low-cost transport.

The Kawasaki line of super sports, sports, touring and custom four-strokes ran on alongside the trail, enduro and off-road machines. Among the custom models, the LTD450 appeared in 1985, using what was effectively half of the Ninja engine. Smaller versions of the Ninja four-stroke appeared with a perimeter frame, while the GT shaft-drive fours became favourites with despatch riders.

There was also a new custom machine for 1985. This was the V-twin VN750, sold as the Vulcan. It featured the best technology on offer at the time; liquid-cooling, double overhead-cam, eight valves, internal balance shafts and rubber mountings, along with shaft drive and the full custom style and trim. At the same time, a new style of machine was appearing: the muscle bike. Long and low, it had its own fans. Kawasaki's ZL900 Eliminator used some of the sports four plus custom parts to cater to this market.

Kawasaki machines continued to develop, becoming increasingly sophisticated. One result was the VN15, a V-twin of 1471cc (90ci), and another a whole series of Eliminator models. At the end of

the 1980s, retro machines became popular. These combined the benefits of new technology with the style of the past.

As the 1990s dawned, the KL types were given the name Tengai while track editions of the race-replica sports models began to appear with aluminium perimeter frames. The super-sports line gained a new code – ZZ-R – and this ran through the line from 250cc (15ci) to 1100 (67ci). The retro range was also expanded, while the ZXR line developed into a limited edition model for racing. This was based on the road version.

The 1992 Estrella model had a simple 249cc (15ci) engine and lines from the 1950s, but it sold best on its home market.

Two years later, the original Ninja was replaced by a new version with many new attributes, but popular demand was such that the original was reintroduced alongside it in 1996.

Kawasaki was now bringing out more revisions and updated versions than new models, adding new features and implementing technical advances to existing designs. One new machine was the ER-5, introduced in 1997. It had a retro look and a 499cc (30ci) twin engine, and was aimed at the no-frills transport market. It was a best seller.

In 1998, Kawasaki produced its first 125cc (8ci) four-stroke, again using a simple specification in an older style for first-time buyers. Meanwhile, at the other end of

scale, the big V-twin was used for a Classic Tourer, sold as the Vulcan Nomad in the USA. In 1999, it was joined by the Drifter, which was available in two engine sizes and had an almost pre-war look about it.

Also in 1999, the retro line was joined by the W650, which drew on the classic looks of the 1966 W1 of 1966. Its engine was overhead-camshaft driven by shaft and bevels, but it had the eight valves of the modern models. Of the two-strokes, there was only one trail model left, but the enduro and motocross range was as competitive as ever.

Kawasaki entered the 21st century with a broad range, from basic commuter transport to superbikes.

JAMATHI

NETHERLANDS 1962–77

Jamathi-Nederhorst was founded in Amsterdam by Jan Thiel and Martin Mijwaart. They were both talented engineers, and it's not surprising that their first machine was a racing special. It was ridden by Mijwaart to take ninth place in the 1962 Dutch TT at Assen on its first outing.

In 1963, the founders were joined by leading Dutch rider Paul Lodewijkx, who achieved several important placings in both the

Netherlands and in Belgium. The best of these included sixth place in the domestic Grand Prix, followed by sixth again in the Belgian Grand Prix just a week later.

The Jamathi success story continued, with Lodewijkx taking second in the 50cc World Championship series despite contesting only three of the five rounds. His 49.6cc (3ci), single-cylinder engine was a liquid-cooled version of the prototype, now

featuring a disc valve and gearbox with no less than nine speeds.

In 1969, Jamathi won three GPs and tied with Derbi for the championship in 1970. The star of this impressive showing was the former Van Veen rider Alt Toerson, whose achievement was in no way lessened by the fact that Derbi was given the title on the grounds that its team had won more races.

Jamathi also built a series of air-cooled street bikes. These were

popular on the home market, but Thiel and Mijwaart decided that they would prefer to work for Bultaco and Cagiva instead.

Jamathi produced some very competitive race machines and a popular range of street bikes. What might have happened had the founders not chosen to work for larger firms instead of pursuing their own efforts?

KREIDLER 50 GRAND PRIX

Kreidler's first 50 Grand Prix machine was developed from Hans-Georg Anscheidt's Renn (Racing) Florett, which won the Coupe d'Europe, and it became available just in time for the first 50cc World Championship. Although based on the production Florett engine, the 1961 winning bike had been somewhat modified. It now boasted rotary-valve induction, twin Dell'Orto carburettors and a six-speed gearbox. Delivering 8hp from its horizontal cylinder, two-stroke engine, the ultra-lightweight 49cc (3ci) Kreidler was capable of 129km/h (80mph).

Led by Johannes Hilber, the race team totally re-designed the engine for the 1962 season and entry into Grand Prix racing. It still employed a horizontal layout and, to gain the maximum possible displacement allowed under the rules, the engine size was increased to 49.9cc (3ci). The cylinder barrel was cast in aluminium and finished with a 'pin-pricked', hard-chrome surface. The idea was that the tiny holes would retain oil for improved lubrication. In fact, Kreidler was the first German motorcycle manufacturer to use this system, which had been developed by Porsche for its high-performance cars.

Modifications did not stop with the cylinders. The Dell'Orto carburettors were replaced by a pair of specially constructed Bing instruments (one for each rotary valve). Power was routed via a 12-speed gearbox. This actually had only four gear ratios, the full range of 12 made available by means of an external, three-speed overdrive controlled by a twistgrip on the handlebars.

The roadster-based 1961 frame was replaced with a lighter version manufactured from high-grade aircraft-quality tubing. The Earles-type front fork was retained, as was the swinging-arm, twin-shock rear suspension. The diameter of the front brake was increased to cope with the superior maximum speed of around 145km/h (90mph). The fairing was also improved. The resulting machine was so light (at 54kg/118lb) that keeping it on the ground was something of a problem.

For 1963, the machine received another new chassis plus stronger (telescopic) front forks, and power output increased to 12hp. In this new configuration, the Kreidler 50 was ridden by Anscheidt again to take the runner-up spot in the championship title race. But Kreidler wanted to win the world title, so the whole machine was thoroughly overhauled for 1964.

The engine was radically updated, gaining a new cylinder, stronger air-cooled clutch and a new expansion chamber exhaust, while the 12 gears had been reduced to six in the engine, with a two-speed, cable-operated overdrive. There was also yet another new chassis (a latticework construction), new forks and more powerful brakes. Now delivering 14hp, the machine could reach 160km/h (100mph).

Despite these impressive efforts, the Kreidler was outclassed by the incredible machines fielded by Suzuki and Honda. In the event, Kreidler did not win the world title until the late 1960s, when the Japanese firms had curtailed their involvement.

ENGINE: 49.9cc (3ci) disc valve to single, 40x39.7mm, air-cooled
POWER: 14bhp at 11,500rpm
GEARBOX: 6-speeds in engine, with 2-speed overdrive, foot-change
FINAL DRIVE: chain
WEIGHT: 58kg (128lb)
TOP SPEED: 160km/h (100mph)

The 50 Grand Prix was a fast and very competitive little machine with an excellent power-to-weight ratio. It put up a spirited challenge for the world title several years running, finally achieving success in the late 1960s.

LAMBRETTA TV 175 SERIES 3 SCOOTER

In 1962, Lambretta launched the world's first mass-produced scooter with a disc brake: the TV 175 Series 3. It was not the first two-wheeler with a disc brake – an obscure US machine, the Midget Motors Autocycle, had one in 1961, as did a 250cc (15ci) Maserati, produced in 1957. However, Lambretta brought the disc brake to the mass market.

The Series 1 TV (standing for Turismo Veloce, or Touring Speed) was introduced in 1957. It was intended as a faster and more upmarket challenge to the Vespa 150 Gran Sport. In essence, this was a good idea, but the machine suffered from lack of development and testing, and quickly gained a reputation for unreliability.

In January 1959, the Series 1 was replaced by the rather better Series 2, which was given a new engine with bore and stroke dimensions of 62 x 58mm (2.4 x 2.3in). Later on, the Series 2 had its 23mm (0.9in) carburettor replaced by a 21mm (0.8in) instrument to promote smoother running.

The Series 3 was the definitive model, however. It had new slimline styling and a smoother ride courtesy of front hydraulic dampers, as well as a 20mm (0.78in) Dell'Orto replacing the TV2's 21mm (0.8in) assembly.

All this aside, though, it was the mechanically operated disc front brake that really attracted attention. Lambretta were making a rather bold move by introducing it – many potential buyers questioned its complexity and reliability. However, it was the right decision; from the mid-1970s, brakes of this kind were the industry standard.

ENGINE: 175cc (11ci) 2s horizontal single, 62x58mm, fan-cooled
POWER: 8.6bhp at 6750rpm
GEARBOX: 4-speed, twistgrip change
FINAL DRIVE: enclosed chain
WEIGHT: n/a
TOP SPEED: 99km/h (62mph)

SANYANG

Sanyang started out assembling chassis parts for Honda, initially using parts supplied from Japan. In time, the firm began undertaking increasingly sophisticated tasks, and eventually moved into the production of complete machines.

The first Sanyang motorcycles were basically Hondas; smaller and older models produced under Sanyang's own badge. Small two-strokes eventually appeared, but the reliable scooterette, with its overhead-camshaft engine and three speeds, remained the favourite on local roads. Other models using the same engine were also available.

As time went by, the range grew in range and sophistication, though the firm remained committed to small models from 50cc (3ci) to 125cc (8ci), which were well suited to the South-east Asian market. Scooters were produced in the same sizes as the motorcycles, and once in production, remained in production for years with little alteration. Technical advances such as electronic ignition, electric start, disc brakes and pump lubrication for the two-strokes were implemented as they became available, but styling changes were minimal and often restricted to paintwork.

MOTO MORINI 250 GRAN PREMIO

Tarquinio Provini joined Moto Morini from MV in 1960. Over the next three years, his talent on the track combined with constant development of the 246.6cc (15ci), twin-cam (gear-driven), six-speed Morini single, created a dramatic race presence. Provini's victory in the 1962 Senior Italian Championship, plus other wins outside Italy, prompted Alfonso Morini to authorize a bid for the 1963 world title.

At that time, the 250cc class was dominated by Honda, which could field massive resources to back up its impressive team led by Jim Redman. All Moto Morini had was a lone hero, yet Provini's challenge was one of the greatest dramas of motorcycle racing.

Tarquinio Provini was plagued by ill fortune along the way. The French GP was cancelled; he could not get a visa for East Germany and thus could not race there; he had mechanical trouble in Holland; and, for various reasons, Moto Morini did not contest the Isle of Man TT. Oh, and his rivals were the very best.

The Honda team, however, had some great four-cylinder bikes, as well as Jim Redman, who won the two races Provini did not enter. But Honda did not have it all its own way. Provini came home ahead of Redman at Monza, Italy; on the Spanish GP circuit at Montjuic Park, Barcelona; on the ultra-fast Hockenheim track in West Germany; and also on the rough Buenos Aires Autodrome in Argentina. Moto Morini's star rider (and his bike) proved that they were both supremely adaptable – and also very, very fast. In the end, Redman won the World Title by just two points, but both he and Honda had been fought hard.

Provini also won the Italian Championship in 1963, but left Moto Morini to ride for Benelli. His replacement for the 1964 season was Giacomo Agostini, who beat Provini for that year's Italian title. The following year, Agostini went to ride for MV Agusta.

Angelo Bergamonti took the 1967 Italian title riding the final incarnation of this machine. This version was modified to deliver more power, with an enlarged bore and stroke. Various experiments with three- and four-valve heads had been carried out, as had trials with Desmodromic valve operation. However, the simpler and conventional two-valve system was the one that won races. The Gran Premio twin-cam single was finally retired at the end of 1967.

ENGINE: 248.36cc (15ci) (early engine 246.6cc/15ci) dohc 2v single 72x61mm, air-cooled
POWER: 36bhp at 10,500rpm
GEARBOX: 6-speed foot change
FINAL DRIVE: chain
WEIGHT: 113kg (249lb)
TOP SPEED: 225km/h (140mph)

A 1963 250 Premio of the type ridden by Tarquinio Provini to within two points of winning the 250cc world title.

PARILLA WILDCAT SCRAMBLER

Parilla built this machine specifically for Cosmopolitan Motors, its US importer. The Wildcat Scramble was constructed around the 247cc (15ci) version of the long-running and highly successful hi-cam engine, and made no pretensions of being a road bike. With an open megaphone exhaust, no lighting equipment, abbreviated mudguarding, long travel, Marzocchi-made motocross front forks, a comprehensive air filtration system, massive rear wheel sprocket, tachometer and knobbly Pirelli 'Motocross' tyres, this was a competition machine to the core. The engine was specially tuned and brake-tested and put out well over 30hp.

The prototype Wildcat Scrambler was shown in the 1961 Milan Samples fair. However, the machine had its problems. Its power characteristics were more suited to road racing than dirt track. It was very impressive in a straight line and decent enough on a dry, fast track, but in the mud and general filth of motocrossing, the Wildcat lacked the low-end torque needed to slog through.

The Wildcat was also too heavy for its intended role. Its frame was developed from a standard roadster with extra bracing, which of course meant increased weight. The result was a machine that could not do what it was built for particularly well, but was pretty good in certain other roles. And there was one thing it did very well indeed – it made a most wonderful sound.

ENGINE: 247cc (15ci) ohv 2v single, 68x68mm, air-cooled
POWER: 31bhp at 8500rpm
GEARBOX: 4-speed foot change
FINAL DRIVE: chain
WEIGHT: 25kg (276lb)
TOP SPEED: 121km/h (75mph)

The Wildcat Scrambler could boast of being the most powerful machine in its class. Unfortunately, it was also heavy, which took the edge off its performance.

BULTACO SHERPA

The awesome Sherpa was one of those machines that just left the competition standing. Light, responsive and with plenty of torque available, it was unbeatable in its day.

Developed by Sammy Miller, the Bultaco Sherpa was designed and put into production in late 1964 after a development period said to have been no longer than 12 days. Its name suggested that it was capable of clawing its way up mountains – and it was. The Sherpa was virtually unbeatable on dirt, and at a stroke rendered most other trials machines obsolete.

The Sherpa was a basic and simple machine. It was built using standard Bultaco parts, including its 18hp, 244cc (15ci) two-stroke engine, plus lightweight aluminium mudguards and alloy brake hub, with a bash plate to protect the underside of the

The Sherpa's success was due to a simple design geared to the rigours of dirt track racing.

machine on rocky ground. The secret of its awesome capability lay in a combination of throttle response, low-down torque and all-terrain ability, coupled with very light weight.

ENGINE: 398cc (24ci) ohv flat twin, 68.5x54mm, air-cooled
POWER: n/a
GEARBOX: unit 4-speed hand change
FINAL DRIVE: chain
WEIGHT: 110kg (243lb)
TOP SPEED: 100km/h (60mph)

CARABELA
MEXICO 1964–85

Carabela was set up, with help from Minarelli, by the Mexican company Acer Mex. At the outset, in 1964, Italian technicians from Minarelli were critical to the marque's operation. However, the Mexicans wanted to stand on their own two feet and gradually reduced the amount of parts that were imported, replacing them with in-house production.

By the mid-1970s, Carabela was offering a full range of models from 60cc (4ci) to 450cc (27ci), with two and three wheels. Engines were bought in from overseas suppliers, including Minerelli and Jawa, and carburettors came from Mikuni in Japan.

The original Carabela line was aimed at the commuter market, but in the early 1970s the firm branched out into sport with off-road models for motocross and enduro competition. These were powered by 125cc (8ci) and 200cc (12ci) two-stroke engines, the former developing around 20hp.

Carabela was able to enter the US market with its sports machines, and in 1974 a landmark was achieved with a new 250cc (15ci) motocross machine. This was the first all-Mexican motorcycle to come from the Carabela works; even the engine was built in-house.

Named the MX5 Moto Cross five-speed, the new machine featured a duplex cradle frame with steeply inclined twin shock rear-suspension units. Power output was 34hp at 8500 rpm. The MX5 was exported to the USA along with a 60cc (4ci) mini-racer complete with fairing and cast-alloy wheels, which was used by Carabela to promote a one-model race series in Mexico.

Carabela was taken over by Yamaha in 1985.

CASAL
PORTUGAL 1964–1990s

Casal began manufacturing its machines, which had a very German style about them, using Zundapp engines. Initial products included a range of 50cc mopeds and motorcycles, which were followed in the early 1970s by 75cc (5ci) and 125cc (8ci) models.

Some of Casal's machines were built for off-road use. Designs tended to follow the style of the period, with front and rear suspension on even the most basic moped, with its single-speed automatic transmission.

There were two- and four-speed sports mopeds with spine frames, an off-road version, and a five-speed sports moped. The last two had duplex frames.

Casal did well out of its range of mopeds, which found a ready market in Portugal and neighbouring Spain, where such machines had become part of popular culture. A 50cc (3ci) water-cooled model appeared in 1982. It featured a six-speed gearbox and a road-racing style using cast-alloy wheels.

Casal continued with the other models, and its style was revised to keep up with trends. A moped in a step-through format was later offered by the firm. In this way, aided by sales of engines to other manufacturers, Casal manged to keep on producing motorcycles until the late 1990s.

DUCATI MACH 1

ITALY 1964

The rivalry between fast Italian (Ducati) and Japanese (Suzuki) production 250cc (15ci) machines was intense. Other machines and other makers were involved, but the fight was led by the Ducati Mach 1 on the European side and, representing Japan, the Suzuki Super Six.

The Ducati arrived first, appearing at Earl's Court in 1964. It was an instant sensation. The Mach 1 was based on the 248cc (15ci) Diana, which had been launched at the 1961 Bologna Motor Show. It used Ducati's well-tried, overhead-cam single

cylinder, with unit construction of the engine and gearbox, bevel-driven camshaft and wet-sump lubrication.

The Mach 1 differed from the Diana in certain important ways. It had a five-speed gearbox, a three-ring Borgo high-compression forged piston, larger valves, stronger springs, a massive 29mm (1.1in) Dell'Orto SS1 racing-type carburettor, rear set footrests, distinctive red and silver paint, and an optional white face Veglia racing tachometer.

The Mach 1 impressed those who tried it. In an article for

Motorcycle News, Pat Braithwaite wrote: 'In a Lightning jet fighter, Mach 1 plus a bit takes you through the sound barrier. The new-for-1965 Ducati Mach 1 takes you through the "ton barrier". And it's only a 250.'

Braithwaite liked the machine a lot, going on to say: 'A fast corner looms up. The gear ratios are as close as a racer's ... change down twice and keel over to sample steering and roadholding second-to-none!'

It is hardly surprising that many Mach 1s found their way on to the race circuit.

ENGINE: 248cc (15ci) oc single, with vertical cylinder, air-cooled
POWER: n/a
GEARBOX: unit 5-speed
FINAL DRIVE: chain
WEIGHT: 128kg (282lb)
TOP SPEED: 161km/h (100mph)

The 1964 Mach I was the first street 250 capable of 160km/h (100mph). It had great handling, excellent acceleration and a high top speed. Unsurprisingly, many Mach Is found their way onto racing circuits.

HODAKA

Hodaka started out in the motorcycle business in 1962, manufacturing engines for Yamaguchi. When Yamaguchi went out of business in 1963, Hodaka took the plunge and began manufacturing complete machines.

Uniquely among Japanese manufacturers, Hodaka was a joint US–Japanese operation selling only to the US market. Development and marketing was done in co-operation with the Pacific Basin Trading Co (Pabatco).

Hodaka's main products were a range of 100cc (6ci) and 125cc (8ci) enduro-style, two-stroke singles with excellent specification and an equally high-build quality. The result was a great deal of word-of-mouth marketing and orders created by recommendation or reputation, creating good sales despite a minimal marketing budget.

For over 15 years, Hodaka was a force to be reckoned with in the on-off road sector. Its 'street scramblers' of the 1960s were renamed 'trail bikes' as the 1970s dawned. However in the mid-1970s, the market became more specialized. Hodaka ceased trading in 1978.

Hodoka's main product line was a range of high-quality 100 (6ci) and125cc (7ci) singles. These machines proved very competitive.

ROYAL ENFIELD CONTINENTAL

The Continental GT was developed from the Crusader 250 of 1956 and Crusader Sports Continental. It went on the market in 1964 and was obviously aimed at the coffee-bar culture of the time.

The Continental GT was taken out of production after Royal Enfield was taken over by Norton Villiers in 1967. However, in its three years of production it was a popular machine for both stylistic and practical reasons. It featured competition-oriented clip-on handlebars, a racing-style fuel tank, a straight-through exhaust and fly-screen. With a top speed of 138km/h (86mph), it could easily outrun any contemporary scooters, and yet it was still learner-legal. The five-speed gearbox was replaced by a six-speed unit in the last year of the machine's life.

ENGINE: 248cc (15ci) air-cooled single-cylinder
POWER: 26bhp
GEARBOX: 5- and 6-speed, foot change
FINAL DRIVE: chain
WEIGHT: 136kg (300lb)
TOP SPEED: 138km/h (86mph)

The Continental GT appeared in 1964, but it can trace its lineage back through a range of over-square 250cc (15ci), unit-construction, five-speed singles to the 1956 Crusader Sports.

CHAPTER SIX

THE BOOM YEARS

1965–1974

Even in the late 1960s, it was still possible to take a rose-tinted view of the British bike industry's future. Motorcycles like the Triumph Bonneville and Norton Commando were powerful and reliable, while offering better handling than the Japanese alternatives, and at a reasonable cost. The US market was fond of the British bikes, and complacent senior management could still dismiss Japanese competition.

1969 is the year when all that changed, with the appearance of Honda's revolutionary CB750. Based round a 67bhp 750cc (46ci) inline-four engine, with cutting-edge chassis technology, and all at a reasonable selling price, this Japanese superbike utterly redefined the market. It is hard now to imagine what a shockwave it created – especially when it was followed by an even more powerful machine from Kawasaki, the 1972 903cc (55ci) Z1. Kawasaki also launched a series of wild two-stroke triples in 350cc (21ci), 500cc (30ci) and 750cc (46ci) capacities, all of which had rather marginal handling.

In Europe, Italian firms were producing superbikes too. MV Agusta was developing 350cc (21ci), 500cc (30ci) machines, in three-and four-cylinder form. Bimota was launched in 1973, and Ducati also released its first Desmodromic V-twin that year. BMW was developing its flat-twin 'R' range too, and these were offering increasing performance, reliability and sophistication.

Left: A classic, 1972 model Honda CB750 is taken for a road test. The CB750 transformed motorcycling by setting a new standard of engineering and technological excellence that other manufacturers struggled to match.

BSA A65 SPITFIRE

ENGLAND 1965–68

Prompted by a similar move by Triumph, the unit construction BSA A50/A65 series followed the non-unit A7/A10 early in 1962. In addition, the new BSA model had better electrics, weighed some 14kg (30lb) less than its predecessor and was significantly less expensive than the competing Triumph. It also featured clean, neat lines, which were perhaps too neat; many considered the styling to be rather bland. And there were a few snags. The first A65 claimed only 38hp, and there was soon some concern about main bearing and oil pump failures.

In terms of performance, the bike to beat at the time was Triumph's T120 Bonneville, while

Norton set the yardstick for handling. BSA twins, on the other hand, were ideal for sidecar work and had a formidable reputation for robustness rather than looks or performance. BSA had created some impressive contenders, notably the A10RGS Rocket Gold Star twin, but these were specialized machines produced in relatively small numbers.

That changed in 1965, with the arrival of the Spitfire. This machine took BSA into the sports twin arena in no uncertain terms. Developed from the twin-carburettor A65L Lightning, the Spitfire was an exhibitionist with bright red paintwork, alloy wheel rims, close-ratio gears,

high-compression pistons and substantially less weight.

The first Spitfire, with racing-style Amal GP carburettors and hot camshafts, delivered a most impressive 55hp, though at the expense of fairly savage engine vibration. Later examples were slightly de-tuned, if less raucous, with Amal Concentric carburettors and slightly lower compression pistons.

The chassis, on the other hand, was only slightly different from more humble BSA twins. The last of the Spitfires was the Mk IV of 1968, with a twin leading shoe front brake and 240km/h (150mph) marked on the speedometer. Although a revised

range of twins with oil-bearing frames appeared in 1970, these were dated and sold poorly.

ENGINE: 654cc (39ci) ohv parallel twin, 75x74mm, air-cooled
POWER: up to 56bhp at 7250rpm
GEARBOX: 4-speed foot change
FINAL DRIVE: chain
WEIGHT: 193kg (425lb)
TOP SPEED: 177km/h (110mph)

The 1968 Spitfire was the final version of this highly successful machine. Less aggressive (and less prone to vibration) than the original, it was nevertheless a very fine machine.

HONGDU

CHINA 1965–PRESENT

Hongdu was one of the first Chinese motorcycle firms, originally producing Japanese designs under license. The first was a small Yamaha two-stroke machine, the YG1, which had already become very successful when Hongdu took it on.

The TG1 had a 73cc (4ci) capacity with the cast-iron cylinder inclined forward and topped by a

light-alloy head. A rotary inlet valve controlled the mixture intake, which was ignited by a flywheel magneto when kick-started. The engine was built in unit with a four-speed gearbox and hung from a spine frame with telescopic front and pivoted-rear forks, wire wheels and drum brakes.

Hongdu did well with their licensed machine, and in due

course it was supplanted by a 100cc (6ci) and later a 125cc (8ci). These designs were similar to the YG1 but received technical upgrades as they became available. Rotary valves were replaced by reeds for the inlet, electronic ignition became standard instead of points, and electric start was added to assist the kick.

The gearbox was upgraded to give a wider range of ratios, tubular frames took over from the spine type for some models, and disc brakes made their appearance.

Hongdu's range ran from 50cc (3ci) to 125cc (8ci) for most years and included mopeds, scooterettes, small motorcycles and scooters in various forms.

MV AGUSTA 350 THREE

The new 343.9cc (21ci) double overhead-cam Three made the world sit up and take note, including the mighty Honda team.

First proposed during the late 1950s, the MV triple was an idea that floated around for a while and was then pushed into reality by outside events. The decision to build this machine was made in response to Honda's entry into the 350cc Grand Prix in 1962 with the 285cc (17ci) Four.

The Hondas outclassed the old four-cylinder 350cc (21ci), which was based on the 500cc (31ci) model, and it was quickly withdrawn. This left rider Mike Hailwood with only the 500cc (31ci), and with it he won the Blue Ribbon Senior class for four years until quitting MV to join Honda in 1965.

Meanwhile, the three-cylinder 350 MV Grand Prix machine made its public debut in 1965, and in the same year MV's owner Count Domenico Agusta achieved a long-standing dream of his – to field an Italian bike with an Italian rider in the larger (350cc and 500cc) racing classes.

And this was no ordinary rider; this was Giacomo Agostini, who had made his name with the tiny Moto Morini factory, winning the 250cc Senior Italian Championship title in 1964. Having beaten no less a rider/bike combination than Tarquinio Provini and the four-cylinder Benelli, he was immediately signed up by MV Agusta.

The new MV was a 343.9cc (21ci) across-the-frame triple with its cylinders inclined forwards at 10 degrees from the vertical. The rest of the machine's specification was impressive too, including a seven-speed transmission, 46cm (18in) wire wheels with Borrani alloy rims, a 16l (4.2 US gallon) fuel tank, and a quad-cam 240mm (9.5in) drum front brake of immense power.

Delivering more than 62hp at 13,500rpm, the new MV triple could mount a serious challenge to the Japanese dominance of the class. With a maximum speed of 241km/h (150mph), it was not only as rapid as its larger, four-cylinder, 500cc (31ci) brother, but because of its lighter weight and superior power-to-weight ratio, it was a superior racing machine.

Agostini and the new MV machine made a truly sensational Grand Prix debut. The race report headline in *Motor Cycling* magazine, on 1 May 1965, summed it up – 'Agostini shatters Redman' – and added the necessary details: 'Undefeated throughout last season's 350cc classic races, Honda team leader Jim Redman met his match in Giacomo Agostini and the new three-cylinder MV.'

The pace of the race was so hot that Redman crashed, while Agostini's team-mate Mike Hailwood, riding one of the old four-cylinder machines, was the only rider to escape being lapped in the 154km (96-mile) race. Agostini went on to win a record 15 world titles in all, the majority of them riding 350cc (21ci), and later 500cc (31ci), versions of this incredible machine.

ENGINE: 343.9cc (21ci) dohc 4v triple, 48x46mm, air-cooled
POWER: 62.5bhp at 13,500rpm
GEARBOX: 7-speed foot change
FINAL DRIVE: chain
WEIGHT: 116kg (256lb)
TOP SPEED: 240km/h (149mph)

VELOCETTE VENOM THRUXTON

ENGLAND 1965

Velocette made its name on the racetrack, and could be relied upon to produce special performance machines whenever possible. The Venom was launched in 1956, and by 1958 it was available with factory extras such as racing wheels, carburettor, ignition, exhaust, rev-counter and close-ratio gears.

This variant came to be known as the 'Thrucky'. It was effectively a factory-built model utilizing the available performance parts, and was in turn derived from the slightly less potent Clubman model, which was itself a tuned Venom. The new name celebrated a similar machine's 1964 victory in the prestigious 800km (500- mile) race at Hampshire's Thruxton circuit. From mid-1965, around 1000 'replica' Thruxtons were built.

The Thruxton was powered by a highly tuned version of the standard 499cc (30ci) Venom overhead-valve engine. Modifications included an Amal racing carburettor, high-compression pistons, special cylinder heads with larger inlet valves, improved gas flow and more radical valve timing. The bike was also equipped with close-ratio gears, uprated forks, clip-on handlebars, rear-set footrests, a humped seat and a long-distance fuel tank.

Although many Thruxtons were raced, others were used on the road. In this role, they were certainly exciting but also totally impractical since they required constant care and attention from the user.

The highest point of the Thruxton's track career was the first 500cc Production TT in 1967. The machine came home first at an average speed of 144.66km/h (89.89mph). In full race tune, a good Thruxton was capable of 193km/h (120mph), which was comparable with even the fastest twins.

ENGINE: 499cc (30ci) ohv single, 86x86mm, air-cooled
POWER: up to 41bhp at 6500rpm
GEARBOX: 4-speed foot change
FINAL DRIVE: chain
WEIGHT: 177kg (390lb)
TOP SPEED: 171km/h (106mph)

The Thruxton Venom was derived from endurance racers and retained many features of race bikes – including, unfortunately, a need for constant maintenance. There were many who found the machine entirely worth the effort.

EGLI

The Egli-Vincent was the creation of Swiss racer and engineer Fritz Egli, who mounted a classic V-twin engine in a modern racing frame, creating a machine with significantly better handling than the original Vincent.

Although the only engines available to Egli were 12 or more years old, he was able to create a racing machine that remained competitive for several years. This was achieved by keeping weight down by every possible design and technical means, including the use of light alloys wherever it was feasible. Egli was world-famous for his ability to wring power out of an engine, and these bikes were tuned to within an inch of their lives.

Egli gave other machines the same treatment. His Honda Red Baron, fitted with a transverse six-cylinder taken out to 1200cc (73ci), weighed only 215kg (473lb). This did not make it a lightweight, but with an engine of such size the results were excellent. The later Egli-Kawasaki Bonneville was also expanded, to 1200cc (73ci) again, and weighed in at only 205kg (451lb).

Egli was an early user of Kevlar-reinforced composites and also experimented with forced induction. He managed to get 300hp out of a Kawasaki-based four-cylinder, which had been taken out to 1425cc (87ci).

Egli's experience with very high power outputs led to Pirelli commissions for tyre research, and he remained in demand to work with machines as disparate as the mighty V-Max and the lowly Enfield Bullet.

A Vincent Black Shadow after getting the Fritz Egli treatment. Egli was famous for taking a machine – ideally a good one to start with, but Egli's magic worked on almost any machine – and turning it into something truly amazing.

HARLEY-DAVIDSON FLH SHOVELHEAD

The fact that the 1213cc (74ci) Shovelhead was still available in 1972, in a 'super sport' hand-shift FLH guise, shows just how different the US market was – and, indeed, is – from the rest of the world. The original 1966 FLH was essentially an Electra-Glide with a new carburettor, higher compression, and a different look to the rocker-box covers. It delivered 60hp, while the less highly tuned FL had a mere 54hp (45hp per litre).

In 1971, the FLH gave rise to the Super Glide FX, which was 32kg (70lb) lighter, owing something to the (relatively) lightweight Sportster series, and the traditional heavyweight models. This was arguably the first 'factory custom' Harley, a concept that later spawned the FXS Low Rider with its 68cm (27in) seat height and 'fat bob' (twin, split) tank in 1977.

In 1980, there were four new models: the Tour Glide, a heavyweight tourer with a full fairing; the Sturgis, a belt drive cruiser; the Wide Glide; and the Fat Bob. All had the same engine and, at last, five-speed gearboxes. These were less urgently needed than on some other designs, as a huge, 'soft' engine with a broad torque range has far less need of extra gears than a small, high-revving one.

ENGINE: 1207cc ohv in-line V-twin, 87x100mm, air-cooled
POWER: 60bhp
GEARBOX: 4-speed foot change
FINAL DRIVE: chain
WEIGHT: n/a
TOP SPEED: 180kph (110mph) approx

ITALJET

Italjet was set up in 1966 by Leopoldo Tartarini, producing machines powered by CZ and Triumph engines. The firm was also involved in the construction of the Indian Velocette, of which around 100 units were made between 1969 and 1970.

This interesting project was the brainchild of former Indian dealer Floyd Clymer. It used the overhead-valve single-cylinder 500cc (31ci) Velocette engine in a twin-loop frame with Marzocchi suspension.

The Indian Velocette might have revived two famous names in one go, but faded away with the death of Clymer in 1970. After this, Italjet, concentrated on producing children's mini bikes such as the 47cc (3ci) Moroni-powered M5B scrambler of 1973, a beautifully executed, scaled-down replica of a full size bike.

The 864cc (53ci) Darmah, released in 1977 by Ducati, was styled by Leopoldo Tartarini and featured a novel duck-tail rear end. Italjet's other work in the 1980s included 350cc (21ci) road-going custom bikes and two- and four-stroke trials machines.

Italjet followed the scooter boom of the late 1990s and early 2000s with its Dragster range, including 50cc (3ci), 125cc (8ci) and 180cc (11ci) machines. The Dragster 50 was capable of only 76km/h (47mph), but it was a very purposeful machine and had some of the most effective brakes in the industry. Based on a sparse Ducati-style trellis frame, the Dragster 50's 50cc (3ci) motor delivered very decent torque, and made the Dragster popular for town riding.

The Italjet Formula F125LC of 1999 used a 114cc (7ci), liquid-cooled, two-stroke twin delivering just 12hp but still capable of 129km/h (80mph). Its very light weight, just 100kg (220lb), was an

When scooters became massively popular from the late 1990s onwards, Italjet was well positioned to take advantage with machines like this Formula 50. Italjet's scooters proved extremely popular in the marketplace.

After a couple of oddball projects, Italjet began producing children's motorcycles. This Junior Cross machine was not a kid's toy – it was a serious bike for riders who happened not to be full grown.

asset in that area. Both the Dragster and Formula machines were extremely popular among

scooter users, while at the other end of the scale, Italjet also produced a custom café racer.

KAWASAKI SAMURAI A1

Although it was not quite as fast as the W1, the Samurai was aimed at the US market and had the acceleration demanded there. Its power came from a 247cc (15ci), twin-cylinder, two-stroke engine with disc inlet valves and a carburettor on each side. This was built in unit with a five-speed gearbox, and the whole was installed in a full cradle frame with suspension for both wire wheels and their drum brakes. Fixtures and fittings were of high quality and typical of Japanese-made bikes of the period.

The Samurai was an effective machine and its impressive acceleration allowed it to leave larger machines behind at the lights, helping establish Kawasaki's reputation for high performance. The A1 was quickly joined by the A1R for road racing and, in 1967, the A1SS street scrambler arrived. This machine had both exhaust systems mounted high on the left, braced handlebars and a sump plate.

A larger twin was also introduced, the 338cc (21ci) Avenger A7, which was faster and had better acceleration. Late in 1967 came the expected A7SS and a limited number of racing A7R twins. All the road twins went on to the end of 1971, but were supplanted by other models well before then.

ENGINE: 247cc (15ci) rotary 2s parallel twin, 53x56mm, air-cooled
POWER: 31bhp at 8000rpm
GEARBOX: 5-speed foot change
FINAL DRIVE: chain
WEIGHT: 145kg (319lb)
TOP SPEED: 160km/h (95mph)

The Samurai was Kawasaki's first real foray into the realm of performance bikes. Building on lessons learned with the W1, it delivered high acceleration and soon established an enviable reputation.

KAWASAKI W1

Based on the earlier Meguro K2 twin, the Kawasaki W1 also bore a considerable resemblance to the BSA A7 twins – at least in general layout. Internally, it differed from the BSA machines, having one-piece connecting rods and a three-part crankshaft that was pressed together, but the valve gear and drives to magneto and dynamo were very similar. This close likeness was also apparent in the separate gearbox, frame, suspension and wheels.

The W1 was a success in Kawasaki's home market of Japan; however, it was to prove a commercial disaster in the USA. The main reason for this was underperformance – the W1 was unable to match competing machines closely enough to carve out a market niche for itself. An attempt to improve matters resulted in the W2SS street scrambler of 1967. This was fitted with twin carburettors and was restyled to distance it from the W1. In 1968 came the similar W1SS and the W2TT with upswept exhaust systems on the left. None lasted beyond 1971, but the next year brought the W3 for the Japanese market, and this ran on to 1975.

ENGINE: 624cc (37ci) ohv parallel twin, 74x72.6mm, air-cooled
POWER: 50bhp at 6500rpm
GEARBOX: 4-speed foot change
FINAL DRIVE: chain
WEIGHT: 180kg (398lb)
TOP SPEED: 175km/h (105mph)

Bearing a marked resemblance to BSA twins of the period, the W1 differed internally. Its performance was not sufficient to impress American riders, though it did well in the home market.

MUNCH

Friedel Munch took the rather odd step of installing a succession of ever-larger and more powerful, air-cooled, in-line, four-cylinder NSU car engines transversely into a motorcycle frame. He thus created a very unattractive machine (the engines were intended to be hidden inside a car rather than put on display), but it was one with a great deal of power and torque available.

Munch's background was with Horex, and most of the components of his original 'Mammut' machines were from Horex, although later they acquired Marzocchi forks and Brembo brakes. It is not clear exactly when the first of these unusual bikes was built, but they

were available off the shelf from 1966 onwards.

The first bikes had 996cc (61ci) engines, and this was followed by an 1177cc (72ci) version, which delivered 88hp. Later still came the 100hp model with fuel injection. The final incarnation of Munch's bikes were assembled to order and had a 1278cc (78ci), fuel-injected engine delivering 104hp at 7500rpm. The exact time that production ceased is not clear, but it was probably during the early 1980s.

Long before that, of course, it was possible to buy much lighter machines whose purpose-built motorcycle engines provided plenty of power without the brute-force approach of the NSU-engined

Munch bikes. This new generation of machines delivered the same sort of acceleration and a higher top speed.

The Munch-4 (as it was known by this time) weighed close to 270kg (600lb) and was as aerodynamic as a brick. There was a prototype 700cc (43ci), two-stroke triple in 1973, but it never entered production. Today, the Munch-4 and the Mammut are sought after as powerful, well-made and very distinctive bikes, although their appeal is limited to a rather small segment of the marketplace.

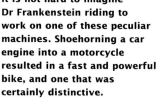

It is not hard to imagine Dr Frankenstein riding to work on one of these peculiar machines. Shoehorning a car engine into a motorcycle resulted in a fast and powerful bike, and one that was certainly distinctive.

SEELEY

Colin Seeley was a motorcycle dealer at the age of 18 and chalked up an impressive array of other achievements as well. He was British sidecar racing champion (twice), a championship-winning team manager, and a constructor of both racing and street bikes (and even Brabham racing cars).

After a successful sidecar-racing career with Matchless- and BMW-powered outfits, Seeley took over

the rights to manufacture AMC's (Associated Motor Cycles) AJS 7R and Matchless G50 racers in 1966. Seeley's firm was never huge; at its peak, it employed 67 workers. However, from the first Seeley-Matchless onwards, the firm built a wide range of machines, culminating in the Seeley-Honda TL200 trials bike of 1980.

Along the way, there were several very interesting machines, such as the Seeley-framed URS

four-cylinder racing solo in 1967. This was followed by the 1968 Mk II Seeley-frame model (again housing either 7R or G50 single-cylinder engines), and the 1969 Kuhn-Seeley with a Norton twin-cylinder engine in a Mk III chassis.

In 1970, there was the QUB (Queens University Belfast) 500cc (31ci) two-stroke single, the engine of which was designed by Dr Gordon Blair. However, the most successful Seeley machine of the

era was the Yamsel, which used a Yamaha two-stroke twin engine in a Seeley frame.

Ducati asked Colin Seeley to build a chassis for its new 500cc (31ci) V-twin GP engine in 1971. Ducati also chose to fit and equip its standard production bikes with a method of chain adjustment developed by Seeley. The same year, a Seeley frame redeemed the previously poor-handling TR500 Suzuki, while the Seeley Condor roadster, which

used a G50 single-cylinder engine, also made its debut.

More commissions came in 1972, with Seeley frames being used for both the 750cc (46ci) Westlake parallel-twin and Kawasaki 750cc (46ci), three-cylinder, two-stroke power units. A year later, the Seeley Monoque, with a Suzuki twin-cylinder engine,

also sported Seeley-made wheels, discs and front-fork assemblies. The same period also saw the 750cc (46ci), three-cylinder Suzuki engine built to complement the earlier TR500-engined machine.

The mid- to late 1970s were spent in co-operation with Honda, resulting in the 1975 big-bore (820cc/50ci), Dixon-Seeley, single

Seely specialized in building frames around other companies' engines, and created a number of very exciting machines in the process. This is a G50, mounting a Matchless engine from the 1950s in a 1970s frame.

overhead-cam Honda four roadster and the 1978 Seeley-Honda Superbike. Success with these machines led to an ambitious scheme to build 1000 Seeley-Honda TL200 four-stroke

trials singles. However, the exercise was a financial disaster. Only 300 machines were built and the resulting money troubles ended Seeley's motorcycle production days.

SUZUKI T20 SUPER SIX

Launched in 1966, the T20 Super Six went to the US market as the X6. In both guises, it was powered by a 250cc (15ci,) air-cooled two-stroke parallel-twin, mated to a six-speed gearbox. It was the latter that provided the model's name. The engine incorporated a sophisticated Posi-Force lubrication system, and developed 29hp at 7500rpm, for a top speed of 153km/h (95mph).

The slant-forward power unit was mounted in Suzuki's first dual-cradle frame, with coil-over telescopic dampers and big drum brakes. The result was a light machine that handled well, and this was coupled to good looks. The chromed tank sides and silencers and two-tone mudguards looked great, though the headlight design was somewhat quirky. For some reason, the Super Six came with a bike pump to inflate the tyres.

The T20 Super Six, Suzuki's first high-performance sports bike. Without the fairing it was good-looking in a fairly conventional way and all versions handled well in addition to delivering good performance.

ENGINE: two-stroke parallel-twin, air-cooled
POWER: 29bhp at 7500rpm
GEARBOX: 6-speed foot change
FINAL DRIVE: chain
WEIGHT: 138kg (304lb)
TOP SPEED: 153km/h (95mph)

ANCILLOTTI

The Ancillotti firm started out as the hobby of Enrico Ancillotti, who was enthusiastic about all forms of motorcycle sport but particularly off-road racing. In the late 1960s, Ancillotti decided to make a business out of this hobby. The result was a successful enterprise that spanned almost two decades until finally becoming a casualty of the motorcycle recession in the early to mid-1980s.

Like many of the smaller Italian marques, Ancillotti machines used bought-in engines from various manufacturers, including Hiro and Franco Morini, and the German

Ancillotti produced a range of trials, motocross and enduro machines using small-capacity engines bought in from elsewhere. This is a businesslike SM50.

Sachs company. All were two-strokes, usually with piston-port induction.

Ancillotti's main products were motocross, enduro and one-day trial bikes. However, to create a market presence, the company had to build reliable bikes that were capable of winning events. Ancillotti was successful right from the start, although almost all its sales were in Italy alone. To exploit fully the relatively small Italian market, the company had to build machines for all levels of riding skill, from novices to national champions.

Ancillotti's bikes were among the best available at any level, and the firm did well out of the Motocross boom of the late 1960s and early 1970s. Then in the mid- to late 1970s, it became fashionable to ride enduro bikes

Ancillotti's specialist market niche was dirt bikes. This FH250 is a typical late 1970s model, produced at a time when the market was very strong and Ancillotti was a class leader.

on the street, which brought further success to Ancillotti.

However, the recession of the early 1980s hit the firm hard

and in 1985, it was forced to close its doors.

LINTO

The first machine bearing the name Linto (in honour of designer Lino Tonti) was a double overhead-cam 75cc (5ci) lightweight in the early 1950s. It was not especially successful. The later Linto was the result

of a collaboration between designer Tonti, racing rider and constructor Umberto Premoli and racing rider Alcide Biotti. This was a 500cc (31ci) machine and was altogether more exciting and much more successful.

The latter Linto was a curious machine, built up of two Aermacchi Ala d'Oro 250cc (actually 248cc/15ci) singles on a common crankcase, creating a 496cc (30ci) twin. Unexpectedly, the engine was not in V formation,

but was instead a (very wide) parallel twin, with the cylinders perhaps 10 degrees above the horizontal. Equally curious was the employment of a pushrod engine at a time when one might have expected overhead-cams.

The Linto was certainly powerful enough: the Ala d'Oro delivered 32hp at 10,000rpm, and Tonti achieved the rare trick of nearly doubling the power by doubling up the engine, with 61hp at 9800rpm.

The bottom end was built in unit with a six-speed gearbox. Suspension was conventional: telescopic at the front, swinging-arm at the rear. The machine had a distinctly vintage look with an enormously long tank that stopped above the front of the rear wheel, just short of a very tight 'bum-stop' seat.

For the 1969 season, Tonti managed to find another 3hp and pared the weight down, from 142kg (312lb) to 134kg (295lb), by switching to a thin fibreglass tank. Alberto Pagani was second in the East German Grand Prix in that year, beaten only by the great Giacomo Agostini on an unbeatable MV Agusta. However, the Linto did not achieve much after this.

Creating a 64bhp engine by coupling two 32bhp units might seem like a simple idea, but it took the genius of Linto Tonti to make it a reality.

MOTO GUZZI V7

ITALY 1967

The V7 got its name from its layout (V) and capacity (7) in decilitres. The idea was to use the engine from the 'mechanical mule' in a replacement for Falcone bikes in police and military hands. The same engine was also considered for use in a 'baby' Fiat, although this came to nothing. The first prototype in a motorcycle frame appeared at the Milan Show in 1965, but financial issues delayed the new machine until 1967, the year that the SEIMM was to take over the firm.

One aim of the design was to create a machine that was extremely easy to maintain. Some of the measures taken were also fairly extreme: plated cylinder bores cannot be re-bored, but they wear very slowly, and can, in the relatively rare cases of damage, be replaced quickly and easily.

Moto Guzzi also borrowed a fair amount from BMW: the V7 is, after all, a BMW with the cylinders bent upwards at 45 degrees each. The alternators on many Guzzi V-twins and BMWs were interchangeable, and the car-type clutch and shaft drive were similar in concept and execution.

The low-stressed engine, with its easy power delivery, was exactly what police and military customers wanted, and civilian users found it to their taste as well. However, it was not long

before they started asking for more power. This was delivered by the V7 Special of 1969, which was given a bigger bore of 83mm to allow 758cc (46ci). Other modifications were also made, and this resulted in a claimed 45hp at 6000rpm.

In 1971, the Special was followed by the V7 Sport, with a slightly smaller bore (82.5mm/3.2in) to bring it inside the 750cc (46ci) racing limits, a hotter cam and 30mm (1.2in) Dell'Orto carburettors for 52hp at 6300rpm. Alongside this model was the long-stroke 850GT, a true 844cc (52ci) delivering 51hp at 6000rpm.

The first 1000cc (61ci) version was the V1000 Convert, with the long-throw crankshaft and an 88mm (3.5in) bore, this time with steel liners. A unique feature of this machine, which became known as the 'Old Grey Goose', was its two-speed automatic transmission. Opinion was rather divided about this system; most people disliked it, but those who liked it, loved it.

ENGINE: 704cc (42ci) ohv transverse V-twin, 80x70mm, air-cooled
POWER: 40bhp at 5800rpm
GEARBOX: 4-speed foot change
FINAL DRIVE: shaft
WEIGHT: 234kg (515lb)
TOP SPEED: 170km/h (105mph) approx

The V7 has been successful with civilian users as well as its target customers: police and military. Later versions delivered a more aggressive performance as a result of minor engine modifications.

AERMACCHI 125 ALA D'ORO

Aermacchi is mainly known for overhead-valve, horizontal, single-cylinder road and racing bikes. However, the firm also built a considerable number of two-strokes, of which one of the most successful was a racer derived from the 1967 M125 Rapido street bike. This machine featured a tuned version of the same 123cc (8ci) piston-ported engine designed by the German engineer, Peter Durr. The original racing prototype developed 20hp, exactly double that of its roadster brother.

Intensive testing at Monza in Italy in June 1967 proved that the prototype, which at that point had a four-speed gearbox, lapped faster than the best private Hondas or Bultacos. This encouraging news led to an early race debut the following month, on the recently opened Zingonia circuit near Bergamo. Alberto Pagani finished third behind a pair of purpose-built factory bikes, but well ahead of the Honda and Bultaco production racers, as well as the Motobi and Morini entries.

For the following year, the bike was considerably modified. Most notable was a specially commissioned, double-cradle tubular frame, a new cylinder head and barrel, and a five-speed transmission. Power increased to 22hp. The machine was renamed Ala d'Oro (Golden Wing) after the factory's four-stroke racers, and proved to be even more competitive than the previous version.

Aermacchi also experimented with an overdrive system, similar to that used on the 1962 Kreidler 50cc (3ci) racer. This allowed a total of 10 gear ratios, five operated by pedal and five by twist grip.

In 1969, the 125 Ala d'Oro delivered more competition results with riders such as Kel Carruthers, Johnny Dodds, Eugenio Lazzarini and Silvano Bertarelli all scoring world championship points. It even won a Grand Prix – something the horizontal single never did – when Dodds rode brilliantly in appalling weather conditions to win the 1970 West German race at the fearsome Nürburgring circuit.

ENGINE: 123cc (7ci) piston-port 2s single, 56x50mm, air-cooled
POWER: 22bhp at 8000rpm
GEARBOX: 5-speed foot change
FINAL DRIVE: chain
WEIGHT: 80kg (176lb)
TOP SPEED: 201km/h (125mph)

BSA ROCKET-3 (A75)

The BSA/Triumph triple appeared to great fanfare in 1968, along with advertising that promised: 'After today, the motorcycle world will never be the same.' The Rocket-3 was certainly very good, and in some ways better than Honda's CB750, which came out a year later. And yet it was the Honda that changed the world, not the BSA machine. Although it handled a lot better, the BSA simply could not match the Honda for sophistication and flamboyance. This came as a surprise to BSA, which had evaluated an early Honda CB750 and dismissed it as 'no threat' when its drive chain broke after less than 160km (100 miles).

The BSA Group had owned Triumph/Ariel since 1951, and initially made two versions of the new machine: the Triumph Trident T150 and the BSA Rocket-3. There were a few differences: the Rocket used forward-inclined cylinders in a tubular twin cradle while the Triumph housed its upright powerplant in a single-downtube, 650-type frame. The BSA also employed a twin-downtube frame compared with the Triumph's single tube chassis.

The powerplant driving these machines was impressive, but in reality it was little more than a stop-gap measure while new systems were under development. It was a concept originally proposed some years earlier by designers Bert Hopwood and Doug Hele, consisting essentially of one-and-a-half Triumph Tigers on a common crankcase. The engine design showed its age, using pushrods at a time when overhead camshafts

Although it was designed as a road machine, the superb handling of the Rocket-3 made it an extremely competitive race machine. In some ways it was a better bike than the Honda 750 that eclipsed it.

were becoming commonplace. The crankcases split vertically, like the twin's, and primary drive was by chain.

In the longer term, Hopwood wanted to develop a modular engine system. However, for the time being, the overhead-valve three would have to suffice against the multis known to come from Japan, and it did so fairly well. A good Rocket was at least as fast as the Honda, its main rival. The first press test Trident recorded almost 210km/h (130mph). This may have been a 'special', as some others struggled to reach 190km/h (118mph). Handling, while better than that of the Honda, was impaired somewhat by the sheer mass that had to be thrown around.

Some features of the Rocket were up to date, and others simply dated. The diaphragm clutch was modern, but the original four-speed gearbox harked back to bygone days. Overall, despite Ogle Design's styling (with 'Ray-gun' silencers and 'Bread-bin' fuel tank), the bike was more a child of the 1960s than the imminent 1970s.

Other components of the Rocket were inadequate, too. The rather feeble twin-leading, shoe-drum front brake fitted to early models was not up to the task of stopping the big 209kg (460lb) machine. Overall, despite a higher price tag, the BSA triple simply was not as refined as the Honda. Improvements were made, but by the time these were ready to be implemented, BSA was in a state of collapse and only Meriden-built Triumph triples benefited. A Lockheed front disc brake was fitted 1973, but by then the triple was already five years old.

Attempts to improve sales resulted in the Triumph X-75 Hurricane, which appeared in 1973. The prototypes wore BSA badges, and the machine looked fabulous. Unfortunately, its appearance was not enough and it was a disaster in the showroom. In 1975, the Triumph T160 electric start version appeared (the competing Honda had always had electric starting). This model delivered more power from an engine leaning forward in the old Rocket-3 manner.

The triple was a success on the track and is fondly remembered by many race fans, partly for the incredible sound it made and partly for the victories it won: first, second and third positions at Daytona in 1971, plus countless other short-circuit victories and a succession of production TT wins.

ENGINE: 740cc (44ci) ohv transverse triple, 67x70mm, air-cooled
POWER: 58bhp at 7250rpm
GEARBOX: 4-speed foot change
FINAL DRIVE: chain
WEIGHT: 209kg (460lb)
TOP SPEED: 190km/h (118mph)

The Ricket-3's engine was something of a throwback. Its pushrod design dated back to 1937, and the four-speed gearbox it drove was hardly cutting-edge technology either.

FANTIC

ITALY 1968–PRESENT

Fantic Motor was founded in 1968 by Henry Keppel Hasselink, a Dutch-Italian. Since then, the firm has grown to become one of Italy's most successful small manufacturers. The firm puts its emphasis on off-road machines, especially trials bikes.

The first model, interestingly, was a small child's bike, the Bronco TXl. This was powered by a four-stroke Aspera engine, as was a prototype tricycle developed at the same time. These were followed by a succession of models, including the Caballero (enduro), Chopper (custom) and Super Six GT (roadster).

During the 1970s, the 125 RC enduro, an air-cooled, twin-shock two-stroke, was extremely successful for works and private

Alongside its range of highly successful conventional trials and off-road bikes, Fantic has produced a number of oddball designs, children's bikes and mini-motorcycles like this Fantic B.

riders alike, and Fantic followed it with a motocross version. However, it was in the world of one-day trials that the firm really made its mark. Since the late 1970s onwards, Fantic machines have often dominated this branch

of motorcycle sport and have gained a string of world and national championship titles along the way.

In the early 1990s, Fantic absorbed the Garelli marque. Back in the 1920s and 1930s, the latter

had been one of the top five Italian bike manufacturers (along with Benelli, Bianchi, Gilera and Moto Guzzi). Indeed, even as late as 1987, Garelli had been the winner of the 125cc World Road-racing Championship title.

Fantic machines have always been strong off-road contenders, but the firm made road bikes too. Among the more conventional offerings from Fantic was the mid-1980s 125c HP1.

KAWASAKI H1

The H1 was sold in the home market (Japan) as the 500-SS, and as the Mach III elsewhere. It was powered by a 499cc (30ci) three-cylinder, two-stroke engine set across the frame, which had conventional porting and was built in unit with its five-speed gearbox. The rest of the bike was fairly standard for Japanese machines of that time.

The H1's performance was better than most other machines, and it was a lot more exciting than just about anything else available. The engine delivered 60hp with a vicious spike in the power curve. This, plus a chassis barely adequate for the job, resulted in a machine that could be very exciting to ride, and which was not for the faint-hearted. The Mach III possessed unbelievable acceleration and a top

speed close to 193km/h (120mph). Over a short distance, it would run away from any opposition, though it was a more than a bit wild through the curves.

Over time, the H1 improved and by its final year of production it was fast rather than crazed. However, by this time it had been joined by other triples: the racing H1R for 1970, then the 249cc (15ci) S1, the 346cc (21ci) S2, and the 748cc (46ci) H2. The latter was raced very successfully by Kawasaki until

about 1975, and the smallest triple, the 400cc/24ci S3 (which had replaced the S2 in 1973), remained in production until 1980.

Fast to the exclusion of all else, the half-wild H1 was an exciting ride but it was not for those of a nervous disposition. Later versions were better behaved.

ENGINE: 498.8cc (30ci) 2s triple, 60x58.8mm, air-cooled
POWER: 42bhp at 7000rpm
GEARBOX: 5-speed foot change
FINAL DRIVE: chain
WEIGHT: 152kg (335lb)
TOP SPEED: 196km/h (118mph)

MORBIDELLI

Giancarlo Morbidelli was born in 1938 and grew up in the 1950s, golden years for the Italian motorcycle industry and its racing teams. He founded a firm in his hometown of Pesaro, making woodworking machinery. His company, located close to the Benelli works, was very successful in the 1960s, but it was motorcycles that were Morbidelli's great passion.

A combination of enthusiasm, finance and the desire to gain publicity for his business saw Giancarlo Morbidelli join the ranks of racing entrants in 1968, when he entered a modified Benelli 60 and a Motobi that Luciano Mele used to win the Italian Junior title. From this relatively small beginning rose a team that went on to win a total of six world championships during the 1970s.

Late in 1968, Morbidelli decided to build a brand-new 50cc (3ci) racer with the help of Franco Ringhini, who had recently left the Guazzoni factory. The machine was first raced in 1969, and featured a single-cylinder 49.8cc (3ci), two-stroke engine with disc-valve induction and liquid-cooling. The following year, again with Ringhini, Morbidelli built a 125cc (8ci) machine. It used the same formula of disc-valve induction and liquid-cooling. Both bikes also featured six speeds.

Most of the next few months were spent with development and race testing. Then, in 1972, Gilberto Parlotti made the racing world sit up and take notice by not only finishing in each of the first four rounds of the World Championship series, but in the process taking a second and a third place.

The next round was in the Isle of Man, which at that time still counted towards the Championship. Parlotti looked set to cause more upset, but the extremely wet conditions brought disaster. Leading the race, he lost control of his Morbidelli and was killed instantly.

The accident was to have profound consequences within the Morbidelli team and for racing as a whole. Parlotti had been secretly testing a new four-cylinder, 350cc (21ci) model, which was then scrapped; only much later did another Morbidelli four-cylinder make an appearance.

His death also meant that the Isle of Man ceased to be a venue for the World Championship.

It was not until 1974 that Morbidelli finally recovered from Parlotti's death. With a new engineer, Jorg Moller, and a new rider, Paolo Pileri, the team finished runners-up in the 125cc title race. Moller's new twin, still with disc-valves, put out 42hp at 14,200rpm.

This resurgence marked the beginning of a period of huge success, starting with Pileri winning the 1975 championship title. This brought demands from private owners for replicas, so a new factory was built by entering into a joint agreement with Benelli Armi, the gun-manufacturing company owned by the Benelli family. The machines made there were sold as Morbidelli-Benelli Armi (MBA). The customer racer was virtually a replica of the works bikes, but the engines were not quite so highly tuned and delivered around 5hp less.

It was team-mate Pier-Paolo Bianchi's turn to be champion in 1976. And by 1977, more than half the grid of any 125 Grand Prix were riding Morbidelli or MBA machines. Bianchi won the championship again, and Morbidelli also took the 250cc title thanks to the consistent riding of Mario Lega.

The 250cc (15ci) machine had first appeared midway through 1976, ridden by Pileri, and had finished runner-up to Walter Villa's Harley-Davidson. The 249.7cc (15.2ci) twin followed the familiar Morbidelli lines with liquid-cooling, disc-valves and six speeds.

Although Eugenio Lazzarini became the new 125cc World Champion in 1978 (now entered as an MBA), the team's fortunes had begun to wane. The new 350cc (21ci) and 500cc (31ci) four-cylinder models were never able to match the performances of their smaller brothers. The 125 MBA production racer was made until the late 1980s, when the FIM brought out a singles-only formula for the class.

Later, in 1994, Morbidelli introduced a new de luxe touring motorcycle with an 850cc (52ci) V8 engine and shaft final drive. However, it was hugely expensive and suffered from extremely bland styling, which further reduced demand. It was redesigned in an effort to improve matters, but the machine was by then doomed to be a total failure in the showroom.

Morbidelli is primarily famous for racing machines, which achieved considerable success despite tragedy in 1972. The best Morbidellis were of small capacity. Later attempts at big tourers were not successful.

NORTON COMMANDO

ENGLAND 1968

As the Dominator engine increased in size (from 500cc/31ci to 600cc/37ci for the 99 and 750cc/46ci for the Atlas), it became ever more prone to vibration. The solution was Isolastic mounting. The engine, gearbox and swinging-arm were assembled as a unit, along with the exhausts and rear wheel, then assembled into a new, single, top tube frame using Isolastic rubber mounts to insulate the frame (and the rider) from the vibration inevitable with any oversized parallel twin.

The resulting machine possessed impressive acceleration and top speed, handled beautifully as long as the Isolastic mounts were in good order – and, above all, it looked great. It soon displaced the Atlas and was followed by variants. The 1969 Commando S (for the US market) had oversize bars, undersize tank and high-level exhausts. The 1970 Roadster was an S with conventional exhausts. The original was designated the Fastback.

From 1970, racing variants were available, delivering 68hp. A year later, Norton came out with the Hi-Rider – something of a monstrosity

with ape-hanger bars. There was also the Fastback LR with a 25l (6.6 US gallon), long-range tank, and this is generally considered the most desirable of all Commandos.

Also from 1971 came the Combat engine; with 65hp, it was a less desirable commodity because it had a tendency to break

down when pushed hard. The 1973 829cc (51ci) 850 was an overbored 89 x 77mm (3.5 x 3in) 750 delivering 60hp with a reduced compression ratio. The Interstate, which used this engine, was road-tested at 194km/h (121mph), but suffered from heavy vibration. After 1974, all Commandos used the 850 motor.

The Commando solved the problem of vibration inherent in big parallel-twin engines, creating a powerful machine.

ENGINE: 745cc (45ci) ohv parallel win 73x89mm, air-cooled
POWER: 49bhp
GEARBOX: 4-speed foot change
FINAL DRIVE: chain
WEIGHT: n/a
TOP SPEED: 185km/h (115mph)

NORTON VILLIERS
Norton

Much the same machine, albeit an earlier model sans fairings and panniers, the Commando was a versatile design that spawned a range of variants for different markets.

VILLA

Villa was the work of brothers Francesco and Walter, who were both world-class race riders. Francesco was also a highly gifted engineer, and an expert on two-stroke engines. He worked for FB Mondial and Montesa, before designing the first Villa machine, a single-cylinder over-the-counter 125cc (8ci) racer with square bore and stroke measurements of 54 x 54mm (2.1 x 2.1in). It was liquid-cooled with disc-valve induction, and produced 30hp at 11,200rpm for a maximum

speed of 190km (118mph).

This machine was quickly joined by seven dirt-bike models. All were orthodox air-cooled singles with piston-controlled induction, and were available in trials or motocross form, ranging from 50cc (3ci) to 250cc (15ci). Villa also produced a disc-valve single-cylinder racer of either 174cc (11ci) or 247cc (15ci), which was suitable for Italian Junior Formula events, a 125cc (8ci) narrow-angle V-twin and a 250cc (15ci) four. The latter was

intended as a Grand Prix competitor but was scuppered by new FIM restrictions, causing Villa to leave the GP scene.

The Villa brothers rode their own machines in competition, as did many others, including Mandolini and Charles Mortimer. The resulting publicity was good for the firm during the early 1970s. Since then, Villa has concentrated its efforts on the manufacture of motocross and enduro bikes, latterly with liquid-cooling as well as monoshock frames.

There were also some street models, notably the 125 Daytona and Italia (roadsters), the 125 Scrambler (trail) and the 350 Rommel (trail). The off-road bikes were imported into Britain during the 1970s by the Cleveland-based John Burdon Engineering concern.

Although Villa built off-the-shelf racers and some street machines, it was their dirt bikes like this Everest that really defined the company.

GORI

Named for its founder, Giancarlo Gori, the Gori marque became famous for excellent dirt bikes: motocross, enduro and trials. The company also produced children's models and two 125cc (8ci) models: a racer and a super sports roadster.

The racer used a specially tuned German Sachs two-stroke engine with a six-speed gearbox, and was very successful in hill-climb events; Guido Valli rode one in his successful 1974 and 1975 bids for the Italian national championships. This success inspired Gori to offer a production machine with the same specification, which included a 125cc (8ci) two-stroke with a 13:1 compression ratio, Motoplat ignition, Marzocchi suspension, a 170mm (6.7in) Fontana double-sided drum front brake and a low-slung expansion chamber exhaust. Producing over 24hp at 11,600rpm, the Gori hill-climber had a maximum speed of almost 185km/h (115mph).

The roadster was named 125 Sport Valli Replica and used the same Sachs unit, though slightly

Guido Vialli's victories made Gori machines famous, and a replica of his race machine soon went on sale. The Vialli Sport Replica was the fastest production 125 in Italy and was (just about) road legal.

detuned. It also featured a full fairing, twin front discs, cast-alloy wheels. At 148km/h (92mph), it was the fastest production 125cc (8ci) in Italy and its excellent styling, coupled with the fact that it was just barely road legal, made it popular in the marketplace.

By 1980, Gori was offering motocross and enduro models of 125cc (8ci) and 250cc (15ci), using Hiro-built two-stroke engines.

Gori made its name with dirt bikes such as the Regolarita, and after 1980 the firm concentrated more or less exclusively on the off-road market.

The 125 RG (enduro) featured a six-speed transmission, Sachs Hydra cross rear shocks, Dell 'Orto 30mm (1in) carburettor with fully sealed air filter, long-travel front forks, Metzeler tyres, Megura levers and unbreakable plastic for the mudguards, tank and side panels. The motocross version had lighting equipment and a more highly tuned motor.

SWM acquired Gori in 1980, but the resulting firm, Go-Motor, was a victim of the recession in the early 1980s. SWM collapsed in 1985, and took Gori with it.

HONDA CB750

The CB750 was instrumental in establishing Honda's reputation for creating luxurious high-performance machines, and took sales away from traditional marques like BSA and Triumph. Its big advantage was that the standard CB750 came with features normally only found on special edition machines or top-of-the-line models.

Although its handling was not all that might be desired at times, the CB750 had many excellent features that more than outweighed such concerns. It was reliable, clean and civilized, and well mannered at low speed. Rather than being a finely tuned racehorse of a bike, with all the temperament that goes with it, the new Honda was actually quite mild, and its 76hp at 8000rpm was well within the engine's limits. This reduced strain and maintenance burdens.

The new engine was an evolution of well-tried principles rather than an attempt at revolutionary advances. Its simple design had just two valves per cylinder, and the single overhead-cam was driven by a central chain. There were four carburettors and four exhaust pipes. Similarly, the frame was a conventional tubular cradle with gaitered telescopic front forks. The five-speed gearbox, electric start and front disc brake that completed the

The CB750 was an experiment for Honda – the firm's first attempt at a big bike. Although not by any means perfect, the resulting machine was highly successful and transformed the motorcycle market by offering as standard many features previously considered to be luxuries.

specification were nice, but not radical – just good components that fitted well into the bike as a whole.

The flexible engine and big comfortable seat made the CB750 practical for touring, but it was also capable of 201km/h (125mph). And all this came in a package that did not need constant fiddling to keep it performing. The concept of a big, affordable, in-line four was so successful that all the Japanese manufacturers built one sooner or later.

The automatic transmission version of the 750cc (46ci), de-tuned to 47hp at 7500rpm and with a torque converter replacing the clutch, was less successful and only sold in small numbers. By 1979, the original single-camshaft 750 (46ci) was outclassed by the opposition. Its replacement was a double overhead-cam, 16-valve machine delivering 77hp. Alongside this came the 95hp CB900, which could reach 217km/h (135mph). This developed into the CB1100R, with a half-fairing and improved handling. All this time the CB750 remained in production – testament to a design that got it right.

ENGINE: 736cc (44ci) transverse-mounted in-line four, 61x63mm
POWER: 67bhp at 8000rpm
GEARBOX: 5-speed, foot change
FINAL DRIVE: chain
WEIGHT: 220kg (485lb)
TOP SPEED: 200km/h (124mph)

JAWA 350 GP V-FOUR

The GP-V four was first prototyped in 1967, though it had a number of teething problems that delayed production. The engine layout was similar to that used in Yamaha fours, though it had been designed independently. Like the Yamaha machines, the Jawa 350cc (21ci) used water-cooling but followed the thermosyphon principle, creating an engine that most observers agreed was much neater than the Japanese models.

The Jawa's two crankshafts were geared and used much of the technology employed on the 125cc (8ci) V-twin. Induction was again by disc-valve, which designer Zdenik Tichy thought necessary for ultimate performance. The 344.5cc (21ci) engine had a compression ratio of 16:1 and power of 9000–13,500rpm. Drive to the rear wheel was by chain, via a seven-speed gearbox.

Initially the new V-four was unreliable, and it was not until mid-1968 that it finished a Grand Prix. Once it could complete the race, it was an impressive competitor. With a top speed of 258km/h (160mph), the Jawa was the only serious competitor to MV and Giacomo Agostini.

Eventually fitted with electronic ignition (replacing four sets of contact breakers), the engine delivered 70hp, resulting in a performance that could challenge the mighty three-cylinder MV. Indeed, at one point it looked like Bill Ivy might take the Jawa to victory over Agostini and MV Agusta. Ivy, though, was killed during a practice run for the East German Grand Prix, bringing Jawa's bid for glory to a tragic end.

ENGINE: 344.5cc (21ci) 2s rotary valve V-four, 48x47.6mm, water-cooled
POWER: 70bhp at 13,000rpm
GEARBOX: 7-speed foot change
FINAL DRIVE: chain
WEIGHT: 265lb (120kg)
TOP SPEED: 258km/h (165mph)

OSSA 250 GP

The GP250's powerful disc-valve, air-cooled, single-cylinder engine delivered race-winning performance but initially suffered from reliability problems. It had not reached its full capability when GP racing was curtailed.

The 250 GP made its race debut at the 1967 Spanish Grand Prix. Carlos Giri rode the new machine to a very decent sixth place, but this did not satisfy the machine's creator, Eduardo Giro. For 1968, Giro signed up Spanish 250cc Champion Santiago Herrero and used that year's racing season as a development exercise for the firm and an opportunity for Herrero to learn the foreign circuits.

The 250 GP moved away from Ossa's traditional piston-port induction, opting instead for the greater performance benefits of disc-valve. The air-cooled 249cc (15ci) featured a seven-fin barrel and head with such large fins that the top end looked more like a 500cc (31ci) than a 250cc (15ci). Its carburettor was a massive 42mm Amal, fitted to the offside crankcase. By 1969, this engine delivered 42hp at 11,000rpm but that was not its only good feature. It delivered over a wide range of throttle settings, and was powerful even at 6500rpm, making the six-speed gearbox quite sufficient.

The new season started well for Ossa and Herrero, who stormed home to win the first race of the season, staged in Madrid. Ignition trouble kept Herrero out of the West German Grand Prix, and he suffered other troubles with his machine. But in between setbacks Herrero and his Ossa were impressive, winning in France and Belgium, taking second place in East Germany and third twice, on the Isle of Man and in Holland.

The Ossa 250 was so fast that Herrero's winning average in Belgium was 188.74km/h (117.96mph) – faster than the runner-up in the 500cc event. However, a crash in Ulster ended his bid for the championship.

In 1970, after experiments including investigations into water-cooling, even more power was wrung out of the machine. Herrero had 45hp under his hand as he took the grid for the Isle of Man TT. However, he crashed on the last lap and subsequently died of his injuries. Ossa ceased competing in GP racing as a mark of respect, so it will never be known what might have been achieved. Perhaps the most impressive point is that Ossa managed to mount a serious GP challenge on a very small budget.

ENGINE: 249cc (15ci) rotary valve 2s 70x65mm, air-cooled
POWER: 42bhp at 11,000rpm
GEARBOX: 6-speed foot change
FINAL DRIVE: chain
WEIGHT: 99kg (219lb)
TOP SPEED: 229km/h (142mph)

BENELLI 500 GRAND PRIX

Benelli produced a four-cylinder race bike, a water-cooled, supercharged 250cc (15ci), in 1940. However, the FIM banned super-chargers before this machine could take to the track, so it faded away. The next four was another 250cc (15ci) race design, this time air-cooled and lacking a supercharger.

The new engine followed the classic engineering layout, with its four cylinders set transversely across the frame. There were double overhead-camshafts with a central gear drive, and a geared primary drive between the first and second cylinders, on the nearside, to reduce overall width.

Originally delivering 40hp at 13,000rpm, the new machine had battery coil ignition, but this was soon replaced by a magneto. A multi-plate dry clutch was employed on the nearside of the

unit construction engine and gearbox assembly, which had six speeds. There was also considerable experimentation with the lubrication system. At first, the oil tank was mounted on the rearside, then it was placed in front of the fuel tank, before finally being relocated under the crankcase.

The new Benelli 250 racer made its debut at Imola in spring 1962. It was fast all right, but it needed more development work. This went on until the end of 1963, when Benelli signed Tarquino Provini from Morini. The 1964 machine was much lighter and had a seven-speed gearbox gears, but Provini was still beaten in the Italian Senior Championship by his replacement at Morini, the young Giacomo Agostini.

For 1964, the four was further improved with new crankshaft,

heads and gearbox. Power output was increased 52hp at 16,000rpm. Later in 1965, the company introduced a larger-engined 322cc (20ci) model. From this came a 343cc (21ci) version, with four valves per cylinder. Provini retired through injury, and his place was taken by Renzo Pasolini for 1967.

Benelli then brought out an even bigger machine, a 494.6cc (30ci) four, which made its debut at Monza in 1968 in the capable hands of Pasolini and Mike Hailwood aboard. Then, in 1969, the firm finally achieved the success such long and hard work deserved when Kel Carruthers won the 250cc World Title – the last victory for a four-stroke in this class. After Carruthers' success, Benelli could no longer race its four in the 250cc category, as FIM rules now permitted a maximum

The 500 Grand Prix was the ultimate development of Benelli's racing fours. This early 1970s model represents 30 years of development. It was raced into the 1970s.

of two cylinders and six gears. The 350cc (21ci) and 500cc (31ci) models continued into the 1970s, making their first appearance with Walter Villa aboard a revamped 350cc (21ci) four in the 1973 Italian GP at Monza.

ENGINE: 494.6cc (30ci) dohc straight four, 54x54mm air-cooled
POWER: 82bhp at 11,000rpm
GEARBOX: 6-speed foot change
FINAL DRIVE: chain
WEIGHT: 120kg (264lb)
TOP SPEED: 264km/h (164mph)

BSA FURY

With the light and middleweight classes dominated by Japanese machines by the mid-1960s, it was clear to BSA that something more sophisticated than overhead-valve singles and twins was needed if they were to compete. The Fury, unveiled to the media in November 1970, was intended to get BSA back into the game.

Designed by Edward Turner, who had created the seminal Triumph Speed Twin some 33 years before, the Fury was the first British roadster to feature double overhead-cams. Its 350cc (21ci) twin engine delivered a claimed 34hp at 9000rpm. In some ways (the chain cam-drive, for example), the design was inspired by the Japanese competition. However,

the crankcases were dry sump and continued to split vertically, as was conventional with British bikes.

The Fury, and its sister, the Triumph Bandit, both had the option of electric starting, though at additional cost. However, although orders were being accepted, development was incomplete and the factory was not ready for production. This

damaged BSA's reputation, and brought bankruptcy a little closer.

ENGINE: 349cc (21ci) dohc parallel twin, 63x56mm, air-cooled
POWER: 34bhp at 9000rpm
GEARBOX: 5-speed foot change
FINAL DRIVE: chain
WEIGHT: n/a
TOP SPEED: n/a

BULTACO ALPINA

The sudden explosion of interest in off-road motorcycling in the early 1970s found Bultaco well positioned to take advantage. The firm brought out a range of trials and motocross machines whose popularity further fuelled the dirt-bike boom.

Bultaco then brought out the Alpina, targetted at the amateur rider who wanted to get a taste of competition. It was more of a trail bike than an enduro machine, but by any standards, it was a good off-roader. The Alpina featured a high-level alloy mudguard, a silencing system, rear dampers, alloy brake hub, leading-shoe front drum brake, and rearward mounted footpegs. The only instrument provided was a rev-counter.

ENGINE: single-cylinder 244cc (15ci)
POWER: 19bhp
GEARBOX: 5-speed foot change
FINAL DRIVE: chain
WEIGHT: 109kg (240lb)
TOP SPEED: n/a

The Alpina was aimed at the serious amateur rather than top-end professionals, and had a price tag to match. Nevertheless, it was a well-put-together machine with good components and found favour in the marketplace.

DERBI WORKS 125

Launched in 1962, the first Derbi Works racer was a very competitive 50cc (3ci) machine with an air-cooled, disc-valve engine and eight speeds. It finished a close second in the opening round. Two years later, Angel Nieto, began riding for Derbi and won five of his 13 world titles on Derbi machines: three 50cc titles in 1969, 1970 and 1972; and two 125CC titles in 1971 and 1972.

The 125cc (8ci) machine first appeared in 1970 at the Belgian Grand Prix, halfway through the season. It was an immediate success, winning the race and three more during the remainder of the season, finishing second in the championship. The Derbi 125 won the next two seasons, both times under the hand of Nieto. This was despite strong competition, and it is interesting to speculate what might have happened in subsequent seasons had Derbi not withdrawn from racing for several years. The final incarnation of the machine delivered 40hp.

Technically, Derbi's 125cc (8ci) racing machines were well designed rather than innovative. All had twin-cylinder engines with the water-cooled cylinders well inclined to reduce overall height. A disc valve went on each side with the drive to the six-speed gearbox built in unit with the engine on the right. Expansion chamber exhausts ran under the unit, which was mounted in a tubular frame with conventional suspension, wire wheels and twin leading-shoe drum brakes front and rear.

ENGINE: 123.97cc (7ci) 2s inclined parallel twin, 43.4x41.9mm, water-cooled
POWER: 34bhp at 14,500rpm
GEARBOX: unit 6-speed foot change
FINAL DRIVE: chain
WEIGHT: 85kg (187lb)
TOP SPEED: 225km/h (135mph)

HERCULES W2000

In 1974, Hercules built the world's first Wankel-engined production motorcycle. The Wankel engine is different from more conventional units, and using it in a motorcycle was something of a gamble. NSU had experimented with such a concept, but it never reached the production stage aboard a two-wheeler. They also licensed other manufacturers to build engines to the design they had developed.

The Wankel engine contains an epitrochoidal chamber; inside, a revolving rotor (piston) shaped like a curved-sided equilateral triangle. This is connected to a gear attached to one of the side housings and supported on an eccentric bearing, which allows it to rotate while keeping its three tips in contact with the chamber.

To prevent gas leakage through the gaps between the rotor and chamber at the tips of the triangle, the Hercules machine used special strips. These were a feature that gave much initial trouble, but by the time the production W2000 model appeared, the rotor seals benefited from the advantages of ceramic technology.

The Hercules' engine was, due to the licence with NSU, limited to a power output of 30hp. It was thus built with a displacement of 294cc (18ci), and the resulting lack of power (27hp at 6500rpm) from the power unit was a problem for both Hercules and W2000. Even with the machine's six-speed gearbox, it was uninspiring at best. However, this machine made it into production and thus made motorcycling history.

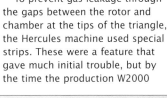

The prototype W2000. This machine made history in 1974 by becoming the first production motorcycle with a Wankel engine, though its performance was less than stellar. The W2000 did not start a revolution – conventional engines continue to reign supreme.

ENGINE: 294cc (18ci) Wankel single chamber, air-cooled
POWER: 27bhp at 6500rpm
GEARBOX: 6-speed foot change
FINAL DRIVE: chain
WEIGHT: n/a
TOP SPEED: 148km/h (92mph)

JAWA MODEL 6 SERIES ENDURO

In 1968, Jawa tried out a new tubular duplex frame and found it to be excellent. The bikes for the Jawa team at the 1969 International Six Day Trial were built on this frame, which had two downtubes curved under the power unit and two top tubes extending rearwards from the steering head to meet the seating supporting tubing. To provide additional support, a third tube ran from the base of the steering head rearwards to join the other at the seat tube area.

The rest of the machine, and notably the front forks and the brake assembly, came mostly from the CZ motocrosser, while the swinging-arm was controlled by conventional twin shocks. To provide maximum strength, the duralumin rear hub was forged, instead of cast.

The massively finned cylinder head (with twin plugs) was of light alloy, as was the cylinder, the latter with a cast-iron liner. Needle rollers were employed for both the small- and big-ends' assemblies. Crankshaft design was unusual in

that it was virtually a one-piece electron casting, with a cover on the nearside for access. On the offside was access to the five-speed in-unit gearbox. Apart from an inherent rigidity, the one-piece casting allowed the crankshaft and gears to be dismantled without removing the engine assembly from the frame.

The Jawa 652, 653 and 654 series of enduro machines totally dominated the 250cc (15ci), 350cc (21ci) and ultimately 500cc (30ci) class sizes, of the 1970s ISDT series. For several years thereafter,

these machines reigned supreme, winning the Trophy team contest in 1970–74, 1977 and 1978, and the Vase contest in 1970–72, 1974, 1976, 1977 and 1979.

ENGINE: 344cc (21ci) 2s single 78x72mm, air-cooled
POWER: 36bhp at 6200rpm
GEARBOX: 5-speed foot change
FINAL DRIVE: chain
WEIGHT: 158kg (347lb)
TOP SPEED: 150km/h (94mph)

MV AGUSTA 350 SPORT

Launched at the November 1969 Milan Show, the 350 twin cylinder series was developed from the earlier 250cc (15ci),

which had entered production in 1967. The larger engine was created by increasing the cylinder bore from 53mm (2in) to 63mm

(2.4in), leaving the stroke at 56mm. This gave a displacement of 348.9cc (21.3ci).

A number of variants of the

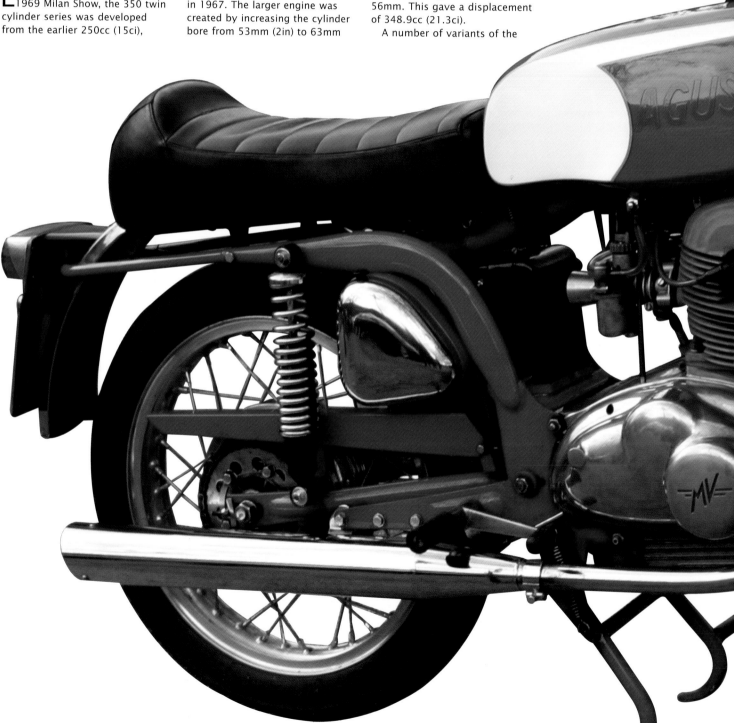

350 B series were produced, the most popular being the 'S' (Sport). Early models featured battery/coil ignition, but a restyled Sport, the Sport Elettronica, with electronic ignition was first shown to the public in 1972.

Also available were the GT (coil ignition) and GTE (Gran Turismo Elettronica, with electronic ignition); the Scrambler with twin hi-level exhausts on the offside; and a GTE police version, with pannier bags, crash bars, windscreen, siren and direction indicator.

The later electronic ignition version of the Sport, along with some of the fours, was available with the option of a fairing that closely resembled the type used by the factory's three- and four-cylinder racing machines. In this and other ways, the 350 had a much more modern and sporty style than the 250 model on which it was based. The touring version also followed this trend, after the initial batch of GT models, which closely followed the 250.

The engine had a very clean appearance, resembling a two-stroke instead of an overhead-valve unit. The cylinder head and barrel were in aluminium, and there were twin Dell 'Orto carburettors.

In traditional MV fashion, lubrication was taken care of by a gear-type pump and was of the wet-sump variety. The five-speed gearbox and wet multi-plate clutch were in unit with the engine, while the foot-operated gear change was on the offside. All models were fitted with full-width drum brakes front and rear.

In 1975, the round-case B series 350 range was replaced by the new Ipotesi, which still employed pushrod-operated valves, but had squared-off outer casings and finning for the cylinders and heads. The 350 S version had a very modern styling job with cast-alloy wheels and triple disc brakes. There was also a GT variant that had twin discs at the front and a drum at the rear, with wire wheels. Production ceased in 1978.

ENGINE: 348.9cc (21ci) ohv 2v parallel twin, 63x56mm, air-cooled
POWER: 28 bhp at 8400rpm
GEARBOX: 5-speed foot change
FINAL DRIVE: chain
WEIGHT: 149kg (329lb)
TOP SPEED: 155km/h (97mph)

The 350cc (21ci) twin-cylinder series reached the market in 1969. A range of versions of the round-case 350B were produced, with the most popular being the S (for Sport). Other variants included tourers and police bikes.

PUCH MAXI

In the 1950s, the top-selling European moped was the German NSU Quickly, but two decades later the bestseller was the Austrian Puch Maxi. This machine went into production at Puch's Graz factory at the end of 1968. The original model had a power output of 1.8hp at 4500rpm and the transmission was single-speed automatic.

The Maxi was well received all across Europe and became not merely the best-selling European moped of the time but the most popular powered two-wheeler overall. Production continued for the next 20 years and encompassed a wide range of models and variants. Even after

Puch was taken over by Piaggio in the late 1980s, the Maxi was licence-built in Austria.

One feature in the success of these machines was their quality of workmanship, which ensured years of reliable service. They were very well put together, using quality parts that not only looked good and performed well, but continued to do so for a long time. The machine itself was good at its job, offering lightweight, nippy urban mobility in conjunction with extremely good fuel mileage – over 2.2l/100km, 130mpg. This made the Maxi a sound investment, which in turn ensured excellent sales figures.

All Maxis used the same basic 48.8cc two-stroke engine with piston-port induction and horizontal cylinder. This drove through an automatic gearbox and centrifugal clutch, and on a machine weighing just 44kg (97lb), it offered very decent performance by moped standards. Maxis were initially built with a rigid frame, though many later models featured swinging-arm and twin rear shock absorbers. Most versions had a single seat, but on some bikes a dual seat was specified as standard equipment.

The Maxi was never considered a status symbol, but for those desiring reliable, usable and economical transport, it was ideal.

Its enormous market success suggests that there were a lot of people like that around.

ENGINE: 48.8cc (3ci) 2s single, 38x43mm, air-cooled
POWER: 2.2bhp at 4500rpm
GEARBOX: single-speed automatic
FINAL DRIVE: chain
WEIGHT: 44kg (97lb)
TOP SPEED: 48km/h (30mph)

The Maxi was unglamorous but it was a best-seller all the same, offering reliable, economical personal transport. This later version has twin shock rear suspension.

YAMAHA YR5 350

Yamahas first 350cc (21ci) twin was the YR1, which led on from the successful 250cc (15ci) YDS models of the 1960s. It was followed in 1970 by the YR5 350, which was powered by an air-cooled parallel-twin producing 36hp. This was good for 153km/h (95mph) and was backed up by good handling and effective brakes.

The YR5 was competitively priced and soon acquired a reputation for reliability. It became very popular and was followed by the six-speed RD350 of 1974 and the 161km/h (100mph) RD400 of 1976. Later developments included the water-cooled, single-shock RD350LC from 1981 and the 1983 YPVS or Power Valve model, whose exhaust power-valve brought mid-range performance to 53hp. The RD350LC F2 was still being made in Brazil in the mid-1990s.

The YR range first appeared in 1967, ushering in a line of larger-capacity two-strokes. These machines were the first to have horizontally split engine cases and fire port cylinder barrels. They were extremely reliable, fairly quick and handled well – and all at a very reasonable price. Not surprisingly, the YR5 had a very long production life.

AERMACCHI 350 TV

Aermacchi's 1971 sports roadster has come to be regarded as the definitive and best Aermacchi model of the type. A 350cc (21ci), overhead-valve horizontal single, the 350 TV benefited in the development stage from Aermacchi's racing experience. Many of its features were worked out on the track, including the TV's hairline steering and super-efficient braking.

The machine boasted Ceriani suspension, a five-speed gearbox and a dry clutch. The 344cc (20.9ci) engine ran on a compression ratio of 9:1 to deliver 29hp at 7500rpm. Carburetion was via a Dell'Orto square slide VHB 30A instrument, with an open polished bellmouth in the best Italian sporting tradition. Although the 6V electrics were not great, the rest of the spec was good.

The 350 TV epitomized the lightweight Italian sports bike with good looks, slick gear change and excellent brakes. The traditional Aermacchi 'open' frame allowed the rider to make full use of the engine's power, while the frame allowed a clear view of the neat, compact unit-construction engine.

However, the full Harley-Davidson takeover of Aermacchi in 1972 resulted in the demise of such machines, since the American owners favoured the much heavier touring machine, the 350SS, and its trial bike brother, the SX.

ENGINE: 344cc (21ci) overhead-valve horizontal single, 74x80mm air-cooled
POWER: 29bhp at 7500rpm
GEARBOX: 5-speed foot change
FINAL DRIVE: chain
WEIGHT: 140kg (309lb)
TOP SPEED: 160km/h (99mph)

CCM

CCM, or Clews Competition Machines, was founded in Bolton by Alan Clews. In 1971, Clews bought up a vanload of spares from the BSA competition shop when it closed, and used them as the basis for a new machine named the Clews Stroka.

The Stroka was a success and orders came in, and the first CCM machines were produced in May 1972, based on the BSA B50 single-cylinder engine unit. Clews made various changes, including cutting away part of the cylinder fins. These machines were either 499cc (30ci), or enlarged to 608cc (37ci). Clews' big four-strokes were successful right through the 1970s, and late in the decade they were joined by a 345cc (21ci) trials model that used an engine based on and developed from the BSA B40. After that came two-stroke scramblers using Italian Hiro engine units of 125cc (8ci) and 250cc (15ci).

The beginning of the 1980s was not a good time to be a motorcycle manufacturer, and CCM was feeling the pressure. The firm was bought out by Armstrong in 1980. Its machines retained the CCM name for 1981 and were rebadged as Armstrong CCM the following year, at which time Armstrong's links with Rotax led to the use of that firm's engines.

Alan Clews bought his firm back in 1987 and spent the next two years rebuilding it by selling spares and Armstrong machines against outstanding orders. CCM returned to the competition field in 1989, still using Rotax engines. For trials, there was a two-stroke engine but the motocross models used the big, four-stroke single with a choice of 500cc (31ci), 560cc (34ci) or 590cc (36ci).

CCM got its start with a vanload of parts bought from BSA, and throughout its history the firm used bought-in engines, modifying them as needed. This early 1970s engine in derived from BSA components.

Only 100 of these four-stroke 345cc (21ci) trials machines were built for sale, plus a handful more for spares. Its engine was developed from the BSA B40 unit.

CCM went on in similar style into the 1990s, and for 1997 added a super moto for use on the road. Based on the motocross machine, it used the metric 598cc (36ci) Rotax four-valve engine in a modern package to offer an excellent, if expensive, model. At the same time, the motocross model was available either in Enduro or Rallye Raid trim, all with the 560cc (34ci) Rotax, so all the CCM machines had a common base.

Plans for the future include a massive V-twin trail model using a 934cc (57ci) Folan engine made in Sweden with double overhead-cams, water-cooling and a high-tech specification. Six speeds, a tubular frame, modern suspension and wire wheels with disc brakes all add up to a spectacular package with further development heralded. However, the initial thrust of the firm for the future lies with the well-established singles, for both road and off-road use.

In 1980, CCM was suffering from financial difficulties but was still producing motorcycles like this 1980 four-valve. A year later the firm was taken over by Armstrong.

LAVERDA 750 SFC

In 1967, Laverda exhibited its new 750 twin at the Milan Show, and within two years the firm had decided to return to racing to garner publicity for the new machine. The bid was successful: in 1970, it won the Oss 24 Hours and the prestigious 500km (311 mile) race for production machines at Monza.

The SF series was joined in 1971 by the 750 SFC (the C stood for Competizione), which was an endurance racing version. It, too, was a success, winning its first-ever event, the Barcelona 24 Horas (Hours), at Montjuic Park.

The 744cc (45ci) SFC differed in several important ways from the SF on which it was based. Its engine was more highly tuned and had a larger oil pump and bigger bearings. Although the frame employed the same basic geometry as the touring SF, with a spine of four 40ml (2.7ci) tubes from which the engine was slung, it was visually distinct from the SF. Its chassis incorporated a revised racing-style, half-fairing seat unit and rear-set controls. The exhaust was a two-into-one affair with virtually an open race pipe exiting on the near side of the machine.

In 1974, a second-generation SFC made its debut. This version mounted triple hydraulically operated Brembo disc brakes rather than the Laverda drum brakes of the original. It also had stronger fork tubes, magnesium rear-wheel hub and revised styling. Initially, discs and wire wheels were used, but a revision soon after launch resulted in the definitive combination of discs and cast wheels. The last major modification to the SFC was the introduction of electronic ignition. A total of 549 machines were built up to 1976.

ENGINE: 744cc (45ci) dohc parallel-twin, 80x74mm, air-cooled
POWER: 70bhp at 7500rpm
GEARBOX: 5-speed foot change
FINAL DRIVE: chain
WEIGHT: 205kg (452lb)
TOP SPEED: 212km/h (132mph)

The last version of the 750 SFC to go to market was the 18000 series, which came out for the 1975–76 season. It featured Bosch electronic ignition, two-into-one exhaust and triple disc brakes.

MV AGUSTA 750S

The 750 S was unveiled to the public at the Milan Show in November 1969, but it did not go on sale until 1971. When it did become available, it was more successful than the preceding 600 and, unlike that machine, had the style to be expected from a four-cylinder MV Agusta.

This was a four-cylinder MV, so the power unit attracted immediate attention. The castings

of the 743cc (45ci), double overhead-cam, four-cylinder engine were in a traditional MV matt 'sand cast' finish, and this was accompanied by great looks in the popular café-racer style of the time.

The machine boasted clip-on bars, bum-stop racing saddle (finished in red), a jelly-mould tank, a four-pipe chrome-plated exhaust with matching

megaphones, and massive Grimeca-made drum brakes, with a 220mm (9in) four leading-shoe device at the front. All this was set off by an abundance of highly polished chrome and stainless steel.

The Type 214, as this machine was officially designated, represented a change of direction for MV Agusta, and a timely one. Perhaps it was the poor sales of

the 600 that suggested to Count Agusta that something was going awry, or perhaps there were other reasons. It will never be known; the Count died in 1971.

It seems likely that the decision to produce the 750S (plus small numbers of the touring GT and super-sporting SS versions) was influenced by Honda's release of the world-beating CB750 in 1968.

MV had released the first modern across-the-frame four-cylinder motorcycle, the 600, but Honda blew it out of the water with its better machine. It is likely, therefore, that the 750S was an attempt to regain lost ground.

However, while production of MV four-cylinder machines (of all types) might just have reached 2000 in the 1960s and 1970s, the CB750 sold more than 61,000 units during its first three years in the USA alone.

ENGINE: 742.9cc (45ci) dohc 2v four, 65x56mm, air-cooled
POWER: 65bhp at 8500rpm
GEARBOX: 5-speed foot change
FINAL DRIVE: shaft
WEIGHT: 230kg (505lb)
TOP SPEED: 201km/h (125mph)

The 750S first appeared at the 1969 Milan show and went on sale for 1971. It was available with or without a fairing. The 750S was good, but it could not really compete with the Honda CB750.

OSSA MICK ANDREWS REPLICA

SPAIN 1971

The Mick Andrews Replica, known as MAR for short, was announced by Ossa's founder Manuel Giro in October 1971. It was named in honour of the British rider Mick Andrews, who took the Ossa trials machines onto the world stage when he and his Ossa scored a hat trick in the famous Scottish Six Day Trial. He also won the British and European Trials Championship titles, and many other international awards.

The MAR featured a 244cc (15ci) engine delivering 17hp at 6500rpm through a five-speed gearbox, and it was very well received. However, just when Mick Andrews' victories were making everyone want an Ossa of their own, the factory was flooded and production severely disrupted. The resulting cash flow problems were the first of many.

Nevertheless, the original MAR remained in production until 1975, and even then the Mk II was little different. A year later, the Mk III arrived and by then the MAR was beginning to show its age.

ENGINE: 244cc (15ci) 2s single 60x72mm, air-cooled
POWER: 17bhp at 6500rpm
GEARBOX: 5-speed foot change
FINAL DRIVE: chain
WEIGHT: 95.5kg (215lb) (with lighting equipment)
TOP SPEED: 105km/h (65mph)

SILK

Based out of Derby, George Silk had always been enthusiastic about Scott bikes, and in 1971 he entered a Scott-engined special in the Manx Grand Prix. This machine was built on a sturdy duplex frame built by the local firm Spondon

Engineering, which was headed by former racer Bob Stevenson.

Silk built a number of Scott-engined bikes before he turned to building his own power unit. Similar in many ways to the Scott, Silk's engine was a water-cooled,

653cc (40ci), two-stroke twin, with deflector pistons and primary drive taken from the centre of the crankshaft. The latter was supported by a combination of two ball bearings and four roller bearings. On the offside of the

crank was sited the throttle-operated oil pump, as well as the infrared triggers of the Lumenition electronic ignition system.

Silk's bike went into production in 1975 under the name 700S, although an early version was

shown at the London Racing and Sporting Show in January 1972. It sold a total of 138 units between 1975 and 1980, with the 100th machine coming off the factory floor in November 1978. Production continued until February 1980,

during which some 140 engine/gearbox units were made, along with 138 chassis. The first 30 were Mk Is, featuring a polished engine, and the remainder were Mk IIs, with engines that were partly black.

Silk also developed a 325cc (20ci) trials engine – virtually a 700S, but air-cooled, with a four-speed gearbox that included a shaft to produce two-speed final drive, giving four low ratios for trials work and four for road use.

A Silk 700S from 1975. This is a Mark I, with an all-silver 653cc (39ci) two-stroke engine. Production ran for five years, though fewer than 150 machines were ever built.

SWM

ITALY 1971–85

Speedy Working Motors (SWM) was another very promising Italian marque that produced good machines but which ultimately fell by the wayside. Its bikes used either German Sachs or Austrian Rotax power units at a time when most other Italian marques bought their engines from domestic suppliers such as Minerelli, Franco Morini or Hiro.

SWM was founded by Pietro Sironi and built a series of extremely competitive off-road machines for both motocross racing and enduro use. The latter also became popular for road use in the mid- to late 1970s, by those who could afford them. This popularity caused the firm to grow rapidly – which proved to be SWM's undoing.

In 1980, with everything going well, SWM bought out Gori, creating an overcapacity in the dirt bike marketplace. At another time, this might have been survivable, but the recession of the early 1980s found SWM overcommitted and without sufficient reserves to struggle through. As the firm's debts mounted, Pietro Sironi was forced to close it down in 1985.

The firm was reformed a few months later under the name SVM, but by 1987 it was gone for good.

This XN350 was built in 1982, at a time when sales were dropping fast and the firm was heavily over-committed. SWM's days were numbered, though it was not the fault of the bikes.

WESLAKE

ENGLAND 1974–PRESENT

Based at Rye in Sussex, Weslake was best known for its work on cylinder heads for major car companies. However, the decision to build a speedway engine was made in the early 1970s, and it was sufficiently successful that the unit was used for grass- and long-track events as well.

The Weslake engine was a 495cc (30ci) overhead-valve single with four valves. It was a tough unit, and it had to be. Not only did it have to withstand its own high

compression ratio but it was intended for use in a very harsh environment. Speedway engines are driven hard, often in several races in quick succession, and there is often little time between meetings. Thus the Weslake engine had to deliver reliability as well as performance.

Although the engine had four valves, there was only one carburettor and one exhaust pipe, the ports joining internally. The tried and tested total-loss

lubrication system was retained, with an external pump bolted to the timing chest, while ignition was either electronic or via battery-powered points.

Weslake's engine was a success from the outset and became dominant in speedway racing, followed by grass- and long-track events. Much later, the firm responded to riders' requests and built single and twin overhead-camshaft engines as well as a 998cc (61ci), overhead-cam V-twin

used for sidecar grass-track events. This engine had five-valve cylinder heads.

In the 1970s, the company built the Weslake Vendetta in collaboration with John Caffrey. The engine was a 492cc (30ci) eight-valve vertical twin and drove a five-speed gearbox installed in a duplex frame. Later came larger versions of the same engine, but in most cases with limited chassis involvement for Weslake, which concentrated on power units.

DUCATI 750 IMOLA

The 750 Imola was the work of Ducati's chief designer, Fabio Taglioni, and used an unusual L-configuration. V-twins in various layouts had been in use for many years, but placing one of the cylinders horizontal was not, according to conventional wisdom, a good idea. It would make for a long wheelbase and consequently poor handling. However, the L-shape did have certain advantages, including smooth running, excellent cooling and a low centre of gravity, and both Moto Guzzi and Aermacchi had built horizontal cylinder machines (albeit singles) that worked well.

When the Imola prototype emerged in 1970, it was apparent that Taglioni had partly solved the problem of length by sticking the front cylinder between the two front downtubes of the frame. The resulting machine handled extraordinarily well, and became a sports bike and even racing bike, even though it had been conceived as a tourer.

The Imola's quality was demonstrated in April 1972, when Ducati riders Paul Smart and Bruno Spaggiari beat the cream of the racing world – Honda, Triumph,

Despite being conceived as a tourer, the Imola 750 was extremely successful as a race bike, taking first and second at Imola in April 1972. The race machine was not significantly modified from the standard version.

ENGINE: 748cc (45ci) sohc, Desmo, 2v, V-twin, 80x74.4mm, air-cooled
POWER: 70bhp at 9000 rpm
GEARBOX: 5-speed foot change
FINAL DRIVE: chain
WEIGHT: n/a
TOP SPEED: 233 km/h (145 mph)

BSA, Moto Guzzi and even the World Champion, MV Agusta with its star rider Giacomo Agostini – to win the inaugural Imola 200. Except for its Desmo heads, larger 40mm (1.6in) carburettors and triple disc brakes, the Imola racer was remarkably similar to the 750 GT tourer, sharing its 748cc (46ci) engine displacement and 80 x 74.4mm (3.1 x 2.9in) bore and stroke. Ducati later offered a replica of the Imola model for sale as the 750 SS. Although it was street-legal, it was a race machine at heart.

The TS1 Imola Replica, a street-legal race bike. The curious L-shape arrangement of the cylinders can be seen here, giving smooth running without the usual long wheelbase and, consequently, awkward handling.

KAWASAKI Z1

JAPAN 1972

The Z1, the 'King of the Road', has lived up to its title, setting the standards for superbikes to follow and establishing Kawasaki's name in the performance world. In layout it was similar to the 1968 Honda CB750, but when it emerged, four years after the Honda, it had more to offer.

The Z1's 903cc (55ci) four-cylinder engine had twin overhead-camshafts, electric start and four carburettors. It was a very tough unit capable of withstanding a lot of tuning, with five speeds and everything else necessary on a bike able to speed at 209km/h (130mph) one minute and to cruise calmly through town the next.

For the home market (Japan), Kawasaki offered the 746cc (46ci) Z2, while for police work both sizes were available with suitable equipment. By 1976, the Z1 had become the Z900 and was joined by a custom version. A year later, they were replaced by the Z1000 series.

ENGINE: 903cc (54ci) dohc transverse four, 66x66mm, air-cooled
POWER: 82bhp at 8500rpm
GEARBOX: 5-speed foot change
FINAL DRIVE: chain
WEIGHT: 230kg (506lb)
TOP SPEED: 220km/h (130mph)

Where the H1 was a lunatic, the Z1 was a well-trained racehorse. Fast when the rider wanted, yet docile enough for urban traffic.

BIMOTA

Bimota was founded by Massimo Tamburini, who had at one time been a central-heating engineer and who had already gained experience of motorcycle manufacture with a 750cc (46ci) Honda-engined racing bike in 1973. The firm's name was derived from the names of the business partners – Bianchi and Morri, plus Tamburini himself.

Bimota set out to build machines that offered the best of the Italian and Japanese worlds – exquisite Italian handling mated to the power and reliability of Japanese engineering. The concept was highly successful, and even when Japanese firms began producing machines that handled like the best of the Europeans, Bimota was able to stay in the

Bimota has always built innovative machines, and the Mantra is no exception. Unusually for a Bimota, the Mantra had no fairing, allowing everyone to see its rather unusual layout.

game, catering for riders who want exclusive sporting machines, often with innovative engineering features built from the best materials and components.

As might be expected, the emphasis was on racing, and

Tamburini created a bike based on the Yamaha TTZ350 two-stroke twin, which was good enough to clinch the 350cc World Championship in 1980. Meanwhile, Charlie Williams proved the Bimota could be just as effective in endurance racing. This success led to the production of road-going frames marketed as kits to be fitted with Japanese engines, and then to a complete machine.

Bimota's first complete road bike was powered by a Suzuki GS750 engine and was named the SB2. At its first appearance in 1977, it was considerably lighter than the standard Suzuki GS750 and a good 32km/h (20mph) quicker as a result. Its handling was also far better, partly due to the advanced monoshock rear suspension and lower centre of gravity gained by moving the fuel tank to a location under the engine.

The Tesi was another radical machine, featuring alloy swing-arm front suspension and steering arm. Unfortunately, it was very expensive and suffered a range of teething troubles.

After the SB2 came the spaceframe KB1, which could be specified with either a 903cc (55ci) or 1015cc (62ci), Kawasaki, double overhead-cam, four-cylinder unit. Unusually, its rear monoshock was horizontally mounted, and it also featured variable steering geometry. This was created by means of eccentric upper and lower steering head bearings, which enabled adjustments of 9.9cm–11.9cm (3.9–4.7in) to be made.

This kind of innovation, and of course the fact that Bimota machines were hand-built to a very high standard, did not come cheap. One result of this was that when the 1980s recession began to bite, Bimota found itself over-extended. Things were not looking good, but Bimota weathered the storm with the help of the DB1, powered by the Ducati V-twin engine. The DB1 was a fairly conventional machine, but it proved popular for a long period and helped Bimota get though the hard times that did for several other manufacturers. Meanwhile, Bimota remained committed to racing success, and achieved it in 1987 when Virginio Ferrari won the Formula 1 Championship aboard a Bimota YB4 powered by a Yamaha FZ750 engine.

Pierluigi Marconi became chief engineer in 1990, after Tamburini departed to join Cagiva. Marconi maintained the company's reputation for producing the unexpected, in particular the T esi (Thesis), which went into production in 1991. The most remarkable feature of this machine was its hub-centre steering, in which the front wheel was mounted within a twin-sided swinging arm that operated a monoshock suspension unit. In common with all hub-centre systems, the idea was that handling benefited from separating braking and suspension forces, which conventional telescopic forks cannot do.

However, the Tesi suffered from teething troubles, and potential buyers, who were put off by the high price, preferred to stick with the more conventional SB6 model, which used the Suzuki GSX-R1100 motor. Meanwhile, Bimota was developing a new innovation, the 500cc (31ci) Vdue engine. Unveiled in 1997, this was a direct-injection two-stroke V-twin mounted in a lightweight frame with 110hp. Typically of Bimota projects, it was radical and clever, but it failed to achieve any real sales success as a result of serious fuel-injection problems.

Although the failed project was withdrawn from sale in fairly short order, there were six other machines on the Bimota stock list. These used more conventional Suzuki, Yamaha and Ducati engines. The company came back with the Mantra, which represented something of a departure for the firm that normally produced bikes with a full fairing. Late in 1998, Bimota was bought by Francesco Tognon, whose formula was to return to Bimota's fundamental product line. The resulting DB4 used the Ducati 900SS engine with the Mantra's ultra-light chassis.

The YB9 was built on a lightweight alloy beam-frame and featured top-end components. The machine was aimed at the conventional sports bike market.

BMW R90S

GERMANY 1973

The 1970s were the dawn of the 'superbike' era, and BMW's contribution was the /6 series. The R90S was the super-sports version of this series, delivering 67hp for a top speed of 200km/h (124mph) – at least in theory. The extra power came courtesy of a move from Bing carburettors to Dell'Ortos, but in truth the main attraction of the bike was its appearance, which was fabulous. The fairing was mainly cosmetic, but that can be forgiven in the light of just how good it looked.

For those that actually pushed the R90S to see how fast it went, there were a few issues to contend with. Very high speeds resulted in a certain amount of weave, a flaw that affected the /5 series as well. However, few

The R90S was available in an elegant grey-on-grey colour scheme or the much more popular 'Bol d'Or' orange-on-yellow version, as pictured here.

riders, especially in the USA, exceeded 161km/h (100mph) on a regular basis, so this did not matter as much as it might have. The /7 series addressed the problem with considerable success.

The other bikes in the /6 line-up were the R90/6, the R75/6 and the R60/6. For some reason, the unfaired R90/6 was supplied with only a single front disk brake. A second brake was available as an option, which was just as well as the single brake was not up to the job. In fact, it was needed on the R75/6 as well.

The /6 machines were the logical successors to the original 'stroke' series, the four-speed, drum-braked /5 models of 1969. They inherited the new engine with a one-piece crankshaft, a common 70.6mm (2.7in) bore, and a single camshaft mounted above the crankshaft. The 498cc (30ci) R50/5 was under-square with a 67mm (2.6in) bore; the 599cc (37ci) R60/5, over-square at 73.5mm (2.9in); and the 745cc (45ci) R75/5 well over square at 82mm (3.2in). Power outputs were 32hp, 40hp and 50hp respectively, giving top speeds of 157km/h

(97mph), 167km/h (104mph) and 175km/h (109mph).

When the /7 series came out, the lack of a small-capacity machine was remedied with the R45 and R65, without a 'stroke' designation because they were not part of the same series. The R45 designation is interesting, as the machine's actual engine size was 473cc (29ci), which meant it could equally have been designated R50 – it is rare for motorcycle manufacturers to understate capacity in this manner.

The R45 was built in both 27hp and 35hp versions, partly

for tax and insurance reasons and partly because some organizations had no need for a bike with more power. The R45 and R65 were good small bikes, but were never a great success with private buyers.

ENGINE: 898cc (54ci) ohv transverse flat twin, 90x70.6mm, air-cooled
POWER: 67bhp at 7000rpm
GEARBOX: 5-speed foot change
FINAL DRIVE: Kardan shaft
WEIGHT: 205kg (451lb)
TOP SPEED: 200km/h (124mph)

An R90S wearing the grey colour scheme. This great-looking bike was theoretically fast but did not behave well at high speeds. The twin front disc brake was very necessary, and wise users of the R90/6 took the option to have one fitted.

MOTO MORINI 3½

Designed by Dianni Marchesini and Franco Lambertini Junior, the 3¹/₂ V-twin prototype was unveiled at the Milan Show in late 1971, but did not go on sale until 1973. It quickly became one of the classic motorcycle designs of the 1970s.

With its cylinders set at an angle of 72 degrees, the 344cc (21ci) V-twin stood apart from its rivals by the use of Heron combustion cylinder heads. These had been used in the Repco Brabham racing car that had won the 1966 F1 world championship and also by the likes of Jaguar and Ford for

their production models, but their use in the 3¹/₂ was a first for the motorcycle industry.

Essentially, the Heron principle uses cylinder heads with a flat face and parallel, rather than inclined, valves, and the combustion recess is formed in the piston crown.

The 3¹/₂ incorporated several other innovations, including the toothed belt to the camshaft, a forged, one-piece crankshaft, transistorized ignition and the generally high level of the aluminium castings. Compared to the Ducati's 90-degree, Morini's 72-degree setup allowed for an engine

The 3¹/₂ incorporated a number of innovations to create a truly world-class machine. This is the Sport 74 model, one of several improved versions of an already great bike.

length that did not over-extend the wheelbase. It was angled so that the camshaft could be located high in the crankcase in the crutch of the vee. Still, it was necessary to space the cylinders apart at the base to allow room for the camshaft, a method of offset known as desaxe; and in the 3¹/₂ the effect was to give a positive bias on one cylinder and a negative bias on the other.

The unit-construction engine, with its helical primary-drive

gears, dry multiplate clutch and six-speed gearbox was housed in a very tidy duplex steel-tube frame. Early production models of both the standard 3¹/₂ and the 3¹/₂ Sport had wire wheels and drum brakes, but by the mid-1970s a Grimeca disc front brake and cast-alloy wheels from the same source were fitted.

Both larger- and smaller-capacity versions (250cc/15ci and 500cc/31ci) of the Morini V-twin were built, plus 125cc (8ci) and 250cc (15ci) singles. All of these machines used the same Heron heads, and there were many other components in common. This made life easier for owners by simplifying maintenance and improving spares availability.

ENGINE: 344cc (21ci) ohv 3v, V-twin, 68x57mm, air-cooled
POWER: 36bhp at 8000rpm
GEARBOX: 6-speed foot change
FINAL DRIVE: chain
WEIGHT: 154kg (340lb)
TOP SPEED: 161km/h (100mph)

Designed by Dianni Marchesini and Franco Lambertini, the 3¹/₂ used a 72-degree angle on the V-twin to avoid a having too long a wheelbase but still gain the vibration benefits of widely offset cylinders.

SIMONINI

The Simonini marque made its home at Maranello, near Modena, which is better known for Ferrari cars. The firm was founded in 1973 by Enzo Simonini, though at that time the company was little more than a workshop, hand-building very small numbers of competition (mainly motocross) bikes.

As demand increased, Simonini moved to Torre Maina, just outside Maranello in 1974. The form continued to build motocross and enduro bikes to the individual specifications of the user, but began offering tuning kits for most Italian dirt-bike engines. Simonini itself used German Sachs engines exclusively, tuning them in-house to create very competitive yet reliable machines.

Simonini did well – well enough in that it had more orders than it could handle. In 1975, with insufficient capital for expansion, the firm joined forces with another local company, Fornetti Impianti SpA, which was based nearby in Maranello. The merged company now had a brand-new factory but retained the older plant as a research and development facility.

During this phase of the marque's existence, the traditional Sachs engines were supplemented by Kreidler and Minerelli units, and an in-house 125cc (8ci) motocross machine called the Mustang was

designed and built. Another new model was the 250 Shadow motocrosser, powered by a seven-speed Sachs engine. This machine featured cast-alloy wheels and disc brakes, both front and rear.

In 1975, Giuseppe Fazioli won the 125cc Junior Italian motocross title on a Simonini. The following year, Sergio Franco contested some of the 125cc World Motocross championship rounds for the marque, while in 1977 the British rider Andy Ainsworth was

signed up. A team of Swedish riders rode Simonini machines in the 1977 International Six Days' Trial (ISDT).

The company expanded further in 1977, introducing new Sachs water-cooled engines for the 50cc (3ci) and 80cc (5ci) models. However, the 1980s brought disaster to Simonini, as they had to so many other firms. Sales fell sharply as the recession began to bite, and Simioni was forced to close down in 1983.

Above: Simonini made its name with motocross bikes, and later a range of off-road sport machines appeared. This is a Shadow 250, a typical Simonini offering.

Below: In the late 1970s, Simonini also produced small numbers of high-performance sports roadsters such as this 125SS single-cylinder two-stroke. However, this was not enough to keep the company afloat.

CAN-AM

The Can-Am 250cc Qualifier was built as a serious enduro model, developed from earlier trail bikes. It led to a series of motocross machines characterized by their tubular frames.

The Canadian Bombardier Group originally manufactured truck-sized, half-track vehicles. With skis in the front and Caterpillar tracks in the rear, these were designed for the worst winter conditions of the Canadian countryside. During World War II, the company produced half-tracks for the Canadian Forces. Afterwards, it experimented with new forms of track systems and developed the Muskeg tractor, an all-tracked heavy-duty vehicle designed for logging and mining operations in extreme wilderness conditions, such as heavy snow or semi-liquid muskeg.

The research for its track base had a welcome and lucrative spin-off. It was now possible to produce a relatively small continuous rubber track, and the teenage dream of the company's founder became a reality – in the shape of the snowmobile. The company created the market, and held its own after it was invaded by Japanese and US competitors in the late 1960s. The group also owned Rotax in Austria, which built both two- and four-stroke

engines in several sizes for it and many other firms around the world.

During the 1970s, Bombardier built the Can-Am brand of off-road competition motorcycles designed for motocross and enduro with Rotax engines. The early bikes had a 175cc (11ci) or 250cc (15ci) single-cylinder, disc-valve, two-stroke engine built-in unit with a five-speed gearbox. Normally, such a type would have the carburettor protruding out from the engine. However, this would be far too wide for off-road work, so Can-Am mounted the instrument behind the cylinder on a long inlet passage, which fed the mixture to the disc valve, keeping the engine narrow. This engine unit went into a tubular frame with long-travel suspension by telescopic front forks and twin rear shocks, wire wheels, drum brakes and off-road tyres. To be street-legal, the machine came with a spark arrestor on the end of the high-level exhaust system that curled over the top of the engine, speedometer, lights, a mirror and turn signals, but also

carried competition plates on each side to show what it could do. The bikes competed successfully in professional racing, Gary Jones winning the 1974 US 250cc American Motorcyclist Association (AMA) National motocross championship.

In 1978, the models already in production were joined by a larger 366cc (22ci) version. This differed in having a reed-valve engine with petroil lubrication instead of the oil injection used by the smaller engines. The range took on a much more serious line with laid-down rear shocks, Marzocchi front forks, more wheel movement and six speeds for the 175cc (11ci) and 250cc (15ci) models, although the 370cc (22ci) model kept to five. In this form, they had become pure enduro models and were listed as the Qualifier. With the enduro line came a two-model motocross series sold as the 250 MX-5 and 370 MX-5 with engines of those capacities. These had

more power, extended wheel travel and no concessions to anything other than fast lap times in competition – thanks to the special detail work incorporated in them.

The range extended for 1980 to include a 125cc (8ci) motocross model, while the Qualifier came in 175cc (11ci), 250cc (15ci), 350cc (21ci) and 400cc (24ci) forms. (The 350cc/21ci was, in fact, a 250cc/15ci bored out to 277cc/17ci and fitted into the 400cc/24ci chassis.) By the 1980s, the emission legislation in the USA began to bite further, so Can-Am turned to Rotax to use the big four-stroke, single-cylinder engine with its overhead camshaft and four valves.

Bombardier, its order book replete with orders for its snowmobile range, eventually outsourced development and production of the Can-Am motorcycles to Armstrong/CCM of Lancashire, England. Thus 1987 was the last model year for Can-Am.

COSSACK

Cossack motorcycles can trace their ancestry back to the 1920s, when Germany was forbidden to manufacture anything that might be used for military purposes. The country therefore entered into a clandestine agreement with the Soviet Union: German firms supplied equipment for assembly in the Soviet Union, and the finished product was then shipped back to Germany. Factories were set up in the Soviet Union for this purpose, one of them being a BMW plant for the manufacture of motorcycles. The name Cossack can be applied to a great many motorcycles of Soviet origin, manufactured in several factories.

In the 1970s, Soviet-manufactured motorcycles bearing the Cossack signature were marketed in Great Britain by the Satra Belarus company. Headed by former Lambretta UK sales manager Alan Kimber, the company tried hard to break into the lucrative UK market. Part of this effort involved spending a considerable amount of money on an advertising campaign.

Satra offered three models: the Voskhod (Sunrise), a 175cc (11ci) twin port two-stroke single; the Jupiter, of IZH manufacture, a 350cc (21ci) twin cylinder two-stroke; and the Ural, an overhead-valve, horizontally opposed twin, based on an obsolete BMW design. Almost immediately, however, their marketing strategy ran into problems.

The first, and most obvious, was that Soviet motorcycle design technology was about 20 years out of date. This was a deliberate aspect of Soviet design technology, which demanded that vehicles should be robust and unsophisticated, enabling their owners to service them at the side of the road if necessary.

The second problem was potentially dangerous. The UK traffic environment was becoming increasingly congested, and the braking performance of these machines was vastly inferior to the mainstream Japanese and European bikes available. All models featured drum brakes, and so, in an attempt to improve matters, the original brake linings were exchanged with British-made Ferodo components. Even so, braking remained a major problem.

Satra eventually went out of business. A new company, Neval, was then formed and continued to market Soviet motorcycles in the UK. Meanwhile, the Cossack Owners Club provides support to owners of Cossack motorcycles. It is an independent club, financed entirely by its members. The club represents owners and other enthusiasts of motorcycles and sidecars made in the Soviet Union or the former Soviet states, including Ukraine, Belarus and Latvia.

These include all models of Ural, Dnieper/Dnepr, Ishevsk (Jupiter & Planeta), Voskhod, Minsk, Riga and their sidecars. These machines are still sold in the UK, either under their original manufacturer's name or under UK trade names, including Cossack, Neval, Britane or Regent and their UK model names, including Soviet Knight, Phoenix and Classic.

Approximately 95 per cent of the club's members are based in the UK.

Although the Russian-built Cossack motorcycles and combinations were sturdy, they were unattractive to western buyers because their design was two decades out of date.

CHAPTER SEVEN

DECLINE AND RENEWAL

1975–1984

In 1973, the British government made a last ditch effort to reform the UK motorcycle industry, forcing a merger between BSA/Triumph and Norton/Villiers. This began the final meltdown for the British bike industry, despite the efforts of workers in the Triumph cooperative experiment in Meriden.

Meanwhile, Japanese firms were having their own problems trying to establish what their bikes should be. Various engine and chassis technologies were being explored in a frantic attempt to optimise power, economy and handling. Large two-stroke engines were considered for a while, especially the Kawasaki KH and Suzuki GT triples, and they gave great power outputs, but with terrible fuel consumption and erratic reliability. Suzuki also experimented with a

Wankel rotary engine in its RE-5 and a turbocharged engine in the XN-85, while Honda and Yamaha also flirted with lacklustre turbo designs. Eventually, the in-line, air-cooled, four-cylinder, four-stroke became accepted as the best solution. Smooth, powerful, reliable and relatively cheap, these engines were fitted in basic steel tube cradle frames, with conventional telescopic forks, dual-shock suspension and disc brakes. The resulting type of motorcycle became known, rather pejoratively, as a Universal Japanese Motorcycle or UJM. Honda's CB range, the Kawasaki Z-bikes, Yamaha's XJ and Suzuki's GS designs all appeared in various capacities from 400cc (24.5ci) to 1100cc (67ci), and enthused millions of bikers with new-found heights of excitement and performance.

Left: One of the great racing bikes of all time, the Yamaha YZR500 won six 500 World Championships between 1975 and 1993.

DERBI CROSS

The Derbi company is a long-standing concern, having been founded in 1922 by Simeon Rabasa Singla as a bicycle repair shop. The business expanded rapidly, and after World War II Derbi began mass production of its first moped, the Derbi SRS – the initials the same as the proprietor's. Matters progressed fairly happily until 1977, when the Japanese floodtide overwhelmed Europe.

In Spain, some firms disappeared, while others were submerged: Suzuki took over Abelló; Honda, Montesa; and Yamaha, Sanglas. Somehow, Derbi managed to survive and pressed ahead with the production of its 50cc (3ci)

The Derbi Cross was an intelligent design, with braced handlebars, high-level exhaust, good ground clearance and flexible mudguards that were positioned well clear of the trail tyres for off-road use.

class motorcycle, models of which were produced for road, trail, motocross and road racing.

The Derbi Cross had a 48.8cc (3cic) air-cooled, two-stroke engine with an alloy cylinder head built-in unit, and the gearbox was driven by helical gears. It had slim-line telescopic front forks and a pivoted-fork rear suspension controlled by twin spring units.

The wire-spoke wheels were fitted with Akron aluminium-alloy rims and had drum brakes front and rear. The machine had braced handlebars, high-level exhaust, good ground clearance, and flexible mudguards well clear of the trail tyres for off-road use.

The Cross had strong links with other 50cc (3ci) models in the Derbi range, such as the Tricampeona, which had a pressed-steel spine frame, low exhaust system, three or four speeds and full road equipment. In both cases, these models

The Derbi Cross engine unit was based on that of the road machines but installed in a tubullar spine frame.

offered good performance and style, and sold well thanks to the firm's racing successes.

ENGINE: 48.8cc (3ci), 2s vertical single, 38x43mm, air-cooled
POWER: 4bhp at 5700rpm
GEARBOX: unit 4-speed foot change
FINAL DRIVE: chain
WEIGHT: 52kg (115lb)
TOP SPEED: 76km/h (46mph)

HONDA GOLD WING

Today, the largest manufacturer of motorcycles in the world, Honda was launched in 1946 by Soichiro Honda. He had a simple aim: to produce a cheap form of transport for a post-war world, where many countries, including Japan, lay in ruins.

The first bikes produced by the firm were powered by surplus army engines. Subsequently, Honda developed a 50cc (3ci) motor and then the Model D, the first all-Honda machine. Honda started to make a name for itself with the introduction of the CB models, starting with the CB72 (250cc/15ci) and the CB77 (305cc/19ci). However, this first series used the old pressed-steel frames, and better road handling came with the introduction of steel tubular frames in the CB92. The CB77 (Super Hawk) was an excellent and reliable motorcycle that outperformed many similar English models.

In 1958, Honda introduced the C100 Super Club as a sports and leisure bike, launching a remarkable advertising campaign that made it the best-selling bike of all time. In the late 1950s, the firm began to build bikes with a bigger engine capacity, starting with the model CB450. The Black Bomber/Black Hawk series represented a serious attack on the British machines that had long dominated this class, although it did not quite match them at this stage.

In subsequent years, Honda modified the Model 450 line to include smaller models, such as the CB500 (1971) and the CB400

(1975). Both bikes were very successful. A larger model was the CB750, introduced in 1969, which was beyond its class at the time. The mass-produced four-cylinder bike was a smooth operator, with excellent handling. It dominated the market at the time and sold very well worldwide, but it was not upgraded and lost popularity towards the end of the 1970s.

In 1975, Honda introduced the Gold Wing. Initially powered by a 1000cc (61ci) four-cylinder motor, the Gold Wing was uprated to

1200cc (73ci) and re-designated the GL1500 in 1988 – and it reigned supreme. In fully dressed format, it metamorphosed through Interstate and Aspencade incarnations in 1980 and 1982. The Gold Wing was built in Ohio, USA, and offered the most lavish specification of seating, equipment and storage for the touring rider and pillion. Only the top Harley-Davidsons could match what the Gold Wing had to offer.

A foot pedal controlled both front and rear brakes, while accessories included cruise

The Honda Super Club was introduced in 1958 as a sports and leisure bike, and was the subject of a massive and well-conducted advertising campaign that turned it into the best-selling bike of all time.

control, a digital clock and radio-casette player. The water-cooled 1.5l (0.4 gallon), flat-six engine made long-distance cruising effortless. In certain markets where its abilities could be fully appreciated – such as the USA, with its expanses of land – it too acquired cult status. In more congested environments like the UK, the ST1100 Pan European with its shaft-drive, transverse-mounted V-four was a more appropriate size. Honda also produced a naked cruiser version of the GL1500 Gold Wing. Called the Valkyrie, or F6C, it was powered by the same six-into-six flat six 1520cc (91ci) engine.

ENGINE: 1520cc (91ci) flat-6, water-cooled
POWER: 100bhp at 5200rpm
GEARBOX: 5-speed, including reverse, foot change
FINAL DRIVE: shaft
WEIGHT: 368kg (811lb)
TOP SPEED: 187km/h (116mph)

The Honda Gold Wing was introduced in 1975 and dominated the market. Produced in the USA, it was aimed at the touring market, for which it was equipped with many lavish features.

MV AGUSTA 125 SPORT

ITALY 1975

The MV Agusta 125 Sport was attractive enough, with its silver frame, red bodywork and black exhaust, and it looked capable of high performance – but owners were to be disappointed. The performance was no better than the earlier pushrod 125 MV roadsters and it had a maximum speed of 115km/h (72mph).

Having introduced the Ipotesi, the new 350 Sport with square-cut lines, triple disc brakes and cast-alloy wheels, MV also put into production a similar and equally modernized 125 Sport overhead-valve single. Like the Ipotesi, the 1975 125 Sport was also available at extra cost with a fairing based on the company's three- and four-cylinder racing models of the era, complete with matching red and silver paint work. The 123.5cc (8ci) engine ran a compression ratio of 9.8:1, with a square-slide Dell 'Orto VHB 22mm (0.8in) carburettor, five-speed gearbox (in unit with the engine), a wet multi-plate clutch, geared primary drive, wet-sump lubrication and a Dansi electronic flywheel magneto ignition system.

Except for its square casings and finning for the top end, the engine was much as before: it used the same 53 x 56mm (2 x 2.2in) bore-and-stroke dimensions that the company had used in its earliest 125cc (8ci) two-stroke, and then continued over the years in its various pushrod-engined machines. However, the rest of the machine was entirely new. The frame, for example, had straight top rails and was of a full duplex cradle type, replacing the open 'banana' sub-frame affair used earlier.

On the 125 Sport, wire wheels were fitted in preference to the cast-alloy ones found on the new 350 S, and the rear brake was a drum, with a single 230mm (9in) disc up front. Other details included: a 19l (5 gallon) fuel tank, a length-adjustable saddle, two-piston Scarab brake caliper and a cast-iron 230mm (9in) disc and a 136mm (5.4in) diameter drum rear brake. The wheel rims were Borrani alloys, with 2.75 section, 46cm (18in) tyres in both the front and rear.

ENGINE: 123.5cc (8ci) 2v single, 53x56mm, air-cooled
POWER: 12bhp at 8500rpm
GEARBOX: 5-speed foot change
FINAL DRIVE: chain
WEIGHT: l03kg (227lb)
TOP SPEED: 115km/h (71.5mph)

BMW R100RS

GERMANY 1976

Pictured is the racing model of the R100S. This turbo machine was quite spectacular, achieving good results against bikes that were optimized for racing.

When the BMW R100RS made its first appearance in 1976, it had an immediate impact: it was unlike both its BMW predecessors and other bikes then on the road. Although technically there had been faster sports-tourers, none could be ridden as far as fast. The 24l (6.5 gallon) tank allowed a range of anything from 280km (175 miles) for really hard riding two-up, to well over 440km (275 miles) when ridden gently. The usable cruising speed was at least 185km/h (115mph); with the rider crouched behind the screen, speeds of well over 209km/h (130mph) were readily attainable.

One of the machine's most attractive features was its fairing, which was developed through testing in a wind tunnel. It cut down drag, reduced lift at high speed, made the bike more stable in crosswinds, gave good protection from weather and buffeting and, as an added extra, looked very smart. Experienced bikers reported that the R100RS took a little getting used to, especially when negotiating town traffic, its weight and considerable proportions sometimes making progress a little tortuous. Acceleration was not a strong point, but then the bike was not designed for ultra-rapid starts. Once on the open road, however, the machine was transformed into an extremely smooth and efficient tourer.

The engine was the most powerful development of the stroke-series pushrod flat twin in a road-going motorcycle, although when the R100RS was reintroduced later, it dropped to 60hp. The other bikes in the line-up were: the R100/7, the 'naked' version; the R100S, the successor to the R90S; the R100RT, with the barn-door fairing, suitable for slow cruising on wide roads; and the R75/7, later the R80/7 (also made as the R80RT), for those who could live without the extra power. Later still came the mighty R80GS and R100GS off-road bikes.

ENGINE: 980cc (59ci) ohv transverse flat twin, 94x70.6mm, air-cooled
POWER: 70bhp at 7250rpm
GEARBOX: 5-speed foot change
FINAL DRIVE: Kardan shaft
WEIGHT: 210kg (462lb)
TOP SPEED: 200km/h (124mph)

Left: The BMW R100S was fast, and it had a long endurance, making it popular as a touring machine. Customers were also very impressed with its fairing, which was developed through wind tunnel testing.

Above: The R100RS could only be described as a beautiful bike. The engine was the most powerful development of the strike series pushrod flat twin in a road-going motorcycle.

CZ175

The CZ marque has a long history, dating back to the days before World War II. It began as a division of the Czech Armaments Factory, Ceska Zbrojovka, and first manufactured motorcycles in 1932. Initally, it offered two-stroke bikes of 75cc (5ci) and 98cc (6ci), but larger two-strokes were soon added. After the war, CZ amalgamated with JAWA, a company founded by Frantisek Janacek in the 1920s to manufacture Wanderer motorcycles. The Name JAWA derives from the first two letters of Janacek and Wanderer.

The CZ first appeared in its modern form in 1946 as a 125cc (8ci). This soon changed, first to 150cc (9ci), next to 175cc (11ci), and then even larger. As a 175cc (11ic), it was also available in trail and enduro forms.

The 175cc (11ci) single had a simple two-stroke engine built-in unit with its four-speed gearbox and multi-task gear lever. It kept the same bore and stroke throughout its life and had a cast-iron cylinder with light-alloy head. In due course, it went over to a pump lubrication system. The carburettor sat behind the barrel with an air cleaner to feed it, and the exhaust ran down to a long silencer on the left. The engine unit went into a tubular frame with telescopic front and pivoted-rear forks for suspension, wire wheels, drum brakes in full-width hubs and, in some years, alloy wheel rims. One of its assets was the fitment of a full case for the final-drive chain so that this was protected from the weather. By the 1970s, the CZ175 was fitted with turn signals as well as the full electric equipment. It served as a basic machine for domestic use.

ENGINE: 172cc (10ci) two-stroke, vertical single, 58x65mm, air-cooled
POWER: 15bhp at 5600rpm
GEARBOX: unit 4-speed foot change
FINAL DRIVE: enclosed chain
WEIGHT: 112kg (247lb)
TOP SPEED: 115km/h (70mph)

For many years, the basic CZ model was the 175, which was also offered with a 125cc (8ci) engine. It was an excellent means of providing low-cost transport.

KRAUSER

The German firm of Krauser GmbH started life in 1924, offering engine repairing, crankshaft regenerating and piston manufacturing. In 1963, it took on the BMW dealership. By 1970, in addition to providing sales, spares and service, it had established a reputation for manufacturing high-quality motorcycle luggage for BMW flat twins. In 1972, Krauser inaugurated an annual motorcycle rally; this event still takes place, attracting some 300 participants. Also in 1972, Krauser developed the first detachable motorcycle pannier in response to a growing demand from a younger generation of bikers, a move that

soon established the firm as a trend-setter. Later, Krauser also produced panniers for smaller motorcycles, topboxes, softcases, innerbags, tank- and leather bags and panniers for pedal cycles.

Mike Krauser's interest in road racing led him to develop a four-valve cylinder head for the BMW Rennsport, and from this work came a conversion for the 1l (0.26 gallon) road engines. The Krauser head for road models kept the qualities of the BMW flat-twin but enhanced these to such an extent that it raised the power. As well as that, the overall engine width was reduced by 35mm (1.75in), thanks to the compact design.

In the early 1980s, Krauser moved on to produce his MKM1000. This was a complete machine with a new tubular frame in trellis form, built up from many tubes welded into a rigid structure that carried the engine 25mm (1in) higher. To this was fitted the stock R100RS BMW engine, complete with its five-speed gearbox and shaft final drive. The wheelbase was increased with BMW telescopic front forks, cast-alloy wheels and double-disc front and single-disc rear brakes. To this assembly was added a 21l (5.5 gallon) fuel tank in aluminium under a body shell that ran back to carry the seat and form a tail, and a fairing that was

The Krauser Domani is a motorcycle based, three-wheeled vehicle developed by Micheal Krauser GmBH and powered by BMW, built for sale in Japan and Europe. The vehicle looks like a motorcycle with sidecar attached. However, the 'sidecar' is structurally an integral part of the frame.

lower than the standard R100RS type. These were all finished in a matching style. Some 200 of these machines were built, either in kit form or complete, and Krauser continued his involvement in racing and special machines for road use.

LAVERDA JOTA

In its heyday, the Laverda Jota was the fastest series production model in existence, and was much prized by motorcycle enthusiasts the world over. The name was coined by Roger Slater, a British importer of Laverda motorcycles, who borrowed it from a flamboyant and energetic Spanish dance. The Jota was a development of Laverda's Model 3C(E), the high-performance version of the standard 3C, and improvements included the fitting of triple discs, alloy wheels, a different seat and tail unit, and needle-roller swinging-arm bearings.

The astonishing thing about the Jota is that it was the product of a small family concern, and was developed without the benefit if substantial funding. The firm devoted many years to refining the 3C(E) until the design was as close to perfection as possible – and when it was road-tested, the testers went into raptures. The first Jota was delivered to

At the height of its production run the Laverda Jota was the fastest series bike in existence, its near-perfect design gradually refined over the years.

Slater's headquarters in Bromyard, Herefordshire, in January 1976. In August that year, *Motor Cycle* magazine conducted a road test in which the Jota test bike achieved a fastest one-way speed of 225.37km/h (140.04mph), with a mean two-way figure of 221.8km/h (137.8mph), making it the fastest bike ever tested by the publication. The resulting publicity instantly transformed the Jota into an icon, making it the envy of almost every rider. Indeed, demand greatly outstripped the firm's ability to supply, and deliveries were consequently slow.

The basic design remained unchanged until 1979, but modification resulted in a number of problems, particularly with the engine. It took the best part of a year to iron out the snags, and in late 1980 Laverda

introduced a hydraulic clutch – a vast improvement over the old manually operated type. Previously the clutch action had been alarmingly heavy, but in truth the Jota had never been the most suitable machine for town use. Its natural habitat was the open road or the race circuit.

The 1982 model year saw the appearance of the Jota 120, using the 120-degree crankshaft from

the RGS model. This provided a smoother, less harsh power delivery. However, with the motorcycle sales depression of the early 1980s, the 120 model never matched the original in terms of numbers sold, and production of the Jota ended in 1982.

ENGINE: 981cc (59ci), triple dohc, 75x74mm, air-cooled
POWER: 79bhp at 8000rpm
GEARBOX: 5-speed foot change
FINAL DRIVE: chain
WEIGHT: 233kg (514lb)
TOP SPEED: 225km/h (140mph)

The Laverda Jota 1000 was the principal production model and its basic design remained unaltered until 1979, when modifications were made. These caused a number of problems that took some time to resolve. Inset shows the Jota 1000's compact engine installation.

QUASAR

The Quasar was a bold attempt to produce a viable and attractive feet-forward (FF) motorcycle, a design that features a low-slung faired body with the rider in a reclining position. FFs have been around since the Wilkinson of 1909, the Neracar of the 1920s and the pioneering Avro Monocar of 1926. Gustav Baumm's record-breaking NSU Flying Hammocks of the 1950s were the first definitive FFs, proving that a recumbent riding position was the most efficient aerodynamically (322km/h, 200mph with 40hp). Since then, all record breakers, from the original 1956 Triumph Bonneville to the present, have been FF.

To date, a number of FF concepts have been tried, but so far nobody has managed to come up with a commercially successful design. In recent times, there has been a considerable revival of interest in the motor scooter as a means of personal transportation, and in some respects these vehicles have features in common with FF motorcycles. Whether the remaining evolutionary step to true FF takes place remains to be seen.

The designer of an FF motorcycle faces a much more daunting task than confronts the designer of a conventional machine. Not the least of the problems is that bikers tend to be a conventional breed, and tend to reject more unusual innovations. To these enthusiasts, an FF motorcycle needs to be seen (and hence marketed) as a two-wheeled car rather than an enclosed motorcycle. Finally, it is worth noting that as the FF design moves the rider from the upright

posture (as on a scooter) to a recumbent posture, the machine becomes lower and may make it harder to see in traffic. There are some engineering problems too, though experimental designs show that these can mostly be overcome. Chief among them is the problem of stability when stationary. FF designs require the rider to stabilize the machine when stationary by putting a foot out of the open side onto the road, which precludes the use of a fully enclosed body.

The all-British Quasar, designed by Malcolm Newell and Ken Leaman in the mid-1970s, was the first modern FF. At first sight, there was a lot going for it. It was fast, reliable and economical, and probably the safest two-wheeler

ever built. The 850cc (52ci) water-cooled engine was from the most pedestrian source imaginable, the Reliant three-wheeler. It had a mere 41hp at 5500rpm, but thanks to the design of the machine and its excellent aerodynamics, even this was good for 176km/h (110mph), with a cruising speed that was very little slower. The four-speed gearbox drove the rear wheel through a twin universal joint Kardan shaft and a spiral bevel. Braking was by triple 241mm (9.5in) discs, two at the front and one at the back, each with Lockheed twin-piston callipers.

With its space frame of Reynolds 531 tubing, specially designed to offer maximum protection in the event of a crash, the Quasar was a

The all-British Quasar was the first modern feet-forward (FF) motorcycle, a design that blends a low-slung faired body with a reclining position for the rider. The FF originated in the 1900s.

heavy machine at 318kg (700lb), but it was also ridiculously economical at 3.75l/100km (90mpg UK gallons).

However, it was not a success commercially; only 20 Quasars were ever built. One reason for its failure was the conservatism of its potential buyers; the Quasar was like a two-wheeled car, not a motorcycle, down to the glass windscreen with windscreen wiper as required by English law. The second problem was that the Quasar was expensive.

The first mass-produced FF was the Honda CN250, launched at the 1985 Tokyo Show as the Fusion and better known as the Helix or Spazio. The Burgman 400, launched in 1999, is the first mass-produced FF to provide enough performance to keep up with conventional motorcycles on the open road, although its seat is still about 15cm (6in) higher than that of a 'true' FF. BMW's new roofed scooter, the seat-belted C-1, also represents a milestone in mass-produced PTW rider protection, even though its seat and centre of gravity are also too high, and its wheelbase too short to qualify as a true FF.

As the rider needs to put his foot out of the open side of the FF to stabilize the vehicle when stationary, it is impossible to feature a fully enclosed body. Plus points included speed, reliability and economy.

HARLEY-DAVIDSON XLCR

Nowadays the Harley-Davidson XLCR (the CR stands for Café Racer) is very much a collector's item, but the model was not a commercial success in its day, and fewer than 3000 were made – a fact that illustrates how Harley-Davidson is constrained by its own success.

The vast majority of buyers are traditionalists, who seem to want big, heavy, tractor-like machines. Designed by Willie G. Davidson, the Harley XLCR 'Cafe Racer' was aimed at the stoplight racers of the West Coast, a fad which started in England and Europe, where the 'ton-up boys' raced from cafe to cafe.

The XLCR was produced in three model years, 1977 (1900 units), 1978 (1200 units) and 1979 (fewer than 10 units left over from 1978).

The all-black steel tank and fiberglass tailpiece coupled with the unique black siamese exhausts (1978 mufflers were larger than 1977) made the XLCR arguably the most attractive bike of its era.

The 'Cafe Racer' was the first Harley with triple disc brakes. A quarter of a century after it was introduced, the Harley-Davidson XLCR is one of the most sought-after vintage Harleys.

When new, however, the XLCR was an unwanted stepchild. Dealers had to discount the bike heavily to move it off the showroom floor, and Harley-Davidson gave up on the idea after only two years.

And so, when the firm offers something else, it sells neither to the traditionalist nor to those who dismiss all Harleys as big, heavy and tractor like. A pity, because Willie G Davidson and his two sons regarded the XLCR as one of the greatest bikes they ever made. The 999cc (61ci) nominal engine was derived from the 1957 XL engine, offering 40hp at 5500rpm.

ENGINE: 997cc (60ci) ohv in-line V-twin, air-cooled
POWER: 61bhp at 6200rpm
GEARBOX: 4-speed foot change
FINAL DRIVE: chain
WEIGHT: n/a
TOP SPEED: 200km/h (125mph)

One of the most collectable of motorcycles on the market, the Harley-Davidson XLCR is in great demand, even though it had little appeal when it was first introduced.

IPREM

The problems faced by smaller concerns in sustaining the high cost of Grand Prix racing were typified by the experience of Iprem, the Italian firm based on the Adriatic coastal township of Pesaro. The company was founded by Enzo Ridolfi, whose principal interest lay in producing road-racing machines and who initially chose to enter the 50cc (3ci) category with a Kreidler-like 49.64cc/3ci (40 x 39.5mm/ 1.6 x 1.5in) horizontal liquid-cooled single-cylinder model. This produced a very respectable

16hp at 16,000rpm. In 1977, ridden by Guido Mancini, it won the prestigious Italian Senior Championship, beating some well-established marques, as well as several top-flight riders. By 1980, the Iprem 50 had been developed into a world-class bike. That year, Iprem's latest signing, Eugenio Lazzarini, was able to take the 50cc World Championship title with victories in Italy and Spain, a second place at Spa Francorchamps in Belgium (the fastest circuit in the calendar) and two third places, in Holland and Yugoslavia.

Also in 1980 a 124.68cc/7.6ci (44 x 41mm/1.7 x 1.6in) liquid-cooled horizontal twin, with disc-valve induction, made its debut. This latest creation was the work of the engineer Paolo Marcheselli, with assistance from Lazzarini. Its first Grand Prix finish came during the French round, when Eugenio Lazzarini came home ninth. Then at the British GP (at Silverstone) the same rider finished an impressive fifth. But the Iprem team's best result with the horizontal twin-cylinder model came in 1981, when

Eugenio Lazzarini, pictured here at Milan, made a considerable input to the design of the Iprem 50. It soon showed itself to be a world-class bike, winning many Grand Prix honours before Iprem found racing too costly.

Lazzarini was fourth in the 1981 Austrian Grand Prix at the Salzburg Ring. However, Iprem could not sustain the costs of GP racing and Lazzarini left at the end of the year to join rivals Garelli.

MAGNI

Arturo Magni was born in 1920 near Arcore, the home town of the famous Gilera marque, for whom he began his working life. With another engineer, Pietro Remor, he left after World War II to join MV Agusta – the company founded by Count Domenico Agusta, the MV standing for Meccanica Verghera. Their brief was to preserve the jobs of employees of the Agusta firm and to meet the post-war demand for

cheap, efficient transportation. They produced their first prototype, the 'Vespa', in 1945. However, given that Piaggio's brand new motorscooter had the same name, this was changed to MV 98.

Throughout the 1950s and 1960s, the company successfully manufactured small-displacement, quintessential Café racer style motorcycles (mostly 125–150cc/ 8–9ci). Then small motorcycle

sales declined, so MV started producing larger displacement cycles in more limited quantities. A 250cc (15ci) and, later, a smart 350cc (21ci) twin were produced, and a 600cc (37ci) four-cylinder evolved into a 750cc (46ci), which is extremely valuable today.

Count Agusta had a passion for mechanical workings and for motorcycle racing. He was determined to have the best Grand Prix motorcycle racing team in the

world, and spared no expense on his passion. He hired some of the best riders of the time, including Carlo Ubbiali, John Surtees, Mike Hailwood, Giacomo Agostini and Phil Read, as well as the best engineers, most notably Arturo Magni. The three- and four-cylinder race bikes were known for their excellent road handling. The fire-engine-red racing machines became a hallmark of Grand Prix racing in the 1960s, winning 17 consecutive 500cc World Championships.

Magni served Agusta as mechanic, engineer and, finally, team manager until MV quit racing at the end of 1976. He then founded the Magni marque in 1977. At first, its main activity was supplying supplying wheels, chain-drive conversion kits, tuning parts and frames for MV owners.

From the early 1980s, Magni began to branch out into other marques, notably Honda, BMW and Moto Guzzi. The first such machine was the Honda-based MHI, which used not only the Japanese CB900 four-cylinder engine, but also Honda forks, swinging-arm, shock absorbers, brakes and exhaust system.

These were built exclusively for export, and in 1981 Magni produced a total of 150 MHIs and the later MH2s. Next came the MB2, powered by a BMW R100 RS flat-twin engine, which made its debut at the Cologne Show in September 1982.

The success of the Magni BMW led to the introduction three years later of the Moto Guzzi-engined Magni, the Le Mans. First displayed at the Milan Show in November 1985, the Magni machine used the power unit from the Le Mans IV. This could be ordered with the standard Moto Guzzi 1000 (948.8cc/58ci) V-twin engine, or exclusively from Magni as an 1100 (1116.87cc/68ci).

The UK price in mid-1986 was £5750 for the 1000 and an additional £300 for the 1100.

Expensive, certainly, but this was one of the world's most exclusive and exciting motorcycles, built by a man who had packed into his life motorcycle experiences that most enthusiasts could only dream about.

The Magni MB2, seen here, was powered by a BMW R100RS flat twin engine with shaft final drive. Making its debut at the Cologne Show in 1982, it was an instant success.

MOTO GUZZI V50

ITALY 1977

Established for more than 80 years, Moto Guzzi is a legend among Italian motorcycle producers. The company was founded by Mandello del Lario in March 1921, and its first motorcycle motorcycle was the now legendary 8 HP Normale. A number of highly successful models followed, including the Guzzi GT (1928), called Norge after the airship flown to the Arctic by Umberto Nobile, and the Airone (Heron) 250 of 1939, which was the best-selling 'middleweight' in Italy for more than 15 years.

The company also achieved deserved success in racing, winning its first victory at the prestigious 1921 Targa Florio.

Moto Guzzi went on to record an impressive series of wins, and by the time the company withdrew from motorcycle racing in 1957, an amazing 14 world titles and 11 Tourist Trophies had been accumulated.

In the years after World War II, Moto Guzzi produced models like the Galletto (1950) and the Lodola 175 (1956). In 1950, Moto Guzzi was the first motorcycle manufacturer in the world to install a wind tunnel at its Mandello del Lario plant, to test and develop the first truly modern fairings. Moto Guzzi's racing team brought together a group of talented individuals, including engineers Umberto Todero and Enrico Cantoni, plus a designer who became a legend in his own right, Giulio Cesare Carcano.

In the late 1960s, Moto Guzzi introduced the first 90-degree V-Twin engine, which was to become the backbone of further development. In one form or another, this unit went on to power many models, including

the famous Guzzi V7, V7 Special and the legendary V7 Sport. Already crowned in glory, this same V twin was later produced in smaller versions for the Guzzi V35 and V50.

While some transverse V-twins got bigger, others got smaller, and 1977 saw the launch of the V50 and its little brother, the 346cc (21ci), 66 x 50.6mm (2.5 x 1.9in) V35. The 350cc (21ci) class had lost the appeal it had once enjoyed, but the 500cc (32ci) offered the same (nominal) horsepower as a Vincent Rapide, even though this was from half the capacity.

At first sight, the V50 was near perfection; and indeed, it handled and went very well, apart from an intractable flat spot. Unfortunately, it also demonstrated a number of faults that often seemed to afflict Moto Guzzi machines, such as flaking paintwork, poor electrics and leaking oil seals, which meant that it missed its chance to become one of the greatest bikes ever.

By the time the much-improved V50III appeared in 1980, the damage to the company's reputation had been done. Increasing the capacity to 643cc/39ci (80 x 64mm/ 3.1 x 2.5in) with the 1981 V65 failed to excite many customers, and when the company tried stretching the capacity yet again to 743cc (45ci) via an increased stroke (74mm/2.9in), the general reaction among consumers was one of indifference. The variants on the small twin that did make a difference, however, were the V35TT and the V65TT – 'TT' for Tutte Terrano (all-terrain). These appeared in 1984, sharing the basic components of the III series, but with most of the bugs removed.

The 750NTX was the V75 derivative of the same series (80 x 74mm/3.1 x 2.9in) but the Quota was based on the bigger engines.

ENGINE: 490cc (29ci) ohv transverse V-twin, 74x57mm, air-cooled
POWER: 45bhp at 7500rpm
GEARBOX: 5-speed foot change
FINAL DRIVE: shaft
WEIGHT: 168kg (370lb)
TOP SPEED: 170km/h (105mph)

Although the Moto Guzzi V50 seemed an excellent machine at first sight, it was let down by a number of adverse features that included flaking paintwork, poor electrics and oil leaks, which combined to rob it of its chance to become a great bike.

AMAZONAS

Locally manufactured motorcycles were a bit of a novelty in Brazil for many years, as bikes and scooters were imported. Indeed, there was little initiative to set up a local manufacturing facility until Amazonas came on the scene. The basic Amazonas is a 1947 Indian Chief bike with a Volkswagen engine mounted in the frame, producing what some critics have called the ugliest motorcycle in the world. The choice of the

Volkswagen engine was not surprising, because in the 1950s the German company had set up a plant in Brazil to manufacture its famous Beetle. Beetle engines were therefore in plentiful supply, and Amazonas used either the 1285cc (78ci) or 1584cc (97ci) versions in their machines. The motor was an air-cooled four with the gear-driven camshaft located beneath the crankshaft to operate inclined valves by rockers. The plugs were

fitted from an angle above and fired by coil ignition via a distributor.

The four-speed (plus reverse) gearbox was retained. The VW single-plate clutch was also kept, and crudely converted to foot change, the drive going to a VW crown wheel and pinion, and then – via a lengthy chain – to the rear wheel. The whole package fitted into a massive duplex frame with telescopic forks at the front and crude plungers at the rear. Cast-

alloy wheels carrying large car-type tyres completed the design.

In summary, the Amazonas machines were large, bulky and far from easy to handle, thanks to car-type tyres, which were quite unsuitable. Considering the size of the engine, performance was poor and the controls, other than the clutch, were very heavy. Despite this, as well as a considerable price tag, the machine remained on the market for over a decade.

BOMBARDIER

The Bombardier Snowmobile Group of Canada began with the dream of mechanic Joseph-Armand Bombardier. He wanted to build a vehicle that could 'float on snow', and in 1937 the roll-out of his first snowmobile from his small repair ship in Valcourt, Quebec, made the dream a reality.

Bombardier, which went on to become one of the world's leading

manufacturing giants, not only built the first snowmobile but was also involved with other forms of transport. For a while, it built motorcycles under its own name, and also under the name Can-Am. In both cases, Austrian Rotax engines were used, since the Group owned Rotax.

The company name was also used to rebadge various 50cc (3ci)

mopeds and motorcycles that came from Puch, another Austrian firm. These were sold through their existing sales outlets.

In 1978, the Group identified a military market for its motorcycles and decided to adapt one of its dirt bikes, the 247cc (15ci) enduro, for military use. The bike had a single-cylinder, disc-valve, air-cooled engine with its carburettor

fitted behind the cylinder to keep the width of the whole unit down. It was attached to a long inlet passage cast as part of the main castings, which also carried the mixture along to the disc-valve and crankcase. The exhaust gases went into a high-level system that ran over the top of the engine and terminated with a spark arrestor. The engine drove a five-speed gearbox built-in unit, and final drive was by an exposed chain – not, perhaps, the best feature for a military model.

The frame and suspension were typical of the period for an off-road machine, with plenty of ground clearance under the duplex tubes. These ran close under the engine unit and into the sub-frame, while the rear fork was controlled by twin spring-and-damper units. Telescopic forks provided front suspension, with a 53cm (21in) wheel at the front and a 45cm (18in) wheel at the back. Both wheels used drum brakes, and the machine came with full road equipment. A rear rack, panniers and extra rear-light were added to this package and the whole machine was finished in khaki. Despite its intended use and customer, the competition side plates were retained on each side.

The Bombardier was ordered in small numbers for service with the Canadian armed forces and subjected to rigorous testing by the US Marine Corps. However, it was in Britain that it found its greatest success, being adopted for use by the British armed forces and manufactured by various surviving components of the BSA group. British-manufactured Bombardiers were also purchased by the Belgian Army.

This Bombardier is an example of machines that were built in Canada and supplied to the British Army. The design was based on the firm's off-road models and proved adaptable to the military market.

CAGIVA

Since its establishment in 1978, the Cagiva company has expanded rapidly to the point where it has become a major participant in the European motorcycle industry, although this swift progress has not been without its share of problems. The factory at Varese, where the firm's machines are manufactured, was originally owned by Harley-Davidson, which sold it to the Castiglioni family. When asked why the family had acquired the plant, Gianfranco Castiglioni, one of the firm's present-day directors replied: 'Because we love motorcycles, of course!'

Gianfranco controls the company with his brother, Claudio. Their father was Giovanno, and the name Cagiva has its origin in the initial letters of the family name, Castiglioni (Ca), the father's name, Giovannin (Gi), and the town of Varese (Va). Although this was their first venture into the practicality of motorcycle production, the Castiglionis' enthusiasm for motorcycles had been apparent for some time, the two brothers having sponsored the heavily modified Suzuki RG500s of Franco Bonera and Marco Lucchinelli. Once Cagiva was in the business, the brothers spent a huge amount of time, money and effort from the late 1970s in a bid to capture the 500cc racing title, but this prize eluded them, even though they had riders such as Randy Mamola and Eddie Lawson. However, Cagiva did have the satisfaction of winning the World 125cc Motocross title on

The Cagiva range of motorcycles is world famous. Pictured here is the Cagiva Mito 125cc, a very popular two-stroke that gave the lie to the tale that Italian bikes were generally unreliable.

more than one occasion, and in 1978 the firm launched a liquid-cooled machine to compete in this sector of the sport. Called the WMXX 125, this 124.6cc/7.6ci (56 x 50.6mm/2.2 x 1.9in) featured reed-valve induction, air- and water-cooling, six-speeds, and magnesium outer engine covers. But what really set it apart was the fact that it was the first production motocrosser to feature a liquid-cooled engine – an innovation that was soon copied by the Japanese. The remainder of the Cagiva range for the first two years consisted of updated designs previously sold under the Harley-Davidson name. All were two-stroke singles, including 250cc (15ci) motocross and enduro mounts.

During its early years, there is no doubt that Cagiva had the advantage of being able to capitalize on the vast stock of spares and former Aermacchi/HD designs that existed at the time of the takeover. One of these, the SST125, became the best-selling motorcycle on the Italian market in the all-important 125cc (8ci) sector between 1979 and 1982. By giving it cast-alloy wheels, better switchgear and finally, in 1982, electronic ignition, Cagiva was able to sell large numbers of these 123cc/7.5ci 6ci (56 x 50.6mm/2.2 x 1.9in), piston-parted, five-speed street bikes on their home market.

Cagiva continued to develop new concepts, and to seek ways of improving current ones, throughout the early 1980s, a period in which the remainder of the Italian industry was content to rest on its laurels. During this period, the Varese factory brought out a succession of new two- and four-stroke models. The figures themselves speak for the amount of work and expertise generated by the firm. Cagiva built 6000

bikes in 1979 and 13,000 in 1980; by 1982, production had tripled to 40,000. The number of staff also increased, from 130 workers in 1978 to 300 at the beginning of 1979, of whom 50 were engaged in research and development.

In 1981, Cagiva made an inroad into the Latin American market with the opening of a new factory in Venezuela, where bikes were assembled from kits produced in Varese. This was followed by several other overseas initiatives, including discussions with the Soviet government about supplying Cagiva expertise to the Soviet Union, just as Fiat had done in the four-wheel sector.

At the 1981 Milan Show, the company displayed its first 'own breed' four-stroke, the Ala Rossa, a 343cc/21ci (82 x 65mm/3.2 x 2.6in) single-cylinder trail bike with chain-driven single overhead-

The Cagiva Elefant 900 is a big, tall bike that handles extremely well on curves. It's not a novice's bike, but can do practically anything under the control of an experienced rider.

cam. There was also a liquid-cooled 250cc (15ci) motocrosser, actually 190cc/12ci (67 x 54mm/2.6 x 2.1in), as well as an all-new 125cc (8ci) trail machine. The Castiglioni brothers, however, had boundless ambition, their aim being to establish a production line encompassing everything from the smallest moped to the most powerful superbike. They realized, however, that to start from scratch in developing their own large-capacity, multi-cylinder models would absorb a great deal of money and a protracted development period lasting several years. So, in a shrewd bid to cut a few corners, they went in search of a European partner to both accelerate the process and broaden the product range. This they eventually found in the shape of Bologna-based Ducati, and at a joint press conference in June 1983, they announced that Ducati would supply Cagiva with engines for seven years. Less than two years later, Cagiva took over its partner firm.

An attempt to break into the North American market presented greater problems than any experienced in the Latin-American venture. This was mainly because the Cagiva name was relatively unknown in the area, and Ducati lacked an efficient dealer network. The Castiglionis found a neat solution by purchasing the world-renowned Swedish Husqvarna concern in 1986. All their

motorcycles would now be developed by Cagiva, bearing the Husqvarna badge and built in Italy. In 1987, Cagiva added Moto Morini to their growing list of conquests.

In November 1987, it was Cagiva, Ducati, Husqvarna, and Moto Morini whose crests dominated the 50th Milan Show, with a massive stand and a prime position. The Cagiva range was impressive in its own right. It included a 50cc (3ci) Cocis, named after a legendary Native American chief (Cochise), and a

125cc (8ci) Tamanaco. Both of these used a hi-tech liquid-cooled, reed-valve single-cylinder motor with Paris-Dakar styling, twin headlamps, disc brakes front and rear, monoshock rear suspension, and a striking multi-colour paint job. Then came the Cruiser, Blues and Freccia. These all used the same basic 124.6cc/7.6ci (56 x 50.6mm/2.2 x 1.9 in) engine from the Tamanaco, but differed in purpose and level of tuning. The Cruiser was a trail bike, the Blues a custom cruiser, and the Freccia a sportster whose styling

was based on the Ducati Paso, with all-enveloping plastic bodywork. In the wake of these came a quartet of trail bikes with either 343cc (21ci) or 452cc (28ci), four-valve, single-cylinder engines, which were developed from the earlier two-valve Ala Rossa. Two Ducati-powered V-twins, the 350 Elefant and 750 Lucky Explorer, completed the street-bike line-up. Finally, there was a pair of full-blown motocrossers, the WMX125 and WMX250, the latter now fitted with a 247cc/15ci (70 x 64.8mm/

2.7 x 2.6 in) engine.

Strangely, after the end of the 1980s, when it built the Freccia – the world's first production roadster to sport seven gears – Cagiva began to splutter. It did sometimes produce an ace, such as the Mito Sportster in 1991 and the Gran Canyon 900 trail bike in the late 1990s. But overall, the company seemed to lose its way, for reasons that were many and varied, ranging from the success enjoyed by Ducati to huge losses encountered in its non-biking generations.

DUCATI NCR 900

ITALY 1978

The NCR company was established in 1967 by three businessmen, whose surnames Nepoti, Caracchi and Rizzi provided the company's initials. Its involvement with Ducati began in 1972 and lasted until the retirement of Giorgio Nepoti and Rino Caracchi in 1995; the third partner, Rizzi, left shortly after the partnership was founded. During these years, NCR co-operated with Taglioni, Farne and the rest of Ducati's experimental department, and provided the support for

Ducati's most successful exploits, including the legendary comeback of Mike Hailwood in the Isle of Man TT in 1978 after a serious accident in Germany in the previous year.

At Silverstone in 1977, Hailwood met Steve Wynne of Sport Motor Cycles Ltd in Manchester, and Wynne let Hailwood try out a Ducati he had prepared. The English champion enjoyed the classic riding position and jokingly offered to race it in the Isle of Man TT next year. They came to an agreement, though Hailwood

initially wanted to race under a pseudonym, so unsure was he of his chances. The contract was quickly drawn up: £1000 for taking part in the event and a new Ducati in his garage.

Wynne bought three bikes from Ducati out of a batch of 20 900s, specially prepared for endurance races. Created at Ducati and, as always, worked on by its best mechanics, the bikes were then assembled by NCR. The machine selected by Hailwood for the race was one of a small batch built by NCR in 1978. Although based

The Ducati NCR 900 is synonymous with the name of Mike Hailwood, who rode it to victory in the 1978 Isle of Man TT after making his comeback from a serious accident in Germany in the previous year.

around the existing bevel 900 SS, these bikes had several differences over the standard production street roadsters.

Items such as the sand-cast crankcases and dry-clutch assemblies came from the NCR endurance racers. There were also special bigger-bore Malossi-modified Dell'Orto carburettors, while the frame was specially fabricated by the Bologna-based Daspa concern. Although similar to the production version, this bike was considerably lighter. The rear suspension units were of British Girling origin. The bike reached 87hp, which was somewhat underpowered compared with Read's official four-cylinder Honda, built just to win the TT1 world championships.

On 2 June 1978, Mike Hailwood lined up at the start against some 100 other riders, including the seven-times World Champion Phil Read. When the gruelling race was finally over, Hailwood and Ducati had become the new Formula 1 World Champions. It was Ducati's first title after many attempts.

ENGINE: 863.9cc (52ci) sohc, Desmo, 2v, V-twin, 86x74.4mm, air-cooled
POWER: 90bhp at 8000rpm
GEARBOX: 5-speed foot change
FINAL DRIVE: chain
WEIGHT: n/a
TOP SPEED: 241km/h (150mph)

HYOSUNG

KOREA 1978–PRESENT

Hyosung Korea was founded in 1978 to produce motor vehicles – not specifically motorcycles at first – and became affiliated with the Suzuki Motor Corporation of Japan in 1978. By 1980, a new factory had been completed at Changwon, and two years later the company was exporting motorcycles and scooters. Its sales philosophy was based on the premise that, throughout the developing world, people were desperate for personal transport yet unable to afford the level of car ownership that was common in other countries.

The smallest-capacity Hyosungs are well represented by the 49cc (2.9ci) Prima scooter: it weighs less than 88kg (200lb), but is still provided with both electric- and kick-starters, automatic clutch and gearbox, suspension at both ends (telescopic forks at the front, coil springs at the rear) and disk front bakes and drum back brakes. The next level provides the 99cc (6ci), 90kg (198lb) Zephyr city scooter, and a steady progression of vehicles follows, up to and including a 250cc (15ci) V-twin.

This diversity explains how Hyosung can export not only to China but also to Brazil and even to Germany, these three countries representing the biggest export markets from the 60 countries into which Hyosung sold at the beginning of the 21st century.

The question is: how long can companies such as Hyosung stay in the motorcycle business, and will they move into other, and more interesting, areas of motorcycling? If two-wheeled transport is merely a transitional stage, they may be expected either to switch to cars or to go out of business.

But, equally, it may be that the rules have changed, and that the sheer expense of cars (and of the fuel to drive them) means that these vehicles cannot flourish in those countries where their use is not already deeply rooted. Today, Hyosung produces at the original Changwon factory and at a second facility built at Daesung in 1990.

The Hyosung Comet 650 is a handsome machine. Upside-down front forks and twin two-pot front brake callipers that seize 300mm (12in) double disks up front give it an very modern aggressive appearance.

LAVERDA V6

ITALY 1978

When Laverda set about developing the V6 in the summer of 1976, the intention was to furnish the company with a new range of modular models. In the event, it appeared only as an endurance racing prototype. It was one of the most ambitious motorcycle designs of all time – too ambitious, it might be said, because its development ultimately landed the company with a financial burden it could not support.

In the beginning, however, everything seemed rosy, as Piero Laverda announced at the launch that he envisaged a range of V-twins, V-fours and V-sixes, covering a displacement spectrum of 350cc (21ci) to 1200cc (73ci). He added that the plan was to create a series of models based around the same set of basic components, and all featuring four-valve heads, liquid-cooling and shaft final drive.

The V6 was developed by a joint design team comprising former Maserati engineer Ing Giulio Alfieri and Laverda's design boss Luciano Zen. Officially, Alfieri was employed by Laverda as a consultant, but in practice he and Zen worked as a team. The 90-degree V6 was an ideal basis for a modular series of engines because the twin and the four could also share the same 90°, thus reducing the cost of tooling. It was soon apparent, however, that the cost of the programme was becoming prohibitive, and the first and only complete type to appear was the V6 endurance racer of 1978, with 995.89cc/61ci (65 x 50mm/2.6 x 1.9in) and almost 139hp.

Its race debut came in that year's Bol d'Or race in France, at the Paul Ricard circuit, where it was timed at an amazing 283km/h (176mph) along the Mistral straight, 32km/h (20mph) faster than any other bike in the event. After eight hours, however, the universal drive shaft failed, forcing its retirement.

Despite this speed, its weight and handling problems were to signal the model's death knell. In technical terms, the V6 proved that Laverda could build the ultimate motorcycle of its era; even so, this exercise placed the company's entire future in jeopardy. The real death-knell for Laverda sounded in the early 1980s, with the European motorcycle industry reeling under fierce and growing competition from the Japanese. This pressure caused many companies, including Moto-Guzzi and NVT (an amalgamation of the British companies Norton, Triumph and BSA), to fail and ultimately disappear.

Laverda attempted to update the product line by introducing the RGS luxury tourer in 1983, a stylish and modern-looking machine with clever features such as integrated but removable luggage, and adjustable riding position; a 1000cc (61ci) SFC sport model; and a smaller 500cc (31ci) entry-level machine named the Alpino.

Unfortunately, this initiative came too late. That said, the company was saved from extinction in 1993 by millionaire Francesco Tognon, and it was eventually absorbed into the Aprilia group.

ENGINE: 995cc (60ci) dohc 4 valve V6 65x50mm, water-cooled
POWER: 139bhp @ 10,000rpm
GEARBOX: 5-speed foot change
FINAL DRIVE: shaft
WEIGHT: 216kg (476lb)
TOP SPEED: 283km/h (176mph)

The Laverda V6 was potentially a good bike, but it was not sufficiently road tested and was too slow in negotiating curves. Its weight and handling problems were the cause of its demise.

SUZUKI GS1000

What amounted to a motorcycle war erupted between Kawasaki, Yamaha and Suzuki in the late 1970s. Kawasaki had already received volumes of praise for its Z1, which had become a legend in its own time, and for the subsequent KZ 1000. Yamaha had recently released the XS11, which was applauded for its awesome power output. Then, in 1978, Suzuki launched the GS 1000. This was capable of outperforming Kawasaki's Z1, and it set new standards for sports bikes of the period, owing to its exceptional handling and powerful 997cc (60ci) four-cylinder engine, whose specification included twin overhead-cams and four valves per cylinder.

The GS 1000 was a simple design that benefited from solid engineering and a light weight. It was only a few pounds heavier than the successful GS 750, its immediate ancestor, and was based on a sturdy tubular-steel cradle frame, with adjustable suspension and twin front disc brakes, running on alloy wheels with ample-sized tyres. The GS1000 proved comfortable and reliable, stable at high speed in a straight line and relatively agile in corners. The straight-ish

handlebars required more of an arms-forward posture than other machines, and styling was unremarkable, despite the

chromed megaphone exhausts. Only marginally slower was the model's 750cc sibling, the GS750 Four, introduced a year earlier and

Above: The GS1000 was based on the successful GS750, the lightest of the 750s, and was just 3kg (7lb) heavier.

Left: Suzuki put a great deal of effort into the GS1000. The redesigned GS750 motor put into the GS1000 was now lighter.

capable of 201km/h (125mph), with a realistic 145km/h (90mph) cruising speed if given a moth screen to improve aerodynamics. In race trim, with cockpit fairing, a Suzuki GS1000 with Yoshimura tuning took Wes Cooley to the 1980 US Superbike title.

Suzuki's design team clearly expended a good deal of effort on the GS 1000. The engine they installed in it, redesigned from the 750's, was actually lighter than the original. Power in 1978 was 83hp at 8000rpm.

ENGINE: 997cc (60ci) 8-valve dohc transverse-mounted four-cylinder, 70x64.8mm, air-cooled
POWER: 87bhp at 8000rpm
GEARBOX: 5-speed
FINAL DRIVE: chain
WEIGHT: 241kg (531lb)
TOP SPEED: 217km/h (135mph)

DUCATI PANTAH

ITALY 1979

One of the top motorcycle magazines is said to have claimed that the Ducati Pantah 500 could not be matched by anything else in the world for power and speed. It was certainly one of the most successful bikes in Ducati's production history. Hardly surprising, as it was designed by a team of unsurpassed talent – Taglioni, Mengoli, Bocchi and Martini. It originated in the mid-1970s, when the Ducati management decided it needed a middleweight parallel twin to take on the Japanese.

Chief designer Fabio Taglioni was against the idea from the start, wanting instead to build a smaller version of his L-shaped 90-degree V-twin. Just as Taglioni had foreseen, the parallel twin proved a massive sales flop, and the result was that he finally got the green light for his project. The product of his work was the ancestor of Ducati's current family of models – the Pantah, with its belt-driven Desmo top end.

The prototype Pantah made its appearance in 1977 and entered production two years later, in 1979. The 1979 model was the 500 SL, which featured bore and stroke dimensions of 74 x 58mm (2.9 x 2.3in) respectively. Ducati sources claimed 50hp at 9050rpm. Other details of the machine's specification included electric starting, a five-speed gearbox, 45cm (18in) cast-alloy wheels, triple Brembo cast-iron discs with two-piston callipers and a racing riding position. A half fairing came as standard equipment, as did a single/dual converter seat.

Incidentally, the 500 SL was not imported to Britain until 1980, and a 'Mark II' version made its debut in 1981. In that year, the 500 was joined by a 600, still coded SL. This was the first Ducati production model to feature a hydraulic clutch.

In 1983, the line continued with a 350 SL, together with the touring-bias 350 XL and 600 TL models, and the 650 SL, the last of the line. Production ceased in 1986. The other Pantah was the 600 TT F2 racer. This version sported a special Verlicchi-made frame, with monoshock rear suspension. The English rider Tony Rutter won no fewer than four world championship titles during the early 1980s on the TT F2 racer, making it Ducati's most successful racing model until the advent of World Super Bike racing in the 1990s.

ENGINE: 498.9cc (30ci) sohc, Desmo, 2v, V-twin, 94x58mm, air-cooled
POWER: 45bhp at 9500 rpm
GEARBOX: 5-speed foot change
FINAL DRIVE: chain
WEIGHT: n/a
TOP SPEED: 193km/h (120mph)

Below and Inset: A leading bike magazine claimed that the Pantah 500 was the fastest, most powerful machine in the world. Designed by an unrivalled team of experts – Taglioni, Mengoli, Bocchi and Martini – it was one of the most successful bikes in Ducati production history.

KAWASAKI Z1300

The Kawasaki Z1300 was developed in response to two principal rivals, the Honda CBX and Benelli Sei, both of which had six-cylinder engines. Kawasaki opted for sheer size, although some critics considered the result to be too extreme. The Kawasaki Z1300 had its 1286cc (77ci) liquid-cooled six-cylinder engine set across the frame, twin overhead-camshafts, five speeds and shaft drive. It rode on cast-alloy wheels with disc brakes.

The result was a massive machine for touring, a job it did extremely well. It featured all the equipment that might be expected in such a comprehensive machine, and therefore had relatively few

changes made to it during its 10-year evolution.

This excellent six-cylinder motorcycle was capable of extraordinary performance, and proved both durable and reliable. In its heyday, to possess a Z1300 brought considerable prestige. Despite its great mass, examples were raced in production class with some measure of success. For example, the 1979 Arai 500 endurance race at Bathurst, Australia saw the debut of the first machine to enter the country – and it won, although the exhausts on both sides were flattened and ground away.

To this day, the record for the fastest run around Australia is held

by the Z1300 – the rider was a police officer. Not for nothing was it affectionately referred to as 'The Thirteen Million'.

In 1980, it was joined by a version with touring panniers and top box, but this was to remain in production for only two years; buyers preferred to make their own choices in terms of extra equipment. However, Kawasaki was undeterred and the year 1983 saw the launch of a similar tourer, the Voyager, which was built for the US market only. Its engine had digital fuel injection, which was fitted to all versions of the bike the following year. This took it on to 1989, its final year of production.

The huge, six-cylinder Kawasaki Z1300 was in some ways the ultimate late 1970s Superbike, the inevitable end product of the Japanese manufacturers' race towards bigger, heavier and more complex machines.

ENGINE: 1286cc (77ci) dohc transverse six, 62x71mm, liquid-cooled
POWER: 120bhp at 8000 rpm
GEARBOX: 5-speed foot change
FINAL DRIVE: shaft
WEIGHT: 295kg (650lb)
TOP SPEED: 225km/h (135mph)

ARMSTRONG

The machine now known as the Armstrong motorcycle was originally developed by SWM of Italy. The firm won several trials championships, including two world championships, before going into liquidation in 1984. Armstrong of Bolton, England, acquired the rights to the SWM XN

Tornado, a Rotax-engined enduro machine of 350cc (21ci) or 506cc (31ci), and developed it into the Armstrong MT500. It was accepted for use by the British Army, which used it in the Falklands. Limited numbers were also supplied to Jordanian and Canadian forces. Total production did not exceed

By 1984, the production of the Armstrong MT500 manual-start model and some electric-start versions for the Jordanian and Canadian military was well under way.

3000, of which fewer than 100 are believed to have had electric start.

The story began with Harry Hooper, chairman of Armstrong Equipment, the automotive

suspension specialist based in Humberside in the north of England. He laid plans to increase his company's product range by expanding into motorcycle manufacture. In 1980, he put in a bid to buy the ailing Triumph Workers co-operative, Meriden, in 1980. The bid failed, but only a month later, Armstrong took over Cotton, which had recently gone into voluntary liquidation.

This was a fortuitous move. Just before Cotton's demise, its boss, Terry Wilson, had forged links with Austrian engine producers Rotax as well as Mike Eatough, the Bolton suspension specialist, aiming to build a race-winning 250cc (15ci) in-line two-stroke twin. After taking control of the company, Armstrong continued this racing development programme and signed up ex-Spartan designer Barry Hart as chief engineer.

Close-up of the chain drive fitted to the Armstrong Army Model. The Armstrong bikes were designed for ease of service and were extremely robust.

Hart's two-stroke expertise and Armstrong's money ensured the new enterprise got off to a winning start, with Steve Tonkin not only winning the 1982 Isle of Man TT Junior (250cc) class, but also taking his third British Championship the same year. Flushed with success, Armstrong announced its intention to enter the road machine market, and envisaged the introduction of 250cc (15ci), 350 (21ci), 500cc (31ci) and 750cc (46ci) street bikes. To compliment the 250cc (15ci) racer, a brand new Hart-designed 350cc (31ci) twin was built. This machine was also an in-line (tandem) twin, but had entirely new horizontally split crankcases, and used 64mm (2.5in) bore aluminium cylinders with a hard chrome lining. Retaining the Rotax 54mm (2.1in) stroke, the new power plant featured Omega pistons, Motoplat electronic ignition and 36mm (1.4in) Mikuni carburettors. Output was an impressive 86hp,

Right: Close-up of the 1985 model's engine. The new motor featured a bore and stroke of 62.5 x 54mm (2.4 x 2.1 in) respectively, and developed 120hp at 11,000rpm.

Below: The Armstrong racing model of 1985 was the brainchild of a formidable design team, with Barry Hart creating the engine.

with 90hp on tap by the time production began in 1982.

As development on the CM 36 350 twin continued and its performance increased, the team thought they had a potential world-beating racer on their hands. Unfortunately, these championship-winning dreams were ended when the sports governing body, the FIM, axed the 350cc (21ci) class at the end of the 1982 season. Armstrong continued with the 250cc (15ci), but it was never quite as good as the 350cc (21ci).

In 1984, a new twin-spar carbon-fibre framed 250 GP bike

was unveiled. It was to be ridden by Niall Mackenzie and Tony Head, with ex-Grand Prix rider Chas Mortimer as team manager. A year later, Armstrong announced a 500cc (31ci,) three-cylinder engine, again the work of Barry Hart. This new motor featured a bore and stroke of 62.5 x 54mm (2.4 x 2.1 in) respectively, and developed 120hp at 11,000rpm. Other features of the triple included rear-facing exhausts, a six-speed gearbox, reed-valve induction and power valves on the exhaust. By 1984, the production of the Armstrong MT500 manual

start model and some electric start versions for the Jordanian and Canadian military was well under way. The Canadian Army took only 90 of the electric start version, known to them as the Armstrong M50. These remained in service until the early 1990s.

In the meantime, Armstrong built a number of off-road bikes, including motocross, enduro and even a trials bike. It tendered for military contracts, but the Canadian-based Bombardier firm won the contract to supply bikes to the British Army. And that was the end for Armstrong.

BENELLI 900 SEI

Towards the end of the 1960s, the influx of Japanese manufacturers caused an unprecedented crisis in the European motorcycle industry. Not the least of the firms affected was Benelli, which had been manufacturing motorcycles since 1911. At this time, Benelli was heavily involved in the American motorcycle market, selling motorcycles under 350cc (21ci) through Montgomery-Ward. However, Benelli products were still largely of single-cylinder pushrod design, and competition from Japan meant that they were now losing popularity. They were perceived as old fashioned in comparison to Hondas, which sported overhead-cam engines with electric starters.

In 1971, the Benelli family sold out to the Argentinian industrialist, Alejandro de Tomaso. This change of ownership introduced a new era of Benelli street bikes. In an attempt to upstage the Japanese and to pull off a publicity coup for his new acquisition, de Tomaso created a flagship six-cylinder model.

This was a 750cc (46ci), built to show the world just what Benelli could do. The Sei (Six) was a typical Italian luxury engineering creation: its single-cam, six-cylinder engine was a logical, almost obvious, choice, resembling the configuration of its four-wheel, 12-cylinder counterparts at Ferrari, Lamborghini and Maserati. Like them, Benelli's 750cc (46ci) was expensive, but lacked style. In fact, apart from six megaphone exhausts that crowded the rear wheel, the Sei's styling was conservative, possibly even bland.

The Benelli's engine design owed more to Tokyo than to Turin, but the prototype still created a sensation when it was launched in 1972. Maximum speed was around 185km/h (115mph), with factory sources claiming 71hp at 8500rpm from the 748cc/46ci (56 x 50.6mm/2.2 x 1.9in), across-the-frame, six-cylinder engine.

By the time the 750 Sei entered production in 1974, Honda's development of its own six, the CBX, was well under way. Benelli responded by bringing out the larger 900, featuring 906cc (55ci) and a bore and stroke of 60 x 53.4mm (2.4 x 2.1in). This was no mere restyling; instead it was virtually a brand new bike. The engine was much stronger, with items such as the crankshaft and gearbox, unreliable on the earlier six, replaced with new components. The appearance of the motorbike was also considerably different, with a six-into-two exhaust and a bikini fairing. Maximum speed was in excess of 209km/h (130mph). Despite such continued innovations, however, the firm continued to lose important market segments, overwhelmed by Japanese competitors. Production of the motorbike ceased in 1987.

ENGINE: 906cc (54ci) ohc straight four, 60x53.4mm, air-cooled
POWER: 80bhp at 8400rpm
GEARBOX: 5-speed foot change
FINAL DRIVE: chain
WEIGHT: 220kg (485lb)
TOP SPEED: 215km/h (133mph)

The Benelli 900 had the benefit of a very compact engine installation, with previously unreliable components such as the crankshaft and gearbox replaced with new items. Top speed was over 209km/h (130mph).

BMW R80GS

People were enthusiastic about the BMW R80GS right from the start, sometimes to the point of euphoria. At first sight, the overall impression is one of size, enhanced by the huge fuel tank. The single-sided rear suspension also surprises. Taking to the road for the first time on the R80GS, the rider has a general feeling of comfort, coupled with an impression of agility and general 'good nature'. The extremely low seat height, in comparison to other contemporary bikes in this class, offers security, while the high, wide handlebar provides a relaxed, upright riding position. Because of the low centre of gravity, the weight (218kg/479lb) of the fully fuelled motorcycle is scarcely noticeable. The only minus point is the poorly designed angular step between the tank and the seat, which interferes a little with the enjoyment of long rides. The R80GS performs very well on secondary roads; in fact, the worse the pavement, the better the bike handles it. Both front

The main picture shows the basic BMW R80GS. The more angular R100GS is on the right in the smaller photo. These were quite large bikes, better handled by a taller rider. Both variants were superb desert racers.

and rear suspension protect the rider from all disturbing influences, yet react softly and sensitively without feeling mushy.

The narrow enduro tyres are particularly beneficial, especially on curvy roads. No wiggling in bumpy curves; barely any tendency to stand up and run wide when braking at a lean; and even at full throttle, running at 170km/h (105mph), the weaving remains within bearable limits.

An off-road motorcycle of this size might seem at first to have limited appeal, simply on the grounds that it is big and heavy, and offers more power than is generally needed on dirt. But the R80GS and the later R100GS were superb desert racers, doing very well in the Paris–Dakar races.

Perhaps more importantly, they were also remarkably good town bikes, with power on tap, good suspension, and enough bulk to be a presence on the road. For these reasons, the GS was, for a considerable period, the only motorcycle to ride. Its only real drawback was that it best suited tall riders. Remarkably, even when the overhead-cam 'new' boxers came out, there were still GS versions: the R1100GS boasted

80hp, an increase of 60 per cent over the original R80GS and 10hp more than the original R100RS.

ENGINE: 798cc (48ci) ohv transverse flat twin, 85x70.6mm, air-cooled
POWER: 50bhp at 6500rpm
GEARBOX: 5-speed foot change
FINAL DRIVE: Kardan shaft
WEIGHT: n/a
TOP SPEED: 185km/h (115mph)

CAGIVA WMX125 MOTOCROSS

ITALY 1980

The WMX125 first appeared in prototype form in 1978 and was notable as the world's first liquid-cooled production motocross bike, entering production in April the following year. It laid a fair claim to being the most competitive dirt racer in its class anywhere in the world at that time, but it could hardly be called well known when it made its racing debut. The machine was designed and developed by Cagiva, and owed nothing at all to Harley-Davidson, from whom Cagiva had purchased its factory in 1978.

Its single-cylinder, 124.6cc/7.6ci (56 x 50.6mm/2.2 x 1.9in) engine was both air- and water-cooled, and made use of magnesium for the outer engine covers and carburettor body. Other notable features included reed-valve

induction, a six-speed gearbox and a 34mm (1.3in) Dell'Orto carburettor. The aluminium cylinder had a nikisel bore, which was more robust than the cheaper chrome system then widely in use. Ignition was a Japanese Nippon Denso electronic unit. Power output was a class-leading 30+hp. It was good enough, in fact, for a Dutch rider to use the WMX engine to break the 125cc world speed record in 1981.

The frame employed chrome-moly tubing, while the suspension was taken care of by 35mm (1.4in), soon replaced by 38mm (1.5in) Marzocchi leading axle forks with magnesium sliders. At the rear were a pair of Corte Cosso gas shock absorbers. A super-lightweight aluminium radiator, and extremely robust, American-made, dual swinging-arm were

further examples of the excellent, and robust, nature of the design.

From mid-1981, the finning of the head and barrel gave way to the more traditional liquid-cooled 'bald' castings. And from the 1983 model year, Cagiva finally bowed to the inevitable and fitted a single shock rear end to the bike, which was marketed as the 'Soft Damp' system. By now, the 35hp and a larger 36mm (1.4in) carburettor size made the Cagiva truly world class, and, by 1983, the factory had begun to take a serious interest in the world championship series. In 1985, Caviga won the 125cc world title for the first time – and scored a major publicity coup. For 1986 a production version appeared, the 'World Champion Replica'. Unlike many efforts, this was more or less exactly what it said it was: with

the exception of the original bore-and-stroke dimensions, the engine was the world champion of the previous year.

After this, Cagiva purchased Husqvarna, and the WMX125 became a Husky rather than a Cagiva. With the help of the WMX125, Cagiva succeeded in overturning the Suzuki monopoly in this class, the Italian machine consistently featuring in the leading group in the principal contests of the late 1980s.

ENGINE: 124.6cc (7.5ci) Reed valve ts single, 56 x 50.6mm, water-cooled
POWER: 37.5bhp at 11,500rpm
GEARBOX: 6-speed foot change
FINAL DRIVE: Chain
WEIGHT: 88kg (194lb)
TOP SPEED: 128km/h (80mph)

MONTESA COTA

SPAIN LATE 1980s

Founded in 1944 by Pedro Permanyer and Francisco Bulto, the Spanish Montesa company at first concentrated on the production of small two-strokes

based on other contemporary designs. These proved an instant success, prompting Bulto to set about designing more advanced machines. The first such design

was an advanced 125cc (8ci) machine, which was the basis of a string of successful road and off-road machines that went on to compete in national and

The small two-stroke bikes produced by the Montesa company were an immediate success.

international events, and of a successful road-racing machine that collected both accolades and prizes at the Isle of Man TT.

The first of the 'Cota' family of bikes made its appearance in 1968, and was one of the machines that established Montesa's position on the world scene. Montesa also developed a range of smaller trials bikes to compliment the Cota 247, in sizes from 50cc (3ci) to 175cc (11ci).

Then, in 1975, with Malcolm Rathmell as the development rider, the bike was stretched to 310cc (19ci) and the Cota 348 for customers in 1976. This was to remain Montesa's flagship until 1979, when the range was revised and brought up to date with all new machines.

The 348 was replaced with an all new 349, which was a full 350cc (21ci) machine, with a new lightweight frame using the alloy bash-plate as the bottom frame rails, and the engine as a stressed member.

Very much a trials competition bike, with no pretensions to road-going, the 1990s Montesa Cota was based on a Verlicchi twin-beam chassis made up of welded aluminium forgings and extrusions.

Front forks were upside-down telescopics, and the rear suspension was by single damper and rising-rate linkage. Disc brakes were fitted front and rear. The frame, ending in an extended rear mudguard, was topped by a fuel tank and a seat of the lowest possible profile. Beneath the mudguard was the silencer for the water-cooled 258cc (16ci) single-cylinder engine.

This unit construction motor was allied to a six-speed transmission. Its all-up weight of 83kg (183lb) reflected its agility.

GILERA CI CROSS

In 1979, the Piaggio engineering company, encouraged by the success of earlier motorcycles produced by its subsidiary Gilera, ordered the firm to build off-road models for demonstration in competitions.

As a step towards achieving this aim, Piaggio engaged the services of one of the finest two-stroke specialists in the world. Dutchman Jan Witteveen joined the firm in 1980 and supervised the design of a new 125cc (8ci) engine with water-cooling. The existing Gilera engine had been used by Elmeca-Gilera to win the 1978 Italian Motocross title in air-cooled form, and Witteveen now developed it to be more efficient, avoiding the need to create a completely new unit from scratch. The 54 x 53.6mm (2.12 x 2.11in) bore and stroke dimensions of the Elmeca-developed engine were retained.

One of the Witteveen water-cooled 125cc (8ci) motocross machines was entered in the 1981 and 1982 Italian and World Championships by factory rider Michele Rinaldi – with some success. The works model, raced by Rinaldi, had Marzocchi single shock rear suspension. The customer version, the CI Competizione Cross, differed by having twin rear shocks (Corte Cosso). An enduro version of the production bike, the EI, was also offered.

For 1983, the customer motocrosser became the C2 with revised styling and the single shock rear suspension that had been pioneered on the works model. Gilera also built a 125cc (8ci) twin motocrosser in 1981, which gave a class-leading 36hp at 12,000rpm.

ENGINE: 122.75cc (7ci) 2s reed vertical single, 54x53.6mm, liquid-cooled
POWER: 32bhp at 10,000rpm
GEARBOX: 6-speed foot change
FINAL DRIVE: chain
WEIGHT: 85kg (187lb)
TOP SPEED: 140km/h (89mph)

The Gilera CI Cross and CI Enduro – the latter seen here – were essentially the same bike with some changes of detail. They were the creations of Dutch designer Jan Wittereen.

MOTO GUZZI 850 LE MANS III

Moto Guzzi's talent for designing 90-degree V-twin engines dates back to 1960, when the original was designed. Engineer Giulio Cesare Carcano was also responsible for the V8 Grand Prix racer. The air-cooled, in-line, V-twin, pushrod engine started out with 700cc (43ci) displacement and 45hp. The engine was designed in response to an Italian government specification for a new police motorcycle, and it won easily, providing the firm with a much-

needed new lease of life. The 1967 Moto Guzzi V7 with the original Carcano engine has been continuously developed into the 1200cc (73ci) 80hp versions offered at the time of writing

Six versions of the Le Mans have been produced, designated I, II, III, IV, V and V11 Le Mans. The I, II and III are 850cc (51ci), the IV and V are 1000cc (60ci) and the V11 Le Mans is 1064cc (64ci). The Mk III of 1982 is seen here.

(2006). Lino Tonti did a redesign of the motor for the 1971 Moto Guzzi V7 Sport, and this formed the basis of the 850cc (52ci), 1100cc (67ci) and 1200cc (73ci) Guzzi engines in use today.

In 1979, a small block version designed by engineer Lino Tonti was introduced as the V35. Further developments based on this design resulted in the 750 Breva and Nevada engines. It was quite radical, cutting the weight from the 249kg (548lb) of the contemporary 850 T3 to the 1175kg (385lb) of the V35.

The horsepower of the original V35 (35hp) was similar to that of other engines of comparable

displacement of the period, but the bigger versions developed later (V50, V65, V75) were rapidly outclassed by the development of water-cooled engines.

Horsepower was increased in the mid-1980s, when Guzzi created four-valve versions of the 'small block' series. Of these, the 650cc (40ci) and the 750cc (46ci) were rated at 60hp and 65hp respectively. The production of the four-valve 'small block' engines ended in the later 1980s.

The Le Mans was the logical development of the V7 Sport and its successors, the 750S (1974) and S3 (1975). It first appeared in 1976 with a claimed 71hp at

Seen here is the Moto Guzzi 1981 Model. Production of the Moto Guzzi Le Mans series continued until right up to the early 1990s.

7300rpm as Moto Guzzi's answer to the BMW R90S; in its later incarnation, it went head to head with the R100RS. The engine was reworked so that, despite a lower compression ratio, it delivered more power at a lower engine speed, while also managing to meet emissions requirements that the earlier machines could not.

The Le Mans 1000 followed in late 1984 with a 949cc (58ci), 88 x 72mm (3.4 x 2.8in) motor with big valves, big carburettors and a higher compression ratio, for a claimed 86hp at the crankshaft

and a claimed 225km/h (140mph) top speed. When it ceased production in the early 1990s, this model could justifiably settle into history as the last of the 1970s 'superbikes'.

ENGINE: 844cc (50ci) ohv transverse V-twin, 83x78mm, air-cooled
POWER: 76bhp at 6200rpm
GEARBOX: 5-speed foot change
FINAL DRIVE: shaft
WEIGHT: 206kg (453lb)
TOP SPEED: 210km/h (130mph)

BARIGO

Founded by Patrick Barigault at La Rochelle, on the west coast of France, Barigo is a small firm with a background in the French supermoto, a combination of road racing and motocross. In an industry associated with small motorcycle production, Barigo produced larger, high-quality machines for sale in niche markets. He bought in an Austrian Rotax unit and, at first, concentrated on

machines for enduro, desert raid and super motard events. The Rotax name was well established with off-road manufacturers. The 500cc (31ci), water-cooled, single-cylinder, four-stroke engine had twin overhead-camshafts and four valves fed by twin carburettors. It was soon enlarged to 598cc (36ci) and drove a five-speed gearbox.

Barigo added top-quality components within a light, strong

frame that offered good handling. This, combined with the tractable engine, made the machine an excellent choice for the longer distance events, such as the tough Paris–Dakar rally.

In 1992, Barigo produced the Supermotard roadster – basically a street legal version of the firm's competition machine with a 600cc (37ci), Rotax single-cylinder engine. It changed the wheels,

tyres and suspension, but kept the alloy frame, upside-down forks, large ground clearance and sump guard for the engine unit. In came better lights, indicators, cockpit fairing and mirrors, as well as a change in the styling. Barigo currently continues to make both models, easily able to update and incorporate alternatives to the standard specification in order to suit customer requirements.

The single-cylinder Barigo Rotax, seen here, was used as the basis for the 53hp 560GRS. Barigo has a reputation for high-quality machines.

GARELLI 125CC TWIN GP RACER

For five years, starting in 1982, the name Garelli was on the lips of every road racing enthusiast. In the first year, Garelli entered both the 50cc and 125cc classes, but it was the latter in which they were ultimately successful. In fact, Angel Nieto and Eugenio Lazzarini finished first and second in the championship title stakes, while Garelli took the constructors' championship.

For many years, the 125cc (8ci) models had been limited by the FIM, the sports governing body, to a twin-cylinder, six-speed formula. Garelli now modified this to

achieve 47hp from a twin-cylinder layout – an amazing result. The 124.7cc/7.6ci (44 x 41mm/ 1.7 x 1.6in) liquid-cooled disc-valve engine had first been conceived by the well-known two-stroke engineer Jorge Moller for the Minerelli company. Under that banner it won its first Grand Prix in 1978, ridden by Pier-Paolo Bianchi. By the time Garelli used the design, it featured six transfer and one exhaust port per cylinder, as well as a pair of 39mm (1.5in) Dell 'Orto magnesium-bodied carburettors. Other features of the 1982 Garelli 125 GP twin

included a duralumin monocoque frame with conventional twin Bitubo gas-filled rear shock absorbers, an aluminium swinging-arm, 32mm (1.2in) Marzocchi front forks with magnesium sliders and a mechanical anti-drive system. The ultra-low dry weight of only 78kg (172lb) was a factor of the tiny dimensions of the bike and the magnesium Campagnolo wheels with narrow-section 44cm (17in) tyres.

Following Nieto's 1982 success, Garelli went on to win the world title another four times. Then the FIM stepped in and ruined the

company's future competition chances by changing to a single-cylinder formula from the 1988 season onwards. Garelli did build a single, but this was never to repeat the glories of its older twin-cylinder brother.

ENGINE: 124.7cc (7.5ci) disc-valve 2s parallel twin, 44x41mm, liquid-cooled
POWER: 47bhp at 12,000rpm
GEARBOX: six-speed foot change
FINAL DRIVE: chain
WEIGHT: 78kg (172lb)
TOP SPEED: 233km/h (145mph)

HESKETH

The Hesketh range of motorcycles was the inspiration of Lord Hesketh, who had a background in F1 racing; his was the last private team to win a F1 Grand Prix, with James Hunt at the wheel. Lord Hesketh wanted to use the skills and facilities built up in that pursuit to greater effect, and a quality motorcycle was born. It was developed on the Easton Neston estate, his home. The prototype ran in the spring of 1980, fitted with a special Weslake engine commissioned for the Hesketh machine. After two years of intense development, it was announced that partners were being sought to help launch the manufacturing process. However, none were forthcoming, so Hesketh Motorcycles PLC was formed. In 1981–82, a modern purpose-built factory began to manufacture the bikes in Daventry. However, a lack of cash, start-up problems and a collapsing market forced it into receivership. It ceased production after manufacturing about 100 V1000 models for the home market.

However, the organization continued to exist in skeleton form in order to service machines already sold, and to build limited numbers of new machines. This was headed by Mick Broom, and in due course he took over the whole operation, which was still based at Easton Neston.

The mainstay of the operation was – and is – the V1000, an unfaired machine of classic looks and impeccable finish. About 200 were built in the first 18 years of production. The Vampire is the faired version and is somewhat rarer, about 50 being built in the same period. Also on the market is the Vortan, a long-stroke but still well oversquare 1100cc (67ci) version (95 x 78mm/3.7 x 3in) with a racing-style frame, and some 27kg (60lb) lighter. The original engine was entirely air-cooled, but later versions incorporated oil-cooling for the rear cylinder, along with programmable electronic ignition.

The Hesketh is, to a large extent, a bespoke motorcycle. For example, it is possible to customize the seat and suspension to suit a rider who is 152cm (5ft 2in) tall; anyone who is more than about 170cm (5ft 7in) should be able to handle the standard seat.

Launched in 1981, the all-British Hesketh V1000 featured Marzocchi suspension and Brembo brakes. Neither it, nor a faired tourer, the Hesketh Vampire, proved popular and they did not sell well.

MOTO MORINI 500 SEI V

ITALY 1982

Moto Morini was very much in evidence at the 1975 Milan Show, with two new designs on display: a 250cc (8ci) single and a 500cc (31ci) V-twin, both directly derived from the 3¹/₂ V-twin. *Moto Cycle* magazine was enthusiastic about it later, describing it as one of the prettiest bikes in the show. 'Pretty' was perhaps not the right word to describe this powerful beast, whose specification included a displacement of 478.6cc (29ci), bore and stroke of 69 x 64mm (2.7 x 2.5in), a compression ratio of 11.2:1 and a power output of 46hp at 7500rpm. The gearbox was a five-speeder and other details included: cast-alloy wheels, triple disc brakes and an ultra-lightweight, 15kg (33lb) dry sump.

The new single was half the capacity of the 500cc (31ci) at 239cc (15ci), and a maximum speed of 129km/h (80mph).

At the beginning of the 1980s, Morini introduced yet more versions of its modular theme, including a 239cc (15ci) V-twin and a 123cc (8ci) single. In 1981, most of the V-twins (except the standard 3¹/₂) were finished in a striking red paint job, black engine casings and exhausts, plus gold cast-alloy wheels. In 1982 came the Sei V, a six-speed version of the 500cc (31ci), in both Sport and Touring guises. The six-speed engine in the 500cc (31ci) had first been used in a factory-entered machine during the 1980 ISDT. Put into production as the Camel (called the Sahara in the UK), it was an

enduro-style trail bike, with leading axle, long-travel front forks and twin-shock rear suspension.

By 1985, the '500' (in trail guise only) had an improved cylinder-head layout. The valves were larger and were set further apart, the carburettor size had increased and the cylinders were bored out by a further 2mm (0.07in) to give 507cc (31ci). In standard form, it was good for 171km/h (107mph), an excellent performance for a dirt bike. It also sported monoshock rear suspension, which had been fitted on the 350cc (21ci) Kanguro dirt bike. However, despite this,

The Morini V twins were introduced in 1973 with the Strada, followed by the 350cc Sport in 1974, a 500cc Strada in 1978 and a 500cc Sport in 1979, which was updated in 1982 to the Sei-V, seen here.

the roadster 500 was only ever manufactured in twin-shock form. The 507cc (31ci) bike was marketed as the 501. Production of the definitive roadster 500, the Sei V, ceased in the mid-1980s. From then on, only custom and dirt-bike versions were offered.

ENGINE: 478.6cc (29ci) ohv 2v V-twin, 69x64mm, air-cooled
POWER: 46bhp at 7500rpm
GEARBOX: 6-speed foot change
FINAL DRIVE: chain
WEIGHT: 140kg (380lb)
TOP SPEED: 177km/h (110mph)

BUELL

USA 1983–PRESENT

Based in Milwaukee, this thriving company was started in 1983 by former racer Erik Buell, who had originally worked as a chassis engineer for Harley-Davidson. In 1981, after hearing of Barton, a small, British-based engineering firm that produced motorcycles, he bought its limited-production racer, powered by a water-cooled, 750cc (46ci), square-four, two-stroke engine. Unfortunately, the bike was poorly manufactured with cheap materials, and the engine was plagued with gremlins to the

point of being unmanageable. However, given his engineering background (and unwaning optimism), Buell felt that he could refine the weak points using his own designs. Slowly, as parts failed, he re-engineered them to increase reliability, and in many cases his modifications brought performance gains. The chassis was a different story, however – Buell deemed it a lost cause from the beginning and designed his own chassis from the ground up. Nonetheless, the engine often failed before completing a race.

Buell first raced a prototype of his bike, still using the mostly-stock Barton engine, in summer of 1982 at AMA National on the Pocono Speedway. He dubbed it the RW750 (RW standing for Road Warrior). During testing at Talladega, AL, the RW750 was clocked at a top speed of 286km/h (178mph). He raced in the 500cc-dominated Formula One class; the Barton engine was designed prior to 1978 and AMA rules forced it into this class. He found some success at the local club levels despite the grossly

overpowered, unrefined engine.

In 1982, Barton closed down and Buell was given the option to purchase the entire stock of spare engines and parts, all drawings and the rights to produce and sell the engine. Buell did so, but the shipment was so delayed that he missed the opportunity to make full use of this new equipment and knowledge for the upcoming 1983 racing season. This stalled the development of the engine to some extent.

The demise of the RW750 persuaded Bluell to design a bike

powered by a Harley-Davidson engine, and this emerged as the RR1000 Battletwin. All Buell's machines displayed an innovative approach to chassis design, particularly when compared to the conservative Harley-Davidsons. From the outset, the machines employed lightweight monoshock chassis with advanced suspension and braking components. Some 50 Buell-Harleys were produced between 1987 and 1988 with overhead-valve XR-1000 engines, before the focus switched to the new Sportster 1200cc (73ci) Evolution powerplant with the RR1200 model. Tuned versions of the same 1200cc (73ci) V-twin have powered all Buell models since. In 1989, following the modest success of the RR1200 (of which 65 were built), came the

first two-seater Buell, the RS1200. The RSS1200, a single-seat sports variant evolved two years later. By this time, inverted telescopic forks and large, efficient disc brakes had become the norm for a marque that was at last gaining credibility in the wider motorcycle community. By the end of 1992, Buell had built almost 450 motorcycles and brought its founder a solid reputation for engineering and design.

In February 1993, Harley-Davidson bought a 49 per cent stake in the Buell company. The merger gave Buell access to development funds and Harley-Davidson expertise, while offering Harley-Davidson a broader model range and a direct line into Buell's creative engineering. Since the merger, Buells have been marketed

in parallel with mainstream Harley machines, using engines made at the 'small powertrains' plant on Milwaukee's Capitol Drive. The current generation of Cyclone, Thunderbolt and Lightning Buell models was first launched in the USA in 1994 and have gradually been developing a good reputation, despite an embarrassing series of recalls in 1998–99. A 492cc (30ci), single-cylinder model, the Blast, was added in 2000. Buell have also taken yet another leaf out of the Harley-Davidson book by founding their own owner's club, BRAG – Buell Riders Adventure Group.

Despite their similar engines, Buells could scarcely be more different in style from Harleys. Buell does not build cruisers, or customs, or tourers in the ElectraGlide sense. Buells are

sports bikes, sports tourers or streetfighter machines – Harleys with attitude. This recipe has been very successful: the 25,000th Buell, a Cyclone M2, rolled off the production line during 2000.

Harley-Davidson bought complete control of Buell Motorcycle in 2003, and currently distributes all Buell motorcycles through selected Harley-Davidson dealerships. Erik Buell remains responsible for the engineering and design of the motorcycles that bear his name.

Belt drives, a Buell design feature, are an alternative to chain drives. Today's belts are made of cogged rubber and operate like metal chains, but do not require lubrication.

CAGIVA 500GP C9

ITALY 1983

Claudio and Gianfranco Castiglioni, directors of Cagiva, spent a good 15 years in the quest for their particular Holy Grail: to win the 500cc Road-Racing World Championship. The goal eluded them, but at least they had the satisfaction of seeing their rider,

Eddie Lawson, victorious for the first time during the 1992 Hungarian Grand Prix.

The following year, the brothers put everything into capturing the 500cc trophy. They were assisted by talents such as engine supremo Ezio Mascheroni and former

Aermacchi works rider Gilberto Milani, both key members of the Cagiva 500cc Race Development Squad. At this point, though, the money dried up.

The first Cagiva 500GP bike was, in fact, a modified Suzuki RG500 square four. This was raced

in 1978 by Marco Lucchinelli, before the brothers took over the Varese factory that summer. It was not until 1980 that a Cagiva-produced bike was ready to be entered for a competition.

The 500GP made its debut at the German Grand Prix in 1980

and was ridden by Cagiva's newest recruit, the 1979 World Championship Runner-up, Virginio Ferrari. The across-the-frame four was housed in a Nico Bakker chassis. For the 1981 season, a completely new engine was designed and built, and this was the first engine to be completely created in house.

Again it was an across-the-frame four, but its rotary-valves were located behind the cylinders and driven by a combination of bevel gears and toothed belts. It was not until the San Marino Grand Prix at Imola at the end of the season that its rider Ferrari finally qualified, but at last Cagiva had raced in a 500cc Grand Prix, and had managed to finish.

That winter, the development team produced a completely new bike, more in the mainstream of Grand Prix design, with a rotary-valve, square-four engine, featuring contra-rotating crankshafts.

Measuring 56 x 50.6mm (2.2 x 1.9in) – as on all Cagiva's 500 Grand Prix machines over the years – this bike delivered 124hp at 11,600 rpm.

By 1983, the square-four specification was coming together. With Ferrari back in the squad (he did not ride in 1982), the basis for a more serious Cagiva challenge in future years was mapped out.

ENGINE: 498.4cc (30ci) 2s square four, 56 x 50.6mm, liquid-cooled
POWER: 125 bhp at 11,200 rpm
GEARBOX: 6-speed foot change
FINAL DRIVE: chain
WEIGHT: 120kg (245lb)
TOP SPEED: 290km/h (180mph)

The 1983 Cagiva C9 500cc Grand Prix racer ridden by Virginio Ferrari. Cagiva failed for 15 years to win the 599cc World Championship.

HARLEY-DAVIDSON SOFTAIL EVO

USA 1984

In 1983, Harley-Davidson introduced its new Evo engine (Evo an abbreviation of evolution). This was an uprated version of the preceding Shovelhead. In fact, it was so uprated that it represented as big an advance over the Shovelhead as the latter had been over its ancestor, the Panhead. Essentially, it was an alloy-barrel version of the Shovelhead, with a lighter valve train and better breathing. It weighed a welcome 9kg (20lb)

less than the preceding all-iron engine. It reportedly delivered 10 per cent more power, but changing ways of calculating power outputs, plus federal and state emission controls, meant that all stated power outputs were suspect.

The Evo was considerably more reliable than its predecessor, and much more oil tight. Perhaps more important was the Softail frame, a bogus hard-tail with the suspension disguised so that the

machine looked like a pre-Duo Glide big Harley. So successful was this strategy that the Heritage Softail (1986) wrapped its Showa forks in huge shrouds for a 1940s Hydra-Glide look. Such cosmetic exercises added to the weight and gave no advantages in handling, but illustrated well the Harley-Davidson ethos.

ENGINE: 1340cc (80ci) ohv in-line V-twin 87.3x100.8mm, air cooled
POWER: 60bhp approx
GEARBOX: 5-speed foot change
FINAL DRIVE: belt
WEIGHT: 273kg (600lb) depending on model
TOP SPEED: 170km/h (105mph) approx

Right: The term 'softail' refers to motorcycles and bicycles that feature a moveable rear suspension system with springs or shock absorbers, but give the appearance of a hard-tail or rigid frame.

KAWASAKI GPZ900R NINJA

In 1984, Kawasaki set about developing a new motorcycle to succeed the well-tried GPZ1100. The new model was intended primarily for the US market, and to take advantage of the martial arts craze then gripping the country, Kawasaki called it the Ninja. A brand new engine design was used: the four cylinders set across the frame were liquid-cooled and closer together; the chain drive to

the twin overhead camshafts was taken from one end of the crankshaft; and the alternator was mounted behind the cylinders. There were 16 valves in the head and a balancer shaft in the crankcase, as the engine unit with its six-speed gearbox was a stressed member of the spine frame, eliminating the need for downtubes. The engine was very compact, and was actually only

25mm (1in) wider than the Honda V-4. Equipped with the latest forks at the front, and Uni-Trak at the rear, the Ninja rode on cast-alloy wheels with disc brakes and had a fairing in the GPZ style.

To achieve the best possible suspension, Kawasaki employed its automatic variable damping system for progressive compression damping, and a three-way adjustable anti-dive

An extremely popular machine, the Kawasaki Ninja was replaced in 1993, but was resurrected three years later.

system. The riding position was biased towards the sport rider, so there were some compromises that affected long-distance comfort. In 1984, the Ninja 900 was the quickest production motorcycle available. The big Ninja was one of the most successful models built by the firm and was later joined by similar machines of other sizes. The original was replaced in 1993, only to return for 1996 and 1997, due to popular demand.

ENGINE: 908cc (54ci) dohc 4v transverse four, 72.5x55mm, liquid-cooled
POWER: 115bhp at 9500rpm
GEARBOX: 6-speed foot change
FINAL DRIVE: chain
WEIGHT: 228kg (501lb)
TOP SPEED: 270km/h (160mph)

Kawasaki went to enormous lengths to create the best possible suspension for the Ninja, using automatic variable damping system.

YAMAHA YZR500

Although the Yamaha YZR500 was the dominant machine in the 500cc Grand Prix championships of the early 1980s, its track record went back to 1973, the year in which it won its World GP debut race. The date was 22 April 1973, and the place was the opening round of the GP series at the Paul Ricard circuit in France. For Yamaha, the race marked its first GP challenge in five years and its first ever in the 500cc class. On that day, Jarno Saarinen of Finland rode the first YZR500 to victory over the 20-lap, 116.2km (72-mile) course in a time of 45 minutes, 57 seconds, beating rival Phil Read on the MV Agusta four-stroke machine by a full 16 seconds. Kanaya followed in third place.

In the second round of the series at the Saltzburg circuit in Germany, Saarinen and Kanaya finished first and second, and in so doing heralded the start of a new era in GP racing.

After winning the manufacturers' championship in 1974, Yamaha competed in GP racing for a further 30 years, using its evolving YZR500 factory machines. During this period, the YZR500 chalked up an enviable record of 115 wins from 20 riders, and a total of 11 rider championship titles and nine manufacturers' titles.

The evolution of the YZR500 has been marked by numerous technological milestones, some of them, like the rear-exhaust system, the consequence of environmental concerns. Other innovations included the Deltabox frame, which contributed to the machine's outstanding handling characteristics, and the electronic-control suspension.

The YZR500 provided the basis for the ROC and Harris-framed privateer V-fours of more recent years. Wayne Rainey took over from Eddie Lawson to win three cups for Yamaha, while Frenchman Christian Sarron triumphed in the 250cc World Championship on Yamaha's TZ twin in 1984. Kenny Roberts captured world titles riding a Yamaha and, more recently, as a team manager.

The Japanese factory's success with 500cc (31ci) V-fours took off with Roberts' disc-valve OW61 of 1982. The YZR, with its crankcase reed-valve induction system, was introduced as the OW81 model in 1984. Its engine used twin crankshafts that were geared together, a layout that had also been adopted by Suzuki and Cagiva, which left only Honda's NSR as a true V-four.

The YZR's power output rose gradually over the years to top 180hp from the most recent 'big bang' unit. Chassis layout remained typical of a Grand Prix 500, based on a thick, twin-beam aluminium frame, with suspension provided by Ohlins, the Swedish specialist firm owned by Yamaha. The YZR may not always have been the fastest bike, but it was tractable and a good all-rounder.

ENGINE: 498cc (30ci) 80-degree reed-valve two-stroke V-four, 56x50.6mm, water-cooled
POWER: 165bhp at 12,500rpm
GEARBOX: 6-speed, foot change
FINAL DRIVE: chain
WEIGHT: 130kg (287lb)
TOP SPEED: 306km/h (190mph)

The Yamaha YZR500 factory machine won its World GP debut race in April 1973 at the French GP. Yamaha then continued to compete in GP racing for 30 years with its YZR500 series.

CHAPTER EIGHT

THE ERA OF THE POWER BIKES

1985–1994

By the middle 1980s, the Japanese hegemony in motorcycling was almost complete. Virtually every area of motorcycling was dominated by the big four firms, and for good reason. In supersports machines, the 1985 Suzuki GSX-R750 set the standards for a 'race-replica' machine, with track-ready chassis and high-output engine. Lightweight sportsbikes like Yamaha's RD350YPVS, Suzuki's RG250 and Kawasaki's KR-1 offered superb handling and big-bike performance in a pocket-sized package.

Full aerodynamic fairings became the norm for mainstream machinery, rather than the preserve of exotica, and frame, suspension, brake and tire technology all began the long-prayed-for catchup with engine power outputs. Whether it was

commuting, touring, trail riding or custom cruising, Japanese firms could meet the biking needs of consumers worldwide better, cheaper and more reliably than anyone else.

Development accelerated in the early 1990s though, with the appearance of two key machines. Honda's CBR900RR FireBlade, and Ducati's 916. The Japanese machine both dominated the present and defined the future: the CBR had class-matching power with unheard-of low weight, and began the move towards controllable full-bore sportsbikes with compact motors and integrated chassis designs. The 916, in turn, guaranteed the future of Ducati, and maintained the Italian bike industry's reputation with its regular World SuperBike race wins, glorious design and superb performance.

Left: The Bimota Tesi had a radical specification for its time, with a Honda V4 engine and a carbon-fibre chassis. Consequently, the Tesi first appeared as a prototype in the early 1980s, but did not go into production until 1990.

SUZUKI GSX-R750

According to some enthusiasts, the racing world will forever be divided into two time periods: before the Suzuki GSX-R750 and after. Suzuki's seminal GSX-R750 is an evergreen favourite with bikers across the world. When launched in 1985, it almost single-handedly kick-started the craze for race-replica machines. Since then, the bike has been one of the leading benchmarks for performance and style, as well as character, in the sports bike class. The GSX-R has stayed in production in its many different forms since 1985 and has also had an enviable race record. Since the bike's launch, more than 40,000 have been sold worldwide.

The GSX-R750 – with the emphasis definitely on the R for 'Race' – was introduced in 1985. It promptly generated a generation of rival bikes that attempted –unsuccessfully – to emulate it. Many riders wish to emulate their racing heroes to a certain extent, and the GSX-R750 was a close approximation of the works endurance bikes from the early 1980s; these had been highly successful under team leader Hervé Moineau. Incredibly fast, with handling to match, the GSX-R750 outperformed all other mass-produced machines, thanks to a specification orientated for high-speed riding.

The powerplant was the 16-valve, oil-cooled, twin-cam four, which had a magnesium cam-cover and developed 100hp at 10,500rpm. It delivered most of its power above 7000rpm, giving a theoretical top speed of 233km/h (145mph). The motor was housed in a new aluminium perimeter frame, which was half the weight of the old GSX750, and the front end consisted of a pair of stout 41mm (1.6in) diameter forks, containing a pair of drilled disc brakes. Much of the bike was concealed by a race-derived fairing, fronted by a pair of headlights and emblazoned with the Suzuki nomenclature.

The road-going machine was equipped with a comfortable pillion saddle, and the four-into-one perforated silencer was set lower than the racer's.

Over the succeeding years, the chassis was refined to give the GSX-R750 even better handling, and in 1992 it was fitted with a water-cooled 116hp engine in a stiffer frame with upside-down forks and sleeker fairings. Although there were few components in common with the original model, the GSX-R750 remained essentially the same in spirit.

ENGINE: 749cc (44.5ci) 16-valve dohc transverse four, 70x48.7mm, oil-cooled (later water)
POWER: 100bhp at 10,500rpm
GEARBOX: 5-speed foot change
FINAL DRIVE: chain
WEIGHT: 176kg (388lb)
TOP SPEED: 233km/h (145mph)

Right: Combining responsive torque and the comprehensive power band of a heavyweight motorcycle with the compact size and easier responsive handling of a middleweight, the Suzuki GSXR750 motorcycle is the leader of its class.

Above: Narrower, lighter and more powerful, the beautiful GSX R750 motorcycle gives the rider high-performance technology in a more aerodynamic, ultra-lightweight frame of aluminium-alloy castings.

JAWA SPEEDWAY MODEL 897

CZECHOSLOVAKIA 1986

The Jawa 897 is a four-valve, air-cooled SOHC motor with a displacement of 493cc (29.5ci). Both the 896 and 897 models have forked rocker arms and traversing wheels rolling on cams of a central camshaft.

Based in the Czech Republic, Jawa takes its name from the initial letters of the name of its founder, Janacek, and of Wanderer motorcycles, first produced in 1929. Historically, Jawa has been very active in racing, and the company sustained a presence in the World Championship until the mid-1960s, putting in performances that were respectable given the fact that it was usually operating within a restricted budget. In Motocross, the firm built an impressive palmares before its four-stroke engines became superseded by two-stroke engines. In Speedway racing, dirt-track racing and ice racing where four-stroke engines were still at an advantage, the firm remained a dominant force, scoring a number of victories that remains unbeaten today. Jawa

Speedway racing motorcycles are now a separate company.

The first Jawa speedway engine was a development of the earlier Eso design, Jawa having absorbed that company during the late 1960s. The engine was a 496cc/30ci (85 x 87mm/ 3.3 x 3.4in), single-overhead-cam, four-valve single with a vertical alloy cylinder barrel and head. A forged two-ring piston was supported by a duralumin, alloy-forged connecting rod, with a pressed-in bronze bush for the gudgeon pin, and a hardened-steel ring for the big-end bearing. The flywheels themselves were specially hardened, which allowed for repeated crankpin replacement. The camshaft was driven by a single row chain. Four different camshafts of different lifts were available to enable riders to

choose the power curve best suited to their particular requirements. Ignition was courtesy of a PAL magneto with a Bosch ignition coil, while carburation was taken care of by an Italian 34mm (1.25in) Dell 'Orto instrument, with a K & N air filter. The carburettor was mounted flexibly; this was to avoid vibration, which could cause loss of performance.

Lubrication was via a dual pump, and the quantity of lubricant could be checked and adjusted. A castor-based oil was recommended, and this was stored in the frame's top tube and drawn down to lubricate the engine components. The used oil then fed to a waste oil tank and was drained after one or two races.

By the mid-1980s, the Czech company had risen to be the

largest producer in the world of both engines and complete motorcycles for speedway and long-track racing events; and 95 per cent of this production was exported around the globe.

ENGINE: 496cc (30ci) sohc V-four single, 85x87mm, air-cooled
POWER: 69bhp at 8800rpm
GEARBOX: none
FINAL DRIVE: chain
WEIGHT: 82kg (181lb)
TOP SPEED: 129km/h (80mph)

YAMAHA FJ1200

The FJ1200's immediate predecessor was the FJ1100, a popular machine that appeared in 1984 and proved extremely popular, competing well against its rivals in the sport-touring motorcycle class. This class is characterized by retaining sportiness while integrating street-friendly ride characteristics, such as greater manoeuvrability, and factors to promote endurance riding, such as a more upright seating configuration that reduces back strain on long trips. Emphasis is placed on a balance of utility and sport, rather than pure performance orientation.

Thanks to the FJ1100's popularity, Yamaha decided in 1986 to boost performance and add upgraded suspension and other components. The result was the FJ1200. Produced virtually the same from 1986 to 1989, a slight update of the bodywork

kept the model line current through 1993, when Yamaha discontinued the FJ. The bike's main competitors during its production years were mainly the BMW's K100RS, Suzuki's 1100 Katana and Kawasaki's ZX-10.

The FJ1200 possessed all of the FJ1100's attributes, plus a huge seat, big tank, half-fairing and belly pan, as well as pulling ability from low and medium revs. In road tests, it frequently outstripped rivals such as the Kawasaki GPZ1100, BMW K1100 and Triumph Trophy 1200. It handled better than the Kawasaki, was faster than the BMW and was less ponderous than the Triumph. Power for the FJ1200 came from a double overhead-cam, air-cooled, in-line, transverse, four-cylinder engine, canted over for optimum porting and a better centre of gravity. This unit gained a reputation for being extremely

hardy, and FJ Owners' Club members cited bikes that had clocked up 193,121km (120,000 miles) for only a routine servicing. Launched in 1986, the big Yamaha was quite at home carrying panniers as well as other luggage. It was no beauty, but it was exceedingly practical.

Although rather long in the tooth by today's technological standards, it still has merit in several areas, especially in terms of handling and ride comfort. The 1200cc (73ci), four-cylinder, 16-valve, DOHC engine is a reliable workhorse geared to provide ample torque even low in the RPM range. The top speed on a stock bike is 257km/h (160mph), but its virtues shine most brightly in the 129–145km/h (80–90mph) range,

where a light twist of the throttle can propel the rider past other traffic even in top gear, largely owing to that ample torque. Rider and passenger are treated well by the wide and comfortable seat, and the frame and rider positioning are suited even to tall riders. Because of the long lifespan of this model, with relatively few changes, parts are plentiful and fan groups are numerous.

ENGINE: 1188cc (71ci), dohc four-cylinder, air-cooled
POWER: 125bhp
GEARBOX: 5-speed foot change
FINAL DRIVE: chain
WEIGHT: 238kg (525lb)
TOP SPEED: 238km/h (148mph)

In 1986, Yamaha decided to boost performance of its FJ 1100 and add upgraded suspension and other components. The result was the FJ1200, which, with updates, was produced until 1993.

CCM

Passionate motorcyclists throughout the world, and especially those with a keen interest in Clews Competition Motorcycles – or, as they are more commonly known, CCM – were delighted when the news broke that the company was back in the hands of its original owner.

Maintaining its heritage as one of Britain's most important motorcycle manufacturers, the famous CCM brand continues to keep its place in two-wheel history some 35 years after it was first conceived. Back in the 1970s, the Bolton-based factory produced some of its most winning machinery. With the company headed by its founder Alan Clews, those original bikes enjoyed some of the biggest successes ever, both on the track and off it, as results were matched by sales.

Clews had a background of success in scrambles, and in 1971 he bought a van-load of parts from the BSA competition shop when it closed. These formed the basis of the first batch of machines, then called the Clews Stroka. This performed well, and riders were soon demanding the bike. In May 1972, the first CCM machines were produced, based on the BSA B50 single-cylinder engine unit. These were either 499cc (30ci), or enlarged to 608cc (37ci), and had a cylinder with the fins part cut away, as well as other changes. These big four-strokes were successful right through the 1970s and, late in that decade, were joined by a 345cc (21ci) trials model that used an engine based on, and developed from, the BSA B40. Later came two-stroke scramblers using Italian Hiro

engine units of 125cc (8ci) and 250cc (15ci).

As a result of financial pressures, CCM was taken over by Armstrong in 1980 and. The machines kept the CCM name for 1981, but by the next year they were labelled Armstrong CCM. At that time, the engine unit was changed to the Austrian Rotax four-stroke single because Armstrong had links with that firm, and the model continued in this form for some years. However, in 1987, Alan Clews was able to buy his old firm back, and over the next two years he built it up by selling spares and Armstrong machines against outstanding orders. CCM returned to the competition field in 1989 with the range still based on Rotax engines. For trials, there was a two-stroke engine but the

motocross models used the big four-stroke single with a choice of 500cc (30ci), 560cc (34ci) or 590cc (36ci).

In 1997, the company added a super moto for use on the road. Based on the motocross machine, it used the metric 598cc (36ci) Rotax four-valve engine in a modern package to offer an excellent, if expensive, model. At the same time, the motocross model was available either in Enduro or Rallye Raid trim, all with the 560cc Rotax, so all the CCM machines had a common base.

Maintaining its heritage as one of Britain's most important bike manufacturers, the CCM brand keeps its place in two-wheel history thirty-five years after it was first conceived.

HONDA CBR600F

Nobody could fail to call the Honda CBR600F a success story. Introduced in 1987, it soon became established as a true multi-role bike, equally at home with commuting, touring and scratching. It built up a rapid reputation for being rider friendly, as well as being comfortable and practical. It proved to be no slouch on the race circuit, either, notching up more Supersport 600 titles by 2000 than any middleweight rival. It struck the right balance for most riders between speed, comfort and practicality, with enough performance boosts over the years to retain a sporting edge, from 83hp with the H-model up to 108hp and 258km/h (160mph). This ranking was called into question in 2000 by Yamaha's R6 and Triumph's T955.

During two decades of evolution, Honda made a number of radical changes to the CBR600F's overall configuration, introducing first one and then another additional model to the range. First came the mechanically identical but dynamically slightly more focused CBR600F Sport, followed by the rather different CBR600RR. The styling of the innovative fairings altered as the bike matured, although the colour scheme, which was changed almost on an annual basis, was always focused on Japanese race-replica imagery.

The year 1991 saw a major change in chassis design, when a smaller, twin-spar steel frame was provided, along with other refinements that included a four-into-one exhaust system. For 1999, a lightweight twin-spar aluminium-beam frame was introduced to enclose the engine, and the swinging-arm pivoted directly on the engine casings. The result was a stronger, lighter chassis that rewarded the rider with masses of feedback. The engine was also 3kg (6lb 9oz) lighter and power was up too. New machines that year also got

The most popular motorcycle in the 600cc Supersport class, the versatile CBR600F provides the cutting-edge power and performance of a racing bike.

a re-designed, direct air-induction system that fed the 36.5mm (1.4in) flat-side carburettors.

ENGINE: 599cc (36ci) dohc in-line transverse four, water-cooled
POWER: 99bhp at 12,000rpm
GEARBOX: 6-speed, foot change
FINAL DRIVE: chain
WEIGHT: 185kg (408lb)
TOP SPEED: 258km/h (160mph)

DUCATI 851

In 1983, Ducati was purchased by Claudio and Gianfranco Castiglioni and became part of the Cagiva Group. With this change of management, the group was in the hands of two great bike and racing fans, who brought a new lease of life to the company, much personal enthusiasm and a great deal of badly needed funding. For some 30 years prior to this takeover, chief designer Fabio Taglioni had been the talent that was Ducati's driving force. He was responsible for a truly vast array of bikes: singles, twins and even, occasionally, four-cylinder machines for both road and track. However, Taglioni chose largely to ignore the development

potential inherent in four-valve cylinder heads.

This omission was more than rectified by Taglioni's successor, Massimo Bordi. The leap ahead began with the appearance of the first prototype of Ducati's liquid-cooled, double overhead-camshaft, fuel-injected, four-valves-per-cylinder V-twin, which made its debut at the 1986 French Bol d'Or 24-hour endurance race.

The vital funds injected into Ducati by the Castoglioni brothers made it possible to develop a new family of bikes. The production model of the 851cc/52ci (92 x 64mm/3.6 x 2.5in) Superbike was unveiled to the public at the Milan Show in November 1987. The Superbikes went on sale early the following year in both Strada street and Kit supersport variants. A total of 500 examples were offered, named the Tricolore after the green, red and white colour scheme.

In 1988, Marco Lucchinelli won the first-ever round of the World Super Bike WSB on a racing version of the 851 at Donington Park, England. Shortly after, the factory built a racer for the general public, the first machines going on sale in 1990. Like Lucchinelli's works' machine, they displaced 888cc/54ci (94 x 64 mm/3.7 x 2.5in).

Frenchman Raymond Roche, aboard another factory-entered machine, won Ducati's first WSB title in 1990. The 851 series was finally discontinued at the end of 1993, to be replaced by the new 916.

ENGINE: 851cc (51ci) dohc, Desmo, 4v, V-twin, 92x64mm, liquid-cooled
POWER:
Strada – 88bhp at 9250rpm
Kit – 100bhp at 10,500rpm
Racing – 888cc (53ci) 120bhp at 11,500rpm
GEARBOX: 6-speed foot change
FINAL DRIVE: chain
WEIGHT: n/a
TOP SPEED:
Strada – 241 km/h (150mph)
Kit – 254km/h (158mph)
Racing – 273km/h (170mph)

Left and below: Prior to the 851, Ducati had relied on a simple, air-cooled, two-valve engine. Massimo Bordi, one of Ducati's engineers, provided a solution in the 851cc (51ci) engine, which had a cylinder head designed with the help of UK engine specialists Cosworth, four valves per cylinder, electronic fuel injection and liquid-cooling. The 851 engine also used Ducati's desmodromic valve-actuation system, meaning valve control was assured even at high rpm.

GILERA NUOVO SATURNO

ITALY 1988

Left: The all-new Saturno model was a lightweight, sporting 500cc (30ci) single with all the attributes of a modern machine. Right: The 1989 Model Nuevo Saturno was one of the new Gilera models released by Piaggio in the late 1980s, trading on the sporting reputation established by Gilera.

First revealed to the public at the 1987 Milan Show, the Gilera Nuovo Saturno (New Saturn) was originally aimed at the Japanese market, but eventually sold throughout the world. It was a classic sports roadster using modern technology. Very much a joint Italian–Japanese project, it was the work of Arcore engineer Sandro Colombo, and the Japanese technician N Hagiwara. Re-inventing the classic Saturno big single in a modern, user-friendly guise, the duo used the 492cc (30ci) Dakota engine to create a compact café racer. Weighing in at 135kg (296lb), the Nuovo Saturno had a purpose-built trellis steel-tube frame and an aluminium swinging-arm with eccentric adjustment for the final drive chain.

The Nuovo Saturno was initially commissioned by the Japanese trading company, C Itoh. After its debut at Milan, the prototype was displayed by Itoh at the Mega Show in Tokyo in December 1987, where critics commented favourably on the high quality of its component parts: the footrests, rear brake and gear-change levers were in aluminium, as was the kick-start lever.

The 40mm (1.75in) front forks had 120mm (4.5in) of travel and were of conventional layout. The rear end was taken care of by an adjustable racing-type single shock absorber, with 130mm (5in) of travel. Other details of the specification included a half-fairing, clip-ons, rear-set foot controls, a single race-type, saddle and a hi-level black exhaust system, which exited into a single silencer.

The engine literally hung in the frame and was readily accessible. Producing 45hp (crank) and 36.5hp (rear wheel), the Gilera single could achieve 178.5km/h (111mph). It was sold in other markets besides Japan and Italy, including Great Britain.

ENGINE: 492cc (30ci) dohc 4v vertical single, 92x74mm, liquid-cooled
POWER: 45bhp (crank)
GEARBOX: 5-speed foot change
FINAL DRIVE: chain
WEIGHT: 140kg (308lb)
TOP SPEED: 178.5km/h (111mph)

In 1992 Gilera returned to the Grand Prix arena and Piaggio continues to produce small-displacement motorcycles with the Gilera name.

NORTON COMMANDER ROTARY

ENGLAND 1988–1992

From 1974 to 1977, Hercules produced a limited number of motorcycles powered by Wankel rotary engines. The tooling was later used by Norton to produce the Norton Commander model in the 1980s. The best-known example of a Wankel-powered motorcycle,

however, was the Suzuki RE5, produced in 1975 and 1976. This 500cc (31ci) (actual) displacement motorcycle could have been a great touring bike except for the poor fuel mileage of 32–36 mpg.

In the Wankel engine, the four strokes of a typical Otto cycle

engine are arranged sequentially around an oval, unlike the reciprocating motion of a piston engine. In the basic single-rotor Wankel engine, a single oval (technically an epitrochoid) housing surrounds a three-sided rotor that turns and moves within

the housing. The sides of the rotor seal against the sides of the housing, and the corners of the rotor seal against the inner periphery of the housing, dividing it into three combustion chambers. As the rotor turns, its motion and the shape of the housing cause

Seen here is the 1988 Model of the Norton Commando Classic. The last-ever Norton racer achieved victory at the Senior in 1992, bringing a proud record of achievement to a close.

each side of the rotor to get closer and farther from the wall of the housing, compressing and expanding the combustion chamber similarly to the 'strokes' in a reciprocating engine.

The history of the last Norton – one of the most famous – is unexpected. Research was initiated by BSA in 1969 and passed to NVT in 1973, who bought the firm. By 1983, it had been developed – almost by accident – into a workable, air-cooled police bike, the Interpol II. It then passed on again to a new company under Philippe Le Roux in 1987, in whose charge it was converted to liquid-cooling for the Commander in the spring of 1988.

Further development led to a racing version giving over 145hp at 10,000rpm (and 304km/h, 189mph). It finally died, only a short time after Norton's last victory at the Senior in 1992.

And that is how Nortons should be remembered: champions at the first ever Isle of Man TT in 1907, and winners in the Senior in 1924, 1926, 1927, 1931, 1932, 1933, 1934, 1936, 1937, 1938, 1947, 1948, 1949, 1950, 1951, 1952, 1953, 1954, 1961, and 1992, the last with their last-ever racer. And that tally does not include further victories, which include – on the Isle of Man alone – the Juniors, the sidecars, the GPs and the Formula 750s. Overall, not too bad a record.

ENGINE: 588cc (35ci) Wankel twin-rotor, liquid-cooled
POWER: 85bhp at 9000rpm
GEARBOX: 5-speed foot change
FINAL DRIVE: chain
WEIGHT: n/a
TOP SPEED: 200km/h (125mph) est.

BMW K1

In 1990, BMW astonished the motorcycling world by demonstrating its latest technology in the revolutionary K1, which featured anti-lock brakes. Named motorcycle of the year by *Motorcyclist* magazine, the model came in avant-garde bodywork with only two possible paint schemes: red and yellow, or blue and yellow. (The yellow driveshaft and special Antera wheels are stock.) The most aerodynamic, mass-produced bike in history, the K1 can reach a top speed of 250km/h (155mph) and run 0–96km/h (0–60mph) in 3.3 seconds with 100 hp. Six thousand K1 bikes were built between 1989 and 1993, with approximately 600 being imported into North America between 1990 and 1993.

The K1 was a long way removed from the BMWs that achieved great popularity in 1960. Very fast, and extremely attractive with its blue bodywork and vivid yellow graphics, it was criticized by some as too big and too heavy to be a true sports bike, but it seems obvious that it was never ridden to its limits by its critics.

The K1 was derived from the original 'brick' of 1983, which had 90hp from the same capacity. The longitudinally mounted straight four was unusual enough. The

Above: In its heyday, the BMW K1 turned heads, because no one had seen such a sleek design before.

Below: The K1 was criticized by some for being too big and too heavy to be a true sports bike.

designers fitted the engine on its side, with the crankshaft on one side and the overhead-cams on the other. This was a master-stroke, though the decision to do this may have been influenced as much by the desire to have a layout that was unique to BMW as any other practical consideration.

The 'brick' was made in plain unfaired guise (K100), with a touring fairing (K100RT) and with a sports fairing (K100RS). The latter could top 225km/h (140mph), and the unfaired K100 was at least as fast as the R100RS. In 1985, a 741cc (45ci) triple was introduced, naked like the K75 or

with a miniature fairing like the K75S. With 74hp and balance shafts to disguise the inevitable vibration that resulted from sawing off one cylinder, it was a nice bike but never really caught on, and was eventually dropped.

The full-sized 'brick' was steadily improved to eliminate a number of faults that were apparent even before it was introduced. Early models produced large volumes of smoke when started, and the petrol tank could get too hot to touch as a result of heat transfer from the cooling system. The four-into-one exhaust was justly decried as ugly, and yellowed with use. There were,

however, many excellent features; the sight glass to check oil levels was one.

The 1987 K100LT was a 'loaded' tourer with ABS brakes; in 1992, the K1100RT and RS appeared with 1092cc (67ci); and the 1997 K1200RS (actually 1171cc/71ci, 75 x 70.5mm/3 x 2.7in) decided to disregard the voluntary 100hp limit that every other manufacturer was also ignoring. It boasted 130hp, a six-speed gearbox and a top speed that few had the nerve to explore. In many ways, it was a more

practical version of the K1, though (as so often with BMWs) there were already faster motorcycles on the road. The K1200LT was the five-speed, 98hp tourer.

ENGINE: 987cc (59ci) dohc 16-valve in-line longitudinal four, 67x70mm, liquid-cooled
POWER: 100bhp at 8000rpm
GEARBOX: 5-speed foot change
FINAL DRIVE: Kardan shaft
WEIGHT: 234kg (515lb)
TOP SPEED: 233km/h (145mph)

Just as attractive in pillar-box red as in its original blue, the K1 has been called the most innovative, exciting bike of the past 50 years.

AMERICAN IRONHORSE

The American IronHorse Motorcycle Company is the nation's largest builder of custom-ordered and -designed touring bikers and performance cruisers.

The machines are clearly inspired by the Harley-Davidson style, with 1573cc (96ci) S & S engines as standard, and 1750cc (107ci) and 1850cc (113ci) available.

However, the products of American IronHorse of Fort Worth, Texas also have interesting features that set them apart – both from the Harleys and from one another. In the case of the IronHorse, this included torsion bar rear suspension, and extreme amounts of plating: brake rotors are not usually candidates for chromium treatment.

Although front and rear wheels were standard 46cm (18in) sizes, an alternative 53cm (21in) front wheel was an available option.

These are macho bikes targeted at macho riders, as the names of the six models revealed at the turn of the century suggest. Slammer, Stalker, Outlaw, Thunder, Classic and Bandit are appellations that give a clear indication of the intended market, though style and weight, rather than technical differences, are what separate the models.

The Slammer and the Classic both weigh an impressive 268kg (590lb), but the Bandit, with its massive mudguards and lockable hard panniers, weighs an enormous 351kg (750lb).

Since the maximum permitted gross vehicle weight for each bike is 500kg (1100lb), this leaves only 159–232kg (350–510lb) for fuel, rider, passenger and luggage. Smaller fuel tanks were the solution to the weight problem, but limited the range to 240km (150 miles).

Above: Stripped down, stylistically the Ironhorse is one of the most distinctive bikes around.

Left: The Ironhorse logo was an attractive pull for the biker fraternity in the United States and elsewhere.

Far left: Although inspired by Harley-Davidson designs, the American Ironhorse machines had many features that set them apart, from both Harleys and from one another. This picture shows the huge Slammer model.

BIG BRUTE

There are a lot of V8 bikes on the market, but the Big Brute may fairly be described as unique. Hitherto, the usual way to produce a bike of this type was to insert large engines into Norton Wideline Featherbed frames. API Racing Inc, the Ontario-based firm, now found a much better alternative – namely to build a motorcycle around a Chevrolet V8. This is the premise upon which the Big Brute was founded.

The company made its name by modifiying Chevrolet engines for dragsters and street rods before it went into the motorcycle business.

The all-aluminium ZZ4 has radical cams, big valves, a 10:1 compression ratio, trick crankshaft and pistons to produce 355hp at 5250rpm from a normally aspirated 5.7l (348ci)

engine. Various kinds of supercharged motors were also available, as were bigger engines, up to 8.25l (503ci).

At 477kg (1050lb), the V8 Big Brute really does live up to its name. Even the 'baby' V6, producing a mere 210hp in its normally aspirated form and weighing only 448kg (985lb), is over twice the weight of a 'normal' motorcycle.

The two-speed automatic transmission is all that anyone could reasonably ask for with so much power on tap, and the Avon 230 38cm x 20cm (15 x 8in) round-section rear tyre means there is some chance of being able to steer round corners, though the manufacturers recommend a square-section tyre for maximum traction, especially with the V8.

The promotional literature issued by the firm tends to concentrate on the Big Brute's appearance rather than its performance, whose good points include nimble handling, light weight and general practicality. Available information on the machine's performance (and even its specification) is sometimes conflicting. For instance, the 'fat bob' tanks are listed variously as 23l (6 US gallons) and 26.5l (7 US gallons).

However, it is not surprising to find such conflicting information for a custom machine that can be ridden as anything from a dragster to a tourer.

Big Brute is, in effect, a drag bike that has been converted to street-legal form. Despite its enormous size, the machine is surprisingly easy to ride.

Seat height may be specified as either 66cm or 71cm (26in or 28in), and ground clearance under the frame is specified as 13cm (7in). Very large twin discs at the front, and a single disk at the rear, mean that it stops as well as goes.

The machine is marketed primarily as a 'cruiser', which for this bike's purposes is probably best defined as a machine that draws admiring glances whether it is moving or not; that has more power than its riders could ever use; and which is not primarily intended as a means of transport.

From an engineering point of view, it is one of the more convincing car-engined V8s. However, due to its size and sheer power, the Big Brute is still a long way from the mainstream motorcycling market.

BIG DOG

Big Dog Motorcycles started production in 1994 and quickly rose to be the largest manufacturer of custom motorcycles in the world, the leading builder of chopper-style bikes and the number two American V-twin company. Like a number of other American manufacturers producing Harley-Davidson lookalikes, Big Dog found that its early fortunes were founded on the failure of Harley-Davidson to meet the burgeoning demand of the early 1990s. Countless 'performance' and 'special' parts were already available for making these machines go faster or turn corners better, or look different, or give a more comfortable ride – and it was easy to start assembling whole bikes from scratch. Big Dog quickly found that they could produce their own designs, while still using an outmoded 45-degree V-twin. The 1750cc (107ci) engines come from S & S and TP Engineering, with Big Dog rocker-boxes, lifter blocks and cam covers. Other components are optional, such as a TP Engineering/Andrews gearbox with oil-bath primary chain drive, S & S carburettor, Works Performance shock absorbers, Performance Machine brake callipers, or Big Dog's own 40cm (16in) wheels, front forks and various cycle parts. As with most of its competitors, Big Dog places great stress on its paint facilities, and on the fact that you can have any colour or design that you want.

In the world of production custom choppers, Big Dog Motorcycles has captured a large slice of the market. Big Dog started building cycles in 1994 and has since been blazing a trail with more models.

There are also a number of clever touches, such as an electronic attachment that flashes the brakelight three times when you first brake, the better to attract the attention of the person behind you.

The Big Dog Vintage Sport, with its rubber-mounted engine, is representative of the six models (the others are Wolf, Bulldog, ProSport, Husky and Pitbull) and weighs an impressive 260kg (615lb) dry. Rather surprisingly, no mention is made in the manufacturers' specifications of the actual power output of the engine with its slightly under-square 108 x 101mm (4.2 x 3.9in)

bore and stroke and 9.6:1 compression ratio. Presumably, like a Rolls Royce, the answer is 'sufficient'; and equally presumably, it is sufficient because large engines can be tuned to produce a lot of power without being particularly stressed. The low seat height and footboards emphasize the bike's low-speed appeal, and although reviews refer to a three-digit top speed, they also talk about 113–130km/h (70–80mph) cruising.

To sum up, the Big Dog is very much an all-American machine, appealing to enthusiasts of the Harley-Davidson.

BIMOTA TESI

ITALY 1990

Bimota, the legendary Italian chassis specialist whose base is at Rimini, went bust in 2000 following the disastrous failure of its then latest product, an ambitious two-stroke 'clean-burning' 500cc (31ci) sports bike. Today, resurrected and under new management, it is marketing the latest version of its famous Bimota Tesi, the 2D.

The Tesi (Thesis) was first revealed in prototype form at the 1982 Milan Show, and appeared on the race track in 1984. The specification was extremely radical, which had been a hallmark of Bimota throughout the company's colourful history. Early versions used Honda V4 power units fitted in carbon-fibre frames – cutting-edge technology at a time when even Formula One racing cars were not yet using carbon-fibre chassis. The steering on the early Tesi was controlled by hydraulics. By the time the Tesi went into production in 1990, the chassis medium had switched to

aluminium alloy, and consisted of a pair of machined plates bolted around the top half of a tuned 904cc (55ci), fuel-injected, eight-valve Ducati V-twin engine. Above this was a subframe composed of small-diameter tubing, which served to support the fuel tank, seat, fairings and handlebar pivot.

With its curious, stripped-down appearance and aluminium swing-arms jutting out at both front and rear, the Tesi looked either like some giant mechanical insect or a part-finished project bike. The double-sided rear unit looked conventional enough, containing an eccentric chain adjuster on the right-hand side, but the front one gave the Tesi a strange appearance. The front wheel rotated around a large-diameter hollow hub, which contained a spindle attached to the swing-arm at either side. At the centre of the spindle was a vertical pin, which was attached to the hub by bearings that provided steering movement, and a steering arm on

the hub was connected to the handlebars via a linkage. To some extent, the width of the front fork as it emerged from the lower part of the fairing restricted the bike's steering lock.

The front brakes were applied by an equally complex-looking torque arm. Suspension damping was by coil-over monoshocks, carried in-board above the frame. The advantage over conventional telescopic forks was that the latter compresses under braking, so that road shocks cannot be absorbed so well, and the steering geometry changes as the machine's attitude alters in corners. The Tesi's set-up passes the forces directly backwards to the frame, whereas a normal steering head that accompanies telescopic forks transmits severe braking forces high up in the frame. The idea was that the Tesi frame could therefore be a more minimal structure, and thus lighter.

The latest version of the Tesi, the 2D, is powered by a 992cc

(61ci) V-twin engine from the Multistrada. The 2D began life as a prototype called the Vyrus, produced by a small, Rimini-based firm called VDM, headed by a former Bimota mechanic named Ascanio Rodrigo. After Bimota had abandoned production of the original Tesi, Rodrigo and his small team continued development, and refined the forkless machine into a racebike, which they named the Vyrus. It was raced with some success, including championship wins in 2002. The basic chassis layout is retained, but almost everything else differs from the original Tesi.

ENGINE: 904cc (54ci) fuel-injected 8v Ducati V-twin
POWER: 118bhp
GEARBOX: 5-speed foot change
FINAL DRIVE: n/a
WEIGHT: 188kg (414lb)
TOP SPEED: 266km/h (165mph)

A Bimota Tesi undergoes trials on a rural race track. The Tesi is today still a popular race bike, especially in its most recent reincarnation as the Vyrus.

The Bimota Tesi 1D's most distinctive feature is its unusual hub centre steering instead of traditional telescopic forks, a feature that was passed over to the later Bimota Tesi 2D. The front suspension is handled by an offset mono-shock concealed by the all-enveloping bodywork.

BOAR

Based in Naples, Florida, Boar Motorcycles was formed in 1997 to manufacture high-performance V-Twin American motorcycles on the Harley-Davidson style, from proprietary components. The main components include Kenny Boyce frames, RC parts, Elite series brakes and wheels, and Sputhe motors. The base option is 1550cc (95ci), but 1700cc (104ci) is available, and the machine can also be ordered with bigger engines such as the enormous 2179cc (133ci) Total Performance Prepared Motor. Less emphasis is placed on performance than on the number of polished components and the extensive use of stainless steel, such as the (stainless steel) brake rotors.

Many owners of BMW twins switched to aftermarket cast iron for better braking.

The tank is light alloy and the wheels are a very traditional 48cm (19in) at the front and 46cm (18in) at the back. The Connolly leather seats can withstand light rain only. As ever with big American cruisers, there is a curious mix of ancient and modern, including 'maintenance-free, self-diagnosing wiring' and a digital display that is, according to the reviews, not too good in bright sunlight but very dramatic in the evenings. At 245kg (540lb) for the base model, Boars could be suitable for heavy solo touring or for light touring, two-up. For heavier touring, two-up, there is the Classic, with a dry weight of 268kg (590lb).

BOSS HOSS

The Boss Hoss Motorcycle Company was founded by Monte Warne in 1990 and is based in Dyersburg, Tennessee. It specializes in manufacturing motorcycles and trikes equipped with General Motors V8 engines and semi-automatic transmissions. By the mid-1990s, Boss Hoss was selling 300 vehicles per year, and by the summer of 2006, total sales had risen to over 4000 machines. In the American

Left and below: The Boss Hoss Motorcycle Company achieved substantial success, its machines having the capacity to travel long distances without imposing undue stress on the rider. The riding position was relatively comfortable compared to many of the other luxury cruisers on the market.

The V8 Model sold well and was later offered with the smaller V6 engine. Like its predecessor, it was vibration free and proved very popular with enthusiasts.

market, there has never been any substitute for cubes on wheels, as big distances between destinations called for large-capacity engines working for hours without stress. For some, stock machines were not enough and so the custom model made its appearance, built to the owner's specifications. One result of this trend was the use of a car engine as a powerplant, combined with a car's transmission and two rear wheels to create a tricycle. Boss Hoss came from that background but differed by being a production model and a solo motorcycle. The company used an enormous 5.7l (1.5 US gallon) Chevrolet V8 with its automatic transmission coupled to a belt final drive.

This all fitted into a massive tubular cradle frame with telescopic front and pivoted-rear forks. Cast-alloy wheels carried fat front tyres and even fatter rear tyres, with disc brakes to bring the bike's considerable weight to a halt. It sold well and was later offered with a smaller V6 engine or a larger 8.2l (2.1 US gallon) V8 offering 500hp to drive its two-speed and reverse automatic transmission.

Wild though the specification was, some owners added twin rear wheels, which made it easier to ride, or with major engine changes to boost the power even further.

Boss Hoss bikes and trikes are noted not only for their power and size, but also for their strikingly minimal vibration, especially when

compared to that of V-twin or single-cylinder motorcycles. The dampening effect of the unusually great mass and relatively high number of engine cylinders combine with the very tall gears of the semi-automatic transmission to provide what is often described as 'vibration-free acceleration'.

This has led to some dealers and riders to describe the Boss Hoss, affectionately, as a 'big scooter'.

Exuding power, the V8 Model was equipped with an enormous Chevrolet V8 engine, which proved to be an excellent powerplant.

CALIFORNIA CUSTOMS

California Customs was established in northern California in 1991. Originally known as a performance and customizing shop, the firm quickly expanded and soon established a reputation for its extremely high attention to detail and personalized customer service. As part of its expansion plans, California Customs introduced a range of four models of custom-built motorcycle platforms, all built to exacting specifications. The first custom-built touring model, the Nomad Convertible RS, was available within a few years and was a collaborative effort between

California Customs and Corbin. This spectacular-looking tourer was fitted with fully integrated, specially made Corbin lockable hard-side panniers. Even then, the manufacturers were at pains to point out that the panniers and the small handlebar fairing could be removed in five minutes to reveal a custom boulevard cruiser underneath.

Machines in the company's model line-up for 2000 were Nomad, Eliminator, Intimidator, Terminator and Dominator – which, for anyone who knows anything at all about motorcycles, is permanently associated with Norton. The motorcycles were

powered by S & S engines with a nominal 96cu in displacement. The actual dimensions were 92mm (3.6in) bore and 117.5mm (4.6in) stroke for a swept volume of 1562cc (95ci), and carburation was also by S & S. Frames were rigid, or conventional or imitations of the Harley-Davidson Softail; some were rubber-mounted, others not. Transmission was assembled by California Customs from Delkron cases with Jims gears, both primary and final drive being by belt.

A single, albeit four-piston, polished stainless-steel brake disc at the front argued that these

were not machines designed to be ridden hard and fast, though the Corbin seats that were fitted as standard are normally very comfortable. Long distances at low speeds should, therefore, have been feasible within the limits imposed by the 18L (5 US gallons) tank, the wide bars and the forward controls. Characteristically, the manufacturers' specifications gave all kinds of information, such as front-fork diameter, but omitted those figures so precious to most motorcyclists – namely, weights, power outputs, and acceleration and top-speed figures, which shows clearly the market being targeted.

COBRA

Based in New Middletown, Ohio, Cobra Motorcycles was founded by Bud Maimone, who originally owned a tool and die shop. Racing with his son, Brent, in the fledgling 50cc class during the early 1990s, he identified a requirement for a bike that could be purchased ready for racing. At that time, the class was made up of highly modified recreational models that absorbed a lot of time and money to become race-ready. After failing to convince several manufactures to produce a race-ready bike, Bud took the plunge himself. The result was Cobra Motorcycles, which today produces premium

race-ready mini motocross bikes for youth riders who are serious about competing. Cobra's three models offer the most competitive performance in the mini category, and Cobras have claimed more than 45 national titles since the company was founded in 1993. Cobra Motorcycles is the only producer of off-road motorcycles that are truly 'Made in the USA'.

Cobra's own publicity material summed up their machines well: 'The first and only motocross bike ever built in the USA. Our parts are 98 per cent American made, we have won the Amateur National

Championships since 1994 and the engine is designed and manufactured in our own shop.'

Cobra has developed a unique set of capabilities that is difficult to match. Based on need and a desire for performance, Cobra does not just assemble bikes; the firm designs and manufactures most of the components that go into the product, including frames and engines. This allows Cobra to continue to improve on its designs, and the firm do everything from its own dynamometer development work to building plastics moulds and cutting its own wheels.

The chosen market – junior motocross, or children's racing – was a very small niche, but the firm attacked it with enthusiasm, originality, skill, and, ultimately, great success. This rested on two similar models, the air-cooled CM50 for children aged four to six, and the liquid-cooled King Cobra for children aged seven to eight. Both were very much 'real' motorcycles, with TIG-welded chromemoly tubular frames, kick-starts, and in-house parts such as hydraulic front forks, 140mm (5.5in) travel on the CM50, 230mm (9in) travel on the King Cobra, remote-reservoir shock absorbers, and more.

CONFEDERATE MOTORCYCLES

Based in Birmingham, Alabama, the Confederate Motor Company, Inc is an American manufacturer of motorcycles, which are distributed by Birmingham Speed of America. Confederate was founded in 1991 by trial lawyer Matthew Chambers, who described it as an 'initiative' seeking 'enlightened design through true American inspiration'. The company opened shop in San Francisco, California in 1992, moving in 1993 to a prototype shop in New Orleans, Louisiana, where its first motorcycle rolled off the production line on 11 November 1994.

Rather oddly, the logo of Confederate Motorcycles was in Fraktur, the German black-letter script much favoured by the Nazis. The names of some of the colours for the 1999 model year – Rebel Black, Combat Grey, Blood Red – were thrown into the realms of bathos by the option of Candy Blue, and one can only conjecture that Officer Yellow was a Vietnam-era

joke. Further colour options were added for the year 2000, including multi-coated metallics. Frames were powder-coated, matched to the paint job, and had a fairly typical wheelbase of 165cm (65in) with a rake of 30 degrees.

As usual, the standard motor was from S & S, this time in the 1852cc (113ci), two-valve-per-cylinder, pushrod guise, with no power output given. With an actual bore and stroke of 114.3 x 101.6mm (4.5 x 3.9in), the true swept volume was 1853cc.

Primary drive to the five-speed Andrews gear set was by belt; the inverted front shocks came from Paioli; and even though there was only one front disc, it was 320mm (12.6in) in diameter with a braking surface of ductile iron, with a six-piston calliper. Fasteners were all nickel-plated hard steel or aircraft-grade stainless steel.

For the 2000 model year, the fuel tank was changed from light

alloy to carbon fibre. Marchesini 43cm (17in) wheels front and rear and Pirelli radial tyres, a two-into-one silencer with an expansion chamber, and a ground clearance of 16.6cm (6.5in) further argued that Confederate motorcycles were, unlike some of their competitors, designed to be ridden. That said, the small size of the fuel tank –

The structure of the Confederate Motorcycles Hellcat, pictured here, is very simple, yet incredibly rigid and light. It is the only backbone downtube, cradle based chassis to utilize the powerplant as a stressed member.

14.5L (4 US gallons) – would not get it far.

The two models, the NBF Hellcat and the REL America GT, were distinguished principally by the GT's pillion seat. Both weighed 227kg (500lb) dry, with a maximum permitted gross vehicle weight of exactly twice that. The Confederate, it seems, looked like an impressive example of a 'Harley-Davidson clone'.

In 2005, Hurricane Katrina caused severe damage to the Confederate Motorcycles plant. Production became virtually impossible, and it was at this point that the firm relocated to Birmingham, Alabama.

Powered by a 1600cc (96ci) S&S 'long block' engine, the Grey Ghost uses a unique crossover, five-speed transmission, combining final-drive sprockets and Big Twins (where the final drive sprocket lives behind the clutch).

TRIUMPH TRIDENT

ENGLAND 1990

The BSA Rocket Three/Triumph Trident was the first true modern superbike, and the last major motorcycle developed by the original Triumph company – Triumph Engineering Ltd. It was effectively badge-engineered to be sold under both the Triumph and BSA marques.

The Rocket Three/Trident was the first-step development of Triumph Motorcycles' plan to move on from the basic vertical twin. The engine was to offer the power required by the US market (750cc/46ci) over the then standard 650cc (40ci), while avoiding the vibration associated with the parallel twin design and the bulk of a four-cylinder layout. This was the only part of the plan to come into production, while the later four-cylinder Quadrant prototype only shows a glimpse of what could have been later.

During its production run (1968–75), BSA fell into financial troubles, and over the course of the official six-year model run, approximately 27,480 Rocket Three/Tridents were produced – the exact number is unknown, because, at the end, the factory did not keep reliable records towards the end. By comparison, a quarter of a million Honda Goldwings were manufactured during its first seven years.

The renaissance of Triumph began in September 1990, when the new range was launched at the Cologne Show. The entry-level model was the unfaired Trident, which was available with two variations of the three-cylinder triple engine – 750cc (46ci) and 900cc (55ci), designated the T375 and T309. All six bikes in the modular range shared many common features, including chassis frames, fuel tanks, engine components and running gear. The three-cylinder triple was a water-cooled twin-cam, with a horizontal joint in the crankcase, and the top section of the casting combined with the wet-liner block. There were four valves per cylinder in the one-piece cylinder head, and these were chain-driven from the right-hand end of the crank via a tunnel in the casting. The electronic ignition was triggered from the same end of the crank, while the oil filter cartridge was underneath the crankcase. The one-piece crank was allied to a vibration-damping balancer shaft ahead of the crankshaft. Compression ratios were 11:1 for the short-stroke engines and 10.6:1 for the long-stroke, while the 36mm (1.4in) Mikuni carburettors used unleaded fuel. Nissin disc brakes were fitted, with twin 296mm (11.7in) discs and two-piston callipers at the front, and a single 255mm (10in) disc at the rear. At the front were Kayaba 43mm (1.7in) telescopic forks, and at the rising-rate rear was a single Kayaba damper.

Pictured here is an unfaired Triumph 750. The renaissance of Triumph began in 1990, with the launch of the 750 Model and others.

By October 1994, the Trident was Triumph's second-best seller after the Trophy. The Trident Sprint, released that year, was essentially a Trident 900 with elegant swooping side and rear panels and a cockpit fairing featuring the contemporary Daytona-style twin round headlights. Both the Sprint and the Trident were later equipped with an aluminium rear-suspension unit that was adjustable for pre-load and rebound damping, making the bikes capable of carrying heavy loads. The Sprint was also available in Executive and Sports formats. Both of these were available with appropriate accessories, such as imitation carbon exhausts and low bars.

ENGINE: (T375) 750cc (44ci) 12-valve ohv triple, water-cooled
POWER: 90bhp
GEARBOX: 5-speed foot change
FINAL DRIVE: chain
WEIGHT: 209kg (461lb)
TOP SPEED: 201km/h (125mph)

The Trident and the Thunderbird were Triumph's only models to come without an adjustable front suspension. Seen here is the 900 model. The Spring rate and damping are perfect for highway cruising.

YAMAHA XT600E

Although it is possible to buy more agile trail bikes with smaller engines that will outperform Yamaha's XT600, none can match it in character or reputation. The doyen of big single-cylinder trail bikes,

Yamaha's XT600E evolved from the DT dirt-trail series of 1976, refined over 25 years into one of the best dual-purpose on/off-road machines available.

Although it could reach 161km/h (100mph) on tarmac, the aerodynamics and riding position mitigated against anything over 121km/h (75mph), with sufficient seating comfort to undertake long journeys. The seat was lower than previous incarnations, and the air-cooled, single-pot motor was slimmer than water-cooled rivals. While not as powerful as the Aprilia Pegaso or Kawasaki KLR650, the XT600E's four-valve twin-carburettor engine possessed a smoother power delivery, with a gear-driven balancer-shaft reducing low-down transmission snatch.

Introduced in 1990, it has been the category leader thanks to its ease of use in around-town riding, its freedom of riding position and enjoyable running performance. In its first 10 years, the XT600E sold a record 92,000 units in the European market, making it the standard of the 600cc (37ci) on-off category. The XT600E has remained especially popular in the southern European countries thanks to the sense of security it brings when riding on cobblestone streets and its ease of use on crowded streets. The reasons most customers give for the XT600E's popularity are its price (affordable), its proven reliability going back to the initial XT500 introduced in 1976, its versatility, and the fact that it is a bike which can be used for many years.

Aftermarket tuning accessories meant that more power could be accessed than the standard 45hp. With suitable tyres such as Avon Gripsters fitted, the XT600E could be cornered with aplomb, on the road. Off-road, it was not as handy as the DT125R. The malleable plastic panels were resilient in spills, and from 1995 improvements were made to the colours, fuel tank and front brake.

ENGINE: 595cc (37ci), ohc single-cylinder, air-cooled
POWER: 45bhp
GEARBOX: 6-speed
FINAL DRIVE: chain
WEIGHT: 155kg (342lb)
TOP SPEED: 161km/h (100mph)

Above and below: Mounting a newly developed liquid-cooled 4-stroke, SOHC single-cylinder, 4-valve, 660cc (40ci) engine with fuel injection on a diamond-type frame, the latest Yamaha XT600E offers an excellent combination of enjoyable ease of use around-town riding plus outstanding high-speed cruising and off-road performance.

APRILIA 650 PEGASO

In the perennial search for niche markets within a niche market, a new variant of motorcycle has been steadily evolving. The basic design parameters of a dirt bike – wide bars, high seat, long suspension, narrow frame, and single-cylinder, four-stroke engine – have been taken and worked into models that owe more to high-tech industrial design than the sand dunes of the Sahara. An excellent example of this is Aprilia's Pegaso 650-3, now into its third stage of the evolutionary cycle.

The Milan Show of 1991 saw the public debut of Aprilia's five-valve single, the 650 Pegaso. It was one of the first modern bikes, along with some of Yamaha's four-cylinder models, to employ five-valve technology in a production model. Like Honda's Dominator, Aprilia designers had wanted to create a motorcycle that retained a visual connection with dirt bikes while also being a good on-road machine. The old four-valve unit (fitted to the original Pegaso and its earlier Tuareg brother) was transformed to a five-valve one, increasing displacement from 562cc/34ci to 652cc/40ci (100 x 83mm/3.9 x 3.3in). The valves (three inlet and two exhaust) featured a radial distribution. Another major development was to change the frame from steel to a light alloy.

Aprilia has been selling large-capacity, dual-purpose machines for more than 10 years. The ETX600 was first and was

Based around a development of the Yamaha 660 single-cylinder engine, the Aprilia 650 Pegaso has been described as an 'agile urban supermotard'. The engine is built in Italy.

followed by the Tuareg, both bikes using the same two-valve engine supplied by Austria's Rotax company. In 1993, the first Pegaso was introduced, with a change of engine to the five-valve, water-cooled Rotax engine that is still featured on the latest version. Brembo disc brakes appeared on the second version of the Pegaso in 1995, along with a quieter exhaust to meet EEC regulations and updated graphics.

The 1995 update was fitted with a more powerful headlamp, as well as revisions to the frame, wheel-rim colour (from silver to bronze) and suspension. In 1996, a new stainless-steel exhaust appeared.

Towards the end of that year, Aprilia launched the Pegaso 3 with an all-new frame, revised riding position, and new styling, camshafts, exhaust system and engine castings. Although heavier, the new Pegaso was a better machine than the one it replaced. As a result of these improvements, the Pegaso became a serious touring bike, so Aprilia introduced a range of accessories, such as panniers, top box, a centre stand and even an optional rear shock with separate adjustment to satisfy owners' requirements.

In 2004, Aprilia announced the all-new Pegaso 650 Strada at the Intermot Munich motorcycle show. Based around a development of the Yamaha 660 single-cylinder engine, the new bike is described as an 'agile urban supermotard'. The engine is built in Italy, not far from Aprilia's Noale factory, and has been breathed on by Aprilia's technicians to achieve the mid- and top-end rush so typical of Aprilia's bikes. Fast steering and an excellent steering lock will make this bike a mean street machine that is also ideal for commuting, and a capable multipurpose motorcycle with 'the emphasis on fun'. KTM's Duke seems to have had some influence here, and it should steal much of the thunder from Ducati's new 620 Multistrada. Power is around 50hp at 6250rpm from the dry sump, four-valve engine, and the weight is a highly respectable 168kg (370lb). The frame is a compact, steel, single-spar arrangement that is said to have class leading rigidity. The Strada's aluminium alloy wheels copy the wheel design of the RSV 1000 R Factory supersports.

ENGINE: 652cc (39ci) dohc vertical single, 100x83mm, liquid-cooled 5v
POWER: 55bhp at 8000rpm
GEARBOX: 5-speed foot change
FINAL DRIVE: chain
WEIGHT: 155kg (342lb)
TOP SPEED: 177km/h (110mph)

BRITTEN

The Britten Motorcycle Company was set up by John Britten in 1992 to develop a design he had been working on for two years.

Actually, the wheels were set in motion some years earlier. In 1986, John Britten decided to redesign his bevel drive Ducati racing bike by creating all his own bodywork, but the motor and chassis proved hopelessly unreliable. John then turned to a New Zealand-made Denco motor in a home-built frame.

This motor also proved to be a weak link. So after much fiddling and rebuilding, he decided to wipe the slate clean and start again, creating a new race bike – motor and all. The bodywork was to be made out of carbon fibre, in two kinds: plain, for use mainly on flat surfaces; and twill, which is more flexible. The woven carbon fibre is wetted out with resin and is then moulded and heat cured.

The high-powered, Christchurch-built Britten V1000 racer has figured among the winners and placegetters at many world-famous racing venues since its introduction in 1990, including victories at Daytona, Brands Hatch and Monza. In 1996, the Britten bike was first overall in the New Zealand National Superbike Championship.

The motor was to be made by casting steel. John Britten did all his own drawings, made his own patterns and designed his own engine. He designed two engines of differing cc ratings because some race events allow a higher cc rating – the Britten V1000 (at 1000cc/61ci) and the Britten V1100 (at 1100cc/67ci) racer versions in four and five valves per cylinder, with power varying between 155hp and 170 hp. The 1100cc (67ci) engine is in the Cardinal bike. The liquid-cooled V-twin engine features two belt-driven cams and four valves per cylinder; a compression ratio of 11.3:1; titanium con-rods and valves (40mm/1.5in inlet, 33mm/1.3in exhaust); and, intriguingly, the option of either cast-iron wet liners or silicon carbide-lined alloy sleeves. Lubrication was wet-sump, with feeds to the big ends, gudgeon pins, camshaft lobes and gearbox shafts. Fuel supply was sequential injection, two injectors per cylinder, with programmable engine management and a history facility to read how the engine behaved in use. The standard gearbox was five-speed, though there was a six-speed option.

The engine is a stressed chassis member, with much of the chassis – the upper part, the girder and the swing-arm – made of a carbon fibre and Kevlar composite. Even the wheels, 43cm (17in) front and rear, were a carbon fibre composite, built in house, but the brake disks were twin 320mm (12.6in) cast-iron rotors at the front and a single 210mm (8.3in) rotor at the back; cast iron affords better stopping power, and better heat dissipation, than stainless steel. The ducted radiator was mounted under the seat. The machine produced 166hp at 11,800rpm with a limit of 12,500rpm, which was a staggering engine speed for a big V-twin. This is also about twice the brake horsepower of a standard Hesketh with a superficially similar engine. This was sufficient to power the 138kg (304lb) machine to about 303km/h (188mph).

Britten's achievement illustrates that, even today, the barriers to designing and building a complete, successful motorcycle – even a race-winner – are small. Although 'backyard specials' built from existing components are common enough, the Britten featured not only its own carbon-fibre cycle parts, but also its own unique, powerful engine. It is an intriguing machine, and as far from a Harley-Davidson clone as can be imagined, though few were built.

The only motorcycle model that ever entered production was the V1000. At the time of writing, the firm was working on at least one new model and on other non-motorcycle projects, despite the death of the company's founder, John Britten, in 1996.

The Brittens have had a very good race history. In 1991, they came second and third in the Battle of the Twins in Daytona, USA. This version of the Britten had a full fairing and was quite different to the Brittens as we know them today. The Daytona version was painted blue and red with the stars from the New Zealand flag painted on the side. One of these two bikes has recently been restored at the factory. To date, the Britten has been placed in nearly every event that it has raced in. The Britten has been so successful because what started out as a hobby in a garage at home became a world class motorcycle, recognized for its brilliance in engineering all over the world. Unlike big established companies that invest huge amounts of money in the development work and are obliged to show a result for the money spent, John Britten persevered on a trial- and-error basis until he was successful.

GILERA GFR 250 GP RACER

Piaggio, who owned the Gilera marque, set up a racing division specifically to design and build racing prototypes, and the Gilera 250 GP Racer was the consequence. The division was under the direction of former Bimota design chief Frederico Martini.

At the Milan Show in 1991, Gilera announced that it would compete in the 1992 250cc World Road Racing Championship series, with riders Carlos Lavado (winner of 19 Grand Prix in the 250cc class) and Jean Philippe Ruggia, on a brand new 75-degree V-twin two-stroke, very similar to its two main rivals, Honda and Yamaha. A more detailed appraisal of the machine revealed twin Mikuni or Dell'Orto carburettors (fuel injection was also tested); reed-valve induction, designed by the Austrian engineer Harold Bartol, with electronically timed exhaust valves; and a six-speed gearbox, balancer shaft and magnesium engine casings. A single crankshaft was used to prevent possible flexing at ultra-high engine revolutions. The chassis was of Delta-box aluminium with Kyaba suspension front and rear. Inverted front forks featured an adjustable steering head rake. However, even though the GFR's power output of 85hp was identical to that of Honda's NSR, it was this rival that clinched the championship, despite the best efforts of Lavado and Ruggia.

The GFR 250 racer was built to challenge Japanese dominance in the 250cc (15ci) racing class.

ENGINE: 249cc (15ci) reed 2s V-Twin, 56x50.7mm, liquid-cooled
POWER: 85bhp at 13,000rpm
GEARBOX: 6-speed foot change
FINAL DRIVE: chain
WEIGHT: 95kg (209lb)
TOP SPEED: 266km/h (165mph)

HONDA CBR900 RR FIREBLADE

From the moment of its launch in 1992, the Honda CBR900 Fireblade was a super-sportster that earned respect. Throughout the 1990s, it took the superbike category higher and on to new levels, its only competent challengers being the Ducati 916 and Triumph T595 Daytona. A really serious threat did not materialize until 1998, with the appearance of Yamaha's R1. FireBlades won the Production TT on three successive occasions in the mid-1990s, and dominated the 1998 British Production Powerbike Championship.

The bike was originally 893cc (54ci), but improvements to the FireBlade's 123hp, 16-valve,

Above: The Honda Fireblade has some excellent qualities. It is very stable in wet conditions and feels safe at high speed. Its powerful delivery is awesome and it will cruise at 193km/h (120mph).

Left: The Fireblade has a motorway range of about 209km (130 miles) before it needs a refill. Although it only weighs 180kg, the Fireblade feels strong and solid, and is stable and easy to handle.

size from 530 to 525. Other components were also made lighter, including the tyres (new Bridgestone BT56, which were designed to warm up to operating temperature more quickly), the cylinder head cover (now magnesium) and even the frame.

The new design of the frame and swing arm means that sections of the frame are now open-backed, instead of closed. The frame is triple-box section, instead of quad-box section as before, but, it is claimed, is more rigid in critical areas.

ENGINE: 893cc (53ci) 16v dohc transverse straight-4
POWER: 123bhp at 12,000rpm
GEARBOX: 6-speed foot change
FINAL DRIVE: chain
WEIGHT: 185kg (407lb)
TOP SPEED: 266km/h (165mph)

transverse four extracted yet more performance, and capacity was lifted to 918cc (56ci), while the lightweight aluminium twin-beam chassis and racy steering

geometry was tweaked to make the bike rather more docile than the tearaway original. The bigger, only very slightly heavier pistons were matched by

larger connecting rods with bigger crankshaft big end journals to match.

To achieve weight reduction, the drive chain was reduced in

HUSQVARNA TC610

In 1986, the Swedish Husqvarna company's motorcycle division was purchased by Cagiva and relocated to Italy, following which it initiated a determined effort to make an inroad into the rapidly expanding market for off-road bikes. The result of their vigorous development programme was the 50hp TC610. This machine was introduced in 1992, and its tubular-steel cradle frame was powered by a state-of-the-art, 577cc (35ci), double overhead-cam, four-valve, water-cooled, two-stroke single, which was allied to a six-speed gearbox. Up front were massive upside-down telescopic forks, and an alloy swinging-arm linked to the rear monoshock. The top half of the machine was clad in the typically sweeping fairings of that period, which incorporated the seat while the trim, high-rise exhausts emerged either side above the knobbly rear tyre.

ENGINE: 77cc (4.5ci) dohc 4v 2s single, water-cooled
POWER: 50bhp
GEARBOX: 6-speed foot change
FINAL DRIVE: chain drive
WEIGHT: 117kg (258lb)
TOP SPEED: dependent on gearing

DUCATI SUPERMONO

The Supermono was conceived by the Argentinean Miguel Galluzzi, almost two decades after the last of the bevel-drive singles had rolled off the Bologna factory's production lines. Intended only for racing, it made its debut in the summer of 1993. Much of the engine design followed 851/888 V-twin practice, including the four-valves-per-cylinder, Weber/Marelli electronic fuel injection, six-speed, dry clutch and Desmo valve system. Ing. Massimo Bordi, who had replaced Fabio Taglioni as mechanical design chief, first tested his 'doppia bielletta' (double con-rod) Supermono engine on the bench in the winter of 1990. This prototype had a displacement of 487cc/30ci (95.6 x 66mm/ 3.7 x 2.6in) with tests revealing 62.5hp. Next came a 502cc/31ci (95.6x70mm/3.7 x 2.8in) version, with power rising to 70hp, before Bordi and his team finally settled on 549cc/34ci (100 x 70mm/ 3.9 x 2.7in) as the definitive

This tremendously refined and elegant four-stroke single was the product of designer Pierre Terblanche in conjunction with the vision of Massimo Bordi and technical expertise of Claudio Domenicali.

layout. The power was now up to 75hp measured at the gearbox output shaft. The second con-rod was, in fact, in place of a conventional balance shaft.

The tubular-steel frame chassis, developed by Claudio Domenicalli, was manufactured at the Cagiva works in Varese from a new high-resistance material coded ALS 500. This provided the same stiffness as the more familiar 25 Cr M4 chrome-moly steel – but at a lower cost. The Bologna-based Verlicchi firm built the aluminium swinging arm, which pivoted on the crankcases like the belt-drive V-twins. The Swedish suspension specialists, Ohlins, were responsible for both the inverted front forks and single rear shock.

Completing the group of experts responsible for the creation of the Supermono was the South African Pierre Terreblanche, who drew out the bike's beautifully sculptured lines. A Series 2 Supermono was built from late 1994 and was known as the 102. This was in reference to its 102mm (4in) bore size, which gave a new engine capacity of 572cc (35ci).

ENGINE: 549cc (33ci) dohc, Desmo single, 4V, 100x74mm, liquid-cooled
POWER: 75 bhp at 11,000rpm
GEARBOX: 6-speed foot change
FINAL DRIVE: chain
WEIGHT: 123.5kg 272lb
TOP SPEED: 241km/h (150mph)

A wide variety of high-tech components and features (liquid-cooling, electronic injection, twin con-rods) on the Supermono combined to create the single most competitive motorcycle in its class.

MUZ SKORPIAN

GERMANY 1993

The MuZ Skorpian was the fruit of a 1990s trend towards 'cross-bred' motorcycles, whereby a smaller company such as Bimota or Buell builds a bike and uses engines made by a larger company such as Harley-Davidson or Suzuki. The result is a custom creation that carefully matches the engine with every other component.

One such cross-breed is the MuZ Skorpian, powered by a water-cooled, 660cc (40ci), five-valve single overhead-cam Yamaha engine. The mainstream model was the Skorpian Sport, with a half fairing, which left both the engine and frame in full view. Three colours were initially on offer: yellow, black and green.

Putting out 48hp, and also built in a restricted 34hp version for novice riders, the Skorpian Sport's specification included a Delta box tubular steel frame, 41mm (1.5in) telescopic front forks, 43cm (17in) cast-alloy wheels, disc brakes front and rear, an electric starter, five-speed gearbox, monoshock rear suspension and a 12V

The MUZ Skorpian Sport has justifiably been described as a German masterpiece, but in fact it was the creation of a UK design team. The Sport is pictured here at the 1994 International Motorshow, Birmingham.

electrical system. This was then followed by other versions, such as the naked Skorpian Tour, an off-road bike and the 'hot' fully faired Skorpion Replica.

This German masterpiece was created by a design team from the UK, Richard Seymour and Dick Powell. The London-based studio came up with several versions of the basic Skorpion theme and also of the prototype-only Yamaha TDM 850 twin-engined Kobra supersports roadster. Besides having more power, the Replica

boasted inverted Dutch-made White Power front forks with no less than 20 possible adjustments for compression damping and eight for rebound. The monoshock rear suspension again came from White Power. Other top brand-name components included: Brembo brakes, with four-piston Goldline callipers and twin 180mm (7in), semi-floating discs at the front, and a dual piston caliper and single 240mm (9.5in) disc at the rear. Compared with the Sport, the Replica also had

wider tyres – 120/60 front and 160/60 rear – whereas the Sport had 110/70 and 150/60 respectively. The factory claimed the Replica could do 200km/h (125mph), or 208km/h (130mph) with the optional tuning kit. Its dry weight was 165kg (363lb), some 5kg (11lb) lighter than the Sport. This was surprising considering that it had a full fairing, rather than the nose-cone type featured on the Sport. A number of Skorpian racing models, which were used by

works-supported as well as private riders, have achieved considerable success throughout Europe in the popular Supermono racing class.

ENGINE: 660cc (39.5ci) ohc 5v single, 100x84mm, water-cooled
POWER: 48bhp at 6500rpm
GEARBOX: 5-speed foot change
FINAL DRIVE: chain
WEIGHT: 170kg (375lb)
TOP SPEED: 174km/h (109mph)

DUCATI 916

ABOVE: In contrast to Japanese in-line, four-cylinder competitors of the time, the Ducati 916's V-twin engine produced less outright power, but a more even torque spread.

BELOW: Released in 1994, the Ducati 916 was admired because of its radical new design and outstanding technical features. It was a water-cooled version of the 888 model.

In 1994, Ducati introduced another winner, the 916. It was the creation of Massimo Bordi, who had succeeded the talented designer Fabio Taglioni. The latter had set Ducati on its path to success by creating the singles and later the V-twins that had already made the company a household name.

The first of the Bordi four-valve-per-cylinder models made its debut at the 1986 Bol d'Or.

Although it retired after eight of the 24 hours, it showed great potential. The Cagiva takeover of Ducati in 1983 provided the funding for the project, and the initial production model, the 851, arrived in 1988, the year that Marco Lucchinelli won the first WSB World Super Bike race at Donnington Park. Ducati subsequently produced many street, supersport and racing four-valvers, including the SP (Sport Production). The 851 was discontinued in 1993, and in 1994 the Corsa Racing model was increased to 926cc (57ci).

The appearance of the 916 ensured the continuation of the great Ducati sports tradition. It was another Ducati-inspired revolution, this time in the high-performance sports motorcycle category. With the 916, technology and style, performance and symmetry reached maximum levels: Ducati once again managed to create a perfect harmony of form and function. From the world's most prestigious bike magazines, the 916 received the title Motorcycle of the Year. The Supermono, one of the most eminent examples of motorcycle design in motorbike history, was also realized at this time.

In 1995, despite product innovation and racing successes, Ducati fell on hard times and a deep financial crisis developed, the firm's cash having been drained by unsuccessful ventures of sister companies within the Castiglioni group. In 1996, Ducati was taken over by Texas Pacific Group, an American investment firm that brought much-needed cash and a new group of international managers. Simultaneously, the launch of the ST family allowed Ducati to enter the Sport Touring segment of the market.

The great success of this period was the Monster Dark, which was the best-selling motorcycle in Italy in 1998 and 1999.

ENGINE: 916cc (55ci) dohc 90-degree V-twin, 4 valves per cylinder, liquid-cooled
POWER: 110bph at 9000rpm
GEARBOX: chain
FINAL DRIVE: 6-speed
WEIGHT: 19 kg (429lb)
TOP SPEED: 259km/h (161mph)

HONDA RC45

The Honda RVF750 RC45 was a fully faired racing motorcycle developed by the Honda Racing Corporation for the superbikes category. Created in 1994, it was Honda's ultimate V-four production bike and was the successor to the VFR750R RC30 (not to be confused

The Honda RC45's finest moments include American John Kocinski winning the 1997 FIM Superbike World Championship.

with the sport touring VFR750). Like its predecessor, the RC45 featured a 749cc (46ci), water-cooled, V-four engine allied to a six-speed gearbox, mounted in a twin-spar aluminium frame with single-sided swinging-arm. To a great extent, the RC45's machinery evolved from the work's racing RVF machines, with mighty four-pot calliper front disc brakes. That said, the RC45 had a completely new engine in which

the camshafts' gear drive was taken off the end of the crankshaft. Electronic fuel injection superseded the previous model's carburettors on the customer model, and performance could be increased to 150hp by fitting Honda's aftermarket race kit, thereby doubling the price of what was already an extremely exclusive machine. The bike was manufactured and sold in limited numbers from 1994 until 1999,

being replaced by the VTR1000R SP-1 RC51 in 2000.

ENGINE: 749cc (45ci) ohv V-four, water-cooled
POWER: 118bhp at 12,000rpm
GEARBOX: 6-speed, foot change
FINAL DRIVE: chain
WEIGHT: 189kg (417lb)
TOP SPEED: 282km/h (175mph) depending on gearing

KYMCO

The Japanese company Kymco established an outlet in Taiwan in 1963 and produced its first motorcycle in 1970. At that time, Taiwan was a popular manufacturing centre for the Japanese motorcycle industry, a trend that continued for many years. Kymco Taiwan carried out sub-assembly work, although the engine units were still put together in Japan. The firm dealt with chassis items such as hubs, wheels, electric wiring harnesses

and handlebars, all of which helped to build up experience, ability and technical knowledge, giving it an understanding of individual parts and how they were assembled, and also of production techniques.

Eventually, Kymco began to produce complete machines, which were sold on their home market and also exported to Italy. The firm's policy was one of simplicity, with 50cc (3ci) two-stroke and 125cc (8ci) and 150cc (9ci) four-stroke engines – derived

from Honda units in the main. These went into mopeds and small motorcycles, styled and finished to meet the demands of the period, plus a range of scooters, most with 50cc (3ci) engines. The scooters had modern lines and specifications with electronic ignition, automatic lubrication and electric start in many cases. Automatic transmission was usual, while front suspension was either trailing-link or telescopic for the scooters, and all had rear

The KYMCO Super 9 is a fully automatic scooter with dual disc brakes and liquid cooling.

suspension. Small disc wheels with drum or disc brakes were used by the scooters, some with a mix of disc front and drum rear.

Names such as Dink, Filly, Heroism, Movie, Vivio, People, Sniper and Top Boy were used to sell this line. Kymco motorcycles and scooters are also assembled in Argentina under the Isma brand.

MITO EVO

Cagiva's Mito Evo was created by Massimo Tamburini, former part-owner of Bimota, and designer of Ducati 916 series and the new MV Agusta F4. In fact, the Mito Evo shared a very similar styling job with the 916: 'letter-box' headlamp, inverted forks and all. The only disappointment for buyers and onlookers came when the engine was started: instead of the booming, four-stroke, V-twin Ducati sound, the Mito Evo offered a 'ring-ting' two-stroke noise. But for buyers who could overlook that this was a small-capacity, single-cylinder 'stroker', instead of a big vee, the rest

of the bike was a sheer delight. And, in SP guise, the Mito could win straight out of the crate, as Dean Johnson was to prove on his Mick Walker Racing Mito SP in the 1995 British Super Teen championship series.

The Mito Evo has the distinction of being the first production roadster to be fitted with the first seven-gearbox in history. Introduced in 1991, the Mito, together with Aprilia's Extrema (subsequently renamed RS125), became the ultimate street-legal 125cc (8ci) sports motorcycle of the 1990s. It offered a combination of

racer-like handling, braking and style, with a 160km/h (100mph) speed potential. Both of these bikes were more than capable of besting the Japanese opposition, including Suzuki's RGV and Yamaha's TZR models.

The Mito's liquid-cooled 124.6cc/7.6ci (56 x 50.6mm/2.2 x 1.9 in), reed-valve, two-stroke engine was a development of the one used in the Freccia, which had been in production during the late 1980s, and it came with many modern two-stroke features, such as an exhaust valve and pump lubrication. Starting was by press button, while the

ignition was of the electronic capacitive type.

The early Mito series, which ran until mid-1994, can be identified by the twin round headlamps, conventional front forks and different styling to the definitive Mito – the EVO (Evolution), which debuted in mid-1994.

ENGINE: 124.6cc (7.5ci) ts single, 56x50.6mm, liquid-cooled
POWER: 30 bhp at 10,000 rpm
GEARBOX: 7-speed foot change
FINAL DRIVE: chain
WEIGHT: 117kg (258lb)
TOP SPEED: 164km/h (102mph)

CHAPTER NINE

REDEFINING PARAMETERS

1995–2007

At the end of the twentieth century, motorcycling was approaching yet another step-change in technology and design. Honda's FireBlade had shown the way forward: less mass, more emphasis on rider control and a focus on chassis design. It took Honda's competitors a few years to catch up, but first Yamaha's 1998 R1 then Suzuki's 2001 GSX-R1000 both redefined open-class performance bike benchmarks. These bikes continued the ever-increasing rise in engine power outputs: the FireBlade made 118bhp in 1992, by 2002, the GSX-R1000 put out nearer 160bhp. But improvements in tires, suspension, brakes and frame design, together with further weight reductions, meant the GSX-R was even easier for most people to ride fast.

The middleweight sector remained vitally important for most manufacturers, with the 600cc (37ci) supersports class most hotly contested. By 2006, bikes like Yamaha's R6 and Honda's CBR600RR had technology levels every bit as high as full-bore superbikes, with power outputs of over 125bhp. Meanwhile, bikes like Ducati's 1098S and MV Agusta's F4 1000 continued to offer moto-connoisseurs a more exotic riding and owning experience. In the UK, Triumph continued its renaissance with the excellent 675 Daytona sportsbike.

Away from the high-octane supersports world, the road market grew in importance. A combination of a more mature market and tougher speeding laws meant top speeds became less relevant, making the experience of a stylish, high-performance bike – like the Triumph Speed Triple, BMW K1200R or Aprilia Tuono – much more appealing. Meanwhile, touring bikes such as Honda's Pan European and BMW's K1200S offered super performance for comfortable, long-distance cruising.

Left: Since its introduction in 1996, the Yamaha YZF1000 'Thunderace' has been one of the most popular race bikes around, with excellent handling and a top speed of 274km/h (170mph).

HONDA CB500 AND 500S

JAPAN 1994–2003

Buy a Honda, and you are not just buying a motorcycle, you are buying reliability. That is very much the key word for the CB500 and CB500S, both trusty little workhorses that were as robust as they could be. In fact, the CB even proved itself at the 1999 Le Mans 24 Hour race, where every team running a CB500 finished without any mechanical issues.

Generally speaking, it was an easy handling commuter; however, it could handle bigger distances too. Averaging 55mpg, the CB gave superb economy and range. With the introduction of Direct Access training, the CB found a new home with riding schools, as it was very easy to deal with and well mannered both in and out of town.

Low seat height and a light weight of 170kg (375lb) made it good for shorter riders. The CB500S was the next development of the original machine; adding a small fairing made motorway riding more bearable. The fairing improved the aerodynamics and gave a greater top speed by 10km/h (6mph) over the naked version without affecting the lively responsiveness of the steering.

To cut down on wear and tear, the engine and wheels were treated to withstand the salt and nastiness of a British winter, and Honda were confident enough in the build quality of the CB500S to offer a two-year guarantee. A lot of smaller machinery does not get the boon of a centre stand, but the CB got the lot, centre stand and all. This was practical for maintenance and for packing up with luggage for a longer trip.

The early CBs were manufactured in Italy, as the bike was aimed at the European market. The only weak area of the CB was deemed to be the suspension, and that was put down to the budget prices. They were replaced in 2004 by the CBF family of machines, which has a lot to live up to if they are to match their predecessors.

APRILIA MOTO 6.5

ITALY 1995

Aprilia are responsible for many machines on the roads these days, and their racing heritage usually comes through in the design of their bikes. 'Race on Sunday, sell on Monday' is an old saying that still cuts it. However, when the firm decided to go for a practical commuter machine, it commissioned Philippe Starck, a designer perhaps best known for his kitchenware and furniture. An interesting decision, and it proved to be an interesting machine: the Moto 6.5 really did break the mould. Aprilia stuck with the design from concept right through to production, a very bold move.

As it was so radical, the Moto 6.5 caused a flurry of press activity when it was launched in 1995. The unusual look was not universally popular, but the bike did sport some interesting features. The deep tank and oval frame gave the Aprilia a curvaceous look, which was continued into the radiator design that wrapped around the liquid-cooled 649cc/40ci (100 x 82.7mm/3.9 x 3.3in) five-valve, double overhead-camshaft, single-cylinder engine. They also opted to run an unusual rear tyre, a 43cm (17in) cross-ply, which was completely different to the low-profile sports radials that most other bikes were sporting at that time.

You either love or loathe its looks, but this bike is a manageable machine. It is ideal in town; the Rotax engine will run forever, although the chassis is a bit unusual. The engine does not provide a huge amount of grunt but not much is needed in town, and its racing pedigree means that it is easy to control.

Sales wise, the Moto 6.5 did not rush out of the show rooms, but it is a radical design. Time will tell if it gains cult status, which would push prices up.

ENGINE: 649cc (39ci) dohc vertical single, 100x82.5mm, liquid-cooled, 4volt
POWER: 45bhp at 8000rpm
GEARBOX: 5-speed foot change
FINAL DRIVE: chain
WEIGHT: 150kg (331lb)
TOP SPEED: 164km/h (102mph)

Not easily recognized as an Aprilia due to Philippe Starck's unique design, the funky city commuter is a capable machine. They broke the mould with the Moto 6.5 but didn't break the market – cult status is the best they could hope for.

APRILIA RS250

Aprilia's crowning glory has to be the RS250. How many would-be-racers have cut their teeth on the 250cc (15ci) V-twin? It has got to be one of Aprilia's top machines ever – bar none.

With the looks and the edge of a race bike packaged for road use, the RS250 was immensely popular until emission regulations got the better of it.

With a successful race history, it made sense to build a race replica for the general public to play with, and that meant furnishing the new creation with a reliable and usable engine. So Aprilia looked to Suzuki and its RGV engine, which was then tweaked to the firm's own specification. Basically, the bike got more mid-range for useful power where its needed, and the firm added its own pipes.

The two-stroke engine is as temperamental as ever and needs lots of revs to keep it happy and howling. It starts to get interested at about 5000rpm; it gets into its stride at 8000rpm and will keep hurtling along at break neck speed until 12,000rpm shows on the clock. At that point, it has reached its limit. The RS sounds the part with the harsh ringing associated with racing two-strokes at full chat.

All the usual two-stroke weaknesses are still present: it needs to be warmed up properly before hitting the road, and the LCD display will stubbornly show 'Cold' until the bike hits a balmy 30 degrees C (86 degreesF). It prefers to be at its operating temperature of 55 degrees C (131 degrees F), and it will show its displeasure by refusing to pull lower revs.

Since the engine cannot be claimed by Aprilia, the firm set out to give the RS250 the best chassis possible. The aluminium beam frame, handed down from its racing siblings, means it holds the road, while its suspension ensures excellent control and feedback. The light weight of the mini racer makes it easy to stop, but it does make it a bit of a handful on a windy day. The bike's agility can also be seen in its light but sharp steering. The firm got the styling more than right on this machine – simple and understated. Are there any down sides? Well, the mirrors could be better placed, and the fuel tank is about as big as a nut shell. But, then, this is very much a race bike, so it is unrealistic to expect all the mod cons to be added as well.

Joe Public and the press loved it from the start; it was pretty much a GP bike for the road. The RS saw some changes for the 1996 version; the twin Mikuni 34mm (1.3in) carburettors were rejetted, and it got a new CDI ignition, which have made it easier to deal with. Sadly, its run of glory ended in 2003 due to tougher emission controls. In terms of 'bang for your buck', that phrase could have been coined with the RS250 in mind – it is the ultimate.

ENGINE: 249cc (15ci) 2s 90-degree V-twin, 56x50.6mm, liquid-cooled
POWER: 60bhp at 12,000rpm
GEARBOX: 6-speed foot change
FINAL DRIVE: chain
WEIGHT: 140kg (309lb)
TOP SPEED: 220km/h (137mph)

Lithe, agile and punchy, the RS delivers as much on track as its sleek looks suggest. The two-stroke engine provides lots of go while the comprehensive chassis makes it usable – the perfect race replica.

PIAGGIO TYPHOON

With city centres now turning into a seething, snarling mess of traffic, the way forward has got to be two wheels instead of four.

To help ease the grid lock, Piaggio launched the Typhoon 125.

It is a typical stylish Italian scooter with a top speed of 100km/h (60mph) supplied by an air-cooled, two-stroke, 123.5cc (8ci), single-cylinder motor. Wide, sturdy 25cm (10in) wheels guarantee its stability, while progressive brakes, excellent handling and automatic transmission make it ideal for the uninitiated.

In true scooter fashion, a full face helmet can be stored beneath the seat. More recent versions also boast a lockable glove and mobile phone compartment as well as an adjustable seat height. You can sail through the gridlock in a blur of Italian chic while thumbing your nose to the stranded car drivers.

ENGINE: 123.5cc (8ci) single-cylinder two-stroke
POWER: 11.9bhp
GEARBOX: n/a
FINAL DRIVE: shaft drive
WEIGHT: 96kg (210lb)
TOP SPEED: 100km/h (62mph)

A modern take on the classic Piaggio scooter, the Typhoon is suitable for commuting or just having fun. It can whip up a storm as it cuts through traffic and even sports a mobile phone holder.

BIMOTA YB11

The YB11 was the fourth in a line of Bimotas motored by the Yamaha Thunderace. It was given the suffix 'Superleggera', or light weight, a reference to the Italian coachbuilder, Touring of Milan, which was responsible for some of the most exquisite car bodies from the 1930s to the 1950s. The coach company had its own exclusive method of using a tubular space frame and aluminium panels to create the lightest possible structure. With similar reasoning, Bimota used the 'Supperleggera' tag for its beautifully detailed YB11, although it might just as easily have been applied to any number of its machines.

Bimota is known for producing lighter, shorter and faster bikes than the competition could manage on a production line.

The Yamaha Thunderace liquid-cooled, 1002cc (62ci), two-cylinder, four-stroke engine was packaged into a rigid frame made up of two diagonal beams with a rectangular cross-section. To this was added an aluminium swing arm and Paioli suspension front and rear for excellent handling. The 51mm (2in) forks can be adjusted by eccentric bushes to further sharpen up the steering, and Brembo brakes provide the stopping power.

The Yamaha FZR100 Thunderace, which donated its engine to the YB11, paled into insignificance next to the Bimota. The Italian interloper out-handled, out-performed and out-priced the humble Thunderace. Indeed, it had the potential to be the fastest production bike of its time. The Bimota was superbly built with tweaks in all the right places. Only 650 of these beauties were built, and riders who could put up with the odd location of the foot pegs – they were set far back – were privy to the handling and awesome power of the YB11 on a twisty road.

ENGINE: 1002cc (60ci) liquid-cooled two-cylinder four-stroke 20v
POWER: 131bhp
GEARBOX: foot change
FINAL DRIVE: chain
WEIGHT: 183kg (403lb)
TOP SPEED: 282km/h (175mph)

The beautiful Bimota YB11, one of only 650 that were manufactured by the unique Italian company. Although based around a Yamaha engine, the Bimota is a far cry from a mass-produced bike.

BUELL M2 CYCLONE

USA 1996

The Cyclone is the base model in the Buell range. Derived from the Harley-Davidson 1200cc (72ci) Sportster engine, it is tuned to perform like no Harley can.

The designer, Eric Buell, has his own take on designing a bike and believes the fun of the actual ride is as important as the destination. With that in mind, the Cyclone

pumps out 86hp, which is more than the biggest Harleys manage. It has a broad swathe of torque, which peaks at 79lb/ft at 5400rpm. The vibration from the

torquey V-twin is reduced using Buell's patented Uniplanar mountings, which uses tie-rods to attach the engine rigidly to the frame. A machine with a rigid

frame results in greater rider control, while the Uniplanar engine mounting system means that the engine adds to the frame rigidity and helps damp out the vibrations.

The Buell is belt drive, which is unusual on a sports-based bike.

Similar to the one used by the Harley range, it is a system that Erik Buell first helped design when he still worked for Harley. Belt drives tend to last much longer than chain drives and require much less maintenance.

Another area that Buell looked to when designing his revolutionary street bike was Mass Centralization. In common terms, this means concentrating the key components near the centre of the bike, which leads to more

responsive handling on the road. The Cyclone runs on slightly less exotic chassis components than its siblings: conventional Showa telescopic forks, rather than the inverted forks of contemporary S1 Lightning and S3 Thunderbolt models; and at the rear, in common with other models, a single White Power shock absorber, which is located under the engine. The result is a bike that handles like a dream.

Low, unsprung weight is one of Buell's specialities, which means minimizing the weight of components not supported by the motorcycle's suspension springs. This is critical to control and the feel of the ride, allowing the tyres to maintain road contact on any irregular surfaces. Although the Cyclone is bestowed with only a single front disc, this offers an enormous friction area swept by a huge six-piston calliper. It is also one of the ways in which unsprung weight has been reduced, saving around 2–3kg (4–6lb) compared with conventional twin disc set-ups. The front brake design means that the braking forces are transferred from the disc to the rim, rather than via the spokes. This allows for the weight-saving design of the front wheel, as well as immense braking power and feel.

With a frame weighing only 12kg (26lb), the Cyclone is 35kg (77lb) lighter and over 10hp more powerful than the latest 1200S Sportster. Cornering clearance, handling, top speed and acceleration are nothing like a Harley. The gear change is clunky – but it adds character – and the clutch can be a touch heavy. The Cyclone turns in easily, smoothly and holds a line well. The bodywork is at a minimum, and with a plastic tank you can forget magnetic tank bags. Like most Harley engines, it takes a few minutes for the motor to warm up, so the Cyclone needs some time before a rider can take it for a whirl.

ENGINE: 1203cc (72ci) ohv longitudinal 45-degree V-twin, 88.9x96.5mm, air-cooled
POWER: 86bhp at 6000rpm
GEARBOX: 5-speed foot change
FINAL DRIVE: toothed belt
WEIGHT: 197kg (435lb)
TOP SPEED: 202km/h (125mph)

With the heart of a Harley, the Buell Cyclone is an interesting take on the iconic American marque. Buell's interesting entry model handles and performs like no other bike on the road because its design is like no other bike.

PANZER MOTORCYCLES

The American Panzer Motorcycle takes its name from the 'Neo-Pan' engine, a revamped, more reliable version of Harley-Davidson's V-twin 'Panhead' engine.

The Panzer can only be described as retro. Look at the advertising surrounding it, and you are whisked back to the 1950s and James Dean, Marlon Brando and Marilyn Monroe.

The Panzer is essentially a Harley wannabe, and is pretty standard in what it provides: a typical big-twin in a cruiser chassis but with a little more in the way of modern reliability and handling. It behaves slightly better than its counterparts in that its throttle response, acceleration and braking are equivalent to a 2000 model year Harley-Davidson.

That means it is pretty good by the standards of big V-twins, though why a modern bike wants to pretend to be an older machine remains a mystery. So pretend it does; meanwhile Harley-Davidsons are the real McCoy.

Above: Looking like an extra from *Easy Rider*, the Panzer is a modern machine that wants to herald from another era. Another big V-twin with tonnes of chrome but nothing that is original.
Below: This bike owner has given his Panzer a customised paint-job.

AMERICAN QUANTUM CYCLES

American Quantum Motorcycles, located in Melbourne, Florida, is a new and innovative company that produces only two machines: the Liberty, a custom style bike; and its touring sister, the Pioneer,

which launched in December 1999.

The Liberty hit the market as an affordable custom bike, which is built largely from aftermarket upgrades for Harley-Davidsons. This innovative company started

out as a study in Best Practices and continues to be so. On its initial expansion, it used prisoners from Wackenhut to polish some parts and fibreglass others.

The Pioneer was just that, not in pure motorcycling terms but in its

production. It was described as 'a product platform', which allows customers to design their own machines by selecting various options at each stage. The Internet is instrumental in this process and can be accessed at dealers' showrooms. The result is a bespoke factory custom bike that is individual to the buyers' requirements.

The unusual manufacturing setup is not the only unique feature of the Quantum machines. Both sport a four-valve head, a system initially designed by Jim Feuling and Feuling Advanced Technology Inc. Jeff Starke, the founder of Quantum, received the rights to patent the design, and continues to develop it to improve the performance and reliability of this unique part.

American Quantum used state-of-the-art 3-D modelling CAD software to design saddlebags that provide maximized interior space while matching the curved lines of the fenders and frame. The futuristic production strategy is more of a talking point than the bikes themselves.

As Harley-Davidson look-alikes, the bikes themselves may not be terribly interesting. However, the company has achieved a lot, with an initial share offering of US$8 million in early 1999. Alongside a network of 61 dealers in 2000, that makes the company a genuine motorcycle manufacturer, rather than just a copy-cat assembler.

DRYSDALE

When Ian Drysdale set out to design his Superbike, the Australian had three requirements in mind. Firstly, he wanted a road-legal machine that offered extremely high performance – in effect, a race bike that could also be ridden to the shops. Secondly, it was to be a unique design, but one using parts that were readily available worldwide. This meant choosing parts from current manufacturers, so any parts that wore out could easily be replaced by the local dealer. And finally, the bike was to be easy to maintain. Both the heads, the clutch, the gearbox, the alternator and the water pump can all be removed with the engine still in the frame – and only the heads oblige the removal of any bodywork. How good is that?

Thus the Drysdale 750-V8 was born. Since it was made up of various machine parts, there were some interesting problems, such as the 1mm gap between the caps of the eight 32mm (1.25in) Keihin flat-slide carburettors initially used – a bit of a tight squeeze. As things progressed, these were replaced with fuel injection, making the throttle action much lighter and the whole engine easier to set up.

Inspired by Moto Guzzi's 500 V8, Ian Drysdale took the idea a step further with his 750 V8. It may be an unusual design but it is reliable and very usable – you can even pop to the shops on it.

The following components were all slotted into the Drysdale: Yamaha FZR 400 heads, a Kawasaki ZZR 250 alternator, Yamaha-Kawasaki gearbox components, Suzuki/Yamaha clutch, Honda CB 1000 oil circulation and a water pump from a Kawasaki ZZR 1100. Custom-made crank cases were made from a light cast alloy, and the crankshaft was honed from billet.

The original underseat radiators proved entirely inadequate for cooling, so they were replaced with two conventionally mounted radiators, one high and one low, in parallel. These proved capable of cooling the V8 monster even in the searing high temperatures of an Australian summer.

Drysdale also opted for a single-plane crankshaft (like an in-line four cylinder). This offered evenly spaced firing impulses along each bank, allowing for optimum exhaust tuning and ensuring the famous V8 'burble.'

The whole pack puts out 161hp, with a rev ceiling of 17,000rpm for street bikes and 19,000rpm for racers. That's an impressive power output compared with the

166hp extracted from an engine nearly one-third bigger in the V-twin Britten, and one that makes clear the advantages of the V8 layout.

A 20l (5.3 US gallon) tank was hardly going to furnish the Drysdale with long-distance touring potential, but it could hold enough fuel to provide

the bike with a reasonable range.

The Drysdale V8 had two inspirations. On the one hand, fast Italian motorcycles – particularly the Moto Guzzi 500 V8. Designed

by Guiliano Carcano, it never really reached its full potential but it did race between 1955 and 1957. Bimota and Ducati also had an influence on the Drysdale. The other inspiration was the reliability of Japanese machines, an area in which the Italians are known to fall short. The Drysdale V8 brought together the best of both worlds.

Based on a race bike, the Australian Superbike is fully road legal but performs like a full-on race bike. The V8 supplies a smooth, powerful ride and is easy to maintain and work on.

GEELY MOTORCYCLES

Cheap and cheerful would be the way to describe the Geely range of scooters. The JL 150 is one of the more powerful with a massive 12 bhp at its disposal.

The Geely Motorcycle group is known primarily in China due to its huge internal market. It produces 132 different scooters and small-capacity motorcycles from 50cc (3ci) up to 250cc (15ci). The country is commonly referred to as the 'Kingdom of Scooters' due to the sheer numbers produced, with annual production capacity hitting 600,000 units.

Geely series models are fashionable, with good performance and, most importantly, a reasonable selling price. This means they are favoured by the Chinese both at home and abroad.

The company name translates to 'auspicious benefit' in Chinese and the firm has certainly benefited from having Li Shufu as chairman. He is a controversial choice, but his innovative ideas have brought success. The company began making refrigerators, but in 1994 Li noted the influx of expensive foreign motorcycles and decided to jump on the bandwagon, producing his own and making them affordable. Some thought he would fail, but he proved them wrong.

Initially, he had to approach the Ministry of Machine-Building Industry (MMBI) for permission to produce motorcycles. The chances of a small private company getting approval were extremely slim, and he did not even make it past the front gate. Undeterred, he went to Hangzhou and bailed out a nearly bankrupt State-owned motorcycle factory. He turned the venture around, and before long Li's motorcycles were being sold in 22 countries, including the USA, Germany and Italy.

In the UK, Geely scooters sell well, the 50cc (3ci) machine being the best-seller. It comes in two guises, a Sportster and a Runner. The Sportster is aimed more at the commuter while the Runner is just that – a runaround. Both are priced under £750 (US$1500), and the Honda-based engine means that they are reliable if well maintained. As with all scooters, they are economical and perfect for getting around in heavy traffic, to and from work. The next model up is a 125cc (8ci) that has been described as the best-value machine. Known as the Commuter, it does look quite sporty and comes in at under £800. The Roadster is the most expensive model, coming in at just under £1300, but it has a more enclosed fairing for a more serious or longer-distance commute. The firm also offers the Wasp for just under £1000. The company is working on 250cc (15ci) and 400cc (24ci) models, which will doubtless be competitively priced and also cheap to run.

As well as a broad variety of two-wheelers, China Geely also offers a range of four-wheelers. The firm makes everything from 'domestic-use economical automobiles' to mini-trucks, and even light buses and travel buses. As if this were not enough, the company also makes decorative fascia materials and provides an education facility.

With a top speed of 40km/h (25mph), the 100T isn't the speediest of scooters, but it is small, easy to ride and ideal for a crowded city. If well maintained, the Geelys are reliable, cost effective runarounds.

KTM 620 EGS-E ADVENTURE

The super tall KTM Adventure arrived in a blur of orange and black in 1997. As the name suggests, it is capable of an all-terrain adventure, but only if the rider is tall enough to ride the massive beast!

With a seat height of 95cm (37in), the rider needs long legs, although a lower after-market seat is available, and this may well be more comfortable, particularly on a long journey.

Sharing its chassis with its LC4 Enduro and Duke siblings, the Adventure is a fun machine with excellent A-road potential, as well as superb off-road capability. For such a big and cumbersome-looking bike, it is noted for its quick steering and fine handling, thanks to its long-travel WP suspension. The swing arm is rather chunky but has a solid look to it, which contributes to a very stable feel for the rider.

This bike handles extremely well, on any given terrain. The ride is firm but soaks up potholes without any hesitation.

It was fitted with screen and hand protectors, and a colossal fuel tank capacity – 28 litres (7.4 US gallons) – which gives plenty of range for the long-distance rider. One criticism is the positioning of the exhausts, which are low slung so that the bike could be equipped with panniers for all-terrain touring. This means that they also tend to get scraped and damaged when the off-roading gets rough.

Most bikes that can be loaded up with luggage come fitted with a centre stand, but not the Adventure, which has a side stand only. It also comes with an intricate dash, which features an electronic competition computer trip master, allowing the rider to calculate distances between comfort stops.

The KTM 620 LC4 Enduro is a sibling of the better-known Adventure model.

This technology is usually used by Paris–Dakar competitors, and this bike is the commercial version of the machine raced by 80 per cent of the entrants in the gruelling desert race. On the production version, it can be used to work out how far to the next services.

The seating position is very upright, which is great for off-road encounters, but a bit problematic on motorways due to the amount of the wind blast. The fairing is small, but does help to reduce the pressure from the oncoming breeze. Being so large a bike means that there is plenty of space to move and adjust the riding position – essential on long trips.

ENGINE: 609cc (36.5ci) single, liquid-cooled
POWER: 50bhp
GEARBOX: 5-speed, foot change
FINAL DRIVE: chain
WEIGHT: 166kg (365lb)
TOP SPEED: 153km/h (95mph)

On-road, off-road, over sand dunes – the KTM can handle the lot. The capable machine takes its heritage from the toughest race on earth, the Dakar Rally. Looks may not be its strong point but it handles like a dream.

RIDLEY

Ridley motorcycles are the brainchild of Clay Ridley, a modern-day inventor and innovator – of which there are few. The fully automatic, scaled-down Ridley Motorcycles are not his only

The Ridley brings a whole new meaning to mini moto. The fully automatic scaled down motorcycle is not a toy, but a fully operational, road-legal bike that is perfect for the new rider.

success or original piece of engineering. When he was only a child, he managed to build a chassis for his very own little car. He then went on to build and fly his own helicopter, a feat that few people have ever achieved. His next achievement was less glamorous but a huge success: a custom production machine to weld polypropylene rope, which led to a new way of making soles for shoes.

When he set up the Ridley Motorcycle company, he intended to bring new and different ideas to motorcycling – and he has certainly achieved that. The bikes

that he produces are a scaled-down version of typical American V-twins. The bikes are three-quarters the size and one-third the weight of Harley-Davidsons. They also have the novelty of being fully automatic, ideal for novice riders or those small of stature.

When the firm started production, the aim was to build 120 units, but in the first year it managed 160. At the time of writing, it produces five automatic machines and has just started manufacturing a more grown-up manual version.

All the bikes have a 750cc (46ci) 90-degree V-twin lay out with

constantly variable transmission (CVT). The Auto–Glide Sport is a slinky, all-black number with a certain monochrome style of its own. The Auto-Glide Classic is just that, a classic based on the original Ridley with classic design and a very easy ride. The Auto-Glide TT is the sporty version with a 48cm (19in) front. The styling of the Auto-Glide Old School is straight out of the 1960s, with super high bars and an old-fashioned bicycle style sprung seat. The final bike in the Auto-glide range is the Chop, and as the name suggests it is a scaled-down chopper – very cute.

The first bike in the range to have full manual transmission is the X88. It has an automatic side stand, which retracts as soon as the rider hooks a gear, and can be put back down at the touch of a button. It runs a Harley 88B engine and transmission, weighs 45kg (100lb) less than others in its class and has a 62cm (24.5in) seat height – hard to beat for shorter people.

Based in Oklahoma City, Oklahoma, the Ridley is a very welcome twist on the standard American V-twin. It is an interesting concept, and a successful one.

TRIUMPH T595 DAYTONA

Triumph likes a challenge, and placing their latest creation firmly in the sports market gave them a lot to live up to. Thankfully, the T595 was accepted and has progressed into a successful venture for the British marque.

The T595 was up against many of the big hitters – namely, Honda's FireBlade and Ducati's 916. However, it was weighing in heavier and felt bulkier than the competition, but it still handled well.

Although it did not offer quick steering, it had a confident feel to it. The engine pulled well; it did have a bit of a flat spot around 5000rpm, but it ran well beyond that.

In 1999, the T595 was superseded by a new model, the 955i. This was a super sports bike powered by the liquid-cooled, double overhead-cam, in-line 955cc (57ci) three-cylinder unit. It contained numerous improvements.

These included a modified exhaust camshaft, revised throttle bodies, a new air bypass system, revised engine management tuning, new exhaust header pipes, a rear suspension unit, an air-box, revised wiring and hoses, and new paintwork.

The engineers at Triumph took on board the feedback from the T595 and worked the improvements into the 955i, putting it on a more level footing with its Japanese counterparts.

When reviving an icon, a company is going to have a lot to live up to. And when it decides to place that icon in the very competitive sports bike market, then it really does have its work cut out. Such was the case for Triumph when it decided to launch the T595 Daytona.

The groundbreaking T595 Daytona was introduced in 1997, and it took Triumph right back to the top of the world's motorcycle manufacturing tree. It differed from its modular predecessors, the T309 and T400 Daytonas, in having as its

basis the curvaceous oval-tube aluminium frame designed by Chris Hennegan.

The perimeter frame allowed more room to manoeuvre in terms of placing the engine, allowing chassis performance to be optimized.

The engine was based on the Hinckley-produced 955cc (58ci) triple, but it was honed down on weight and boosted in capacity to give that sporty feel.

It produced 128hp at 10,200rpm, with a massive 72.3ft/lb of torque. Magnesium was used for the engine casings

and crank, and the gearbox and clutch were also lightened.

The single-sided swing-arm allowed the three-into-one exhaust system to be tucked in tightly on the right-hand side, thus showing off the three-spoke Brembo wheel, which was shod with sticky Bridgestone BT56 tyres. Showa suspension soaked up the undulations of a normal road and does not suffer too much from dive under braking. Nissin four-piston callipers at the front and two-pistons at the rear were in place for stopping the fast Daytona.

ENGINE: 955cc (57ci) fuel-injected ohv triple, 79x65mm, water-cooled
POWER: 128bhp
GEARBOX: 6-speed foot change
FINAL DRIVE: chain
WEIGHT: 198kg (436lb)
TOP SPEED: 257km/h (160mph)

YAMAHA FAZER 600

In the late 1990s, the market opened up to a whole type of bike – namely, the naked middle weight, prompted by the success of the Ducati Monster. Yamaha's equivalent was the FZS600 Fazer.

The firm was already in possession of a robust engine in the form of the Thundercat motor, so this was used in the early Fazers. Its claim to fame was that it also used the same brakes as the much sought-after R1, plus it

Originally fitted with a detuned Thundercat engine, the more recent machines benefited from the R6 lump. The fine pedigree, along with sure-footed agility, has made the Fazer a popular track tool.

had a small fairing that made it much more user friendly than the competition. Due to emission regulations, the original Fazer bit the dust in 2003 to be replaced by an even livelier piece of kit: yes, the new Fazer was given a detuned R6 engine.

The new Fazer was now known as the FZ600 and was a very capable bike with good acceleration and top speed. It handled well due to its firm chassis; throw in light agile steering and first class brakes, and it was a great all rounder. It was also fairly easy on the motion lotion, averaging 50mpg, ideal for commuting.

The Fazer is happy under any conditions, open roads or clogged-up cities. The unfaired

version may mean that wind blast is a problem on motorways. The styling has a funky edge to it, appealing to a wide audience. It does not have the most comfortable seat, a problem for long-distance riders. It is an ideal bike for a beginner or for a more experienced rider who prefers to avoid spending time in a racing crouch.

While the 600cc (36ci) was taking the bike world by storm, Yamaha introduced a 1000cc (60ci) version that used the R1 engine in a detuned form. This arrived in 2001 with a top-notch motor and cutting-edge performance running gear, all built into one easy-to-handle package. Like its smaller capacity sibling, the 1000cc (60ci)

Fazer was well behaved and had a heady mix of performance, handling and usability.

When a sports bike engine is used elsewhere in a detuned form, it is sometimes criticized for not being punchy enough. In this case, the retuning gives superb low- to midrange power, which is more usable in day-to-day situations. It was carried out by fitting smaller carburettors, which help to increase fuel economy and provide more torque lower down the rev range. A heavier crankshaft was also added for better, low-down drive, while a re-mapped ignition finished things off nicely. The chassis is precise but not overly stiff like a sports machine, giving an easier

ride. The suspension is sporty enough to handle, and the R1 brakes are ideal for hauling the big Fazer to a halt.

The small fairing offers decent protection from wind blast, so longer rides are no problem. The Fazer has taken its headlamps from the R1, and when slotted into the fairing it gives it a very mean stare. Equipped with a 21l (5.5 US gallon) tank, it can run for 290km (180 miles) between fuel stops. There is even a very sensible centre stand, ideal when packing up with luggage for a long trip. The seat is comfortable with plenty of space for both the rider and a pillion.

The Fazer family has been a successful venture for Yamaha,

bridging the gap between sports bikes and general commuters. The machines work for a wide range of riders of varying ability.

The fine-handling Fazer tackled the sports bikes and did a good job of usurping them in many cases. It is capable of touring, commuting and hooning on highways.

ENGINE: 600cc (36ci) in-line four dohc 4-stroke 65.5 x 44.5mm
POWER: 98bhp
GEARBOX: 6 speed
FINAL DRIVE: chain
WEIGHT: 191kg (423 pounds)
TOP SPEED: 217km/h (135mph)

APRILIA RSV MILLE

In 1998, Aprilia completed its motorcycle range by adding the RSV Mille to their line up, giving them the accolade of being the only European company with machines from 50cc (3ci) to 1000cc (61ci). It was unveiled in a flurry of excitement at the Milan Show at the end of 1997.

With oodles of Italian flare and a rich race pedigree of wins in the 125cc and 250cc Grand Prix classes, Aprilia upped the ante against its main rival, Ducati. As an Italian marque, it will always be measured against Ducati, and

the Mille stood up to the test.

The firm's rapid growth meant that Aprilia was in a strong position to start working on its first big bike. At the end of 1996, its turnover was some 800 billion lire (a 32 per cent increase over 1995), selling an amazing 231,000 vehicles, 45 per cent of which were exported. On the track, it had picked up eight world championships by the end of 1997, which helped to promote its image around the world: 'Race on Sunday, sell on Monday' is an adage that still rings true. It also

enabled the company to transfer the technical innovations gained from its racing programme to its standard production models.

The chassis of the new superbike was excellent, as would be expected from a company with a wealth of racing experience behind it. However, the real surprise came with the quality of the engine: at that point, Aprilia was known for producing much smaller power plants, so to pull off a superb 1000cc (60ci) motor was a considerable achievement. Where other manufacturers, such as

Ducati, Honda and Suzuki, were fixing their cylinders at 90 degrees, Aprilia set its cylinders at 60 degrees, enabling it to create a compact, lightweight design. To quell the extra vibration from the narrower cylinder angle, the machine sports dual balancer shafts, offering as smooth a ride as possible.

Aprilia gave the RSV Mille a dry, not wet, sump lubrication. This allowed the company drastically to reduce the size of the oil container area below the crankshaft, thus enabling the engine to be positioned much lower in the frame. This, in turn, lowered the centre of gravity, producing a bike that handled and performed superbly.

When Aprilia designed the Mille, it tapped into what riders want from a sports bike. This has meant that the RSV has received numerous awards from specialist magazines. During its first few years of life, it became the benchmark for performance, rideability and track success. With the Aprilia race pedigree behind it, as well as top-notch technology, it has won over a huge legion of fans worldwide.

ENGINE: 997cc (60ci) dohc 60-degree V-twin, 97x67.5mm, liquid-cooled
POWER: 128bhp at 9500rpm
GEARBOX: 6-speed foot change
FINAL DRIVE: chain
WEIGHT: 189kg (417lb)
TOP SPEED: 266km/h (165mph)

With a huge amount of racing know-how behind them, it was about time Aprilia broke into the big sports bike market. The Mille took on the competition and came out with lots of awards – they obviously got this one very right.

BMW R1100S

The BMW boxer engine has been around since the beginning of time, or so it seems. In 1998, BMW decided to slot it into the R1100S, a sports tourer with unique telelever suspension.

BMWs are notoriously quirky and the R1100S was no exception. The sporty motor kicks left as all boxers do, but the size of the engine makes the movement more noticeable. The sturdy engine pulls well from 3000rpm and works well up to 6000rpm. It redlines at 8000rpm, but is capable of pulling all the way through the rev range, although the vibration kicks in towards the top of the range.

The R1100S was the sportier version of the four-valve-per-cylinder, fuel-injected boxers that first turned up in 1992. Krauser had made four-valve heads for the older boxers, but these were not well regarded. Thus the new bikes had factory-installed four-valve heads, as well as a single, chain-driven overhead-cam per cylinder.

In common with the makers of a number of other big twins, BMW decided not to take the conventional liquid-cooled route, but to take advantage of the cooling properties of the lubricating oil instead. Whereas oil-coolers (and deep, high-capacity sumps) were popular accessories for the old boxers, oil-cooling was an integral part of the new boxers right from the beginning.

The most radical feature of the R1100S had to be the patented front suspension; the telelever effectively eliminated dive on braking and twist under any conditions. It is most obvious on the unfaired models, looking like a mudguard that has unaccountably extended back to the engine.

A monoshock behind the headstock provides the springing and damping for the telelever arm. The front telelever has a fairly short suspension travel, but it gives riders enough feedback to know they have hit the brakes.

At least as important in a very conservative market is the fact that the telelever does not look too unusual. The design works well when cornering in a spirited fashion, giving good feedback. Although a bit on the heavy side

The boxer engine is reinvented yet again by BMW, this time as the heart of a very well-rounded Sports Tourer. The engine has lost none of its unique appeal and copes well with the more modern design of the R1100S.

for a sports bike, it turns well into corners and holds a strong line, the weight keeping it planted.

The main concern when cornering with a boxer engine is the cylinder heads touching down. However, on the R1100S there are other features that touch down before the rocker-box covers. The crash bars and the centre stand hit the deck early on, as soon as the pace picks up.

The new boxer line-up soon showed more variation and popular appeal than its predecessor. Known as the 'brick', this off-road R1100GS was launched in 1994, offering 'only' 80hp, alongside an R850R offering only 69hp.

This was followed by an R1100R and R1100RT tourer in 1995. Then, in 1996, came an R1200C cruiser, with an 1170cc (71ci) version of the big twin, delivering a mere 61hp for very relaxed power delivery, but it had a very unusual look; in fact, traditional motorcyclists thought it looked a bit strange. Interestingly, despite its impressive performance, the R1100S has only an 18l (5 US gallon) fuel tank, the smallest of the Rs. The biggest, the R1100RT, boasts 26l (6 US gallons). Since the R1100S considers itself a tourer, a larger fuel range would have been expected.

BMWs have always been seen as safe, conservative options, but that changed with the sports tourer, which can hold its own on or off the track.

ENGINE: 1085cc (65ci) ohv 8volt four-stroke transverse flat twin, 99x70.5mm, air/oil-cooled
POWER: 98bhp at 7500rpm
GEARBOX: 5-speed foot change
FINAL DRIVE: Cardan shaft
WEIGHT: 229kg (504lb)
TOP SPEED: 225km/h (140mph)

Grinding the cylinder heads is the biggest concern for anyone trying to hustle with the BMW R1100S. Considering it is a Sports Tourer, ground clearance is not as good as it could be, but the touring aspect makes up for this particular lack.

CANNONDALE

USA 1998–PRESENT

From bicycles to motocross bikes, Cannondale has done an excellent job of producing both. They did not go for a copy-cat job either: the Cannondale machines have their own unique design, which makes them even more specialized.

These days, it is unusual for a manufacturer of one successful product to branch out into the unknown. In the late 19th and early 20th centuries, it was not unusual for bicycle manufacturers to take up motorcycle manufacture as cheap forms of transport were required; by the late 1990s, it was very unusual indeed. Mountain-bike manufacturers Cannondale were not deterred, however, and began producing an off-road motorcycle that made its racing debut early in 1999.

Cannondale made the point of bringing in outside talent early in the project, ensuring a suitable level of knowledge and expertise. The result was a machine that proved remarkably competitive and innovative from day one.

The engine that powered both the motorcycle line-up and later

the quad bike was a 432cc (26ci), double overhead-camshaft, four-valve, liquid-cooled single, hooked up via a five-speed gearbox. Bore and stroke were 95 x 61mm (3.7 x 2.4in) and heavily over square. The Cannondale took on some interesting design concepts, one of which is that the engine actually breathes through the frame, thanks to a unique design of steering-head bearing. Not only does this mean that the air is cleaner, but it is also cooler, and therefore denser, which means that more fuel-air mixture goes directly into the cylinder. The design also features a long inlet tract, which is muted to improve low-speed throttle response.

Design peculiarities did not end there, however. The cylinder head was mounted 'backwards', with the inlet at the front and the

exhaust at the back. Cooling the exhaust-valve is usually the problem with such machines, but this was solved by the adoption of liquid-cooling overall. Taking no chances on the cooling front, Cannondale carried out extensive wind-tunnel testing of the ducted cooling design during development.

The reversed head also allowed the repositioning of the cylinder, thereby lowering the centre of gravity. It also shortened the exhaust pipe by nearly 30.5cm (12in), rendering it less susceptible to damage in an accident, and the rider less susceptible to burns from the exhaust pipe in the event of a spill. The shorter exhaust also created a wider range of usable power. Reversed heads are usually seen as bad news, but as technology advances, it is often

a good idea to challenge the norm. How else can new discoveries be made?

Considering the Cannonade was a limited-production motorcycle, the firm really went to town on development, For example, frame flex was actually measured via numerous tiny strain gauges, mounted all over it. Depending on the state of trim, the bikes weighed 110–113kg (242–249lb), with the heavier version being fully equipped with lights and instruments. Of the two lighter versions, one had no provision for lights, while the other could be fitted with a lighting coil for off-road racing. Tall, skinny tyres, in the usual off-road mould, made steering more precise, as did a modest degree of rake and a short wheelbase. Years of experience in manufacturing bicycles has translated into motorcycles with a low weight and manoeuvrability.

The fascination people have for the Cannondale lies in its contrariness. Most new American manufacturers make copy-cat versions of Harley-Davidson V-twins, but Cannondale broke the mould with a genuinely original and competitive motorcycle. It found a niche in the market for a four-stroke motocross bike, and got it into the market place ahead of the big players who have a wealth of experience behind them.

For a company that started out in a loft above a pickle factory, Cannondale have come a long way, and much of the time they have led the way. It is a unique company and a unique motorcycle.

EMB LECTRA

USA 1998

With the environment increasingly becoming an issue of concern as the 1990s progressed, one company decided to do its bit. EMB produced the Lectra and, as the name suggests, it was an electric motorbike.

The usual concern with an electric bike is its speed, or lack of it. The Lectra performed well on the handling front and had as much performance as could be expected. Acceleration was enough to keep up with traffic in built-up areas, with a top speed of 80km/h (50mph). In terms of handling, it had the characteristics

of a scooter but was much more stable, like a motorcycle.

It was launched at a price of around $4000 in 1998 – which later went up to $4500. The small-wheel chain drive machine was rather heavy at 104kg (340lb), because of the 104 Ah (lead-free) batteries that were needed to propel it. Due to the weight,

This bike is as environmentally friendly as they come. Powered by a variable reluctance motor, the VR24, with a top speed of 80km (50mph), is anything but reluctant.

substantial brakes had to be added – ironic given that it was such a slow vehicle. A dual-calliper, 190mm (7.5in) floating disc at the front, and a 100mm (4in) drum at the back were fitted as standard.

The 24V extremely advanced 'variable reluctance' motor and controller was rated at 3hp continuous, and 8hp peak for acceleration. This technology was used, as it has high efficiency, robustness, good power density and low manufacturing costs. The 24V motor offered regenerative, anti-lock braking, and a very unique 'growling' sound. In September 1999, at the Woodburn Electric Drag Races, the Lectra actually set a couple of (highly specialized) world records: it completed the standing 200m (0.125 mile) in 15 seconds, at a terminal speed of just over 64km/h (40mph).

EMB claimed that the battery system would not spill or leak, and, with proper care, would last for 14,484km (9000 miles). A full recharge for the Lectra took just

over four hours and cost only pennies. It could be charged easily with an extension cord from under the seat, which could be plugged into almost any electrical power outlet (90–260V, 47–63Hz). The bike lasted about 40–64km (25–40 miles) without a re-charge, and it was fitted with a 'fuel gauge' that tracked the level of stored energy. Like a normal motorcycle, there was even a reserve to help riders to reach the nearest power outlet.

Running at top speed would be likely to effect a significant reduction in the claimed range of 64km (40 miles), even though it was fitted with regenerative braking, which fed power back into the battery when rolling downhill or slowing down. Most users reckoned that a distance of 40km (25 miles) between charges was nearer to the mark.

Although the bike itself did not belch out any fumes, the label 'zero emissions' is a bit of a misnomer. The electricity to power the Lectra has to come from somewhere, and

that somewhere is a fossil-fuel burning power station, or even a nuclear power plant.

Claims that this is the world's first electric motorcycle are incorrect. Ome (1920), Bullo (1924–26), Socovel (1938) and Solo (circa 1950s) all made electric bikes. Nevertheless, this is a bold attempt to produce a modern machine, incorporating interesting

There are not many bikes that can have their fuel levels topped up simply by plugging them into the mains. The Lectra does just that and saves the planet at the same time.

and innovative ideas, to take motorcycle development away from the oil-leaking combustion engine and onto a different plane.

EXCELSIOR-HENDERSON SUPER X

The Excelsior-Henderson comeback began in 1993, when the Hanlon Manufacturing Company paid a visit to Sturgis, and was struck by the fact that individuality was missing from the many machines on show. Every machine seemed to be a copy.

With that in mind, as well as the necessary funding, the firm started to look back through the history books to see where to start. Excelsior-Henderson was chosen as a name because the Schwinn Company had allowed it to lapse.

Design work on the new Excelsior-Henderson started in earnest, its makers taking inspiration from the 1931 Super X. The prototypes were unveiled in 1996 at the Sturgis rally; a year later, running prototypes were unveiled at Bike Week in Daytona Beach, Florida. In July 1997, Excelsior-Henderson became a publicly traded company.

After five years of careful planning, financing, designing, engineering and marketing, the first production bike arrived. It had unique features, the engine being the main one. Instead of the 'knife-and-fork' type, the 50-degree, 1386cc/85ci (93 x 102mm/3.7 x 4in), air-cooled V-twin was a modern, offset design with the two con rods running side by side on a forged crankshaft. Both the offset and the increased cylinder angle allowed significantly better cooling.

Better still, each cylinder head had twin, chain-driven camshafts

and four valves. Unexpectedly for an overhead-camshaft design, the actual valve operation was reportedly hydraulic. Fuel injection was included in the design from the start, and was made easier by that small increase in cylinder angle. Given these specifications, the actual power output was surprisingly low given that 45–50hp/l had been achieved on plenty of road-going bikes, even big V-twins, by the end of the 1920s.

Another brand on a comeback mission that sadly did not last. The Excelsior-Henderson did its best on styling and design, but it was not enough to keep the fledgling company afloat.

There were numerous mechanical innovations, some technically interesting and some imposed by the styling requirements of the American 'big cruiser' market. For instance, the cam chains are concealed within the oversized cylinder outline, which looks very clean but is of dubious merit from an engineering viewpoint: it is an

invitation to distortion if the machine is ridden very hard, although this may not be an issue given the low power output of the engine. Test riders reported bad vibrations around 2200rpm and again after 3500rpm, all the way up to the point where the rev-limiter comes in and cuts the spark to one cylinder at

5500 rpm. Not ideal when cruising at speed.

Another unusual feature is a hydraulic clutch. In theory, this reduces maintenance and potentially makes clutch operation easier. However, it costs more, weighs more and is more difficult to service – a case of pros and cons cancelling each other out. In order to pass the Californian emission regulations,

the Excelsior-Henderson had only to add an evaporative emission canister, two valves and some extra hoses.

On the styling front, the designers tried to re-create the look of the old Excelsiors, including the rigid rear end, which was a sprung monoshock. They even went for the front forks through the front mudguard, a design that was more successful

in the 1930s, when forks and tyres were much skinnier.

A lot of the other features were conventional, like the five-speed, foot-change gearbox with belt final drive. The footboards are in the American cruiser style, which were reportedly all too easy to ground, and the machine'was, to European eyes, grossly overweight at 314kg (690lb). A single 29cm (11.5in) front disc (with four-pot callipers)

Despite all its innovative design, the Excelsior put out very little power. In fact, it was on par with bikes from the 1920s. A big vibration at certain revs did not help matters.

was typically American: elsewhere in the world, twin, smaller discs were more usual. Unexpectedly, the rear brake is the same size as the front brake.

The top speed of this machine is not stated. It is perhaps academic anyway, because the vibration problems would make everything a blur at speed – for all the wrong reasons.

The Super X was built from December 1998 through August 1999, with production not breaking the 2000 mark. Sadly, production stopped in September 1999 and the company filed for bankruptcy court protection in December 1999. It looked like it would survive under the supervision of a group of investors, but they simply returned the company to bankruptcy – so that was that.

A truly beautiful machine but one where form won over function. 1930s styled forks were fine in the 1930s, but perhaps don't quite cut it these days.

GILERA RUNNER SCOOTER

When Gilera set about designing the Runner Scooter, it decided that the bike needed to be given more of a motorcycle edge; indeed, the firm went as far as saying that it had given the design the soul of a motorcycle. Perhaps this is why the Runner has been such a hit with streetwise youngsters.

For Gilera fans, it seemed that their favoured marque had bitten the dust at the end of 1993. However, Gilera rose from the ashes by building an entirely new range of machines, heading the class-leading range of liquid-cooled Runner scooters.

The scooter might not be a model easily associated with Gilera, but at the dawn of the 21st century, scooter sales are actually booming. With roads getting busier, a traffic-busting scoot is the way forward.

Gilera's PR went into overdrive when it announced the all-new Runner series. Available in three engine sizes – 50cc (3ci), 123.5cc (8ci) and 175.8cc (11ci) – it combined 'for the first time, the practicality and ease of use of a scooter, with rigidity, and handling of a fully fledged motorcycle'. It is a lot to ask from any vehicle, since bikes and scooters are inherently different, and several machines from the past have already attempted to bridge the gap between the two, such as the Moto Guzzi Galletto.

But what sets the new Gilera apart from the earlier efforts of the 1950s is the advantages of modern technology. The Runner's specification includes features such as super-rigid frame construction, inverted front forks, alloy wheels with low-profile tyres, a powerful hydraulically operated disc front brake and a sleek fairing with flowing lines. The 50cc (3ci) models use upside-down front forks and a rear monoshock, whereas the 125cc (8ci) has conventional forks and twin hydraulic shock absorbers at the back. Gilera claim that they have quicker acceleration and sharper braking than their rivals, and also offer low fuel consumption and emissions.

The VX 125 has enough grunt to compete in traffic, and also has near to instant pick-up, progressing to 80km/h (50mph) in a smooth and brisk fashion. The handling is good and has plenty of potential for the sort of stunt-riding that young scooter fans so enjoy.

The largest Runner – coded the 180 – is capable of 120km/h (75mph). All three employ liquid-cooled, single-cylinder engines with automatic oil pumps, electronic capacitive ignition (CDI) with variable advance and a choice of kick- or push-button electric and 12V batteries.

The Runner has sharp contours and the signature Gilera headlight, in which twin lamps are covered by a single transparent sheet. The back-lit, analogue, digital instrument panel is pretty comprehensive for a machine of this lever.

All three Runners have their fuel tanks under the central tunnel, which helps to create a low centre of gravity. That, combined with a rigid tubular steel frame, makes for excellent agility and precise handling.

It also explains why, since 1999, the Runner 50cc (3ci) and 125cc (8ci) scooters have provided the base for the Gilera Runner Trophy, an international one-model race series that involves more than 200 riders from all over Europe. The series is organized in two engine sizes (70cc/4ci and 180cc/11ci), in collaboration with engine-tuning specialists Malossi.

The Gilera Runner has tapped into the teen market and has a big following among young riders. It even has its own owners club, offering tips on customizing the scooter and tuning it for maximum performance.

ENGINE: 175.8cc (10.5ci) 2s horizontal single, 65.6x50mm, liquid-cooled
POWER: 21bhp at 8000rpm
GEARBOX: automatic CVT variator with torque convertor
FINAL DRIVE: gears
WEIGHT: 115kg (254lb)
TOP SPEED: 120km/h (75mph)

The Gilera Runner has won over legions of fans, it has an owners club, a one-make race series and even a computer game. Gilera hit the right market with the Runner.

HARLEY-DAVIDSON TWIN CAM

Most big manufacturers produce a new engine every few years or rework an old one on a regular basis. But Harley-Davidson likes to do things differently. The Twin Cam was the first new engine it produced since the Evolution Sportster motor of 1986. It is also the first new Big Twin motor since the original Evolution, which was released in 1984.

In a Harley time frame, 15 years between engines is not really that long; the Evo's predecessor, the Shovelhead, lasted 19 years. When the Twin Cam was announced, everyone was expecting an overhead-cam design. In fact, it was simply a bigger and better version of the preceding Evo V-twin, albeit with the same primitive knife-and-fork bottom end.

The new engine was built in two versions, one for rubber mounting and the other with balance shafts for rigid mounting and three per cent less power. The rationale behind the under-square engine appears to have been to offer bigger and bigger displacements as factory options and also to take the opportunity to address shortcomings in the previous engine. The Twin Cam 88 is a 45-degree V-Twin. The total displacement landed at 1450cc (87ci), 110cc (7ci) more than the Evolution's 1340cc (82ci). The Twin Cam is named because it has two chain-driven cams, which have been designed to give the pushrods a straighter run at the rockers for higher potential performance. The new engine should respond much

more positively to performance enhancements; that said, it is no slouch in stock form. In standard, EPA-regulated trim, its claimed peak torque at the crank is 86ft/lb at 3500rpm.

Twin Cam featured on all the Touring and Dyna models during its first year in production, with the Softails following later. Initial reactions ranged from predictable slavish admiration of anything Harley-Davidson does to the equally predictable condemnation from traditionalists who regard all change, for whatever reason, as always being for the worse.

As things move on, at the time of writing, Harley was introducing

its lastest machinery for 2007: the Twin Cam 96, due to power all models in the Harley Dyna, Softail and touring-based machines. They will also benefit from a 6-speed Cruise Drive transmission. No doubt, these new era Harleys will continue to stir the soul of new converts with their presence, expression and passion.

ENGINE: 1450cc (87ci) ohv in-line V-twin, 95x102mm, air/oil-cooled
POWER: 65bhp est.
GEARBOX: 5-speed foot change
FINAL DRIVE: belt
WEIGHT: 278kg (612lb)
TOP SPEED: 177km/h (110mph) est.

It's just a new engine, so what is all the fuss about? Harley has not had a new engine since the mid-1980s, as it likes to make them last. The Twin Cam has been used on the bulk of the Harley range.

INDIAN

America's oldest motorcycle brand, the Indian Motorcycle Manufacturing Company, was founded way back in 1901, two years ahead of Harley-Davidson. So it is a real shame that it did not manage to continue in seamless production. However, it was finally resurrected successfully in 1998 after a number of failures.

Attempts to revive the marque included badge-engineering Royal Enfields, Velocettes and even Ehler Industries. Then came a Vindian, which was an Indian running on a Vincent engine. Who had the rights to the name was the main sticking point, and the situation grew increasingly murky as lawsuits flew in all directions. Once the deal was settled, however, the 'new' Indian Motorcycle Company, with its headquarters in Gilroy, California, seemed to have full rights to the name, and planned the production of 11,000 machines a year.

The comeback model was based around a newer version of the Chief, which was originally introduced way back in the 1920s. This was followed up by the Scout and Spirit models, which started production in 2001.

In order to come into the marketplace as quickly as possible, the firm decided not to design its own motor. Instead, it went for the readily available S&S 1441cc (88ci) nominal displacement V-twin, actually 1436cc/88ci (108 x 92mm/ 4.3 x 3.5in). Many other great motorcycle marques started out with someone else's engine: Brough Superiors built their reputations on bought-in V-twins, initially JAP and later Matchless, while the original Indian engines were built by Thor.

The finished product was built to look as similar as possible to a 1953 Indian Chief, from the last year of full production. Deeply valanced mudguards, a fringed

The Scout is the little brother to the Chief; it is lighter, faster and handles better than its bigger, older sibling. America's oldest motorcycle brand is still hoping to make a further come back in 2007.

saddle and an Indian Head running light all gave it the distinctive Indian look.

This 'new' Indian was not a true Indian but was more of an assembled machine. Thus a great deal hinged upon the promise of the in-house engine, which was due to appear in 2000. Other parts were supplied by established names in motorcycling: Supertrapp made the exhausts; Showa, the front forks; Arlen Ness, the headlights; and Corbin, the seat. Not the lightest of bikes to hit the market at a dry weight of 295kg (650lb), it was as portly as it was handsome, with a tendency to ground the floorboards during anything other than the most sedate cornering. This did not deter customers, who knew that it was the first of a new breed of Indians and that all these issues could be addressed.

Sadly, the in-house engine was never completed as the company succumbed to bankruptcy once again in late 2003, after a major investor backed out. At the time of writing, there is some hope that the production will resume in 2007. On 20 July 2006, the newly formed Indian Motorcycle Company, owned largely by Stellican Limited, a London-based private equity firm, announced its new home as Kings Mountain, North Carolina.

This is where it hopes to breathe life back into the iconic Indian Motorcycle Brand. This new company is aiming to be producing a new Chief by mid-2007. It has raised $30 million for the relaunch and is currently working to a business plan to get the mighty Indian back on its feet over the next two years.

MV AGUSTA F4

Any machine that develops from a collaboration between Cagiva, Ducati and Ferrari is going to be a special motorcycle, and the MV Agusta F4 is exactly that. It has been hailed by many as

the ultimate Superbike; indeed, the MV Agusta F4 could easily have been produced as a Cagiva, a Ducati, or even a Ferrari. It began as the result of conversations between two

men – Claudio Castiglioni, the Cagiva boss, and his chief designer, Massimo Tamburini. Help also came from Piero Ferrari, son of Enzo Ferrari, and Ferrari's owners, Fiat.

Rumours of a brand new Cagiva-masterminded Superbike began to surface at the beginning of the 1990s. These went into overdrive at the launch of the new Ferrari 465 GT car, when a photograph of the new engine was shown – a mistake or a perfect PR stunt? Either way, Claudio Castiglioni was forced to confirm that the engine was being developed in conjunction with Ferrari, and that both Castiglioni and Pieri Ferrari had actually tested the prototype machine.

Cagiva's financial difficulties during the mid-1990s stalled development at the company's hilltop research centre in San Marino. However, in spring 1998, the first examples of this long-awaited and exotic machine arrived. It was badged as an MV Agusta since Cagiva had purchased the brand name in the 1980s, thus reviving an iconic brand. Having earlier sold Ducati to the American TPG finance house, it could not have used the Ducati name.

With such a high-level design team, it is little wonder that the F4 was hailed as a work of art. Indeed, the F4's styling put it ahead of every other series production sports bike in the world. And there were innovative technical features to match. With four cylinders and

four valves per cylinder, the double-overhead-cam, across-the-frame, liquid-cooled, 749.8cc/45.7ci (73.8 x 43.8mm/2.9 x 1.7in) engine had the advantage of the very latest Weber-Marelli electronic fuel injection and ignition systems. It had also a removable (cassette-type) six-speed gearbox and

a radical radial valve cylinder head.

The F4's frame is made up of a 'mixed' steel and aluminium structure, while the single-sided swinging-arm is cast in aluminium and the frame's steering head angle is multi-adjustable. Front suspension is a specially built inverted Showa fork assembly.

The Ohlins hydraulic steering damper mounted across the frame and an exhaust that exits under the seat are typical of designer Massimo Tamburini.

His team also came up with a particularly innovative front light. The twin-stacked polyellipsoidals give the F4 an unmistakable

A work of art on wheels is the only way to describe the stunning MV Agusta. With the F4 having been spawned from three top Italian manufacturers, namely Cagive, Ferrari and Ducati, how could it be anything else?

appearance, while also allowing for a very narrow fairing for maximum aerodynamics.

Although the bike is compact, it is comfortable to ride. Its limited steering lock makes three point turns good fun. It provides it rider with a lot of feedback through the front end, instilling confidence.

The chassis is taut and the suspension flexible enough to deal with hard hits. When cornering, it is unstoppable and will handle whatever the road throws at the rider, holding a rock-solid line.

The 750cc (46ci) engine needs to be worked to get the most out of the MV, but is worth the effort.

The same goes for handling, which needs a bit more body language than a regular Japanese bike.

Throughout, the detailing on the F4 is superb. Coupled with the flamboyant style and performance – just over 272km/h (170mph) – this makes it a 'must own' for the serious sports rider.

ENGINE: 749.4cc (45ci) dohc 4v straight four, 73.8x43.8mm, liquid-cooled
POWER: 126bhp at 12,200rpm
GEARBOX: 6-speed foot change
FINAL DRIVE: chain
WEIGHT: 180kg (397lb)
TOP SPEED: 272km/h (170mph)

YAMAHA YZF-R1

Six years after Honda launched the highly successful Fireblade, Yamaha decided it was time to retaliate with the R1. This was powered by a four-stroke, in-line, four-cylinder motor with five valves per cylinder, which was slotted into a state-of-the-art chassis sporting telescopic front forks and a monoshock at the rear.

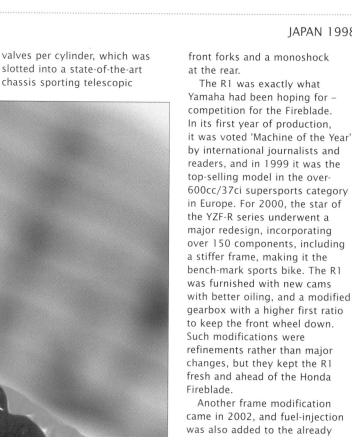

The R1 was exactly what Yamaha had been hoping for – competition for the Fireblade. In its first year of production, it was voted 'Machine of the Year' by international journalists and readers, and in 1999 it was the top-selling model in the over-600cc/37ci supersports category in Europe. For 2000, the star of the YZF-R series underwent a major redesign, incorporating over 150 components, including a stiffer frame, making it the bench-mark sports bike. The R1 was furnished with new cams with better oiling, and a modified gearbox with a higher first ratio to keep the front wheel down. Such modifications were refinements rather than major changes, but they kept the R1 fresh and ahead of the Honda Fireblade.

Another frame modification came in 2002, and fuel-injection was also added to the already successful mix. These lightened the R1 and improved its handling – important, as they were now facing competition from the mighty GSX-R1000. More advanced fuel injection was included, as well as new sleek bodywork for improved aerodynamics.

Further revamps appeared in 2004 and were so extensive that few, if any, parts fitted the earlier versions. The changes worked their magic: the R1 made it to the top of the sales charts and was declared by many to be the best sports flagship of the year.

The R1 is less extreme than most other sports bikes on the market making it much more user-friendly with a more comfortable riding position. This has helped with its popularity and a huge amount of sales.

ENGINE: 998cc four-stroke in-line four-cylinder, 20 valves, 74mmx58mm, liquid-cooled
POWER: 150bhp at 10,000rpm
GEARBOX: 6-speed foot change
FINAL DRIVE: chain
WEIGHT: 175kg (386lb)
TOP SPEED: 286kph (178mph)

Yamaha's R1 was the CBR busting machine that they had hoped for. The slightly less extreme sports machine won fans left, right and centre giving it massive sales potential.

BUELL X1 LIGHTNING

When launched back in 1999, the X1 Lightning set about replacing and surpassing the S-series Lightning at the head of the Buell range. The bike shared its name with a 4800km/h (3000mph) experimental rocket plane, which seems appropriate for this muscular, 'streetfighter' sports machine, whose power and handling are vastly superior to more traditional cruising Harley-Davidson machines.

It is a difficult bike to try to describe. It is not really a sports bike by comparison to a Yamaha R1. Nor is it a commuter bike, as it is a bit too much of a handful for cruising around town. It may have a Harley motor, but it is too sporty for most Harley fans, and sports bike fans think it is too Harley to be sporty.

Powering the X1 is a tuned 'Thunderstorm' version of the familiar 1203cc (72ci) Sportster V-twin, with higher compression pistons, larger valves and ports re-profiled for improved gas flow. Lighter flywheels improve both

gear selection and quicken engine response. The motor is lively considering that it came from a Harley, but may still be found wanting by comparison to Japanese machinery. It has a huge swathe of torque, but that is centred around a narrow power band. The real power appears only between 4000 and 6300rpm. Anything below 3200rpm and the rider can feel the pulsing of the two huge pistons. The X1 has a lazy, low revving feel, which pulls well from 2000rpm and can hike the front wheel up on power alone at 3000rpm in first gear – fun, fun, fun.

Most striking of all, however, is the X1's Dynamic Digital fuel injection, which employs sophisticated computer control to ensure that the big V-twin delivers its best under all conditions. The result is one of the crispest 'Harley's' ever built, and perhaps the most powerful. The fuel injection also improved the fuel economy and exhaust emissions.

Another Buell creation that does not seem to have a niche. It performs well with lots of usable torque, but as it doesn't quite fit into any category, it will have to make its own placing.

The gearbox is reassuringly clunky and, for a sporty bike, it requires a lot of gear changing. Like all Harley twins, the engine is hugely flexible – but potent, too. Top speed is reached at around 220km/h (135mph), although this varies since some markets normally receive models with raised gearing to help meet local noise limits.

The chassis is a tubular steel trellis, with a cast-aluminium alloy rear sub frame and high-quality Japanese Showa suspension components at both ends. The inverted front forks are adjustable for pre-load, compression and rebound damping, as is the single underslung rear shock absorber. The front disc brake boasts a 340mm (13.4in) rotor gripped by a huge six-piston 'Performance Machine' calliper. A simple single piston calliper and 230mm (9in) disc adorn the rear.

With a wheelbase of only 1410mm (55.5in) and just 89mm (3.5in) of trail, the X1 turns quickly by Harley standards, yet its stability is also surprisingly good. The thinly padded seat and overall ergonomics fall a long way short of the Electra Glide, say, but the X1 is aimed at owners who will not mind.

Overall, the bike's ergonomics have improved, and are by no means as crippling as other sports machines. The bars are well placed and the seat is a big improvement on the 1998 Buells.

ENGINE: 1203cc (72ci) ohv longitudinal V-twin, 88.9x96.5mm, air-cooled
POWER: 95bhp at 6000rpm
GEARBOX: 5-speed foot change
FINAL DRIVE: toothed belt
WEIGHT: 199kg (439lb)
TOP SPEED: 217kph (135mph)

KAWASAKI KX250

This motocross model has a long history dating all the way back to 1974, when it replaced the 1968 models. Kawasaki's dirt bike legacy started before that in 1963, when the company produced the B8M Motocrosser, which established Japanese bikes in motocross.

This is the bike from which the KX developed, and which it subsequently replaced. The early KX250 bore little relation to the modern one, as it had a piston-ported, air-cooled engine, with a low-level exhaust and twin units for the rear suspension. A reed valve engine, with high-level exhaust and improved suspension all arrived in 1978. This led to success on the motocross front.

The rear suspension had a major revamp in 1980, when the Uni-Trak type appeared on both the KX250 and the smaller KX125. It was later used on many other models across the range. Both motocross machines adopted a disc front brake in 1982. In the same year, the KX125 went over to liquid-cooling, which was adopted by the KX250 one year later.

A revamped engine landed in 1985, a disc rear brake arrived in 1986, in 1987 a longer stroke engine was installed, and upside-down forks appeared in 1989. The next big change was the perimeter frame in 1990; more engine modifications were included in 1992 with an even longer stroke, and a revised

Uni-Trak came in 1994. These additions kept the KX at the front of the field.

Bringing the KX250 right up to date, the 2006 model features engine, chassis and braking revisions. The engine has KIPS valves that operate independently, for strong, linear power through the rev range. At the time of writing, the 2007 model has received a very powerful 249cc (15ci), liquid-cooled, two-stroke engine, in an ultralight perimeter frame for improved acceleration and agility.

The aluminium sub-frame and the rear shock with dual compression adjustability allows a wide variety of tuning options. New petal-style disc brakes have

been added, and these are lighter than traditional discs, while their shape helps to clean the brake pads for more efficient braking performance when the mud gets too much.

The KX now has a four-stroke counterpart in the KX250F. The 2007 model also has a revised engine spec to give better bottom-end and midrange power.

ENGINE: 249cc (15ci) reed 2s single, 66.4x72mm, liquid-cooled
POWER: 54bhp at 8500rpm
GEARBOX: 5-speed foot change
FINAL DRIVE: chain
WEIGHT: 97kg (213lb)
TOP SPEED: n/a

KTM DUKE II

KTM first hit the road with the 620cc (38ci) Duke back in 1996, transforming its big Supermoto traillie into a road bike. The second incarnation appeared in 1999, named Duke II.

Powered by the water-cooled 640cc (39ci) LC4 engine, the Duke II used a chrome-molybdenum double cradle frame and was equipped with 12-spoke alloy wheels rather than the traditional wire spokes fitted on the bulk of off-road machines.

The styling is unique. Reminiscent of a praying mantis,

it looks like an insect about to pounce. The bodywork is minimalist as is to be expected for any off-road machine. The front-fairing containing the headlight, which contributes to the insect look, is matched at the tail with a pointed rear light like a bee sting. A pair of high-rise mat-alloy silencers flank both sides.

The Duke II is equipped with full instrumentation and lighting, with relatively comfortable seating. The WP suspension is top notch, and the handling is superb,

suitable for a variety of terrains. KTM build sturdy machines and their build quality rivals Honda.

The power is not quite what might be expected, but it has a dirt bike feel to it. The Duke will start shaking its head around 121–128km/h (75–80mph) depending on the surface, and steering damper can be added to counteract that. The brakes on the Duke are 320mm (12.6in) with 4-piston Brembo callipers, with stainless lines. Overall styling and build quality means the Duke II is headed for the top of its class.

ENGINE: 248cc (15ci) single, air-cooled
POWER: 50bhp
GEARBOX: 5-speed, foot change
FINAL DRIVE: chain
WEIGHT: 145kg (319lb)
TOP SPEED: 145km/h (90mph)

If you want to liven up a dull commute, get a KTM Duke II. The supermoto based road machine has the benefit of being tall for seeing over traffic, while its slim proportions make it perfect for filtering.

KTM 200 EGS

The KTM 200 EGS was a road-going version of KTM's 200 EXC enduro. The EGS had the basics added to make it road legal.

The biggest difference between these two machines was that the EGS had a gear-driven oil pump and a bit more stuffing in the seat. The lightweight machine – which weighed in at just 98kg (216lb) – was powered by a 193cc (12ci), two-stroke, single-cylinder engine. This explains the oil pump, used to avoid running premix in the temperamental two-stroke. The machine derived much of its agility and surefootedness from its in-house manufactured WP suspension.

All KTMs are well built and can handle the terrain that is thrown in front of them. The responsive 200 has superb suspension, which makes it ideal for off-roading.

The KTM motorcycles are not cheap, but this is typical of specialized machinery.

The barely road-legal KTM 200 EGS is basically an off-road bike with a headlamp fitted. It is ideal for riding to an off-road location for some fun in the mud and then riding home on the road.

ENGINE: 193cc (12ci) single, liquid-cooled
POWER: 80bhp
GEARBOX: 5-speed foot change
FINAL DRIVE: chain
WEIGHT: 98kg (216lb)
TOP SPEED: 129km/h (80mph)

PIAGGIO HEXAGON

The Hexagon is Piaggio's big-engined scooter offering. Ideal for a longer commute, with the added benefit of weather protection that only a scooter can offer.

Quite a few motorcycle manufacturers have branched out into scooter production. Triumph made the 249cc (15ci) Tigress TW2 overhead-valve twin and BSA the identical Sunbeam in 1959, but the modern super-scooter was born when Yamaha came out with its 250cc (15ci) Majesty in 1997.

Piaggio are best known for the traditional Vespa-styled scooters, but they have recently made a move into plastic-bodied scooters. Concern for the environment is now top of every manufacturer's

agenda, and Piaggio has been carrying out research work into eco-friendly town transport with combined four-stroke, battery machines and small, light delivery vehicles.

Following the Japanese lead, Piaggio popped Honda's 250cc (15ci), four-stroke single into its Hexagon in 1999 and joined the big-bore scooter bandwagon. Small scooter wheels with wide expanses of bodywork coupled with a relatively hefty 140kg (300lb) were not ideal on a wind-blown motorway. However,

creature comforts such as a mobile phone socket and rain protector for the seat were novel touches, which make up for the disadvantages of riding a scooter.

Storage space was minimal, with just a rear boot and space behind the fairing, and none under the seat – unusal, given that this is perhaps one of the best advantages of a scooter. Another option was the Hexagon's smaller 125cc (8ci) sibling, which could equal the 250's 100km/h (62mph) top speed, but lacked the larger machine's novelties.

The Hexagon underwent a trial period in London as a taxi scooter. However, the feedback from the Pan European riding courier was poor, and its taxi abilities were never exploited to the full.

ENGINE: 250cc (15ci) single-cylinder four-stroke
POWER: 18bhp
GEARBOX: n/a
FINAL DRIVE: shaft drive
WEIGHT: 140kg (300lb)
TOP SPEED: 100km/h (62mph)

SUZUKI GSX1300R HAYABUSA

JAPAN 1999

At its debut in 1999, the distinctive but chunky looks of the Suzuki GSX1300R Hayabusa belied its potential as the fastest road-going bike on its debut. Sensationally, it was suggested that the magic 'double ton' – 322km/h (200mph) – would be possible to achieve on this machine. Under the right circumstances, road-testers showed that it was.

At the time, the world's fastest production motorcycle was Honda's 1100XX Blackbird; with a top speed in excess of 275km/h (170mph), it just beat Kawasaki's ZX1100, which ran 5–6km/h (3–4mph) slower. Suzuki raised the bar with a top speed 32km/h (20mph) over other heavyweight sports bikes.

The Hayabusa was powered by a 1299cc (79ci) transverse four-cylinder motor with 16 valves, developing 173hp. Engine timing was by eight 'trigger poles' at the end of the crank, doubling the number found on the 750cc (46ci) model. The water-cooled engine was based on Suzuki's latest 750cc (46ci) range rather than the outdated 1100cc (67ci). Fuel injection was controlled by maps individual to each cylinder, improving the balance between each cylinder and making cold starts and high temperatures less power-sapping.

A computer-activated flapper valve in the air box monitored the air flow through the rev-range, shutting at under 4000rpm and reducing air intake; above 4000rpm, it was wide open, giving maximum air flow.

Weighing 218kg (480lb), it put out over 155hp (rear-wheel – 16hp more than any other stock sports bike at the time. Out of the box, the 'Busa was capable of a sub-10-second quarter-mile (0.4km) and would top out in excess of 315km/h (196mph). Despite the high state of tune and fuel injection required for high-speed antics, the bike has great

Above and top: Two Hayabusas are put through their paces on the racetrack by professional riders. If you fancy a 322km (200mph) blast, then the Hayabusa is the bike for you. With the world's fastest production bike, you can cruise at speed all day without feeling it, thanks to excellent aerodynamics.

town manners and is capable of accelerating cleanly from low down in sixth gear.

Like the GSX-R750, the Hayabusa made use of SRAD (Suzuki Ram Air Direct) to boost top-end power. The narrow, stacked headlight allowed the top fairing air intakes to be placed as close to the centre line of the bike as possible, in order to pass the greatest volume of air through. At the other end of the combustion cycle, to cope with emission laws,

the model carried twin catalysts in the main pipe work just ahead of the cams, and PAIR (Pulsed-secondary AIR), which introduced air downstream of the exhaust valves, diluting the unburned hydrocarbons and carbon monoxide.

The Hayabusa was based on a twin-spar aluminium frame, with fully adjustable inverted 43mm (1.7in) front suspension and progressive monoshock at the rear. Suzuki claimed 15 per cent higher

rigidity in both frame and swing-arm for the Hayabusa over the GSX-R750. Bridgestone extended its BT56 range to suit the Hayabusa, having submitted 15 different combinations of tyre, based on the 190 rear. Suzuki engineers favoured the BT56 type J, which became the only recommended tyre for this bike. Its actual width is 198mm (7.8in) with a more shallow crown radius, and in 1999 it had the distinction of being the flattest, fattest rear

tyre yet seen. For a big bike, the Hayabusa hides its bulk well; it turns in quickly but can be hard to get back up on its feet. Once in a corner, it likes to stay there, a fault that can be blamed on the long wheelbase or its heavy weight. However, the smaller, lighter bikes will be left for dust by the Hayabusa's power as soon as a straight appears.

The riding position is good, and comfortable. The foot pegs are low and have 2.5cm (1in)

This three-view photograph of the Hayabusa demonstrates well the sleekness and well-balanced weight of the bike. For a big bike, the Hayabusa handles like a smaller machine. Its mass is well placed to keep it feeling balanced and for a sports bike it has a comfy riding position.

of rubber on them to kill engine vibes. The dash board is clean and completely enclosed; it has a tachometer and speedometer of equal size, a clock and two trip meters, which also give average fuel consumption in mpg.

To achieve the goal of a potential 322km/h (200mph) top speed, aerodynamics were a big consideration when the bike was designed.

The machine had to be able to slice cleanly through the air;

hence the sculptured, sleek bodywork. Suzuki engineers used their wind tunnel to define the most 'slippery' shape, and the front mudguard was critical for initial penetration. With its deep sides, the mudguard channelled the passing air onto the fairing sides, which stretched as far forward as possible to keep air moving to the back of the bike.

The belly-pan extended up to the rear wheel to clear the air flow under the bike, while the top

fairing benefited from the shaped headlight, and even the mirror backs were contoured for maximum slice. The Hayabusa's fairings culminated in a TL1000R-style hump at the rear, although it failed to offer similar storage potential as the twin. Suzuki did not classify the GSX1300R Hayabusa as a true 'R' model, so the 'R' was placed only at the end of the bike's designation. The traditional GSX-R blue-and-white paintwork was also absent.

With all the aerodynamic work, the Hayabusa provides excellent wind protection and also helps to keeps the rider dry while slicing through the air at top speed.

ENGINE: 1299cc (79ci) 16-valve transverse four, 81x63mm, liquid-cooled
POWER: 173bhp at 9800rpm
GEARBOX: 6-speed
FINAL DRIVE: chain
WEIGHT: 215kg (474lb)
TOP SPEED: 322km/h (200mph) est.

YAMAHA YP125 MAJESTY

As the new millennium kicked in, so did the craze for scooters. An odd way to greet the future, perhaps, but a development that Yamaha noticed and for which it produced the YP125 Majesty.

Its sharp handling qualities made it a strong competitor against its main rivals, namely the Honda and Piaggio offerings. Top speed was 105km/h (65mph), and for a scooter it was equipped with a relatively high seat height of 774mm (30.5in). The increased seat height sets it apart from the competition, giving the rider an elevated riding position for a good view of the road ahead.

The 125cc (8ci) four-stroke has enough grunt to pull you along at 80km/h (50mph) on a clear run and has enough acceleration to cut through traffic with confidence. The Majesty is very stable for a scooter and the 1480mm (58in) wheelbase helps its stability especially under braking. Stopping power is provided by a 220mm (8.6in) disc at the front and a 190mm (7.5in) disc at the back.

The Majesty was not made to look like a scooter for your Mum; instead, it was styled with an appealingly aggressive attitude, ideal for hanging out at street corners. With more weight forward than the Honda Pantheon, it could be turned into corners with greater enthusiasm. As well as the seat being high, it is also wide, which means that it is comfortable and can accommodate a passenger.

There is also a lot of storage space under the ample seat – 32L (7.5 US gallons) in fact – which is more than enough for a weekend away! There is also a glove box that locks to protect valuables.

The Majesty, according to the Yamaha blurb, 'symbolizes liberty, luxury and contentment'. The fully automatic 125cc (8ci) engine allows you to get out and about, while comfort is provided by a little machine that sports a wide fairing and an equally wide, spacious seat. It is a capable all-rounder, and it can carry two people with luggage off into the sunset. It is a capable scooter – fast enough for a spirited commute but roomy enough to take on longer rides.

The latest Majesty has been updated for 2007 with a striking new fairing with distinctive 'fox-eye' headlamps, more chrome and much improved passenger grab handles. It is comfortable enough and powerful enough for an adventure and not just the daily grind of city commuting.

ENGINE: 125cc (7.5ci) ohc four-stroke single-cylinder
POWER: 10bhp at 8000rpm
GEARBOX: automatic
FINAL DRIVE: n/a
WEIGHT: 128kg (282lb)
TOP SPEED: 105km/h (65mph)

Majestic by name, majestic by nature, the Yamaha Majesty took the comfort of a scooter to a higher level – raising the seat height and allowing extra leg room for longer trips.

SUZUKI SV 650

Suzuki is well known for its ultra-fast GSX-Rs, so when the firm produced a mid-range 650cc (40ci) V-twin, a lot of people were taken by surprise. The SV 650 and SV 650S (the faired version) were instant hits, for they offered it all: character, good looks and outstanding handling.

The SVs slipped nicely into the Bandit area of the market and started to steal it away. The short frame promoted responsive handling, and slotting in a 90-degree V-twin motor meant that keeping the frame short was no easy task. Suzuki then added a long swingarm and this, coupled with the short frame, made the SV handle impeccably. The 654cc (40ci) liquid-cooled engine, with double overhead camshafts tops out at 192km/h (119mph) for the SV650 and 201km/h (125mph) for the 650S.

The two SVs have very different riding positions and gearing to suit their look and layout. The SV650 has higher and had wider handlebars and lower overall gearing than the faired S, which has lower-slung clip-on handlebars. Both models appeal to experienced riders looking for good value, but are manageable enough for a beginner.

With bike theft on the up, Suzuki have given the little SV an ignition lock with a tamper-proof steel ring, and attempts at hot-wiring simply shut the ignition down. Suzuki supply the 650 engines to Cagiva, which means there are no worries about reliability. Both bikes are cheap to buy, and Suzuki also had the forethought to make the SV available in a version that conforms to direct access license specification.

With the success of the 650 in 2003, Suzuki decided it was time to unleash the SV1000. With the SV650 already trouncing bigger sports tourers, it was time to step up to the mark, and so the SV 1000 and SV 1000s were born. Both have plenty of luggage hooks and passenger grab rails, so touring is very much in mind with this bike.

An all-new aluminium alloy truss frame houses the TL1000 motor – enough oomph to pop wheelies but still comfortable enough for touring or commuting. The big-bore engine pumps out masses of torque like any classic V-twin; power delivery is refined by the same dual-throttle valve electronic fuel injection system that is fitted to the class-leading GSX-R1000.

Suzuki used a short-stroke 90-degree V-twin which is a shorter engine; this reduces seat height and lowers the centre of gravity. The SV 1000 has been as popular as the SV 650 and has turned out to be a very civilized machine. Since it is not an out and out sports monster, it can tour well and bump along at 56km/h (35mph) if necessary when commuting.

Being a Suzuki V-twin rather than an Italian one, it has a much smoother transmission. And so, although it is a bigger machine, it feels as nimble as the 650 version. The big SV can handle on-track action as well as general all-day comfort, so it definitely slots into the all-rounder slot. The frame is based on Ducati's trellis design, but in a much more substantial guise of alloy sections and cross-bracing.

The faired S version still manages to look aggressive due to the styling of the fairing, and it is quite good at keeping the wind blast off the rider. It is fitted with a 17l (5 US gallon) tank, which is good for about 160–190km (100–120 miles) before the warning light appears. The SV1000 is well made, good value for money and fun to ride just about anywhere.

ENGINE: 654cc (40ci) 4 stroke dohc v-twin 81.0 x 62.6mm
POWER: 68 bhp
GEARBOX: 6 speed
FINAL DRIVE: chain
WEIGHT: 165kg (363.8 pounds)
TOP SPEED: 201km/h (125mph)

BENELLI 900 TORNADO

The Benelli Tornado heralded the return of a famous Italian marque that had been absent from our roads since the 1960s. Benelli began life in 1911 as a family garage in Pesaro in Italy. It produced its first motorcycle in 1920 and, a year later, produced one using an engine it had built.

Tonino Benelli raced its 175 Benelli, winning four Italian championships. By the early 1960s, Benelli was producing 300 bikes a day. However, the Japanese began to flex their muscles in Europe and that hit sales, leading to the demise of the Benelli motorcycle.

A revival looked likely in 1989, but it was not until 1995 that Benelli got back on its feet, under

The rejuvenated Italian marque made a pleasant return to the world of bikes in 1995. The three-cylindered goddess took everyone's breath away with unique styling and design.

the influence of Andrea Merloni. The result was the 900 Tornado.

The Tornado was a famous Benelli model name from the early 1970s. The earlier machine used a 650cc (40ci) overhead-valve parallel twin engine, but the heart of the new Tornado boasts more cubic capacity and an extra cylinder as well.

Benelli's 900 runs an in-line three-cylinder engine. Like an in-line four, the triple can spin over at much higher speeds than a V-twin – which is vital for higher horsepower figures. However, the triple configuration provides better torque than a four, and is also more compact. It is the ideal compromise between the classic V-twins and straight fours.

Although the first production Tornado features an 898.4cc/54.8ci (85.3 x 52.4mm/3.4 x 2.1in)

The Tornado gets its narrow dimensions from the radiator being relocated to the back of the bike. It took its design lead from F1 and has its weight evenly distributed for superb handling.

engine size, Benelli is planning an entire family of units, of various displacement sizes. The cylinders are vertical, and the 12 valves (four per cylinder) are inclined at 15 degrees and driven by a chain on the nearside (left) of the cylinder block. The crankshaft is timed at 120 degrees to provide a natural 'big bang', enabling optimal traction for the rear wheel for both street and racing uses. A balancer shaft is fitted to iron out vibration, while the integrated ignition and injection system has been developed to use either three or six injectors. The engine has a gorgeous exhaust note, which matches the beautiful Italian styling.

Benelli looked to F1 for advice on where to mount its radiator, and decided to put it at the back – hence those unusual yellow fans in the tail section. Most bikes have the radiator fitted at the front, close to the exhaust manifold, which heats up the coolant. Bikes with front-mounted radiators need a larger radiant surface to compensate, which limits streamlining. The rear radiator, unaffected by heat coming from

the engine, can be 20 per cent smaller than a traditional frontal radiator – so a winner in more ways than one.

The lack of a front-mounted radiator offered the design team greater freedom to create a large 13L (3 US gallon) air box without intruding on the petrol-tank capacity. The absence of a front radiator also helps to achieve optimum weight distribution, which aids handling. The engine is a stressed member of the frame structure, contributing to considerable overall rigidity. The frame itself is made in chrome-moly steel (front) and cast aluminium (rear), providing attachment for the single rear shock absorber. The steering head angle is adjustable.

Other details include: 43cm (17in) tyres, triple discs, racing-quality helical five-spoke wheels, an aluminium swinging arm, and a wet multi-plate clutch with anti-locking device. The anti-lock slipper clutch means that the back wheel will not lock up if the rider moves down a couple of gears and lets the lever out before engine revs match road

The Benelli just oozes with Italian style and flare, with crisp well-defined lines. Benelli has come a long way from the family garage in Italy way back in 1911, and long may it continue.

speed. The six-speed cassette gearbox can be removed without taking the engine out of the bike, which is very useful for riders wanting to use the Tornado as a track machine.

The Tornado weighs 198kg (437lb) – some 11kg (24lb) more than a 998S Ducati and 19kg (42lb) more than a GSX-R1000. It is also down on top speed, topping out at around 250km/h (155mph). But the Tornado can be let off because it is beautiful.

ENGINE: 898.4cc (54.8ci) dohc triple 85.3x52.4mm, liquid-cooled
POWER: 140bhp at 11,500rpm
GEARBOX: 6-speed foot change
FINAL DRIVE: chain
WEIGHT: 185kg (408lb)
TOP SPEED: 280km/h (174mph)

BUELL BLAST

USA 2000

The Buell Blast was added to the Buell range in 2000, as an entry-level machine aimed at newcomers to motorcycling. This was an area Harley-Davidson had always found difficult, the nearest previous 'starter' model being the very traditional 883cc (54ci) Sportster.

Harley enlisted Erik Buell to build a bike that was easy to learn to ride and looked funky too, in the hope of bringing more new riders into the motorcycling fold. The firm opted for a lightweight,

single-cylinder powered motorcycle that is easy to ride, instilling any newcomer with confidence.

The single cylinder – which is unusual for Harley-Davidson, the V-Twin master – is a 492cc (30ci) two-valve engine producing 206.8kPa (30lb/ft) of torque at a modest 3500rpm.

Like the other models in the range, it has a five-speed transmission, while toothed belt final drive is retained, along with vibration-damping Uniplanar engine mounting. The frame

was a first for Buell, a lightweight backbone constructed of high-strength, low-alloy steel with wide-beam construction. The wide beams help to reduce the overall height of the Blast and keep the centre of gravity low while providing a solid, rigid chassis. The frame itself is also fitted with integral engine oil reservoir. Protecting it from damage, the Blast bodywork is made from Surlyn, the same material used on the outside of golf balls.

Another issue examined by

Harley and Buell was that of maintenance – or the lack of it. Maintaining a bike is the last thing a newcomer wants to worry about, so the Blast was fitted with a valve train that utilizes self-adjusting hydraulic lifters, which eliminate any need for mechanical tuning. The carburettor is equipped with an automatic fuel enricher that eliminates cold-starting issues and the need for a choke

Eric Buell always does things in his own way and the same goes for the Buell Blast. This is a bike aimed at beginners in every way possible. From damage-resistant paint to minimal maintenance, Buell has considered every aspect of new bike ownership that could be a potential problem.

knob. Two seat heights are available (699mm/27.5in or 648mm/25.5in), so short riders need not feel intimidated.

The suspension on the Blast comes courtesy of Showa, both front and rear. Since this is a beginner bike, the preload and rebound are preset by the factory. Both the gas-charged rear shock and the 37mm (1.5in) front forks offer 101.6mm (4in) of travel. Unlike other Buells, the Blast's progressive rate spring shock is mounted in a more conventional position.

Buell's Blast was fitted with an extremely light clutch, unlike its Sportster counterpart. It does live up to its name, as it is exciting to ride, easy to handle and can take very tight turners with out any qualms. First gear is very short and needs to be shifted quickly up to second, but for a beginner that is not an issue; a taller first would need more clutch work, which is difficult for a novice.

Harley-Davidson and Buell appear to have hit their target of a usable but unusual entry-level big bike. It has plenty of character, but nothing that will deter a new rider. It sounds good, looks good and behaves, well, perfectly.

ENGINE: 492cc (30ci) ohv single, 88.9x79.4mm, air-cooled
POWER: 34bhp at 6500rpm
GEARBOX: 5-speed foot change
FINAL DRIVE: toothed belt
WEIGHT: 163.3kg (360lb)
TOP SPEED: 167kph (104mph)

CSA

Keeping options open is always a good move, and that is what Confederate did when it decided to set up CSA. It is debatable whether CSA should be regarded as a separate brand from Confederate Motorcycles, but it was conceived as a 'second string' for Confederate, offering equal quality but at a cheaper price – a cost-effective Confederate.

There were just the two models, the PLC Wildcat and JPB Confederado with starting prices at $19,800. The intended

production run for the 2000 model year was 500 machines. To keep costs down, both models came in the proverbial 'Any colour you like, as long as it's black'.

The engine was from engine specialists S & S, and a similar specification to the Confederate machines, but of 1638cc (100ci) instead of 1852cc (113ci). The 101.6mm (4in) 'square' engine had an actual swept volume of 1647cc (101ci). Many other components were similar to those on the original machines: Paioli

upside-down forks, five-speed Andrews gear-sets, and so on.

The weight of the PLC Wildcat dropped a useful 13.6kg (30lb) to 214kg (470lb), while retaining a 227kg (500lb) load-carrying capacity. This was still no lightweight by European standards, but not bad for a machine with such a big engine.

The other model, the JPB Confederado, stayed the same weight as the earlier machines at 227kg (500lb), but the load-carrying capacity was upgraded

to an impressive 318kg (700lb). To handle the braking, twin, 220mm (8.7in), ductile-iron disks with four-piston callipers were fitted at the front. Instead of the 43cm (17in) Marchinesi wheels and Pirelli tyres on the Confederates and Wildcats, the Confederado came with spoked wheels with stainless spokes and light-alloy rims, and Avon bias-belted tyres, 40cm (16in) at the front and 38 (15in) at the back. The fuel tank held a modest 15L (4.2 US gallons).

HONDA FES PANTHEON 125

The Honda Pantheon had a lot of competition when it was first catapulted into the market back in 2000. However, this powerful, comfortable scooter was effortless to ride, and was the cream of the crop of the trendy new scooters flooding the market.

It was the smaller and younger sibling of the FES250 Foresight, which arrived on the scene in 1998. Although it was one of the heaviest scooters of its type, it carried its weight in all the right places, making it more stable than some of its competitors. Due to

their small wheels and long wheel base, scooters are notoriously unstable at speed, so well-placed weight is a boon.

Compared with a traditional machine like the Aprilia Habana Custom 125, the Honda was no beauty. However, the seat was relatively low and allowed for a good range of positions for the rider's feet, and accommodated smaller riders. It ran with a two-stroke engine – the Active Radical Combustion motor, which supplied power smoothly from low revs to provide better acceleration than its rivals from other manufacturers such as Peugeot or Yamaha.

The Pantheon was equipped with the Combined Braking System (CBS), a hand-me-down from Honda's sports bikes. When either brake lever is applied, a proportion of its pressure is applied to the other brake. It is a facility that is not universally popular, but Honda's market research evidently showed that commuters were not fussy. For those two-up dashes to the office or a weekend away

(a brave move on a 125cc/8ci scooter), the Pantheon's broad pillion seat was a few inches higher than the driver's. It was considered to be one of the most comfortable, although the grab handles were sharp-edged.

The Pantheon includes all of Honda's most advanced scooter design and development in a high-class, high-quality commuter style. It is ideal for busy commuters who want more comfort on their travels. As part of Honda's new Executive Class Commuter range, it takes comfort, convenience, economy and security to an all-time high. It is also perfect for newcomers to the two-wheeled world, as it matches 125cc (8ci) licence regulations.

ENGINE: 125cc (8ci) ohv 2s single, liquid-cooled
POWER: 15bhp
GEARBOX: V-matic
FINAL DRIVE: chain
WEIGHT: 145kg (319lb)
TOP SPEED: 113km/h (70mph)

The Pantheon 125 has been well received as a utility scooter, especially among urban commuters.

MOTO GUZZI CALIFORNIA JACKAL

The Moto Guzzi California Jackal is an excellent illustration of the Moto Guzzi as toy, slotting into the Sports Cruiser category quite nicely. It is essentially a stripped-down California, with bars that are slightly smaller than a fully dressed machine but a little too high and wide for serious fast riding; a full wind blast greets the rider on the open road.

It may be possible to touch the claimed 200km/h (124mph) top speed. However, cruising for any length of time at even 100mph (160mph) would be hard on the neck, arms and bottom, thanks to the somewhat minimal saddle.

The company's promotional material describes the Jackal as being 'targeted at the more fashion conscious younger market'. This means that it is, in short, a machine for posing, rather than either serious touring or serious fast riding.

On the Sport Cruiser front, the Jackal has a big dollop of sport: the 90-degree, across-the-frame V-twin is the same basic design that powers Moto Guzzi's other sports bikes. The fuel-injected 1064cc (65ci) engine has more oomph than a typical 1100cc (67ci) V-twin and will pull away from some V-twins with more capacity.

Most cruisers are criticized for not handling well, so the J ackal has addressed that issue. The firm, heavily damped suspension combines with a rigid chassis to produce a bike that is extremely stable in corners at all speeds and road surfaces. The steering is responsive and predictable, and this Guzzi offers more ground clearance that other sporting cruisers.

The traditional floorboards have been replaced by pegs that are mounted higher and further back. Moto Guzzi have decided not to include linked brakes on the Jackal. The bike does have

some vibration about it, but is comfortable at cruising speed.

The Jackal has clean-cut look to it, with a simple tank and a single instrument – a speedometer. There is a lack of chrome, which is a good thing, meaning less cleaning.

ENGINE: 1064cc (65ci) ohv transverse V-twin, 92x80mm, air-cooled
POWER: 74bhp at 6400rpm
GEARBOX: 5-speed foot change
FINAL DRIVE: shaft
WEIGHT: 264kg (581lb)
TOP SPEED: 200km/h (124mph)

HONDA GL1800 GOLD WING

In the world of heavyweight tourers, Honda's Gold Wing is king. From its original 1974 inception as a flat-four, 1000cc bike, the Wing has increased in size and complexity through the decades, finally evolving into the ultimate luxury tourer that is the GL1800. First seen in 2001, the 1800 improved massively over the previous GL1500 model, with a stiff new aluminium frame reducing weight and improving handling. The engine was also heavily updated, although it remained a flat-six design. Fuel injection was fitted to increase efficiency, while power increased by 20 per cent to 117bhp. Mass was slightly reduced, from 372kg to 363kg, and the Wing's performance was transformed.

However, it is the GL1800's equipment that most impresses. Massive luggage space is built-in, and a CD/radio unit, heated grips and seats, adjustable windscreen, reverse gear, cruise control and a huge list of optional extras make Honda's Gold Wing the luxury way to travel on two wheels.

ENGINE: 1832cc (112ci), l/c flat six, 12-valve, SOHC
POWER: 117bhp at 5,500rpm
GEARBOX: 5-speed (plus reversing aid)
FINAL DRIVE: shaft
WEIGHT: 363kg (799lb)
TOP SPEED: 225km/h (140mph)

Above and inset: The GL1800 includes two massive luggage compartments fully integrated into the rear of the bike, making it the ideal tourer. The latest GL1800 also includes built-in satellite navigation on control panel.

Below: Honda fitted two side-mounted radiators to improve cooling efficiency and keep heat away from the rider, making this the ultimate comfortable ride.

APRILIA TUONO

ITALY 2002

Aprilia's Tuono first appeared in 2002, and it was a pretty simply design. The Aprilia design team had simply taken the firm's RSV Superbike, removed the plastic bodywork and fitted some higher, flat handlebars. The resulting upright riding position, radical naked styling and very high specification chassis components immediately marked the Tuono (Italian for thunder) out as a pretty special machine. The 60-degree V-twin engine wasn't detuned from its superbike installation, and the instant, strong pulses of power it provided when the throttle was opened made for an incredibly exciting machine. The track-ready suspension was fully adjustable for the ultimate racetrack setup, while lightweight aluminium wheels and grippy race tyres let

the rider get the most from the engine. Race Brembo brakes meant the Tuono stopped as hard as it accelerated.

Later versions of the Tuono offered a more refined package, but Aprilia also developed extreme track variants of the bike. The 2006 Tuono Factory was a limited-edition version, with Ohlins race suspension, a more powerful 139bhp engine and carbon-fibre body panels.

ENGINE: 998cc (61ci), l/c 60° V-twin, 8-valve, DOHC
POWER: 133bhp at 9,500rpm
GEARBOX: 6-speed
FINAL DRIVE: chain
WEIGHT: 185kg (407lb)
TOP SPEED: 256km/h (160mph)

The Tuono 'streetfighter' is a powerful, sporty bike that is often modified by owners, with different exhausts, tyres and brakes. It makes an ideal track or stunt bike.

DUCATI 999R

ITALY 2003

Ducati began using the 'R' suffix to denote its ultimate race-replica models in 2001, with the 996R. These models are the limited-edition variants built as 'homologation' models for entry in Superbike racing.

As such they have chassis and engine designs aimed directly at top-class racing: carbon-fibre fairings, lightweight wheels, ultra-high-performance engine parts and

race suspension and brakes.

The 999R fulfils all these criteria completely. An extremely short-stroke engine layout, with titanium internals, allows a high rev ceiling, while magnesium and carbon engine covers cut weight. The chassis is based on a welded steel-tube trellis frame, with Ohlins fully adjustable race suspension and radial-mount Brembo race brakes. Wheels are forged

aluminium and the bodywork is made from light carbon fibre.

The 999R was the ultimate Italian sportsbike of its time, its 150bhp engine and superb chassis giving amazing performance. It also won the World Superbike title in 2003, 2004 and 2006'

ENGINE: 999cc (61ci) l/c 90-degree V-twin, eight-valve, DOHC desmodromic
POWER: 150bhp at 9,750rpm
GEARBOX: 6-speed
FINAL DRIVE: chain
WEIGHT: 181kg (398lb)
TOP SPEED: 281km/h (175mph)

Ducati's 999R was designed purely for racing, with high-end chassis and engine components. It was also produced in a 'Xerox' version, with WSB replica paintwork, decals and race exhausts.

HONDA CBR600RR

Honda's CBR600F had dominated the middleweight sportsbike class for much of the 1990s. But as the 21st century dawned, its essentially roadbike-biased design was making it harder to compete with increasingly radical designs from Yamaha and Suzuki.

So in 2003, Honda released the CBR600RR – an unabashed race-replica. It had an all-new super-compact engine with dual injectors per cylinder, and a peaky, 115bhp power output. The RR's chassis owed several design and styling cues to Honda's MotoGP bike, the RCV211V, while its geometry and weight distribution were optimized for track performance. Fully adjustable suspension, sports tyres and brakes and a committed, aggressive riding position underlined its intentions.

On track, the CBR's stability and communicative front end made it a superb handler, although its engine was not as strong as some competitor machines. Nevertheless, the CBR600RR won every World Supersport championship from 2003 to 2007. On the road, its lack of comfort was a handicap, but despite that drawback, it still made an excellent sportsbike.

ENGINE: 599cc (36.5ci), l/c inline-four, 16-valve DOHC
POWER: 115bhp at 13,000rpm
GEARBOX: 6-speed
FINAL DRIVE: chain
WEIGHT: 163kg (359lb)
TOP SPEED: 265.5km/h (165mph)

KAWASAKI Z1000

Kawasaki's Z1000 was an inspired idea: take the ZX-9 engine, bore it out to 1000cc (61ci) and off you go. As far as naked bikes go, it is one of the funkiest and user friendly around.

With gold anodized forks at the front and four silencers stacked like a double-barrelled shot gun at the rear, it certainly looks different – very retro, which you will either love or loathe. The re-worked ZX-9 engine is torquey although it can be a touch busy. It is slotted into a compact frame, which gives it fine handling too. These aspects of the bike, combined with good brakes and slim dimensions, made the Z1000

a big success on the sales front.

Fitted with upside-down 41mm (1.6in) front forks, and with the swing arm stolen from the ZX-9R, the Z1000 hangs onto the road like it owns it. The 300mm (11.8in) discs up front and with four-pot callipers are ample for pulling up the Z1000.

Since the 1000cc (61ci) version was such a hit, Kawasaki decided to go for the smaller Z750, which was introduced in 2004. Like its older sibling, the Z750 handles well; it looks good and has been built to a budget price. It lacks the double-barrelled exhaust of the Z1000, but is fitted with an oval end can and stainless pipe work.

The Z1000's streetfighter styling is perfect for urban riding and occasional track work. But the lack of bodywork makes high-speed distance riding hard work for the rider – especially tall ones.

It does have its own unique personality, combining responsive power and lightweight handling. The power is supplied by a 748cc (46ci), liquid-cooled, in-line four with electronic fuel injection. Kawasaki did cheat a little bit on both machines by running an old-style steel cradle, which was hidden behind plastic covers. This is not necessarily a bad thing, as the steel frame adds rigidity to the already sharp handing pair.

The 750 also runs 300mm (11.8in) front discs but with two

pots and a rear single pot caliper and 220mm (8.6in) disc. Both bikes have a relatively low seat height; combined with a slim seat and narrow tank, this means they represent no challenge to short riders. The wide, flat bars make for a comfortable riding position, as well as giving lots of manoeuvrability, especially at low speed.

This is a fierce, naked machine that handles and behaves as well as it looks.

KAWASAKI ZX-10R

Like Kawasaki's middleweight sportsbike range, its litre-class sportsters were rather lacklustre in the 1990s. The ZX-9R couldn't match machines like the Honda FireBlade on performance, but its replacement was much more capable.

The ZX-10R was released in 2003, and its huge power output and tiny all-up weight immediately marked it out as something special. Styled like the firm's ZX-RR MotoGP racebike, the ZX-10R was marketed as for 'experienced riders only' – and that was backed up by its frankly brutal performance on track and the street.

Although its statistics were exceptional, the 10R's design was fairly straightforward. Its fuel-injected, 16-valve engine was compact and light, and used dual-valve throttle bodies to improve drivability.

The frame rails passed over the top of the engine to cut width, and the suspension units were fully adjustable, top-specification parts. Race-type, radial-mount brakes were fitted up front, and a minimalist fairing and instrument package finished off the ZX-10R's impressive design.

ENGINE: 998cc (61ci), l/c inline-four, 16-valve, DOHC
POWER: 182bhp at 11,700rpm (with ram-air assistance)
GEARBOX: 6-speed
FINAL DRIVE: chain
WEIGHT: 175kg (386lb)
TOP SPEED: 298km/h (185mph)

Hurtling around a high-speed racetrack on the limit – the perfect way to sample the ZX-10R's massive power and accomplished chassis package.

DUCATI 749R

JAPAN 2004

Ducati's smaller superbike range was designed to compete in the Supersports race class – where 750cc (46ci) twins race against 600cc (37ci) fours. Externally similar to its bigger sibling, the 999, the 749 first appeared in 2003 to replace the elderly 748 desmoquattro.

Like the 748, the 749 used a smaller 748cc (46ci) version of the trademark Ducati eight-valve,

water-cooled, 90-degree V-twin engine. But the 749 motor was heavily revised to allow higher revs and increased peak power.

The 749R followed in 2004, and boasted an even higher level of engine tune, with lighter, tougher internals, wider bore and shorter stroke. This allowed higher maximum engine speed and a power boost to 121bhp.

Like its 999 sibling, and all

other 'R' Ducatis, the 749R's chassis had a peerless specification.

The steel-tube trellis frame combined stiffness with lightness, and the fabricated aluminium swing arm was based upon the 999F world superbike factory race bike design. Ohlins supplied the top-spec suspension, and the brakes were Brembo superbike radial calipers.

ENGINE: 749cc (46ci), l/c 90-degree V-twin, 8-valve, DOHC desmodromic
POWER: 121bhp at 10,500rpm
GEARBOX: 6-speed
FINAL DRIVE: chain
WEIGHT: 183.5kg (405lb)
TOP SPEED: 265.5km/h (165mph)

The smaller Ducati 'R' superbike has just as much style, sophistication and performance as its 999cc (61ci) sibling, but in a middleweight package that's eligible for Supersport racing.

HONDA CBR1000RR FIREBLADE

JAPAN 2004

The original 1992 CBR900RR FireBlade revolutionized the sportsbike world when it first appeared. But by 2003, Honda's flagship sportsbike needed a serious overhaul to compete with competition from Suzuki's GSX-R1000 and the Yamaha R1. The result was the CBR1000RR Fireblade – a much more racetrack-oriented design, with a host of

advanced design cues, a new 170bhp engine, and completely revised chassis. Honda had put huge efforts into 'centralizing' the bike's mass – all the major components were positioned as close to the bike's centre of gravity as possible. This, together with new upside-down front forks and Unit Pro-Link rear suspension (borrowed from Honda's RC211V

The sharp nosecone, underseat exhaust and sleek bodywork give the CBR1000RR excellent aerodynamic performance. Its 170bhp engine and race-ready chassis make it a formidable track and road contender.

MotoGP bike), improved handling and stability.

The CBR1000 also had a novel computer-controlled steering damper. It had an electronically variable damping circuit, which stiffened up the steering damper as the bike's speed increased. This gave a light steering feel at slow speeds, while preventing instability at high speeds.

ENGINE: 998cc (61ci), l/c inline-four, 16-valve, DOHC
POWER: 170bhp at 11,250rpm
GEARBOX: 6-speed
FINAL DRIVE: chain
WEIGHT: 179kg (395lb)
TOP SPEED: 281km/h (175mph)

Honda produced the CBR1000RR in this 'Repsol' replica paint, as a tribute to the firm's RC211V and RC212V MotoGP bikes. The Honda factory team has been sponsored by Repsol for many years.

BMW K1200S

For a firm with such strong performance in the automobile world, BMW's two-wheeled sportsbikes have generally failed to inspire. Until 2005 that is, when the Bavarian firm released the K1200S. It was a totally new design, incorporating a 'conventional', transverse-mounted, in-line-four engine, with a twin spar aluminium frame and full fairing.

But the rest of the bike was far from conventional. The front suspension used a unique 'Duolever' setup, based on a design by British designer Norman Hossack. This used a cast-aluminium wheel carrier to mount the front wheel, the carrier being joined to the frame via a dual wishbone and monoshock. The rear suspension was BMW's Paralever system, revised to drastically reduce mass.

The result was BMW's highest-performing bike ever. The 226kg mass was only around 11kg more than Suzuki's Hayabusa, the class leader, and the modern engine made a massive 167bhp. For high-speed sport-touring fans, BMW finally had a credible contender.

ENGINE: 1157cc (71ci), l/c inline-four, 16-valve DOHC
POWER: 167bhp at 10,250rpm
GEARBOX: 6-speed
FINAL DRIVE: shaft
WEIGHT: 226kg (498lb)
TOP SPEED: 290km/h (180mph)

With its optional semi-hard luggage, the K1200S makes an excellent long-distance fast tourer. This bike has also had an aftermarket exhaust fitted, increasing power and style.

BMW K1200R

Following on from the success of its K1200S, BMW was keen to capitalize on the engine and chassis design. The result was the K1200R – a naked version of the S.

Many riders in Europe prefer a naked bike – without plastic bodywork fitted – for its more relaxed riding position and reduced maximum speed. But the K1200R hadn't lost any of the power or sophistication of the S.

The engine remained the same in-line, four-cylinder, 16-valve design, with high compression ratio, angled cylinders and advanced engine management. Peak power output is slightly reduced by the lack of an integrated ram-air system,

but is still a massive 163bhp – enough to make it the most powerful naked bike available.

The lack of bodywork allows a better view of the unique chassis layout. The aluminium frame can be seen passing over the top of the engine, and the Duolever front suspension linkages are also more easily seen.

ENGINE: 1157cc (71ci), l/c in-line-four, 16-valve DOHC
POWER: 163bhp at 10,250rpm
GEARBOX: 6-speed
FINAL DRIVE: shaft
WEIGHT: 211kg (465lb)
TOP SPEED: 265km/h (165mph)

BMW's K1200R has brutal styling to match its brutal performance. Its naked design, without protective plastic bodywork, shows off the unusual chassis and engine designs to the full.

BMW R1200GS

BMW pretty much invented the 'large trailbike' class with its R80GS in 1980, and it has dominated the class ever since. The R1200GS, first shown in 2005, was the first of the modern Boxer designs that had drastically reduced weight and much stronger performance than before. It replaced the R1150GS, and it offered a much sleeker,

lighter, and more dynamic ride. The engine had numerous internal revisions, including lighter pistons and a new six-speed gearbox, while remaining an air-cooled flat twin. The chassis was also the same basic layout, but careful design had reduced the all-up weight by 30kg. This improved

acceleration and handling, and added agility for off-road or town riding.

But the GS's main role remains the same – a long-distance touring machine that's able to tackle occasional off-road work with relative ease. Equipped with optional accessories like hard luggage, sat-nav and heated grips, the R1200GS lives up to its

popular and intended 'adventure sport' image.

ENGINE: 1170cc (71ci), a/c flat-twin, 8-valve SOHC
POWER: 98bhp at 7,000rpm
GEARBOX: 6-speed
FINAL DRIVE: shaft
WEIGHT: 199kg (439lb)
TOP SPEED: 209km/h (130mph)

Although the BMW R1200GS is styled to look like an off-road enduro machine, only expert riders can get the most from it away from the Tarmac. For most riders, it's best used as a touring machine.

BMW F800

When it first appeared in 2006, the F800 filled a gap in BMW's range between its large-capacity twins and fours, and the single-cylinder F650 range. The 800cc (49ci) parallel twin was initially produced in two variants: an 'S' sportsbike and an 'ST' sports tourer with larger fairing. The engine used a novel balancing system, with a reciprocating 'balance bar' pivoting at the back of the crankcase, and operated by an additional small connecting rod between the two piston con-rods. This bar moves up and down, opposing the piston's motion and balancing out their movement.

The F800 uses a conventional chassis design, with an aluminium twin-spar frame, telescopic forks and a monoshock rear suspension. However, the single-sided rear swing arm, Kevlar belt final drive and underseat fuel tank mark it out as something a little out of the ordinary.

On the road, the F800 is a lively, spirited performer that is ideal for novice riders and commuters, as well as more advanced riders.

Launched in South Africa in 2006, the F800S gave a real boost to BMW's middleweight range. Lively and fun, it was a real challenger to bikes like Honda's Hornet 600.

ENGINE: 798cc (49ci), l/c 360° parallel twin, 8-valve, DOHC
POWER: 85bhp at 8,000rpm
GEARBOX: 6-speed
FINAL DRIVE: Kevlar belt
WEIGHT: 182kg (401lb)
TOP SPEED: 201km/h (125mph)

BMW R1200S

Light, powerful and technologically advanced, the R1200S is BMW's flagship sporting twin. It can't match pure sportsbikes on paper, but does offer an exhilarating alternative to Japanese or Italian machines.

BMW has long been associated with the air-cooled, flat-twin engine layout, which it has optimized and perfected for roles in enduro, touring and roadster models. It's less suited for outright performance machinery, but BMW persevered and the result was the R1200S. Launched in 2006 to replace the aging R1100S, it had a heavily revised sporting version of the 1170cc (71ci) flat-twin engine used in the firm's R1200GS. High-performance cylinder heads, pistons, exhaust and fuel-injection systems raised peak power by 24bhp, to a heady 122bhp. The chassis was also modified with racing suspension units from Ohlins, wide, lightweight aluminium wheels and sports tyres. Careful attention to detail meant a weight loss over the R1100S of over 30kg (66lb) to 190kg (418lb), which played a big part in the hugely improved performance. On track, the BMW's unique suspension systems can feel strange to a rider used to more conventional designs. It's a strong performer off the track though, and makes a fast, capable, sporty road bike.

ENGINE: 1170cc (71ci), a/c flat-twin, 8-valve, SOHC
POWER: 122bhp at 8,250rpm
GEARBOX: 6-speed
FINAL DRIVE: BMW Paralever shaft
WEIGHT: 190kg (419lb)
TOP SPEED: 257km/h (160mph)

DUCATI MONSTER S4RS

ITALY 2006

Ducati's Monster range started life in 1993 with the 900 Monster. But as the years passed, its 900cc (55ci) air-cooled, four-valve engine fell behind opposition from Japanese and other European manufacturers. Ducati had a ready-made replacement in the form of its 916 superbike engine, so this eight-valve watercooled powerplant was fitted to the Monster, to create the 2001 Monster S4. The strong, torquey desmoquattro engine complemented the naked chassis perfectly, and made for a sophisticated, powerful roadster.

By 2005, even the updated S4 – the 996cc S4R – had been left behind, so Ducati launched the S4Rs with a 999 superbike engine, Ohlins track suspension and Brembo race brakes.

Finished in classic Ducati colours chemes, with offset race stripes, the S4Rs was Ducati's finest naked roadster. The 'Testastretta' engine borrowed from the 999 gave instant punch and perfect fuelling, while the top-specification chassis components provided precise, fluid handling. For track or road riding, few competitors could offer the class or sophistication of the S4Rs.

With an engine basically lifted straight from Ducati's 999 superbike, and a chassis specification to match, the Monster S4Rs has performance to match many pure sports bikes on track.

ENGINE: 998cc (61ci), l/c 90° V-twin, 8-valve desmodromic, DOHC
POWER: 130bhp at 9,500rpm
GEARBOX: 6-speed
FINAL DRIVE: chain
WEIGHT: 177kg (390lb)
TOP SPEED: 249km/h (155mph)

The S4Rs evolves the classic Monster styling with a new swing arm and gorgeous paint schemes. It's a fantastic modern interpretation of a timeless icon.

DUCATI MULTISTRADA 1100

ITALY 2006

Despite its unconventional style, Ducati's Multistrada is actually intended to be a practical, everyday, all-round motorcycle. The clue is in its name – 'Multistrada' is Italian for 'all roads', and it's the class of all-round 'adventure sport' bikes that Ducati specifically had in mind with the Multistrada.

The heart of the bike is Ducati's long-running air-cooled 90-degree V-twin, in a 1078cc (66ci) version, with fuel injection, two valves per cylinder and desmodromic valve operation, which uses a cam to positively close as well as open the poppet valves.

The Multistrada chassis is similar to the firm's Monster range, but with longer travel suspension, to soak up bumps and potholes in less-than-perfect roads. The rear swing arm is also a single-sided design, similar to the company's iconic 916 range of superbikes.

The Multistrada's final quirk is in the bodywork – its screen rotates with the steering, and is separate from the rest of the fairing.

ENGINE: 992cc (60.5ci), a/c 90°V-twin, 4-valve, SOHC desmodromic
POWER: 92bhp at 8,000rpm
GEARBOX: 6-speed
FINAL DRIVE: chain
WEIGHT: 196kg (432lb)
TOP SPEED: 225km/h (140mph)

Although it has many exotic ingredients, including sports suspension, a classic Ducati engine and deep red paint, the Multistrada is a strong performer.

KAWASAKI ZZR1400

JAPAN 2006

Kawasaki is considered by many to be the inventor of the 'hypersports' class with its 1990 ZZ-R1100. This class of motorcycle is marked out by large-capacity, sporty bikes with comfortable accommodation and incredible top speeds. Kawasaki's massive ZZR1400 meets all these criteria perfectly.

Producing nearly 200bhp from its inline-four 16-valve engine, it is little surprise that the ZZR is incredibly fast: its 299km/h

Long, low, and lithe – Kawasaki used all its aerodynamic design know-how to make the ZZR1400 slice through the air at high speeds, while protecting its rider from windblast.

(186mph) top speed is a factory-limited figure.

What is more surprising is how well it handles at all speeds. Weighing in at 215kg (474lb), the ZZR1400 is no lightweight, but a combination of modern chassis design and sporting suspension and tyres means it handles like a good 1,000cc (61ci) sportsbike of the late 1990s.

Powerful brakes and reasonable ground clearance further underline the bike's outstanding performance potential.

The ZZR1400 is also very practical. It has a modern digital dashboard with large LCD screen, comfortable seating for rider and pillion, and for fast, long-distance sports-touring, it is a difficult act to beat.

ENGINE: 1352cc (82ci), l/c in-line four, 16-valve, DOHC
POWER: 190bhp at 9,500rpm (198bhp with ram-air)
GEARBOX: 6-speed
FINAL DRIVE: chain
WEIGHT: 215kg (474lb)
TOP SPEED: 299km/h (186mph) (factory limited)

A full-bore hyperbike engine producing nigh-on 200bhp makes the ZZR1400 the undisputed king of the road. When launched in 2006, it was by far the most powerful production bike available.

SUZUKI GSX-R600

JAPAN 2006

Suzuki's GSX-R range has always stood for ultimate racetrack performance, and the GSX-R600 is no exception. From the first SRAD model of 1996 to the K6 2006 model, the GSX-R was generally accepted as amongst the most extreme, focused track bike in the 600 class. Marked out by a compact chassis, powerful if rev-hungry engine and full race bodywork, the K6 model was based heavily on the GSX-R750. Suzuki had moved the bike's silencer box underneath the engine, centralizing mass and improving aerodynamics. This required some major rearranging though: a new, smaller, engine was needed to mount higher up in the frame. This engine featured dual-valve, dual-injector fuel injection, a first for the class, while a catalyst and butterfly valve in the silencer cut noise and emissions while boosting power and drivability. The rear shock offered separate high- and low-speed damping adjustment, a feature previously only found on exotic race machinery, while radial-mount front brakes and upside-down forks gave a superbly controlled front end.

ENGINE: 599cc (36.5ci), l/c inline-four, 16-valve DOHC
POWER: n/a
GEARBOX: 6-speed
FINAL DRIVE: chain
WEIGHT: 161kg (355lb)
TOP SPEED: 265.5km/h (165mph)

SUZUKI GSX-R750

JAPAN 2006

First launched in 1985, the GSX-R750 is the longest-running supersports bike still on sale, and it's a bike Suzuki is extremely proud of. It was born in order to compete in the top-class racing of the time, which was generally based on 750cc (46ci) machines. Race regulations change though, and by 2004 the 750cc (46ci) class was no longer a major race class. But the GSX-R750 remained a strong seller for Suzuki.

The 2006 model was an incredibly sophisticated development of the original GSX-R – but it was based on the same principles: light weight, strong power and sharp handling. The in-line four engine used titanium valves to reduce internal losses, and advanced electronic engine management to improve rideability while cutting emissions. An underslung exhaust system optimised mass distribution, and a fabricated aluminium frame and swing arm gave stiffness without excess weight. Sophisticated suspension units offer a wide range of adjustment, allowing riders to achieve the optimal setup for their weight and riding style.

ENGINE: 749cc (46ci), l/c inline-four, 16-valve, DOHC
POWER: 148bhp at 12,500rpm
GEARBOX: 6-speed
FINAL DRIVE: chain
WEIGHT: 163kg (359lb)
TOP SPEED: 282km/h (175mph)

The last of the three-quarter litre superbikes, and for many the perfect sportsbike, Suzuki's GSX-R750 combines the precision of a 600 and the power of a 1000 in a supremely controllable package.

YAMAHA R6

Crammed with high-tech engineering, then wrapped in MotoGP-derived bodywork, Yamaha's 2006 R6 took the 600cc (37ci) sportsbike class to new levels of sophistication on track.

One look at the sharp lines of Yamaha's 2006 R6 is enough to tell you that this is an extremely radical motorcycle. From the yawning ram-air intake between the sharp-edged headlights, back to the ultra-minimalist tail unit and vestigial passenger seat, this is clearly a focused, razor-sharp track bike. A closer look reveals exotic suspension units with separate high- and low-speed compression damping adjustment, radial-mount front brake calipers and sticky race tyres already fitted.

Underneath the supremely aerodynamic bodywork, even more technology lurks. The 599cc (36.5ci) engine has a unique 'fly-by-wire' fuel injection system, where the rider's twistgrip operates a computerized sensor rather than directly opening the throttle valves. The computer then opens the throttle via an electric motor, giving optimum power delivery.

The result of this focused design is an extremely sharp track bike, at its best in the high-rpm frenzy of circuit riding. However, everyday road riding is rather compromised as a result of the race focus.

ENGINE: 599cc (36.5ci), l/c inline-four, 16-valve DOHC
POWER: 133bhp at 14,500rpm
GEARBOX: 6-speed
FINAL DRIVE: chain
WEIGHT: 161kg (355lb)
TOP SPEED: 265.5km/h (165mph)

SUZUKI GSX-R1000

JAPAN 2007

Between 1996 and 2001, Suzuki relied on its venerable GSX-R750 to compete in the open sportsbike class. Good though it was, the 750 couldn't really match Honda's CBR900RR FireBlade or Yamaha's 1,000cc R1, so Suzuki fans were ecstatic when the firm released the GSX-R1000 in 2001. Based on the legendary GSX-R750, the new bike had the statistics to dominate the open class, with over 150bhp driving its 172kg. At its world launch in America, journalists found a hugely powerful sportsbike, with excellent handling. More importantly though, the new bike offered excellent levels of rider control – an area bike firms were increasingly having to focus on.

Later updates in 2003, 2005 and 2007 further improved the GSX-R's handling and power. But Suzuki also managed to retain exquisite levels of control – control that became ever more vital if normal riders were to handle its stunning performance in safety.

ENGINE: 999cc (61ci), l/c in-line four, 16-valve, DOHC
POWER: 175bhp at 9,800rpm
GEARBOX: 6-speed
FINAL DRIVE: chain
WEIGHT: 166kg (366lb)
TOP SPEED: 299km/h (186mph) (restricted)

MINOR MANUFACTURERS

Since the 1880s, there have been literally thousands of motorcycle manufacturers. However, many justify only a few words because their bikes were either rare or simply did not survive for very long. Below, we have attempted to cover every minor manufacturer and every model not mentioned elsewhere in the book.

ABAKO
Germany (Nurnberg) 1923–25: This was a manufacturer of 129cc (8ci) single-cylinder machines with their own two-stroke engines, Sturmey Archer gearboxes and chain drive.

ABBOTSFORD
England 1919–21: Single-cylinder scooter with two-stroke engine and chain drive.

ABC
England (Birmingham) 1920–24: This assembler used Villiers two-stroke engines, first 296cc (18ci), and then 247cc (15ci)

ABC
Germany 1922–25: Lightweights with their own 149cc (9ci) two-stroke single.

ABENDSONNE
Germany 1933–34: This assembler used two 98cc (6ci) Villiers two-stroke singles coupled together.

ABERDALE
England 1947–59: This was a manufacturer of Lightweight/Autocycles with 98cc (6ci) and 123cc (8ci) Villiers and Sachs two-strokes engines. It was taken over by Bown in 1959.

ABE-STAR
Japan 1951–59: Maker of two overhead-valve four-stroke singles, originally 338cc (21ci), then 148cc (9ci).

ABIGNENTE
Italy 1926: Maker of 345cc (21ci) two-stroke motor; manufactured in very limited numbers.

ABINGDON
England 1903–33: The original Abingdons had proprietary engines (Fafnir, Kerry, Minerva, MMC) but later the company used its own singles and V-twins. Also known as AKD, Abingdon King Dick, after 1925.

ABJ
England 1949–54: A.B. Jackson made unremarkable lightweights, initially 98cc (6ci) and later 49cc (3ci) and 123cc (8ci), all powered by Villiers two-stroke singles. They also produced an auxiliary cycle-motor from 1952 onwards.

ABRA
Italy 1923–27: This manufacturer used 149cc (9ci) DKW single; it later switched to using its own 132cc (8ci) single.

ACCOSSATO
Italy (Moncalieri near Turin) 1973–unknown: This company made limited-production, small-capacity motocross enduro single-cylinder two-strokes with high performance. Models included the CE 80 (1985), producing 21 horsepower at 12,000rpm from a water-cooled engine.

ACHER
France 1926: This firm was the manufacturer of a 500cc (31ci) water-cooled two-stroke twin engine.

ACHILLES
Austro-Hungary, later Czechoslovakia (Ober-Politz a.d. Nordbahn) 1906–12: This company made four-stroke singles and V-twins with engines from Fafnir and Zeus.

ACHILLES
Germany 1953–57: The founder of the Austro-Hungarian Achilles, above, moved to Germany after WWII. The new firm began with two-strokes using 147cc (9ci) and 174cc (11ci) Sachs engines, then made a 48cc (3ci) two-stroke single.

ACMA
France (Fourchambault) 1948–62: Built Vespa scooters under licence: 123cc (8ci), 147cc (9ci) and 173cc (11ci) motors.

ACME
England 1902–22: Until 1918, this firm used bought-in Minerva engines. After this, they built their own 348cc (21ci) singles and 997cc (61ci) V-twins. Merged with Rex in 1922.

ACS
France 1980: A builder of racing machines, it began with a 999cc (61ci) four-stroke triple that delivered 150 horsepower at 11,000rpm, with the engine a stressed frame member.

ACSA
Italy (Bologna) 1954: A moped with 75cc (5ci) engine, which was a total commercial failure.

ADER
France 1901–06: Manufacturer best known for a long-stroke transverse-mounted V-twin delivering four horsepower; also made a single with half the power.

ADM
Spain 1987–: Builds small capacity two-stroke models, including road racing machines up to 125cc (8ci).

ADONIS
France (Neuilly-s-Seine) 1949–52: This company made scooters and mopeds of 48cc (3ci) and 999cc (61ci) with VAP engines.

ADRIA
Germany 1912–29: Began with an auxiliary cycle-motor, then, around 1921, introduced a 276cc (17ci) single-gear machine, and in 1923 a 282cc (17ci) three-speed. All had belt drive.

ADS
Belgium 1949–54: This firm assembled 98cc (6ci) autocycles with Sachs and Ilo two-stroke single engines.

ADVANCE
England (Northampton) 1906–12: A range of singles and V-twins made by Smart and Gainsforth fiited with engines of their own manufacture.

AEL
England (Birmingham) 1919–24: This company was a typical small assembler – actually a motorcycle dealer – making motorcycles from 147cc (9ci) to 348cc (21ci) with Blackburne, JAP and Villiers proprietary engines.

AEOLUS
England (London) 1903–05: Short-lived shaft-drive machine with 492cc (30ci) four-stroke single-cylinder engine of their own manufacture.

AEOLUS
England (Birmingham) 1914–16: This company made machines fitted with their own single-cylinder two-stroke of 269cc (16ci). They went on to make the Bown.

AER
England 1931–50: The earliest bikes from A.E. Reynolds were Scott-based specials, but from 1938 to 1940 the AER was a distinct make with 180°, two-stroke parallel twins of 246cc (15ci) and 346cc (21ci).

AEROPLAN
Germany (Kohlfurt) 1922–25: This company made crude two-strokes with DKW engines of 125cc (8ci) and 175c (11ci).

AEROS
Czechoslovakia (Kaaden, Bohemia) 1927–29: Assembler of machines with four-stroke 348cc (21ci) and 498cc (6ci) overhead-valve Kuchen engines, and 250cc (15ci) Bekamo two-strokes.

AEROSCOOT
France 1953–54: This company made scooters with proprietary 98cc (6ci) motors.

AETOS
Italy (Turin) 1912–14: This firm manufactured a 492cc (30ci) V-twin capable of delivering three-and-a-half horsepower.

AFW
Germany (Brake, Westphalia) 1923–25: The grandly-named Allgemeinen Fahrzeugwerk assembled 246cc (15ci) four-stroke singles using Hansa engines.

AGF
France 1948–56: Made lightweights and scooters powered by Ydral engines of 123cc (8ci) and 173cc (11ci).

AGL
France 1950: A 250cc (15ci) racing four-stroke single built by Monsieur A. (presumably G.) Loupia

AGON
Germany (Augsburg) 1924–28: Assembler using a range of single-cylinder and twin-cylinder engines, including Bradshaw, Kuchen, JAP and Paque from 172cc (1oci) to 996cc (61ci).

AGRATI
Italy 1958–61: This moped manufacturer became better known after its merger with Garelli.

AGS
The Netherlands 1971–unknown: Two-stroke motocross bikes with Sachs, Puch, Zundapp and other engines.

AIM
Italy (Florence) 1974–unknown: Made off-road, motocross, successful 50cc (3ci) to 250cc (15ci) machines with off-beat model names such as Mini Girls, Cross Boy, Jumbo. Despite this, they have won many competitions.

AIROLITE
England 1921–23: Made a lightweight with a 110cc (7ci) two-stroke Simplex engine, and an auxiliary cycle-motor.

AJAX
Belgium 1949–53: Lightweights with Sachs and NSU two-stroke engines.

AJAX
England 1923–24: This firm assembled machines with 147cc (9ci), 247cc (15ci) and 269cc (16ci) Villiers two-stroke engines, or a 346cc (21ci) Blackburne four-stroke.

AJR
Scotland (Edinburgh) 1925–26: A.J. Roberston personally tested every one of the machines that bore his name; fitted with JAP 350cc (21ci) and 500cc (31ci) four-stroke engines.

AJW
England (Exeter and Wimborne) 1926–70s or later. In Exeter from 1926 to 1945, Arthur John Wheaton used various proprietary engines up to 1000cc (61ci), including a 750cc (461ci) four-cylinder Austin and supercharged machines.

AKD
England (Birmingham): see ABINGDON.

AKKENS
England 1919–22: Thomas and Gilbert actually built most of this 292cc (18ci) two-stroke.

ALATO
Italy (Turin) 1923–25: This company made a single, high-quality model with 131cc (8ci) two-stroke motor.

ALBA
Germany (Stettin, now in Poland) 1919–24: This firm made good, basic bikes with their own 198cc (6ci) four-stroke engines and a choice of belt or chain drive.

ALBATROSS
England 1954: An interesting scooter with a 224cc (14ci) Villiers two-stroke engine and four-speed transmission.

ALBERT
Germany 1922–24: One of many German manufacturers of the mid-1920s, it made a 183cc (11ci) two-stroke machine.

ALBERTUS
Germany 1922–24: A patented two-stroke motor made in capacities of 113cc (7ci), 142cc (9ci) and 176cc (11ci), it could be switched from petrol to diesel once warm.

ALDBERT
Italy (Milan) 1953–59: Specialized in sporting two-stroke lightweights like the 175c (11ci) Gran Sport, which claimed 160km/h (100mph). Also made mopeds and four-strokes.

This photograph shows the split single engine of the Austrian-built Allstate Puch SES250.

ALECTO
England (London) 1919–24: This company built their own 295cc (18ci) and 345cc (21ci) machines, initially with belt drive and, from 1921 for the 345cc/21ci, with chain drive.

ALERT
England (Coventry) 1903–06: Smith and Molesworth, the makers, used Belgian Sarolea engines.

ALEU
Spain (Barcelona) 1953–56: Built two-stroke singles of 198cc (12ci) and 247cc (15ci), with three-speed transmission.

ALFA
Germany 1925–28: Former BMW engineer Alexander von Falkenhausen built motorcycles with a 172cc (10ci) Villiers two-stroke and a 344cc (21ci) twin of unverified performance.

ALFA
Italy 1923–27: This began with 125cc (8cii) and 175c (11ci) Norman engines before moving onto a 350cc (21ci) Sport in 1927; apparently used Blackburne and Bradshaw engines.

ALFA-GNOM
Austria (Wiener Neustadt) 1926–28: Sports racer with 598cc (6ci) single-cylinder engine; made by Franz and Anton Rumpler, the same firm built the FAR.

ALGE
Germany 1923–31: Motorenfabrik Alfred Geissler built a 173cc (11ci) two-stroke and four-strokes of 200cc (12ci), 250cc (15ci), 350cc (21ci) and 498cc (6ci). Also used Blackburne and Villiers engines.

ALIPRANDI
Italy (Milan) 1925–30: Used proprietary 175cc (11ci) and 350cc (21ci) engines from Moser, JAP and Sturmey-Archer.

ALLDAYS/ALLDAYS ONIONS
England (Birmingham) 1900–15: After starting with De Dion Bouton-engined three-wheelers in 1898, this firm entered the two-wheeler market in 1903 with the Matchless (no relation) using their own engine. Renamed Allon in 1915.

ALLEGRO
Switzerland (Neuchatel) 1925–27 and late 1940s to 1950s: The early series were Villiers-engined two-strokes and MAG or Sturmey-Archer four-strokes of 250cc (15ci) and 350cc (21ci). Post-war machines were mopeds and lightweights.

ALLELUIA
France 1920s and 1950s: In the 1920s, it made 175c (11ci) lightweights. In the 1950s, it rebadged other firms' mopeds.

ALLON
England 1915–24: The successors to Alldays, Allon built big V-twins (798cc/49ci and 988cc/60ci), good-size singles (499cc/31ci and 539cc/33ci) and a 292cc (18ci) two-stroke.

ALLSTATE
Austria 1953–63: These were Steyr-Puch scooters and mopeds labelled 'Allstate' for Sears, Roebuck in the United States.

ALLWYN
India 1972–88: A Lambretta by any other name, 125cc (8ci) to 200cc (12ci).

ALMA
France 1949–59. It began in 1949 with lightweight 125cc (8ci) and 175c (11ci) two-strokes and later made mopeds, lightweights and scooters with (from 1953) Sachs motors.

ALMIDI
Belgium c.1950s: Moped made in the same place that made the bodywork for Dyna-Panhard.

ALMORA
Germany 1924–25: Julius Lowy-designed lightweights with two-stroke engines of 113cc (7ci), 138cc (8ci) and 176cc (11ci) that could be switched to diesel oil once warm.

ALP
England 1912–17: This firm built Moto-Reve machines under licence, and a variety of other motors: 199cc (12ci) four-stroke, 348cc (21ci) two-stroke and twins of various sizes.

ALPA PICQUENOT
France c.1956: Two mopeds/autocycles, 49cc (3ci) and 80cc (5cci), with two-speed transmission.

ALPHA CENTURI
England c.1967: This company made racing two-stroke parallel twins of 250cc (15ci), reputedly capable of 190km/h (118mph).

ALPHONSE THOMANN
France 1908–23: This firm made two-stroke autocycles.

ALTA
Wales 1968–71: This company made motocross and trials bikes powered by Suzuki two-stroke singles.

ALTEA
Italy (Milan) 1939–41: Fixed-head 196cc four-stroke unit-construction single capable of 75km/h (47mph).

ALTER
Italy 1955–56: Mopeds and lightweights (49cc/3ci and 70cc/4ci two-strokes) with two-speed transmission.

The 1983 Armstrong Rotox 250. This Armstrong had no connection with the earlier firm of that name.

AMAG
Germany (Berlin) 1924–25: This firm was an assembler of lightweights with 149cc (9ci) Bekamo two-stroke singles.

AMBAG
Germany (Berlin) 1923: This firm used a single-cylinder 155cc (9ci) Gruhn side-valve in their own frames.

AMC
USA (Chicago) 1912–15: The Allied Motor Corporation built a 980cc (60ci) inlet-over-exhaust V-twin with advanced suspension.

AMC
France 1942–50s: The Ateliers de Mecanique du Centre built a 99cc four-stroke with a bought-in motor, then tried various engine sizes (108cc/6.5ci, 118cc/7ci, 123cc/7.5ci, 125cc/8ci and 170cc/10ci) before introducing a 250cc (15ci) in 1953, followed by 125cc (8ci), 150cc (9ci) and 175c (11ci) four-strokes and 99cc (6ci) and 125cc (8ci) two-strokes.

AMERICAN
USA (Chicago) 1911–14: Singles (550cc/33ci) and V-twins, four-stroke.

AMERICAN-X
USA 1910–30: American Excelsior V-twins (996cc/61ci), rebadged as American-X for the UK.

AMI
Germany (Berlin-Schoneberg) 1921–25: Auto-Moto-Industrie GmbH made 49cc (3ci) auxiliary cycle-motors.

AMI
Switzerland 1950–54: Scooter with 98cc (6ci), later 123cc (8ci), two-stroke engine.

AMMON
Germany (Berlin) 1921–25: Fitted motors from various sources, including DKW, Bekamo, Baumi and a four-stroke Paque, into an unusual pressed-steel frame.

AMO
Germany (Munich) 1921–24: Their 146cc (9ci) two-stroke delivered less than one horsepower; the motor which they used was apparently bought in.

AMO
Germany (Berlin) 1950–54: This company made two-stroke mopeds with 48cc (3ci) Westendarp & Pieper engines.

AMR
Italy (Carsarza Ligure) 1970–83: Competitive motocross bikes with Sachs engines from 125cc (8ci) to 350cc (21ci) in high-class frames.

AMS
Spain (Malaga) 1954–65: Began in 1954 with Hispano-Villiers two-stroke engines of 125 (8ci), 148cc (9ci) and 248cc (15ci) before moving on to a 247cc (15ci) parallel twin.

ANCON
Argentina 1958: Lightweight with a 100cc (6ci) Sachs two-stroke.

ANCORA
Italy 1923–40: Ancora began with 147cc (9ci) Villiers two-strokes, then built other capacities up to 247cc (15ci) and 350cc (21ci), in road, sport and race trim. By 1940, engine sizes ranged from 60cc (4ci) to 175c (11ci).

ANDRE
France 1920s: Andre made lightweights with a choice of engines: a 175c (11ci) two-stroke and 249cc (15ci) and 337cc (21ci) four-strokes.

ANDREAN
France 1924: An advanced overhead-valve 225cc (14ci) four-stroke single delivering 10 horsepower.

ANDREES
Germany (Dusseldorf) 1923–29: This firm began with sporting machines powered by a variety of four-strokes: Blackburne, Bradshaw flat twin, JAP and MAG V-twin. Adding its own 198cc (12ci) two-stroke in 1928 over-stretched the company.

ANGLIAN
England 1903–12: As well as their own two-and-a-half Anglian motors, these early bikes were available with two-and-three-quarter horsepower engines from De Dion Bouton, MMC, Fafnir and Sarolea, and later with JAP and Blumfield.

ANGLO-DANE
Denmark 1912–14: As the name suggests, these assemblers used English motors (JAP and Villiers).

ANKER
Germany (Bielefeld, then Paderborn) 1949–58: This firm were assemblers of lightweights with Sachs and Ilo engines from 98cc (6ci) to 250cc (15ci).

ANTOINE
Belgium (Liege) 1900–10: This firm built singles of three to four horsepower and twins of four-and-a-half and five horsepower, first with Kelecom engines and then with its own.

ANZANI
France 1906:Best known as a supplier of proprietary engines, Anzani made an improbable propeller-driven motorcycle in 1906, when President of the Union of French Aero-clubs.

APACHE
USA (Denver) 1907–11: Braun & Beck made a 597cc (36ci) inlet-over-exhaust single with a 'backwards' engine where the exhaust was situated at the rear of the engine.

APEX
Germany (Cologne) 1925–26: Made Sporting two-strokes with 247cc (15ci) and 348cc (21ci) Blackburne engines.

API-LAMBRETTA
India 1965–88: Another Indian Lambretta (150cc/9ci and 175c /11ci), built under licence.

APOLLO
Sweden (Varnamo) 1950s: Began in 1951 by assembling two-strokes with 123cc (8ci) Villiers and 198cc (6ci) Zundapp engines. It went on to a 128cc scooter (1955) and 50cc mopeds (Sachs and Zundapp) and ended up part of Volvo.

AQUILA
Italy (Bologna) 1927–35: Firma Cavani began with 132cc (8ci) DKW engines, then (in 1934) Rudge Python 250cc (15ci) and 350cc (21ci).

AQUILA
Italy (Turin) 1927–35: Sporting machines with two-stroke and four-stroke engines, including Rudge Python, Kuchen and OBM.

AQUILA
Italy (Rome) 1953–58: Moto Aquila made 48cc (3ci), 123cc (8ci) and 158cc (10ci) two-strokes and 98cc (6ci) and 174cc (11ci) four-strokes.

ARAB
England (Birmingham) 1923–26: This firm assembled bikes with 147cc (9ci) Villiers two-strokes.

ARBINET
France 1927–34: This company made their own two-stroke singles in many cacities from 98cc (6ci) to 497cc (30ci).

ARC
Spain 1954–56: Lightweight with 123cc (8ci) Hispano-Villiers two-stroke.

ARCO
Germany (Speyer am Rhein) 1922–30: Water-cooled, overhead-valve singles (246cc/15ci, 346cc/21ci), built 'backwards', carburettor at the front, exhaust at the back.

ARDEA
Italy (Cavaria Oggiona) 1928–33: At first a 175c (11ci) horizontal single, then (1931–34) a 350cc (21ci) (21ci).

ARDEN
England (Coventry) 1912–20: This assembler used various engines (even, unusually, it own), notably 269cc (16ci) Villiers.

ARDENT
France (Cannes) 1950–57: This firm made mopeds of 48cc and 49cc (3ci) and, from 1953, a 65cc (4ci) scooter.

ARDILLA
Spain (Barcelona) 1951: Lightweight with 125cc (8ci) two-stroke delivering four-and-a-half horsepower.

ARDITO
Italy (Stradella, Pavia) 1951–54: Offering 48cc (3ci) to 125cc (8ci) lightweights and an auxiliary cycle-motor, S.I.M.E.S. made a sports model in 1953 with 100cc (6ci) two-stroke or 175c (11ci) four-stroke, and a 49cc (3ci) mini-scooter.

ARES
Germany (Zittau) 1922–28: Built by Heros.

ARGENTRE
France (Paris) 1927–32: This firm offered its own 250cc (15ci) and 350cc (21ci) two-strokes or a 350cc (21ci) JAP.

ARGEO
Germany (Berlin) 1924–27: Made its own 198cc (12ci) and 246cc (15ci) two-stroke singles in a conventional frame.

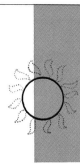

MOTOR SCOOTER SR 59 *Berlin*

An advertisement for East Germany's Berlin SR59 scooter.

ARGUL
Germany 1923–26: Argul used DKW and Bubi two-strokes, and Alba four-strokes, in their own frame.

ARI
Germany 1924–25: Ari mounted 146cc (9ci) DKW engines in their own frame.

ARIZ
Italy (Milan) 1952–54: Sold for use with the Garelli Mosquito auxiliary cycle-motor.

ARLIGUE
France 1950–53: An assembler that used proprietary engines, especially Ydral and AMC (France).

ARMAC
USA 1911–13: This firm made one engine (four horsepower single), fitted into many models, 14 in total.

ARMIS
England (Birmingham) 1920–23: Used a range of proprietary engines (298cc/18ci to 654cc/40ci): JAP, MAG and Precision.

ARMOR
France (Paris) 1910–57: An offshoot of Alcyon, Armor made lightweights with 98cc (6ci) two-stroke engines and 173cc (11ci) four-stroke engines; added a 498cc (6ci) four-stroke single in the late 1920s; closed in 1934; and after 1945 made 48cc (3ci), 98cc (6ci), 125cc (8ci) and (in 1953) 250cc (15ci) machines before being re-amalgamated with Alcyon.

ARMSTRONG
England (London) 1902–05: The first 'Armstrong' name put 211cc (13ci) Minervas in Chater-Lea frames.

ARMSTRONG
England (London) 1913–14:Unconnected to the first firm, this Armstrong used 269cc (16ci) Villiers two-strokes.

ARMSTRONG
England 1980–87: Briefly owned both COTTON and CCM.

ARNO
England (Coventry) 1906–15: Bright yellow motorcycles with engines of 250cc (15ci), 350cc (21ci) and 500cc (31ci).

ARROW
USA (Chicago) 1909–14: Quiet lightweights with their own engine of one or one-and-a-half, depending on the source.

ARROW
England (Birmingham) 1913–17: Used Precision and Levis 211cc (13ci) two-strokes.

ASAHI
Japan (Tokyo) 1953–65: Established in 1909, Asahi made its first side-valve machines (Asahi HA, then Golden Beam FA/2, both 249cc/15ci) in 1955, an overhead-valve of 344cc (21ci) in 1956 and a 500cc (31ci) twin in 1960. There was also a 125cc (8ci) two-stroke twin.

ASCOT
England 1905–06: An assembler that used Minerva and Antoine engines.

ASHFORD
England 1905: This firm installed motors from various manufacturers in their own frames.

ASL
England (Stafford) 1907–15: Associated Springs Ltd fitted proprietary engines into their own frames which featured pneumatic springing front and rear.

ASPES
Italy 1967–82:Typical manufacturer of high performance, lightweight 49cc (3ic) to 123cc (8ci) motocross machines, with their own engines as well as Franco-Morini and Minarelli.

ASPI
Italy 1947–?1951: Manufacturer of three-wheeler delivery vehicles (Società Attrezzature Servizi Pubblici Industriali) who also made 125cc (8ci) and 175c (11ci) flat twin two-stroke motorcycles and an auxiliary cycle-motor.

ASSO
Italy 1927–31: Sporty overhead-valve 174cc (11ci) (one source says 157cc/10ci) single with its own engine.

ASSO
Italy 1947–early 1950s: Single cylinder two-stroke auxiliary cycle motor.

ASTER
France (St. Denis-s-Seine) 1898–1910: The well-regarded Atelier de Construction Mechanique supplied engines to other manufacturers as well as building its own complete motorfirm cycles, including a 355cc (22ci) single.

ASTON
England (Birmingham) 1923–24: This firm built their own 142cc (9ci) two-stroke and offered a choice of one-speed, two-speed and three-speed models. Most had belt drive.

ASTRA
Italy (Milan) 1931–51: Astra made mostly Ariel-based machines from Max Turkheimer with engines from 123cc (8ci) to 498cc (6ci).

ASTRAL
France (Puteaux-s-Seine) 1919–1923: This company made 98cc (6ci) and 122cc (7ci) two-stroke bikes.

ASTRO
Italy 1950: Auxiliary 47cc (3ci) cycle motor with friction drive.

ATALA
Italy 1925–34: Set up in 1906, this bicycle manufacturer offered, for a decade, Blackburn and JAP engines of 174cc (11ci), 346cc (21ci) and 498cc (6ci) in their own frames.

ATALA
Italy (Padua) 1954–unknown: Lightweights from 49cc (3ci) to 124cc (8ci).

ATLANTA-DUO
England (Portsmouth) 1935–37: JAP-engined machines: 248cc (15ci) and 490cc (30ci) overhead-valve singles, 746cc side-valve twins.

ATLANTIC
France 1929–32: This firm set proprietary engines (98cc/6ci two-stroke, 347cc/21ci and 497cc/30ci four-stroke) in their own frames.

ATLANTIC
Germany 1923–25: Powered by 193cc (12ci) side-valve singles.

ATLANTIK
Germany 1925–26: Atlantik made small numbers of 150cc (9ci) two-stroke machines.

ATLANTIS
Germany (Kiel) 1926–32: First used its own two-strokes, then moved to proprietary engines from many manufacturers: 348–990cc (21–60ci) or 250–600cc (15–37ci) engines.

ATLAS
England (Coventry) 1913–14: Sporty machines with 492cc (30ci) JAP and 496cc (30ci) Blumfield engines.

ATLAS
England (Birmingham) 1922–25: Aston Motor and Engineering made this 142cc (9ci) two-stroke.

ATLAS
Germany 1924–29: Built for hill-climbs, with its own 350cc (21ci) and possibly also 250cc (15ci) two-stroke singles.

ATTOLINI
Italy 1920–23: With rear suspension, the belt-drive Attolini was powered by a 269cc (16ci) Villiers two-stroke single.

AUBIER DUNNE
France 1926–50s: Began with a 175c (11ci) two-stroke before moving to a four-stroke in 1929. Postwar models included 100cc (6ci) to 175c (11ci) lightweights.

AUGUSTA
Italy (Turin, then Bologna) 1926–31: Augusta made 348cc (21ci) overhead-cam singles initially, later 123cc (8ci) and 174cc (11ci) singles.

AURORA
England (Coventry) 1902–07: These were pioneering machines with proprietary engines from Condor (UK), Coronet, MMC, Whitley and possibly others.

AURORA
Isle of Man (Douglas) 1919–21: One of two Isle of Man motorcycles, this had a 318cc (19ci) two-stroke from Dalm.

AUSTEN
England (London) 1903–06: An assembler using Kelecom two-and-a-quarter horsepower motors, and possibly others.

AUSTISA
Spain 1985-:Focuses on machines of 100cc (6ci) and below. Raced in 80cc (5ci) world racing championships during late 1980s; riders included Alex Barros and Juan Bolart.

AUSTRAL
France 1908–32:First, they made 211cc (13ci) two-strokes, then in 1918 enlarged the engine to 246cc (15ci) and bought in Zurcher and JAP sv and overhead-valve four-strokes.

AUSTRIA
Austria (Vienna) 1903–07: Early auxiliary four horsepower cycle-motor.

AUSTRIA
Austria (Trautmannsdorf) 1930–33: Ardie built the light alloy frames, then Austria installed Villiers and Sturmey-Archer 246cc (15ci) and 347cc (21ci) engines, some water-cooled.

AUSTRO-ALPHA
(Some sources say Austria-Alpha) Austria 1933–52: Pre-war, sporting machines with a 30˚ 348cc (21ci) overhead-cam V-twin and a 498cc (6ci) single. Postwar, the firm used 250cc (15ci) proprietary two-strokes: Puch split-single, Ilo, Rotax.

AUSTRO-ILO
Austria 1938: Production of these Ilo-engined 120cc (7ci) two-strokes was stopped by the Anschluss.

AUSTRO-MOTORETTE
Austria 1924–27: Began with an 82cc (5ci) two-stroke auxiliary cycle-motor delivering one horsepower; moved on to 144cc (9ci) two-stroke vertical twins. Also made 173cc (11c) double overhead-cam parallel twins for racing in 1926.

AUSTRO-OMEGA
Austria 1932–39: Even good manufacturers used proprietary engines: the firm built race-winning overhead-valve singles (348cc/21ci Sturmey-Archer and 498cc/6ci JAP) and road and sports bikes with JAP singles and twins to 746cc (46ci).

AUTINAG
Germany (Dusseldorf) 1923–25: Most of the few Autinags ever built were 127cc (8ci) and 198cc (6ci) two strokes: some used an inlet-over-exhaust MAG 496cc (30ci) single.

AUTO-BI
USA 1902–12: Made small bikes and enclosed-engine machines with one-and-a-half and two-and-a-half horsepower E.R. Thomas engines.

AUTOBIROUE
France 1957: Lambretta-based scooter, which may have entered series production.

AUTO-BIT
Japan 1952–62: Overhead-cam 250cc (15ci) single.

AUTO-ELL
Germany (Stuttgart) 1924–26: Light sports bikes with a 142cc (9ci) Grade two-stroke.

AUTOFAUTEUIL
France 1905: Precursor of the scooter, with enclosed 427cc (26ci) two-and-three-quarter horsepower motor and chain drive.

AUTOFLUG
Germany (Berlin) 1921–23: Initally a step-through with 117cc (7ci), 122cc (7ci) two-stroke engines, then a conventional machine with 129cc (8ci), 146cc (9ci) Bekamo two-strokes.

AUTOGLIDER
England (Birmingham), 1919–22: A Villiers 289cc (18ci) two-stroke single sat above the front wheel of this scooter-like machine.

AUTOPED
USA 1915–21: A 155cc (9ci) four-stroke single sat above the front wheel of the American original. Also built under licence by CAS (Czechoslovakia) and Krupp (Germany), the latter with 200cc (12ci).

AUTOSCO
England (London) 1920s: Scooter built by Brown and Layfield. Sources give the engine size as 117cc (7ci) or 180cc (11ci).

AUXI
Switzerland early 1920s: Auxiliary cycle motor of 135cc (8ci), with belt or chain drive.

AVADA
The Netherlands 1950s: This company built 49cc (3ci) mopeds and may have survived until 1964.

AVAROS
Netherlands, late 1950s: This company made a 150cc (9ci) fully enclosed scooter and 49cc (3ci) mopeds.

AVANTI
India 1982–93: 49cc (3ci) mopeds and a 150cc (9ci) scooter.

AVENIR
Belgium 1956–unknown: Mopeds with 49cc (3ci) two-stroke engines.

AVIS-CELER
Germany (Hannover), 1925–31: Made sports machines, first with Villiers two-strokes of 172–346cc (10–21ci), then with 347cc (22ci) and 497cc (30ci) MAG engines. The racers used JAP 248cc (15ci), 348cc (21ci) and 498cc (6ci) engines.

AVOLA
Germany (Leipzig) 1924–25: Avola used frames from Defa (Deutsche Fahrradbau GmbH) and engines from DKW (145cc/9ci and 173cc/11ci).

AVON
England (Croydon) 1919–20: Villiers 347cc (21ci) two-strokes powered these machines.

AWD
Germany (Dusseldorf) 1921–69: For production motorcycles (he also built racers), August Wurring used a wide range of proprietary engines before World War II, and Sachs and Ilo engines afterwards. There was also a scooter in the 1950s.

AWO
East Germany (Suhl) 1950–61: The AWO 425 was a 250cc (15ci) overhead-cam single. Later came a 49cc (3ci) scooter (1955) and the 425S, a 250cc (15ci) two-stroke (1957), and finally 250cc (15ci) and 350cc (21ci) overhead-cam singles. In the 1950s, the name changed to Simson.

AYRES-HAYMAN
England (Manchester) 1920: This was an unusual machine with a 688cc (42ci) Coventry-Victor side-valve flat twin. Inadequate finance led to its demise.

AZA
Czechoslovakia 1924–26: Lightweights powered by 147cc (9ci) two-strokes.

AZZARITI
Italy 1933–34: A pioneer of desmodromic valve operation, these had 173cc (11ci) and 344cc engines, the latter with a 180° crankshaft.

BABEL
France 1957: This model used a triple for its power unit.

BABYMOTO
France 1952–54: This company was a manufacturer of mopeds and a 123cc (8ci) two-stroke scooter.

BABY STAR
Germany 1950s: This was produced as a moped with odd-looking 49cc (3ci) single-cylinder engine: the second 'cylinder' was the exhaust stub.

B.A.C.
England (Blackpool) 1951–53: B.A.C. stands for the Bond Aircraft and Engineering; it made the Gazelle scooter with 98cc (6ci) and 123cc (8ci) Villiers two-strokes, and a lightweight with the same 98cc (6ci) engine.

BADGER
USA, dates uncertain: Autocycle with 163cc (10ci) four-stroke single in rear wheel. Either 1920–21 or 1951–55.

B.A.F.
Czechoslovakia (Prague) 1927–30: This firm produced two-strokes with 125cc (8ci) and 250cc (15ci) Bekamo engines. It also produced four-strokes with 346cc (21ci) side-valve and overhead-valve Kuhne or overhead-cam Chaise engines.

BAIER
Germany (Berlin) 1924–30: This company initially made 173cc (11ci), 198cc (12ci) and 240cc (15ci) two-strokes, then from 1927–30 a 500cc (31ci) split-single.

BAILIEUL
France (Levallois) 1904–10: This company used Peugeot and Buchet engines.

BAKER
England 1927–30: F.A. Baker began with Cleveland, and moved on to Precision/Beardmore Precision. He then made his own bikes with Villiers two-strokes (147cc/9ci, 198cc/ 12ci, 246cc/15ci), until being taken over by James in 1930.

BALALUWA
Germany (Munich) 1924–25: This company manufactured unusually robust, well-made frames, fitted with 350cc (21ci) and 500cc (31ci) JAP side-valve and overhead-valve engines, hub brakes and three-speed gearbox.

BALKAN
Bulgaria (Lovech) 1958–75: Balkan initially made a 48cc (3ci) moped and a 250cc (15ci) two-stroke lightweight with a pressed steel spine frame. Later added a 73cc (4ci) model.

B.A.M.
Germany (Aachen) 1933–37: The Berliner-Aachener Motorenwerk was a front to allow the sale of Belgian FN motorcycles in the Third Reich. All were singles: 198cc (6ci) two-strokes, 346cc (21ci) side-valve and 500cc (31ci) side-valve and overhead-valve.

BAMAR
Germany 1923–25: This company assembled small numbers of motorbikes using engines from companies such as Alba, Baumi, DKW, Gruhne and possibly others.

BAMO
Germany 1923–25: The initials stand for Bautzener Motorradfabrik Staubingen & Klingst; this company assembled bikes with 148cc (9ci) and 173cc (11ci) DKW engines.

BANSHEE
England (Bromsgrove) 1921–24: Banshee used several proprietary engines including Blackburne 347cc (21ci) and 497cc (30ci), Bradshaw oil-cooled 346cc (21ci), sleeve-valve Barr & Stroud 347cc (21ci), and Villiers 269cc (16ci).

A lovingly-restored 1950s two-stroke Bernadet BM250 scooter.

BARDONE
Italy (Milan) 1938–39: Bardone manufactured heavy 499cc (30ci) overhead-valve unit-construction singles.

BARNES
England (London) 1904: Barnes was an obscure firm that used proprietary engines from MMC and Minerva.

BARON
England (Birmingham) 1920–21: This assembler used Villiers 269cc (16ci) and Blackburne 348cc (21ci) engines.

BARONI
Italy 1958: Officine Meccaniche Moto Baroni made mopeds and lightweights with 50cc (3ci) engines, and a 175c (11ci) four-stroke.

BARRY
Czechoslovakia 1932–39: J. Friedrich Drkosch built a 248cc (15ci) racing overhead-valve single. A 100cc (6ci) two-stroke lightweight, launched in 1938, was overshadowed by the war.

BARTALI
Italy (Florence) 1953–61: In 1953, Bartali made a 158cc (10ci) two-stroke and in 1955, they made a sports version, as well as a racer. In 1956, they produced a moped and a 175c (11ci) four-stroke and in 1957 they went on to produce a 124cc (8ci) two-stroke. In 1958, came a motocross version.

BARTER
England 1902–05: There was no conventional crankshaft on this engine, and the con rod went straight to the rear axle.

BARTISCH
Austria 1925–29: Production of these advanced singles, the first of which (1925) was a chain-drive overhead-cam 348cc (21ci), and the second (1928) a bevel-drive overhead-cam 498cc (6ci), was limited by lack of financial resources.

BASIGLI
Italy (Ravenna) 1952: This was a water-cooled triple, which probably did not proceed much beyond prototype stage.

BASTERT
Germany (Bielefeld) 1949–55: Bastert made lightweights, mopeds and scooters using 49cc (3ci), 98cc (6ci), 125cc (8ci) and 150cc (9ci) two-stroke engines from Ilo and Sachs.

BAUER
Germany (Klein-Auheim am Main) 1936–54: Pre-war, this company made bicycles with cycle motors; postwar, 123cc (8ci), 147cc (9ci) and 173cc (11ci) Sachs and Ilo two-strokes.

BAUGHAN
England (Stroud) 1928–c.1936: Produced Blackburne-powered trials bikes, in overhead-valve and side-valve, at 247cc (15ci), 347cc (21ci) and 497cc (30ci) capacities, and some with sidecars with driven wheels (but no differential).

BAYERLAND
Germany (Berlin/Munich) 1924–30: JAP engines from 248cc (15ci) to 490cc (30ci) powered this firm's production bikes.

BAYERN
Germany (Munich) 1923–26: Bayern first used licence-built Bosch-Douglas engines from SMW. After 1924, it chose MAG V-twin engines: 498cc (30ci), 747cc (46ci) and 988cc (60ci).

BB
Germany (Stettin, now Poland) 1923–25: BB was an assembler that used Alba 197cc (12ci) side-valve singles.

BB
Italy (Parma) 1925–27: Ugo Bocchi was the designer of this 123cc (8ci) two-stroke flat single.

B.C.R.
France (Le Frentin Bicebre) 1923–30: The frim fitted a range of capacities of proprietary engines, mostly from JAP and Chaise, two-stroke and four-stroke, into early spring frames.

BD
Czechoslovakia (Prague) 1927–29: Breitfeld & Danek built high-quality 490cc (30ci) and later 350cc (21ci) unit-construction double overhead-cam singles. Production continued after 1929 as Praga, with shaft drive.

BEADING ENGINE CO
USA (Farmington, Michigan) 1949: This company made an auxiliary cycle-motor.

BEASLEY
England 1955: This motorbike was a racer with double overhead-cam 125cc (8ci) engine twin.

BEAUFORT
England (South Twickenham) 1923–26: The Argson Engineering Company made invalid carriages, and also used their 170cc (10ci) two-stroke single engine in a motorcycle.

BEAU-IDEAL
England (Wolverhampton) 1905–06: Beau-Ideal was an assembler which used Clement, JAP and Minerva engines.

BEAUMONT
England (Leeds) 1919–23: This firm used Wall 269cc (16ci) two-stroke engines and Blackburne 349cc (21ci) side-valves. They may also have built several prototype(s) with a Redrup three-cylinder radial, effectively a transversely mounted flat twin with a single sticking up from in the middle.

BE-BE
Germany (Berlin) 1923–27: The Berlin-Burger-Eisenwerk built its own 112cc (7ci) two-stroke.

BECCARIA
Italy (Mondovi) 1924–28: Beccaria and Revelli made bikes with Villiers 350cc (21ci) two-strokes or side-valve and overhead-valve Blackburne engines, and Sturmey-Archer gearboxes.

BECCARTA
Italy 1925–28: This firm has a similar history to Beccaria; the name may be a misprint.

BECKER
Germany (Dresden) 1903–06: Pioneer using Fafnir V-twins and its own singles.

BEFAG
Germany 1922–24: The Badischen Albertus Fahrzeugwerke was one of several who failed to make a success of the Julius Lowy engine that could (in theory) run on diesel after warming up on petrol: the engine was of 113cc (7ci) and 176cc (11ci).

BEHAG
Germany 1922–25: The Bremener Eisenhandels AG, an iron and steel works, made a limited number of motorcycles with JAP side-valve engines of 348cc (21ci) and 490cc (30ci).

BEISTIGUI HERMANOS (BH)
Spain 1956–unknown: This moped was unchanged for years.

BEKAMO
Czechoslovakia 1923–30: Subsidiary of Bekamo (Berlin), initially with smaller (124cc/8ci) engines and the petrol tank in a big top tube. A 174cc (11ci) engine arrived in 1927, and a 247cc (15ci) engine arrived in a conventional frame in 1929.

BENOTTO
Italy 1953–57: This firm began with 49cc (3ci) mopeds. In 1954 came the 150cc (9ci) Dragon and 100cc (6ci) Condor; in 1955, the Vulture 125cc (8ci)and Centauro Gran Sport 160cc (10ci). All two-stroke engines, some or all from Ilo.

BERCLEY
Belgium (Brussels) 1905–09: An advanced machine and one of the earliest vertical parallel twins, this was a 616cc (38ci) with mechanically operated inlet and exhaust valves.

BERESA
Germany (Munster) 1923–25: Beresa built small numbers of singles with JAP and Blackburne 350cc (21ci) and 500cc (31ci) engines.

BERGFEX
Germany (Berlin) 1904–09: This company installed single and twin cylinder Fafnir and Minerva engines or four to five horsepower in their own strong, well-made frames.

BERGO
Germany 1924: Assembler using 145cc (9ci) DKW engines.

BERINI
The Netherlands (Rotterdam) 1949–81: Berini began with a 25.7cc (1.5ci) two-stroke auxiliary cycle-motor, which later came in 32cc (2ci) and 48cc (3ci) forms. The company moved into moped construction in 1955 and in 1959, added the Solex-like M13 with 32cc (2ci) motor over the front wheel. In 1970, they had nine machines, fitted with Anker and Suzuki motors.

BERLICK
England 1929: Unusually, these three-speed machines with their 247cc (15ci) Villiers two-strokes had shaft drive.

BERLIN
East Germany (Berlin-Ludwigsfelte) 1958–65: This company used 150cc (9ci) MZ engines in its motorcycles and scooters.

BERNARDET
France (Chatillon-sous-Bagneux) 1930–34: Assembled small numbers of unremarkable machines with engines of 100cc (6ci) to 500cc (31ci) from both Train and Chaise.

BERNARDET
France (Chatillon-sous-Bagneux) 1949–57: These scooters had 123cc (8ci) and 246cc (15ci) two-stroke engines.

BERNEG
Italy (Casalecchio di Reno, Bologna) 1954–61: Jewel-like, fast overhead-cam parallel twins, initially 158cc/10ci (100km/h, 62mph) then 185cc (11ci) in 1957.

BERO
Germany 1924–25: This firm assembled small numbers of machines with 145cc DKW engines.

BERTAUD
France 1963: This company produced advanced, relatively powerful 50cc (3ci) two-stroke mopeds.

BERTIN
France (St Laurent Blangy) 1955–58: 49cc (3ci) two-stroke moped.

BERTONI
Italy 1954: The Bertoni was a short-lived sporting 160cc (10ci) two-stroke lightweight.

BERVA
Hungary 1958: A 48cc (3ci) two-stroke moped with front and rear suspension.

BERWICK
England (Tweedmouth) 1929–30: These shaft-drive two-strokes used Villiers singles of 246cc (15ci) and 346cc (21ci).

BESSONE
Argentina 1960s: Made 125cc (8ci) DKW lightweights and 125cc (8ci) and 150cc (9ci) DKW scooters under licence; also, in 1963, made an Italian-designed 150cc (9ci) scooter.

BETTOCCHI
Italy (Poretta Terme) 1950s: Bettocchi installed Demm engines in their own frames, and sold them as Beccaccinos.

BEUKER
Germany (Bocholt, Westphalia) 1921–29: As well as bicycles and two-stroke auxiliary cycle-motors, Beuker made two-stroke motorcycles, initially 231cc (14ci), later 145cc (9ci), 173cc (11ci), 198cc (2ci) and 246cc (15ci).

BEZDEZ
Czechoslovakia 1923–26: This firm manufactured auxiliary cycle-motors, and motorcycles with their own 145cc (9ci) side-valve four-stroke engines.

BFG
France 1978–83: BFG (Boccardo, Favrio and Grange) built small numbers of a 1299cc (79ci) Citroen car-engined Superbike, using a five-speed gearbox.

BH
Spain 1956–60: Made two-stroke 49cc (3ci) mopeds.

B & H
England 1923: This firm specialized in engine building, but made a few complete 996cc (61ci) side-valve motorcycles.

BICHRONE
France (Paris) 1902–07: Made complete V-twin two-strokes of two-and-a-quarter to two-and-three-quarters horsepower.

BIKOTOR
England 1951: An auxiliary 47cc (3ci) two-stroke cycle motor.

BIM
Japan (Tokyo) 1956–61: This Japanese firm made BMW copies with engines of 250cc (15ci), 350cc (21ci), 500cc (31ci) and 650cc (40ci).

BIMA
France 1952–unknown: Initially making an auxiliary cycle motor, this firm then manufactured 49cc (3ci) mopeds with horizontal cylinders. A Peugeot trademark.

BIMM
Italy (Montemurlo) 1968–79: This firm, which became Bimotor in 1979, made two-stroke trials and motocross bikes with 49cc (3ci) and 123cc (8ci) Minarelli engines.

BIMOFA
Germany 1922–25: Hansa side-valve engines propelled these Gustav Kunstmann-designed machines.

BIMOTOR
Italy 1979–unknown: BIMM (q.v.) made two-stroke trials and motorcross bikes, changing its name to Bimotor in 1979.

BINKS
England (Nottingham) 1903–06: One of the first straight-fours, and probably the first transverse four. The 385cc (23ci) side-valve four-stroke was fitted in both orientations.

BINZ
Germany 1954–58: Binz made scooters with 47cc (3ci) Ilo and 49cc (3ci) Sachs engines, then in 1956 produced a lightweight with a 150cc (9ci) Sachs engine.

BIRCH
England (Nuneaton) 1902–06: Birch incorporated the cast crank-case and bottom bracket into their frame, with direct belt drive from the two, two-and-a-half and three horsepower engines to the rear wheel.

BIRD
USA c.1970: This comapny made mini-bikes with four-stroke Tecumseh motors of 120cc (7ci) and 148cc (9ci).

BIRMA
France (Lyon) 1949–late 1950s: This company was known for making lightweights with 98cc (6ci) Aubier Dunne motors.

BISMARCK
Germany 1904–56: From 1904 to 1908, Bismarck made V-twins with capacities up to 1300cc (79ci) using engines from Anzani, Fafnir and Minerva. From 1908 to 1931, it made autocycles of 75cc (5ci) and 98cc (6ci). After 1945, it used two-stroke Ilo and Sachs engines in 98cc (6ci), 147cc (9ci) and 173cc (11ci) lightweights.

BISON
Austria (Liesing) 1924–26: This Austrian firm built modest numbers of longitudinal-engine flat twins with motors from Bosch-Douglas (293cc/18ci), BMW (493cc/30ci), Coventry-Victor (678cc/41ci) and possibly others.

BITRI
The Netherlands 1955–60: Bitri was an early manufacturer of 147cc (9ci) scooters.

BJR
Spain (Algemesi) 1939–61: BJR built very few scooters in 1939, but resumed production in 1955 with at first a 125cc (8ci) engine (MX125), then a 175c (11ci) two-stroke (VZ175).

BLACKFORD
England (London) 1902–04: This company fitted Minerva 211cc (13ci) engines in Frank Blackford's frame.

BLAIR
Ireland (Belfast) 1970: This firm was known for a racing 246cc (15ci) two-stroke twin, which they built at Queen's University Belfast and installed in a Seeley frame, hence they were also known as QUB-Seeley.

BLANCHE HERMINE
France 1950–53: An assember of 100cc (6ci) machines.

BLEHA
Germany (Neiheim-Ruhr) 1923–26: This company used 247cc (15ci) DKW two-strokes and its own 247cc (15ci) side-valve four-strokes in its own motorbike frames.

BLERIOT
France 1920–23: Parallel twins of 498cc (6ci), in side-valve and overhead-valve guises, came from the aircraft manufacturer.

BLOTTO
France (Dijon) 1951–55: This assembler used 123cc (8ci) to 348cc (21ci) proprietary two-strokes.

BLUMFIELD
England (Birmingham) 1908–14: These were short-lived machines, but nevertheless they were big enough to compete in TT races. Some engines were water-cooled.

BM
France 1954: Powered by its own 250cc (15ci) flat twin, this may not have entered commercial production.

BM
Italy 1928–31: Side-valve and overhead-valve 490cc (30ci) JAP engines powered these three-speed Italian motorcycles.

BM
Italy 1950–early 1980s: Made a bewildering range of mopeds, minibikes, scooters, lightweights, and motorcycles up to 250cc (15ci) with engines from Ilo, NSU and Minarelli, as well as its own overhead-cam singles.

BMG
Hungary 1939–44: Two-stroke lightweights with their own 98cc (6ci) single came from BMG.

BMG
Italy 1950: The Bicomosquito Garelli moped used a Garelli motor by Industrie Mecchaniche Meridionali, which was set in a frame by Metalmeccanica Meridionale of Pomigliano d'Arco.

BMM
Italy (Zola Predosa) 1983: This was an unusually late introduction date for a 48cc (3ci) auxiliary cycle motor.

BMP
Italy 1920–25: Made four-speed two-strokes with their own 240cc (15ci) motors.

BMP
France (Paris) 1933: Buraglini, established in 1911, made motorcycles with JAP and Rudge Python engines in 1933 and maybe for some time after.

BNF
Germany (Bielefeld) 1903–07: Fafnir singles and V-twins powered most machines from this pioneering company.

BOASSI
Italy 1950: Made the 'Gazella' auxiliary cycle motor, 60cc (4ci) single-speed or 65cc (4ci) two-speed.

BOCK & HOLLANDER
Austria (Vienna) 1905–11: Better known for four-wheelers and Regent cars, this firm also made singles and V-twins of three-and-a-half and six horsepower. They were eventually taken over by WAF, which was known as a car company.

BODO
Germany (Thale) 1924–25: For a few months, Fritz Kindermann assembled two-stroke lightweights with engines from DKW and Villiers.

BOGE
Germany 1923–27: Built bikes with Blackburne 246cc (15ci) and 346cc (21ci) singles, overhead-valve and side-valve. Enjoyed some racing success but better known for their shock absorbers.

BOGEY
Germany 1929: Unusual 350cc (21ci) engine with gear-driven valve actuation and a piston with a 'nose' to increase the compression ratio.

BOHME
Germany 1925–30: Martin Bohme's water-cooled horizontal two-stroke singles of 123cc (8ci), 129cc (8ci), 173cc (11ci) and 246cc (15ci) had stepped pistons, in the Dunelt style. The rigid frames had an elegant tubular top tube and tank.

BOLIDE
France (Pantin) 1902–10: This firm were pioneers using their own one-and-a-quarter horsepower engine.

An Indian Bond Capella scooter, from around 1959.

BONANZA
America 1970s: The manufacturer of minibikes with 100cc (6ci) two-strokes or four-strokes of 127cc (8ci), 148cc (9ci), 172cc (10ci) and 200cc (12ci).

BOND
India 1990s: Bond made Morini-engined sports mopeds, similar to BSA India. The 'Bond' was from 'Brooke Bond' tea.

BONZI & MARCHI
Italy (Milan) 1913–14: The original belt-drive model had a three horsepower 330cc (20ci) engine from Moser and weighed just 50kg (110lb); the second had chain drive, with a two-and-three-quarters horsepower Moser; and there were also two V-twins.

BOOTH
England (London) 1901–03: Initially used Minerva and De Dion Bouton proprietary engines, then their own two-and-three-quarter, three-and-a-half and four horse-power motors.

BORD
England (London) 1902–06: Built lightweights with their own singles, variously described as one-and-a-half and one-and-three-quarter horsepower.

BORGHI
Italy (Milan) 1951–63: This firm assembled mopeds and lightweights with 38cc (Mosquito), 49cc (3ci) (Cucciolo) and 123cc (8ci) (BSA Bantam) two-stroke motors. There may also have been a 175c (11ci) Bantam-based bike. All were sold as 'Olympia'.

BORGO
Italy 1906–26: Confusingly, there were two Borgo factories, founded by three brothers. One, founded by A.B. Borgo and C. Borgo built four-stroke singles, initially, in 1906, a 497cc (30ci) inlet-over-exhaust, then later 453cc (28ci), 493 (30ci), 693cc (42ci) and 827cc (50ci), while the other, founded by E.M. Borgo, started in 1915 with a belt-drive 996cc (61ci) V-twin. In 1921 came a race-winning eight-valve 477cc (29ci) V-twin capable of 6000rpm, followed by a 496cc (30ci) overhead-valve with a two-speed unit-construction gearbox.

BORHAM
England 1902–05: Borham was an early bike assembler using Minerva engines of two and two-and-a-half horsepower.

BOTTARI
Italy 1951: Carlo Bottari's two-stroke was made as a 100cc (6ci) and a 125cc (8ci), and also sold as an Eolo made by Omea in Milan.

BOUCHET
France (Saint-Cheron) 1902–05: An acetylene-driven machine.

BOUGERY
France 1896–02: This was a pioneering machine with the engine between the pedal bracket and the rear wheel.

BOUNDS-JAP
England (London) 1909–12: This assembler used JAP 345cc (21ci) singles and 492cc (30ci) V-twins.

The 1919 British-made Black Prince carried a flat-twin, two-stroke engine with shaft final drive.

BOVY

Belgium (Liege) 1906–32: These sturdy machines used a range of proprietary engines: initially side-valve and overhead-valve JAP and Blackburne, then MAG and Aubier Dunne, then Villiers two-strokes, and finally a 250cc (15ci) overhead-cam Anzani. Capacities ranged from 100cc (6ci) to 1000cc (61ci).

BOWDEN

England (London) 1902–05: The same Frank Bowden who founded Raleigh Sturmey Archer also made motorcycles with FN two horsepower engines, and with motors of his own manufacture.

BOWDEN

England 1922: This Bowden was an assembler with no relation to the firm above. It made a 116cc (7ci) machine.

BOWN

England (Birmingham) 1922–24: This company was an assembler that used 248cc (15ci) and 348cc (21ci) JAP and Blackburne engines, and later used 147cc (9ci) Villiers.

BOWN

Wales (Tonypandy) 1950–58: Built mopeds, autocycles and lightweights with Villiers 125cc (8ci) and, later, 123cc (8ci) engines, Sachs 49cc (3ci), and possibly 98cc (6ci) engines.

B&P

Italy 1926: Della Ferrara two-strokes powered this short-lived line of autocycles and lightweights.

BPR

Switzerland 1929–32: Moser and Motosacoche singles of 347cc (21ci) and 497cc (30ci) powered these machines made by former employees of Moto-Reve and Motosacoche.

BPS

France 1973–unknown: These lightweights, listed with trials and motocross styling, were powered by Sachs, Aspes, Franco-Morini and Minarelli engines (49cc/3ci to 123cc/8ci).

BRAAK

Germany 1923–25: Used 129cc (8ci) and 198cc (6ci) Heilo and Namapo engines in frames from Gruhn of Berlin.

BRAECKMANN

France (Nanterre) 1946: A rotary valve gear was built into the head of this light-alloy 11cc (0.6ci) four-stroke machine.

BRAND

Germany (Berlin) 1925–30: Used horizontal two-stroke Bekamo-licence singles of 123cc (8ci), 147cc (9ci) and 173cc (11ci) capacity.

BRAVIS

Germany 1924–26: As well as its own 175cc (11ci) and 297cc (18ci) two-stroke singles, Bravis used a 293cc (18ci) Bosch-Douglas flat twin.

BREDA

Italy 1946–51: These were autocycles with a 65cc two-stroke engine from the former aircraft factory.

BREE

Austria (Vienna) 1902–04: This was an early manufacturer of two-stroke one-and-a half horsepower engines, which where all fitted in a lightweight but sturdy frame.

BRENNABOR

(Brandenburg am Havel) Germany 1902–40: From 1902–12, this company built motorcycles with engines of its own manufacture as well as Zedel, Fafnir, Peugeot, Minerva and others. From 1933 to 1940, it produced autocycles with 73cc (4ci) and 98cc (6ci) Sachs and Ilo engines. They also built cars until 1933.

BREUIL

France 1903–08: This firm built singles and V-twins with their own engines as well as those of Peugeot, Aster and Zurcher.

BRIBAN

France 1950s: This company began with a 50cc (3ci) auxiliary cycle-motor, then 98cc (6ci) and 123cc (8ci), and later a fan-cooled 123cc (8ci) for scooters.

BRIGGS & STRATTON

USA 1919–20: The manufacturer of stationary engines built the Briggs and Stratton Flyer auxiliary cycle motor. One model drove the rear wheel; another was built into an interchangeable front wheel.

BRILANT-ALCYON

Czechoslovakia (Zuckmantel) 1932: The Fuchs factory built a few Alcyon-licensed 98cc (6ci) two-stroke machines, which were named 'people's motorcycles'.

BRITISH-RADIAL

England (London) 1920–22: A radial side-valve triple with a 120° Redrup engine; the frames were from Chater-Lea.

BRITISH-STANDARD

England (Birmingham) 1919–23: Assemblers who used a wide range of bought in engines, such as Villiers, TDC, JAP, Bradshaw, Blackburne and Barr and Stroud and produced them in a wide range of capacities (147cc/9ci to 548cc/33ci).

BRM

Italy 1955–57: BRM made auxiliary cycle motors and mopeds of 48cc (3ci).

BROCKHOUSE

England 1948–55: Manufacturers of the Corgi folding scooter, they were also involved in the early 1950s with Indian, for whom they made the 248cc (15ci) side-valve single Brave.

BRONDOIT

Belgium 1924–29: This company began with a 250cc (15ci) two-stroke, added a 350cc (21ci) version in 1927, then in 1928, made a 500cc (31ci) MAG overhead-valve single four-stroke.

BROOKLANDS

England 1981–86: The Brooklands was an attempt to build and market a modern caf-racer with the looks of a Max Norton, and powered by an Austrian-made overhead camshaft Rotax engine.

BROWN

England (London) 1902–19: This firm built machines with its own 348cc (21ci) and 498cc (6ci) singles and 498cc (6ci) V-twins. After 1919, it was to become known as VINDEC.

BROWN-BICAR

England 1907–13: Enclosed three horsepower singles and five horsepower twins characterized this bike. Not a great success, it was also made under licence in the United States.

BRUNEAU

France (Tours) 1903–10: After briefly using Zedel engines, M. Bruneau turned to his own 500cc (31ci) parallel twins.

B & S

Germany (Berlin) 1925–30: Bekamo-licensed two-strokes powered these machines from B & S (Brand und Sohne).

BSA

India c.1980–89: This company made Morini-engined sports mopeds, which were sold under the BSA name.

BSM

Germany 1926: A short-lived, small assembler.

BSU

Italy 1923: Ugo Siniscalchi built a small number of Blackburn-engined 350cc (21ci) machines.

BUBI

Germany 1921–24: This company was a bicycle manufacturer that strengthened its frames to fit a one-and-a-half horsepower two-stroke engine.

BUCHER

Italy 1911–20: This firm was successful for almost a decade with in-house overhead-valve singles and V-twins of 342, 499, 568cc. It was also known as Bucher-Zeda.

BUCKER

Germany (Oberursel im Taunus) 1922–58: Before World War II, this assembler made four-strokes from Bark, Blackburne, Cockerell, Columbus, JAP, MAG and Rinne, at 98cc (6ci) to 996cc (61ci). Postwar, it used Ilo or Sachs two-strokes.

BUGRE

Brazil (Sao Paulo) 1954: This Brazilian firm began with a 48cc (3ci) auxiliary cycle motor, then made the first South American motorcycle engine, a 124cc (8ci) two-stroke single.

BULLDOG

England 1920: An assembler using the 269cc (16ci) Villiers engine.

BULLO

Germany (Bremen) 1924–26: This was an electric motorcycle with a 120Amp-hour battery and a 0.7 horsepower engine.

BULOW

Germany 1923–25: Lightweights with their own two-stroke engines of two, two-and-a-half and three horsepower.

BUMBLEBEE

England c.1920: Granville Bradshaw designed this improbable 90°, 100cc (6ci) V-twin delivering three-and-a-half horsepower at 5000rpm.

BURFORD

England (London) 1914–15: The inscrutably named Consolidated Alliance Ltd. made a few side-valve 496cc (30ci) singles with direct belt drive, to sell at 29 guineas, before World War I stopped production.

BURGERS-ENR

The Netherlands (Deventer) 1897–24: This company began producing with its own technically advanced engines; then later switched to a 680cc (41ci) JAP V-twin and a Blackburne 497cc (30ci) single. In 1922, it used a two-stroke Vitesse, but it closed down in 1924. Some sources suggest it continued to 1961, but this seems unlikely.

BURKHARDTIA

Germany (Magdeburg) 1904–08: Hans Grade designed the early two-strokes, which were a 165cc (10ci) single and a 244cc (15ci) twin that powered these pioneering machines.

BURNEY

England 1923–25: This English firm built mostly a 497cc (30ci) single with external flywheel, plus a few 680cc (41ci) V-twins. The full name of the company was Burney, Baldwin & Co, Burney being Cecil Burney, late of Burney & Blackburne, and Baldwin being the racing rider O.M. Baldwin.

BURNOR

Argentina 1960s: This company assembled machines using 150cc (9ci) two-stroke engines.

BUSI

Italy (Bologna) 1950–53: Starting in the 1940s as a frame manufacturer, Athos Busi also built sporting two-strokes of various capacities, from 125cc (8ci) to 200cc (12ci).

BUSSE

Germany 1923–26: A small assembler using Grade motors, and later DKW two-strokes of 175cc (11ci) and 206cc (13ci).

BUYDENS

Belgium 1950–55: This company built 125cc (8ci)lightweights, first with Ydral, then Sachs, engines.

BV

Czechoslovakia (Prostejov) 1923–30: Karel Balzer (B) and Jaroslav Vernola (V) built machines with their own engines: a 173cc (11ci) two-stroke, 346cc (21ci) side-valve single, 496cc (30ci) overhead-valve (and overhead-cam for racing) single, and 746cc (46ci) side-valve V-twin.

BVR

England 1985–91: BVR (Brian Valentine Racing), builder of limited production five-valve single-engined machines for competition or fast road use.

BYVAN

England 1949: These were fully enclosed machines of extremely unconventional design. The horizontal 148cc (9ci) two-stroke was rubber-mounted on the front fork, with the drive divided two ways, having a chain drive to the rear wheel.

CABTON

Japan 1954–61: Mizuho [or Mizubo] built two-stroke singles (125cc/8ci and 50cc/3ci), and overhead-valve parallel twins (250cc/15ci to 650cc/40ci), under the name Cabton.

CACHARO

Spain 1919: A surprisingly old-fashioned belt-drive 750cc (461ci) twin.

CAESAR

England 1922–23: This company assembled lightweights, which were fitted with the ubiquitous Villiers 269cc (16ci) two-stroke.

CALCATERRA

Italy (Milan) 1926–27: This firm manufactured a 175c (11ci) two-stroke lightweight.

CALCOTT

England (Coventry) 1909–25: Calcott began in 1904 as motor-car manufacturers but branched out in 1909 with motorcycles powered by White and Poppe 292cc (18ci) singles and their own 250cc (15ci) and 292cc (18ci) engines. In 1923, they also built a 1460cc (90ci) four with cone clutch, three-speed gear and shaft drive.

CALVERT

England 1899–1904: A pioneer that used their own engines of two-and-a quarter to three-and-a-quarter horsepower, as well as bought-in Minerva motors.

CAMBER

England 1920–21: Precision 492cc (30ci) side-valve engines powered Cambers; built by (or for) a once-prominent dealer.

CAMBRA

Germany (Berlin) 1921–26: This firm made its own 180cc (11ci) and 198cc (6ci) side-valve engines but was otherwise a typical short-lived Berlin company of the postwar era.

A close-up of the French BFG 1300cc No 218 (1983). Just 400 were produced.

CAMILLE-FAUCEAUX
France 1952–54: Built mini-scooters with 65cc engines.

CAMPION
England (Nottingham) 1901–26: Well known in the first decade of the twentieth century, Campion supplied frames to many other manufacturers, as well as building its own bikes with a variety of bought-in engines, initially Fafnir and Minerva. The last models used 1000cc (61ci) JAP engines.

CAPELLO
Italy (Turin) 1912–14: This firm began with three models: a two horsepower vertical single, a two-and-three-quarters horsepower and a three-and-a-half horsepower V-twin. Others followed, but the last new introduction was apparently a three-and-a-half horsepower single in 1914.

CAPPA
Italy (Turin) c.1905: This advanced water-cooled single had cone clutch, a three-speed gearbox and full suspension.

CAPPONI
Italy 1924–26: Built small numbers of machines powered by its own three-port 173cc (11ci) two-stroke engine.

CAPRIOLO
Italy 1948–63: Aircraft manufacturer that switched to light motorcycles after World War II. Initially 73cc (4ci) overhead-valve engines in pressed-steel frames; later 123cc (8ci) and tubular frames. Also built a 149cc (9ci) transverse flat twin with a pressed-steel frame, presumably inspired by the Velocette LE.

CAPRONI-VIZZOLA
Italy 1953–59: NSU-based machines of 173cc (11ci),198cc (121ci) and 248cc (15ci).

CARCANO
Italy (Milan) 1899–1902: A very early cycle-motor/motorised bicycle, mounted inside the diamond frame, delivering three-quarters horsepower and driving the rear wheel by belt.

CARDA
Italy (Bologna) 1950: Cyclemotor mounted over the rear wheel and driving it by chain.

CARDAN
France 1902–08: A De Dion-Bouton motor drove the rear wheel via a shaft. The original Cardan or Kardan shaft.

CARFIELD
England 1919–24: Carfield put proprietary engines in spring frames, beginning with 269cc (16ci) Villiers two-strokes, then moving on to 350cc (21ci) Villiers and a Coventry Victor 688cc (42ci) flat twin.

CARGNELUTTI
Italy 1926: A 125cc (8ci)four-stroke with unique valve gear.

CARLEY
France 1950–53: This was a French mini-scooter with horizontal 49cc (3ci) two-stroke motor and friction drive.

CARLTON
Scotland (Glasgow) 1922: Lightweight with 269cc (16ci) Villiers two-stroke single.

CARLTON
England 1938–40: Founded by the racer and record-breaker D.R. O'Donovan of Norton renown, this company made lightweights with a 125cc (8ci) Villiers engine.

CARNITI
Italy 1953: An improbable 186cc (11ci) two-stroke triple – with still more improbable rubber-roller drive system – powered this long, odd-looking machine.

CARPATI
Romania (Bucharest) 1960–unknown: This company was the manufacturer of the 67cc (4ci) two-stroke Carpathi scooter.

CARPIO
France 1930–35: This firm was the assembler of lightweights which were fitted with 98cc (6ci) and 125cc (8ci) engines; these were bought in from Aubier-Dunne and Stainless.

CARREAU
France (Puteaux) 1903–10: A pioneer that used a remarkably low-powered one horsepower engine.

CAS
Czechoslovakia (Prague) 1921–24: The early scooter was based on the (American) Autoped but featured a seat instead of standing room, and flat twin engines of 129cc (8ci) and 149cc (9ci). There were also lightweights with 173cc (11ci) and 225cc (14ci) two-stroke engines.

CASALINI
Italy 1958–: The 50cc (3ci) David scooter had suspension front and rear, but the company was better known afterwards for producing mopeds and three-wheel delivery vehicles.

CASOLI
Italy (Milan) 1928–33: This company made sporty two-stroke bikes that were fitted with 172cc (10ci) engines from Villiers and also fitted with engines of their own manufacture.

Capriolo
WORKSHOP MANUAL

CAPRIOLO LTD.,
66-68 SOUTHBRIDGE ROAD.
CROYDON, SURREY.
Telephone CRO 6550.

Capriolo started making motorbikes straight after World War II. The company had been an Italian aircraft manufacturer.

CASTADOT
Belgium (Liege) 1900–01: This firm was the producer of small numbers of motorcycles that used one-and-a-half horsepower Swiss Zedel motors.

CASTELL
England (London) 1903: Pioneer using Sarolea and Minerva engines, and possibly their own as well.

CASWELL
England (London) 1904–05: Installed Minerva motors of two-and-a-half to three-and-a-half horsepower in their own, quite basic, cycle-type frames.

CAYENNE
England 1912–13: A technically interesting 497cc (30ci) water-cooled overhead-valve V-twin fitted with a radiator.

CAZALEX
France 1951–55: Lightweights and autocycles with 49cc (3ci) to 125cc (8ci)motors.

CAZANAVE
France 1955–57: This moped manufacturer later added two-stroke lightweights of 110cc (7ci) and 125cc (8ci).

CBR
Italy (Turin) 1912–14: Signore Cigala, Barberis and Ruda lent their initials to this machines when they began with a belt-drive of 250cc (15ci). They switched to chain drive, then added a three horsepower two-stroke and then bigger engines of up to eight horsepower.

CC
England (Blackpool) 1921–24: Charles Chamberlain catalogued machines from 147cc (9ci) to 1000cc (61ci) with JAP and Blackburne engines.

CEDOS
England (Northampton) 1919–29: Initially produced 211cc (13ci) and 249cc (15ci) two-strokes with open 'ladies' frames, later overhead-valve singles with Blackburne and Bradshaw engines, and eventually a 1000cc (61ci) JAP.

CENTAUR
Germany 1924–25: This firm installed one-and-a-half horsepower side-valve Gruhn motors in their own frames.

CENTAUR
England (Coventry) 1901–15: This firm built a 500cc (31ci) side-valve single and a 350cc (21ci) side-valve V-twin; early models had the silencer (muffler) built into the frame.

CENTER
Japan 1950–62: Sporting overhead-valve singles.

CENTRUM
Sweden 1933: This firm installed CZ motors with three-speed gearboxes in frames with tele-forks.

CENTURY
England (London) 1902–05: This firm was an assembler that used Minerva and MMC engines. The front wheel was apparently spoked in an odd way.

CF
Italy 1928–71: Castelli and Fiorani (C and F) built racing overhead-cam singles of 173cc (11ci) and 248cc (15ci). Fusi bought the company in 1937. Production was not continuous from 1928 to 1971, and the later productions were mopeds.

CFC
France (Boulogne) 1903–06: The Compagnie France du Cycles used a one-and-three-quarters horsepower engine in its diamond-frame machines.

CHAMPION
USA (St. Louis) 1911–13: Champion built the air-cooled Militaire under licence, with wood-spoked main wheels and small 'trainer wheels'.

CHAMPION
Japan (Tokyo) 1960–67: A Bridgestone trademark for two-stroke mopeds and lightweights, 50cc (3ci) to 175c (11ci).

CHAPUIS
France 1950–60: Just one of the countless French moped manufacturers.

CHARLETT
Germany (Berlin) 1921–24: This firm built side-valve singles of 147cc (9ci)and 198cc (6ci), but had the misfortune to set up business at the beginning of postwar soaring inflation.

CHARLKRON
Germany 1925: This firm installed 348cc (21ci) and 498cc (6ci) three-valve Kuechen proprietary singles in its own frames.

CHARLTON
England 1904–8: Charlton was an early English maker that used 402cc (25ci) Buchet motors.

CHASE
England (London) 1902–6: These sporting machines with low, light frames, were powered by engines from MMC, Minerva, Precision and others. The Chase brothers who made the machines were well-known cycle racers.

CHAY
Argentina 1953–unknown: This firm made a scooter, initially with 125cc (8ci)horizontal two-stroke single, later 175c (11ci).

CHELL
England (Wolverhampton) 1939: Short-lived lightweight with 123cc (8ci) Villiers engine.

CHIANALE
Italy (Cuneo) 1927: This lightweight machine was fitted with a 350cc (21ci) Chaise overhead-cam motor.

CHIORDA
Italy (Bergamo) 1954–unknown: Initially, it produced a lightweight machine with a 100cc (6ci) four-stroke twin then, in 1957, the Arlecchino 48cc (3ci) moped.

CHRISTOPHE
France (Neuilly s/Seine) 1920–30: Christophe produced two-stroke lightweights and 350cc (21ci) and 500cc (31ci) four-strokes in 1920, as well as an overhead-cam 498cc (6ci).

CICALA
Italy 1952: This big-wheeled, fully enclosed scooter with 49cc (3ci) two-stroke power was built by Costruzioni Meccanice G. Vivani.

CICCA
France 1949: A 50cc (3ci) Veloreve motor drove the rear wheel of this scooter via a friction roller.

CIE
Belgium (Herstal) 1900–05: The Compagnie International d'Électricité made this belt-drive, magneto-ignition single that claimed a top speed of 84km/h (50mph).

CIMA
Italy 1924–27: Sporting machines with side-valve and overhead-valve Blackburne engines of 247cc (15ci) and 347cc (21ci).

CITA
Belgium (Liege) 1922–25: This firm was a short-lived maker of 175cc (11ci), 200cc (12ci) and 350cc (21ci) machines.

CITO
Germany (Suhl) 1905–27: Began with Fafnir singles and V-twins; after c.1923, it made its own 346cc (21ci) two-stroke.

CITYFIX
Germany (Osnabruck) 1949–53: This was a scooter with a Sachs engine, initially 48cc (3ci), later 98cc (6ci).

CL
Germany 1951: This was a producer of a mini-scooter with a 34cc (2ci) engine.

CLAES
Germany 1904–08: Fafnir engines of three-and-a-half and five horsepower in frames from a well-established bicycle company. These were also sold under the Pfeil name.

CLAEYS FLANDRIA
Belgium 1955–unknown: This firm produced mopeds (1955), a scooter (1956) and a lightweight motorcycle (1957), all powered by Ilo two-strokes.

CLARENDON
England (Coventry) 1901–11: This company built bicycles, cars and motorcycles, the latter with a three horsepower side-valve single. Engines were made in-house or bought in.

CLAUDE DELAGE
France (Clichy s/Seine) 1925: This firm assembled tiny numbers of cars and motorcycles in the few months of its existence.

CLESS & PLESSING
Austria (Graz) 1903–6: Its own two-and-a-half horsepower engine powered these machines, initially with shaft drive, then belt drive. Later engines were a three-and-a-half horsepower single and a five horsepower V-twin. Also sold as Noricum.

CLEVELAND
England (Middlesborough) 1911–14: These sporting machines were fitted with Precision engines, and possibly others.

CLUA
Spain (Barcelona) 1954–64: Four-speed gearboxes and up-to-date suspension graced these 125cc (8ci) and 175c (11ci) two-strokes from the start. Later came a 49cc (3ci) moped.

CLYDE
England (Leicester) 1898–1912: This firm fitted carburettors built under a Simms licence to early engines of their own manufacture. The engines were two-and-three-quarters, six-and-a-half, seven and eight horsepower V-twins, later with JAP engines. Tehcnically advanced, they used water-cooling as early as 1903.

CMK
Italy 1950s: This was a surprisingly advanced four-speed scooter with 50cc (3ci) two-stroke, having a chromium-plated bore and delivering 4.2 horsepower at 6700rpm.

CMM
England (Coventry) 1919–21: The initials CMM stand for Coventry Motor Mart. The company made a few machines with the inevitable 292cc (18ci) two-stroke motor, even though they were bought in from Union, and not Villiers.

CMP
Italy (Padua) 1953–56: Producer of machines that initially used two-stroke Ceccato engines of 75cc (5ci), 100cc (6ci) and 125cc (8ci); then 49cc (3ci) Sachs and, finally, a 125cc (8ci) four-stroke Ceccato.

CMR
France 1945–48: These French-built BMW copies were made with many R12 and R71 parts, probably to get around the non-availability of new BMWs.

COCYMO
France late 1950s: This firm produced first the Cocynette moped, then later a 125cc (8ci)two-stroke lightweight.

CODRIDEX
France (Lyon) 1952–56: This French company built two-stroke mopeds with 49cc (3ci) and 65cc (4ci) engines.

COFERSA
Spain (Madrid) 1953–60: Made basic 100–175cc (6–11ci) two strokes, latterly powered by Hispano-Villiers engines.

COLELLA
Italy (Rome) 1981–unknown: This was a 'mini-moped' of just 1100mm (43in) in length and weighing 37kg (81lb) with a 49.9cc (3ci) two-stroke motor of the company's own design.

COLIBRI
Austria 1952–54: A scooter with a 123cc (8ci) DKW motor.

COLIBRI
Germany (Munich) c.1950s: This firm was the producer of the Colibri, which means humming bird.

COLIBRI
Sweden 1920: This was an obscure make powered by a four-stroke 96cc (6ci) engine of the company's own design.

COLOMB
France 1950–54: A small-scale assembler of mopeds and lightweights.

COLONIAL
England (Nuneaton) 1911–13: This firm built a few machines fitted with its own 450cc (27ci) two-stroke single.

COLUMBIA
USA 1900–05: This US firm installed Pope single and V-twin motors in diamond cycle-type frames.

COLUMBIA
France 1922–26: This was an early producer of side-valve singles of 198cc (12ci) and 250cc (15ci) capacity.

COLUMBUS
Germany (Oberursel – Frankfurt/Main) 1923–24: This firm produced overhead-valve 250cc (15ci) singles as well as 600cc (37ci) and 800cc twins. It also offered an overhead-valve 49cc (3ci) cycle motor. The company was renamed Horex when it was bought out by the Kleeman factory.

COLUMBUS
USA 1960: Columbus made the Rocket, a small scooter fitted with a two-and-a-half horsepower single-cylinder engine.

COM
Italy 1926–28: This company produced lightweights with 123cc (8ci) and 173cc (11ci) engines.

COMERY
England (Nottingham) 1919–22: This was an English assembler that used Villiers and Blackburne engines.

A mid-1950s model Capriolo 150cc (9ci) ohv flat twin.

COMESA
Spain 1957: A licence-built FB-Mondial machine.

COMET
England (London) 1902–07: Minerva engines and BSA-based frames are characteristic of these pioneers.

COMFORT
Italy (Milan) 1923–27: This up-market assembler used overhead-valve motors bought-in from Bradshaw (later Barr & Stroud), with Sturmey Archer gears.

COMMANDER
England 1952–53: The General Steel and Iron Company built the Commander, a remarkably ugly 1930s-style machine. It was fitted with a chrome-plated cage to conceal its 99–123cc (6–8ci) Villiers engine.

CONDOR
England (Coventry) 1907–14: This firm built a large 96x112mm (810cc) single.

CONDOR
Germany (Braunschweig) 1953–54: This firm produced scooters and lightweights with 50cc (3ci) two-stroke engines.

CONNAUGHT
England (Birmingham) 1910–27: Bordesley Engineering began with a 293cc (18ci) two-stroke engine, later enlarged to 347cc (21ci). In 1925, the firm switched to 350cc (21ci) Blackburne side-valve and Bradshaw overhead-valve motors.

CONSUL
England (Norwich) 1916–22: A Villiers 269cc (16ci) two-stroke powered this machine from Burton & Theobald Ltd. There may also have been a 247cc (15ci) model.

COOPER
Mexico 1972–73: Made in Mexico but sold principally in America, these were 246cc (15ci) two-stroke singles in both trials (enduro) and moto-cross form.

COPPI
Italy 1958: This firm was the builder of mopeds, which were with 48cc (3ci) two-stroke motors.

The distinctive triangular-framed Cotton Blackburne.

CORAH
England (Birmingham) 1905–14: This was a company that initially made machines with bought-in JAP motors. It went on later to manufacture machines using its own overhead-valve 498cc (6ci) singles and 746cc (46ci) twins.

CORONA
England (Maidenhead) 1901–04: Corona was the name of this assembler, which used Minerva and Clement engines.

CORONA
Germany (Brandenburg) 1902–24: Until 1907, Fahrradwerk & Metallindustrie produced unremarkable machines with Zedel and Fafnir singles and V-twins of two and two-and-a-half horsepower, but they were also known for a special tandem model. The later series (1922–24) had 346cc (21ci) side-valve singles of uncertain provenance.

CORONA-JUNIOR
England 1919–23: A long stroke of 100mm (3.9in) characterized this company's 450cc (27ci) two-stroke single.

CORRE
France (Neuilly) 1901–10: This firm fitted Zuercher, Peugeot and Zedel proprietary motors to its machines. It was better known for automobiles.

CORYDON
England (Croydon) 1904–08: Bradbury Brothers built a two-and-a-half horsepower single, and three and three-and-a-half horsepower V-twins.

COSMOS
Switzerland 1904–07: This firm constructed bicycle-type frames that were fitted with Zedel and Fafnir engines.

COTTEREAU
France (Dijon) 1903–09: Cottereau was actually better known for building automobiles, but it also constructed motorcycles with engines of its own make, as well as with those bought in from Minerva and Peugeot.

COULSON
(London, later Birmingham) England 1919–24: Also known as Coulson-B, this firm initially made machines with 347cc (21ci) and 497cc (30ci) Blackburne engines; later, 497cc (30ci) overhead-valve JAP-powered twins and an oil-cooled Bradshaw 346cc (21ci).

COVENTRY-B & D
England (Coventry) 1923–25: Barbary and Downs (B & D) catalogued JAP-engined machines in various capacities, from 350cc (21ci) to 1000cc (61ci), and also made the Coventry B & S with a Barr and Stroud 350cc (21ci) motor.

COVENTRY-CHALLENGE
England (Coventry) 1903–11: Bicycle dealer Edward O'Brian assembled machines with Fafnir and Minerva engines.

COVENTRY-MASCOT
England (Coventry) 1922–24: Made 350cc (21ci) singles with Barr & Stroud sleeve-valves and oil-cooled Bradshaws.

COVENTRY-MOTETTE
England (Coventry) 1899–1903: Starting with three-wheelers, this company introduced a Ladies' Model in 1901 with the engine fitted behind the pedals. A Miss De Veille became famous for riding one of these from Coventry to London.

COVENTRY-STAR
England (Coventry) 1919–21: This was a firm of assemblers that used Coventry and Liberty engines in the machines.

COVENTRY-VICTOR
England (Coventry) 1919–36: A leading maker of flat-twin engines, which were also supplied to other manufacturers.

CPC
France 1931–37: This firm built lightweights with 100cc (6ci) two-stroke motors.

CP-ROLEO
France (Paris) 1924–39: The firm fitted JAP, Voisin, Chaise and MMC engines into pressed-steel frames, which incorporated the petrol tank.

CR
Germany 1926–30: A firm of assemblers using Villiers 172cc (10ci) two-strokes.

CRESMA
Spain 1950: This was a machine with a steel frame housing a 197cc (12ci) two-stroke motor, with a four-speed gearbox.

CREST
England 1923: This assembler used Barr and Stroud sleeve-valves and small-capacity Villiers two-stroke engines.

CROFT
England (Coventry) 1923–26: This firm made high-end sports machines in small numbers, with British Anzani overhead-valve V-twins of 992cc (61ci) or, occasionally, 1078cc (66ci).

CROWNFIELD
England (London) 1903–04: This firm produced an open-frame Ladies' Model with engines from Givauden and Kerry.

CRT
Italy (Treviso) 1925–29: Cavasini & Romin, Trevino (hence CRT) built side-valve tourers and overhead-valve sports bikes with Blackburne 250cc (15ci) and 350cc (21ci) engines.

CRYPTO
England (London) 1902–08: This firm showed a machine with the motor over the front wheel at the 1901 Stanley Show. It entered production with two-and-a-half horsepower MMC and three-and-a-half horsepower Peugeot and Coronet singles. In 1906, the firm launched V-twins of four and five horsepower.

CSEPEL
Hungary (Csepel) 1932–51: Own-make 98cc (6ci), 123cc (8ci) and 146cc (9ci) two-strokes gave power to these machines which came from the Manfred Weiss steelworks. In 1951, the name Csepel was dropped from the models and the same bikes were branded Pannonia and Danuvia.

CUB
USA 1950s: A small two-speed automatic scooter that was hard-pressed to reach a speed of 40km/h (25mph).

CUDELL
Germany 1898–1905: Pioneering machines powered by De Dion Bouton engines of 402cc (24ci) and 510cc (31ci).

CURWY (CURSY)
Germany (Frankfurt a. d. Oder) 1923–31: A series of 350cc (21ci) and 498cc (6ci) side-valve and overhead-valve singles, and a 348cc (21ci) overhead-cam. The name changed to Cursy in 1927.

A 1933 Carlton Motors C776, which had a powerful 500cc (31ci) JAP engine.

English firm housed the usual motors. These motors were bought-in from Villiers with 269cc (16ci), and also bought-in from Blackburne with 350cc (21ci) and 500cc (31ci).

DELAPLACE
France 1951–53: This company was responsible for the installation of 173cc (11ci) and 247cc (15ci) engines from Ydral and fitting them into several Delaplace frames.

DELIN
Belgium (Leuven) 1899–1901: This firm built De Dion-Bouton machines under licence. Later in its shortlived production span, it was to switch to the use of Fafnir engines.

DELOMA
Germany (Magdeburg) 1924: This was one of several machines under production during the mid-1920s to be partial to using the Julius Lowy light-oil two-stroke engine.

DE LONG
USA c.1901: This was a pioneering machine, which was unique in that it was offered with a coil-and-battery ignition.

DELTA
Germany 1924: This machine was fully enclosed. It was also distinctive in that it had been fitted with a 499cc (30ci) two-stroke three-port single engine.

DE LUXE
USA (Indianapolis) 1912–15: The F.W. Spacke Machine Company was the supplier of the engines (both singles and twins) for these machines. It also supplied several other mechanical parts for these motorcycles, built by Excelsior.

DE LUXE
England (Birmingham) 1920–24: 269cc (16ci) two-stroke engines from Villiers and 350cc (21ci) four-stroke engines from Barr & Stroud powered these machines. The 350cc (21ci) models were offered with a free side-car chassis.

DENE
England 1903–22: This company made relatively few machines, considering the fact that it was manufacturing over a fairly long period of time. The machines were fitted with a variety of bought-in engines from such companies as Fafnir, Precision, Green-Precision (their water-cooled engines), Abingdon and JAP.

DENNELL
England (Leeds) 1903–08: As well as using the usual JAP, Minerva and NSU engines, Herbert Dennell built an early triple, which was an air-cooled in-line 660cc (40ci) from JAP with belt drive.

DERBY
England (London) 1902–10: This obscure pioneer was fitted with MMC engines.

DERONAX
Belgium late 1950s: Two-stroke engines from Ilo with two-speed gearboxes powered these lunmemorable machines, produced amongst the fierce competition of the 1950s.

DERONZIERE
France (Lyon) 1903–14: This firm used Peugeot and Zedel engines in the early years, as well as fitting its own 282cc (17ci) engines with automatic inlet valves into some machines.

DESPATCH-RIDER
England (Birmingham) 1915–17: A 269cc (16ci) Villiers two-stroke engine powered this unsuccessful assault on the military market.

DE TOGNI
Italy (Milan) 1932–40s: This was effectively an armchair on a motorcycle frame. It was fitted with outrigger wheels and a 175c (11ci) DKW motor, which must have felt the need for its three-speed gearbox. After the end of World War II, De Togni switched to light delivery vehicles fitted with Sachs engines.

DETROIT
USA c.1903: An upper frame tube was the oil tank, and a lower frame tube was the silencer, in these early machines. One version of the bike was started by magneto ignition, while the other version was started by coil ignition.

DFB
Germany 1922–25: The 159cc (10ci) engine manufactured by this company was sold both as an auxiliary cycle motor and on complete machines.

DFR
France (Neuilly) 1921–33: Desert et De Font Reault began by building motorcycles with Train two-stroke engines and Bradshaw oil-cooled four-stroke engines, with chain primary drive and belt secondary. Then in 1925, or thereabouts, it produced a pump-charged 250cc (15ci) two-stroke single engine and then 350cc (21ci) MAG engines. It then progressed to 175cc (11ci) and 250cc (15ci) two strokes, overhead-valve and other machines. It raced a supercharged machine with an engine from Bradshaw with some success between 1925 and 1927. The frim was eventually taken over by Dresch in about 1930.

CYC-AUTO
England (London) 1934–56: An autocycle with a Scott 98cc (6ci) two-stroke engine. The 1956 Bantamoto was a 38cc (2ci) two-stroke cycle motor.

CYCLE-SCOOT
USA (New Jersey) 1953–55: This was a scooter that had a two-and-a-half horsepower four-stroke engine.

CYCLE-STAR
Netherlands (Rotterdam) 1952: This moped was fitted with a 38cc (2ci) two-stroke engine mounted under the pedals and friction drive to the rear wheel.

CYCLETTE
France 1920s: This was an autocycle fitted with a 91cc (6ci) motor, in two versions: the Gentlemen's (conventional) and the Ladies' (open frame).

CYCLEX
France 1946: Cycle motors, one a 48cc (3ci) weighing 10kg (22lb), the other a 98cc (6ci) twin weighing 16kg (35lb).

CYCLOLUX
France 1950s: This was a cycle motor that was fitted with a 49cc (3ci) two-stroke engine with friction drive.

CYCLON
Germany 1901–5: After a few years of making motorcycles with engines from De Dion-Bouton, Werner and Zedel, this firm changed to producing three-wheelers (the Cyclonette).

CYCLONETTE
Belgium 1958–late 1960s: These machines were, in fact, mopeds fitted with 49cc (3ci) Zundapp engines.

CYCLOP
Germany 1922–25: This assembler used a wide variety of two-stroke and four stroke – mostly obscure – engines such as Kurier, Bubi, Teco and Namapa, amongst others.

CYCLOTRACTEUR
France 1918–22: Early 100cc (6ci) moped/cycle motor that must have been one of the last designs to use an automatic inlet valve. The motor was mounted over the front wheel, driving it by friction.

CYKELAID
England 1919–26: This was a two-stroke cycle motor of 131cc (8ci), for mounting over the front wheel, with chain drive.

CYMOTA
England 1950: This was an all-enclosed cycle motor of 45cc (3ci) for mounting over rear wheel, with friction drive.

CYRUS
The Netherlands (Vento) 1952 (or 1931)–71: Pressed-steel frame moped fitted with various engines, such as Anker, Fichtel and Sachs, Ilo and Villiers.

DAK
Germany (Pinneberg) 1923–25: These were lightweight deflector-piston two-stroke engines of 117cc (7ci) and 147cc (9ci) capacity, bought in from Ilo. The enterprise was started in 1923 by an association of several German car dealers.

DALESMAN
England 1969–74: These were lightweight, successful competition machines, several of which were fitted with 98cc (6ci) and 123cc (8ci) engines from Puch.

DALL'OGLIO
Italy c.1926: Guido Dall'Oglio, founder of GD (reference below), bestowed his name upon a horizontal single 125cc (8ci) engine with a bronze cylinder head. This Italian engine was equipped with a two-speed transmission.

DALTON
England (Manchester) 1920–22: This company was a small assembler of machines with 348cc (21ci) and 498cc (6ci) singles from Blackburne and the 688cc flat twin from Coventry Victor.

DANE
England 1919–20: This was an English firm of assemblers who had two-stroke and four-strokes in a variety of capacities – 350cc (21ci) to 1000cc (61ci) – with engines bought in from Precision, JAP and others. These included overhead-valve engines.

DANUBIUS
Germany (Ratibor) 1923–24: Ganz were the firm responsible for making this conventional 198cc (6ci) side-valve machine.

DANUVIA
Hungary 1955–63: This model was a two-stroke 123cc (8ci) lightweight, manufactured by the Hungarian firm CSEPEL.

DARLAN
Spain (Zarauz) 1958–60: These lightweights were manufactured with in-house 94cc (6ci) two-stroke engines.

DARLING
Switzerland (Bern) 1924–26: This company built small numbers of machines powered by an in-house 250cc (15ci) two-stroke three-port single engine.

DART
England (Coventry) 1923–24: This was a rare overhead-cam machine of 74x81mm (348cc/21ci), designed by A.A. Sidney and delivered a creditable seventeen-and-a-half horsepower.

DART
England (Kingston) 1901–06: Built by Frank Baker (not the same Baker as Precision engines and motorcycles), these two-and-a-half horsepower machines were fitted with Minerva and MMC engines.

DAUDON
France 1950s: Daudon were responsible for the production of two-stroke mopeds, as well as several four-stroke mopeds.

DAVENTRY
Belgium 1951–55: This company produced lightweights with bought-in 125cc (8ci) and 175c (11ci) engines. The engines were supplied by such companies as Sachs and Puch, as well as several other firms.

DAVID
Spain 1950s: This was a motor tricycle with drive to front wheel. The tricycle was fitted with a 350cc (21ci) two-stroke unit-construction single engine.

DAVISON
England (Coventry, later London) 1902–08: This was a pioneer company which used engines from Simms and Minerva of two and two-and-three-quarters horsepower in the production of its various machines.

DAW
England (Coventry) 1902–05: This Coventry-based company produced Minerva singles. They manufactured these singles under licence bought from other firms.

DAW
Germany (Munich) 1924–25: Diana-Werk built a 405cccc (25ci) two-stroke single with full enclosure. However, this machine was not widely produced, and was manufactured only in small numbers. It failed to do as well as other two-stroke singles, hence the brevity of its life-span: only one year.

DAX
France (Clichy) 1932–39: This firm built machines of original design with 100cc (6ci) and 175c (11ci) two-stroke engines, and overhead-valve four-strokes, in various capacities: 125cc (8ci), 175cc (11ci), 250cc (15ci), 350cc (21ci) and 500cc (31ci). The firm was an early user of foot-change gearboxes.

DAY-LEEDS
England (Leeds) 1912–14 (or –1917): Job Day and Sons made an inlet-over-exhaust 500cc (31ci) single engine.

DAYTON
England (London) 1913–20: Charles Day used the Dayton name for auxiliary cycle motors of 162cc (10ci). He then did the same for a 269cc (16ci) Villiers-powered lightweight.

DAYTON
England (London) 1954–60: This was a scooter, initially powered by 198cc (6ci) Villiers engines – which were later to become 175cc (11ci) and 259cc (16ci) engines.

DECA
Italy 1954–57: This firm initially produced a 48cc (3ci) four-stroke moped. From these ordinary beginnings, it went on to produce a 100cc (6ci) lightweight that could top 90km/h (55mph). It was also responsible for manufacturing 48cc (3ci) cycle motors. However, the firm was to disappear, despite the announcement of new 100cc (6ci) and 125cc (8ci) machines in 1958. The name is also occasionally found with a variant spelling, under the reference DE-CA.

DECLARET
England (Stevenage) 1962: This firm, based in Kent, southern England, produced several mopeds.

DE-DE
France (Courveboie) 1923–29: This firm wasshortlived. They underwent a limited production of, initially, 100cc (6ci), 125cc (8ci) and 175cc (11ci) models. They were later responsible for the production of more machines, including several 250cc (15ci), 350cc (21ci) and 500cc (31ci) JAP-powered models.

DEFA
Germany 1921–24: This was a firm of frame builders who were also responsible for manufacturing a complete 198cc (6ci) side-valve motorcycle.

DEFY-ALL
England 1921–22: These unusual spring frames from this

DGW

Germany (Zschopau) 1927–28: These were DKWs but were badged as DGWs when exhibited at the 1927 London Olympia Show.

DIAG

Germany (Leipzig) 1923–31 (or 1921–28): DIAG produced double-cradle frames and in-house side-valve motors of various capacities: 175cc (11ci), 250cc (15ci) and 350cc (21ci). The firm also made an overhead-valve version of the 350cc (21ci) and manufactured 83cc (5ci) and 101cc (6ci) auxiliary cycle motors.

DIAGON

Germany 1923: This firm assembled a machine notable mainly for the fuel tank positioned in the top frametube.

DIAMOND

England 1969: This was a lightweight machine fitted with a Sachs engine.

DI BLASI

Italy (Francofonte) 1970–unknown: These machines were lightweights and mopeds. Their advanced design and high-quality manufacture owed much to aircraft design expertise. At a weight of less than 32.5kg (72lb), the R7 – which was fitted with a 50cc (3ci) engine – gave endurance of over 100km/2.5litres (about 110mpg).

DIEM

France early 1950s: These were cycle motors of 48cc (3ci), which featured chain drive and a two-speed gearbox.

DIESELLA

Denmark 1954: This Danish machine was a moped with a 50cc (3ci) two-stroke motor. The motor was mounted under the pedals. In later versions, the motor was fitted behind the saddle, with friction drive to the rear wheel.

DIETERLE-DESSAU

Germany 1921–25: This company made 350cc (21ci) two-stroke engines but suffered in the harsh financial climate of the interwar Weimar Republic. The firm was eventually wiped out by inflation.

DIFRA

Germany (Frankfurt a.d. Oder) 1923–25: These lightweights were produced with 198cc (6ci) Namapo motors.

DIHL

Germany (Berlin) 1923–24: This firm initially made a partially enclosed machine with 269cc (16ci) two-stroke motor. They went on later to manufacture lightweights which were fitted with 125cc (8ci) and 150cc (9ci) engines.

DIK-DIK

Italy 1950: Vanzango built this 43cc (3ci) auxiliary cycle motor with friction drive to the rear wheel. The petrol tank sat atop the rear mudguard, with the engine more or less hanging below, on the right, with a tiny silencer. It allowed a top speed of up to 35–40km/h (22–25mph).

DILECTA

France 1920–39: This was a firm of assemblers who used motors bought-in from numerous sources. These sources included Soyer, Aubier-Dunne, Chaise, JAP and Villiers.

DISA

Denmark 1954: These machines were lightweights and they were put into production under the direction of the Dansk Industri Syndicat.

DISSELHOF

Netherlands 1956: These machines were scooters fitted with 150cc (9ci) engines bought in from the Ilo company.

DIXON-HONDA

England 1972–unknown: This company were manufacturers of 'go faster' frames. They fitted these frames around Yoshimura-tuned twins and fours from Honda.

DIXOR

France 1951–56: This French firm was responsible for the manufacture of limited numbers of mopeds with 49cc (3ci) engines.

DJOUNN

Germany (Berlin) 1925: This unusual single-cylinder 500cc (31ci) was not particularly well-developed. It had been designed by a former pilot from Russia. It's hard to tell whether or not it entered series production. However, if it did, it failed to make a great impression, and not many were sold.

DKF

Germany 1923–24: The initials DKF stand for Deutsche Kleinmotoren und Fahrzeugwerk ('German small-engine and vehicle works'). Under this name, the firm made single engines of 148cc (9ci) and 198cc (6ci) in the 1920s.

DKR

England (Wolverhampton) 1957–66: This was a firm of manufacturers who were responsible for the production of scooters with names such as the Dove, Manx, Pegasus and Capella. These scooters were on the whole fitted with Villiers two-stroke single engines. The company also manufactured several vertical twins, although these were still two-stroke.

DMF

Belgium 1948–50: This company made 125cc (8ci) to 200cc lightweights and 49cc (3ci) mopeds. They were usually two-stroke, and were fitted with a variety of bought-in motors from various firms, such as Villiers, Ilo, and Puch, as well as Fuchs.

DMF

The Netherlands 1951–57: The initials stand for Driebergse Motoren Fabriek. The company made a range of small-capacity machines. These included the Nestor, fitted with a 50cc (3ci) Ilo engine, and the Olimpia, fitted with 125cc (8ci) two-stroke engine (motor brand unknown).

DMG

Germany (Berlin) 1921–24: The grandly named Deutsche Motoren Gesellschaft (German Motor Society) built its own 197cc (12ci) engine for the few machines it manufactured. It also produced 147cc (9ci) side-valve auxiliary cycle motors.

DNB

Japan (Tokyo) 1957–61: This Japanese company built two-stroke singles of 125cc (8ci), 200cc (12ci) and 250cc (15ci).

DOBRO-MOTORIST

Germany (Berlin) 1923–25: This model was noted for having a silencer attached directly to the cylinder of the 145cc DKW motor. Also noteworthy were the clean lines of the triangular frame. There was also a 350cc (21ci) JAP four-stroke version.

DOGLIOLI & CIVARDI

Italy (Turin) 1929–35: This Italian assembler was typical of the period, using English motors from 175cc (11ci) to 500cc (31ci) bought in from firms such as Norman, New Imperial, JAP and Rudge.

DOLF

Germany (Frankfurt am Main) 1922–25: These 114cc (7ci) two-strokes bikes were surprisingly fast, in part because of their eight transfer ports and rotary crank-case valve. They delivered three horsepower, which would have been a considerable figure for a small two-stroke in that era.

DOLLAR

France (Joinville-le-Point) 1925–39 (or –1928): This company was an adventurous manufacturer of machines. They were powered by singles, twins and fours, which were either bought-in from Chaise or built in-house. Some machines had shaft drive, whereas others had overhead-cams. The company was also responsible for building two-strokes.

DOMINISSIMI

Italy (Pordenone) 1924–28: The Dominissimi brothers made four models in the four years they were in business during the 1920s. They fitted the machines with 172cc (10ci) and 248cc (15ci) engines, which they bought in from DKW.

DONISELLI

Italy (Milan) 1951–73: This manufacturer of delivery bicycles moved into the production of auxiliary cycle motors and light delivery vehicles. After that, it produced 50cc (3ci) scooters. All machines which left the assembly line were fitted with proprietary motors bought-in from companies such as Ilo and Alpino.

DOPPER

The Netherlands 1904: An early overhead-valve engine of 269cc (16ci) gave power to this pioneering machine.

DORION

France (Boulogne) 1932–36: This French assembler used 123cc (8ci) Aubier-Dunne two-stroke motors.

DORMAN

Hungary 1920–37: This assembler used proprietary engines from such companies as Villiers, MAG and also JAP. However, the company ultimately made few machines.

DORNIER

Germany 1949–57: This famous aviation company manufactured the Pearle moped with an aluminium frame. The firm also produced three-wheelers, but it returned to its roots, recommencing aircraft.

DOTTA

Italy (Turin) 1924–26: These lightweights and delivery vehicles which were produced in the Italian city of Turin were fitted with 125cc (8ci) two-stroke motors bought in from Piazza.

DOUE

France 1903–10: This French firm was responsible for the installation of one-and-three-quarter horsepower motors into strengthened bicycle frames.

D-RAD

Germany (Spandau) 1921–33: Deutsche Industriewerk AG began life as a weapons factory, and in 1923 introduced a 393cc (24ci) side-valve flat twin motorcycle. They followed this three years later with a 500cc (31ci) side-valve single engine, which had been designed by Christiansen and then had undergone refinements under the direction of Martin Stolle. Overhead-valves were to appear in the R10 model. This was introduced for 1929, which was just prior to the union with NSU. The last machines were fitted with two-stroke engines which came from Bark. The D-Rad name would continue in production right up until 1933.

Built in 2006, the CF Moto CF250T5 CVT had automatic transmission.

DREADNOUGHT

England (Birmingham) 1915–39 (or –1925): Despite the splendid name, these machines had a rather tedious specification: they were powered by the ubiquitous Villiers 269cc (16ci) two-stroke. They were built by Williams Lloyd Cycle, who was also responsible for making Quadrant and LMC machines.

DREVON

France 1946–53: These were lightweights fitted with engines bought in from Ydral and Aubier-Dunne.

DRS

Italy 1967: This 125cc (8ci) Grand Prix racer was produced in relatively small numbers and bought only by privateers. The machine was a horizontal single two-stroke and featured a water-cooled cylinder and an air-cooled head. It was recorded as delivering 22 horsepower at 19,800rpm.

DS

Sweden (Hedemora) 1924–28: This short-lived 742cc (45ci) V-twin was fitted with an engine from MAG. In its conception, it was aimed primarily at buyers from the Swedish military market. Over the years, the Swedish military market has been responsible for sponsoring a number of unusual vehicles on two and four wheels.

DSH

Austria 1924–32: Three Austrian men, Doller, Seidl und Hauler, lent their initials to the name of this firm. From 1924, it built unremarkable road machines. These machines were powered by imported British engines from firms such as Villiers and JAP, and then later on from MAG. The firm enjoyed some competition success with their racers. However, the tragic death of Rupert Karner on a 350cc (21ci) DSH at the Hungarian TT in 1928 brought things to a halt for a year.

DS-MALTERRE

France (Paris) 1920–58: Deblades et Sigran made 500cc (31ci) overhead-valve bikes that seemed as if they were quite advanced when first introduced in 1920. However, they looked distinctly less advanced when compared to other makes at the outbreak of World War II in 1939. In the postwar years, the company made lightweights with overhead-valve AMC engines (124cc/8ci and 246cc/15ci) and 123cc (8ci) and 247cc (15ci) Ydral two-strokes.

DUCATI (MOTOTRANS)

see MOTOTRANS (below).

DUCSON

Spain 1956–early 1970s: These machines of fairly enduring success were two-stroke 50cc (3ci) engined mopeds.

DUMO

Germany 1924–25: This shortlived German model was, in fact, a sports version of the two-stroke 198cc (6ci) Autinag.

DUNJO

Spain (Barcelona) 1952: Although this was an interesting 32cc (2ci) two-stroke diesel with variable compression ratio, it failed to emerge from the drawing board to make it into series production.

DUNKLEY

England (Birmingham) 1913–20 and 1957–?60: The first series from this company began life fitted with motors of 199cc (12ci), 499cc (30ci), 750cc (46ci) and 988cc (60ci)

from Precision, before moving on to singles and twins from 300cc (18ci) to 700cc (43ci) from JAP. A 350cc (21ci) two-stroke engine was also available. After a long absence from the motorcycle market, the company returned and introduced the Whippet line of lightweights and scooters.

DUNSTALL

England 1967–unknown: This company was essentially a frame builder, responsible for making 'beefed up' frames. These frames were used to enclose high-output derivatives of engines from various manufacturers. Dunstall also made frames for engines where the manufacturer's standard frame was not able to withstand the power of its motor, and needed to be enclosed by something more durable.

DURAND

France 1920–23: This firm was an assembler who used two types of engine – side-valve and overhead-valve – which were supplied by Zurcher.

DURANDAL

France (Dijon) 1925–32: These machines – which were self-proclaimed as 'The Indestructible Motorcycle' – had a pressed-steel frame. They were fitted with engines from JAP, Zurcher and Chaise. There was also a works racer which was fitted with a Velocette KTT 348cc (21ci) to give the 'Indestructable Motorcycle' its power.

DURYEA

USA 1897: Charles E. Duryea was well-known in the USA during the last decade of the twentieth century as a pioneer in the automobile trade. However, in 1897, he entered the new field of motorcycles and patented a design of one of these vehicles. It left the production line complete with a flat twin in the front wheel.

DUVAL

Belgium 1950–55: This firm was an assembler that used mostly 123cc (8ci) two-stroke engines from Royal Enfield.

DUX

England (Coventry) 1904–06: This company was one of the first to set up business in Coventry, using Rex frames and singles, as well as twins from Minerva, MMC, and Sarolea, amongst engines from other manufacturers.

DUX

USSR (Moscow) 1908: This company was possibly the earliest manufacturer of motorcycle engines in the country, setting up during the first decade of the twentieth century. The firm produced a Moto-Reve engine fitted with twin cylinders.

DUZMO

England 1919–23: These English machines were designed and intended as sporting bikes. They were overhead-valve 500cc (31ci) singles and they had some input from the famous racer Bert Le Vack during the design process.

This 250cc (15ci) Hungarian-made Csepel Pannonia motorcrosser dates from 1968.

DWB

Germany 1924–26: This company, set up during the 1920s, was the successor to Juho. It was responsible for manufacturing the same 195cc (12ci) side-valve engine. Within its short production period, it was also responsible for the manufacture of a 269cc (16ci) two-stroke engine.

DYNACYCLE

USA 1900–40: These were auxiliary cycle motors which came from the USA. The machines had a long life-span compared to other machines of the same type. The Dynacycles were fitted with a 100cc (6ci) four-stroke engine.

DYSON-MOTORETTE

England 1920–22: The English Dyson-Motorette model was an auxiliary four-stroke cycle motor that generated one-and-a-half horsepower.

EAGLE

USA 1910–15: These machines had Spacke four horsepower singles and seven horsepower V-twins.

EBE

Sweden (Amal) 1919–30: In 1925, this firm was making 172cc (10ci) and 598cc (6ci) overhead-valve singles and their 173cc (11ci) auxiliary cycle motor.

EBER

Germany (Einbau-Ebersach) 1924–28: This firm assembled a range of 350cc (21ci) and 500cc (31ci) engined machines.

EBO

England (Leicester) 1910–15: Edward Boulter used Precision engines and some JAP V-twins.

EBS

Germany (Berlin) 1924–30: This firm built side-valve and overhead-valve machines, using their own singles of 198cc (12ci) to 496cc (30ci), and a 796cc (49ci) V-twin.

EBU-STAR

Japan 1952–55: These 250cc (15ci) V-twins were unusual; one cylinder pointed forward, the other up.

ECHO

Japan (Tokyo) late 1950s–early 1960s: Echo made 123cc (8ci) and 148cc (9ci) two-stroke lightweights and a scooter, the Pandra.

ECONOMIC

England 1921–23: This 165cc (10ci) flat twin was mounted in line in early machines, and transide-valversely in later ones.

EDETA

Spain (Barcelona) 1951–60: These were two-stroke 173cc (11ci) lightweights.

EDMONTON

England 1903–c.1910: This pioneer assembler used Minerva and Fafnir engines.

A DKR Manx scooter undergoes a road test in 1959.

EDMUND

England (Chester) 1907–24: This firm installed engines from various manufacturers — Barr & Stroud, Blackburne, Fafnir, JAP and MAG — in its own well-made frames, some of which were sprung.

EFA

Netherlands 1950s: This 34cc (2ci) auxiliary cycle motor weighed 6kg (13lb) and gave three-quarters horsepower at 4000rpm, and a speed of 24km/h (15mph).

EGA

Germany 1922–26: The Gaggenau iron works built these deflector-piston, three-port two-strokes of 246cc (15ci) and 346cc (21ci).

EICHLER

Germany 1920–25: The biggest producer of lightweights, Eichler used DKW engines (119cc/7ci to 173cc/11ci), and Bekamo engines of 129cc (8ci) and 149cc (9ci), and the Golem and Lomos scooters, with 145cc (9ci) DKW motors.

EISLER

Czechoslovakia 1920–26: This firm supplied its 148cc (9ci) engine as an auxiliary cycle motor installed in a bicycle.

ELAND

The Netherlands 1955–60: These were lightweights with Sachs engines of 123cc (8ci) and 158cc (10ci).

ELFA

Germany 1926–39: The Saxon Elstwerdaer Fahrzeugwerk installed 198cc (12ci) and 298cc (6ci) DKW two-strokes, and 346 (21ci) and 497cc (30ci) Kuchen four-strokes in their own frames. In the 1930s, they made autocycles with 100cc (6ci) Fichtel and Sachs engines.

ELI

England 1911–12: These machines had Precision motors of three-and-a-half horsepower.

ELIE-HUIN

France (Clermont-Ferrand) late 1950s–early 1960s: These unusually modern assembled machines had Ydral, AMC and other 125cc (8ci) to 250cc (15ci) engines.

ELITE

Germany (Brand-Elisdorf) 1926–40: This firm's motorcycles were made with 348cc (21ci) and 498cc (6ci) overhead-valve Kuhne engines. In 1929, Opel took over; and continued with 100cc (6ci) Sachs engines.

ELLEHAM

Denmark (Copenhagen) 1904–09: A complex 734cc (45ci) twin-cylinder engine of their own design powered this, the first Danish motorcycle.

ELMDON

England (Birmingham) 1915–21: This firm entered small-scale production of 269cc (16ci) Villiers-engined machines.

ELSA

Italy (Brescia) 1920: This two-stroke cycle motor of 75cc (5ci) was very forward-looking, allowing 50km/h (25 mph).

ELSINORE

Japan 1973–: This brand of Honda motocross machine had 123cc (8ci) and 248cc (15ci) engines.

ELSTAR

England 1968–71: Various engines powered these competition machines.

ELSTER

Germany (Mylau) 1924–26: As well as 198cc (6ci) singles of their own design, Elster used 175cc (11ci) and 206cc (13ci) DKW motors. All were two-strokes.

ELSWICK

England (Barton on Humber) 1903–20: The well-known bicycle works also made motorcycles with Precision engines of 348cc (21ci) and 498cc (6ci).

ELVE

Belgium 1958–63: This firm made mopeds with their own engines and with 49cc (3ci) Sachs engines.

EMA

Germany (Aalen) 1922–26: Eduard Molitor Motorenfahrzeugbau used 148cc (9ci) DKW engines.

EMBLEM

USA 1909–25: A pioneer of dual seats, these machines had a 1245cc (76ci) V-twin. The 1915 single was 653cc (40ci).

EMMAG

Hungary 1924–27: This firm built a 495cc (30ci) air-cooled two stroke and a 670cc (41ci) water-cooled two-stroke twin.

EMPO

Netherlands 1955–c.1970: This firm manufactured mopeds with 47cc (3ci) TWN motors.

EMURO

Japan 1953–late 1950s: This firm built 90cc (5ci) to 250cc (15ci) two-stroke singles.

EMW

East Germany (Eisenach) 1945–56: This firm's sole model, a shaft-drive 346cc (21ci) overhead-valve single, was essentially a 1934 BMW.

EMWE

Germany 1924–25: They did it their way, with an in-house 293cc (18ci) single in a pressed-steel frame.

ENAG

Germany (Nurnberg) 1924–25: Erle and Nestler AG built a 348cc (21ci) two-stroke with water-cooled barrels. Early machines were belt-drive, then later, chain.

ENDRICK

England (Birmingham) 1911–15: Peco motors of 346cc (21ci) and Precision 496cc (30ci) engines powered most Endrick machines.

ENDURANCE

England (Birmingham) 1909–24: C.B. Harrison built these two-strokes, initially with Villiers 269cc (16ci) engines and later with their own 259cc (16ci) and 297cc (18ci) engines.

ENERGETTE

England 1907–11: J.L. Norton designed the Energette, with a 274cc (17ci) licence-built Moto-Reve V-twin.

EOLE

Belgium c.1900–07: This, one of the first Belgian motorcycles, used Fafnir engines.

EOLO

Italy (Milan) 1950: Eolo mopeds from 1953 had a horizontal single 46cc (3ci) two-stroke motor and were built by ICEM.

ERIE

USA (Hammondsport) 1905–11: This assembler used Spacke, Minerva and Curtiss engines.

ERIOL

France 1932–39: These autocycles had 98cc (6ci) two-stroke motors.

ERMAG

Germany 1923–30: This firm made various machines – stepped-piston two-stroke, overhead-valve single and side-valve – with various capacities (246cc/15ci, 497cc/30ci and 547cc/33ci).

ERNST-MAG

Germany (Breslau) 1926–30: These sports and racing machines used MAG singles and V-twins in 350cc (21ci), 500cc (31ci), 750cc (46ci) and 1000cc (61ci) capacities.

ESCH-REKORD

Germany (Cologne) 1927–30: These racers used JAP and other engines, from 350cc (21ci) to 500cc (31ci).

ESCOL

Belgium (Chatelet) 1925–38: The Escol brothers used Villiers 147cc (9ci) engines, JAP and Python engines of 250cc (15ci), 500cc (31ci) and 600cc (37ci), and their own 250 (15ci) and 350cc (21ci) two-strokes.

ETOILE

France 1933–39: These were two-strokes with Aubier-Dunne engines of 98cc (6ci) and 198cc (6ci).

EUROPA

Germany (Munich) 1931–33: Schliha two-strokes of 147cc (9ci)and 198cc (6ci), and Villiers two-strokes of 98cc (6ci) and 147cc (9ci), powered these lightweights.

EVANS

USA 1919–33: This firm began with a 91cc (6ci) two-stroke machine but made its name with a 119cc (7ci), reincarnated in Germany as a Stock.

EVART-HALL

England (London) 1903–5: This firm originally made singles in a bicycle-type frame, then a Charles Binks-designed in-line air-cooled straight four.

EVYCSA

Spain (Barcelona) 1954–60: This firm made a pleasant pushrod overhead-valve lightweight of 173cc (11ci), later supplementing it with bought-in 169cc (10ci) and 250cc (15ci) Fita-AMC four-strokes.

EXCELSIOR

Germany (Brandenburg) 1901–39: An established bicycle manufacturer that bought in assorted English side-valve and overhead-valve single engines of 198cc (12ci), 246cc (15ci) and 346cc (21ci), and later Bark engines of 198cc (12ci) (two-stroke) and 196cc (12ci) to 496cc (30ci) (side-valve).

FABULA

Germany (Bielefeld) 1922–1924: This firm made a 246cc (15ci) two-stroke engine with shaft drive.

FAGAN

Ireland (Dublin) 1935–37: Fagan used a 123cc (8ci) Villiers single.

FAGGI

Italy (Milan) 1950–53: Two-strokes from Ilo (125cc/8ci and 175c/11ci) and Villiers (125cc/8ci and 198cc/6ci) powered these motorcycles and delivery vehicles.

FAINI

Italy 1923–27: This 1925 light motorcycle was a 198cc (6ci) side-valve.

FAIRBANKS-MORSE

USA 1956: A three-wheeled machine reaching 7km/h (4mph).

FAIRFIELD

England (Warrington) 1914–15: Alfred Forster built this 269cc (16ci) two-stroke before World War I struck.

FAKA

Germany (Salzgitter-Bad) 1952–57: Kannenberg's scooters had 147cc (9ci), 174cc (11ci) and 197cc (12ci) Ilo two-stroke engines.

FALCO

Italy (Vercelli) 1950–53: Erminio di Giovanni used Fichtel and Sachs two-stroke engines of 98cc (6ci) and 147cc (9ci).

FALCOKE

Germany 1923–25: This assembler used 142cc (9ci) Grade ad 145cc (9ci) DKW deflector-piston engines.

FALTER

Germany (Bielefeld) 1952– : This firm's scooter (1954–1959) had a 49cc (3ci) Fichtel & Sachs engine; mopeds had 49cc (3ci) Sachs, Ilo and Zundapp engines.

FAM

Italy 1951–69: Benelli built 115cc (7ci) singles and 195cc (12ci) flat twins.

FAMA

Germany 1923–25: Built in-house singles of 190cc (12ci) and 420cc (26ci).

FAMA

Netherlands (Utrecht) 1938: This lightweight had a 125cc (8ci) Villiers motor.

FAMAG

Germany (Schweinfurt) 1923–25: This was a 420cc (26ci) side-valve, then a 197cc (12ci) side-valve with belt drive.

FAMO

Germany 1923–26: These had 127cc (8ci) two-strokes and triangular frames.

FAR

Austria 1924–27: FAR fitted machines with 346cc (21ci) and 496cc (30ci) JAP and Blackburne singles.

FARNELL

England (Birmingham) 1901–05: Farnell used Minerva engines in strengthened bicycle frames.

FAVOR

France (Clermont-Ferrand) 1919–59: This firm used JAP 350cc (21ci) singles, then 100cc (6ci) to 250cc (15ci) two-strokes and, post 1945, Aubier-Dunne two-strokes and AMC four-strokes to 250cc (15ci).

FAVORIT

Germany (Berlin) 1933–38: Favorit began with a 996cc (61ci) side-valve JAP V-twin, but then used 100cc (6ci) and 125cc (8ci) two-strokes.

FB

England (Birmingham) 1913–22: Fowler and Bingham built 206cc (13ci), 269cc (16ci) and 411cc (25ci) two-strokes.

FB

Germany (Breslau) 1923–25: FB began with 269cc (16ci) two-strokes, then used a 250cc (15ci) two-stroke and 348cc (21ci) and 496cc (30ci) JAP and Blackburne singles.

FB-MONDIAL

See Mondial (below).

FEDERATION

England (Birmingham) 1919–37: (also Federal) These had either Villiers two-strokes (147cc/9ci to 250cc/15ci) or JAP four-strokes (250cc/15ci to 500cc/31ci).

FEILBACH LIMITED

USA (Milwaulkee) 1912–15: Singles (550cc) and V-twins (990cc/60ci and 1130cc/69ci) characterized this make.

FERBEDO

Germany (Nurnberg-Doos) 1954: Betthauser built this basic scooter with a 49cc (3ci) Zundapp motor.

FERRARIS

Italy (Milan) 1903: This strengthened bicycle frame had a Peugeot engine.

This Dollar bike features a single cylinder with a Chaise overhead valve engine.

This Follis Type FY 175cc (11ci) dates from 1954.

FHG
Germany 1927–29: AJS importer Pleus sold the FHG 173cc (11ci) two-stroke.

FIAM
Italy 1923–25: An auxiliary cycle motor of 110cc (7ci).

FIAMC
Italy (Parma) 1952–53: This firm made a 125cc (8ci)two stroke for a motorcycle and scooter.

FIDUCIA
Switzerland 1902–5: In-house 450cc (27ci) motors ran these pioneers.

FIMER
Italy 1952–57: This was a 125cc (8ci) two-stroke scooter, later in a 'Luxus' version and a lightweight motorcycle of the same capacity.

FINZI
Italy 1923–25: This flat twin became a 598cc (6ci) overhead-valve transverse V-twin with a 36° included angle.

FIORELLI
Italy 1951–68: Made a three-speed 125cc (8ci) two-stroke, then Sport and Touring models and, in 1957, a 175c (11ci) model; later came 49cc (3ci) mopeds and bicycles.

FIT
Italy 1950–54: This assembler installed 123cc (8ci) and 147cc (9ci) Ilo engines.

FIX
Germany (Bremen) 1922–26: Lloyd Maschinenfabrik GmbH owned this firm, which used its own 150cc (9ci) two-stroke engines, and 250cc (15ci) and 350cc (21ci) side-valve singles.

FKS
Germany (Berlin) 1922–26: This firm began with a 147cc (9ci) two-stroke single, over the front wheel, then inside the frame. It then built a 298cc (6ci) two-stroke flat twin.

FLANDERS
USA 1911–14: The rear-facing exhaust did not improve the cooling of this 500cc (31ci) single.

FLINK
Germany 1920–22: This forerunner of BMW motorcycles made a 148cc (9ci) two-stroke single with a Kurier engine.

FLM
England 1951–53: This firm built lightweights with Villers and Jap 123cc (8ci) and 198cc (6ci) engines.

FLOTTWEG
Germany (Munich) 1919–37: This firm's first product was a 119cc engine, over the front wheel. Then came 183cc (11ci) overhead-valve and 350cc (21ci) side-valve engines and a 95cc (6ci) four-stroke. From 1928 to 1931, it used JAP 198 and 346cc (21ci) engines, then its own designs with a 198cc (6ci), before being taken over by BMW.

FLY
Belgium (Brussels) 1940s: Villiers 98cc (6ci) engines powered these lightweights made with pressed-steel and conventional frames.

FM
Italy (Milan) 1925–54: This firm installed 346cc (21ci) MAG singles and then 348cc (21ci) Bradshaw oil-cooled singles in a cast-light-alloy frame. After a long gap (1927–50), it brought out the FM scooter, a 125cc (8ci) two-stroke.

FMT
Italy (Treviso) 1929: This firm built a two-stroke lightweight of 132cc (8ci) with two- and three-speed gearboxes.

FOCESI
Italy 1952–55: This firm made Gloria mopeds and lightweights; 49cc (3ci) and 160cc (10ci) two-strokes, and 98cc (6ci) overhead-valves, Touring and Sport.

FOCHJ
Italy 1954–57: This firm used a wide range of NSU four-stroke engines, from mopeds to the 250cc (15ci) Max.

FOLLIS
France (Lyon) 1903–60: This firm used bought-in engines (JAP, Python, Blackburne, Ydral and AMC).

FORELLE
Germany (Bad Wildungen) 1955–58: These mopeds had 49cc (3ci) Ilo and Sachs engines.

FORONI
Italy (Modena) 1975: These mopeds and mini-scooters had 48cc (3ci) Morini engines.

FORSTER
Switzerland (Zurich) 1921–32: This firm made two-stroke singles of 140cc (9ci), 200cc (12ci) and 250cc (15ci).

FORTUNA
Germany (Nurnberg) 1921–28: These were three-port two-strokes of 150cc (9ci), 175cc (11ci) and 200cc (12ci), with external flywheels.

FORWARD
England 1909–15: These were small capacity V-twins (350cc/21ci and 500cc/31ci) in very light frames.

FOX
France 1931–late 1940s: This was a 100cc (6ci) lightweight.

FRANCAIS DIAMANT
France 1931–35: This small manufacturer made two- and four-strokes of 100cc (6ci) to 500cc (31ci).

FRANCE
France 1931–35: These two-stroke lightweights had in-house 98cc (6ci) to 245cc (15ci) engines.

FRANCHI
Italy (Milan) 1950–58: Franchi made lightweight motorcycles from 1950 with Sachs 98cc (6ci) and 150cc (9ci) engines, in 1954 a Sachs-engined 49cc (3ci) moped, and a 125cc (8ci) and a 175c (11ci) Gran Sport.

FRANZANI
Germany (Nurnberg) 1923–32: This firm used a 283cc (17ci) two-stroke engine, then JAP engines of 198cc (12ci) to 490cc (30ci), and 497cc (30ci) Kuchen engines.

FRECCIA AZZURA
Italy 1951–52: The original Freccia Azzura (Blue Arrow) scooter had a Puch 125cc (8ci) twin and three speeds and, in 1952, a 147cc (9ci) Sachs engine and four speeds.

FRECO
Germany (Hanover) 1923–25: Blackburne 173cc (11ci) and 247cc (15ci) engines powered their sport and racing machines, but the everyday lightweights had 145cc (9ci) and 173cc (11ci) DKW two-strokes and 197cc (12ci) Runge side-valve engines.

FREJUS
Italy (Turin) 1960–68: These were mopeds and lightweights with Rex, Sachs and Minarelli engines of 48cc (3ci) to 198cc (6ci).

FREYER & MILLER
USA (Cleveland, Ohio) 1902–05: This was a big single with the engine behind the saddle-tube.

FRISCHAUF
Germany (Offenbach) 1928–33: This assembler used JAP and Blackburne 198cc (6ci) engines, and an overhead-cam Kuchen 497cc (30ci).

FRISONI
Italy (Gallarate) 1952–57: This firm made a 160cc (10ci) fully enclosed scooter, later fitted with a Villiers 123cc (8ci).

FUBO
Germany (Stuttgart) 1923–25: Fuchs & Borner made its own 170cc (10ci) and 269cc (16ci) two-strokes but later offered Blackburne-powered machines of 247cc (15ci) and 348cc (21ci).

FUCHS
Italy (Milan) 1949–57: This firm produced a Sachs-engined 98cc (6ci) two-stroke scooter; then in 1955, 50cc (3ci) and 75cc (5ci) models and lightweights with 125cc (8ci) two-strokes or 150cc (9ci) four-strokes.

FUJI KIKAI
Japan 1961: The Queen Sunlight was a 123cc (8ci) two-stroke single of 90km/h (55mph).

FVL
Italy 1926–35: FVL set world speed records in the first decade of the twentieth century and then built lightweights, initially with 124cc (8ci) and 174cc (11ci) overhead-valve Moser engines, later with its own 174 cc (11ci) and (in 1932) 248cc (15ci) engines.

GA
Italy (Milan) 1925–1927: Franci Azzara of Casa Brevetta Azzara put 678cc (41ci) overhead-valve Blackburne V-twins in his sporting machines.

GABBIANO
Italy 1954–1956: This lightweight had a two-stroke flat-twin of 123cc (8ci).

GABY
England (Birmingham) 1914–1915: Metro two-strokes powered this short-lived marque.

GADABOUT
England 1948–1951: This was a Villiers-engined 123cc (8ci) scooter built by the Swallow sidecar works.

GAIA
Italy (Forno Canavese) 1922–1932: This firm built motorcycles using a 125cc (8ci) two-stroke and 150cc (9ci) overhead-valve engines from Moser; later came 173cc (11ci) Ladetto & Blatto overhead-valve engines.

GALATOR
Italy (Turin) 1933: These were Sachs-powered 74cc (5ci) and 98cc (6ci) machines from Silvio Gagliacco.

GALBAI
Italy (Tradate) 1921–1925: Made a range of two-stroke singles, a 276cc (301cc) in 1923 and 350cc (21ci) in 1924, and 348cc (21ci) racers and 492cc (30ci) racing V-twins.

GALF FLYER
Canada 1920: Although Canada is a minor producer of motorcycles, they do it with style. This air-cooled straight four had shaft drive and suspension front and rear.

GALLMOTOR
Italy c1953: Galimberti and Chiarini designed this original 42cc (3ci) multi-fuel auxiliary cycle motor.

GAMAGE
England c1905–1924: A variety of machines, from several makers, were sold under its own label by the London department store. The makers were Radco, Wulfruna, and Omega. They included 269cc (16ci) two-strokes and side-valve singles of 250cc (15ci), 350cc (21ci) and 500cc (31ci).

GAR
Germany 1924–1926: These limited-production machines had REmpp-designed 499cc (30ci) overhead-valve singles.

GARAVAGLIA
Italy 1904: In this monocycle, the rider and single-cylinder engine were contained in a 2m (79in) wheel.

GARIN
France (Lyon) 1950–1953: This firm produced mopeds and 98cc (6ci) lightweights.

GARLASCHELLI
Italy (Milan) 1922–1927: Angelo Garlaschelli made 65cc (4ci) and 123cc (8ci) two-strokes, and a choice of two-stroke or overhead-valve 175cc (11ci) models.

GASSMAN
Germany early 1950s: These were scooters and lightweights.

GASUDEN
Japan late 1950s–late 1960s: These were re-badged Fujis.

GATTI
Italy (Modena) 1904–1906: Initially, these were De Dion Bouton one-and-three-quarter horsepower motors in strengthened bicycle frames; later, other motors were used.

GAZDA
Austria 1924–1927: Anton Gazda invented Gazda leaf-spring handlebars. The firm made a 147cc (9ci) two-stroke auxiliary cycle motor, then a 246cc (15ci) two-stroke motorcycle.

GAZELLE
The Netherlands (Dieren) 1903–1958: A bicycle maker, this company motorized a few machines in the pioneer days; resumed motorcycle production with Ilo and later Villiers engines of 60cc (4ci) to 250cc (15ci) in 1932 and then made mopeds after the war, ceasing in 1958.

GAZZI
Italy (Milan) 1929–1932: This firm made an advanced 175c (11ci) overhead-valve single of their own design.

GB
England 1905–1907: Minerva engines of three-and-a-half, four-and-a-half and five-and-a-half horsepower moved these pioneers, noted for their long wheelbase.

GECO-HERSTAL
France (Jeumont) 1924–1928: Etablissements Gerkinet & Co – Geco – built its own 175cc (11ci) and 350cc (21ci) side-valve singles, and Belgian Gillet machines under contract.

GEER
USA (St Louis, Missouri) 1905–1909: The Harry R. Geer company put tits own singles and V-twins into strengthened bicycle frames.

GEHA
Germany 1920–1924: These were two-stroke lightweights with their own one-and-a-half horsepower engines.

GEIER
Germany (Lengerich) 1934–early 1960s: This manufacturer dabbled in Ilo- and Sachs-engined autocycles and lightweights.

GEKA
Germany 1924–1925: These lightweights had 173cc (11ci) DKW engines.

GE-MA-HI
Germany (Magdeburg) 1924–1927: These machines were powered by 131cc (8ci) to 175c (11ci) two-strokes from a variety of suppliers: Esbe, Bekamo, Grade, DKW and Villiers.

GEMINI
Taiwan 1970– : Yamaha two-strokes, built under licence.

GEMS
Italy (Milan) 1921–1923: Galazzi & Moroni built a 269cc (16ci) two-stroke vertical single.

GENIAL-LUCIFER
France 1928–1956: Assemblers of lightweights from 49cc (3ci) to 250cc (15ci).

GENTIL
France (Neuilly) 1903–1904: Initially an autocycle with the engine in front of the pedalling gear, this later became 98cc (6ci) autocycles and a bigger V-twin.

GEORGES RICHARD
France 1899–1905: This pioneer used Buchet, Minerva, Peugeot and Zedel engines. It was later known for Unic cars.

GEORGIA KNAPP
Germany late 1890s: This model offered direct drive from an engine mounted over the front wheel.

GEPPERT
Germany (Magdeburg) 1925–1926: This assembler used 147cc (9ci) DKW and Grade two-strokes.

GERALD
France (Paris) 1927–1932: Assembled Aubier-Dunne 175c (11ci) two-strokes, a 250cc (15ci) overhead-valve JAP, and 350cc (21ci) and 500cc (31ci) overhead-cam Chaise engines.

GERARD
England (Birmingham) 1913–1915: This model was powered by the ubiquitous 269cc (16ci) Villiers engine.

GERBI
Italy 1952–1953: These machines were lightweights with Sachs engines of 98cc (6ci), 125cc (8ci) and 175c (11ci).

GERHART
USA (Summerdale Station) 1913–1915: This firm made commercially unsuccessful fours.

GERMAAN
The Netherlands 1935–1966: This firm made lightweights from a cycle factory before World War II using, Fichtel & Sachs, Ilo and Villiers engines of 98cc (6ci) to 147cc (9ci) and afterwards, Czepel and Ilo engines, up to 350cc (21ci).

GERMANIA
Germany (Dresden) 1901–1908: Seidel & Neumann built typewriters and Laurin & Clement machines under licence: singles and V-twins of two-and-a-half to four horsepower.

GERRARD
England 1914–1915: Probably a misprint for Gerard (see above) or an abbreviation cum misspelling of Clement-Garrard (see above).

GERVO
Germany 1924–1925: This firm produced lightweights with 173cc (11ci) DKW two-strokes as well as unspecified 198cc (6ci) lightweights.

GH
Czechoslovakia 1924–1925: Gustav Heinz fitted 172cc (10ci) Villiers engines to his machines.

GHIARONI
Italy 1970s– : Efrem Ghiaroni founded a bicycle factory in 1966 and went on to build mopeds such as the Bimbo Bip Bip and the Camel with Morini motors.

GIACOMASSO
Italy (Vignola) 1926–1935: This firm produced initially a 175c (11ci) two-stroke, later (1927) an overhead-valve Moser of the same capacity, then (1933) 489cc (30ci) and 595cc (36ci) overhead-valve twins with shaft drive using Felice Giacomasso's own engines.

GIANOGLIO
Italy 1932: This firm made 70cc (4ci) autocycles.

GIANT
Japan 1924: Murato Iron Works built their first bike in 1924.

GIGANT
Austria (Vienna) 1936–1938: Side-valve and overhead-valve JAP engines powered roadgoing Gigants of 500cc (31ci), 600cc (37ci) and 750cc (461ci). Racers used JAP and Husqvarna.

GIGUET
France (St Denis) 1903: This was a pioneer with Minerva and De Dion Bouton engines.

GIMA
France (Puy de Dome) 1947–1956: These were lightweights of 108–250cc (7–15ci) fitted with various bought-in engines.

GIMSON
Spain 1956–1964: This was a bicycle maker that diversified into 49cc (3ci) and 65cc (4ci) mopeds.

GIRARDENGO
Italy 1951–1954: These lightweights were fitted with bought-in 123cc (8ci), 147cc (9ci) and 173cc (11ci) two-stroke engines.

GITANE
France 1953–1980: This firm was another bicycle maker that diversified into mopeds and lightweights of 49cc (3ci) to 175c (11ci). It became part of Renault in 1980.

GIULIETTA
Italy (Peripoli) 1959–1980: This firm produced mostly mopeds, and some 98cc (6ci) lightweights.

GIVAUDAN
England 1908–1914: This assembler used singles and V-twins from Villiers, Precision and others.

GKI
Russia 1955: This was a Russian flat-twin two-stroke racer of 343.5cc (21ci), delivering 48 horsepower at 7000rpm thanks to supercharging; it was based on a pre-war DKW.

GL
France (Argenteuil) 1919–1921: This assembler used many British components: 1000cc (61ci) JAP V-twin, Sturmey-Archer gear box and Binks carburettor.

GLENDALE
England 1920–1921: The almost inevitable Villiers 269cc (16ci) and Blackburne 350cc (21ci) powered these machines.

GLIDER
Canada 1931: This 75cc (5ci) auxiliary cycle motor could be installed over either the front or the rear wheel.

GLOBE
England (Coventry) 1901–1911: Clarke, Cluley and Co, used their own three-and-a-half horsepower, as well as Minerva, MMC and Sarolea engines.

GLOCKNER
Austria 1953–late 1970s: These mopeds were fitted with HMW and other motors.

GLORIA
England 1924–1925: Campion built the frames, and Train supplied the two-stroke engines for these machines.

GLORIA
England 1931–1933: This was a Villiers-engined 98cc (6ci) lightweight.

GLORIA
Italy 1948–1955: Focesi built mopeds and a 123cc (8ci) lightweight.

GN
Italy 1920–1925: Giuseppe Navone assembled 346cc (21ci) two-strokes from mainly English components.

GNADIG
Germany 1925–1926: Franz Gnadig built a 500cc (31ci) overhead-valve machine with shaft drive; the power unit reputedly formed the basis of the first Kuhne proprietary engines.

GNOM
Germany 1921–1923: This was an auxiliary 63cc (4ci) cycle motor.

GODIER GENOUD
France 1980s: This firm produced racers and high-performance sports machines with Kawasaki and Honda motors up to 1300cc (79ci): the 1135 R delivered 120 horsepower at 8500rpm, weighed 241kg (530lb) and could top 260km/h (160mph).

GOEBEL
Germany (Bielefeld) 1951–1979: These mopeds were fitted with 49cc (3ci) Sachs engines.

GOETZ
Germany 1925–1935: These were in limited production (79 machines in total) with a wide variety of engines.

GOGGO
Germany (Dingolfing) 1951–1954: Ilo two-strokes of 123cc (8ci), 147cc (9ci) and 173cc (11ci) powered scooters from Hans Glas, better known for his later Goggomobil micro-cars.

GO-KART
USA 1959: Tiny, light (25kg/55lb) mini-bike, the Big Bear Scramble.

GOLD-RAD
Germany (Cologne) 1952–1981: These mopeds were fitted with 49cc (3ci) proprietary engines.

GOLEM
Germany 1921–1923: More a model than a marque: this was a scooter-like machine built first by DKW and then by Eichler.

GOLO
Austria 1923–1925: JAP and Bradshaw 350cc (21ci) and JAP 500cc (31ci) engines powered these machines.

GORI
Italy 1969–1983: These motocross and trials machines were of 50cc (3ci) to 250cc (15ci).

GORICKE
Germany 1903–unknown: This motorcycle division of a bicycle works began with singles and V-twins. It moved on to Villiers, MAG and Blackburne engines of 172cc (10ci) to 496cc (30ci); then after World War II, to two-strokes of 125cc (8ci) to 250cc (15ci) (Ilo and Fichtel & Sachs motors); and for many years made mopeds.

GORRION
Spain 1952–1955: Sachs engines powered the 49cc (3ci) mopeds and the 125cc (8ci) and 175c (11ci) lightweights.

GOUGH
England 1920–1923: This assembler used 292cc (18ci) JAP and 498cc (6ci) Blackburne motors.

GOUVERNEUR
Germany 1903–1907: This obscure German machine had a three-and-a-half horsepower GN engine.

GR
Italy (Turin) 1925–1926: Count Gino Revelli built a few JAP-engined 500cc (31ci) machines with triple valve springs.

The Gilera Saturno was made between 1946 and 1958. Only 6026 were produced.

Follis G26 sport 125cc (8ci): French firm Follis (1903–60) used popular bought-in engines for all their motorbikes.

GRADE
Germany (Magdeburg) 1903–1925: Built two-stroke singles, twins and fours, and supplied engines to other manufacturers.

GRANDEX-PRECISION (GRANDEX)
England (London) 1906–1917: Began with Precision engines of two-and-a-third to six horsepower. Dropped the name 'Precision' to use JAP engines of two-and-a-half horsepower (225cc/14ci) to six horsepower (750cc/461ci V-twin).

GRAPHIC
England (Wolverhampton) 1903–1906: This assembler used Minerva, MMC and Sarolea engines.

GRASETTI
Italy 1952–1965: These were two-strokes with in-house 123cc (8ci) and 148cc (9ci) motors.

GRATIEUX
France 1919–1921: These two-stroke radials came from a firm better known for aircraft engines.

GRAVES
England (Sheffield) 1914–1915: The Graves Speed King was an 'own-brand' machine built for Graves by Omega at Wolverhampton with 293cc (18ci) JAP side-valve.

GREEN
England (London, later Bexhill) 1919–1923: This firm built water-cooled engines, mostly singles; and later converted air-cooled engines to water-cooling.

GREYHOUND
USA (Buffalo, New York) 1907–1914: These singles were rated at four-and-a-half horsepower and built by Thor.

GREYHOUND
England 1905–1907: Fafnir, Minerva and MMC engines powered the machines from this small assembler.

GRG
Italy (Turin) 1926–1927: Two 175c (11ci) Della Ferrera singles were coupled together to give a 350cc (21ci) twin.

GRI
England 1921–1922: G.R. Inshaw designed these 350cc (21ci) and 500cc (31ci) machines, built by MacRae & Dick.

GRIGG
England 1920–1925: After beginning with a 200cc two-stroke scooter, Grigg built a variety of machines up to 1000cc (61ci) with proprietary engines, both two- and four-stroke.

GRIMSHAW
England (Sunderland) 1908: This monster 2596cc (158ci) V-twin rated at 20 horsepower; it weighed only 150kg (330lb).

GRINGO
USA 1973–unknown: Motocross and flat-track machines with 248cc (15ci) and 358cc (22ci) two-stroke singles.

GRITZNER
Germany 1903 and 1950s–1970s: This sewing-machine factory briefly built Fafnir-engined machines in the pioneering period, then returned after World War II with Sachs-powered machines of 100cc (6ci), 150cc (9ci) and 175c (11ci).

GRIZZLY
Czechoslovakia (Pardubice-Skrivanek) 1925–1932: Matyasch & Polak built 250cc (15ci) two-strokes with in-house engines, and after 1929, MAG motors including overhead-cam racers.

GROSE-SPUR
England (London) 1934–1939: Grose was a dealer; and these Villiers-engined 125s were built by Carlton.

GROTE
Germany (Berlin) 1924–1925: Two or three of this firm's 307cc two-stroke singles (70x80mm) could somewhat improbably be coupled together to make a 614cc (37ci) twin or a 921cc (56ci) triple.

GRUCO
Germany 1924–1925: Kuhne engines were put into simple frames by this assembler.

GRUHN
Germany (Berlin) 1923–1932: Richard Gruhn built lightweight side-valve machines of 197cc (12ci); then two-strokes; then overhead-valve 175cc (11ci) and 197cc (12ci) machines with shaft drive.

GRUHN
Germany 1920–1926: Hugo Gruhn, brother of Richard (above), also built motorcycles.

GRUTZENA
Germany 1925–1926: Kuhne 350cc (21ci) singles powered these heavy assembled machines.

GS
Germany 1920–1924: Gustav Schulze built a 129cc (8ci) two-stroke auxiliary cycle motor that could also be supplied ready-fitted to a complete machine.

GS
Germany (Berlin) 1923–1925: Georg Schroff's machines were heavily Gruhn-based.

GS MOTORI
Italy c.1950: The Gioello two-stroke cycle motor was also sold complete with a bicycle.

GSD
England (Coventry) 1921–1923: R.E.D. Grant built two shaft-drive models: one with a White and Poppe 350cc (21ci) two-stroke, the other with a transverse-mounted Bradshaw 496cc (30ci) flat-twin.

GUARALDI
Italy 1905–1916: Began with a Fafnir (four horsepower), later other engines (two-and-three-quarters to four horsepower).

GUIA
Italy (Milan) 1950–1954: Ettore Buralli put small two-strokes (98cc/6ci to 147cc/9ci) in both conventional tubular frames and pressed-steel frames.

GUIGNARD
France (Lyon) 1933–1938: These were lightweight two-strokes of 100cc (6ci) and 125cc (8ci).

GUILLER
France 1950–late 1950s: These mopeds and lightweights, both two-stroke and four-stroke, up to 250cc (15ci), had engines from AMC, Aubier-Dunne, Junior, Vap and Ydral.

GUIZZARDI
Italy (Turin) 1926–1932: These lightweights had 125cc (8ci) and 175c (11ci) overhead-valve machines, including an overhead-cam model.

GUIZZO
Italy (Bologna) 1955–1962: Palmieri & Gulinelli made a 48cc (3ci) moped and a 150cc (9ci) scooter.

GULDNER
Germany 1925: Guldner built 350cc (21ci) and 50cc (3ci) singles that were sufficiently similar to contemporary Nortons to allow interchange of many parts.

GUSTLOFF
Germany (Suhl) 1937–1940: These mopeds were designed by Martin Stolle with 98cc (6ci) engines.

G&W
England (Liverpool) 1902–1906: Guy and Wheeler used Fafnir, Minerva and Peugeot engines.

GYS
England early 1950s: Mopeds and auxiliary cycle motors of 49cc (3ci).

HAB
Germany 1926: These German machines – which had a very shortlived career – were fitted with overhead-cam single engines of 250cc (15ci) and 350cc (21ci) capacity as their powerbase.

HACK
England 1920–23: This particular English machine from the 1920s had the appearance of a cross between a scooter and a ladies'-frame bicycle. It was fitted by the manufacturers initially with a 110cc (7ci) Simplex motor, which was in later times to become a motor of 103cc (6ci) capacity.

HADEN
England (Birmingham) 1920–24: This 1920s machine from Birmingham, England was a single model fitted with a 350cc (21ci) Precision two-stroke engine as its powerplant.

HAGEL
Germany 1925: This was a short-lived machine of the 1920s from Germany which was fitted with an in-house 247cc (15ci) capacity two-stroke engine as its powerbase.

HAI
Austria 1938: These machines were fitted with low-cost 110cc (7ci) two-stroke engines. One report suggests that these models were manufactured by using a pressed-steel frame, while another source refers to a cast frame.

HAJA
Germany 1924–25: These German machines featured Hansa single engines as their powerbase and these had been fitted into simple frames.

HAKO
Germany 1924–25: These were German motorbikes which had JAP 350cc (21ci) and 500cc (31ci) engines as their powerbase. These engines were fitted into a close copy of contemporary HRD machines. The company name came from the first two initials of the name Hans Korn.

HALUMO
Germany 1923–26: In-house engines, which were initially a 147cc (9ci) two-stroke, later 146cc (9ci) and 198cc (6ci) overhead-valve, provided the source of power for these German machines from the Weimar Republic era.

HAM
The Netherlands 1902–06: These machines from the first decade of the twentieth century were pioneer singles, fitted with two horsepower Altena motors to provide their power.

HAMILTON
England 1901–07: This firm was known as an engine-maker, and manufactured singles of two-and-a-quarter to four horsepower as well as manufacturing V-twins of four-and-a-half horsepower. It also made complete machines.

HAMPTON
England (Birmingham) 1912–14: Cross 500cc (31ci) engines were fitted into these machines as the powerbase. These machines were unusual in that they were some of the earliest users of the foot-change gearbox.

HANFLAND
Germany (Berlin) 1920–25: The in-house 147cc (9ci) two-stroke engine fitted to power these machines was supplied to the company by Flink.

HANSA
Germany (Bielefeld) 1922–26: This make was characterized by a side-valve engine of 197cc (12ci) capacity and an overhead-valve of 298cc (6ci) capacity.

HANSAN
England 1920–22: This was a firm of assemblers who were known for using Arden two-strokes and Blackburne 346cc (21ci) side-valve engines to fit into their machines. The company is also listed in some sources (probably incorrectly) under the name Hansa.

HAPAMEE
Germany 1925–26: These machines were fitted with in-house deflector-piston engines of 198cc (12ci) and 246cc (15ci) capacity as their powerplants.

HARDING–JAP
France (St Cyr) 1912–14: Englishman H.J. Harding went to live in France, where he built English-style motorcycles from English components. In particular, he was known for using the 500cc (31ci) JAP V-twin engine to power his machines.

HAREWOOD
England 1920: Two-stroke engines from Villiers and side-valve motors from Precision, which were of 269cc (16ci) and 346cc (21ci) capacity respectively, powered these machines assembled by this firm.

HARLETTE
Austria 1925–28: Puch built these split-single two-strokes of 125cc (8ci) and 175c (11ci) capacity. These machines were also sold under the name Harlette-Geco when they were assembled at Jeumont in France by Gerkinet & Co.

HARPER
England 1954–55: The Scootamobile was manufactured by this English firm, and was fitted with a 198cc (6ci) motor from Villiers as its powerbase.

HARRAS
Germany (Berlin) 1919–26: These lightweights were fitted with a Bekamo engine of 150cc (9ci) and 200cc (12ci) capacities. These engines were designed by Ruppe.

HASCHO
Germany 1923–26: Engines of 150cc (9ci) and 175c (11ci) capacities bought in from Villiers were fitted to provide the power for these lightweight machines.

HASCHUT
Germany 1929–31: These shortlived machines were fitted with Villiers engines, as was typical of many from that period. The engines were of 175c (11ci) capacity and were ensconced in a conventional frame.

HASTY
France (Aix en Provence) 1930–34: This company from the south of France was responsible for the manufacture of an auxiliary cycle motor which had a capacity of 100cc (6ci).

HAVERFORD
USA 1909–14: These American machines were primitive singles that had automatic inlet valves.

HAWEKA
Germany (Hamburg) 1923–26: These were sporting machines from Hamburg which were fitted with engines of 350cc (21ci) to 678cc (41ci) capacities bought in from JAP and MAG.

HAWKER
England (Kingston-on-Thames) 1920–23: Harry Hawker, the aviation pioneer, used a 348cc (21ci) side-valve engine from Blackburne, as well as his own 293cc (18ci) two-stroke engine to provide the powerbase for these machines.

HAXEL-JAP
England 1911–13: This was an English assembler who admitted his debt in its name to the 293cc (18ci) engine that had been fitted to power his machines.

HAZEL
England (London) 1906–11: Cripps Cycle and Motor Co. from London, England, began manufacturing its machines in the first decade of the twentieth century with singles and V-twins from Peugeot, before moving on to engines which had been bought in from JAP.

HB
England (Wolverhampton) 1919–24: The Hill Brothers used 350cc (21ci) and 500cc (31ci) side-valve and overhead-valve Blackburne engines to act as the powerbase for their motorcycles.

The Henderson four, which from 1920 had a side valve engine mounted on a heavier frame.

HEC
England 1922–23: Two-stroke engines bought in from Villiers with a capacity of 250cc (15ci) powered these machines. Despite the reliability of the engines, the machines had a shortlived career in the early 1920s.

HEC
England 1939–55: These were autocycles manufactured in England which had been fitted with 80cc (5ci) Levis two-stroke engines in order to provide the powerbase.

HECKER
Germany (Nurnberg) 1921–56: This firm followed a common path of that period, beginning manufacturing machines with its own two-stroke engines of 245cc (15ci). It went on to produce its own 350cc (21ci) overhead-valve engines; then used four-stroke singles from JAP and MAG and V-twins up to 750cc (461ci). It fitted Sachs two-strokes engines into its smaller machines. After World War II had come to an end, the company fitted its machines with Sachs and Ilo engines of various capacities, ranging from 100cc (6ci) to 250cc (15ci).

HEDLUND
Sweden 1963: This model made during 1963 seems to have been shortlived. It was a long-stroke (80x99mm/3.1x3.8in) double overhead-cam 499cc (30ci) motocross machine.

HEIDEMANN
Germany (Hanover) 1949–52: This German company produced lightweights which were fitted with engines from Fichtel & Sachs. These engines were of 98cc (6ci) capacity.

HEILO
Germany 1924–25: This firm were responsible for the manufacture of machines that were fitted with in-house two-stroke engines. These engines were produced in capacities of 120cc (7ci) and 150cc (9ci).

HELI
Germany 1923–25: This product was fitted with an in-house water-cooled 246cc (15ci) two-stroke engine, which was equipped with belt drive.

HELIOS
Germany 1921–22: This shortlived machine was lucky enough to be powered by the original 500cc (31ci) BMW M2B15 flat-twin engine, which was mounted along the frame.

HELLA
Germany (Munich) 1921–24: This south German company produced horizontal two-stroke single engines of capacities of 147cc (9ci) and 183cc (11ci).

HELLER
Germany 1923–26: This firm began manufacturing machines fitted with the 500cc (31ci) BMW M2B15 flat-twin, like the Helios. After 1924, the company used the similar, but larger, 750cc (461ci) MJ side-valve engine to power their vehicles.

HELO
Germany 1923–25: This was a two-stroke with a pumping cylinder in its crankcase, and was of a 149cc (9ci) capacity.

HELVETIA
Switzerland 1928: Universal AG from Switzerland built this 170cc (10ci) lightweight machine.

HELYETT
France (Sully-sur-Loire) 1926–55: Before World War II, this company were responsible for the manufacture of a good range. Capacities were from 100cc (6ci) upwards, and their machines included interesting V-twins (some of which were mounted transversely) of up to 750cc (461ci), as well as racers. After World War II and its commerical and logistical constraints had come to an end, the firm manufactured various mopeds and lightweights.

HEMY
France 1946: These were auxiliary cycle motors, which initially came in a capacity of 34cc, and later, in 48cc (3ci) capacity.

HENKEL
Germany 1927–32: This company took over responsiblity for the production of the 500cc (31ci) Krieger Gnadig (KG) machines after they had been dropped by Allright. Allright bought Cito, who in turn purchased the rights to manufacture the KG from the designers. After 1929, a 198cc (6ci) side-valve single engine bought in from Blackburne was used as a powerbase for the Henkels.

HENLEY
England (Birmingham, then Oldham) 1920–29: The early machines from this company were fitted with 269cc (16ci) two-strokes from Villiers and 497cc (30ci) side-valves from Blackburne for their powerbase. They were then fitted with side-valve and overhead-valve JAPs and Blackburnes of various capacities – such as those of 248cc (15ci), 293cc (18ci) and 346cc (21ci). The company name eventually changed to become New Henley in 1927, two years before production ended.

HERBI
Germany (Bad Liebwerde) 1928–32: This company offered potential customers either a machine fitted with the 198cc (6ci) side-valve engine bought in from Blackburne, or a 498cc (6ci) overhead-cam three-valve engine which had been bought in from Kuhne.

HERCULES
England (Derby) 1902: H. Butler used MMC and Minerva engines to power their machines. Other sources suggest that White and Poppe engines were possibly used as a powerbase, as well as those mentioned above.

HERDTLE-BRUNEAU
France 1902–14: Of an adventurous turn of mind, this company from France built a 264cc (16ci) parallel twin that had the advantage of being water-cooled. This appeared as early as 1913. The firm also built two-stroke V-twins, as well as one of the earliest overhead-cam singles in motorcycle history.

HERKO
Germany (Bielefeld) 1922–25: This firm was originally an engine builder who also supplied complete machines. These appeared in various capacities and types; initially a 158cc (10ci) four-stroke, and later also 122cc (7ci) and 150cc (9ci) two-stroke engines.

This is thought to be the only remaining example of the 1929 FVL 125cc (8ci).

HERKRA
Germany 1922–23: In-house 141cc (9ci) two-stroke engines powered this obscure, shortlived brand of motorcycle.

HERMA
Germany (Augsburg) 1934: These were auxiliary cycle motors of 148cc (9ci), which were manufactured by this firm in both front-wheel and rear-wheel versions.

HERMES
Germany 1922–25: This machine was fitted with a horizontal two-stroke single engine, with a capacity of 142cc (9ci).

HERMES
Germany 1924–25: JAP side-valve engines of 348cc (21ci) to 678cc (41ci) powered these shortlived machines.

HERO
India 1978– : This company were originally responsible for the manufacture of Peugeot mopeds under licence. It has been manuacturing Hero-Puch mopeds since 1988, after it bought the plant from Peugeot. The company has also been producing 98cc (6ci) Hondas, under licence.

HEROS
Germany (Zittau) 1921–29: This firm from the 1920s was responsible for the manufacture of belt-drive machines. These machines were fitted with a variety of in-house two-stroke and four-stroke engines, which included several inlet-over-exhaust designs. The swept volumes of these machines included 155cc (10ci), 185cc (11ci) and 247cc (15ci).

HEROS
Germany 1923–24: The popular DKW 142cc (9ci) two-stroke powered what was seen at the time as the 'other' Heros.

HERTHA
Germany 1924–25: These machines were produced as lightweights with 142cc (9ci) DKW motors.

HESS
Germany (Eberstadt) 1925: Germany's only air-cooled in-line four, 780cc (48ci).

HEXE
Germany (Bamberg) 1923–25: Conflicting reports when writing about these machines refer to a 500cc (31ci) side-valve single as the company's sole product, but also refer to a range that includes a cycle motor, two-strokes of 142cc (9ci) and 269cc (16ci), and a belt-drive 246cc (15ci) single.

HIEKEL
Germany (Leipzig) 1925–32: Various sources agree that these were fitted with the 350cc (21ci) three-port engine, but differ on whether the frame was a tubular or a pressed-steel one.

HILAMAN
USA (Moorestown, New Jersey) 1906–15: The initial single which this company was responsible for producing in 1906 was later supplemented by a V-twin after 1912.

HIRANA
Japan 1951–61: Hirana (also reported as Hirano) Seisakusho was responsible for the manufacture of the 78cc Popet scooter from 1951 until 1957. They also produced the 125cc (8ci) Pop Manlee from 1956 onwards; and the 175c (11ci) Earles-fork Pop Super De Luxe from 1960 onwards. Other models to come from this company ranged down to 50cc (3ci). All were two-strokes.

HIRO
Italy (Milan) late 1960s– : This firm began production of motorcycles with motocross, trials and similar machines. It soon offered a range up to capacities of 350cc (21ci).

HIRONDELLE
France (Courbevoie) 1921–26 and early 1950s: This armaments manufacturer made two-strokes, then, after a long gap in production, mopeds and a 125cc (8ci) scooter.

HIRSCH
Germany (Berlin) 1923–24: This firm from the 1920s is variously reported as using an in-house 150cc (9ci) engine to power their machines, or otherwise their own 128cc (8ci) engine and a 142cc (9ci) from DKW.

This Gori MR500 motorcrosser dates from 1980–81.

HIRTH
Germany (Stuttgart) 1923–26: These machines were built for racing. They were fitted with water-cooled two-strokes of 123cc (8ci) and 244cc (15ci) capacity, and had the advantage of ultra-light alloys.

HJ
England (Birmingham) 1920–21: Howard & Johnson used 269cc (16ci) engines in their machines. These engines were bought in from the firms Villiers and A.W. Wall (Liberty).

HJH
Wales (Neath) 1954–56: H.J. Hulsman was responsible for fitting two-strokes of 147cc (9ci), 197cc (12ci) and 247cc (15ci) into conventional frames. The engines used to power their machines were bought in from Villiers.

HKR
Germany 1925–26: The company Hako (see reference above) was later known as HKR, these initials standing for Hans Korn, Rothenburg.

HM
Sweden late 1960s: Sven Hakanson designed this extremely unusual water-cooled 500cc (31ci) (69.4x54mm) V-twin, of about 60°, with the lower cylinder pointing straight forward.

HMK
Austria 1937–38: This pre-World War II company was the manufacturer of English-style JAP-engined machines. They came in a range of capacities, of 250cc (15ci) and, possibly, even larger.

HMW
Germany 1923–28: This firm manufactured side-valve singles fitted with in-house engines.

HMW
Austria 1946–64: The Halleiner Motorenwerk began production with 49cc (3ci) auxiliary cycle motors. It later made mopeds, lightweights and even a scooter (the 75cc/5ci Bambi-Roller). All were fitted with two-stroke engines.

HOCHLAND
Germany 1926–27: This 496cc (30ci) overhead-valve flat-twin was shortlived, and made in only small numbers.

HOCKLEY
England (Birmingham) 1914–16: Two-strokes that were fitted with 269cc (16ci) engines bought in from Liberty and Villiers.

HOCO
Germany (Minden) 1924–28: Wood-framed machines made in a factory that normally produced furniture. They were fitted either two-strokes from Villiers 150cc/9ci and 250cc/15ci, or side-valves of 300cc (18ci) and 350cc (21ci) from JAP.

HOENSON
The Netherlands 1953–55: Like many firms based in the Netherlands, this began as a bicycle factory and took on a side-line in motorcycles. These were powered by 147cc (9ci) singles bought in from Sachs and 198cc (6ci) singles bought in from Ilo, as well as a 248cc (15ci) twin from Ilo.

HONE
Germany 1950s: An auxiliary two-stroke cycle motor of 48cc (3ci) capacity.

HOFFMANN
Germany (Düsseldorf) 1949–54: Hoffmann began manufacturing machines fitted with Fichtel & Sachs and Villiers two-stroke engines. After it moved on to using Ilo 250cc (15ci) engines, it was briefly responsible for making 250 and 350cc (21ci) overhead-valve flat-twins with shaft drive, which were very similar to the miniature BMWs. The firm eventually ended up making Vespas under licence.

HOLLEY
USA (Bradford, Pennsylvania) 1902–late 1910s: These machines featured belt-driven single engines with a rear-leaning cylinder. The engines were fitted by the company into a bicycle frame which had been strengthened.

HOLROYD
England 1922: This company produced sporting machines, with JAP 250 and 350cc (21ci) machines. The firm was built under the impetus of Jack Holroyd, the well-known racing motorcyclist.

HOOCK
Germany (Cologne) 1926–28: As well as importing engines from Villiers for distribution, this company were responsible for the installation of some of these engines into tits own motorcycle frames.

HORAK
Czechoslovakia 1969: This shortlived company were responsible for the manufacture of machines for motocross use. They were fitted with 250cc (15ci) desmodromic singles. The company also built a desmodromic four.

HORSY
France 1952–53: This machine was one of many scooters being produced at that time. The scooter would have been fitted with motors of 85cc (5ci) capacity.

HOSK
Japan 1955–57: The firm Nikon Kosusu Kikan was responsible for the manufacture of the 235cc (14ci) Hosk SS and the 143cc (9ci) Hosk BC-CA. Both these machines were equipped with three-speed gearboxes and both featured full suspension.

HOSKISON
England 1919–22: This company manufactured three models, and used engines bought in from three different engine-makers: a 269cc (16ci) from Villiers and 292cc (18ci) two-strokes from Union, and Blackburne 497cc (30ci) side-valves. All were fitted in conventional open frames.

HOVY
Belgium 1954: These machines were lightweights that were powered by engines bought in from Villiers. The engines came in a range of capacities, of 125cc (8ci) and 150cc (9ci), as well as 200cc (12ci).

HOWARD
England 1905–07: This machine was a fairly typical two-and-a-half horsepower pioneer. Where it was not typical was in its early attempt to employ the method of fuel injection.

H&R (R&H)
England (Coventry) 1922–25: Messrs Hailstone & Ravenhall also went under the shorter name R&H. The company was responsible for the manufacture of a 147cc (9ci) machine, which had a Villiers engine as its source of power.

H&R
Germany 1921–25: The company Hartman & Richter of Heros was responsible for the manufacture of motorcycles that were fitted with in-house engines. These engines came in various capacities, namely 155cc (9ci), 185cc (11ci) and 250cc (15ci).

HT
England 1920–22: An early, fully enclosed scooter, this was initially powered by a 292cc (18ci) Union two-stroke engine, and later a 350cc (21ci) Barr & Stroud sleeve-valve.

HUC
Germany (Berlin) 1924–25: The usual DKW two-strokes of 145cc (9ci) and 172cc (10ci) capacities powered these Max Hecker-designed machines.

HUCKE–RINNE
Germany 1924–26: Max Hucke, the racing motorcyclist, used Rinne two-stroke engines. These engines were in capacities of 124cc (8ci) and 174cc (11ci), as well as 247cc (15ci): the latter engines were noted during that period of motorcycle history for their 'total loss' method of evaporative cooling.

HUFFER
Germany 1923–25: These shortlived lightweight machines were fitted with a variety of proprietary engines in capacities of 150cc (9ci) to 200cc (12ci).

HULBERT-BRAMLEY
England 1903–06: A motorcycle powered by the Binks four-cylinder was Hulbert-Bramley's best-known product of the early days of the twentieth century. However, the company were also repsonsible for the manufacture of lightweights and three-wheelers.

HULLA
Germany (Hagen) 1925–32: This company fitted proprietary engines into their machines to provide their power. These engines were mostly two-strokes of 200cc (12ci) and 300cc capacities bought in from DKW, but the company were also known to use bought-in JAP side-valves as a powerbase.

HULSMANN
The Netherlands (Rotterdam) 1939–60s: This was yet another Dutch bicycle-maker who had a sideline in lightweight motorcycles. Their machines were powered by 123, 198 and 225cc (14ci) engines, which had been bought in from Villiers. Other sources suggest that the firm maybe also used other makers' power units in their machines.

HUMMEL
Germany 1951–54: This shortlived company is best known as a manufacturer of scooters. It has been quoted as using anything from 58cc (4ci) to 149cc (9ci), apparently bought in from Ilo. It was also responsible for the manufacture of lightweights of capacities of up to 248cc (15ci).

HURIKAN
Czechoslovakia 1947–49: Jaroslav (one source cites the name Vladislav) Vlk was responsible for the manufacture of a very nice overhead-cam 250cc (15ci) machine. Other sources suggest that the company also made machines of 350cc (21ci) capacity.

HURRICANE
Japan late 1950s–61: A 350cc (21ci) overhead-valve single was the biggest machine to come from this company. Its line-up included two-stroke lightweights of up to 250cc (15ci) capacity, as well as the Rabbit scooter of both 90 and 125cc.

HURTU
France 1903–58: This firm had a long history. It was initially better-known for the production of lightweight cars. However, before World War II it also built lightweight motorcycles, and went on to produce auxiliary cycle motors after the war.

HUSAR
Germany (Munich) 1923–25: Sources vary on the engine size used by this company: some quote either 300cc (18ci) side-valve, or 350cc (21ci) and 500cc (31ci). Whichever size was used, few of these particular machines, with their leaf rear-springs, were built.

JAC
Czechoslovakia (Horadzovice) 1929–32: J.A. Cvach built this interesting, unorthodox shaft-drive 500cc (31ci) single with pressed-steel frame and petrol tank under the saddle.

JACKSON-ROTRAX
England 1949–66: These machines had JAP 500cc (31ci) overhead-valve speedway engines in frames designed by speedway rider Alec Jackson.

JACK SPORT
France 1927–31: These machines had JAP Jack 350cc (21ci) and 500cc (31ci) singles.

JAK
Germany 1922–25: DKW (119cc/7ci to 173cc/11ci) and Bekamo 129cc (8ci) engines powered these lightweights.

JALE
Germany (Munich) 1923–25: Motorradbau Jakob Lehner built 170cc (10ci) deflector-piston machines with air- and water-cooling.

JANOIR
France c.1905–1920s: This was initially a 995cc flat-twin (in line with the frame) with three-speed gear. In 1921, it became a new, fully enclosed version.

JAVON
Germany (Nurnberg) 1929–32: J.A. Vogler was a small assembler who used 142cc (9ci) two-strokes and JAP 200cc (12ci) and 500cc (31ci) four-strokes in his own original frames.

J-BE
USA 1950s: Joe Berliner had motorcycles built in Europe, with Fichtel & Sachs engines of 100cc (6ci) and 125cc, for sale under this name. The name is also rendered Je-Be in some places.

JB-LOUVET
France (Argenteuil) 1926–30: This assembler used two-stroke Aubier Dunne engines (175cc/11ci and 250cc/15ci) and four-strokes from JAP (350cc/21ci and 500cc/31ci).

JCM
France (Vesoul) 1980s: These were original trials bikes, such as the 303 (82x58mm/3.2x2.3in) with the tank under the saddle, which used Italian TAU motors.

JD
England 1920–26: Equipped with both pedals and a clutch, this 116cc (7ci) machine was made in ladies' and gents' models.

JEAN THOMANN
France 1920–30: The smaller 100cc (6ci) and 250cc (15ci) two-strokes were fitted with Alcyon, and there was also a 500cc (31ci) overhead-valve engine with external flywheel.

JEECY-VEA
Belgium 1923–27: King Albert favoured these in-line flat-twins with proprietary engines: Coventry Victor 498cc (6ci) overhead-valve and 688cc side-valve, and Watelet 750cc (461ci) side-valve.

JEHU
England 1901–c.1910: This firm offered normal pioneer fare with MMC, Minerva and possibly their own engines of two-and-a-quarter, two-and-a-half and three horsepower.

JELINEK
Czechoslovakia (Prague) 1904-07: As well as the usual Minervas and Fafnirs, this firm also fitted Czech Orion engines.

JES
England (Birmingham) 1910–24: Before World War I, this firm produced 116cc (7ci) and 189cc (12ci) overhead-valve singles. After the war, it produced 169cc (10ci) and 247cc (15ci) two-strokes, Blackburne 250cc (15ci), 350cc (21ci) and possibly 500cc (31ci) side-valve and overhead-valve engines. It was eventually taken over by Connaught.

JESMOND
England 1899–1907: This was a typical pioneer model: strengthened cycle frames and De Dion Bouton, Sarolea and MMC engines.

JEUNET
France 1950s: This firm produced 50cc (3ci) mopeds.

JFK
Czechoslovakia 1923–26: J.F. Koch, a noted designer, manufactured this 350cc (21ci) single under his own name.

JH

England 1913–15: James Howarth used JAP and Villiers 269cc (16ci) two-strokes and a MAG V-twin.

JHC

Germany 1922–24: In-house 183cc (11ci) two-strokes powered these machines.

JNU

England (Preston) 1920–22: J. Nickson installed a 318cc (19ci) Dalm two-stroke in an open frame.

JNZ

New Zealand 1960–63: The name, Jawa New Zealand, gives the game away.

JOERNS

USA (St Paul, Minnesota) 1910–15: The Joerns-Thiem Motor Co was once well known for making singles and V-twins and, with the 1000cc (61ci) Cyclone, probably the first series-production overhead-cam V-twin.

JOHNSON

England 1920s: This auxiliary cycle motor was notable chiefly for being a 140cc (9ci) two-stroke flat-twin.

JOHNSON

USA 1923: This was an obscure 155cc (9ci) two-stroke.

JOOS

Germany 1900–07: This firm started with flat-twins then switched to singles and V-twins.

JORDAN

Canada (Toronto) 1950: Albert Jordan built this double overhead-cam 500cc (31ci) single, which does not seem to have been widely taken up in the commercial market.

JOUCLARD

France 1903–07: This conventional pioneer had a one-and-a-half horsepower single engine.

JOYBIKE

England (Birmingham) 1959–60: This was an early cross between a moped and a scooter, powered initially by a 70cc (4ci) JAP two-stroke, then later by a 50cc (3ci) Trojan.

JSL

Germany (Liegnitz) 1923–25: J. Schatzle used a 206cc (13ci) DKW engine as well as his own engines for which various capacities are reported: 132cc (8ci), 180cc (11ci) and 197cc (12ci) side-valve.

JUCKES

England (Wolverhampton) 1910–26: These were well-made machines with in-house engines, two-strokes of 269cc (16ci), 274cc (17ci) and 399cc (24ci), and a 350cc (21ci) overhead-valve single, the last of which had a form of hub-centre steering.

JUDENNE

France 1950s: These were mopeds, and the Scot scooter with its 70cc Lavelette two-stroke engine.

JUERGENSEN

Denmark 1904–World War I: This firm built Humbers under licence, which were themselves licensed from Phelon and Moore.

JUERY

France 1931–39: Before World War II, Juery built 350cc (21ci) and 490cc (30ci) machines with in-house four-strokes, and a 175c (11ci) two-stroke. Sources differ as to whether these were side-valve or overhead-valve; the firm may also have bought in Chaise engines.

JUHO

Germany 1922–24: Julius Hoflich built his own engines. One source reports 148cc (9ci) side-valve and 195cc (12ci) two-stroke, and another reports 147cc (9ci), 174cc (11ci) and 248cc (15ci) side-valves.

JULES

Czechoslovakia 1929–34: These auxiliary cycle motors of 120cc (7ci) were also sold as a package with the (otherwise unrelated) Praga bicycle.

JUNCKER

The Netherlands 1932–35: This was yet another Dutch bicycle manufacturer with a sideline in lightweights, namely 98cc (6ci) to 198cc (6ci), with Ilo and Villiers engines. This firm merged with Gazelle after World War II.

JUNCKER

France 1935–37: These were lightweights with Aubier-Dunne and Stainless two-strokes of 124cc (8ci) and 147cc (9ci) (one source gives 98cc/6ci, 123cc/8ci and 147cc/9ci).

JUNIOR

Italy (Antignano) 1924–35: Eduardo Mascagni began with his own two-stroke 350cc (21ci) single, then moved on to Blackburne 250cc (15c) and 350cc (21ci) and then JAP. Production ceased after his death in Abyssinia.

JUNO

England 1911–23: Sun made most of the frames for these machines, and engines were from Villiers, Precision, JAP or (to order) from anyone else. Capacities ranged from 147cc (9ci) (Villiers) to a 770cc (47ci) V-twin (JAP).

JUPP

England 1921–24: This 269cc (16ci) Liberty-engined machine was what might today be called a 'step through'.

JURISCH

Germany 1926–30: This firm built a water-cooled, split-single 248cc (15ci) two-stroke racer.

K

Germany (Baden-Baden) 1925: Schiele & Brucksaler built overhead-cam 350cc (21ci) and 500cc (31ci) engines with fixed heads.

K125

Russia (Kovrovsk): This was a copy of the pre-war 125cc (8ci) DKW two-stroke single.

K&K

Germany (Hanover) 1924–25: Kuhlmann & Konecke built 197cc (12ci) side-valve machines.

KADI

Germany 1924–30: This firm's big bikes used the three-valve overhead-cam 498cc (6ci) Kuchen single; their small machines used a 198cc (6ci) side-valve.

KANNON

USA 1990s–: This company were responsible for the production of the monster V6 and V8 machines with Ford and Chevrolet V6 and V8 powerplants; it used its own patented automatic transmission.

KANTO

Japan 1957–60: This machine was a modest 124cc (8ci) two-stroke.

KAPISCOOTER

Spain 1950s: This three-speed scooter was fitted with a pushrod 174cc (11ci) engine.

KAPTEIN

The Netherlands 1938–51: Originally an importer of French machines, Kaptein later produced machines with 49cc (3ci), 125cc (8ci), and 175c (11ci) engines heavily based on Motobecane. It also produced mopeds.

KARU

Germany (Stockdorf) 1922–24: These flat-twins were fitted with licence-built Bosch-Douglas or BMW engines.

KATAKURA

Japan c.1960–late 1960s: This motorcycle company built auxiliary cycle motors, mopeds and lightweights, albeit with some interesting engines (for the period), such as the Silk Sel with a 124cc (8ci) two-stroke twin.

KATAYAMA

Japan 1956: This company's only model, the Olympus King KS, had a 346cc (21ci) overhead-valve motor.

KAUBA

Austria 1953–55: This company produced scooters with 98cc (6ci) and 124cc (8ci) Rotax-Sachs engines.

KC

Germany (Magdeburg) 1921–24: Sources vary about KC: one says that Kirchheim built 114cc (7ci) two-strokes and a 500cc (31ci) machine with a BMW engine, while another refers to a 105cc (6ci) auxiliary cycle motor and a 257cc (16ci) flat-twin, both two-strokes.

KELLER

Switzerland 1930–32: Easy to work on, but old-fashioned in appearance, the 347cc (21ci) Keller with its in-house engine was not a great commercial success.

KELLY

England (Brighton) early 1920s: An odd-looking cross between a ladies'-frame bicycle, a step-through and a moped, with belt drive.

KEMPTON

England 1921–22: This firm produced lightweights and

A first generation English Kerry (1902) with a belt final drive.

scooters with 125cc (8ci) ABC engines; some sources suggest that they may have been built by ABC.

KENI

Germany (Berlin) 1921-23: This company produced two-stroke lightweights, fitted with engines of sizes given (variously) as 145cc (9ci), 158cc (10ci) and 164cc (10ci).

KENILWORTH

England 1919–24: This firm produced a belt drive scooter/step-through fitted with engines reported variously as Norman 142cc (9ci) overhead-valves, Villiers 269cc (16ci) two-strokes and JAP 293cc (18ci) side-valves. Kenilworth may also have made a conventional machine with the JAP motor.

KENZLER WAVERLEY

USA (Cambridge, Wisconsin) 1910–14: Early use of overhead-valve engines characterized these singles and V-twins, which were associated with Jefferson.

KERRY

England 1902–15 and c.1960: The first generation of these machines (1902–10) was reputedly made in Belgium with Kelecom (and possibly FN) engines for the East London Rubber Company. The next generation (1910–15) was built by Abingdon with 499cc (30ci) singles and 670cc (41ci) V-twins, and the third generation (late 1050s) were Italian-built 49cc (3ci) mopeds.

KESTREL

England 1903–04: Minerva and (possibly) MMC engines of 211cc (13ci) powered this short-lived brand.

KG

Germany (Suhl, then Cologne, then Mabendorf) 1919–32: The Krieger brothers and Franz Gnadig began with shaft-driven 503cc (31ci) inlet-over-exhaust singles, then moved on to the 499cc (30ci) overhead-valve of advanced design. These were built by the Cito works, and were followed in 1923 by a belt-drive flat-twin. Then in 1924 Cito had financial problems and were taken over by the Köln Linderthaler Metalwarenfabrik, giving rise to the Allright-KG. When production of this stopped, ex-Cito man Paul Henckel bought the machinery and rights and created the Cito-KG from 1927.

KIEFT

England (Wolverhampton) 1955–57: These 150cc (9ci) and 200cc (12ci) Sachs-engined two-stroke scooters were actually built by Hercules of Nurnberg. As a company, Kieft was better known for small, light sports and racing cars.

KILEAR

Czechoslovakia (Brno-Malomerice) 1924–26: These were largely unremarkable 250cc (15ci) two-strokes.

KINETIC

India 1972– : This firm began with licence-built Vespas and then moved on to its own-brand two-stroke mopeds, finally adding a licence-built Honda 100cc (6ci) in 1986.

KING

England 1901–07: This company used a range of engines in their machines: De Dion Bouton (shared with three wheelers, which they also made), Minerva, MMC, DAW, Antoine, Sarolea and maybe others.

KING FRAM

Sweden 1957–early 1960s: These mopeds were fitted with 49cc (3ci) engines, all from a variety of sources.

KING-JAP

Germany (Augsburg) 1928–31: This was an assembler that fitted JAP engines.

The Horex Regina was the German firm's best-seller in the immediate postwar era.

KINGSBURY

England 1919–23: This firm, a former aircraft engine works, briefly made motorcycles with its own two-stroke engines, variously described as 216cc (13ci) or 261 (16ci) and 350cc (21ci). The company also made light cars and a scooter.

KINGSWAY

England (Coventry) 1921–23: JAP 293cc (18ci) side-valve engines powered these unremarkable machines.

KITAGAWA

Japan 1955–unknown: The original four-speed overhead-valve twin shaft-drive TW 247cc (15ci) produced by this firm was similar to a Sunbeam S7, but was a smaller machine at 247cc (15ci). Kitagawa's 1956 Liner 250 was a 248cc (15ci) overhead-valve single, again with shaft drive, and Earles forks; and the Liner Crown was a 125cc (8ci) model.

KLOTZ

Germany (Stuttgart) 1923–26: These up-to-date two-strokes (variously reported as 200cc/12ci and 246cc/15ci) were promoted by racing successes. However, despite receiving this attention, they never sold very well.

KM

Germany 1924–26: KM produced two-stroke machines fitted with 142cc (9ci) and 159cc (10ci) engines built in-house.

KMB

Germany (Cologne) 1923–26: The Kölner Motorradwerk Becker built motorcycles with its own 249cc (15ci) two-stroke and 350cc (21ci) and 500cc (31ci) JAP and Blackburne motors, although one source contradicts this and says that all motors were four-stroke, and all were in-house.

KMS

Germany 1922–24: Unusually, the in-house 196cc (12ci) overhead-valve single was the bigger machine, while a bought-in Grade 142cc (9ci) two-stroke completed the range.

KOBO

Germany (Barmen-Hatzfeld) mid–1920s: Kohler and Bolenkamp were a well-known chain manufacturer who briefly made a machine powered by an in-house 276cc (17ci) two-stroke engine.

KOCH

Czechoslovakia 1934–35: These machines were advanced 348cc (21ci) overhead-cam singles that came from J.F. Koch, who had been formerly employed as chief designer at Praga (see also JFK).

KOEHLER–ESCOFFIER

France 1912–57: The first company to build overhead-cam V-twins in large numbers, with its own in-house 996cc (61ci), it also made an in-house overhead-cam 500cc (31ci) single and bought-in 350cc (21ci) and 500cc (31ci) Chaise and MAG overhead-valve engines, a 300cc (18ci) side-valve and 250cc (15ci) Villiers two-strokes. After World War II, it brought out Villiers-powered models of 100cc (6ci) or 125cc (8ci), 175cc (11ci) and 250cc (15ci).

KOFA

Germany 1923–25: This assembler used bought-in 283cc (17ci) two-stroke engines.

KOHOUT

Czechoslovakia 1904–06: This company was the first Czech motorcycle maker, using two-and-three-quarters horsepower Minerva and Fafnir engines to power its machines.

KOLIBRI

Germany 1923–30: The Kolibri (Hummingbird) was an auxiliary two-stroke cycle motor of 110cc (7ci), and was also available ready-built into a bicycle.

KOMAR

Poland c.1958–68: These machines were 50cc (3ci) mopeds.

KOMET

Germany 1902–05: This company was originally a bicycle manufacturer which branched out into motorcycles. Under licence, it was responsible for manufacturing Ixion two-stroke engines of one to four horsepower.

KOMET

Russia 1950s: These were racers with 500cc (31ci) flat-twins and shaft drive. The Komet 2 was solo; Komet 3, chair.

KONDOR

Germany 1924–25: These machines were available with a choice of Ideal side-valve (3 horsepower) engines or Simplex two-stroke (three-and-a-half horsepower) engines.

KOSTER (KS)

Germany (Schwerin) 1923–25: This was an odd looking machine with a hybrid tubular/pressed-steel frame, powered by 123cc (8ci) Bekamo or 144cc (9ci) Cockerell two-strokes.

KOVROVETZ

Russia (Kovrov) early 1960s: This had a hybrid tubular/pressed-steel frame and two-stroke power: the 175c (11ci) engine gave eight horsepower at 5000rpm. There was also a 125cc (8ci) model.

KR

Germany (Munich) 1924–25: This company produced flat-twins with BMW engines, and an MAG 998cc (6ci) V-twin. Sources suggest it was related to Karu.

KR

Germany (Munich) 1922–24 or 1930–33: Karl Ritzinger

---

assembled limited numbers of machines. Sources differ on the dates and motors. Once source says 150cc (9ci) two-stroke; another, 200cc (12ci) and 250cc (15ci) four-strokes.

KRAM-IT

Italy (Arcore) late 1970s–unknown: These were trials and similar machines with engines from Minarelli (50cc/3ci and 80cc.5ci) and Rotax (125cc/8ci and 250cc/15ci, and later 300cc (18ci)). The firm later adopted the HRD name to make sporting machines.

KRASNY-OKTOBR

Russia 1930–34: Sold under this name, the Red October was heavily based on the contemporary DKW, with a 296cc (18ci) engine. They were the first large-production machines in the history of Soviet motorcycles.

KRIEGER (ORIGINAL KRIEGER)

Germany 1925–26: The Krieger brothers of KG fame built various KG-like machines. These included their own shaft-drive 500cc (31ci) and a Blackburne 350cc (21ci). They were also known to have supplied frames to other manufacturers.

KROBOTH

Germany (Seestal-Lech) 1949–54: These were scooters with Sachs engines of 100cc (6ci) to 175cc (11ci) and were built by Czech ex-racer Gustav Kroboth.

KRS

Germany (Berlin) 1921–26: This company was yet another small assembler among many at that time. Sources differ on exactly which proprietary engines were used by this firm.

KRUPP

Germany (Essen) 1919–21: An unsuccessful scooter, with 185cc (11ci) and 198cc (6ci) engines mounted over the front wheel, from the famous steel and weapons group.

KSB

Germany 1924–29: This firm of assemblers installed various engines (including DKW, Kuhne, Blackburne and JAP) of capacities from 150cc (9ci) to 500cc (31ci) in its own frames.

KUHNE

Germany 1928–29: This firm produced overhead-valve 350cc (21ci) and 500cc (31ci) engines, and later produced a desmo.

KULI

Germany (Berlin) 1922–24: This firm was a typical assembler of 150cc (9ci) and 200cc (12ci) two-strokes.

KUMFURT

England (Rise) 1914–16: Villiers 269cc (16ci) two-strokes and Precision singles and V-twins powered these Berkshire-built machines.

KURIER

Germany (Berlin) 1921–24: Unusually, this firm built its own 150cc (9ci) two-strokes and also supplied engines to assemblers.

KURRAS

Germany 1925–27: Bekamo 173cc (11ci) two-strokes powered these slightly sporty machines.

KV

Germany 1924–27: In-house overhead-valve singles of 200cc (12ci) and 250cc (15ci) powered these unremarkable bikes.

KYNAST

Germany (Quackenbruk) c.1950s: These machines were robust mopeds with two-speed auto transmission.

KYNOCH

England (Birmingham) 1912–13: This firm, a manufacturer of ammunition, may have used its own engines, but probably

---

bought them in; singles (500cc/31ci) and V-twins (770cc/47ci).

KZ

Germany 1924–25: Franz Gnadig (KG, above) designed these machines with 200cc (12ci) side-valve engines from Alba and 348cc (21ci) overhead-valve engines from Kuhne.

L-300

Russia 1932–1940s: The military favoured these DKW-based 294cc (18ci) and 346cc (21ci) two-strokes and 350cc (21ci) four-strokes.

L&C

England (London) 1904–05: Engines from De Dion Bouton, Minerva and Antoine powered these assembled machines.

LABOR

France 1908–60: Initially a 350cc (21ci) single, the name resurfaced with Alcyon, with two-stroke lightweights, a four-stroke moped and, in 1954, an overhead-cam 250cc (15ci).

LADETTO (LADETTO & BLATTO)

Italy (Turin) 1923–32: Emilio and Giovanni Ladetto began with 125cc (8ci) two-strokes. After Angelo Blatto joined them in 1927, other engines were added, including a 175c (11ci) overhead-valve four-stroke and a 250cc (15ci) side-valve.

LADIES PACER

England (Guernsey) 1914: A Gloucester-built JES engine powered this open (ladies') frame machine.

LADY

Belgium (Sainte Mariaberg) 1925–38: Conventional machines fitted with various proprietary engines: Blackburn, JAP, MAG, Rudge Python and Villiers, from 175cc (11ci) to 500cc (31ci).

LAFOUR & NOUGIER

France (Nimes) 1927–36: This company's own frames had 100cc (6ci) to 500cc (31ci) engines from Aubier-Dunne, JAP, Train, and Villiers.

LA FRANCAISE

France 1936–50s: Before World War II, this firm made lightweights and machines of 100cc (6ci) to 350cc (21ci), two- and four-stroke; afterwards, a 100cc (6ci) lightweight; then (in 1948) a 49cc (3ci) pushrod engine; four-stroke lightweights of 169cc (10ci) and 175c (11ci), in 1949; and in 1953 a 250cc (15ci) overhead-cam motorcycle.

LAG

Austria 1921–29: Liesinger Motorenfabrik AG began with 118cc (7ci) and 148cc (9ci) auxiliary cycle motors, moved on briefly to a 250cc (15ci) two-stroke motorcycle; and then made a 350cc (21ci) two-stroke from 1927.

LA GALBAI

Italy 1921–25: All machines were powered by in-house two-strokes: 276cc (17ci), 301cc (18ci), 347cc (21ci) singles and a 492cc (30ci) V-twin.

LAGONDA

England (Staines) 1902–05: This firm made three-wheelers, then motorcycles with De Dion Bouton and Minerva engines, then cars.

L'ALBA

Italy (Milan) 1924–26: Versions of 198cc (6ci) side-valve machines came from Alba.

LA LORRAINE

France 1922-25: Unusually, this firm's own two-strokes powered these 98cc (6ci) to 250cc (15ci) lightweights.

LAMPO

Italy 1925–30: Initially this firm produced two-stroke 98cc

First made in 1946, the rigid-framed Indian Chief was outdated in the post-war market.

(6ci) lightweights; then, after 1926, two- and four-strokes of 125cc (8ci), 175cc (11ci), 200cc (12ci) and 250cc (15ci). In 1928, a new pushrod 250cc (15ci) in Comfort, Supersport and Super Comfort versions appeared.

LANCER

England (Coventry) 1904–05: This firm used two to three-and-a-half horsepower Minerva and MMC engines.

LANCER

Japan 1957–early 1960s: First a two-stroke lightweight, then a 250cc (15ci) transverse pushrod V-twin with shaft drive.

LANCO

Austria (Vienna) 1922–26: The Erdburger Maschinenfabrik was better known for steam reciprocating engines and turbines. MAG motors up to 1000cc (61ci) V-twins supplemented its own 569cc (35ci) single, in side-valve Touring and pushrod Sports versions.

LANDI

Italy 1923–26: Lamberto Landi used either a Train engine, or his own 122cc (7ci) and 172cc (10ci) two-strokes.

LANGFORD

America 1915: This was an late steam-motorcycle; the con-rods worked directly on the rear wheel.

LA PANTHERRE

France 1928–32: JAP engines of 350cc (21ci) and 500cc (31ci) powered these conventional machines.

LAPIERRE

France 1950s: These were mopeds with 50cc (3ci) engines.

LAPIZE

France 1930–37: Assembling used Aubier-Dunne, LMP, JAP and possibly other engines of 100cc (6ci) to 500cc (31ci).

LARDORI

Italy (Castellina) 1925: This firm assembled from Train 350cc (21ci) motors, Ideal three-speed gearboxes, and Druid forks.

LATSCHA

France 1948–53: This firm fitted Aubier-Dunne two-strokes (98 and 123cc (8ci)) or JAP four-strokes (350cc/21ci and 500cc/31ci).

LAURENTI

Italy (Bologna) 1956–unknown: An overhead-cam 173cc (11ci) engine of its own design powered their machines.

LAVALETTE

France 1952–unknown: This firm produced mopeds of 48cc (3ci) and 65cc (4ci), and 70cc (4ci) scooters and lightweights, often with automatic transmission.

L'AVENIR

Belgium 1959– : These mopeds had HMW or Fichtel & Sachs engines.

LAZZATI

Italy (Milan) 1899–1904: An early Italian manufacturer, fitting De Dion Bouton engines into strengthened bicycle frames.

LDR

Germany 1922–25: This basic 548cc (33ci) side-valve had an external flywheel. It was chain/belt drive, then later all-chain.

LEA FRANCIS
England (Coventry) 1911–26: Until 1920, this firm used JAP and MAG V-twins; after that, MAG only. Capacities of 500cc (31ci) to 750cc (461ci). George Bernard Shaw rode a Leaf.

LEBELT
Germany 1924–25: These were powered by two-strokes and four-strokes of up to four-and-three-quarters horsepower.

LECCE
Italy 1930–32: The head of Lecce, Otello Albanese, modified 173cc (11ci) Moser engines with 'go-faster' cylinder heads and put them in his own sporting frames.

LE FRANCAISE-DIAMANT
France 1912–59: This firm was a part of Alcyon: 100cc (6ci) to 500cc (31ci) models came before World War II, two-strokes up to 250cc (15ci) after it.

LEGNANO
Italy (Milan) 1954–68: This firm initially made mopeds with Sachs, Minarelli and Mosquito motors, later (1967) supplementing them with a 175c (11ci) motocross machine.

LE GRIMPEUR
France (Paris) c1900–32: This firm made large-capacity machines, V-twins with engines from Aubier-Dunne, Chaise, JAP, MAG and Stainless. Some smaller machines were also made until tit was bought out by Dresch.

LEIFA
Germany 1924–25: Improbably, a former shipyard built these 148cc (9ci) side-valve lightweights.

LELIOR
France 1922–24: This firm made a 174cc (11ci) flat-twin and a two-stroke single resembling the Evans.

LEM
Italy 1974: These were mopeds and mini-bikes for young riders.

LENOBLE
Belgium 1954: Built the fully enclosed Kontiki scooter.

LEONARD
England (London) 1903–06: Fafnir, Minerva and MMC engines powered these typical pioneers.

LEONARDO FRERA
Italy (Tradate) 1930–34: Typical JAP-engined machines of 173cc (11ci) to 348cc (21ci) in Italo-English style.

LEONE
Italy (Turin) 1948–mid-1950s: This firm produced initially a 50cc (3ci) two-stroke, later a 75cc (5ci) lightweight.

LEOPARD
Germany (Magdeburg-Neustadt) 1921–26: This is variously reported as a one-model company making a 300cc (18ci) two-stroke, or as offering a choice of 250cc (15ci) and 350cc (21ci), initially two-stroke, later four-stroke.

LEPROTTO
Italy (Turin) 1951–54: These were singles of 125cc (8ci), 160cc (10ci) and 200cc (12ci), two-stroke and four-stroke.

LETHBRIDGE
England 1922–23: These were Villiers-powered assembled two-strokes of 247cc (15ci) and 269cc (16ci).

LETO
Germany 1926–28: Rinne two-strokes of 173cc (11ci) and 198cc (6ci) powered these Lehmann-designed machines with their pressed-steel frames.

LE VACK
England 1923: Bert Le Vack, the racer, built these JAP-powered overhead-valve 350cc (21ci) singles.

LEVANTE
Germany (Hamburg) 1954: Five hundred of these 38cc (2ci) Rex-engined scooter-type mopeds were built.

LEVRON
France 1951–53: This was a two-stroke lightweight.

LFG
Germany 1921–25: Luftfahrzeug GmbH switched from airships to a 164cc (10ci) auxiliary cycle motor and a streamlined 305cc (19ci) two-stroke.

LGC
England (Birmingham) 1926–32: Known for three-wheel light delivery vehicles, the Leonard Gundle Motor Co used Villiers engines (247cc/15ci) and JAP singles (293cc/18ci) side-valve, 346cc/21ci side-valve and overhead-valve) in its bikes.

LIAUDOIS
France 1923–27: These were lightweights with Train 100cc (6ci) and 175c (11ci) engines.

LIBELLE
Germany 1950-52: These scooters were powered by Ilo 98cc (6ci) or 118cc (7ci) engines.

LIBERATOR
France (Paris) 1902–20: This firm began with Sarolea engines and later switched to JAP.

LIBERIA
France (Grenoble) 1920–65: This firm made lightweights with Aubier-Dunne engines up to 250cc (15ci), then mopeds.

LILIPUT
Germany 1923–26: This assembler used a range of proprietary engines: DKW, Baumi, Gruhn, and Namapo.

LILLIPUT
Italy 1899–06: These were strengthened bicycle frames with 285cc (17ci) motors.

LILY
England 1906–14: Assembled 270–500cc (16–31ci) bikes with Villiers, Cross (TDC) and possibly Minerva engines.

LINCOLN-ELK
England (Lincoln) 1902–24: Kirby & Edwards singles had 349cc (21ci), 402cc (24ci), 499cc (30ci) and 597cc (36ci); there was also a 770cc (47ci) V-twin, more successful before World War I than after it.

LINER see KITAGAWA

LINSER
Austria-Hungary, later Czechoslovakia (Reichenberg, later known as Liberec) 1904–10: This firm began with its own 500cc (31ci) single of three-and-a-half horsepower, and later used a 620cc (38ci) V-twin of four-and-a-half horsepower, under the trademark Zeus.

LINSNER
Germany 1922–24: This assembler bought in in-line Bosch-Douglas and BMW engines.

LINTO
Italy 1965–68: Lino Tonti based his six-speed road-racing 500cc (31ci) twins on the Aermacchi Ala d'Oro 250 single.

LION–RAPIDE
Belgium 1936-53: The smaller bikes (98cc/6ci to 247cc/15ci) were powered by Villiers engines, and the 350cc (21ci) by a 347cc (21ci) FN.

LITO
Sweden (Helsingborg) 1959–65: These motocross machines had modified BSA and Husqvarna 500cc (31ci) overhead-valve singles.

LITTLE GIANT
England 1913–15: This assembler used Precision engines: 225cc (14ci) two-stroke, 199cc (12ci) four-stroke.

LLOYD
Germany 1923–26: Initially an auxiliary cycle motor of 137cc (8ci), they became JAP-engined motorcycles of 293cc (18ci), 346cc (21ci) and 490cc (30ci).

LLOYD
The Netherlands 1930–31: This assembler used DKW 198cc (6ci) two-stroke engines and Hulla pressed-steel frames.

LMP
France 1921–31: As well as supplying engines to others, LMP made complete motorcycles: two-strokes of 173cc (11ci) and 248cc (15ci), and side-valve and overhead-valve singles of 250cc (15ci) to 500cc (31ci).

LMS
Germany 1923: This manufacturer made odd-looking machines with 142cc (9ci) DKW engines.

LOCOMOTIEF
The Netherlands 1957–66: These were mopeds with Pluvier and Sachs engines of 49cc (3ci).

LOHNER
Austria 1950–58: This firm made scooters and mopeds from 49cc (3ci) to 200cc (12ci) with engines from Ilo, Sachs and Rotax.

LOMOS
Germany 1922–24: This scooter had a pressed-steel frame and 142cc (9ci) DKW motor.

LORD
Germany (Munich) 1929–31: The name of this 200cc (12ci) JAP-engined lightweight reflected the high regard in which British machines were held in Europe.

LORENZ
Germany 1921–25: This auxiliary cycle motor, a two-stroke flat-twin, was also supplied as a complete machine.

LOUIS CLEMENT
France 1920–32: Overhead-cam V-twins of 600cc (37ci) and 1000cc (61ci) of its own design gave way after 1928 to 100cc (6ci) two-strokes.

LUCIFER
France (Paris) 1928-56: Mestre & Blatge built the other Prince of Darkness with a range of proprietary engines up to 500cc (31ci) bought-in from Train, MAG and Chaise.

LUGTON
England 1912–14: Precision and JAP engines powered these 500cc (31ci) singles.

LUTRAU
Germany (Walldorf) 1924–33: Ludwig Traunspurger GmbH built two-strokes of 200cc (12ci), 250cc (15ci) and 350cc (21ci), and side-valve machines of 350cc (21ci) and 500cc (31ci), with in-house engines.

LUTZ
Germany (Braunschweig-Kralenreide) 1949–54: This firm produced scooters and motorized bicycles of 50cc (3ci) and 60cc (4ci), and an Ilo-engined 175c (11ci) scooter.

LUWE
Germany (Freiburg) 1924–28: Ludwig Weber's frames carried bought-in 150cc (9ci) singles to 750cc (461ci) V-twins from Blackburne, JAP, Kuhne and MAG.

LVOVJANKA
Soviet Union 1962– : This firm produced two-stroke mopeds of 49cc (3ci) capacity.

MABECO
Germany (Berlin) 1923-27: Max Bernhard & Co. began with more or less straight copies of the Indian Scout at 600cc (37ci) and 750cc (461ci), with engines built by Siemens & Halske, but after a lawsuit from Indian the company was dissolved and reformed as Mabeco. In this guise it made 996cc (61ci) overhead-valve V-twins for racing and Garelli-licensed 350cc (21ci) split singles.

MABON
England (London) 1904–10: These were pioneer fare with MMC and Fafnir engines in strengthened bicycle frames.

MACAL
Portugal 1980s: These were mopeds and lightweights, including trials-type machines with 50cc (3ci) engines.

MABRET
Germany 1927–28: This assembler used Kuhne side-valve and overhead-valve engines of 350cc (21ci) and 500cc (31ci).

MACKLUM
England 1920–22: This scooter was fitted with a Union (or possibly Peco) two-stroke engine of 292cc (18ci) capacity.

MACO
Germany 1921–26: Maco made two-stroke machines with DKW engines, and side-valve machines with its own 200cc engine.

MACQUET
France (Paris) 1951–54: Ydral two-strokes powered these 125cc (8ci) and 175cc (11ci) machines.

MADC
Switzerland 1901–05: This firm was the manufacturer of the Motosacoche auxiliary cycle motor, which was known as the forerunner of MAG.

MAFA
Germany (Marienberg) 1923–27: This German firm was a bicycle factory that diversified into motorcycles with 120cc (7ci) to 250cc (15ci) two-strokes from DKW and 350cc (21ci) and 500cc (31ci) four-stroke engines from Kuhne.

MAFALDA
Italy 1923–28: This company manufactured sports machines powered by in-house two-stroke engines, and possibly four-strokes, of 125cc (8ci) and 175cc (11ci).

MAGATY
France 1931–37: This auxiliary cycle motor was a 200cc (12ci) two-stroke.

MAGDA
France 1933–36: This firm made lightweight motorcycles with 100cc (6ci) and 125cc (8ci) Train and Stainless two-stroke power units.

MAGNAT-MOSER
France (Grenoble) 1906–14: Moser engines (up to 750cc/461ci) were fitted in frames from this branch of Magnat-Debon.

MAGNEET
The Netherlands 1955 to early 1970s: These mopeds were fitted with 50cc (3ci) Sachs motors.

The Koëhler-Escoffier 350cc (21ci) 4-speed Model KPS 47.

The Levis Model K. Levis was an English company which produced bikes from 1911 to 1940.

MAGNET

Germany (Berlin) 1903–24: This firm produced unusual-looking machines with low frames and smaller-than-usual wheels. Their machines were powered by Adler, Minerva and Fafnir motors as well as Magnet's own V-twins. The company never really recovered from the economic hardships produced by World War I.

MAGNI

Italy 1928–30: Luigi Magni built a 500cc (31ci) vertical single and a 350cc (21ci) overhead-cam parallel twin with the cylinders pointing forwards.

MAINO

Italy (Alessandria) 1902–10 and 1945–50s: Initially, Giovanni Maino used Souverain two-and-a-quarter horsepower engines, then engines of his own manufacture. After a 35-year gap, he re-entered the market with lightweights that were powered by Mosquito, Sachs and NSU engines, from capacities of 38 to 150cc (9ci).

MAJESTIC

Belgium 1928–31: JAP 350cc (21ci) and 500cc (31ci) engines powered these English-style machines.

MAJESTIC

France (Chutenay) 1929–33: Original pressed-steel frames from this firm housed JAP and Chaise singles, JAP twins up to 1000cc (61ci) and the 500cc (31ci) Chaise four-cylinder.

MAJESTIC

England (Birmingham) 1931–35: These were basically pre-Matchless AJS machines that were assembled at the OK Supreme factory from parts left over after the Matchless take-over.

MAJOR

Italy (Turin) 1947–48: Salvatore Majorca used a 350cc (21ci) engine of his own design to power this shaft-drive, fully enclosed machine.

MAMMUT

Germany (Nurnberg, later Bielefeld) 1923–32, then 1952–60: Originally, Mammut made lightweights with 200cc (12ci), 250cc (15ci) and 300cc (18ci) two-stroke engines. Then, at the new Bielefeld works, they produced mopeds of 49cc (3ci) and lightweights and scooters of 125cc (8ci) to 198cc (6ci) fitted with Fichtel & Sachs and Ilo motors.

MAMOF

Germany 1922–24: As well as 150cc (9ci) Grade and DKW two-strokes, Mamof lightweights were also powered by its own 155cc (9ci) side-valves.

MANET

Czechoslovakia (Povazska Bystrica) 1948–67: Initially, this company produced a lightweight with a 90cc (5ci) split single engine which had been designed by Vincenz Sklenar. Later, they manufactured two-stroke scooters of 125cc (8ci).

MANON

France (Courbevoir) 1903–06: This firm produced the usual pioneer stuff: strengthened bicycle frames, and a one-and-a-quarter horsepower engine.

MANTOVANI

Italy (Milan) 1902–10: This firm produced lightweight machines with engines of its own make from one-and-a-half horsepower to four horsepower, some water-cooled.

MANUFRANCE

France 1951–55: This company manufactured lightweights of 125cc (8ci) and 175c (11ci) and two-stroke 125cc (8ci) scooters.

MANURHIN

France 1955–62: This company took over (and improved) the DKW Hobby scooter, fitting a 75cc (5ci) two-stroke.

MARATHON

USA 1910: This was a two-stroke with shaft drive; however, sources differ on whether it was a single or a twin.

MARC

France (Vincennes) 1926–51: This firm produced English-looking machines of 250cc (15ci) to 500cc (31ci) with Staub-JAP, JAP and LMP engines.

MARCK

Belgium 1904–08: In-house 500cc (31ci) inlet-over-exhaust singles powered these pioneers.

MARIANI

Italy 1930–34: Mariani was a 500cc (31ci) side-valve of unique design, in two-valve and three-valve versions, and for petrol or diesel.

MARIANI

Italy 1924–28: This was a two-stroke lightweight: however, sources differ on whether it was 125cc (8ci) or 175c (11ci).

MARLOE

England (Birmingham) 1920–22: This was a small assembler of 350cc (21ci) Precision- and Blackburne-engined machines, and 500cc (31ci) machines with Blackburn engines.

MARLOW

England (Warwick) 1920–22: These machines were mostly Villiers 269cc (16ci) powered, but 350cc (21ci) and 500cc (31ci) JAP engines were available to order.

MARMAN

USA 1940s: A belt-drive, two-stroke flat-twin 110cc (7ci) moped.

MARMONNIER

France (Lyon) 1947–51: These two-stroke lightweights were fitted with 125cc (8ci) and 175c (11ci) Aubier-Dunne engines.

MARS

England 1905–08: These machines were essentially Fafnir and Minerva engines in strengthened bicycle frames.

MARS

England (Coventry) 1923–26: These well-made and assembled machines were fitted with a saddle tank as early as 1923. Engines came from Villiers, JAP, Barr & Stroud and Bradshaw, and maybe others, and were mostly 250cc (15ci) and 350cc (21ci).

MARSEEL

England (Coventry) 1920–21: This scooter had a horizontal 232cc single.

MARSH

USA (Brockton, Massachusetts) 1901–20: From the start, in these machines, the engine and the frame were considered as a whole, and in the 1902 model, the 244cc (15ci) single was integrated with the saddle-post tube in a machine that weighed 40kg (88lb). After the company took over Metz, its machines were known as MM, which stood for Marsh-Metz.

MARTIN

England (London) 1911–22: Harry Martin, the racer, put 97km (60 miles) into the hour with a 250cc (15ci) JAP-engined bike at Brooklands in 1909 and went into production a few years later with engines up to 500cc (31ci) from JAP and Precision.

MARTIN

Japan 1956–61: This firm manufactured motorcycles up to 250cc (15ci); the 250H was a 244cc (15ci) two-stroke twin.

MARTINA

Italy (Turin) 1930s: JAP 175c (11ci) engines were fitted as standard, but others could also be ordered.

MARTIN-JAP

England (London) 1929–57: A maker of speedway machines, fitted with JAP 350cc (21ci) and 500cc (31ci) motors.

This photograph shows the 1975 model offroad 50cc (3ci) Milani Metro Cross.

MARTINSHAW

England 1923–24: The Bradshaw oil-cooled 350cc (21ci) engine powered this rare machine from England.

MARVEL

USA 1910–13: Singles and V-twins supplied by Glenn Curtiss.

MAS

Germany 1923–24: Made small (183cc/11ci) two-stroke engines.

MASCOTTE

France 1923–24: These were lightweights fitted with in-house, 175c (11ci) side-valves.

MASON & BROWN

England 1904–08: Mainly Minerva engines – but also De Dion-Bouton and Antoine – powered these pioneers.

MASSARINI

Italy (Piacenza) 1923–24: These were lightweights fitted with 125cc (8ci) and 175c (11ci) four-strokes.

MASSEY (MASSEY-ARRAN)

England 1920–31: E.J. Massey, who also designed the first HRD machines (see above), assembled bikes under his own name using Villiers, JAP, Bradshaw and Blackburne engines.

MAT

Czechoslovakia (Prague) 1929–30: This was a four, consisting of two coupled twins, like a Square Four. The 500cc (31ci) MAT also had shaft drive.

MATADOR

England 1922–27: Bert Houlding designed these 350cc (21ci) machines fitted with bought-in oil-cooled engines from Bradshaw and air-cooled engines from Blackburne.

MATADOR

Germany 1925–26: These lightweights were fitted with in-house, 269cc (16ci) motors.

MATRA

Hungary 1938–47: Laszlo Urbach used 100cc (6ci) and 200cc (12ci) two-strokes from Fichtel & Sachs and Ardie.

MAURER

Germany (Nurnberg) 1922–26: Ludwig Maurer began with an auxiliary cycle motor, then moved on to a 250cc (15ci) two-stroke single and a 500cc (31ci) two-stroke, water-cooled flat twin, mounted in line. On the latter, lengths of the inlet tracts from the single carburettor to the two cylinders were unequal.

MAV

Italy 1951 to mid-1960s: Motori Ausiliari Velocipedi built auxiliary cycle motors: these were initially the 45cc (3ci) Jolly, then, after 1955, a 49cc (3ci) model.

MAVISA

Spain (San Cugat) 1957–60s: This two-stroke 250cc (15ci) twin had shaft drive and automatic transmission.

MAWI

Germany (Swinemunde) 1923–30: The Norddeutsche Motor-Fahrradwerk Marquardt & Winter used JAP singles of 200cc (12ci), 300cc (18ci) and 500cc (31ci), and 750cc (461ci) and 1000cc (61ci) V-twins from the same firm, or, according to one source, 142cc (9ci) and 175c (11ci) DKW two-strokes and JAP singles (not twins) up to capacities of 546cc (33ci).

MAX

England 1907: Claude Johnson, later of Rolls-Royce, installed a two-and-a-half horsepower Triumph engine in this forerunner of a scooter, with belt drive.

MAX

Germany (Berlin-Schoeneberg) 1924–25: Auto-Motor-Industrie built its own 180cc (11ci) two-stroke and 446cc (27ci) side-valve singles to power its bikes.

MAX

France 1927–30: This assembler used engines of 100cc (6ci) to 500cc (31ci) from a variety of sources.

MAXIM

England (London) 1919–21: A Dalm two-stroke of 318cc (19ci) powered this unremarkable machine.

MAXIMA

Italy (Voghera) 1920–25: The Firma Nazionale Motocicli Maxima, also known as Officine Meccaniche Carminati, began with a 680cc (41ci) flat twin mounted in line, and added a 750cc (461ci) shortly before its disappearance.

MAXWELL

Netherlands 1954: These mopeds were fitted with 50cc (3ci) HMW engines.

MAY BROS

England (Wolverhampton) 1903–06: These were pioneers who installed De Dion-Bouton, Minerva and other engines.

MAZOYER

France 1950–54: The only model from this firm seems to have been an English-style 500cc (31ci) overhead-valve single capable of delivering a comfortable 25 horsepower at 5000rpm.

MAZZILI

Italy (Milan) 1970s: These were off-road 125cc (8ci) racers which were fitted with Sachs two-stroke engines.

MAZZUCHELLI

Italy 1925–28: A 198cc (6ci) Alba powered this lightweight machine.

MB

Czechoslovakia (Prague) 1927–28: Milos Bondy built this rotary-valve 500cc (31ci), which was supplanted by the Mat (see reference listed above).

MB

USA (Buffalo, NY) 1916–20: This machine was an early 750cc (461ci) parallel twin with shaft drive.

MBA

Italy 1976–80s: Morbidelli of Pesaro and Benelli of Urbino collaborated first on a 125cc (8ci) racer, then a 125cc (8ci), along with Sachs-engined mopeds.

MBM

Italy (Cesena) 1974–81: These were mopeds and light scooters which had been fitted with 50cc (3ci) engines.

MBR

Italy (Bologna) 1924–26: This machine was a motorized bicycle fitted with a 124cc (8ci) two-stroke engine.

MC

Czechoslovakia (Prague) 1924–27: This was a heavy, well-built side-car hauler which was powered by a 1000cc (61ci) side-valve JAP V-twin engine.

MCB

Sweden 1960–75: Monark Crescent Bolaget could trace its ancestry back to 1902 through various company incarnations, but it made mainly mopeds and lightweights with two-stroke engines from Sachs and Franko-Morini.

MCC

England (London) 1903–10: Motor Castings Ltd built engines under Minerva licence, and bought in engines from other manufacturers as well.

MCKECHNIE

England (Coventry) 1922: A Coventry-Victor 688cc (42ci) flat twin powered this well-made machine.

MCKENZIE

England (London) 1921–25: Although McKenzie was based in Shaftesbury Avenue, its 169cc (10ci) two-strokes were manufactured in Coventry by Hobart.

MDS

Italy (Milan) 1955–60: The Scoccimaro brothers began manufacturing an 65cc (4ci) overhead-valve lightweight. They then progressed to 70cc (4ci), 75cc (5ci) and even 80cc (5ci), as well as making a 65cc (4ci) scooter.

MEAD

England (Birmingham) 1922–24: Engines from Precision, Villiers and Wall, of one-and-three-quarters horsepower to three-and-three-quarters horsepower drove these assembled machines.

MEAD
England (Liverpool) 1911–16: Precision supplied 200cc (12ci), 500cc (31ci) and 600cc (37ci) singles; JAP provided 300cc (18ci) singles; and the 750cc (46ci) and 1000cc (61ci) V-twins were fitted with Premier engines. Premier may also have built the machines for the company.

MECCANICA NVB
Italy (Milan) 1956–57: These machines from this Italian firm were lightweights with two-stroke motors of 50cc (3ci) and 150cc (9ci) capacity, and also 125cc (8ci) four-strokes.

MEIHATSU
Japan 1953–61: These Japanese machines of the 1950s were fitted with two-stroke singles and twins of 125cc (8ci) and 250cc (15ci).

MEISTER
Germany (Bielefeld) 1949–59: This firm produced lightweight machines fitted with Ilo or Fichtel & Sachs engines of capacities of 100cc (6ci), 125cc (8ci), 150cc (9ci) and 175c (11ci). It also made a scooter fitted with a 50cc (3ci) engine.

MEIYER
Netherlands (Korbgeflecht) c. 1901: This machine was a scooter that was equipped with hand-start and belt drive.

MELDI
Italy 1927–37: These machines were racers that were powered by JAP and Rudge Python engines of capacities of 250cc (15ci), 350cc (21ci) and 500cc (31ci).

MEMINI
Italy 1946–47: In-house, 175c (11ci) two-strokes sustained this Italian undertaking, which was also known by the name Memini Electra.

MENON
Italy (Veneto) 1930–32: This bicycle factory was founded in 1875 but did not make motorcycles until much later. JAP singles powered its 175cc (11ci) and 200cc (12ci) machines.

MENOS
Germany (Berlin) 1922-23: This was a fully enclosed machine powered by a 618cc (38ci) water-cooled flat twin.

MERCER
England 1961: A.C. Mercer built a two-stroke, six-cylinder radial that appears to have found no commercial takers.

MERCIER
France 1950–62: This company made lightweight and mini-scooters that were fitted with Ydral and Villiers engines of 100cc (6ci) to 175c (11ci), as well as manufacturing Lavalette-powered mopeds.

MERCO
Germany (Berlin) 1922–24: This company (full name Mercur-Motoren-GmbH) made 150cc (9ci) and 200cc (12ci) two-strokes with in-house engines.

MERCURY
England (Dudley) 1956–58: This firm produced mopeds and scooters fitted with Villiers engines of 50cc (3ci) to 100cc (6ci). Model names included Dolphin, Whippet and Pippin.

MERLI
Italy 1929–31: Train 175c (11ci) two-stroke engines powered these assembled machines.

MERLIN
Spain 1982–unknown: This company produced off-road and trials machines that were fitted with Cagiva two-stroke singles of 125cc (8ci), 350cc (21ci) and 400cc (24ci).

MERLONGHI
Italy (Tolentino) 1927–30: This was a two-stroke engined machine of 132cc (8ci).

MESSNER
Austria (Vienna) 1928–33: These were racers, which were initially fitted with a JAP 250 and later, an in-house overhead-cam, of the same capacity.

METEOR
Czechoslovakia 1909–26: This company, when situated in the boundaries of the Austro-Hungarian empire, manufactured a 211cc (13ci) auxiliary cycle motor. It later went on to produce 147cc (9ci) and 169cc (10ci) two-strokes.

METEOR
Germany 1925–26: Despite the name, these were largely unremarkable 185cc (11ci) side-valve machines.

METEOR
Germany (Hanover) 1924–26: These German machines were fitted with two-stroke engines from Thumann, which had a capacity of 172cc (10ci).

METEORA
Italy 1953–66: These were mopeds, lightweights and trials-styled machines, which were fitted with both two-stroke and four-stroke engines of 49cc (3ci) to 148cc (9ci).

METEORE
France 1949–54: These French machines were lightweights fitted with 125cc (8ci), 150cc (9ci) and 175c (11ci) engines.

METISSE (RICKMANN)
England 1959–unknown: Rickmann-made frames made a lot of engines go faster. Some examples of these were BSA, Honda, Kawasaki, Norton, Triumph, Weslake and Zundapp.

METRO
England (Birmingham) 1912–19: This was a cheap, solid 269cc (16ci) two-stroke: a two-speed gearbox cost £30 instead of £25. See also METRO-TYLER.

METROPOLE
France 1950s: This company produced mopeds that were fitted with 50cc (3ci) engines.

METRO-TYLER
England (London) 1919–23: The Tyler Apparatus Co. bought out Metro (above) and thereafter offered a choice of two-speed (L80) or three-speed (L85). This serves as a reminder not only of postwar inflation but also of technical progress. The company also offered a 350cc (21ci) with Blackburne engine and a 696cc (42ci) V-twin.

MEXICO
Belgium 1932–35: This firm offered a choice of machines which were powered by 350cc (21ci) Villiers engines, or 350cc (21ci) and 500cc (31ci) JAP engines.

MEYBEIN
Germany (Hamburg) 1922–26: Willibald Meyheim built primitive machines which were fitted with 119cc (7ci) and 147cc (9ci) DKW engines and had direct belt drive.

MEYBRA
Germany 1923–25: A 186cc (11ci) two-stroke engine, which was built in-house, powered this basic lightweight machine.

MEZO
Austria 1923–26: Medinger was a leading racer who cashed in on his name by offering assembled machines with Villiers and JAP engines. However, production was hampered by the injuries he sustained in the 1924 Austrian TT.

MF
Germany (Nurnberg) 1922–25: This firm, the Fahrzeugfabrik Max Fischer, offered machines powered by the 500cc (31ci) BMW flat twin engine or Blackburne singles of 350cc (21ci) and 500cc (31ci).

MFB
Germany (Hamburg, later Munich) 1923–24: Wooden frames characterized these machines, powered by Nabob 198cc (6ci) and JAP 293cc (18ci) engines. After the original firm collapsed, Hoco – based in Munich – took over production.

MFB
Italy (Bologna) 1957–64: These were mopeds and lightweights, the latter fitted with 75cc (5ci) and 125cc (8ci) two-stroke singles and a 175c (11ci) overhead-valve single.

MFZ
Germany (Berlin-Kopenick) 1921–28: These were excellent but unexciting machines fitted with in-house engines of up to 350cc (21ci). The 175cc (11ci) and 250cc (15ci) singles from this company may have been the first German overhead-valve engines of those capacities.

MGC
France 1927–29: Ets. Marcel Guignet et Cie. used light-alloy in its frames and cycle parts, and powered their machines with Chaise and JAP engines of 250cc (15ci), 350cc (21ci), 500cc (31ci) and 600cc (37ci).

MGF
Italy (Milan) 1921–25: Motocicli Garanzini Francesco mostly used overhead-valve engines of 250cc (15ci), 350cc (21ci) and 500cc (31ci), which had been bought in from Blackburne, as well as its own 142cc (9ci) two-stroke engine.

MGF
Germany (Berlin) 1923–31: The Gesellschaft fur Verbrennungsmotoren Muhlbauer & Co made its own three-port two-stroke engines of 122cc (7ci), 140cc (9ci), 173cc (11ci) and 198cc (6ci), as well as Bekamo-licensed, pumping two-strokes. They supplied engines to other manufacturers as well as building complete machines in their factory in Berlin.

MG-TAURUA
Italy 1933–50s: Vittorio Guerzoni began with 175c (11ci) Train two-strokes and moved on to his own 250cc (15ci) and 500cc (31ci) overhead-valve (later, overhead-cam models), as well as manufacturing Sachs-engined autocycles. After World War II, engines ranged from 75cc (5ci) to 200cc (12ci), and were available in a mixture of four-strokes and two-strokes.

MIAMI
USA 1905–23: This rather basic machine came with a rear-leaning 298cc (6ci) single engine and pedalling gear.

MICHAELSON
USA (Minnesota) 1910–15: In-house inlet-over-exhaust singles of 500cc (31ci) capacity and 1000cc (61ci) twins powered these all-chain-drive machines.

MICROMA
France 1947: Messrs Mignob, Croleak and Malaprade lent their names to this three-valve single (one inlet, two exhaust), which they designed for Gillet.

MIDGET
USA 1950s–early 1960s: Models included the Autocycle, which was the second production powered two-wheeler to sport a disc front brake as original equipment.

MIDGET-BICAR
USA (Lynbrook) 1908–09: The Walton Motor Company built this curious British design (by John T. Brown) under licence. What appears to be a substantial enclosure is, in fact, the monocoque frame. Engines used were in-house and from various other companies and types: Fafnir singles, or in-house V-twins.

MIELE
Germany 1933–58: Miele motorcycles were of the same very high quality as its domestic appliances. Pre-war bikes were Sachs-powered (75cc/5ci and 98cc/6ci) while postwar production (1951–58) comprised 50cc (3ci) mopeds and lightweights of 98cc (6ci), 124cc (8ci) and 147cc (9ci), which were fitted with Fichtel and Sachs engines.

MILANI
Italy (Cesena) 1970–81: This firm manufactured Minarelli-powered 49cc (3ci) and 125cc (8ci) two-strokes. Their machines were aimed at the market for off-road sport.

MILLER
USA c. 1903: Of this short-lived pioneer, no machines are known to survive.

MILLET
France (Paris) 1890s: Felix Millet built his first three-wheelers in 1892, and offered a motorcycle with electric ignition a year later, in 1893. The engine delivered two to three horsepower at 180rpm and drove the rear wheel directly by belt.

MILLIONMOBILE
England (Cheltenham) c.1902: This was an auxiliary cycle motor for mounting over the front wheel, and was capable of delivering one-and-three-quarters horsepower.

MIMOA
Germany (Achern) 1924: Bruno Felbers & Sohn were among those who used the 142cc (9ci) Julius Lowy light-oil two-stroke, which unfortunately did not work well.

MINETTI
Italy (Turin) 1924–27: This was an everyday 125cc (8ci) two-stroke machine.

MINEUR
Belgium (Herstal) 1924–28: This Belgian firm assembled 350cc (21ci) and 500cc (31ci) machines which were fitted with proprietary engines, including the Bradshaw 'oil-boiler'.

MINIMARCELLINO
Italy (Milan) 1969: This company manufactured one of the better folding lightweights, named the Super America.

MINIMOTOR
Italy (Turin) 1945–50s:Built two-stroke auxiliary cycle motors from 49cc (3ci) to 88cc, and the 49cc (3ci) Motominima mini-bike. Engines were also built under licence in England.

MINISCOOT
France 1960–62: This machine was a small folding scooter which was fitted with a 75cc (5ci) two-stroke engine.

MINNEAPOLIS
USA (Minneapolis) 1901–15: This company were the manufacturers of surprisingly advanced singles (and possibly V-twins) with two-speed gear and chain drive. They also made three-wheeler delivery wagons.

MIRANDA
Germany (Dortmund) 1951–54: This machine was a scooter fitted with 173cc (11ci) Sachs or 198cc (6ci) Kuchen engines.

MISHIMA NAINENKI
Japan 1955-late 1950s: These motorcycles were advanced machines compared to those produced by others in the 1950s. They were a 250cc (15ci) overhead-valve and, later, a 125cc (8ci) two-stroke.

MISTRAL
France 1902–early 1960s: This company was the astonishingly long-lived manufacturer of lightweight machines. After World War II, it specialized mostly in the manufacture of mopeds, also supplying 49cc (3ci) engines to other manufacturers.

This proud ownder is showing off his 1974 Moto Villa 125cc (8ci) Viper MX.

MITCHELL
USA (Racine, Wisconsin) 1901–06: As well as being involved in the manufacture of cars, this company built motorcycles with a rear-leaning 345cc (21ci) engine. This engine was fitted in a strengthened bicycle frame.

MIYATA
Japan 1909–64: This was an old-established Japanese company that was responsible for the manufacture of a wide range of machines with engines of up to 500cc (31ci).

MJ
Germany 1924–25: This company built 600cc (37ci) and 750cc (461ci) flat twins, both air- and water-cooled, and supplied engines to several assemblers; as well as this, they also manufactured substantially experimental 249cc (15ci) two-strokes.

MJS
Germany 1924–25: In-house 245cc (15ci) two-strokes powered these simple machines.

ML
Argentina 1970s: This machine was initially produced as a 100cc (6ci) two-stroke; then it became a 125cc (8ci); then a 175c (11ci), and finally it used a Jawa motor.

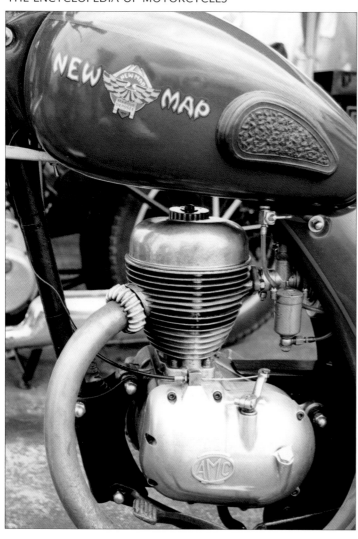

This 1950s era New Map features an AMC engine.

MM
USA 1905–c1914: The American Motor Company began producing machines fitted with Thomas singles, before moving on to singles and V-twins from a number of other manufacturers.

M&M
England 1914: The ubiquitous Villiers 269cc (16ci) two-stroke powered these assembled machines.

MMM
Germany 1925–27: MMM produced two-stroke singles of 148cc (9ci).

MMV-Z
Soviet Union (Minsk) 1951–unknown: MMV-Z were responsible for the manufacture of basic machines, initially the M1A and in 1975 the surprisingly powerful Minsk, which had a capacity of 125cc (8ci) and produced 12 horsepower at 6000rpm. MMV-Z also made this model in versions suitable for off-road sports riding.

MOAG
Germany (Berlin) 1924: This was a remarkably advanced machine compared to others being manufactured at that time. It had an Electron frame, overhead-valve engine, five-speed gearbox, all-chain drive and a choice of air- or water-cooling.

MOBILE
England 1913: A.V. Roe of aviation fame (AVRO) manufactured this scooter, which was fitted with a 350cc (21ci) Villiers motor.

MOCHET
France 1950–55: This French company produced two-stroke lightweights with 125cc (8ci) and 175cc (11ci) Ydral motors, as well as manufacturing light delivery wagons.

MOFA
Germany 1920–25: These were auxiliary cycle motors of 70cc (4ci) and 148cc (9ci), which were also fitted into the firm's complete lightweight machines.

MOHAWK
England (London) 1903–05 and 1920–25: In the pioneer years, this bicycle manufacturer fitted two-and-a-half horsepower and three horsepower motors. Later on, it fitted singles from Villiers (269cc/16ci), JAP (350cc/21ci) and Abingdon (500cc/31ci), V-twins from JAP (300cc/18ci and 77cc/5ci) and an American-built, two-stroke twin.

MOLTENI
Italy 1925–27: The machines produced by this company came with light-alloy frames and forks; the prospective buyer also had a choice of a 348cc (21ci) Bradshaw oil-cooled engine, or a 500cc (31ci) MAG engine.

MONACO-BAUDO
Italy (Turin) 1927–28: Augusto Monaco and Antonio Baudo collaborated on a 500cc (31ci) single with a characteristic big external flywheel, as well as buying in 350cc (21ci) Blackburne and JAP singles. The original Monaco doesn't appear to have been sold commercially.

MONARCH
USA (New York State) 1912–15: The Ives Motorcycle Corporation installed in-house, 500cc (31ci) singles and 1000cc (61ci) V-twins in spring frames. The smaller bikes were fitted with chain-cum-belt drive, while the larger bikes were all-chain.

MONARCH
England (Birmingham) 1919–21: R. Walker and Son, who also made Excelsior machines, bought in 269cc (16ci) Villiers and 300cc (18ci) JAP engines to fit into its Monarch brand.

MONARCH
Japan 1955–62: These machines closely resembled Nortons as they were fitted with their overhead-valve engines of both 350cc (21ci) and 500cc (31ci).

MONFORT
Spain (Esparaguerra) 1957–59: These Spanish lightweights were fitted with 200cc (12ci) two-stroke motors, and possibly also 125cc (8ci) engines.

MONOPOLE
England (Coventry) 1911–24: Before World War I, this firm fitted 500cc (31ci) Precision motors and a 269cc (16ci) Villiers; afterwards, engines up to 350cc (21ci) from Abingdon and Villiers, and a JAP 680cc (41ci) V-twin, were fitted.

MONOTO
France 1935–38 and 1951: This machine was a two-stroke lightweight with (somewhat improbably) shaft drive. Before World War II, it was fitted with a two-speed 98cc (6ci) capacity engine; after, it was 125cc (8ci) with four-speeds.

The 496cc (30ci) four cylinder Nougier racing motorcycle made its debut in 1953.

MONOTRACE
France 1926–28: This machine was the Mauser (below), built under licence with a 520cc water-cooled engine.

MONTEROSA
Italy 1954–58: This company was responsible for the production of 49cc (3ci) mopeds, which were fitted with Itom engines as their powerbase.

MONTLHERY
Austria 1926–28: JAP 350cc (21ci) side-valve and overhead-valve engines gave the power to these rare machines.

MONVISO
Italy (Savigliano) 1951–56: These machines were light motorcycles with Fichtel & Sachs engines of 100cc (6ci), 125cc (8ci), 150cc (9ci), and 175c (11ci) capacities.

MOONBEAM
England (London) 1920–21: The M.R.P. Trading Company sold these low-cost, Villiers-powered, 269cc (16ci) two-strokes.

MOORE CAR
England 1917: This was very similar in appearance to a two-wheeled motor-car, with bonnet (hood) and running boards, as well as retractable outrigger wheels.

MORETTI
Italy (Turin) 1934–52: Before World War II, this firm produced 125cc (8ci) and 250cc (15ci) lightweights with DKW, JAP and Ladetto engines. After, it produced overhead-valve machines, including a shaft-drive 246cc (15ci) parallel twin.

MORRIS
England 1902–05: William Morris, later Lord Nuffield, experimented with motorcycles in the pioneering days, fitted his machines with two-and-three-quarters horsepower De Dion-Bouton and MMC singles.

MORRIS
England (Birmingham) 1913–22: This was a well-finished but basic 247cc (15ci) two-stroke single.

MORRIS-WARNE
England 1922: This rare two-stroke single, which was fitted with a 248cc (15ci) engine, was manufactured in both vertical and horizontal configurations.

MORS (SPEED)
France 1951–56: This famous pioneer of motorcars was briefly responsible for the manufacture of 60cc (4ci), 115cc (7ci) and 125cc (8ci) two-stroke scooters.

MORSE-BEAUREGARD
USA (Detroit) 1912–17: This was a 500cc (31ci) parallel twin machine, mounted in-line with unit, two-speed gearbox and offered by the company with a choice of chain or shaft final drive.

MORTON-ADAM
England (Coventry) 1923–24: Harry Sidney designed the overhead-cam 250cc (15ci) and 350cc (21ci) models.

MOSER
Switzerland (St. Aubin) 1905–35: Well known as suppliers of motors, from auxiliary cycle motors up to 598cc (6ci) (85x106mm/3.3x4.2in), this company also built complete motorcycles. These came in a predictably wide range of capacities and went on to enjoy considerable success in racing, especially those fitted with the 123cc (8ci) and 173cc (11ci) overhead-valve singles.

MOSER
Austria 1953–54: Rotax 98cc (6ci) and 123cc (8ci) engines powered these predecessors of KTM.

MOTAG
Germany 1923–24: The frame of this machine is described by various sources as cast-alloy and pressed-steel; it may be both. Its engines are variously described as 125cc (8ci), or as a choice of parallel twins, air- or water-cooled, and in capacities of 514cc (31ci), 642cc (39ci) and 804cc (49ci).

MOTAUTO
Italy (Sesto Callende) 1955: This was an unlikely looking, fully clad 250 machine fitted with a 125cc (8ci) two-stroke single, from Vittorio Monaco, in '1950s futuristic' style.

MOTA-WIESEL
Germany 1948–52: This was a small-wheel step-through which was fitted with a 75cc (5ci) or 100cc (6ci) engine.

MOTEURCYCLE
France 1921–24: The 206cc two-stroke engine which gave power to this machine was mounted behind the saddle, and it drove the rear wheel by friction.

MOTOBIC
Spain 1949–65: After kicking off with an 80cc lightweight, this company's product range in 1957 included 50cc (3ci) mopeds, and lightweights of 60, 75, 82 and 100cc (6ci). By the early 1960s the staples of their range were a 75cc (5ci) lightweight and a scooter, which came with a choice of 75cc (5ci) and 95cc engines.

MOTOBIMM
Italy 1969–71: These were Minarelli-powered 49cc (3ci) off-road sports machines.

MOTO BIROS
Italy (Cesena) 1970s: Giancarlo Biondi and Vincenzo Rossi elided their surnames to christen these 50cc (3ci) reed-valve mopeds and off-road sports machines.

MOTOBLOC
France (Vichy) 1948 to late 1960s: This company is probably best known for the 65cc (4ci) SE-engined, two-stroke Sulky scooter. However, it was also responsible for the production of mopeds as well as lightweights with Aubier-Dunne and Villiers two-strokes of 125cc (8ci) to 200cc (12ci) and AMC 125cc (8ci) and 250cc (15ci) overhead-valve four-strokes.

MOTO-B.M.
Italy (Rastignoro Pianoro) 1952–c. 1960: This company began production of motorcycles in 1952 with Ilo-engined 125cc (8ci) and 160cc (10ci) two-strokes; a year later, it added 75cc (5ci) and 100cc (6ci) four-stroke lightweights with NSU engines; then produced 125cc (8ci) and 250cc (15ci) four-strokes; and finally Minarelli-engined mopeds.

MOTO-BORGO
Italy (Turin) 1906–26: The famous piston-manufacturing brothers, Carlo and Alberto, also manufactured and raced complete motorcycles. At first, these motorcycles were singles from 500cc (31ci) to 827cc (50ci), then they were followed by V-twins of 990cc (c. 1917), 746cc (46ci) (c. 1919) and 500cc (31ci) (1921: 477cc/29ci; 1925: 492cc/30ci).

MOTOCLETTE
Switzerland 1904–15: This assembler used Zedel and then Moser proprietary (but still Swiss) engines.

MOTODELTA
Italy (Florence) 1970–unknown: These off-road sporting machines were fitted with 125cc (8ci) engines.

MOTO EMILIA
Italy (Bologna) 1953: This was a short-lived, four-stroke machine with an engine of 175c (11ci) capacity. The machine was available in three different forms: Touring (pushrod), Sport (single overhead-cam) and Super Sport (double overhead-cam). The last could top – so it was claimed by the company's publicity material – a speed of 114km/h (70mph).

MOTOFLASH
Italy 1957–unknown: Small (50cc) motors from this company powered a variety of machines: these were mopeds, scooters and also lightweights.

MOTO GELIS
Argentina c. 1960: Sachs and, some sources claim, possibly Italian engines of up to 250cc (15ci) capacity, as well as imported Italian cycle parts, made up these machines. Dates for their production are given in various sources as 'from 1963', and between 1955 and 1962.

MOTO GORI
Italy 1960s–68: This firm started its production of motorcycles with scooters, then went on to off-road sports machines; and linked up with Moto Bimm (above) to make Gori-Bimm. After this point, they concentrated on off-road sports vehicles.

MOTOLUX
France 1933–38: This was a bicycle manufacturer that offered an optional 100cc (6ci) auxiliary motor.

MOTOMEC
Italy (Longiano) 1985–unknown: The unique thing about the Jobby moped was that it could drive separate accessory pumps, a feature that proved useful for the small farmer.

MOTOMETEORA
Italy 1953–mid 1980s: Mopeds, lightweights, scooters, off-road sports bikes: this Italian firm Motometeora made them all. They were manufactured for the most part with 50cc (3ci) engines (from NSU, Morini and Minarelli) although the company's first and biggest engine was a 125cc (8ci)OMS four-stroke single.

MOTO MONTE
France 1932–39: These were lightweight machines, which were variously reported as having capacities of 100cc (6ci), 175c (11ci) and 250cc (15ci).

MOTOPEDALE
France 1933–39: This company produced mainly Aubier-Dunne-powered two-strokes machines, of 100cc (6ci) and 125cc (8ci) capacity. However, it also manufactured bigger machines fitted with Rudge Python and JAP four-strokes of 250cc (15ci), 350cc (21ci) and 500cc (31ci).

MOTOPIANA
Italy (Florence) 1923–31: Working backwards, this company produced an in-house 250cc (15ci) overhead-valve; a side-valve version of the same motor (1927); and assembled machines with Villiers and JAP engines, the former 150cc (9ci) to 250cc (15ci), the latter, 250cc (15ci) to 500cc (31ci).

MOTORFLY
France (Voisin) 1920: This was an auxiliary, two-stroke cycle motor, 157cc (10ci), weighing 317kg (697lb), which had friction drive to the rear wheel.

MOTORMEYER
The Netherlands 1949–51: Two-stroke split-singles with 350cc (21ci) capacity powered these machines from the Netherlands.

MOTOSOLO
Belgium 1920s: These machines were middleweights with chain-cum-belt drive.

MOTOTECNICA DELL'ITALIA CENTRALE
Italy (Florence) 1953–86: These machines were initially 125cc (8ci) lightweights, and later of 80cc (5ci) capacity, and the firm also produced mopeds. Most of these machines were pretty utilitarian, save for the occasional off-road sport model.

MOTO-V
Italy (Turin) 1927: From this Italian company, a pressed-steel frame was offered which housed a 325cc (20ci) motor. The 'V' stands for Vandone, which was the constructor.

MOTO VILLA
Italy 1960s to (at the least) the 1980s: This company were responsible for the production of racing and off-road competition machines, from the initial 125cc (8ci) two-stroke to as much as 500cc (31ci) in one direction, and children's mini-bikes of 50cc (3ci) in the other direction.

MOTOX
Switzerland 1951: This was an auxiliary 50cc (3ci) two-stroke cycle motor.

MOTRA WIESEL
Germany 1949–52: This machine was a scooter, with engines variously reported as being Sachs or Matra, in capacities of 75cc (5ci) or 100cc (6ci).

MOTRON
Italy (Modena) 1961–unknown: This company were responsible for producing mopeds with 50cc (3ci) engines.

MOTTE
Germany 1955–59: Two-stroke motors of 50cc (3ci) to 120cc (7ci) powered these mopeds, scooters and lightweights.

MOUNTAINEER
England (Marsden) 1902–26: Before World War I, this company fitted various Fafnir, Minerva and MMC motors; afterwards, they used the omnipresent 269cc (16ci) Villiers.

MOVEO
England c.1907: This was a firm of assemblers, who used JAP singles and V-twins.

MOVESA
Spain (Vitoria) 1952 to early 1960s: Motocicletas y Vehiculos SA built vehicles that were all but indistinguishable from the contemporary 173cc (11ci) Peugeots and were also fitted with the same engine.

NAGAS & RAY
Italy: Allesandro Nagas and Tullio Ray were the Italian importers of Indian and Zundapp machines; they also manufactured their own 350cc (21ci) side-valve single engines. The name appears with the variant spelling of Negas & Ray in some sources.

NAMAPO
Germany (Stettin) 1921–24: Bernhard Nagl's Namapo was a side-valve single of 197cc (12ci) and 194cc (12ci). The latter was also available as an auxiliary cycle motor. Stettin where the company was based, became a part of Poland after the end of World War II.

NARCISSE
France 1950–53: This company began manufacturing machines that were fitted with 100cc (6ci) engines from Aubier-Dunne and Sachs. It went on to add 48cc (3ci) mopeds in 1953. The top tube was the fuel tank, and the machinery was fully enclosed.

NARCLA
Spain (Gerona) 1955–60: This company was responsible for the production of four-speed 125cc (8ci) lightweight machines which came with better-than-average specification.

NASSETTI
Italy 1951–57: Ettore Nassetti began with the Pelegrino 49cc (3ci) friction-drive auxiliary cycle motor but moved on to 49cc (3ci) mopeds in 1954, including the Sery and Dilly.

NASSOVIA
Germany 1925: A two-and-three-quarter horsepower Anzani engine powered these shortlived lightweight machines.

NAVONE
Italy (Turin) 1928: This company was responsible for the production of an Italian version of the 175c (11ci) French PM auxiliary cycle motor.

NAZZARO
Italy (Turin) 1926–28: Eugenio Nazzaro, the brother of the Italian motor-racing champion Felice Nazzaro, built a 175c (11ci) overhead-valve pushrod machine in limited numbers.

NEALL
England (Daventry) 1910–14: This was a firm of assemblers which used Precision motors.

NEANDER
Germany 1924–29: Ernst Neander catalogued Villiers two-strokes and JAP, MAG and Kuchen four-strokes in a cadmium-plated Duralumin frame, which were subsequently licensed to Opel. Swept volumes ranged from 122cc (7ci) to 1000cc (61ci), and other engines were available to order.

NECCHI
Italy 1951–53: This firm produced everyday lightweight machines, which were powered by Villiers 98cc (6ci) and 125cc, and Sachs 150cc (9ci) motors.

NECO
Czech Republic 1922–27: Neco was responsible for the production of machines that were powered by JAP motors of 350cc (21ci) and 500cc (31ci), of side-valve and overhead-valve types.

NEEDHAM
England 1928: This was a lightweight motorcycle which had been fitted with a 170cc (10ci) two-stroke motor and (unusually) a unit four-speed gear box.

NEGAS & RAY
see NAGAS & RAY

NEGRINI
Italy (Vignola) 1954–: This firm produced mopeds (including sporting off-road models) fitted with 49cc (3ci) engines, as well as lightweights of 75cc (5ci) and 125cc (8ci).

NEKO
Hungary 1921–28: This Hungarian firm produced British-inspired singles that had been fitted with Blackburne engines of 350cc (21ci) and 500cc (31ci) capacity.

NEMALETTE
Germany 1924–25: Hardly a motorcycle at all, this machine seems to have been an enclosed three-wheeler, with one wheel at the front. It was powered by a 175c (11ci) motor which had been bought in from DKW.

NENCIONI
Italy (Florence) 1926: This was a motorized bicycle fitted with a 125cc (8ci) Ferrera motorcycle, by Carlo Nencioni.

NERA
Germany 1949–50: This scooter was fitted with either a 123cc (8ci) Ilo or a 150cc (9ci) Sachs motor.

NERGINI
Italy 1954–: This firm produced lightweight two-strokes of 125cc (8ci), and later, mopeds with a 49cc (3ci) engine.

NERVOR
France 1930–60: Sources vary in their reports of this company. Nervor probably began manufacturing life with single-cylinder and V-twin two-stroke engines, and moved on after World War II to four-strokes from AMC and NSU, including a parallel twin with a capacity of 250cc (15ci).

NESTOR
England (Blackpool) 1913–14: This firm was responsible for the production of lightweights, with a choice of 269cc (16ci) Villiers two-stroke engines or 300cc (18ci) and 350cc (21ci) (two-and-three-quarter and three-and-three-quarter horsepower) Precision four-stroke engines.

A rarity today: a 1919 Premier with single vertical cylinder.

NESTORIA
Germany (Numberg) 1923–31: Initially between 1923 and 1925, this firm produced machines with 300cc (18ci) and 350cc (21ci) two-stroke engines of its own manufacture, then, after taking over the Astoria factory, it produced four-strokes from 200cc (12ci) to 500cc (31ci) with engines bought in from a range of makers, especially Kuchen.

NETTUNIA
Italy 1950–53: These machines were good but unexciting two-strokes of 125cc (8ci) and 160cc (10ci) capacities.

NEVA
France 1926–27: These French machines were singles fitted with 350cc (21ci) engines bought in from Anzani.

NEVAL
Soviet Union 1945–: This machine was one of the Soviet copies of the pre-war BMW; there are similarities between it and the Ural, Cossak and Dneipr.

NEVE
Germany (Neumunster) 1924–26: This German firm was also known as Neve-Ilo, after the 132cc (8ci) and 170cc (10ci) Ilo engines fitted into its conventional frames.

NEW COMET
England (Birmingham) 1905–32: Before World War I, this firm used a range of engines bought in from JAP, Peco, Precision and Villiers. Afterwards, there was a hiatus, variously given as 1918–1931 and 1924–1931; then machines with 293cc (18ci) Climax and 198cc (6ci) Villiers motors were built.

NEW COULSON
England 1923–24: Formerly known as Coulson (see above), this company revived itself in 1923 and made a few more motorcycles with characteristic leaf-sprung rear end. Most had 269cc (16ci) Liberty two-stroke engines, although some 350cc (21ci) and 500cc (31ci) road models were also available, with air-cooled Blackburne engines and Bradshaw oil-cooled motors, as well as JAP-engined racers.

NEW DEAL
France 1951–54: This shortlived French firm were responsible for producing mopeds.

NEW ERA
USA (Dayton, Ohio) 1908–13: The engine lived under the seat and the fuel tank over the rear wheel in this progressive but eccentric machine. It featured a frame which was semi-open.

NEW ERA
England 1920–22: The standard engine in these machines was a 311cc (19ci) Dalm two-stroke: JAP and Precision motors could be ordered.

NEW GERRARD
Scotland (Edinburgh) 1922–40: Jock Porter, the Scots racer and 1923 TT Lightweight winner (175cc/11ci and below), made these light, sweet-handling machines, initially with Blackburne engines, later JAP. Most production was of 350cc (21ci) overhead-valve engines, although arange of capacities was sold in the early years (175–500cc/11–31ci), and a few very early models had Blackburne sleeve-valve engines. Some were built or part-built in Nottingham, England.

NEW HENLEY
England (Birmingham, then Oldham) 1927–29: The Clarke brothers of Birmingham re-organized Henley (see above) in 1927, without actually changing the machines. Shortly afterwards, the racers Arthur Greenwood and Jack Crump bought the name and transferred production to Oldham, but they did not prosper.

NEW KNIGHT
England (Bedford) 1923–27?: Villiers two-strokes of 150cc (9ci) to 300cc (18ci), and JAP 300cc (18ci) side-valves, were assembled into small numbers of machines by this company.

NEW MAP
France 1920–58: This surprisingly prolific factory followed a fairly typical course. Before World War II it assembled big four-strokes, with engines of up to 1000cc (61ci) from Blackburne, Chaise, JAP, MAG and Zurcher. After the war, it was noted for mopeds and lightweights up to 250cc (15ci), both two-stroke and four-stroke, from AMC, Aubier Dunne, Mondial, Kuchen, Sachs and Ydral.

NEW MOTORCYCLE
France (Chatenay) 1925–30: As commonly happened, the base model from this company was an in-house two-stroke (in this case 250c/15ci), which was supplemented with overhead-valve and even overhead-cam Chaise, JAP and MAG engines of 350cc (21ci) and 500cc (31ci) capacities.

NEWMOUNT
England (Coventry) 1929–33: The frames, and the four-valve Rudge Python 350cc (21ci) and 500cc (31ci) engines used in the more powerful machines, were English but many models which came from this company were powered by Zundapp two-strokes of 200cc (12ci), 250cc (15ci) and 300cc (18ci).

NEW PARAGON
England 1919–23: These distinctive machines had their own leaf-sprung frames and their own two-stroke singles of 235cc (14ci), 347cc (21ci) and 500cc (31ci). They were also known simply as 'Paragon'.

NEW RAPID
The Netherlands 1933–36: This firm was an assembler that used a wide range of two-stroke and four-stroke engines, from the lowly 98cc (6ci) Villiers to the mighty 500cc (31ci) four-valve Rudge Python.

NEW RYDER
England (Birmingham) 1913–22: Before World War I, this firm used Precision singles and V-twins in their machines, and afterwards they used the (almost ubiquitous) Villiers 269cc (16ci) two-stroke engines.

NEW SCALE
England (Manchester) 1909–25: Harry Scale built Scale motorcycles before World War I, and New Scale afterwards. They were all conventional assembled machines of 350cc (21ci) and 500cc (31ci), with Precision, Blackburne and Bradshaw engines, or (for the racer) an overhead-cam 350cc (21ci) Dart.

NEWTON
England (Manchester) 1921–22: This machine was essentially a Villiers 269cc (16ci) two-stroke in a cheap frame.

NFK
Germany 1924–25: Variously reported as being named NFK and NKF, these machines used a 123cc (8ci) Bekamo pumping two-stroke which was built under licence.

NIBBIO
Italy (Milan) 1949–53: These Italian scooters were produced initially with 98cc (6ci) and 125cc (8ci) two-stroke motors. However, the 98cc (6ci)-engined model was quickly dropped.

NICHOLAS
England 1911–15: This English firm was an obscure assembler of one-and-a-half horsepower machines.

NICKSON
England (Preston) 1920–24: As well as 350cc (21ci) and 500cc (31ci) engines from Bradshaw (overhead-valve) and Blackburne (side-valve), this English company also fitted Villiers two-strokes with capacities of up to 269cc (16ci).

NIESNER
Austria 1905–11: Fafnir and Minerva singles and V-twins powered these pioneers from Austria.

The King Scorpion 250cc (15ci) was made by Spanish firm Montesa.

NINON
France 1931–35: This was a firm of assemblers responsible for fitting JAP overhead-valve singles.

NIS
Germany 1925–26: One of many short-lived 1920s assemblers, this firm was marked chiefly by using JAP 300cc (18ci) side-valve engine, as well as 269cc (16ci) two-strokes.

NISSAN
Japan 1951–56: Better known for producing cars, Nissan also made some scooters with a capacity of 60cc (4ci).

NKF
see NFK

NLG
England 1905–12: North London Garage believed in manufacturing powerful V-twins. Although it made 500cc (31ci) singles and 750cc (461ci) V-twins for road use, it also used a 2913cc JAP engine in a 1907 (or possibly 1909) racer, while a 944cc (58ci) Peugeot powered another racer.

NMC
Japan early 1950s–early 1960s: These were conventional lightweights of 125cc (8ci) and 175cc (11ci) capacity.

NOBLE
England (London) 1901–06: An early convert to the New Werner engine position (in the pedal bracket), Noble used its own engines as well as some from De Dion-Bouton, Minerva, MMC, and Coronet, from two-and-three-quarters to four-and-a-half horsepower.

NORBRECK
England (Wellingborough) 1921–24: The standard engines fitted into its machines by this company were 269cc (16ci) Villiers or Arden two-strokes; 350cc (21ci) and 500cc (31ci) Blackburnes were added as an option. The pressed-steel forks were unusual features for that period.

NORDSTERN
Germany 1922–24: This company was yet another short-lived German producer of small two-strokes, which were built with in-house engines.

NORICUM
Austro-Hungary (Czech Republic) 1903–06: These were re-badged Cless and Plessing machines (see above) which were for sale in Czechoslovak territory.

NORLOW
England 1919: This English machine was a true standing-room-only scooter, with the engine over the front wheel.

NOUGIER
France 1947–c.1960: This company were responsible for producing fast, advanced designs, initially 250cc (15ci) and then 350cc (21ci) double-overhead-cam singles, followed by pushrod engines, twins, and even an air-cooled four. The 1957 175c (11ci) racing single could almost reach 160km/h (100mph): top speed was given as 155km/h (96mph).

NORVED
Germany 1924–25: This was an assembler that used Kuhne 350cc (21ci) and 500cc (31ci) engines or (to special order) Blackburne motors.

NOVA
Hungary 1925–28: This firm of assemblers produced sporting 250–500cc (15–31ci) machines from – mostly – British parts, using Blackburne and JAP engines.

NOVICUM
Austro-Hungary/Czech Republic (Prague-Smichov) 1904–08: This Czech pioneer used the customary engines of that period, including those from Fafnir and Minerva.

NOVY
Belgium (Courtrai/Kourtrijk) early 1930s–early 1960s: These were well-thought-out assembled machines, mostly with Ilo 125cc (8ci) to 250cc (15ci) two-stroke engines.

NSH
Germany (Hersfeld) 1923–28: A. Nodling u. Sohne of Hersfeld (hence NSH) began producing a 185cc (11ci) overhead-valve single machine with an engine from Paque of Augsburg, rising to 198cc (6ci) in 1924. When Paque ceased production, NSH switched to JAP (350cc/21ci and 500cc/31ci), Blackburne (250cc/15ci to 500cc/31ci), and Villiers (125cc/8ci to 350cc/21ci) engines, the latter capacity both as a single and, in the final year of production, as a parallel twin.

NUX
Germany 1924–25: Given the date and the place, one might guess (accurately) that this firm made small, simple two-strokes. The engine was 170cc (10ci), and built in house.

NV
Sweden (Uppsala) 1926–60: Nymanbolagen AB started with an excellent 246cc (15ci) single but then switched to 98cc (6ci) mopeds in about 1932. After World War II, it resumed production with machines of 50cc (3ci) to 250cc (15ci), with a variety of two-stroke engines, eventually standardizing on DKW and Sachs. They also manufactured a 38cc (2ci) moped.

NYMAN
Sweden 1955: This appears to be NV (see above) under a different name.

OCM
Italy early 1960s: Franco-Morini engines powered these mopeds and light delivery vehicles.

OD
Germany (Dresden, later Sulzbach-Rosenberg) 1927–35: OD began with MAG-engined machines up to 1000cc (61ci) (JAP for the racers), adding 200cc (12ci) and 250cc (15ci) two-strokes with Bark motors; then (after 1935) Ilo three-wheeled delivery vehicles.

OGAR
Czech Republic (Prague) 1934–50: Frantisek Bartuska designed the very sporty 250cc (15ci) two-stroke that made this firm's name. When Ogar was absorbed into Jawa, it made a 350cc (21ci) two-stroke twin.

OLMO
Italy 1951–61: These were mopeds and ultra-lightweights with 38cc (2ci) Mosquito and 49cc (3ci) engines.

OLYMPIA
France 1949–54: These were primitive mopeds with friction drive from a front-wheel motor.

OLYMPIQUE
France (Courbevoie) 1922–58: These unmemorable but longlived two- and four-stroke machines were of 100cc (6ci) to 350cc (21ci) before 1939, and postwar from 100cc (6ci) to 250cc (15ci), with various bought-in engines.

OMEA
Italy (Milan) 1950–53: The monoshock rear end was an interesting feature of this 125cc (8ci) two-stroke lightweight.

OMEGA
England (Coventry) 1919–27: As well as its own two-stroke engines of 170cc (10ci) and 350cc (21ci), these machines used a variety of other engines: initially Villiers 269cc (16ci) and Blackburne 500cc (31ci), then later Barr & Stroud, Bradshaw and JAP.

OMEGA
Japan 1960s: This firm built off-road sport bikes of 90cc (5ci), 125cc (8ci) and 151cc (9ci), and street parallel twins of up to 500cc (31ci).

OMNIA
Germany (Bad Godesberg) 1931–33: The Imperia works built these low-cost two-strokes with 100cc (6ci) and 150cc (9ci) Villiers engines, and a 200cc (12ci) Bark.

OMNIA
Italy 1949–53: This firm produced rebadged MT 250cc (15ci) overhead-cam parallel twins. It is also reported as being named OMT.

ONAWAY
England 1904–08: This unusual-looking machine had a basketwork bucket seat and a low frame, and was powered by a five horsepower Kelecom V-twin or Berkley parallel-twin.

ONOTO
France 1934–38: These were unexciting two-strokes of 100cc (6ci) to 175cc (11ci) with Aubier Dunne engines.

OPRA
Italy (Rome) 1927–29: The Officine di Precisione Romani Automobilistiche built what may have been the world's first transverse air-cooled four, just 490cc (30ci), delivering 32 horsepower at 6000rpm; a water-cooled version had just 30 horsepower. It was subsequently developed into the Rondine 4 and the Gilera 4.

OR
Italy (Milan) 1928–31: The Officine Riunite di Costruzioni Meccaniche began with an auxiliary cycle motor and moved on to a 175c (11ci) lightweight.

ORAM
Italy 1949: The Officine Ricostruzione Automobili e Motocicli built a 125cc (8ci) lightweight.

ORBIT
England (Wolverhampton) 1913–24: Before 1914, this firm built a 350cc (21ci) side-valve; after the war, it built a 261cc (16ci) two-stroke. Also, it fitted on request the motors of other manufacturers, as long as they began with a B: Barr & Stroud, Blackburne and Bradshaw.

OREOL
France (Puteaux) 1903–14: This firm made mainly V-twins, with Moto-Reve, Zedel and other engines. The 333cc (20ci) single-cylinder record-breaker ridden by Cissac seems to have been their own.

ORIENT
USA 1900–06: The Waltham Manufacturing Co. built these very early machines with Aster engines behind the steering head and a petrol tank over the rear mudguard. They may have stayed in production as late as 1910.

ORIGAN
France 1929–mid-1950s: This firm produced two-strokes of 100cc (6ci) and 175cc (11ci) – bought in mostly from Aubier-Dunne – and an AMC four-stroke.

ORION
Czech Republic (Slany) 1902–33: In the pioneering years, this company built singles and V-twins. After 1918, it built a 350cc (21ci) two-stroke single and a 596cc (36ci) split-single; after 1927, it made 500cc (31ci) side-valve and overhead-valve machines, as well as a 600cc (37ci) side-valve machine. All engines were designed and built in house.

ORIX
Italy (Alessandria) 1949–54: This firm produced scooters of 125cc (8ci) and 175cc (11ci), and a 175c (11ci) lightweight, all with Ilo two-stroke engines.

ORMONDE
England 1900–06: Kelecom and Antoine engines powered these pioneers, some of which featured partial enclosure.

ORUK
Germany 1922–24: The direct shaft drive from the 189cc side-valve single, mounted beside the rear wheel, explains the name: Ohne Riemen Und Kette (without belt and chain).

OSA-LIBERTY
France (Argenteuil) 1926–32: As well as in-house two strokes of 175cc (11ci) and 250cc (15ci), this firm used JAP 350cc (21ci) and 500cc (31ci) engines built under licence by Staub in France.

OSCAR
Italy (S. Andrea di Sesto) 1965–82: This firm produced mopeds and ultra-lightweight motorcycles.

OSMOND
England (Birmingham) 1911–24: Before World War I, this firm made 500cc (31ci) Precision-engined singles and postwar, two-stroke lightweights with proprietary engines, reported as 102/108cc (6/7ci) and 200cc (12ci), plus a 239cc (15ci) two-stroke of its own.

OVERSEAS
England (Birmingham) 1909–15: Designed (as the name suggests) for use in the then British Empire and colonies, these solid, substantial machines had an in-house 842cc (51ci) V-twin engine.

PA
Belgium (Liege) 1921–29: Initially, Praillet used Blackburne engines of 250cc (15ci), 350cc (21ci) and 500cc (31ci), but in 1925, made his own engines: a 250cc (15ci) two-stroke and a 350cc (21ci). For the last two years JAP and MAG engines of 350cc (21ci) and 500cc (31ci) could be ordered.

PAGLIANTI
Italy 1954–62: This firm produced 49cc (3ci) mopeds, and in 1959, mini-scooters with 75cc (5ci) engines; all were two-stroke.

PALLION
England 1905–14: This firm was an early assembler, fitting Fafnir, JAP, Minerva and Villiers engines.

PALOMA
France early 1950s to late 1960s: At first and throughout, this company made 49cc (3ci) mopeds. In 1954, it made a 70cc (4ci) big-wheel scooter and in 1955, scooters with 75cc (5ci) and 125cc (8ci) engines, and a 60cc (4ci) moped/lightweight.

PAM
USA 1923: This American firm made two four-strokes, a 225cc (14ci) single and a 200cc (12ci) twin.

P & P
England (Coventry) 1922–30: Packman & Poppe built both sporting machines (with JAP engines of 250cc/15ci to 1000cc/61ci) and the unusual Silent Three, with an extremely well-muffled Barr & Stroud sleeve-valve engine, substantial enclosure, and good rider protection against road dirt. The designer was Ealing Poppe, son of the firm's owner.

P&S
see PEARSON & SOPWITH

PANTHER
Germany 1903–07: These typical pioneer machines had Fafnir singles in strengthened bicycle frames.

PANTHER
Germany (Braunschweig) 1933–mid-1970s: Before 1939, this firm made Ilo and Sachs two-strokes of 73cc (4ci) and 98cc (6ci). Postwar, it made mopeds and lightweights (including a 175c/11ci Sachs, sold in England as the 'Leopard'). Towards the end, there were only 49cc (3ci) mopeds.

PAQUE
Germany (Augsburg) 1921–25: After beginning with a 140cc (9ci) auxiliary cycle motor, Paque made a range of machines including 150cc (9ci) and 200cc (12ci) overhead-valve, 200cc (12ci) overhead-cam, and 497cc (30ci) side-valve, all singles. Paque engines were also used by other makers.

PARAGON
England 1919–23: A 350cc (21ci) two-stroke single.

PARAMOUNT-DUO
England 1926–27: This was a scooter-like machine with two bucket seats and a 490cc (30ci) single or 990cc (60ci) V-twin engines from Blackburne and JAP.

PARIS-FRANCE
France (Paris) 1934–59: These were run-of-the-mill lightweight machines of 100cc (6ci) and 175c (11ci).

PARVUS
Italy (Milan) 1921–26: The early two-stroke auxiliary cycle motors of 104cc from this firm were of an unusual design; from 1923, it also made 125cc (8ci) lightweights.

PASCO
Australia (Melbourne) 1919–22: McRae and Pasco built heavy, solid machines for Australia's uneven roads, with JAP 550cc (34ci) singles or 750cc (461ci) V-twins, all side-valve.

PASQUET
France 1932–39: Aubier-Dunne two-stroke engines of 100cc (6ci) and 125cc (8ci) drove these scarce machines.

PATRIA
Germany (Solingen) 1925–50: Sports-racers with 250cc (15ci) and 350cc (21ci) overhead-cam Rocanova motors made this firm's name by 1927. From then to 1949, it made only mopeds; it then added new 100cc (6ci) and 123cc (8ci) models with Imme and Sachs engines to their range. Hans May, the owner, died in 1950.

PAUVERT
France (Lyon) 1933–40: This company produced two-stroke lightweight machines of 100cc (6ci) to 200cc (12ci) capacity.

PAWA
Germany (Berlin) 1922–23: This strange-looking design had a great deal of sheet metal covering the frame, bucket seat, long wheelbase, and a 226cc (14ci) two-stroke engine that worked badly, driving the chain to the rear wheel through a multi-plate oil-bath clutch.

PEARSON & SOPWITH
England 1919–21: Tom Sopwith, aviation designer of the Sopwith Camel, made motorcycles. He used a Dalm 318cc (19ci) two-stroke, or 293cc (18ci) JAP side-valves, or 499cc (30ci) side-valve Blackburnes.

PEBOK
England (London) 1903–09: In-house engines of various horsepowers drove this once-prominent make.

PEERLESS
USA (Boston) 1913–16: This was when American machines led the world, and Peerless singles and V-twins had their own inlet-over-exhaust engines of four to eight horsepower drive.

PEERLESS
England (Birmingham) 1913–14: The International Manufacturing Co used Veloce 292cc (18ci) and 499cc (30ci) engines in its machines.

PEGASO
Italy 1956–64: The Societa Italiana Motori built these 48cc (3ci) lightweights in large numbers.

PEM
USA 1910–15: Unusually, this company built only singles, with an in-house, four horsepower overhead-valve engine.

PENNINGTON
England 1897: E.J. Pennington was an American engineer-cum-confidence trickster who sold a worthless design to a consortium of gullible and greedy Britons for a reported £100,000 (half a million dollars).

PENTA
Czech Republic 1992–94: This machine was a water-cooled 125cc (8ci) designed for off-road competitions.

PER
Germany (Stockheim) 1924–26: Kurt Passow developed the Per from the Pawa (above). The pressed-steel frame incorporated a good deal of enclosure; the twin seats were big 'tractor-pan' types; and the 308cc (19ci) two-stroke was enlarged after its introduction to 342cc (21ci).

PERIPOLI
Italy 1957–: Mopeds with Demm motors were supplemented in 1962 with the Giulietta 100cc (6ci) lightweight, although most later machines (including the subsequent Giulietta scooter) reverted to 50cc (3ci).

PERKS & BIRCH
England 1899–1901: Also known as Perks, these pioneers used a 222cc (14ci) single to propel two- and three-wheelers.

PERMO
Germany 1952–54: This firm manufactured mopeds which were propelled by 32cc (2ci) Victoria engines.

PERNOD
France 1899–1905: This French pioneer fitted its own one horsepower engine behind the rear wheel.

PERNOD
France c.1980: This pastis-maker sponsored a 250cc (15ci) racer.

PERSCH
Austria (Graz) 1922–25: These auxiliary cycle motors of 110cc (7ci) also came with matched Krammer frames.

PERUGINA
Italy (Castel del Piano) 1953–62: Giuseppe Menicucci, who was also responsible for BMP, built attractive 125cc (8ci), 160cc (10ci), 175cc (11ci) and 250cc (15ci) machines with in-house two-stroke and four-stroke motors.

PERUN
Czech Republic 1904–24: Before World War I, this firm made big singles and V-twins rated at three-and-a-half to four-and-a-half horsepower; after, it built auxiliary cycle motors.

PETERS
England (Isle of Man, later London) 1919–25: The engine in this machine formed the front downtube, and the petrol tank (fully enclosing the steering head) was the top tube. The belt drive was variable-ratio, the in-house engine was a 76mm (2.9in) square two-stroke with a capacity of 346cc (21ci).

PG
Italy 1927–31: Giuseppe Parina designed these overhead-valve singles, the short-lived 125cc (8ci) and the longer-lived 175cc (11ci).

PGO
Taiwan 1964–: Lightweights and scooters made from technology used under licence from Peugeot and Vespa.

PHANOMEN
Germany 1903–40: In the pioneer era, this firm briefly built V-twins and possibly singles of four and six horsepower. After a long hiatus, it resumed production of two-wheelers in the 1930s, first with 74cc motorized bicycles, and later with 100cc (6ci) and 125cc (8ci) Sachs-engined lightweights.

PHANOMEN
Germany 1950–58: This firm seems to be unrelated to the earlier undertaking. It began with lightweights powered by engines of 125cc (8ci), 150cc (9ci) and 175c (11ci) from Fichtel & Sachs, and later used a 200cc (12ci) Ilo, as well as producing mopeds.

PHANTOM
Germany 1921–28: For the first five years, this firm used its own 150cc (9ci), 200cc (12ci) (12ci) and 250cc (15ci) side-valve single engines, then later added JAP side-valve engines of 175cc (11ci) to 500cc (31ci) capacity.

PHASAR
England 1980s: A derivative of the futuristic Quasar, the Phasar enjoyed about as much success as its forebear.

PHILLIPS
England 1954–64: This subsidiary of Raleigh built mopeds.

PHOENIX
England 1900–08: As well as using Minerva engines of 211cc (13ci) and 345cc (21ci), this firm, founded by the well-known racer J.V. Hooydonk may have built in-house motors.

PHOENIX
England 1955–64: These were scooters with a surprising range of Villiers engines from 150cc (9ci) to 323cc.

PHONIX
Germany (Neuheim an der Ruhr) 1933–39: see RMW: the machines were identical.

PIANA
Italy 1923–31: Gualterio Piana began with Villiers two-strokes of 147cc (9ci), then later added bigger Villiers engines and JAP four-strokes of 250cc (15ci) to 500cc (31ci). After 1928, an in-house overhead-valve 250cc (15ci) was also used.

PIATTI
Belgium 1955–58: The Piatti scooter was built in England to the design of the Italian Vincenzo Piatti, for sale in Belgium. The engine was a 125cc (8ci) two-stroke single.

PIAZZA
Italy 1924–34: Antonio Piazza began with two- and four-stroke auxiliary bicycle motors, initially 125cc (8ci), later 175c (11ci). It moved on, in about 1927, to 175c (11ci) lightweights, at first overhead-valve, later with an optional single-valve layout. A 500cc (31ci) overhead-valve JAP engine may also have been offered.

PIERTON
France 1922–25: This assembler offered a wide variety of engines from 100cc (6ci) to 500cc (31ci) from Aubier Dunne, Blackburne, JAP, Train and Villiers. It was also called Pietron.

PILOT
England 1903–15: This firm began with JAP and Precision engines of 200cc (12ci) to 600cc (37ci), later offering its own 318cc (19ci) two-stroke.

PIOLA
Italy 1919–21: A rare 620cc (38ci) single-valve flat twin.

PIRATE
USA (Milwaukee) 1911–15: These old-fashioned machines had pedals, although the engines themselves – inlet-over-exhaust singles and V-twins of three to eight horsepower – were modern.

PIROTTA
Italy (Milan) 1949–55: This firm built mopeds of 40cc (2ci) to 75cc (5ci), then in 1954, a 160cc (10ci) lightweight capable (in late Sport guise) of over 115km/h (70mph) claimed.

The 1955 Radior Bison featured a 250cc (15ci), 2-stroke, twin-cylinder engine.

Made in Japan, the Rabbit 90 was a two-stroke single cylinder scooter.

PITTY
East Germany 1955–late 1960s: MZ two-strokes of 147cc (9ci) powered these scooters.

PMC
England (Birmingham) 1908–15: The Premier Motorcycle Company of Birmingham (distinct from the one in Coventry) seems to have used only JAP engines, up to 1000cc (61ci).

POINARD
France 1951–56: Two-strokes from Aubier Dunne and Ydral, and four-strokes from AMC, powered these scooters and lightweights of up to 250cc (15ci).

POINTER
Japan 1946–62: Once a significant player, this now-forgotten company specialised in two-strokes up to 250cc (15ci).

POLENGHI
Italy 1950–55: This shortlived firm produced mopeds.

POSDAM
Italy (Turin) 1926–29: The Possi brothers teamed up with Da Milano – hence the name – to build a 150cc (9ci) belt-drive machine, then a 125cc, followed by a 175c (11ci) with chain drive. They were as much motorized bicycles as lightweights.

POTTHOFF
Germany 1924–26: Unusually for the time and place, this firm used overhead-valve 185cc (11ci) Norman engines instead of two-strokes.

POUNCY
England 1930–38: Villiers two-stroke singles of up to 350cc (21ci) powered these assembled (but charmingly named) machines.

POUSTKA
Czech Republic 1924–34: A Czech equivalent of the Pouncy, with the same 150cc (9ci), 250cc (15ci) and 350cc (21ci) Villiers motors.

POWELL
England 1921–26: After a Blackburne-engined single, Powell moved on to 170cc (10ci) and 250cc (15ci) two-strokes and (in 1924) a fully-enclosed 200cc (12ci) motorcycle.

POWELL
USA late 1940s: This firm produced both a scooter and a miniaturized motorcycle, the latter powered by a 400cc (24ci) single-cylinder engine.

POWER WHEEL
England 1951: No less a firm than Tube Investments built this Cyril Pullin-designed 40cc (2ci) two-stroke auxiliary cycle motor which delivered 0.7 horsepower at 3600rpm.

POW WOW
USA c.1945: This was an auxiliary cycle motor, similar in concept to the Powerbike, with its own small driving wheel.

PRAGA
Czech Republic 1929–35: When the Praga car works merged with Breitfeild Danek in 1929, theytook on a 500cc (31ci) overhead-cam single, sold initially as BD and later as Praga. In 350cc (21ci) form, with the same 90mm (3.5in) stroke but a reduced bore, it powered a shaft-drive version with a pressed-steel frame after 1932.

PRECISION
England 1912–19: Before World War I, F.E. Baker's Precision machines were for export only; postwar, the new 350cc (21ci) two-stroke for the home market was produced for a short while under the Precision name before Beardmore took over and it became Beardmore-Precision.

PREMIER
England (Coventry) 1908–15: In the early years of the twentieth century, Premier claimed to be the biggest bicycle factory in the world. After beginning with White & Poppe engines, it developed its own 548cc (33ci) 90° V-twin, in 1910 a 499cc (30ci) single, in 1912 a revised 548cc (33ci) engine, and in 1914 a 998cc (6ci) V-twin based on a doubled-up single, Vincent-fashion. Premier lightweights were used by the Allies in World War I. It also made three-wheeled light delivery vehicles until the early 1920s, although after 1914 they were known as Coventry-Premier.

PREMIER
Austro-Hungary/Czech Republic (Eger) 1913–33: The German Premier factory was moved in 1913. After the 350cc (21ci) single, 1923 saw a 269cc (16ci) two-stroke along with 350cc (21ci) and 500cc (31ci) JAP-engined machines. After 1927, Premier's own 350cc (21ci) and 500cc (31ci) singles and an in-house 740cc (45ci) V-twin were used.

PREMO
England (Birmingham) 1908–15: Premier/PMC used this trademark for some of its machines, initially with Minerva engines, later with JAP singles and twins.

PRESTER (JONGHI)
France 1926–late 1950s: Prester began with Aubier-Dunne two-strokes up to 250cc (15ci), and Chaise shaft-drive four-strokes up to 500cc (31ci). It merged with Jonghi in 1939, and built 350cc (21ci) four-stroke and double overhead-cam racers up to 350cc (21ci). After World War II, it made lightweights up to 250cc (15ci), and a 125cc (8ci) scooter.

PRESTO
Germany (Chemnitz) 1901–40: Better known for cars, Presto made pioneering machines with Zedel, Minerva and Fafnir engines, and later Alba. In the 1930s, it concentrated on 75cc (5ci) and 100cc (6ci) Sachs-powered mopeds.

PRIDE & CLARKE
England 1938–40: The well-known London dealer briefly offered a 63cc (4ci) ultra-lightweight under its own name.

PRINA
Italy (Asti) 1949–54: This bicycle manufacturer brought out a 125cc (8ci) two-stroke scooter in 1949; the Sport lightweight with the same engine, in 1950; and in 1952, a 175c (11ci) scooter. Engines were from Ilo.

PRIORY
England 1919–26: This assembler, used Villiers engines of 150cc (9ci) to 250cc (15ci), Arden 269cc (16ci) engines and Union 292cc (18ci) engines, all two-strokes.

PROGRESS
Germany 1901–14: This firm began with proprietary singles and V-twins from Zedel and Fafnir, later graduating to its own 532cc (32ci) singles and 700cc (43ci) V-twins.

PROGRESS
Germany 1951–57: This Scooter was initially sold as 'Strolch' with Fichtel & Sachs two-stroke engines of 100cc (6ci) to 200cc (12ci).

PROMOT
Poland late 1968–73: These were Puch-engined two-stroke trials machines.

PSW
Germany 1924–29: As well as in-house 250cc (15ci) two-strokes, this firm bought in JAP and Blackburne engines up to 500cc (31ci).

PUMA
Argentina 1954–early 1960s: Two-stroke 98cc (6ci) motors powered these mopeds and lightweights.

PV
England (London) 1910–25: This small firm hedged its bets with a mix of engines: JAP 292cc (18ci) to 1000cc (61ci), Villiers two-strokes of 250cc (15ci) to 350cc (21ci), or Barr & Stroud 350cc (21ci) sleeve-valves and Bradshaw 350cc (21ci) oil-boilers.

QUAGLIOTTI
Italy 1902–07: The founder of this short-lived firm was a man named Carlo Quagliotti. His firm built machines fitted with Peugeot engines as their powerplants. Various sources note that Quagliotti used two types of engine. What is clear is that heused singles, and it is possible that he also used V-twins. The common feature was their all-chain layshaft drive.

This Raynal Auto 98cc (6ci) autocycle has a Villiers engine.

RENNER-ORIGINAL
Germany 1924–32: JAP side-valve 350cc (21ci) singles and 678cc (41ci) V-twins were the mainstay of this company, although other engines could be fitted to special order.

RENNSTEIG
Germany (Suhl) 1925–30: These machines had Krieger-Gnading-style frames with Blackburne and Sturmey Archer engines of 250cc (15ci) to 600cc (37ci) (one source has 200cc/12ci to 500cc/31ci).

REPUBLIC
Austro-Hungary/Czech Republic 1899–1908: Laurin & Klement used this name for machines exported to Europe and the Americas.

REVERE
England 1915–22: The ubiquitous Villiers 269cc (16ci) engine was fitted into Sparkbrook frames by Whitehouse & Co.

REX
Germany (Munich) 1948–64: This firm made auxiliary bicycle motors, and complete mopeds, initially 31cc, then 34cc (2ci), and finally 49cc (3ci).

REX
Sweden 1908–57: After some success with Motosacoche engines, Rex went on to its own V-twin but soon dropped that in favour of Villiers and JAP engines from 150cc (9ci) to 750cc (461ci): all this was before World War I. Later, it moved on to 100cc (6ci) lightweights, and after World War II, a range of machines with Ilo, Husqvarna and Sachs two-strokes from 125cc (8ci) to 250cc (15ci).

REX-JAP
England (Birmingham) 1908–15: Predictably, this firm produced JAP engines of 300cc (18ci) to 1000cc (61ci) in frames made – possibly – by Rex.

REYNOLDS-RUNABOUT
England 1919–22: This rather elegant scooter had mid-size wheels – about 33cm (13in) – and a bucket seat atop a fully enclosed engine. It was propelled by a choice of Liberty 269cc (16ci) or (later) JAP 350cc (21ci) engines.

RHONSON
France 1952–58: These mopeds and lightweights went up to 123cc (8ci).

RHONY-X
France (Lyon) 1924–32: Wonder how many of their catalogued machines they sold? There were two-strokes of 100cc (6ci), 185cc (11ci), 250cc (15ci) and 350cc (21ci), and four-strokes of 250cc (15ci), 350cc (21ci) and 500cc (31ci), with engines from LMP, Stainless, Chaise and JAP.

RIBI
Germany (Berlin) 1923–25: These were relatively advanced overhead-valve singles of 200cc (12ci) and 250cc (15ci).

RIEJU
Spain 1952–: The firm began with a lightweight powered by a 175c (11ci) AMC four-stroke. It moved on to a 125cc (8ci) step-through, then mopeds and sub-100cc (6ci) machines.

RILEY
England 1901–08: Riley's three-wheelers and motorcycles began in 1901 with a one-and-a-quarter horsepower model that grew to three-and-a-half horsepower: a three-wheeler used the nine horsepower engine. Most engines were their own, though some were De Dion-Bouton, Minerva and MMC.

RINNE
Germany 1924–32: This was a more than usually successful make, powered by in-house two-stroke motors of 125cc (8ci), 175cc (11ci) and 250cc (15ci).

RIP
England 1905–08: The distinguishing features of this firm – presumably 'Rip' rather than 'R.I.P.' – was its sprung frames. Engines came from Peugeot, Stevens and White & Poppe.

RIVARA
Italy (Colorno) 1975–: This firm produce mopeds, including the collapsible Beach.

RIZZATO
Italy (Padua) 1972–: These mopeds and lightweights go up to 125cc (8ci).

RMW
Germany (Neuheim an der Ruhr) 1925–55: The smaller engines were in-house two strokes (132cc/8ci, 148cc/9ci and 198cc/6ci) while the bigger engines (up to 500cc/31ci) were bought-in four-strokes from Bark, Blackburne, JAP, Kuchen, MAG, Moser and Sturmey-Archer.

ROA
Spain (Madrid) 1952–early 1960s: Industrias Motorizadas Onieva used Hispano-Villiers in mopeds, in motorcycles of 200cc (12ci) and 325cc (20ci), and in three-wheeled delivery vehicles.

ROC
England (Guildford, then Birmingham) 1904–15: A.W. Wall designed these machines with an unusually long wheelbase. Most had Precision V-twins up to three-and-a-half

horsepower, although there were also in-house Roc engines. Wall was an unusually early devotee of the free engine, and made one of the first four-speed gearboxes for a motorcycle.

ROCKET
Japan 1952–late 1960s: The firm's range began with a 150cc (9ci) side-valve and expanded to embrace two-strokes of smaller capacity and four-strokes of greater capacity.

ROCKET
Italy 1953–58: An attractive, intriguing, but unfortunately overly expensive machine with a 200cc (12ci) transverse flat twin and shaft drive.

ROCKET
USA 1960: One of the rash of automatic (and rather crude) scooters of the time, from the Columbus Cycle Company.

ROGER BARBIER
Switzerland 1920s: Their overhead-valve 250cc (15ci) machine was capable of almost 110km/h (70mph) but it was overshadowed by an oil-cooled four-valve overhead-cam 500.

ROHR
Germany (Landshut) 1952–58: This firm made an Ilo-powered 200cc (12ci) two-stroke scooter with a prepossessing appearance.

ROMEO
Italy 1969–75: Minarelli-engined 48cc (3ci) tiddlers.

ROMP
England 1913–14: A Precision 500cc (31ci) single powered these rare machines.

RONDINE
Italy 1923–28: Train-engined 100cc (6ci) two-stroke lightweights.

RONDINE
Italy (Rome) 1934–35: The most famous Rondine engine was the supercharged, liquid-cooled 500cc (31ci) straight-four from Compagnia Nazionale Aeronautica. Gilera bought the design in 1936.

RONDINE
Italy (San Martino) 1952–57: These Sachs-engined lightweights were of 125cc (8ci) and 150cc (9ci) capacities.

RONDINE
Italy 1968–early 1970s: These were off-road two-stroke competition machines of 48cc (3ci).

ROSSELLI
Italy 1899–1910: The original Lilliput had a one horsepower engine in front of the pedal bracket. Later machines went up to two-and-three-quarters horsepower.

ROSSLER & JAUERNIGG
Austro-Hungary (Aussig) 1902–07: These machines were powered by in-house singles and V-twins of two to four horsepower and had sprung frames.

ROTARY
Japan early 1950s–1961: Two-strokes of 125cc (8ci).

ROUSSEY
France 1948–56: This firm made an auxiliary cycle motor and lightweights up to 175c (11ci) and a water-cooled scooter.

ROVETTA
Italy (Brescia) 1900–06: Giovanni Rovetta devised several machines, including water-cooled engines and an auxiliary cycle motor.

ROVIN
France 1920–34: Raoul de Rovin began with two-strokes of 100cc (6ci), 125cc (8ci) and 175cc (11ci), and in 1924 designed a pumping-action three-piston two-stroke for racing. In 1929, he took over San-Sou-Pap and added four-strokes to his line-up, with JAP and MAG engines of 500cc (31ci).

ROVLANTE
France 1929–35: These were lightweight two-strokes of 100cc (6ci) and 125cc.

ROWILL
France (Rouen) 1950s: These mopeds were fitted with Vap and Scoutex motors.

ROYAL
Italy (Milan) 1923–28: JAP and Blackburne 350cc (21ci) and 500cc (31ci) four-strokes added glamour to the basic 132cc (8ci) in-house two-strokes from this firm.

ROYAL
Switzerland (Basle) 1900–08: Made a few one-and-a-quarter to two horsepower machines, with Zedel engines.

ROYAL-AJAX
England (London) 1901–08: The British Cycle Manufacturing Co built two-and-a-half horsepower machines.

ROYAL-MOTO
France 1923–33: Massardier provided the engines, first 175cc (11ci) and 250cc (15ci) two-strokes, and later 350cc (21ci) and 500cc (31ci) and possibly 250c/15ci four-strokes.

ROYAL NORD
Belgium 1950–early 1960s: Villiers and Maico two-strokes powered the 125cc (8ci) and 250cc (15ci) 'big' bikes; there were also 50cc (3ci) mopeds.

RABBIT
Japan 1946-68: These scooters were made with 90c (5ci) to 200cc (12ci) in-house engines.

RADCO
England 1913–32: A range of machines with two-stroke and four-stroke engines, from 211cc (13ci) to 500cc (31ci), came from this firm. Engines came from JAP and Villiers.

RADEX
Germany 1951–late 1950s: This firm made re-badged Express machines.

RADIOLA
France 1933–39: Auxiliary 98cc (6ci) cycle motors came from this firm.

RADIOR
France 1904–60: This company began with Peugeot and Antoine engines in the pioneer days and in the 1920s moved to bread-and-butter in-house two-strokes of 100cc (6ci) to 250cc (15ci), plus JAP and Chaise four-strokes of 250cc (15ci) to 500cc (31ci). Postwar, it produced mopeds, also 125cc (8ci), 175cc (11ci) and 250cc (15ci) two-strokes and a 250cc (15ci) four-stroke. Engines came from Nervor, AMC and NSU.

RADMILL
England 1912–14: This was a firm of assemblers of two-strokes with Villiers 269cc (16ci) and Precision 350cc (21ci).

RAGLAN
England 1909–13: This company is variously reported as making only 500cc (31ci) singles, or 300cc (18ci), 350cc (21ci) and 500cc (31ci) machines, with various Precision, or in-house, motors.

RAMBLER
USA 1903–14: This was a fairly typical manufacturer of V-twins and big singles.

R & F
Germany 1924–26: Unusually for the time and place, an in-house 348cc (21ci) overhead-valve engine powered this short-lived marque.

RANZANI
Italy (Milan) 1923–31: After starting with 175c (11ci) side-valve Heros engines (German) and 170cc (10ci) overhead-valve Norman engines (British), Ranzani moved on to an in-house overhead-valve 175c (11ci) engine. Both two-speed and three-speed options were offered.

RAP
Netherlands 1955–70s: This company produced mopeds, with engines from Rex, and later Puch.

RASSER
France 1922–23: This was a 100cc (6ci) two-stroke in an unusual pressed-steel frame.

RATINGIA
Germany 1923–25: These were 170cc (10ci) and 195cc (12ci) lightweights, but were side-valve instead of two-stroke.

RAVAT
France (Saint Etienne) 1898–1950s: This firm built four-strokes of up to 500cc (31ci), and small two-strokes.

RAY
England (Nottingham, later Leicester) 1922–25: This firm initially manufactured an in-house side-valve 193cc (12ci), and later (from 1924) also a 172cc (10ci) Villiers-Jardine.

RAYNAL
England 1914–53: Initially, this firm produced machines with Precision and Villiers engines and in the 1920s, the ubiquitous Villiers 269cc (16ci). From the late 1930s, it made a machine with a Villiers 98cc (6ci).

READY
Belgium 1924–39: Belgian Readies offered a ange of engines up to 500cc (31ci), variously reported as JAP, Blackburne, MAG and Rudge Python as well as a Villiers two-stroke.

REBRO
England 1922–28: This was a basic 150cc (9ci) Villiers-powered two-stroke lightweight.

RED STAR
Belgium (Antwerp) 1902: This machine was a Minerva-powered 211cc (13ci) pioneer.

REFORM
Austria (Vienna) 1903–05: Thein & Goldberger (see below) are variously reported to have used Monarch engines (from Birmingham) and Fafnir for their Reform machines. Both primary (layshaft) and secondary drive were by chain.

REGINA
England (Ilford) 1903–15: Initially (until 1907) this firm produced the usual pioneer engines: Minerva, MMC, Fafnir, from one-and-three-quarters to two-and-three-quarters horsepower. Then, after a gap, tit made an in-house 292cc (18ci) two-stroke.

REGINA
France 1905–15: Buchet, Peugeot, Zurcher and possibly other proprietary engines were fitted by this pioneer.

REIMA
Switzerland late 1960s: This racing 500cc (31ci) pushrod twin delivered 50 horsepower at 9500rpm.

ROYAL-RUBY
England 1909–30s: Highly regarded, especially in their early years, Royal Ruby supplemented its own 350cc (21ci) and 375cc (23ci) singles with Jap V-twins up to 1000cc (61ci).

ROYAL SCOT
Scotland (Glasgow) 1922–24: The frame (from Victoria) and the 350cc (21ci) sleeve-valve engine from Barr & Stroud were made in Scotland; they were built with an assortment of English and Scottish parts by Royal Scot.

ROYAL STANDARD
Switzerland 1928–32: A bike powered by a 400cc (24ci) parallel twin built by Zurcher, to a Royal Standard design and only for Royal Standard. Mounted in line with the frame.

ROYAL SUPER
Italy 1923–28: This was another name for the 132cc (8ci) two-stroke Royal from Milan.

R&P
England 1902–06: This firm was an advocate of the 'New Werner' engine position, built into the pedal bracket. In-house 350cc (21ci) singles powered most or all of these machines.

RTV
Australia 1998–: This 'updated Vincent' with a 1200cc (73ci) V-twin seemed at the time of writing to be put on hold.

RUBINELLI
Italy (Milan) 1921–27: Two-stroke lightweights of 125cc (8ci) and 175cc (11ci) came from this firm; the engines were also supplied to assemblers.

RULLIERS
Czech Republic 1924–29: Ladislaw Fischer & Spol seem to have used Villiers and possibly also JAP engines of 150cc (9ci), 175cc (11ci) and 350cc (21ci), although sources vary widely on detail.

RUPP
Germany 1928–32: This firm produced as a staple product an in-house 200cc (12ci) side-valve, and for glory, a 500cc (31ci) overhead-valve three-valve Kuchen.

RUPPE
Germany (Berlin) 1925–28: This was an auxiliary cycle motor of 98cc (6ci).

RUSH
Belgium 1922–34 or 1921–34: Mijnheer Van Geert won the Monza 250cc (15ci) with one of his own (Blackburne-engined) overhead-valve 250cc (15ci) machines in 1924; a Blackburne 350cc (21ci) was also available. He later made his own side-valve and overhead-valve engines, at least 350cc (21ci) and 500cc (31ci), and possibly 600cc (37ci) as well.

RUSPA
Italy (Turin) 1926–29: The Ruspa brothers, Luigi and Franco, brought out their first 125cc (8ci) early in 1926, and the pushrod 175cc (11ci) later in the same year. Their overhead-cam 350cc (21ci) was built in very limited numbers.

RUSSELL
England 1913: This was an obscure manufacturer of 175cc (11ci) and 500cc (31ci) machines – altogether an unlikely combination of sizes.

RUT
Germany 1923–24: This firm made the usual basic two-strokes, but unusually with an outside flywheel.

RUTER
Spain 1957–60: Hispano-Villiers two-strokes of 100cc (6ci) and 125cc (8ci) powered these lightweights.

RUWISCH
Germany 1948–49: Victoria 38cc (2ci) auxiliary-cycle motors were adapted for these mini-scooters.

RWC
Austria 1949–60: A Rotax-Sachs 100cc (6ci) motor was used by this bicycle manufacturer to build a lightweight.

R.W. SCOUT
England (London) 1920–21: As well as building Blackburne-powered Weatheralls, R. Weatherall used two-strokes – 318cc (19ci) Dalm and possibly 269cc (16ci) Villiers – in the R.W. Scout.

SACHS
Germany 1930s: Fichtel & Sachs began making engines for other motorcycle manufacturers in the early 1930s. Massive production figures. Took over several marques, including Hercules and Victoria at the end of the 1950s. Built its first own-brand bike in 1980.

SACI
Brazil (Sao Paolo) 1959–60s: Costrucciones Mecanicas Grassi built a motor scooter with a 175c (11ci) Sachs engine, and a trials bike.

SADRIAN
Spain 1956–63: This firm produced Hispano-Villiers-powered lightweights of 125cc (8ci) and 200cc (12ci), and three-wheeled delivery vehicles.

SALIRA
Belgium 1955–early 1960s: Villiers engines powered most of these 100cc (6ci) to 200cc (12ci) machines.

SALSBURY
USA 1946–mid-1950s: One of the rash of postwar scooters, this had a fan-cooled 150cc (9ci) side-valve motor.

SALTLEY
England 1919–24: This assembler produced machines with the 269cc (16ci) Villiers, 500cc (31ci) Blackburne and the novel 350cc (21ci) Vulcanus.

SALVE
Italy (Milan) 1925–26: The Societa Automotociclette Lombardo Veneto-Emilia put an in-house 496cc (30ci) side-valve of advanced design into a modern frame.

SANCHOC
France 1922–24: As was common, this firm fitted two-strokes for the smaller bikes (100cc/6ci to 250cc/15ci) and side-valves for those up to 350cc (21ci).

SAN CHRISTOPHORO
Italy 1951–54: This firm produced two-stroke lightweights of 125cc (8ci) typical of the period.

S & G
Germany (Nurnberg) 1926–32: Scharer & GroB made bikes with 350cc (21ci), 500cc (31ci) and 600cc (37ci) side-valve and pushrod singles; later bikes had 175cc (11ci) and 200cc (12ci) two-strokes, and they made three-wheeled delivery vehicles.

S & N
Germany 1901–08: Laurin & Klement licensed its machines to this firm, supplying some parts ready-made.

SAN-SOU-PAP
France 1923–36: 'Sans soupapes' ('without valves') was true of the early Train-powered two-strokes of 100cc (6ci) to 250cc (15ci), but not of the later JAP and MAG four-strokes of 250cc (15ci) to 500cc (31ci).

SANTAMARIA
Italy 1951–63: These mopeds and lightweights went up to 150cc (9ci) with Ilo, Sachs and Zundapp engines.

SANYO
Japan 1958–62: In-house 250cc (15ci) overhead-valve motors powered these sporting lightweights.

SAR
Italy (Reggio Emilia) 1920–25: The Societa Reggiana Motocicli began with a 500cc (31ci) flat twin in Sports (overhead-valve) and Touring (side-valve) guises, the former capable of over 150km/h (90mph). It added a single in 1924.

SAR
Germany 1925–30: Two-strokes of 125cc (8ci) and 200cc (12ci); also reported as having began production in 1928.

SARACEN
England 1967–73: Off-road competition machines with Sachs engines up to 200cc (12ci), and Mickmar 250cc (15ci).

SARENKA
Poland 1961–c.1970: This was a 123cc (8ci) DKW-engined two-stroke in a pressed-steel frame from WSK.

SARTORIUS
Germany 1924–26: Kuhne supplied the engines to this small assembler: 197cc (12ci) side-valve for utility, 350cc (21ci) overhead-valve for the flagship.

SATAN
Czech Republic 1929: An in-house 550cc (34ci) 'sloper' powered this bike, which neither went nor sold like the devil.

SATURN
England 1925–26: This firm made modest numbers of machines with an in-house 350cc (21ci) two-stroke single.

SATURN
Germany 1921–27: An interesting array came from this firm, a 150cc (9ci) side-valve auxiliary cycle motor to a 250cc (15ci) two-stroke to a 350cc (21ci) overhead-valve and a 500cc (31ci) side-valve V-twin.

SAUND
India 1962–88: DKW-inspired machines werer based ever more loosely on the 100cc (6ci) original.

SCARAB
Italy 1967–85: These were off-road competition machines from Ancilotti, with engines of 50cc (3ci), 125cc (8ci) and 250cc (15ci) from Sachs, Hiro and Franco-Morini.

SCARABEO
Italy (Noale) 1968–: These typical Italian off-road competition machines came from Aprilia, with engines of 50cc (3ci) and 125cc.

SCHEIBERT
Austria (Vienna) 1911–13: The engine was built into the steering head, after the fashion of the Original Werner.

SCHICKEL
USA (Stanford, Connecticut) 1912–15: The cast light-alloy frame of this machine housed a big two-stroke single.

SCHLIHA
Germany (Berlin) 1924–33: Predictably, this was a 175c (11ci) two-stroke at first. Later models offered 200cc (12ci), 300c (18ci), 350cc (21ci) and 500cc (31ci).

SCHMIDT
Germany 1921–24: Its own in-house side-valve motors powered this 200cc (12ci) lightweight; there was also an auxiliary cycle motor.

SCHNELL-HOREX
Germany 1952–54: 'Schnell' refers both to the speed and to Roland Schnell, the racer/designer. Based on Horex parts, these 250cc (15ci), 350cc (21ci) and 500cc (31ci) singles had gear-driven overhead-cams and were sold to privateers.

SCHURHOFF
Germany 1949–53: Mopeds with 50cc (3ci) Sachs and Ilo engines, and lightweights up to 175c (11ci), with Ilo engines.

SCHUTT
Germany 1933–34: Paul Schutt's 200cc (12ci) two-strokes were set in a Duralumin frame.

SCHUTTOFF
Germany 1924–33: This firm produced 250cc (15ci), then 350cc (21ci) and 500cc (31ci) in-house engines, both side-valve and overhead-valve. It was taken over by DKW in 1933.

SCHWALBE
Germany (Aalen) 1922–24: The Spiegler brothers made a 125cc (8ci) or 150cc (9ci) flat-twin, as a lightweight and an auxiliary cycle motor, then added a 200cc (12ci) lightweight.

SCHWALBE
Switzerland 1901–05: These machines featured Zedel two-and-three-quarters horsepower engines in strengthened bicycle frames.

SCHWEPPE
Germany 1949–50: This Ilo-powered scooter, with 143cc (9ci) to 184cc (11ci) engines, was the precursor of the Pirol.

SCOOTAVIA
France 1951–56: These were AMC-powered overhead-valve 175c (11ci) scooters.

SCORPION
England 1951–56: Villiers 200cc (12ci) (12ci) and 250cc (15ci) motors in pressed-steel frames ensured that these had less sting than their name implied.

SCOTO
France 1949–early 1950s: Mosquito 38cc (2ci) engines powered these mini-scooters.

SCOTT-CYC-AUTO
England 1934–50: This long-lived moped had an in-house 98cc (6ci) motor.

SCYLLA
France 1931–37: These were two-stroke lightweights with 100cc (6ci) and 125cc (8ci)Aubier-Dunne motors.

SEAL
England 1912–23: Was this a motorcycle or a three-wheeled car? The driver and passenger sat in the large, permanently attached sidecar, and steering was by wheel. Power came from a six horsepower 1000cc (61ci) JAP V-twin.

SEILIG
Italy 1938–39: These were rather handsome machines, with the single 250cc (15ci) or 350cc (21ci) side-valve cylinder set well back in the frame.

SEMIOR
Spain 1952: This was quite an advanced 175c (11ci) two-stroke lightweight, with good suspension.

SENIOR
Italy 1913–14: Moser singles (300 and 330cc) and V-twins (500cc/31ci) powered these sporting machines.

SERVICE
England 1900–12: Connaught, and Wartnaby & Draper, actually built these machines, sold as Service.

SESSA
Italy (Milan) 1951–53: These were two models of Ilo-powered 150cc (9ci) lightweight.

SETTER
Spain 1954–56: These ultra-lightweights had an in-house 60cc (4ci) motor.

S-FORTIS
Czech Republic 1929–31: These English-looking 600cc (37ci) pushrod singles had Sarolea engines.

SFW
Germany 1924–26: As well as a 200cc (12ci) two-stroke of their own manufacture, this company also offered a 500cc (31ci) with the BMW proprietary flat twin.

SGS
England (Macclesfield) 1926–33: Gleave Engineering built Sid Gleave Special racers and sporting roadsters with JAP 250cc (15ci) and 500cc (31ci) four-strokes, and 175cc (11ci) and 250cc (15ci) Villiers two-strokes.

SHANGHAI
China 1964–unknown: This firm began with two machines copied from others' designs. One was a 750cc (461ci) BMW-like sidecar hauler, the Donghai 750 A, and the other was a CZ-based 250cc (15ci) two-stroke single.

SHARRATT
England 1920–30: These machines were fitted with JAP engines of 300cc (18ci) to 1000cc (61ci), and some Villiers and MAG engines.

This French-made Rovin dates from 1927 and has a JAP ohv engine.

431

This Scott CYC autocycle 98cc (6ci) DeLuxe dates from the early 1950s.

SHAW
England 1898–1909: Sidney Shaw built his first 250cc (15ci) chain-drive Gazelle motorcycle in 1898 but he seems not to have kept ahead of the times; production ended in 1909.

SHAW
USA 1909–23: These were simple, direct-drive machines with single-cylinder in-house engines, giving two-and-a-half and three-and-a-half horsepower.

SHAW
England 1918–22: This auxiliary 115cc (7ci) cycle-motor was actually made in Galesburg, Kansas.

SHIN MEIWA
Japan 1955–mid-1960s: The 250cc (15ci) Pointer Ace was followed by the Pointer of the same capacity, the 123cc (8ci) Senior, 60cc (4ci) Junior, 175c (11ci) Pointer Comet and Pointer 90. In 1960, the line-up was restructured. The last model, the Pointer Sports KS1 of 1963, made 130km/h (80mph) from its 16 horsepower (at 8500rpm), 125cc (8ci) motor.

SHL
Poland (Kielec) 1935–: Before 1939, Villiers 125cc (8ci)two-strokes powered these machines; postwar, they had 125cc (8ci), 150cc (9ci) and 175c (11ci) two-strokes.

SHOWA
Japan mid-1950s–early 1960s: In the 1950s, this firm built mopeds of 50cc (3ci), 125cc (8ci) lightweights, and a 250cc (15ci) scooter, then in 1961, a 125cc (8ci) scooter, all two-strokes.

SIAMT
Italy 1907–14: Luigi Semeria was 26 when the first machine to bear his name appeared, a 260cc (16ci) single. Later came 350cc (21ci) singles and 500cc (31ci), 688cc (42ci) and 731cc (45ci) V-twins.

SIAT
Italy (Senegallia) 1924–26: The Societa Italiana di Applicazioni Techniche built a 75cc (5ci) auxiliary cycle motor, then lightweights of 100cc (6ci) to 200cc (12ci), both two- and four-stroke.

SIATA
Italy 1954: This automobile pioneer also made the 160cc (10ci) two-stroke Dinghi lightweight and the Cucciolo moped.

SIC
France (Paris) 1921–25: Initially Aubier-Dunne, Train, Zurcher and possibly other motors powered these machines, in capacities from 100cc (6ci) to 350cc (21ci); the firm switched to a DKW 160cc (10ci) two-stroke just before the end.

SICRAF
France 1947–53: These assembled machines of 50cc (3ci) to 250cc (15ci) had Ydral and AMC (France) motors.

SIDEMOTOR
France 1925: This was an integral combination of sidecar and motorcycle, with the engine alongside the frame and driving between the two rear wheels (one motorcycle, one sidecar).

SIEG
Germany 1922–30: Success was not prolonged for Jungst's ambitious machine that could be had with a variety of engines from 110cc (7ci) to 600cc (37ci), from many different manufacturers.

SIGNORELLI
Italy 1928–30: These models had in-house 175c (11ci) two-strokes.

SIL
India 1978–: These were Lambrettas for which Sil bought the tooling when Lambretta ceased production.

SILVER PIDGEON
Japan early 1950s–1965: This improbably-named scooter, with its choice of 87cc (5ci) two-stroke or 192cc (12ci) side-valve engines, was a separate marque within the Mitsubishi group.

SILVER PRINCE
England 1919–24: This assembler had a 350cc (21ci) Blackburne for a flagship and Villiers two-strokes from 150cc (9ci) to 269cc (16ci) for the lesser models.

SILVER STAR
Japan 1953–58: In-house 125cc (8ci) and 150cc (9ci) overhead-valve engines powered these lightweights.

SIM
Italy (Milan) 1955–60s: The Societa Italiana Motori began with a 48cc (3ci) four-stroke moped, and the Pegaso with a pressed-steel frame.

SIMCA
France 1935–39: From a choice of 250cc (15ci), 330cc (20ci) and 350cc (21ci) prototypes, the French War Department ordered 40,000 350cc (21ci) two-stroke, shaft-drive twins. Only about 250cc (15ci) were built before Hitler interfered with the delivery schedule.

SIMONCELLI
Italy 1927–35: These 175c (11ci) lightweights were initially powered by Train strokes, then by JAP four-strokes.

SIMPLEX
Italy (Turin) 1921–50: Luigi Pellini (of Pellini & Ferrari) began with a 124cc (8ci) auxiliary cycle motor and in 1927 moved on to 150cc (9ci) and 175c (11ci) overhead-valve lightweights. Enclosed valve gear followed in 1930, along with bigger engines.

SIMPLEX
USA 1935–75: The popular Clinton 200cc (12ci) industrial engine powered these small-wheeled runabouts, designed for factory messengers and the like.

SINGER
England 1904–15: This firm began by licensing the Perks & Birch Motorwheel, but followed with more conventional machines, mostly with its own engines. It produced exotica for racing and record-breaking but the road-going machines were less exciting. Later, they became better known for cars.

SIROCCO
Czech Republic 1925–28: These Moravian machines used Villiers two-strokes of 175cc (11ci) to 250cc (15ci).

SIRRAH
England (Birmingham) 1922–25: Alfred Wiseman (who also built the Verus) built these machines, with a choice of six engine sizes from four manufacturers.

SIS
Portugal 1950–: These mopeds and lightweights went up to 98cc (6ci) with Sachs engines.

SITTA
Germany 1950–55: Ilo engines powered all Sitta's 49cc (3ci) mopeds, 119cc (7ci) and 123cc (8ci) scooters, and lightweights from 125cc (8ci) to 250cc (15ci).

SJK
Japan 1956–early 1960s: These were mopeds and lightweights of up to 250cc (15ci) capacity.

SKF
Russia 1961–65: These double-overhead-cam racers of 350cc (21ci) were not sold publicly.

SL
England 1924–25: The in-house 345cc (21ci) single powering the SL had two inlet valves and one exhaust.

SLAVIA
Austro-Hungary/Czech Republic 1899–1908: This was another Laurin & Klement trade mark.

SM
Poland 1935: This was an advanced shaft-drive overhead-valve 350cc (21ci) unit-construction single.

SMART
Austria (Wiener Neustadt) 1925–c.1930: JAP engines, side-valve and overhead-valve, powered this machine.

SMART
France 1922–27: This 200cc (12ci) side-valve lightweight had an in-house engine.

SNOB
Germany 1921–25: These direct-drive lightweights had inlet-over-exhaust 154cc (9ci) in-house engines, although there were also overhead-valve racing versions.

SOCOVEL
Belgium 1938–60: After a brief pre-war play with electric motorcycles, Socovel returned in 1947 with lightweights and middleweights. Some had pressed-steel frames and fully enclosed 123cc (8ci) and 197cc (12ci) Villiers engines.

SOLO
Germany 1949–82: These were mopeds, including an electric one.

SOUPLEX
Belgium 1947–53: After beginning with a conventional Villiers-powered 123cc (8ci) two-stroke, Souplex offered a more interesting transverse flat twin with a 300cc (18ci) Coventry-Victor engine.

SOUTHEY
England 1905–25: As well as supplying frames to other makers, Southey made motorcycles with engines from Villiers (250cc) and Blackburne (side-valve 350cc/21ci).

SOYER
France (Coulombes, later Levallois) 1920–35: In-house two-strokes powered most Soyers, initially 250cc (15ci), later 100cc (6ci) and 175c (11ci). Four-stroke options from 250cc (15ci) to 500cc (31ci) were provided courtesy of Chaise, JAP and Sturmey-Archer.

SPARKBROOK
England 1912–25: Before World War I, these were big JAP V-twins of 750cc (46ci) and 1000cc (61ci). Postwar, the biggest machines were 350cc (21ci) singles from various engine manufacturers.

SPARTA
Netherlands 1931–: Sparta moved from bicycles into lightweights, initially (and to this day) with auxiliary cycle motors and later 49cc (3ci) mopeds, but also until about 1960 Sachs, Villiers, Ilo and Victoria engines, from 100cc (6ci) to 250cc (15ci).

SPARTON
Wales (Caernarfon) 1976–unknown: These were limited production racers, four-cylinder four-strokes of 500cc (31ci) and 750cc (461ci), and two-strokes of 500cc (31ci) and 525cc, all water-cooled.

SPHINX
France 1933–39: This assembler used Stainless engines.

SPIEGLER
Germany (Aalen) 1923–32: The successor to Schwalbe, Spiegler made a pressed-steel box section, incorporating the tank, stretched from the steering head to the rear wheel: the rest of the frame was tubular. As well as its own engines, JAP and MAG were used. All were singles; capacities varied from 200cc (12ci) to 600cc (37ci).

SPRITE
England 1965–unknown: These off-road two-stroke competition machines came in kit form, up to 400cc (24ci).

STADION
Czech Republic 1958–66: Mopeds fitted with Jawa engines.

STANDARD
Germany and Switzerland 1925–52: Wilhelm Gutbrod set up Standard in Germany in 1925, and in 1929 bought Zehnder in Switzerland. From JAP 250cc (15ci) and 350cc (21ci) overhead-valve motors, the firm switched to MAG 350–1000cc (21–61ci) engines of varying types. In 1930, the firm introduced its own 200cc (12ci) and 250cc (15ci) engines.

STAR
England 1898–1914: Star were early motorcycle producers, first using De Dion-Bouton engines, and then JAP 625cc (38ci) singles and 770cc (47ci) V-twins.

STAR
Germany 1920–22: In-house 400cc (24ci) flat twins powered these precursors of the D-Rad.

STEFFEY
USA (Philadelphia, Pennsylvania) 1902–10: The Steffey's engines, some water-cooled, some air-cooled, were their own manufacture.

STELLA
Belgium 1921–36: JAP-licensed Staub engines of 350cc (21ci) and 500cc (31ci), and 100cc (6ci) two-strokes, powered these machines, some with pressed-steel frames.

STELLAR
England 1912–14: The Stellar was surprisingly advanced: a 750cc (461ci) water-cooled two-stroke unit construction parallel twin with free engine, two gears and shaft drive.

STERZI
Italy (Palazzolo sull'Oglio) 1939–early 1960s: Only a few Sachs-powered 100cc (6ci) and 125cc (8ci) machines were built before the war. From about 1948 came a range that began with 125cc (8ci) and went on to include 160c (10ci) and 175c (11ci) (1954), all two-stroke, an overhead-valve four-stroke moped (Pony 49, 1955), a 60cc (4ci) lightweight (1957) and a 160cc (10ci) two-stroke scooter (1958).

STILMA
Italy (Turin) 1948: The Societa Torinese Industrie Lavorazione Meccaniche e Affini built an interesting 500cc (31ci) single with partial enclosure, telescopic forks and parallelogram rear suspension.

STIMULA
France 1902–30s: As well as using Buchet, Minerva and Peugeot engines in the pioneering days, Stimula later made its own 350cc (21ci) and 500cc (31ci) engines.

STOCK
Germany 1924–33: This firm began with a licence-built Evans of 119cc, but moved on to 200cc (12ci), 300cc (18ci) and 350cc (21ci) two-stroke singles with shaft drive. It also built water-cooled racers in the late 1920s.

STROLCH
Germany 1950–58: These were Sachs-engined scooters of 98cc (6ci) to 198cc (6ci), later renamed Progress.

STUART
England 1911–12: The Stuart was a 300cc (18ci) two-stroke single from the same firm that built Stellar.

STURM
Germany 1923–25: More of a light shower than a full-blown storm, these were Alba-powered 150cc (9ci) two-strokes.

STYLSON
France 1919–39: This idiosyncratic assembler used JAP (and Staub-built JAP-licensed) engines up to 1000cc (61ci). Some were shaft drive; some had transverse-mounted V-twin engines.

STYRIA
Austria 1905–08: Fafnir singles and V-twins powered these pioneers.

SUBLIME
France 1954: This motorcycle was a 350cc (21ci) pushrod twin with four-speed box and telescopic forks that was reasonably up-to-the-minute.

SUDBRACK
Germany 1949–51: Ilo engines were used by this bicycle factory to make 98cc (6ci) and 123cc (8ci) lightweights.

SUECIA
Sweden 1928–40: JAP engines of 250cc (15ci), 350cc (21ci) and 500cc (31ci) powered these assembled machines. Two-strokes built by Sparta were also sold as Sucias.

SULKY
France 1954–57: These were mini-scooters with AMC (France) engines of 100cc (6ci) to 125cc.

SUMITA
Japan 1951–55: In the Japanese style, these machines had in-house 125cc (8ci) and 150cc (9ci) overhead-valve engines.

SUPERBA
Italy 1928–35: JAP and Piazza engines, both 175c (11ci), powered these sporting lightweights.

SUPERB-FOUR
England 1920–21: This was a longitudinally mounted overhead-cam straight four of 1000cc (61ci) made, sadly, in very small numbers.

SUPERIA
Germany 1925–28: These sporting machines were mostly overhead-cam Kuchen-powered with 350cc (21ci) and 500cc (31ci) engines, plus 500cc (31ci) ECE side-valve machines.

SUPERIA
Belgium 1957–70: These mopeds had engines bought in from numerous suppliers.

SUPER-X
USA 1924–30: These American machines were Schwinn inlet-over-exhaust V-twins, similar to Excelsior/American-X.

SUPPLEXA
France 1922–32: JAP engines up to 1000cc (61ci) powered these machines, which were noted for their long wheelbase.

SUPREMOCO
England 1921–23: This assembler used 250cc (15ci) to 350cc (21ci) engines from a wide variety of suppliers. The same factory made Defy-All.

SUQUET
France 1929–34: These Aubier-Dunne powered lightweights were of 100cc (6ci) and 125cc (8ci) capacities.

SUT
Germany 1921–27: Lightweights powered by In-house side-valve and inlet-over-exhaust engines of a range of capacities – 148cc (9ci), 172cc (10ci), 197cc (12ci), and 247cc (15ci).

SUZY
France 1932–33: An overhead-cam 500cc (31ci) Chaise powered this enclosed-engine machine.

SWAN
England 1911–13: This was an unconventional machine with a rivetted chassis of steel and light alloy, part of which concealed the 500cc (31ci) side-valve Precision that drove it.

SWIFT
England (Coventry) 1898–1915: With links to Starley and Ariel, Swift illustrates the closeness of the British motorcycle industry. From De Dion-Bouton engines, it moved on to White & Poppe engines, also using its own V-twins to 768cc (47ci).

SYMPLEX
England 1913–22: Dalm 311cc two-strokes powered these assembled machines.

SYPHAX
France 1952–53: These were lightweights with AMC and Aubier-Dunne two strokes of 100cc (6ci) to 175cc (11ci), and AMC overhead-valve engines of 125cc (8ci) and 175c (11ci).

TANDON
England 1948–57: Villiers two-strokes of 123cc (8ci) to 322cc (20ci), mostly singles but vertical twins for the two largest sizes powered these unremarkable machines. Tandon also made the Talbot moped with a Trojan motor.

TAPELLA-FUCHS
Italy 1953–57: These mopeds were fitted with Fuchs engines.

TARBO
Italy (Bologna) 1967–unknown: Tartarini combined his name with the place where he built his machines – actually Italianized Jawas, from mopeds to a 350cc (21ci) twin.

TAS
Germany (Saargebiet) 1924–31: As well as 200cc (12ci) two-strokes (one source has 173cc/11ci and 248cc/15ci), TAS used 350cc (21ci) and 500cc (31ci) four-strokes, initially from Gnome et Rhone and later from MAG.

TAU
Italy (Milan): 'Hot' two-strokes (of 125cc/8ci and later 100cc /6ci) were made for off-road use, and later supplemented by a 250cc (15ci) twin delivering 38 horsepower at 8000rpm.

TAURA
Italy (Turin) 1927–30: Giulio Doglioli began with 175c (11ci) JAP-powered lightweights, moving on in 1929 to 500cc (31ci) side-valve JAP and 350cc (21ci) overhead-valve Blackburne.

TAUTZ
Germany 1921–23: This neat 'step-through' had a DKW engine of 120cc (7ci) and possibly also 200cc (12ci).

TAVERNIER
France 1921–23: Blackburne, JAP and Zurcher engines of 175cc (11ci) to 500cc (31ci) powered machines from this small assembler.

TECNOMOTO
Italy 1968–unknown: Minarelli 50cc (3ci) engines powered these tiny machines.

TECO
Germany (Stettin) 1920–26: Based in the 'Polish Corridor' this Polish manufacturer of Alba-powered 200cc (12ci) lightweights also made a Kuhne-powered 350cc (21ci) single.

TEDDY
France 1922–24: A 203cc (12ci) side-valve engine, apparently of its own manufacture, powered these lightweight machines.

TEE-BEE
England 1908–11: This company apparently used its own engines as well as 300cc (18ci) JAPs.

TEHUELCHE
Argentina (Santa Fe) 1958–62: These small machines – initially 75cc, later 100cc (6ci) – had overhead-cam engines.

TEMPLE
England 1924–28: Claude Temple, record-breaker, racer and tuner, lent his name to these machines from the OEC stable, mostly 350cc (21ci) and 500cc (31ci) singles, but also 1000cc (61ci) Anzani V-twins.

TEMPO
Norway 1949–: There mopeds of 49cc (3ci) and lightweights of 123cc (8ci) had a range of bought-in two-stroke motors.

TERRA
Germany 1922–24: Simple three-port two-strokes, Terra's in-house engines were 125cc (8ci), 150cc (9ci) and 175cc (11ci).

TERROT
Czechoslovakia 1933–35: This short-lived subsidiary of the French company built 350cc (21ci) singles.

TETGE
Germany 1923–26: This firm made MAG 600cc (37ci) V-twins at the top of the line, and 150cc (9ci) and 175cc (11ci) singles for everyday fare.

TGR
Italy (Bologna) 1980s: This electric moped with 60 Amp-hour batteries had a top speed of 30km/h (20mph).

THIEM
USA (St Paul, Minnesota) 1903–14: These typical US singles (550cc inlet-over-exhaust) and V-twins (900cc/55ci and 1000cc/ 61ci) came from that brief era when US motorcycle design led the world.

THEIN & GOLDBERGER
Austria 1903–05: These were typical pioneers with Fafnir and Minerva engines of two-and-a-quarter to three horsepower.

THOMANN
France 1912–39: This was part of the Alcyon group, which built two-stroke machines of 100cc (6ci) to 250cc (15ci).

THOMAS
England 1904: The usual pioneering bought-in engines – Minerva, Sarolea, maybe others – powered these rare machines.

THOMAS
USA 1907–08: The Thomas automobile works built three-horsepower singles with its own in-house engines.

THOROUGH
England 1903: MMC and Coronet engines powered these assembled pioneers.

THREE-SPIRES
England (Coventry) 1931–32: The three spires is a common Coventry logo: these lightweights had a 147cc (9ci) two-stroke engine, priced at 18 guineas (£18 and 18 shillings).

THUMANN
Germany (Hanover) 1925–26: In-house 250cc (15ci) and 350cc (21ci) side-valves powered the small firm's bikes.

THUNDER
Italy 1952–54: Offering more of a loud buzz than rolling thunder, this was a well-made, fast, and overly expensive 125cc (8ci) overhead-valve parallel twin.

TICKLE
England 1967–73: John Tickle bought the right to make Manx Nortons after they were discontinued by Norton.

TIGER
1903–14: These were uncannily reminiscent of Allright and Vindec machines of the same period.

TIGER
USA (Chicago, Illinois) 1915–16: Unusually for the US, this was a 241cc (15ci) two-stroke lightweight.

TIGLI
Italy 1950: Twenty-three years after his last 125cc (8ci) Italian championship win, racer Amedeo Tigli (in partnership with Franco Morini) offered a 75cc (5ci)two-stroke.

TIKA
Germany 1921–24: This assembler of lightweight four-strokes used Herko 150cc (9ci) and 200cc (12ci) side-valve engines.

TILBROOK
Australia 1950–53: Villiers two-strokes of 125cc (8ci) and 200cc (12ci) powered Rex Tilbrook's advanced but short-lived machines.

TILSTON
England 1919: This assembler used 225cc (14ci) Precision two-stroke engines.

TINKLER
England 1920s: Almond Tinkler, a maker of timepieces, built his first 'bitsa' in 1914 and announced the Tinkler Special in 1927. His machines – including a three-cylinder radial – do not appear to have entered series production.

TITAN
Austria (Puntigam, near Graz) 1927–33: After the two-stroke 144cc (9ci) twin Austro-Motorette, Titan introduced a reed-valve 350cc (21ci) of its own design as well as offering 350cc (21ci) and 500cc (31ci) JAP and Blackburne four-strokes.

TITAN
San Marino 1975–: These mopeds in various guises came from Curio Rinaldi and Gianfranco Mularoni.

TIZ-AM
Russia (Kharkov) 1931–40: As well as a solid 600cc (37ci) side-valve single in a sprung frame, Tiz-Am sold a two-horsepower lightweight.

TM
Italy (Pesara) 1968–92: Typical – but successful – Italian lightweight machines for off-road competition, with 48cc (3ci) (Franco-Morini, Zundapp) to 125cc (8ci) (Yamaha) engines.

TOMASELLI
Italy 1931–39: These JAP engines of 167 to 500cc (31ci) were fitted into sporting assembled machines.

TOMMASI
Italy 1926–27: One Della Ferrera 123cc (8ci) powered the smaller machine: two, coupled together, powered the 246cc (15ci) machine.

TOREADOR
England (Preston) 1924–26: Although JAP and Blackburne

singles, and even a 500cc (31ci) MAG V-twin, were used in these bikes, most Toreadors were powered by Bradshaw oil boilers, including the rare double overhead-cam 350cc (21ci).

TORPADO
Italy (Padua) 1950–70: This firm produced 50cc (3ci) mopeds with a Minarelli engine.

TORPEDO
Austro-Hungary/Czech Republic (Kolin) 1903–12: This unusually self-sufficient company even made its own carburettors. Engines were singles of three-and-a-half and four horsepower, and V-twins of six and eight horsepower.

TORPEDO
England (Barton on Humber) 1910–20: F. Hooper used Precision singles and twins of 300cc (18ci), 350cc (21ci) and 500cc (31ci).

TORPEDO
Germany (Geestemunde) 1901–07: Ernst Weichelt used the usual proprietary motors, including Fafnir, Minerva and Zedel.

TORPEDO
Germany (Rodelheim bei Frankfurt) 1928–56: Before World War II, these were fitted with Blackburne 200cc (12ci) side-valves, and after it, Sachs and Ilo 125cc (8ci), 150cc (9ci) and 175c (11ci).

A 1960 Moto Sterzi with a two-stroke 160cc (10ci) engine.

TORROT
Spain 1960–85: This firm produced mopeds. The name is a Spanish readjustment of Terrot, of which the company started as a subsidiary.

TOWNEND
England 1901–04: These were pioneer singles.

TOYOMOTOR
Japan 1957–early 1960s: Adler apparently provided the inspiration for these 250cc (15ci) two-stroke twins.

TRAFALGAR
England 1902–05: Trafalgar was a pioneer in sidecar manufacture, originally to accompany its own machines with MMC and Minerva engines.

TRAFFORD
England 1919–22: The famous 269cc (16ci) Villiers two-stroke was found in this company's only model.

TRAGATSCH
Czech Republic 1946–49: The author of the famous Complete Illustrated Encyclopaedia of the World's Motorcycles built JAP-engined track racers of 350cc (21ci) and 500cc (31ci).

TRANS AMA
Italy (Pesaro) 1970s: These off-road sporting vehicles were mostly 50cc (3ci) (Minarelli), 125cc (8ci) and 250cc (15ci) (Hiro), but the firm also made a 320cc (Hiro), as well as mopeds and road-going derivatives of the racers, and children's mini-bikes.

TREBLOC
England 1922–25: The 63cc (4ci) engine that powered these machines was remarkable for its unusual swept volume and for the fact that it was manufactured in-house.

TREMO
Germany 1925–28: Unusually, given the time and place, these featured in-house 308cc (19ci) side-valve and overhead-valve engines.

TRENT
England 1902–06: This was common pioneer fare: a 207cc (13ci) engine in a strengthened bicycle frame.

TRESOLDI
Italy (Milan) c.1980–: These were off-road sports machines for children, with 50cc (3ci) and 80cc (5ci) engines.

TRESPIDI
Italy 1926–30: Paolo Trespidi designed and built two-strokes with in-house engines, initially 250cc (15ci), later 175cc (11ci).

TRIANON
Germany 1922–26: This bicycle manufacturer built motor-cycles fitted with an in-house 232cc (14ci) two-stroke engine.

TRIBUNE
USA 1903–14: This was an obscure pioneer, apparently with Aster and Thor engines.

TRIPLE-H
England 1921–23: Hobbis, Hobbis and Horrell used a 250cc (15ci) John Morris two-stroke for their simple lightweight.

TRIPLETTE
England 1923–25: This machine was a Villiers 150cc (9ci) two-stroke fitted in a low-cost frame.

TRIPOL
Czech Republic 1925–26: This bicycle manufacturer also built motorcycles with a Villiers 250cc (15ci) two-stroke engine.

TRIUMPH
USA (Detroit, Michigan) 1912: This branch factory of the English make turned out 550cc side-valve singles.

TROBYKE
England 1958–60s: This was a very small-wheeled scooter with a 98cc (6ci) Clinton two-stroke engine.

TROPFEN
Germany (Osnabruck) 1923–24: Tropfen, an airship firm, built an airship-shaped motorcycle with full enclosure and a choice of motors: sources refer to 250cc (15ci), 300cc (18ci), 350cc (21ci) and 770cc (47ci) capacities, most (or all) two-stroke.

TSUBASA
Japan 1950–60: This company produced mostly an overhead-cam 250cc (15ci) single, and later also a 125cc (8ci), both with in-house engines.

TURKHEIMER
Italy (Milan) 1902–05: As well as importing others' machines, Max Turkheimer also assembled one-and-a-quarter horsepower machines under his own name.

TULA
Soviet Union c.1970s: This scooter was fitted with a 200cc (12ci) two-stroke single engine.

TUNTURI
Finland 1956–: This bicycle (and exercise bicycle) manufacturer also built Puch-engined 50cc (3ci) mopeds, some of which were very well styled.

TVS
India 1976–: This firm first buit Batavus 50cc (3ci) mopeds under licence; later (1980s) it licensed Suzuki technology; and from 1993, built a 60cc (4ci) scooter of its own design.

TX
Germany 1924-26: These Bekamo-engined 132cc (8ci) and 174cc (11ci) two-strokes had a massive top tube that acted as a fuel tank and incorporated the steering head.

TYLER
England 1913–23: Before World War I, this manufacturer used the 269cc (16ci) Villiers and possibly 198cc (6ci) Precision engine; afterwards, as Metro and Metro-Tyler, its own 269cc (16ci) engine.

TYM
Taiwan c.1970–: A scooter-cum-moped of 50cc (3ci).

TYPHOON
Sweden 1949–51: This well-designed 200cc (12ci) two-stroke had an in-house engine, from the pen of Folke Mannerstaedt, famous for Husqvarna racers.

TYPHOON
The Netherlands 1955–early 1960s: These mopeds had 50cc (3ci) engines from various makers.

The LE 'Noddy Bike' exemplified all that was unconventional about Velocette.

ULTIMA
France (Lyon) 1908–c.1960: This firm began with JAP singles and twins, also fitting others from Aubier Dunne to Zurcher. The 1930s line-up included 250cc (15ci) and 350cc (21ci) singles, and a 500cc (31ci) V-twin. After 1945, it focused on lightweight two-strokes of 125cc (8ci), 175cc (11ci) and 200cc (12ci) with in-house engines.

UNDERSLUNG
USA 1912: A bizarre machine with a low frame of two parallel tubes, a low seat, steering with a car-type wheel, and 'training wheels' on either side of the rear wheel to stop it falling over.

UNIBUS
England 1920–22: This fully-enclosed scooter had a 269cc (16ci) Precision four-stroke engine built by the Gloster Aircraft Co. using aircraft materials and techniques.

UNION
Sweden (Charlottenberg) 1943–52: JAP engines of 350cc (21ci) and 500cc (31ci) powered this sporting marque.

UNIVERSELLE (UNIVERSAL)
Germany 1925–29: These were powered by an in-house engine that grew from 183cc (11ci) to 197cc (12ci) and finally 247cc (15ci).

URAL
Russia 1976–: Brand name used by the Irbit works to market its range of BMW-inspired horizontally-opposed twin cylinder models in Western countries.

URANIA
Germany 1934–39: Lightweights from a bicycle-maker.

UTILIA
France 1929-36: Sachs, Duten and Train supplied two-strokes (and Utilia built some themselves), while Chaise, JAP and LMP supplied the four-strokes in this firm's ambitious line-up from 100cc (6ci) to 500cc (31ci).

VAGA
Italy (Milan) 1925–35: These machines were fitted with English four-strokes. These engines had a 175c (11ci) displacement and were bought in from various sources; these included Blackburne, CF (overhead-cam) and possibly JAP. However, one source also refers to the company being responsible for the production of a machine fitted with a 125cc (8ci) two-stroke engine.

VAL
England (Birmingham) 1913–14: Principally the manufacturers of sidecars, the firm is also noted in some sources as a manufacturer of a few motorcycles fitted with JAP 500cc (31ci) engines. These motorcycles, however, were very much the subsidiary interest of the company.

VALENTI
Italy (Milan) 1978–unknown: This firm was one of the many Italian manufacturers of small sports machines designed for off-road use, which were to come from the prolific decade of the 1970s. The company fitted Honda engines of 80cc (5ci) capacity into their machines to serve as their powerplant.

VALIANT
USA 1964–65: Clinton motors of 125cc (8ci) capacity – which bore similarities to the motors installed in lawn mowers – were fitted as a powerplant for this shortlived lightweight.

VALLS
Spain (Barcelona) 1955: The only model of motorcycle manufactured by this firm was given the name the V125. It was a two-stroke lightweight, and it was fitted with an engine that had a 125cc (8ci) displacement. A 'flat' single cylinder served this machine, but it only lasted a year.

VALMOBILE
France 1956: Manufactured during the 1950s, this bike was a handy scooter, which was designed to be collapsible. The scooter was fitted with an engine of 125cc (8ci) capacity.

VAP
France 1949–early 1970s: This company had a long and varied career, which spanned four decades. The firm was responsible for the manufacture of mopeds, and its machines were initially fitted with engines of 98cc (6ci) displacement. However, the firm later went on to reduce the capacity of their motors and manufactured machines fitted with 50cc (3ci) engines. In addition to this, the firm was responsible for the production of auxiliary cycle motors.

VAREL
Germany 1952–53: This firm produced mopeds and mini-scooters. Some of their machines were lightweights which had been fitted with engines of 100cc (6ci) displacement, and all of them had two-stroke engines. The firm's 43cc (3ci) engines were manufactured in house; however, the 100cc (6ci) capacity engine was bought in from Mota.

VASCHETTO
Italy (Turin), no dates given: Engines which were bought in by this Italian company from Mercury acted as the powerplants to Giuseppe Vaschetto's machines. These engines were of two capacities: they were either 250cc (15ci) or 500cc (31ci).

VASCO
England 1921–23: These single-cylinder two-strokes were fitted with obscure engines. They were initially 269cc (16ci) displacement engines that had been bought in from Orbit, but these were later to become engines of 349cc (21ci) displacement which were bought in from Broler.

VASSENA
Italy 1926–29: This bicycle, which came from Pietro Vassena, was motorised. Its powerplant was an engine that had a capacity of 125cc.

VATERLAND
Germany 1933–39: This firm produced a heavyweight name, but was responsible for the production of lightweights. These were powered by motors of 100cc (6ci) and 120cc (7ci) displacement which had been bought in from Sachs.

VAUXHALL
England 1922–24: The famous automobile manufacturer also dabbled in motorcycle production, making an in-line shaft-driven straight four with an engine displacement of 931cc (57ci). A notable feature was its enormous running boards.

VECCIETTI
Italy 1954–57: These were fitted with 40cc (2ci) engines which had been bought in from Victoria.

VELAMOS
Czech Republic 1927–30: Gustav Heinz was responsible for the design and for the manufacture of these two-stroke singles. They had a shortlived career of only three years. As a powerbase, the machines were fitted with in-house motors of three different capacities, namely 250cc (15ci) and 350cc (21ci), as well as 500cc (31ci).

VELOX
Czech Republic 1923–26: These lightweights were initially fitted with two-stroke engines with a capacity of 150cc (9ci) which had been bought in from Villiers. However, the motorcycles were later fitted with Bekamo engines of two different capacities: 125cc (8ci) and 175c (11ci).

VENUS
England 1920–22: This company offered for sale a choice of their own engine – which was a 300cc (18ci) side-valve – or an engine from Dalm – which was a two-stroke – to be fitted into their machines.

VENUS
Germany 1920–22: This motorcycle was a scooter which was fitted with choice of two-stroke engines from Fichtel & Sachs. These engines had capacities of either 100cc (6ci) or 150cc (9ci) as well as 175c (11ci).

VERGA
Italy 1951–54: These were lightweight machines powered by engines of 73cc (4ci) capacity.

VERKHOVINA
Soviet Union (Lvov) c.1970s: The exact dates for this company are unknown, but it offered for sale mopeds, which were also manufactured as versions designed for off-road use.

VERLOR
France 1930–38: These lightweights were powered by either 100cc (6ci) or 125cc (8ci) capacity engines, which had been bought in from Aubier-Dunne and Stainless.

VEROS
Italy 1922–24: Oresete Garanzini both imported and renamed Verus machines, before then going on to slightly modify them. All models seem to have had the 350cc (21ci) Blackburne engine option available.

VERUS
England (Birmingham) 1919–25: Wisemann, who was also responsible for the manufacture of Sirrah and Weaver machines, manufactured the Verus. The cheaper models of this make had in-house two-strokes of 211cc (13ci) and 269cc (16ci) capacity, while the more expensive models had four-strokes of 250cc (15ci) to 1000cc (61ci) which had been bought in from Blackburne and JAP

VESTING
Netherlands 1956: This machine is another moped manufactured and sold during the 1950s that is interesting only for having the feature of rear suspension.

VESUV
Germany 1924–26: This machine was predictably yet another basic 250cc (15ci) two-stroke in an open frame. The engine was manufactured in house.

VIATKA
Soviet Union 1956–79: From (unlicensed) Vespa copies, the company Viatka moved on to the manufacture of their own V150 two-stroke scooter.

VIBERTI
Italy 1955–late 1960s: This firm were responsible mostly for mopeds with a 50cc (3ci) capacity, as well as for lightweights with a capacity of 125cc.

VICTA
England 1912–13: This assembler used Precision singles of 500cc (31ci) capacity to act as a powerbase.

VICTORIA
Scotland (Glasgow) 1902–26: This firm was responsible for the production of high-quality machines. They used a variety of single and V-twin two- and four-strokes of 125–700cc (8–43ci) capacity, bought from English firms such as Villiers, JAP, Blackburne and Precision.

VICTORY
Italy 1950–55: These Italian lightweights were Villiers-engined machines of 100c and 125cc (8ci) capacity.

VILLOF
Spain 1951–61: As well as using two-strokes which were bought in from Hispano-Villiers, Villof were also responsible for the manufacture of their own motors. These had capacities of 75cc (5ci) to 125cc (8ci).

VINCO
England 1903–05: These pioneers were powered by an engine with a capacity of 211cc (13ci), which had been bought in from Minerva.

VINDEC-SPECIAL (VS)
England 1903–14: Surprisingly, these were no relation to Vindec: the VS name was adopted in 1909 in order to avoid confusion. The South British Trading Co. imported what were in effect rebadged Allrights, above, which were manufactured in Cologne, Germany.

VIPER
England 1919–22: Despite its name, the 293cc (18ci) side-valve engine which was bought in from JAP meant that this assembled machine lacked bite.

VIRATELLE
France 1907–24: This individualistic French assembler used a very wide variety of bought-in engines in the production of motorcycles.

VIS
Germany 1923–25: The in-house 250cc (15ci) two-stroke single from this company was more successful than its other machine, the in-house longitudinally mounted 500cc (31ci) two-stroke flat twin. In the latter machine, the rear cylinder overheated.

VITTORIA
Italy 1931–80: Before the outbreak of World War II, this was an assembler that used a wide variety of engines in different capacities, from 100cc (6ci) to 500cc (31ci): these engines were bought in from Sachs, JAP, Kuchen and Rudge Python. Postwar, the company produced for the most part small two-strokes of capacities of under 100cc (6ci).

VOLLBLUT
Germany 1925–27: These motorcycles were full-blooded machines designed for sporting use. They had been fitted with 250cc (15ci) and 350cc (21ci) overhead-valve engines, bought in from Blackburne.

VOMO
Germany 1922–31: These machines had a relatively successful career span in terms of their longevity, as they lasted through the 1920s and into the 1930s. They were, in effect, ultra-lightweight motorcycles fitted with two-stroke engines as their powerbase.

VON MEYERBERG
Germany 1893: This very early example of a powered cycle was actually a steam-powered machine. The single cylinder was positioned under the saddle.

VORAN
Germany 1921–24: This machine, which was manufactured for a few years during the 1920s, was a lightweight two-stroke three-port model. It had been fitted with an engine of 143cc (9ci) capacity as its powerbase.

VOSKHOD
Russia 1966–: Marketing name for two-stroke models built by the Kovrov company. Early models based on German DKW RT125. Later capacity was increased to 175c (11ci).

VOYAGER
England c.1990: This machine was yet another attempt at the Quasar/Phasar, and was fitted with a Reliant engine as its powerbase. Although the machine was extremely practical, it was nonetheless too radical for the market, despite its feature of open seating.

VULCAN
Czech Republic 1904–24: These machines appear to have been identical to Perun, above.

VULCAN
England 1922–24: A choice of engines characterized this rare machine. Engines available were two-stroke or four-stroke, the former being of a 250cc (15ci) capacity and the latter of 300cc (18ci).

WADDINGTON
England 1902–06: This pioneer used a range of bought-in engines such as MMC and Minerva.

WAG
England 1924–25: This was a rare 500cc (31ci) two-stroke V-twin.

WAGNER
USA 1904–14: Starting dates for this concern are variously given as 1901, 1904 and 1909: it built singles and parallel twins of up to four horsepower. The 18-year-old Clara Wagner, daughter of the manufacturer, rode a single from Chicago to Indianapolis in 1910.

WAGNER
Czech Republic 1930–35: No examples of the machines made by this company – 100cc (6ci) to 500cc (31ci), two-stroke and four-stroke, with a variety of valve layouts – are known to exist.

WALLIS
England (Bromley) 1925–26: Very long wheelbases, twin-tube frames, and hub-centre steering distinguished these machines with JAP 350cc (21ci) and 500cc (31ci) engines.

WALTER
Czechoslovakia 1900–27: Former pedal cycle manufacturer. Josef Walter began producing 346cc (21ci) single-cylinder motorcycles with belt final drive. Later built larger V-twin models with 750cc (461ci) engine.

WALTER
Germany (Muhlhausen) 1903–42: This firm initially produced Fafnir, and then, from World War I to the mid-1930s, Villiers 175cc (11ci) to 350cc (21ci) machines. Until its demise, they made Ilo and Sachs 98cc (6ci) mopeds.

WASSELL
England 1970–75: These off-road competition machines were fitted with 125cc (8ci) Fichtel & Sachs two-stroke motors.

WATNEY
England 1922–23: Blackburne 350cc (21ci), JAP 300cc (18ci) and the ubiquitous Villiers 269cc (16ci) engines powered these assembled machines.

WAVERLEY
England (Birmingham) 1921–23: This assembler offered a choice of Peco 269cc (16ci) two-strokes and Blackburne 350cc (21ci) and 500cc (31ci) side-valve four-strokes.

WD
England 1911–13: In-house inlet-over-exhaust 500cc (31ci) singles powered this marque.

WEARWELL
England (Wolverhampton) 1901–06: Wearwells were built in the same Wearwell Motor Carriage factory as Wolf and Wolfruna. The engines came from Stevens Brothers, later A.J.S., and were of two-and-a-half to three-and-a-quarter horsepower.

WEATHERELL
England 1922–23: These sporting machines were fitted with Blackburne overhead-valve engines: 250cc (15ci) and 350cc (21ci) singles, and a big V-twin (676cc/41ci or 696cc/42ci).

WEBER-MAG
Germany 1926–37: MAG singles of 350cc (21ci) and 500cc (31ci), and V-twins of 750cc (461ci), all inlet-over-exhaust, powered these scarce machines.

WEBER & REICHMANN
Czech Republic 1923–26: The pressed-steel frames were made under DKW licence; the engines (142cc/9ci and 172cc/10ci) were DKW.

WECOOB
Germany 1925–30: This was a typical 'big catalogue, small numbers' firm offering JAP engines from 350cc (21ci) to 1000cc (61ci), Villiers from 175cc (11ci) to 350cc (21ci), and a Rinne 142cc (9ci) two-stroke.

WEE MCGREGOR
England (Coventry) 1922–25: This lightweight was made by the Coventry Bicycle company: the early 170cc (10ci) engine was later enlarged to 202cc (12ci).

WEGRO
Germany 1922–23: A 452cc two-stroke parallel twin powered this unusual long-wheelbased machine.

WELLER
England 1902–05: In-house one-and-three-quarters and two-and-a-quarter horsepower engines drove the machines that came from this pioneer, also known for cars.

WELS
Germany 1925–26: Kuhne 350cc (21ci) and JAP 500cc (31ci) overhead-valve engines powered these machines with their clean, elegant lines.

WELT-RAD
Germany 1901–07: Their own singles of three-and-a-half horsepower, and V-twins of seven horsepower, were used in these sturdy and (for the time) reliable machines.

WESTFALIA
Germany 1901–06: These pioneers used the customary engines: De Dion-Bouton, Fafnir and Zedel, of one-and-three-quarters and two-and-a-half horsepower.

WIGA
Germany 1928–32: These were good assembled machines with JAP and Kuchen engines, the latter three-valve.

WILHELMINA
Netherlands 1903–15: A variety of engines, most notably the two-and-a-half horsepower Precision, powered these machines from this leading importer.

WILIER
Italy 1962–c.1970: This mini-bike was powered by a 48cc (3ci) motor.

WILKIN
England (Sheffield) 1919–23: An enclosed drive chain was the principal remarkable feature of these 350cc (21ci) and 500cc (31ci) Blackburne-powered machines.

WILLIAMS
USA 1912–20: The power unit for this machine was built into the rear wheel.

WILLIAMSON
England (Coventry) 1912–20: For most of their career, Williamson used 996cc (61ci) flat twins, both water- and air-cooled, specially built for them by Douglas of Bristol, but in the last year or so, they used a 770cc (47ci) JAP V-twin.

WIMMER
Germany 1921–39: This bicycle factory started out with an overhead-valve 175c (11ci) engine, then switched to a 200cc (12ci) two-stroke, supplemented with 250cc (15ci), 300cc (18ci) and even 500cc (31ci) singles. All were built in house. Bicycle production, but not motorcycle production, was resumed after World War II.

WIN
England 1908–14: Precision singles of 500cc (31ci) and 600cc (37ci) were the choices for this assembled machine.

WITTLER
Germany 1924–53: This was yet another two-stroke manufacturer, albeit with in-house engines of 249cc (15ci). After World War II, it produced mopeds with Zundapp or Fichtel & Sachs engines, and a 175c (11ci) Sachs-engined lightweight.

W.M.R.
Germany (Rottenburg am Neckar) 1926–32: The Wurtttemburger Motorfahrzeug Werke began with side-valve and overhead-valve Kuchen engines of 500cc (31ci), later adding 250cc (15ci) and 350cc (21ci) Blackburnes, initially side-valve but then (for the Sport models) overhead-valve.

WOLF
England (Wolverhampton) 1901–39: From the same factory as Wearwell, this was a wide range of machines with engines from 100cc (6ci) to 750cc (461ci), all powered by proprietary engines. Early models had engines from Moto Reve, Blackburne, JAP, Peco, Stevens Brothers (later of AJS) and Villiers: later machines (after a break in production) mostly used 250cc (15ci) Villiers two-strokes.

WOTAN
Germany (Chemnitz) 1921–22: This was a rare 600cc (37ci) V-twin.

WURRING
Germany 1921–59: August Wurring (also of AWD) used a wide variety of proprietary motors of 150cc (9ci) to 600cc (37ci) from Bark, Columbus, DKW, Ilo, Kuchen, Kuhne, Sachs and Villiers.

WURTTEMBERGIA
Germany 1925–33: Good frames characterized these solid Blackburne-powered 200cc (12ci) to 600cc (37ci) machines, which came from this agricultural machinery manufacturer.

X-ALL
England 1902–c.1906: Accounts of this machine vary in their details: not only are there several slight variations in the dates during which the machine was manufactured, but the name of the model is also reported as being XL-All. What is clear is that it was a V-twin. It may have been the first engine to offer the option of shutting down one cylinder when the full power of the engine was not absolutely necessary. Alternatively, the second cylinder may have been a spare, to which ignition and carburation were transferred in the event of a failure of the first cylinder. Reports suggest that there may have been two models offered, one of which had a power output of two horsepower, and the other a power output of four horsepower. However, these figures might have referred to the power output, the former on one cylinder and the latter on two.

XL
England (Worthing) 1921–23: Reports of this machine conclude that it was strong and well-made, and fitted with a side-valve engine of 500cc (31ci) capacity.

X-TRA
England 1920–22: This machine was accompanied by a sidecar. Unusually, this sidecar was so firmly incorporated into the machine's design that it was effectively a three-wheeled car which had handlebar steering of one wheel, and chain drive to another.

YALE
USA 1902–15: Initially, this company was responsible for the manufacture of a single. In this machine, the engine was mounted over the pedals within a strengthened bicycle frame. Later, the company was responsible for the manufacture of an all chain-drive V-twin which was a two-speed with a capacity of 950cc (58ci).

YAMAGUCHI
Japan 1953–64: Always confusingly named, Yamaguchi models began with the Super 200 and Super 100 two-strokes. These machines had capacities of 83cc (5ci) and 60cc (4ci) respectively. However, the 1956 Model 600cc (37ci) was fitted with an engine of 147cc (9ci) capacity. The biggest engine produced was the 250cc (15ci) four-stroke T92, which appeared shortly afterwards, while the Super 350cc (21ci) had a capacity of 125cc (8ci) and the AP10 moped a capacity of 50cc (3ci). The commencement of production is reported as being as early as 1941.

YANKEE
USA 1922–23: This primitive model had a two-stroke engine with a capacity of 296cc (18ci) with belt drive.

YANKEE
USA 1970–74: This was an Ossa-based machine and was made by the US Ossa importer. It was fitted with a 488cc (30ci) capacity two-stroke parallel twin as its powerbase.

A2
AMC, 125 cm³, 4 temps, 4 vitesses par sélecteur incor-
ge et éclairage par volant magnétique — Suspension :
à balancier ; AR : oscillante — Moyeux AV et AR : gros
e 130 m/m. — Équipement : Commandes par poignées
mpteur dans le phare. Réservoir 15 l. environ. Garde-
pants. Carter de chaine, selle à ressorts, porte-bagages
nage avec boite à outils incorporée. Rétroviseur ,outillage,
biplace en supplément.

The Thomann A2. Thomann built two-stroke machines up to 1939.

YORK
Austria (Vienna)/Germany 1927–30: These machines were fitted with JAP engines with capacities which ranged from 350cc (21ci) to 750cc (461ci), and which were singles and V-twins. They featured frames from Britain, either assembled in the UK to Robert Sturm's design, or assembled from British parts in Vienna. The company moved to Germany in 1929.

YOUNG
England 1919–23: The Young was an auxiliary cycle motor that had been designed for mounting over the rear wheel. The original 269cc (16ci) version, which was a four-stroke, was manufactured by the Mohawk Cycle Company. There was a later two-stroke, which was manufactured by the Waltham Engineering Co Ltd in 1922 or 1923.

YVEL
France 1921–24: These machines featured in-house side-valve engines in capacities of 175cc (11ci) and 233cc (14ci). In their frame construction, they were lightweights.

ZEDEL
France 1902–15: Zurcher und Luthi were renowned as engine suppliers but their division, Zedel, built up whole motorcycles of two to three-and-a-half horsepower, which were fitted with both single and V-twin engines.

ZEGEMO
Germany 1924–25: A 248cc (15ci) Baumi two-stroke powered this design by Hans Knipp, who was formerly of Zetge, below.

ZEHNDER
Switzerland 1923–39: The firm's name was made by these fast, horizontal two-strokes of 110cc (7ci), 150cc (9ci) and 250cc (15ci) capacity. The German Standard undertaking bought it out in 1928 and continued to make motorcycles.

ZEHNER
Germany 1924–26: Otto Dehne designed this 197cc (12ci) side-valve.

ZENIT
Italy 1954–56: AMC (France) engines of 125cc (8ci) and 175c (11ci) powered these assembled machines.

ZEPA
Italy (Reggio Emilia) c.1950s: The exact dates of this machine are unknown, but the 38cc (2ci) engine that powered it was also available as an auxiliary cycle motor.

ZEPHYR
England 1922–23: This 131cc (8ci) two-stroke, was sold in two forms: as an auxiliary cycle motor, and already installed in a lightweight.

ZETA
Italy 1947–54: This scooter, with its 33cm (13in) wheels, was initially powered by a 48cc (3ci) Cucciolo motor and possibly later by a 60cc (4ci) Ducati engine.

ZETGE
Germany 1922–25: One source reports this machine as having two-stroke engines of 150cc (9ci) and 175c (11ci), another reports side-valve singles of 500cc (31ci) and twins of 600cc (37ci) and 750cc (461ci).

ZEUGNER
Germany 1903–06: This assembler used the usual range of pioneering proprietary engines: Fafnir, FN, Minerva, Peugeot and Zedel.

ZEUS
Austro-Hungary (Czech Republic) 1902–12: These machines were singles of three and three-and-a-half horsepower and V-twins of four and four-and-a-half horsepower. They were also sold as Linser, after the name of the designer, Christian Linser.

ZEUS
Germany 1925–27: Kuchen 350cc (21ci) and 500cc (31ci) three-valve engines powered these well-designed machines.

ZIEJANU
Germany 1924–26: This common story featured 211cc (13ci) and 246cc (15ci) two-strokes, which were produced in-house and were supplemented by bought-in 350cc (21ci) and 500cc (31ci) four-strokes, from JAP.

ZIRO
Germany 1919–24: These two-strokes of 150cc (9ci) and 350cc (21ci) had rotary valves in the crankcase. Albert Roder, the designer, later worked with Ermag, Zundapp and Victoria, before becoming chief designer at NSU.

ZM
Poland 1959: Zakladt Motolowa built a 49.8cc (3ci) two-stroke, which was called the S38.

ZURTZ-REKORD
Germany (Darmstadt) 1922–26: This shortlived assembler used a variety of engines as powerbases. They were two-stroke and four-stroke, and were bought in from firms such as DKW, Paque and Columbus, as well as from JAP. The JAP engines went up to a capacity of 500cc (31ci).

ZWEIRAD-UNION
Germany 1958–74: Three motorcycle firms amalgamated in 1958; these were DKW, Express and Victoria. The Hercules company was to join later, in 1966. These four concerns were combined and went on to end up as part of Fichtel & Sachs. They were responsible for the manufacture of two-strokes – mainly of 50cc (3ci) and 100cc (6ci) capacity – which were enclosed in their pressed-steel frames.

ZWERG
Germany 1924–25: This shortlived firm was yet another manufacturer of that period responsible for the production of in-house two-stroke lightweights. The company used engines with capacities of 147cc (9ci) and 187cc.

ZWI
Israel (Tel Aviv) 1952–55: This shortlived make was based in Israel during the early 1950s. It was founded by the Hungarian racer Stefa Auslaender. He used two-strokes which were bought in from JAP and Villiers. These engines were of 123cc (8ci) displacement.

ZZR
Poland 1960–unknown: Exact dates of this company are difficult to obtain, but what is clear from various sources is that they were responsible for the production of mopeds.

HHV54CK

The Polish WSK 175c (11ci) single-cylinder trail bike was first made in 1977.

GLOSSARY

ABS Anti-lock braking system

AC Alternating current (as produced by an alternator)

ACCELERATION Rate of change of speed, commonly expressed in terms of standing-start quarter mile times

ACCELERATOR PUMP Carburettor feature that enriches the fuel/air mixture when the throttle is opened quickly

AIR-COOLING Cooling in which the passage of air over the engine takes away combustion heat

AIR-BOX A pre-chamber of still air feeding the engine, surprisingly important for performance

AISE An engine with an Auto Inlet, Side Exhaust valve

ALTERNATOR The electricity generator on most motorcycles, producing alternating current, which must be rectified to DC

AMMETER Instrument that measures electrical current flow

AUTOMATIC Gear-less transmission, favoured on commuter machines, in which some sort of fluid drive or variable belts transmit power to the rear wheel

AUTOMATIC INLET VALVE Early type of valve in which the suction of the piston opened and closed the inlet valve

AUTOMATIC TENSIONER Spring-loaded self-adjusting tensioner, normally used on cam chains or belts

BEADED-EDGE TYRES Early tyre in which a hard edge (the bead) is located into a channel on the wheel rim

BELLMOUTH Trumpet-shaped tube designed to improve air-flow into a carburettor

BELT DRIVE Flexible toothed belt that takes the drive to the final wheel (e.g. modern Harleys) or drives the camshafts (Ducati), or other components such as superchargers. Many early machines used a simple leather belt from the final drive

BEVEL DRIVE Drive in which drive is turned through 90° from one shaft to another via bevel gears

BHP Brake horsepower, the horsepower developed by an engine

BIAS-BELTED Tyre construction with two or more fabric belts at different angles, effectively a half-way house between cross-ply and radial construction

BIG END The eye in the lower end of a connecting rod and its associated crankshaft journal

BORE The diameter of the cylinder in which the piston travels

BUTTERFLY Rotating disc acting as a throttle valve in some carburettors and most fuel injection inlets

CALLIPER Disc brake component in which one or more pistons press friction pads against the disc rotor

CAMSHAFT Shaft, usually with several cam lobes that control the opening of valves, either directly or via some intervening mechanism

CAPACITY The displacement of an engine

CARBON FIBRE Very strong, light composite of fine filaments of carbon, woven and bonded in a matrix such as epoxy resin

CARBURETTOR Device, usually working on the Venturi principle, for mixing fuel and air in the correct quantities to enable combustion

CARDAN SHAFT The final drive shaft in shaft driven motorcycles

CABLE On a motorcycle, a Bowden cable with a stiff outer and flexible steel inner, which transmits linear movement (e.g. clutch cable) or rotation (speedometer cable)

CASTOR See 'rake'

CC Cubic centimetres, the units for measuring engine displacement (1 cu.in (cid) = 16.4cc)

CHOKE Refers both to the carburettors venturi diameter (or fuel injector trumpet bore), and to any mechanism for richening the mixture for cold starts

CLUTCH Device for controlling the transmission of power from engine to gearbox, usually by means of friction plates

COIL Electrical windings that turn a low-voltage current into the high voltage required by the spark plugs

COMBUSTION CHAMBER The space (usually in the cylinder head) above the piston at top dead centre in which combustion begins.

COMPRESSION RATIO The ratio of maximum cylinder and combustion chamber volume at bottom dead centre to that at top dead centre

CONNECTING ROD (Con rod) Metal rod that joins the piston to the crankshaft

CONTACT BREAKER (Points) Pairs of mechanically controlled electrical contacts which, with high-tension coils, create the current for the spark plug

CRANKCASE Commonly split in two, the cases in which the crankshaft (and often the gearbox) are located

CRANKSHAFT Shaft (one-piece or pressed up) which turns the up-and-down motion of the pistons into rotational movement.

CROSS-PLY Tyres having fabric layers with cords lying crosswise, as opposed to radial tyres

CV Constant Vacuum, Constant Velocity: carburettor in which the choke is controlled by depression rather than a direct mechanism such as in a conventional slide-type carburettor

CYLINDER The usually cylindrical chamber in which the piston travels

CYLINDER HEAD The crown of an engine. In two-strokes, it's little more than an inverted metal dish with a spark plug; in four-strokes, it contains the valves and usually the camshafts.

DAMPER Device for slowing the movement of components relative to each other. Usually hydraulic, but friction dampers were once common

DESMO (Desmodromic) Valve system in which a cam rather than a spring controls the closing of the valve, such as on many Ducatis

DISC BRAKE Brake in which pads of friction material are squeezed against a spinning rotor

DISC VALVE Type of valve using a rotating disc with a window to permit flow, sometimes seen on two-stroke inlet ports

DOHC An engine with a Double Overhead Camshaft

DRAG RACING Sprint-type racing, usually over a measured quarter mile

DRUM BRAKE Brake in which shoes of friction material are moved radially against the inside of a cylinder (the drum)

DRY SUMP Four-stroke engine in which the lubricating oil is contained in a special tank rather than in the crankcases

DRY WEIGHT The weight of a motorcycle without fluids

DUPLEX Literally, double. Used of frame design and double-row chains, etc

DYNAMO Simple device for converting rotation of a shaft into electricity, now almost unknown on motorcycles

DYNAMOMETER (Dyno) Instrument for measuring engine torque (from which power can be extrapolated).

EFI Electronic fuel injection

ENDURO Off-road motorcycle racing over an unseen course

ENGINE BRAKING The braking effect of an engine when the throttle is closed

EOI An engine with Exhaust Over Inlet valve, as on some Indian fours

EXPANSION The characteristic of almost all materials to grow larger as they are heated.

EXPANSION CHAMBER Bulbous portion of two-stroke exhaust system, designed to maximize exhaust pressure-pulses and so improve engine efficiency

FADE Lose effectiveness, especially of overheated brakes

FEELER GAUGE Precision metal strip of marked gauge used to measure fine clearances

FENDER American expression for mudguard

FIN/FINNING Cooling extensions, on cylinder, crankcase, brake drums and some electrical components

FISHTAIL SILENCER Silencer with flattened, wedge-shaped end portion

FLATHEAD Cylinder head offering flat combustion chamber face, such as many sidevalves and 'Heron' head ohv

FLAT TWIN Boxer engine layout with two cylinders opposed at 180, e.g. BMW, Douglas

FLOAT Bouyant object in carburettor used to actuate a petrol cut-off valve

FLYWHEEL Rotating mass, commonly in crankshaft assembly, used to store energy and smooth power delivery

FLYWHEEL MAGNETO Magneto mounted directly on the crankshaft, rather than driven remotely

FOOTCHANGE Gearchange mechanism operated by the foot (early bikes were hand-change)

FOOTREST Fixed or hinged rest for the rider or passengers' foot

FORCED INDUCTION Engine using a supercharger or turbocharger

FOUR STROKE Engine operating on the Otto cycle requiring four piston strokes for each power stroke

FUEL INJECTION Positive metering and introduction of fuel by mechanical or electro-mechanical means, now often integrated into comprehensive engine management systems

The 2006 Yamaha YZF-R6 boasts an ultra-precise throttle control and aluminium Deltabox frame for intense cornering performance.

GAITER Flexible protective shroud, usually around a suspension unit or control linkage

GAP Space between two elements, especially contact breaker points or spark plug electrodes

GASKET Sealing between two joint faces. May be of paper, metal, composite or 'plastic'

GAS TIGHT Seal or joint which is impervious to gas, used especially of cylinder head to barrel face

GAS WELDING Joining materials by heating with burning gases, usually oxygen and acetylene

GAUGE Measuring device; measure of thickness

GEAR RATIO Ratio of turning speeds of a pair of gears, or the aggregate ratios of a train of gears

GEAR TOOTH Projection on a gear designed to mesh with a complementary indent on another gear

GEL COAT Thin, uppermost coat used in glass-fibre lamination to give a smooth finish, with or without colour

GIRDER FORK Front suspension comprising rigid beams, movement being allowed by links at the steering head

GIRDRAULIC Vincent's proprietory form of girder forks employing light alloy blades and hydraulic damping

GLAND Joint, usually in a pipe, with either jointing material or a preformed seal

GLASS FIBRE Fine strands of spun glass, usually pressed or woven into sheets and treated with a chemically-setting resin

GP Grand Prix; type of Amal racing carburettor

GRAND PRIX Blue-riband motorcycle road racing competition, began in France in 1913 but was not incorporated into a world championship until 1949

GRASS TRACK RACING 'An accident looking for a place to happen' on an oval grass circuit

GREASE Stabilized mixture of a metallic soap and a lubricating oil

GRINDING PASTE Abrasive compound of carborundum powder and oil, used to bed-in valves and mating surfaces

GROMMET Doughnut-shaped item, usually rubber, preventing chaffing of control and electrical cables passing through a hole

GROUND CLEARANCE The distance between the lowest sprung point of a motorcycle and the ground

GROUND JOINT Face joint made by lapping two surfaces together

GUDGEON PIN (wrist pin in USA) Hard steel tube linking the piston to the small-end

GUIDE Component that directs, aligns or positions another, e.g. valve guide

GUSSET Piece used to strengthen any open structure, such as steering head assembly

GYROSCOPIC PRECESSION The effect in which gyroscopic forces give a rotating wheel both a self-centring effect and the capacity for counter-steering

HAIRPIN SPRING Commonly a valve spring, hairpin-shaped but often with coils at the closed end

HALF TIME PINION Crankshaft gear or sprocket sized to drive ignition or camshaft at half engine speed

HALOGEN BULB Light bulb using one of the halogen family of gases, e.g. iodine, to increase light output

HANDLEBARS Projections from the steering column used for mounting controls and steering by the hands

HEAD ANGLE Angle of the steering axis with reference to the horizontal or vertical

HEAD STEADY Tie-bar between cylinder head and frame

HEAT SINK Usually metallic mass that absorbs heat away from another component (e.g. brake, rectifier) until it can be shed

HELICAL GEARS Gears with spiral or part-spiral meshing faces

HELICOIL Brand name for a type of threaded female insert, used in alloy to repair or strengthen a fastening

HEMI HEAD Hemispherical head, favoured in some older engines, in which the combustion chamber is roughly half a sphere

HERON HEAD Type of cylinder head in which combustion chamber is formed in the piston rather than the head itself, e.g. Morini

HIGH TENSILE Material, commonly steel, of high 'stretch' strength

HIGH TENSION 'HT', the high-voltage secondary phase in an ignition system

HILL CLIMB Standing-start speed competition over a twisting uphill course

HONING Achieving a fine finish to precise size by abrasion, typically in cylinder bores

HORIZONTALLY OPPOSED Engine layout with pairs of cylinders opposed at 180°, e.g. BMW Boxer, Honda Gold Wing

HOSE Any flexible pipe, e.g. hydraulic brake lines

HOT SPOT Area of a combustion chamber which gets too hot, causing pre-ignition. Often caused by incandescent carbon deposits

HOT TUBE IGNITION Primitive ignition system in which a platinum tube is heated by spirit burner

H-SECTION Shaped like a letter 'H' in cross-section

HT LEADS High tension cables, from coil to spark plug or coil to distributor to spark plug

HUB Centre part of a wheel

HUB CENTRE STEERING Steering system in which the axis of wheel movement lies within the wheel hub

HUGGER Lightweight, racing-style rear mudguard, which moves up and down with the wheel; Harley-Davidson models with very little ground clearance

HUNTING Erratic tickover, often caused by incorrect carburation

HYDRAULIC Mechanism using the flow or pressure of a liquid through valves and orifices, such as with motorcycle brakes and suspension dampers

HYDROMETER Instrument for measuring specific gravity of a liquid, e.g. to test state of charge of a battery

HYGROMETER Instrument for measuring humidity, such as to calculate jetting for racing engines

HYGROSCOPIC Substance that attracts water, such as (most) brake fluids

HYSTERESIS Literally, lag. Of tyre rubber, high-hysteresis compounds (invented by Avon) have less internal bounce and more grip

ICE RACING Racing on oval ice tracks with speedway-like machines fitted with metal-spiked tyres

IDIOT LIGHT Slang for an instrument warning light

IDLER GEAR Gear interposed between two others to avoid using overlarge working gears

IGNITION ADVANCE Extent to which the ignition spark precedes TDC, necessary because combustion is not instantaneous but takes a finite time to occur

IMPORT, GREY motorcycle imported into a country that does not officially import that model

IMPORT, PARALLEL motorcycle that is imported in direct competition with official imports

INDEX MARK Vehicle identification number (VIN) of a vehicle; also reference point for adjustment, e.g. of wheel alignment or ignition timing

The BMW R1200GS is 30kg (66lb) lighter than the R1150GS, its predecessor, and has a new boxer engine with improved power output of 100bhp.

INDUCTION Drawing-in of fuel-air to an engine, although correctly it is mainly pushed in by atmospheric pressure

INERTIA The tendency of all things to carry on moving in the same direction once started. Everything in an engine – the pistons, even the air in the carburettor – has inertia

INJECTOR Pressurized nozzle for squirting fuel or oil into engine

INLET Place of entry, as in inlet valve, inlet tract

INSTANT GASKET Plasticized substance, sometimes hardening, for sealing joint faces

INSTRUMENT Device that measures or controls a function

INTAKE Inlet

INTEGRAL Belonging to a complete whole

INTER 'Between', as in inter-cooler

INTERNAL COMBUSTION ENGINE Any heat engine in which energy is developed in the engine cylinder and not in a separate chamber

INVERTED FORKS Upside down forks, in which the sliders are at the top rather than the bottom. Theoretically stiffer than conventional forks, and with less unsprung weight

IOE Inlet Over Exhaust – engine with overhead inlet valve and side exhaust valve

ISDT Former name of the ISDE, the International Six Day Enduro (Trial), an international team off-road endurance event

ISOCHRONOUS Occurring at the same time, e.g. two-stroke induction and exhaust phases

ISOLASTIC Proprietary name for the rubber-mounted engine/swinging fork system of Norton's Commando

JAMPOT Slang for the fat rear dampers of 1950s AJS and Matchless machines.

JET An orifice through which fuel passes

JET NEEDLE Tapered needle in a carburettor which rises and falls to vary fuel flow at medium throttle openings

JIG Cradle used to manufacture or check the dimensions of an assembly such as a motorcycle frame

JOINTING COMPOUND Material applied to joint faces to assist sealing

JOURNAL Accurately machined portion of a shaft on which a bearing (e.g. big end) engages

JUBILEE CLIP Originally branded hose clips, the term is now generic

KADENCY Effect, using pressure waves to enhance cylinder filling and scavenging

KEIHIN Japanese brand of carburettor

KEVLAR A synthetic (para-Aramid) fibre with enormous tensile strength, used in exotic motorcycle components and protective clothing (including bullet-proof vests)

KICK BACK Brief but often fierce reverse rotation of an engine during starting

KICKSTARTER Foot-operated crank for starting an engine

KILOWATT kW, now becoming the standard ISO measure of horsepower. 1kW equals 1.3596PS or 1.341bhp

KNEELER Usually a low-profile sidecar outfit in which the rider kneels; more rarely special solos such as the 1953 Norton kneeler

KNEE SLIDER Slippery attachment to racing leathers, allowing the rider to drag his inside knee on the ground in corners

KNURLING Machine tool rolling process for cross-hatching components

LAMINAR FLOW The tendency of fluids near a solid surface to stick with the surface and lubricate the movement of fluids farther away. The principle relates to mixture in an inlet tract as much as to motorcycle aerodynamics

LAP Complete circuit of racetrack; bed-in by lapping with abrasive compound

LATENT HEAT Heat needed to change a solid to liquid or liquid to gas. Methanol's high latent heat gives excellent engine cooling

LATHE Machine tool with rotating workpiece and fixed cutter

LAYSHAFT Gearbox shaft parallel to the mainshaft, carrying the laygears

LEADED Petrol bearing tetra-ethyl lead, an anti-knock compound and neuro-toxin

LEADING LINK Form of front suspension using a pivoted link with the wheel spindle in front of the pivot

LEADING SHOE In a drum brake, the brake shoe with its actuating cam at its leading edge

LEAF SPRING Suspension spring comprising one or more narrow strips of spring steel

LEAN Ingoing fuel-air charge that has too little fuel

LEAN-OUT Make fuel-air mixture more lean; extent to which the steering head leans away from the vertical in a sidecar outfit

LEVEL PLUG Plug, usually screw-in, which marks the desired upper level of fluid in a chamber

LEVER Handle for achieving a mechanical advantage, typically a brake or clutch lever

LIFT Amount something is raised, e.g. a valve off its seat

LIGHT ALLOY Loose expression for a multitude of aluminium alloys

LINER Detachable insert, commonly a steel cylinder liner in an alloy barrel

LINKAGE Typically an articulated joint, such as in a gearchange mechanism

LOBE Raised part of a cam

LOCK (Maximum) steering deflection

LOCKHEED Generic term for hydraulic fluid, taken from the company of the same name

LOCKING WIRE/LOCKWIRE Strong, usually stainless steel wire used for securing items against loosening

LOCKNUT Nut tightened hard against another to prevent loosening

LOCK STOP Abutment to the steering gear limiting amount of steering lock

LOCK WASHER Washer with anti-loosening feature

LOCKWIRE PLIERS Special pliers with jaws capable of locking onto and twisting lockwire

LOCTITE Proprietary liquid used for securing threads, bearings, etc

LONG REACH A spark plug of 3/4in (19mm) reach

LONG STROKE Undersquare engine, in which the stroke exceeds the bore

LUBRICANT Any substance interposed between rubbing surfaces to reduce friction

MAGIC BOX Anything electrical which you don't understand

MAGNESIUM Metal (36 per cent lighter than aluminium) expensively used for some motorcycle castings

MAGNETO Ignition spark generator requiring no external electrical power source

MAIN BEARING Any principal bearing, but usually those carrying the crankshaft

MAIN JET The principle fuel jet in a carburettor

MAINS Crankshaft main bearings

MAINSHAFT Principle shaft, usually in gearbox

MANIFOLD Branched system conducting mixture to, or exhaust from, an engine

MARQUE Another word for make of motorcycle

MARSHAL Usually unpaid safety official at race meeting

MASTER CYLINDER Reservoir and pump at the operator end of a hydraulic system

MAUDES TROPHY ACU trophy infrequently awarded for feats of unusual machine endurance

MEGAPHONE Megga, outwardly tapering four-stroke exhaust chamber capable of increasing power and power spread

METALASTIK Flexible bush acting as both pivot and vibration insulation

MIKUNI Japanese carburettor manufacturer, began making Amals under licence

MIXTURE Ingoing fuel-air charge

MON Motor octane number, arrived at by a more severe test than RON and more relevant for racing purpoes

MONOBLOC Amal carburettor with float bowl and mixing chamber formed in one casting; any such carburettor

MONOGRADE OIL Oil with a viscosity defined by a single SAE number

MONOSHOCK Rear suspension system employing a single shock absorber. Although a Yamaha trade name, now commonly used

MOPED Pedal-assisted motorcycle

MOTOCROSS Off-road circuit racing, formerly called scrambles

MOTOCROSS DES NATIONS Annual international team motocross championship

MUDGUARD Shroud designed to prevent road dirt being flung from wheels onto machine and rider

MULTIGRADE OIL Oil with viscosity characteristics encompassing two or more SAE numbers

MULTI-RATE A spring that changes length unequally for different increments of load

NEEDLE ROLLER A bearing roller very much longer than its diameter

NEGATIVE EARTH Connecting the negative battery terminal to earth; the usual convention

NGK Nippon Geika Kaisha, Japanese spark plug manufacturer

NIKASIL Proprietary process for applying a thin, hard coating to alloy cylinder bores

NIMONIC Nickel-rich iron alloy favoured for exhaust valves

The Ducati Multi 1100S has a larger 1,078cc (66ci) desmo engine giving out 95bhp – 11bhp up on its 992cc (60.5ci) predecessor.

NIPPLE Boss with a hole in it for admitting grease

NITRIDING Process for hardening steel

NITRO Nitro-methane, an oxygen-rich fuel of low calorific value

NON-UNIT Engine layout in which the powerplant and transmission as separate units

NORMALLY-ASPIRATED Engine charged by atmospheric pressure, rather than forced induction

NYLOC Nut with a nylon insert which resists loosening through vibration

NYLOCABLE Bowden cable with 'self-lubricating' nylon inner sheath

OBSERVED SECTION Part of a trials course in which penalties can be incurred

OBSERVER Official stationed at observed section to monitor competitors' performance

OCTANE RATING Measure of the knock resistance of fuel, higher numbers being more knock resistant. Usually given as average of MON and RON

ODOMETER Mileage recorder, usually inset into the machine's speedometer

OHC An engine with an Overhead Camshaft

OHV An engine with an Overhead Valve

OIL Natural or synthetic fluid with good lubricating properties

OIL BATH Protective oil reservoir into which a component dips

OIL COOLER A radiator containing engine oil rather than water

OIL COOLING Where oil is used to collect engine heat and transport it to cooling surfaces. Although all engines are partially oil cooled, Suzukis GSX-R series has taken this to extreme lengths

OIL PUMP Mechanical device for pressurizing oil in an engine

OIL SEAL Lipped, semi-elastic oil barrier on a shaft

OIL THROWER Shaped ring or plate designed to throw oil away from a particular site

O-RING Rubber sealing ring, typically in oil feeds

O-RING CHAIN Final drive chain using O-rings to seal in grease

OTTO CYCLE The four-stroke cycle

OUTSIDE FLYWHEEL Flywheel carried outside the crankcases, where it can be wider and thus more effective with less weight

OVERLAP Time when the inlet and exhaust valves are simultaneously open

OVER-SQUARE Engine in which the bore is greater than the stroke, as in most modern engines

PANNIER Component hanging down either side of a motorcycle, as in luggage bags or fuel tanks

PATENT Protection granted by the state to an inventor

PATTERN PARTS Replacement parts not authorized by the original manufacturer

PAWL Catch meshing with a ratchet wheel

PEAK Highest point, as of cam lobe, power output, revs

PEAK REVS Maximum safe revs for a particular engine

PENETRATION Consistency of a grease; infiltration of a freeing agent; depth of a weld

PENT ROOF An efficient combustion chamber form in multi-valve heads, shaped like a pitched roof

PETROIL Petrol and oil mixture used in some two-stroke engines

PETROLEUM JELLY Waxy petroleum product used to protect battery terminals; 'Vaseline'

PHASED PISTON Large 'supercharging' piston in machines such as DKW and early EMC racers

PHILLIPS Proprietary form of crosshead screw, often wrongly used generically

PHOSPHOR-BRONZE Copper-tin alloy with excellent bearing qualities, often used for small-end bushes

PIGGY-BACK Often used of the pressurized gas reservoir attached to a modern suspension unit

PIGTAIL Short length of conducting wire connected to a pickup brush

PILGRIM Simple type of double-ended pump using a single plunger to supply and scavenge

PILLION Seat behind the rider; person on it

PILOT JET Auxilliary jet in a carburettor, which governs fuel flow at small throttle openings

PILOT LIGHT Small, low-wattage bulb; parking light

PINCHBOLT Bolt pinching two elements of a part together, such as on a fork yoke

PINKING Metallic tinkling noise produced by pre-ignition

PISTON Moving plunger in a cylinder, accepting or delivering thrust

PISTON RING Springy metal hoops in groove on a piston, designed to promote gas seal or scrape oil from bore

PISTON SLAP Audible contact of piston skirt against cylinder bore, worse in cold or worn bores

PITCH Distance between two repeating characteristics, such as rollers on a chain or teeth on a gear

PLAIN BEARINGS Plain metal bearings (such as some big-ends and mains) which effectively suspend the moving components on a microscopic oil film

PLATING Electrolytic deposition of a metal onto a dissimilar material for protective or cosmetic purposes

PLUG CAP Spark plug cover acting as protection, HT conductor and often radio suppressor

POCKETING Valves sunk into the cylinder head by repeated hammering effect, to the detriment of performance

POLARITY Positive or negative, as of electrical connections

POLYCARBONATE Lightweight, resilient plastic used for crash helmets

POP RIVET Deformable metal pin used for joining two components

POPPET VALVE Reciprocating valve (as in cylinder head), essentially a disc on a stick

POPPING BACK Spitting back through the carburettor

POROUS Material allowing the passage of fluids. Often this is unwanted, as in porous castings

PORT Any opening, now commonly applied to two-stroke's cylinder windows and their associated tracts

POSITIVE EARTH Electrical system in which the battery's positive terminal is connected to earth

POT Slang for cylinder

POWER The rate of work, as measured in horsepower; more loosely, an engine's peak power output

POWER BAND The range of rpm in which an engine is making useful power

POWER-SLIDE Cornering with deliberate power-induced wheelspin, as in speedway

POWER VALVE Two-stroke exhaust mechanism that alters the height (and thus duration) of the exhaust valve, usually known by manufacturers trade names

PRE-IGNITION Spontaneous combustion of the fuel-air mix before sparking

PRE-LOAD Compression applied to a spring in installation. It has no bearing on the spring's rate

PRE-'65 Class of trials and motocross competition for machines built before 1965

PRESSURE GAUGE Instrument for measuring air or oil pressure

PRE-UNIT Description of a layout with separate engine

and gearbox, but of a model type which later had them in unit

PRIMARY CHAIN Chain transmitting drive from crankshaft to gearbox

PRIMARY GEARS Gear train transmitting drive from crankshaft to gearbox

PROGRESSIVE RATE Spring compressing at a rate that decreases with load

PROP-STAND Retractable side-stand

PS Widely used German measure of horsepower (equivalent to French cv). 100PS equals 98.6bhp

PTFE Poly-tetra-fluoro-ethylene, a low-friction plastic often used for bushes

PUDDING-BASIN Early, abbreviated form of crash helmet, cork-lined with leather temple protection

PULLING POWER Slang term for an engine's ability to work under heavy load at low rpm

PUSH ROD Metal rod used to transmit motion, such as from cam follower to rocker arm or in a clutch mechanism

QUENCH To cool; used of metal treatments, and combustion chambers in which a large area of metal is in contact with combustion gases, restraining pre-ignition

QUIETENING RAMP Gradual slope between base circle of a cam and the lobe proper

RADIAL TYRES Radials have plies lying across each other radially (c.f. cross ply), allowing greater flexibility and grip.

RADIAL VALVES Multi valves radiating from the centre of the head rather than in parallel pairs

RADIATOR Device for dissipating heat through a large surface area, usually used for engine coolant

RAKE Effective slope of the front forks relative to the vertical. Also known as castor. Usually, but not necessarily, the same as head angle

RAM AIR The use of forward-facing air-scoops to pressurize an air box. At most speeds, the intake air's coldness is of more benefit than its supposed pressure

RAMP CAM Cam fitted with quietening ramps

REAMER Fluted tool used to cut a hole to an exact final size

REAR WHEEL STEERING Steering a motorcycle by deliberately drifting the rear wheel

REBORE Machine a cylinder to accept an oversize piston

REBOUND DAMPING The damping that resists the spring's tendency to recoil after compressing

RECIPROCATING Moving backwards and forwards along a single path, such as a piston

RECOIL The bouncing back of a spring to its unloaded position

RECTIFIER Electrical device passing current in one direction only, thus converting AC to DC

REED VALVE A 'flapper' valve in a two-stroke's induction system, comprising flexible plates housed in a reed cage

REFLECTOR Polished bowl of a light unit; passive safety reflector in rear light units; element in some exhaust systems designed to maximize exhaust wave harmonics

REGULATOR Electronic component that maintains the desired voltage; sometimes the voltage control unit

REV COUNTER Tachometer: Instrument for measuring the rotational speed (rpm) of an engine

REVERSE CONE Extension to some megaphones having a steep taper in the opposite direction to the megaphone

RIFFLER Small fine-toothed file, especially used in porting work

RICH (mixture) Fuel-air mixture with excess fuel

RIM Edge of a wheel carrying the tyre

RING GEAR In engines with a longitudinal crankshaft, the gear engaging with the starter motor

RING PEGS Small metal keepers preventing piston rings from rotating, especially in two-strokes

RISING RATE Suspension in which linkages cause the rate of movement to decrease as wheel travel increases

ROCKER Pivoting arm translating rotational cam action into linear valve movement

ROCKERBOX Closed compartment housing the rocker gear

ROCKING COUPLE Lateral rocking motion set up in some types of multi-cylinder crankshaft

ROLLER BEARING Bearing having cylindrical rollers rather than balls

RON Research octane number

ROTARY Spinning, rather than reciprocating. Usually applied to Wankel engines

ROTARY VALVE Rotating, rather than piston-port or poppet valve, which opens and closes gas passageways as it spins

RPM Revs per minute, the rotational speed of a shaft or engine

RUMBLE Low-pitched noise emitted, especially, by worn crankshafts

RUNNING ON Phenomenon of an engine continuing to run after the ignition has been switched off, usually due to local hot spots

RUN-OUT A shaft or wheel that is out of alignment

SAND CASTING Metal component made by pouring molten metal into pre-formed sand mould

SAND RACING Racing on beaches, often on speedway-type courses

SCAVENGE Clear away, especially of exhaust gases from a combustion chamber

SCHNURLE LOOP Two-stroke scavenging process in which transfer ports direct gases up and away from the open exhaust port, propelling exhaust gases ahead of them

SCHRAEDER Design of tyre valve core, also used for air suspension

SCRAPER Tool for scraping; piston ring designed to clear oil from bores

SEALED BEAM Light unit with lens, filament and reflector in one piece

SECURITY BOLT Clamped rubber pad designed to prevent creep of tyres running at low pressure

SEIZURE Binding together of inadequately lubricated parts, especially pistons in cylinders

SELECTOR FORK Fork-shaped prong, controlled by a cam-plate or drum, able to slide gearbox pinions and change gear

SHOCK ABSORBER Device for smoothing transmission impulses; also applied less correctly to suspension dampers

The Testastretta engine on the Ducati 999R chassis is designed for heavy track use.

The 2005 Ducati Monster uses the engine from the 999 model with Öhlins suspension front and rear and radial front brakes.

SOCKET Cylindrical spanner fitted with a positive square drive

SOCKET HEAD SCREW Fastener with a recessed head taking hexagonal 'Allen key'

SODIUM-FILLED VALVE Hollow valve containing sodium, which melts at working temperature, aiding heat transfer to the cooler end of the valve

SHORROCK Brand of rotary, vane-type supercharger

SHORT REACH Spark plug hole of half-inch depth

SHORT STROKE Markedly oversquare

SHOT BLASTING Bombardment of parts to de-scale or work-harden them. Bead blasting is similar but less destructive

SHUTTLE VALVE Valve free to move to and fro, often found in telescopic forks

SIAMESE Two pipes joined into one, especially in exhausts

SIDEVALVE Engine with valvegear at the side and below the combustion chamber, rather than above

SIDEWALL The part of a tyre between the tread and the bead

SILENCER (Muffler in USA) Portion of an exhaust system concerned with reducing its noise, now very sophisticated with modern noise limits

SILENTBLOC Proprietory part made from rubber block bonded to metal

SILVER SOLDER Solder with high silver content giving much stronger joint than ordinary tin solder

SIMMONDS NUT Precursor of the nyloc nut, with fibre anti-loosening insert

SINGLE LEADING SHOE (SLS) Drum brake with one actuating cam, and hence one leading and one trailing shoe

SINTERED Formed by heat and pressure, usually of metallic powders

SKIMMING Removing metal to achieve a flat or straight surface, e.g. of cylinder head face

SKIRT Hanging portion, particularly of the piston below the gudgeon pin

SLAVE CYLINDER The end of a hydraulic system remote from the operator

SLICK Treadless racing tyre

SLICKSHIFT 1950s Triumph gearchange mechanism that automatically disengages the clutch. Not to be confused with the modern racing mechanism that cuts the ignition momentarily between gearchanges

SLIDE Moving piston in a slide carburettor, which both opens the venturi and governs the flow of fuel through the main jet

SLIDER The moving lower part of a telescopic fork leg

SLIPPER PISTON Piston with its skirt cut away to reduce weight and friction

SLIPPER TENSIONER Tensioning device employing a synthetic blade, typically on a cam drive chain

SLIP RING Rotating part of a magneto on which the brushes bear

SLUDGE Accumulation of oil-insoluble material in an engine, sometimes centrifuged into a sludge trap

SMALL END Bearing on a con rod through which passes the gudgeon pin, sometimes called little end

SNAIL CAM Chain adjustment eccentric

The 2006 Suzuki GSX R750 pushes the supersports motorcycle category towards a new advanced standard. Narrower, lighter, and more powerful than ever before, the new GSX R750 motorcycle gives the rider high-performance technology in a more aerodynamic, ultra-lightweight frame built entirely of aluminium alloy castings.

SOHC Single Overhead Camshaft

SOLDER Tin alloy of low melting point, typically used to join electrical components

SOLENOID Electrical device using a magnetic field to move a soft iron core and thus engage a mechanism

SPARK ARRESTOR Silencer component designed to reduce fire risks from some off-road motorcycles

SPARK EROSION Process for discreet removal of hard components from softer ones by bombardment with high tension sparks

SPARK PLUG Device for arcing HT current across two electrodes to initiate combustion

SPECTACLE HEAD Cylinder head with iron element comprising valve seats and spark plug boss, onto which is cast a skull of light alloy

SPEEDOMETER Instrument for measuring speed

SPIGOT Protrusion, e.g. of cylinder liner into crankcase mouth

SPINDLE Fixed rod about which another part turns, e.g. wheel spindle

SPINE Backbone, especially of spine-type frame

SPLAYED HEAD Four stroke twin cylinder head with widely splayed inlet and/or exhaust valves

SPLINE Grooved shaft allowing longitudinal but not radial movement of a complementary part

SPLIT SINGLE Two-stroke engine with two pistons sharing a common combustion chamber

SPRING Anything that deforms to permit movement and recoils elastically

SPRING WASHER Spring steel washer of interrupted circle, designed to prevent loosening

SPRUNG HUB 50s Triumph suspension with the springing located in the rear hub

SQUARE FOUR Cylinder layout using two crankshafts to place four parallel cylinders at the corners of a square; Ariel Square Four

SQUAT Extent to which the rear suspension of most motorcycles sags under power. Anti-squats are designed-in features intended to reduce this

SQUISH BAND Area of cylinder head almost touched by the piston at TDC, promoting quenching and turbulence of combustion gases

STAINLESS Corrosion-resistant steel, often non-magnetic, having some 25 per cent of alloyed metals such as chromium

STALL Stop an engine by overloading it

STANCHION Rigid structural member; in telescopic forks, the static tube clamped by the yokes

STEERING DAMPER Friction or oil-damped device for combatting tank-slappers

STEERING HEAD The section of frame into which the front forks engage

STICTION 'Static friction' — initial resistance to movement especially in suspension systems

STINGER Relatively narrow-bore pipe to the rear of two-stroke exhaust systems, important in exhaust resonance control

STOICHIOMETRIC RATIO Theoretical air:fuel ratio for perfect combustion at molecular level, 15:1 by weight

STOPPIE Monowheeling on the front wheel under extreme braking

STRAIGHT (OIL) Mineral grade oil without additives, and thus monograde

STROBOSCOPE an instrument using an intermittent bright light to freeze rotating markers and so determine ignition timing

STROKE Linear travel of any component, especially a piston

SUBFRAME Framework secondary to the main frame, usually at the rear of a motorcycle

SUMP Oil reservoir, below or integral with the crankcase, in wet sump engines

SUPERCHARGER Mechanically driven air pump for used in forced induction engines, now rarely used

SUPPRESSOR Electrical resistance in a spark plug to suppress TV and radio interference

SV An engine with a Side Valve

SWAN NECK S-shaped tube linking sidecar to motorcycle

SWARF Scrap metal from machining processes, sometimes present destructively in new engines

SWEPT VOLUME The volume covered by a piston's travel, cylinder displacement

SWG Standard Wire Gauge, a measuring convention in which smaller numbers refer to thicker wire

SWINGING ARM Pivoting rear suspension member carrying the wheel at its free end. More accurately called a swinging fork unless single-sided

SYNTHETIC Substance such as oil or paint based on artificial rather than organic materials. Synthetic oils can be finely tuned and offer greater performance and longevity

TAB WASHER Washer with one or more tabs capable of being bent to secure a nut

TACHOMETER Rev counter

TANK RAIL Frame tube on which sits the petrol tank

TANK-SLAPPER Violent lock-to-lock wobble of a moving motorcycle

TAPER A narrowing, especially of a shaft onto which another component is pressed

TAPER ROLLER Tapered roller bearing, adjustable and able to take loads radially and axially, such as at the steering head

TAPPET Part interposed between cam and valve or pushrod, often with provision for valve clearance adjustment

TAPPET CLEARANCE The free play allowed at a cold tappet to allow for thermal expansion

TDC Top Dead Centre, the highest position reached by the piston, opposite of BDC

TELESCOPIC Paired tubes, one able to slide within the other, as in telescopic forks

TERMINAL A battery post to which connections are made

THACKARAY WASHER Spring washer with three coils

THERMAL EFFICIENCY Ratio of an engine's output to the potential energy of the fuel it consumes

THERMOSTAT 'Switch' responding to temperature, typically one that opens a valve in a water-cooling system in the engine

THERMO-SYPHON Water-cooling system using convection rather than a pump

THROTTLE A variable restriction in, usually, a carburettor; the twistgrip

THRUST BEARING Bearing whose working face takes up the thrust and any rubbing action of associated shaft

THRUST WASHER Washer that operates as above.

TIMING The opening and closing points of valves, and of spark occurrence, expressed in degrees of crankshaft rotation or distance from TDC; adjusting the same

TIMING COVER Access cover to the valve timing mechanism

TIMING GEARS Gears driving the valvegear and/or ignition

TITANIUM Strong, grey metal, 43 per cent lighter than steel, used in exotic motorcycle applications

TOE-IN Extent to which the path of a sidecar wheel converges with that of the motorcycle

TOLERANCES Allowable variations in manufacturing dimensions

TOOTH Meshing projection on a sprocket, gear or rack

TORQUE The twisting force exerted by the crankshaft. Horsepower is a measure of torque over time

TORQUE CONVERTER A fluid coupling using oil and rotating vanes in some automatic transmission systems

TOTAL LOSS System of lubrication, usually in two-strokes, in which the oil is lost after delivery to the working surfaces; racing ignition systems with a battery but no charging system

TRACT Passageway in an engine, as in 'inlet tract'

TRACTION CONTROL Electronic system that reduces power to the driven wheels in the event of wheelspin. Rare on motorcycles

TRAIL The distance by which the steering axis, extended to the ground, lies in front of the tyre's contact patch. Its effect is to make the bike run straight when upright, but to turn the bike in the direction of lean when cranked over

TRAILING LINK Form of front suspension using a pivoting link with the wheel spindle behind the pivot

TRAILING SHOE Brake shoe with a cam at its trailing edge

TRANSMISSION The general term for the drive chain from crankshaft to final drive, including clutch and gearbox

TREAD Part of a tyre intended to clear water from the road

TRIAL Motorcycle competition over off-road hazards in which penalty points are incurred by a rider putting his feet down, falling or failing a section

TRICKLE CHARGE Slow charge given to a battery

TRIGONIC Triangular-section race tyres developed by Dunlop in the 1960s

TRIPLEX CHAIN Chain with three parallel rows of rollers

TRUMPET Inlet tube (bellmouth), typically applied to fuel injection applications

TUBELESS Tyre needing no inner tube

TUNGSTEN Rare metal used as alloy with tough steels and as filament in a conventional light bulb

TURBOCHARGER A forced air pump, broadly similar to a supercharger, but driven at very high speed by exhaust gases, rather than mechanically

TURBULENCE Agitation in a fluid, especially of inlet charge, where it can promote combustion

TWIN LEADING SHOE (2LS) A brake with two actuating cams and hence two leading shoes

TWISTGRIP Rotary throttle control on the right handlebar

UNDER-SQUARE Engine with stroke greater than the bore

UNIT CONSTRUCTION Engine in which the powerplant and transmission are formed in one integrated unit

UNIVERSAL JOINT (UJ) The double knuckle joint in shaft drive which allows play in the driven shaft to permit suspension movement

UNLEADED Petrol devoid of tetra-ethyl-lead, deriving its anti-knock capability from other ingredients

UNSPRUNG WEIGHT That part of the wheels, brakes and suspension which lies the road side of the springs

VALVE Any device for regulating flow

VALVE BOUNCE Destructive condition where a poppet valve is travelling faster than its spring can control it

VALVE GEAR The timing gear, cam(s), pushrods, rockers, valves and associated parts in a four-stroke engine

VALVE LIFTER Mechanical device, sometime automatic, for reducing compression during starting of a four stroke single

VALVE SEAT Insert of harder material into an aluminium cylinder head on which the poppet valve sits when closed

VENTURI A narrowing in a gas passage, especially in a carburettor

VENTURI PRINCIPLE The basis on which carburettors work: gas moving through a narrowing creates a partial vacuum able to lift fluid (fuel) into the venturi

VERNIER Precision measuring device comprising parallel-jawed sliding caliper

VETERAN Any motorcycle made before 1915

VINEY BONES Rubber bands cut from old inner tubes, named after trials ace Hugh Viney

VINTAGE Any machine made before 1931

VISCOSITY Runniness, indicated by SAE number. Higher number denotes more viscous

VOLUMETRIC EFFICIENCY Ratio of the mass of charge drawn into an engine to that which the cylinder could hold at atmospheric pressure. Can exceed unity in racing engines

V-TWIN Twin-cylinder engine having its cylinder axes arranged in a 'V' formation, both big-ends usually sharing a common crankpin

WANKEL Rotary engine invented by Felix Wankel, operating on four-stroke cycle but without reciprocating parts

WASHER Disc of, usually, metal, placed under a nut or bolt head to prevent scouring, loosening or to seal

When launched in 2004, the 165bhp put out by BMW's K1200R made it the firm's most powerful BMW motorcycle to date by a large margin.

WATER-COOLING liquid cooling; transmission of heat from an engine to atmosphere via a liquid intermediary

WATT Unit of electrical 'volume' — volts times amperes

W-CLIP 'W'-shaped clip securing headlamp unit to shell

WEIGHT DISTRIBUTION Ratio of a vehicle's weight, which bears on the front and rear wheels respectively

WELLER TENSIONER Self-adjusting spring-loaded blade tensioner, such as used on camchains

WELD Join materials by melting

WERNER POSITION The (now) usual site for a motorcycle engine in a frame; the name of two brothers who first put one there in 1897

WET LINER Cylinder liner that bears directly against the cooling liquid

WET SUMP Engine in which the oil is carried in a well below the crankcase, rather than in a remote tank

WHEEL Any circular object rotating on an axle at its centre

WHEELBASE The distance between front and rear wheel spindles

WHEELIE Monowheeling on the rear wheel under excess acceleration.

WHITE METAL Applied to various alloys of a whitish colour, typically used in plain bearings

WHITWORTH Type of thread of coarse pitch

WINDING Coil of wire around a core in a solenoid or generator

WIRE-WOUND PISTON Vintage piston with split skirt wrapped in coils of steel wire, eliminating differential expansion with an iron bore

WOODRUFF KEY Half moon-shaped piece of hard steel locating a component onto a shaft

WORM GEAR A uni-directional gear set in which a gear-wheel meshes with a screw-type thread, such as in speedometer drives

WRIST PIN (gudgeon pin in USA) Secondary big end pin found in radial and some V-twin and split single engines

Y-ALLOY Hidiuminium, a brand of light alloy that casts well and retains strength at high temperatures

YOKE Component connecting two or more others, usually called a fork yoke

ZENER DIODE Voltage regulator allowing excess voltage to leak to, commonly, an associated finned heat sink

ZINC Grey metal used in galvanising

ZOLLER A Vane-type supercharger

INDEX

PICTURE CREDITS

PIRANESI

PIRANESI

Etchings and Drawings

Selected and with an Introduction by
ROSELINE BACOU

NEW YORK GRAPHIC SOCIETY
BOSTON

Translated from the French *Piranèse: gravures et dessins*

International Standard Book Number: 0–8212–0577–3
Library of Congress Catalog Card Number: 73–9113

First published in 1975 in the United States by
New York Graphic Society Ltd.,
11 Beacon Street,
Boston, Massachusetts 02108

Printed and bound in France

CONTENTS

To Jean Prinet

INTRODUCTION

In 1740 a young architect from Venice entered Rome for the first time; his name was Giovanni Battista Piranesi; he was twenty years old. From this first encounter till his death in Rome in 1778, the history of Piranesi would be that of his passion for this city; Rome would direct his ambitions, would even justify his mistakes, would finally come to dominate his every thought and his whole life. The convergent point of his multiple activities as architect, decorator, archaeologist and etcher/engraver was the city of Rome; it became the centre of an immense and diversified oeuvre, all dedicated to glorifying the city's *magnificenza*. This outstanding Roman by adoption never ceased to recognize his debt to Venice, however. When, in 1750, Felice Polanzani engraved the portrait (p. 8) of his friend Piranesi he inscribed on the plate: *Jo. Bat. Piranesi Venet. Architettus.* On the frontispieces of his works, the artist himself followed his name with the title 'Venetian architect', thus stressing the debt he felt was owed by him to the city which was the setting of his youth and which had determined his profession.

Along with the eulogy which G. L. Bianconi dedicated to Piranesi after his death, the major source of information on the artist is without doubt the *Notice historique sur la vie et les ouvrages de J. B. Piranesi*, compiled in 1799 by Jacques-Guillaume Legrand, architect and professor of architecture. For his *Notice*, which was 'to be placed as a foreword to the new edition of the Works of Piranesi in Paris in the year VIII and the year IX [of the Directoire]', Legrand made use of 'notes and fragments communicated by his sons, his

Portrait of Piranesi by Felice Polanzani,
1750

companions and those who continued his numerous works', also what was recounted to him by Francesco and Pietro Piranesi (the artist's sons), who by this time had set up in Paris their own 'Chalcographie Piranesi'. Though this document, which is preserved in the Département des Manuscrits of the Bibliothèque Nationale, may not be exact in recording the chronology of the events of Piranesi's life, and as such must be clarified by reference to other sources, the personality of the artist comes through with remarkable power, whatever the truth of the numerous anecdotes which Legrand thought fit to include.

Born near Mestre, baptized and brought up in Venice, Piranesi took up architecture as a profession through his father, the stone-mason Angelo Piranesi. His mother's brother was the architect Matteo Lucchesi, to whom, it is said, the education of the young Piranesi was entrusted. Lucchesi was also employed as engineer by the Magistrato delle Acque, a body whose functions in maintaining the sea-walls were important in a city traditionally threatened by water; this fact is interesting in the light of the attention which Piranesi later gave to the solutions adopted by the Romans to control water and combat erosion. Smitten with polemics, as was every Venetian in the eighteenth century, Lucchesi took part in a debate on Etruscan remains, maintaining the theory that Greek art originated in Etruscan art, which his nephew, some years later, was to make one of the tenets of his own archaeological convictions. Piranesi is said to have studied perspective with Carlo

Zucchi, and, as an essential complementary subject, stage-design with the famous Bibiena family and their rivals, the celebrated Valeriani brothers. Legrand specifically states that Piranesi painted with the Valeriani brothers in Venice and Bologna; this stay in Bologna has not been proved, but the work of Piranesi from the beginning does suggest an intimate knowledge of the art of stage-design and a definite influence of the Bibiena family.

An older brother – a Carthusian monk – taught the young Piranesi Roman history. 'Piranesi,' Legrand relates, 'was very pleased to be taught by him, and applied himself to reading and explaining the main outlines of that history; he dreamed about it at night and conceived a violent desire to travel, and above all to go to Rome . . .' (fol. 130). In 1740 he managed to have himself engaged as designer in the retinue of the Venetian ambassador, Marco Foscarini, who went to Rome to take up his appointment to the new Pope, Benedict XIV; hence, Piranesi's first lodging in Rome was in the Palazzo Venezia, in the heart of the city. He discovered Rome, the modern city with its palazzi, its churches and baroque fountains, also the ancient city, the remains of which were everywhere, abandoned among brambles or providing the setting for the everyday life of the inhabitants. He found fellow Venetians in Rome – the sculptor Corradini, who was lodged with him in the Palazzo Venezia, and soon afterwards Felice Polanzani, who arrived there in 1742; he no doubt also became acquainted with certain *pensionnaires* of the French Academy, whose director, from 1738, was Jean-François De Troy.

Tail-piece, 1762 (Focillon, cat. no. 426)

There was little place in Rome for a young Venetian architect, however. The example of Giovanni Paolo Pannini, in 1740 at the height of his fame, certainly inspired Piranesi to try his luck in the genre which had made Pannini famous – the *veduta*; this might be a precise view of an existing monument or a romantic combination of real and invented elements, and the different types of *vedute*, widely disseminated through engravings, were then in great vogue among the numerous visitors to Rome, whether amateurs or simple tourists. Piranesi decided to perfect himself in the art of engraving, and entered the studio of Giuseppe Vasi, a Sicilian architect, ten years his senior, who had received lessons from S. Conca and P. L. Ghezzi, and instruction from Filippo Juvara; Vasi's major work, the plates of the *Magnificenze di Roma antica e moderna*, was published from 1747 to 1761. It was from this architect turned engraver that Piranesi learned his craft; there he made rapid progress, which aroused, it is said, the jealousy of the master, who would have preferred to see in his pupil less fire and more patience. 'Also,' Legrand recounts, 'he was constantly telling him, "you are too much a painter, my friend, ever to be an engraver" ' (fol. 130 v.); if this is not in fact true, it nevertheless deserves to be. He perfected himself at the same time in the art of perspective, copying in particular the stage-designs of Juvara and studying the work by Giuseppe Bibiena, *Architetture e Prospettive*, which appeared in 1740.

The results of his attempts are the plates of the *Prima Parte di architetture e prospettive* (pp. 25–28), published in Rome in 1743; the proposed second part never saw the light of day, but in 1750 the artist produced a second augmented edition of the *Prima Parte* under the title *Opere varie* (p. 41). The themes of this first work are the result of a somewhat traditional inspiration, but certain essential qualities of Piranesi are already evident: the amplitude of the architectural conceptions, the free and creative imagination which attempts to reconstruct the most ambitious of antique monuments, a very personal use of shadows and light to underline his intentions. One of the plates, *Carcere oscura* (p. 28), directly inspired by stage-design, is of particular interest, for it was to appear in 1743 as a prelude to the most celebrated of the artist's suites, the Prisons (*Carceri*; pp. 44 ff.).

Legrand places a first trip to Naples at about this time. In company with Corradini, who had received a commission from the Court of Naples, Piranesi went to this city to study painting, particularly that of Luca Giordano. During his visit to the Portici Museum, where the first objects found during the excavations of Herculaneum were preserved, the director, Carlo Maderna, advised him to devote himself to making engravings of Roman antiquities.

A period of crisis followed. Deprived of his lodgings at the Palazzo Venezia, and weakened by illness, Piranesi decided to return to Venice. He could certainly rely on important support in Rome, in particular that of the architect Nicola Giobbe, to whom he dedicated the *Prima Parte*, and that of Mgr Bottari, who had charge of the Vatican Library, and whom he thanked for his help in a letter addressed from Venice on 29 May 1744; however, because of lack of financial resources he could not take advantage of the support offered him.

Piranesi remained in Venice for about a year, and during this time his work underwent a development of considerable importance. The engraving of *vedute*, which had been initiated by Luca Carlevaris at the beginning of the century, was brilliantly developed in Venice by Marco Ricci, Michele Marieschi, and above all by Canaletto, whose etchings of luminous simplicity Piranesi no doubt admired. The studio of Giovanni Battista Tiepolo was then the centre of attraction for young artists; tradition holds that Piranesi worked there; at any rate he knew Tiepolo's decorative schemes for Santa Maria dei Gesuati and the church of the Scalzi, and above all the etchings of the *Capricci*, which are today thought to have been published in 1743. The revelation was profound; in the four plates of his *Capricci* (pp. 31–34), which Piranesi engraved in Venice, or shortly after his return to Rome, depicting the ruins of architecture, lying in heaps as though wrecked by some ancient cataclysm, the influence of etchings by Tiepolo is clearly discernible – a palm-tree rising above a ruin, the smoking altars and the bones of the dead recalling unknown rites, the hour-glass and the skull on the ground. But in these images of fascinating funereal grandeur there is also to be seen a triumphant new freedom of line, now arabesque, supple and controlled, which takes in the light and causes transparent shadows to rise from the white page. It may fairly be said that in this respect Piranesi was never more Venetian.

Legrand relates that Piranesi executed various architectural and decorative works in Venetian palazzi, but 'boredom took hold of him, Rome and his lofty memories were forever present in his mind' (fol. 131 v.). He had now found a way to make a living there; Giuseppe Wagner, the Venetian printseller, needed an agent in Rome. Piranesi left Venice, never to return. It was after this final move to Rome that his great period of activity began. In the studio he rented in the Corso, opposite the French Academy, he sold the stock of engravings which Wagner had entrusted to him; he attempted at the same time to make a name for himself as an original engraver. His beginning may have been modest in contributing to the anthology of *Varie Vedute di Roma* (p. 68), but he was to become, ten years later, the renowned author of the *Antichità Romane* (pp. 73–92), a huge undertaking, the four volumes of which were published in the same year, 1756; from 1748 there appeared, on separate sheets, his most important suite, the *Vedute di Roma* (pp. 136 ff.).

Carceri

It may seem paradoxical that the date of the execution of the Prisons and that of the first edition cannot be fixed exactly. Towards 1760–61, Piranesi, having reworked his copper plates and added two supplementary plates (II and V), published a second edition under the title of *Carceri d'invenzione*; he himself printed it, for Plate II bears his address at the time 'a strada Felice, vicino alla Trinità de' Monti' (p. 63). We are certain of the fourteen plates of

Study of a Man, pen and brown ink. 17·0×7·0 cm. (6¾×2¾ in.)

down of the subject, rapidly done, with guidelines for proportions and measurements, without any thought of the final effect, which was to be achieved by etching. There is nevertheless a notable evolution from the drawings of his youth, for example, in connection with the Prisons and the *Opere Varie*, which are very Venetian in inspiration, the colour wash exalting or dramatizing the subject, to the drawings of his maturity, from *c.* 1750, which are objective and synthetic in character. If we leave aside certain drawings, the purpose of which demanded a fine precision – the presentation drawings for San Giovanni in Laterano or designs delivered to those responsible for the renovation work on the Aventine church – the major quality of this draughtsman, one of the greatest ever, is his exceptional power to seize a theme in its totality, and, with a supreme mastery, to reduce it to its essentials. There is nothing intellectual in such a drawing, however; the sanguine sketch, sometimes strengthened with vigorous pen strokes, suggests not only the structure of a wall, but also, as if with a sort of sensual tenderness, the diversity of the materials employed, their substance, the roughness of their surfaces, even their coloration.

Piranesi's inner passion, and also the very awareness he had of the importance of his labours, made it a duty for him not to start a plate before having tested, in front of the subject, those profound impressions which alone would give the finished work its value both as testimony and instruction. All the remarkable effects of his plates are due, writes Legrand, 'to the exact observation which he made of nature each day, sometimes in brilliant sunlight, sometimes by moonlight, when the masses of architecture acquire great force, and have a solidity, a softness and a harmony often much superior to the image seen in the dazzle of daylight. In this way he learned effects by heart, by studying them from close to, from far, and at every hour . . .' (fol. 135 v.). Then, alone, with the help of his memory and his preparatory drawings, he set to work; after having worked on his copper plate coated with hard varnish and blocked out his highlights in varnish with a brush 'as one touches up a drawing with white', he then applied the acid 'with more care and patience than one would have thought possible, grading his tonalities, returning in this way ten or twelve times to certain plates. It must be done slowly, he would say to himself, I am doing three thousand drawings at a time' (fol. 135 v.). He used all the resources of the bite of the acid, even its surprises; to those who were taken aback by the unfinished character of his drawings he said, 'If my drawing were finished, my plate would only be a copy; on the contrary, I create the effect on the copper, and make of it an original' (Legrand, fol. 146 v.). The plates executed *c.* 1745 are done in a light and luminous style, the spaced strokes reminiscent of the etchings of B. Castiglione and G. B. Tiepolo; later, Piranesi accentuated the effects, perhaps under the influence of Rembrandt; when the artist took back his copper plates for the second edition of the Prisons, he enhanced the clear parts with new elements and multiplied his strokes to obtain a deeper black. In the same way, in the *Vedute*, the limpidity of the first views gives way to an intensity of contrasts between shadow and light, which was accentuated more

15

*Osservazioni . . . sopra la Lettre de
M. Mariette*, 1764 (Focillon, cat.
no. 967)

after 1770; in the Paestum suite (pp. 192, 193), published in 1778, the very year of his death, the columns of the temples in the foreground are dealt with in a broad, dark, flat manner, the columns hardly penetrated by a gleam, standing out in a mass against the brilliant background of the sky.

At a time when people travelled often and far, Piranesi never crossed the frontiers of Italy; moreover, he never left Rome and the Roman Campagna after 1745 except for brief excursions to Etruscan sites or the excavations of Herculaneum or Pompeii. His knowledge of the world was reduced to this restricted domain, but such was his genius that he abolished the limits of space and time.

Content and style

The earliest of the *Vedute di Roma* show a contemporary city as seen by a contemporary tourist; between 1748 and 1754, the artist engraved the monuments and the sites which were then, as they are now, the most frequently visited: St Peter's and the Basilicas, the Quirinale and the Capitol, the Piazza Navona and the Trevi Fountain, the banks of the Tiber. . . . A picturesque animation rules the streets; stalls are set up in the Piazza Rotonda; at the Ripa Grande the boats are being moored at the quaysides. At first glance, the *vedute* do not differ noticeably in treatment from the traditional engravings; the placing is usual, with an oblique view of the monuments to show them in their entirety, and downward views of piazzas, which engravers of *vedute* in the seventeenth century already conveyed with skill.

Piranesi, however, imposed new proportions on this real world; the people are reduced to little figurines, and their scale makes the grandness of the façades and the elevations of the interiors startling; this pygmy population seemingly inhabits a city conceived for giants.

The first collection of views, devoted to the monuments of the ancient city, dates from 1748; in a subsequent edition this was given the title *Alcune Vedute di Archi trionfali*. These plates were printed in the same small format and in the same spirit as those of the anthology to which Piranesi contributed on his return from Venice, the *Varie Vedute* of 1745. Around 1754, the artist's conception of his work changed profoundly; he prepared the *Antichità Romane*, studying the structure of monuments, making an inventory of the tombs along the Via Appia, visiting excavations where more remains were constantly being brought to light; the documents he assembled, his readings, his conversations with erudite scholars and with antiquaries helped to deepen his culture. The engraver of *vedute* gave way to the architect-archaeologist; thereafter, his engraved suites had as an end not only to represent what exists, but to demonstrate what once existed. The format grew; all effects of perspective were put to the service of this demonstration. The plate showing the foundations of the Mausoleum of Hadrian (p. 91), in the *Antichità*, is a typical example. The composition, of an exceptional boldness, with only a corner of the sky appearing at the right, concentrates one's eye on the mass of colossal blocks, the top of which is not visible; the light, softly stroking the surface, emphasizes with its shadows

16

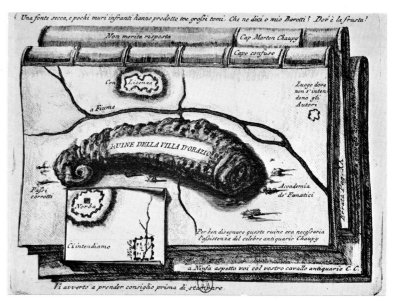

Satirical vignette against Capmartin de Chaupy, 1769 (Focillon, cat. no. 856)

the joins between the stones, to show the different construction techniques employed; the tiny people appear giddy at the side of this immense monster. It was also important to the architect in Piranesi to know in what manner and with what tools the ancient Romans were able to accomplish what they did; in the *Antichità*, the views of monuments alternate with technical plates, which, in their rigorous precision, are masterpieces; here the impassioned attention of Piranesi confers on the least important object, treated in isolation, a presence and a mysterious radiance: 'the practice of treating grand things,' writes Legrand, 'made him always give an imposing and majestic aspect, which Italians call *il grandioso*, to the most ordinary and least exalted of objects . . .' (fol. 138).

The *vedute* executed between 1754 and 1765 reflect this evolution; the images of the contemporary city are replaced by views of ancient monuments, which, together, could form a supplement to the *Antichità*. For in the same period the archaeologist had become a theoretician, and soon after a formidable controversialist when it came to defending the ideas expressed in his essay of 1761, *Della Magnificenza*; irritated by the vogue of Greece and the success of works recently devoted to Greece, as that of J.-D. Leroy, *Ruines des plus beaux monuments de la Grèce*, published in 1758, Piranesi upheld the theory, in fact rather ill-considered, of the Etruscan origin of Greek art, thus asserting the national and original character of Roman art. The learned Parisian collector, Mariette, expressed some reservations and took up the defence of Greek art in a letter to the *Gazette littéraire de l'Europe* in 1764;

having heard that Piranesi was working on an answer to him, Mariette wrote to their mutual friend, Mgr Bottari: 'He is most assuredly the master, but I desire only that he should not insist with such severity; he would have little enough reason to act as he does, given that the difference of our opinions on this point in no way diminishes the esteem I hold for his talents.' Despite these precautions, the *Osservazione* of Piranesi were published, being notable for their singular bitterness. Piranesi's violence was unleashed against Leroy, and Legrand regretted that 'he did not know how, in this contest which he fought with frenzy, to keep the measure of a discussion among learned men' (fol. 135). Later, in a satirical vignette, he ridiculed Capmartin de Chaupy, the director of excavations at the country villa of Horace, calling him 'Capo Confuso' (muddle-head). The entire production of the artist during these years was motivated by the defence of this sacred cause, the grandeur of ancient Rome; the *vedute* constitute his documentary evidence.

From 1761, in *Le Rovine del Castello dell' Acqua Giulia*, Piranesi became interested in the different methods used by the ancient Romans to conserve and canalize water; indeed, these subterranean installations appeared to him proof of the genius of the ancient architects for the same reasons that the monuments above ground did. But soon this thesis developed to become rather more than a demonstration of ancient works; it became a kind of *leitmotiv* in his own work. Vast sea-green cisterns where one can just make out strange shapes, stairways leading nowhere, the last steps of which

17

disappear under water, gloomy vaults supported by pillars covered with moss or half-submerged columns, grille-covered air-holes through which filter faint rays of light: we are once again in the closed and suffocating space of the Prisons. The world of stone and silence of the Prisons is echoed in this subterranean world of water, in which the murmurings and the currents in the deep canals reverberate above in the galleries. The small agitated figures of the Prisons served to emphasize the rhythms of the opposing composition; contrasting with the vertical walls are the curves of vaults and the ascending spirals of the stairs. By the pools of Albano and Castel Gandolfo, the characters live independent lives and, with their tattered clothes, their interrupted dance-like movements, and their gestures of desperation, they constitute another race of humanity which no longer resembles our own. Bianconi tells how, during his youth, Piranesi 'began to draw the cripples and the hunchbacks he saw by day in Rome, the holy refuge of the choicest specimens that Europe could produce in this genre. He also liked to draw ulcerated legs, broken arms, all the miseries of sickness, and when he found examples in a church, it appeared as if he had encountered a new Apollo Belvedere or a Laocoön, and he hurried to draw them . . .'. This society of Piranesi may bring to mind certain creations of the Mannerists of the sixteenth century, and also those of a Callot, a Salvator Rosa, or a Magnasco, but they are more directly inspired by the *Commedia dell'arte*; among the Piranesi ruins the mountebanks and the mimes of the Venetian stage are revived. The critics of the eighteenth century were severe towards these non-academic characters who turn one's attention, they said, away from the true subject; but for us these deformed and dancing beings become the interpreters of the most secret dreams of the visionary. Even more, in the view of the Via Appia (p. 119) the poetic power of the image comes from the presence of a little man on this ancient way – the scene of so many triumphs – his back turned, walking away.

The imagination of Piranesi knew no limits; it tried to create for his contemporaries a new setting for life, all the elements of which were taken from an ancient repertoire. Examples of comparable attempts are known, as the cell of Father Le Sueur at the Trinità dei Monti, transformed by Clérisseau into picturesque ruins, or, again, the burial grounds of Bailli de Breteuil in Rome. In his *Diverse maniere d'adornare i cammini* (pp. 126–133) of 1769, Piranesi imagined elaborate fireplaces, the composite style of which was inspired not only by Roman and Etruscan art but Egyptian art; the statues and bas-reliefs brought from Egypt to adorn Hadrian's Villa were the inspiration for these reconstructions. In these plates the taste for top-heavy masses is triumphant – a style already evident in the illustrations of *Parere sull'architettura* (pp. 106–108). The inventions of *Diverse maniere* helped to spread the neoclassical style throughout Europe, and, in particular, influenced styles of decoration and ornamentation in the Napoleonic period.

Among the *vedute* executed *c*. 1770, the most significant are assuredly those of the admirable suite of Hadrian's Villa. The remains of the palaces and the temples of the Villa were then shrouded in vegetation. 'As Piranesi and

G. B. Piranesi, engraving by F. Piranesi after a portrait by J. Cadès, 1779

Clérisseau were among the first to clear and draw Hadrian's Villa at Tivoli,' writes Legrand, 'they were obliged to back their way through the brambles, and then set fire to them to frighten away the snakes and scorpions . . .' (fol. 138 v.). They were regarded as sorcerers. The spell cast over Piranesi during the days and nights spent at these favourite places is reflected in the images he has left us. The roots of trees have split the vaults of the temple of Canopus, the bomes of the Baths have fallen in and, in their place, creepers create a transparent and illusory architecture. In the face of this victory of the ephemeral, Piranesi's meditations on the grandeur of the past were never more serious; time had destroyed the creations of man; all that remained, standing in solitude, were sections of walls which were eroded and crushed by vegetation. As Marguerite Yourcenar wrote, 'the edifice is sufficient in itself; it is at once the drama and the background to the drama, the setting of a dialogue between the human will yet inscribed on the massive stonework, the inert mineral energy, and irrevocable Time.'

In the last of the *vedute*, the visionary genius of Piranesi is expressed with a freedom so great that the artist seems to step back from his subject to study it in greater spaciousness. Monuments are no longer placed in the forefront, in a proximity which would allow them to be studied; they are at a distance, as, in the plate of 1775, the last arches of the aqueduct of Nero (p. 185) disappear beyond the horizon. The last view of the Colosseum is a bird's-eye view (p. 183); in this the immense monument is made to appear like the gaping crater of some extinct volcano.

In 1777, already ill, Piranesi went to Paestum to study its temples, whose harmonious proportions contradicted all the theories he had so ardently upheld; the engraved suite appeared in April 1778 (pp. 192, 193), a few months before his death on 9 November. He died at the age of fifty-eight, in the city of Rome, a man who one day had said to a student: 'I must produce grand ideas and I believe that if I were commissioned to produce plans for a new world, I would be mad enough to undertake the task'.

Roseline Bacou

CHRONOLOGY

1720   October 4
Birth of Giovanni Battista Piranesi, son of Angelo Piranesi, stonemason, and his wife, Laura (*née* Lucchesi), at Mogliano, near Mestre.

1720   November 8
Baptism at S. Mosè, Venice.

1730/1740
First apprenticeship in Venice. Architecture probably taught to him by his maternal uncle, Matteo Lucchesi, architect and assistant engineer at the Magistrato delle Acque, and by the architect Scalfarotto; studies perspective with Carlo Zucchi and stage-design with members of the Bibiena family and the Valeriani brothers.

1740
Arrives in Rome, in the retinue of Marco Foscarini, Venetian ambassador to Pope Benedict XIV, probably as draughtsman.

1740/1743
First period in Rome. He works with the engraver Giuseppe Vasi and becomes friendly with the Venetian Felice Polanzani. Among his first supporters, the architect Nicola Giobbe, and Mgr G. G. Bottari, the erudite keeper of the Vatican Library.

1743
Publishes in Rome his first suite of engravings under the title *Prima parte di architetture e prospettive, inventate ed incise da Gio. Batta Piranesi architetto veneziano*, printed by the Pagliarini brothers, and dedicated to Nicola Giobbe. According to Legrand, he travels to Naples where he starts to paint, he visits the Portici Museum, where the director, Carlo Maderna, urges him to reproduce in engravings the antiquities of Rome.

1744   March 29
Writes to Mgr Bottari to inform him of his return to Venice and to thank him for his support. In Venice he perhaps works with Giovanni Battista Tiepolo, whose first suite of etchings, the *Capricci*, was published in 1743. During, or shortly after, this stay in Venice, he engraves the fourteen plates of the *Carceri* (Prisons), which will be published, without date (*c.* 1745), in Rome, by J. Bouchard.

1744/1745
He moves to Rome, where he will spend the rest of his life. He starts as agent to Giuseppe Wagner, printseller in Venice, and at the same time begins to become known in Rome as an original engraver.

1745
Publishes views in a small format in the anthology *Varie Vedute di Roma*; his

name will be cited in *Raccolta di varie vedute di Roma . . .* (1752), evidence of his rapid rise to fame.

1748

Publishes *Antichità romane de' tempi della Repubblica*, with a dedication to Mgr Bottari.

He begins to engrave the first plates of his celebrated suite *Vedute di Roma*, his monumental series of Roman views, the production of which would be ended only by his death in 1778.

1750

Republishes the *Prima Parte* with additional complementary plates and the *Capricci*, under the title *Opere varie*.

1752

Marries in Rome Angela Pasquini. There are three children, Laura, Francesco and Pietro, all of whom will be associated, in different ways, with the work of their father.

1756

Publishes the four volumes of the *Antichità romane*, with his portrait by F. Polanzani (1750) at the beginning of the first volume, and a dedication to Milord Charlemont, later omitted.

1757 February 24

Elected honorary member of the Society of Antiquaries of London. He circulates his *Lettere di Giustificazione scritte a Milord Charlemont*, dated 15 August 1756, and February and 31 May 1757.

1758

Cardinal Carlo della Torre Rezzonico becomes Pope, taking the title Clement XIII. He grants Piranesi his protection, and commissions certain architectual projects, e.g. for the apse of San Giovanni in Laterano (1764).

1760

Probable date of the second edition of the *Prisons*, sixteen plates published under the title *Carceri d'invenzione di G. Battista Piranesi*.

1761

Elected member of the Academy of Saint Luke in Rome. He publishes *Della Magnificenza ed Architettura de' Romani*, the text of which, illustrated by a portrait of Pope Clement XIII and thirty-eight plates, sums up his theories of Roman architecture. He establishes his own printing house in the Palazzo Tomati, Strada Felice.

1762

Publishes the *Lapides Capitolini*, with a dedication to Clement XIII, and

Il Campo Marzio dell'antica Roma, with a dedication to the architect Robert Adam.

1763/1764
Visits Chiusi and Corneto to study Etruscan art.

1764
Publishes the *Antichità d'Albano e di Castel Gandolfo* and the *Antichità di Cora*. Cardinal Giovanni Battista Rezzonico, nephew of the Pope and Grand Prior of the Order of Knights of Malta, entrusts him with the conversion of the church of Santa Maria Aventina, which will be finished for the Pope's visit on 20 October 1766.

1765
Keeps up a controversy with a number of learned men on the subject of his theories contained in *Della Magnificenza*, particularly with the French collector P. J. Mariette, who, in a letter in the *Gazette littéraire de l'Europe* of 4 November 1764, had refuted his opinions about ancient Greece. He prepares the *Osservazioni . . . sopra la Lettre de M. Mariette* and *Parere sull'architettura*.

1767   January 16
Receives from Clement XIII the title of Cavaliere degli Sproni d'Oro. He presents to Cardinal G. B. Rezzonico a series of projects drawn up for San Giovanni in Laterano.

1768
Begins publication of *Vasi, Candelabri . . .*, the plates of which appear separately until 1778, and are then brought together in two miscellanies.

1769
Publishes his most important collection on the decorative arts, *Diverse maniere d'adornare i cammini*.

1777/1778
Visits Paestum; he engraves seventeen of the twenty plates of the collection *Différentes Vues de quelques restes de trois grands édifices qui subsistent encore dans le milieu de l'ancienne ville de Pesto*. He had visited Pompeii and Herculaneum; his son Francesco would use his drawings in the *Antiquités de la Grande Grèce*, the first volume of which would appear in 1804.

1778   November 9
Dies in Rome at the age of fifty-eight. His protector Cardinal G. B. Rezzonico would erect his tomb in Santa Maria Aventina with this epitaph: *Cineribus et Memoriae | Joan Baptistae Piranesi Domo venetiis | Sculptoris Linearis aere caelando | Plastae sigillari Architecti.*

The Plates

Prima Parte di Architetture e Prospettive inventate ed incise da
Gio. Batta. Piranesi architetto veneziano . . ., 1743

Frontispiece. 35 × 25 cm. (13¾ × 9¾ in.)   Frontispiz. 35 × 25 cm.

Vestiggi d' antichi Edificj fra i quali evvi l' Urna Sepolcrale tutta d' un pezzo di porfido di Marco Agrippa che oggi serve per il Sepolcro di Clemente XII. Si vede anche un pezzo di Guglia con caratteri Egizj, ed in lontano un Vestibulo di antico Tempio rovinato.
Gio. Batta. Piranesi Architetto inventò, et incise di Roma.

Prima Parte di Architetture e Prospettive inventate ed incise da
Gio. Batta. Piranesi architetto veneziano . . ., 1743

Plate 5, Remains of Antique
Edifices. . . . 33×25 cm. (13×9¾ in.)

Tafel 5, Überreste antiker Gebäude.
33×25 cm.

*Ruine di Sepolcro antico posto dinanzi ad altre ruine d'un Acquedotto pure antico;
sopra gli archi del medesimo v'è il canale, per cui si conduceva l'acqua in Roma.*
Gio. Batta. Piranesi Architetto inventò. ed incise in Roma.

*Prima Parte di Architetture e Prospettive inventate ed incise da
Gio. Batta. Piranesi architetto veneziano . . ., 1743*

Plate 6, Ruins of an Ancient Tomb.   Tafel 6, Ruinen eines antiken
. . . . 36×24 cm. ($14\frac{1}{4} \times 9\frac{1}{2}$ in.)   Grabes. 36×24 cm.

27

Carcere oscura con Antenna pel suplizio dè malfatori. Sonvi da lungi le Scale, che conducono al piano e vi si vedono pure all' intorno altre chiuse carceri.

*Prima Parte di Architetture e Prospettive inventate ed incise da
Gio. Batta. Piranesi architetto veneziano . . . , 1743*

Plate 2, Dark Prison. . . . 36×24 cm.
(14¼×9½ in.)

Tafel 2, Düsteres Gefängnis mit
Folterwerkzeugen. 36×24 cm.

Tempio antico inventato e disegnato alla maniera di quelli che si fabbricavano in onore della Dea
Vesta; quindi vedesi in mezzo la grand'Ara, sopra della quale conservavasi dalle Vergini Vestali l'inestingui-
bile fuoco sacro. Tutta l'opera è Corintia ornata di statue e di bassi rilievi, e di altri ornamenti ancora.
Il piano di questo Tempio è notabilmente elevato dal suolo: vedesi in mezzo la Cella rotonda, come lo è
pure tutto il gran Vaso del Tempio stesso: quattro loggie portavano ad essa, e per altrettante scale vi si
ascendeva. Le parieti del gran Tempio hanno due ordini, sopra il secondo s'incurva una vasta Cupola con
isfondati, e rosoni, e termina in una grande apertura, dalla qle dipende il lume alla Cella che le sta sotto. 15.
Gio Batta Piranesi Arch.º inv, ed inciso in Roma l'Anno 1743.

Antique Temple . . . in the style of the
Temple of Vesta. 1743, 34×25 cm.
(13¼×9¾ in.)

Tempel, entworfen und gezeichnet in der
Art antiker Vestatempel. 1743,
34×25 cm.

30

Frontispiece, pen and brown ink, brown wash, over a black
chalk sketch. 39×51 cm. (15½×20 in.)

Frontispiz. Federzeichnung, braun getuscht und laviert und
Schwarzstift. 39×51 cm.

Capriccio. 39× 54 cm. (15½× 21¼ in.)

Capriccio. 39× 54 cm.

32   *Capriccio.* 39×54 cm. (15½×21¼ in.)   *Capriccio.* 39×54 cm.

Capriccio. 39×54 cm. (15½×21¼ in.)   *Capriccio.* 39×54 cm.   33

34   *Capriccio.* 39×54 cm. (15½×21¼ in.)   *Capriccio.* 39×54 cm.

Ruins with Statue of Pallas Athene. 49×63 cm. (19¼×25¾ in.)   *Ruinen mit Statue der Pallas Athene.* 49×63 cm.   35

Scene of Sorcery, pen and brown ink, brown wash, over sanguine outlines, signed bottom right 'Piranesi'. 25×18 cm. (9¾×7 in.)

Hexenszene. Federzeichnung, braun getuscht und laviert, mit Rötel. Signiert rechts unten. 25 × 18 cm.

Group of Masqueraders, pen and brown ink, brown wash, over black chalk outlines, signed bottom right. 25 × 18 cm. (9¾ × 7 in.)

Skizze mit Maskierten. Federzeichnung, braun getuscht und laviert und schwarze Kreide. Signiert rechts unten. 25 × 18 cm.

Fragments of Antique Architecture with Figures,
pen and brown ink, brown wash, over black chalk outlines,
signed bottom right 'Piranesi'. 18×25 cm. (7×9¾ in.)

Ruinen antiker Architektur mit Figuren. Federzeichnung,
braun getuscht und laviert und Schwarzstift.
Signiert rechts unten. 18×25 cm.

Triumphal Arch, pen and brown ink, brown wash, over a
sanguine sketch. 14×21 cm. (5½×8¼ in.)

Triumphbogen. Federzeichnung, braun getuscht und laviert,
mit Rötel. 14×21 cm.

40

Study for the plate opposite, pen and brown ink, over a
sanguine sketch. 47×74 cm. (18½×29 in.)

Skizze zum folgenden Blatt. Federzeichnung, braun getuscht
und laviert, mit Rötel. 47×74 cm.

Parte di ampio magnifico Porto all'uso degli antichi Romani, ove si scuopre l'interno della gran Piazza pel Comercio superbam.te decorata di colonne rostrali, che dinotano le più segnalate vittorie marittime. Le Pareti, che sono d'intorno alla gran Piazza vanno formando molti Archi trionfali ornati parim.te di trofei navali, quali Archi si uniscono dalla parte opposta al Tempio della Fortuna, sopra la cui cima sta collocato il gran Fanale per guida de' naviganti. Le dette Pareti sono difese ed alternate da Contraforti, che gli fanno argine e nel medesimo tempo gli servono di solido maestoso ornam.to Sopra di questi forti in qualche distanza sonovi distribuiti i posti di guardia per le sentinelle con a' piedi de' mascheroni, per espurgo delle immondizie. Le grandi Scalinate, che veggonsi, portano alla gran Piazza ornata di Portici, Basilica, e d'altri nobili edifici con l'ara di Profumi inestinguibili dedicata a Nettuno Dio del mare. Si vedono ancora sepolcri ed urne colle ceneri de' benemeriti Capitani, estinti ne' conflitti navali, situate a miglior vista del Porto per eccitamento di gloriosa emulazione. Questa vasta Fabrica tutta di soda architettura composta e nobilitata di Statue, Fontane, Trofei, Bassirilievi, e di tutto ciò, che può servire non meno d'ornamento, che di comodo per la navigazione, resta molto bene difesa dagl'insulti del mare per mezzo del Molo, de' Lazzaretti e Magazini, che la circondano.

Opere varie de architettura, prospettive, grotteschi, antichità sul gusto degli antichi Romani
inventate ed incise da Giambattista Piranesi architetto veneziano . . ., 1750

Partial view of a Magnificent Harbour. . . . 40 × 55 cm.
(15¾ × 21½ in.)

Teilansicht eines prunkvollen, grossen Hafens. . . . 40 × 55 cm.

Palace Interior, pen and brown ink, brown wash, over a
sanguine sketch. 16×22 cm. (6¼×8½ in.)

Inneres eines Palastes. Federzeichnung, braun getuscht und
laviert, mit Rötel. 16×22 cm.

Palace Interior, pen and brown ink, brown wash, over a
sanguine sketch, signed bottom right. 51 × 76 cm. (20 × 29¾ in.)

Inneres eines Palastes. Federzeichnung, braun getuscht und
laviert, mit Rötel. Signiert rechts unten. 51 × 76 cm.

43

Invenzioni capric. di Carceri all'acquaforte datte in luce da Giovani Buzard . . ., c. 1745
2nd edition: *Carceri d'invenzioni di G. Battista Piranesi archit. vene., c. 1760*

Frontispiece. 54×41 cm. (21¼×16¼ in.)   Frontispiz, erste Fassung. 54×41 cm.

Carceri

Plate III, first state. 54×41 cm. (21¼×16¼ in.)   Blatt III, erste Fassung. 54×41 cm.   45

Carceri

Plate IV, first state. 55×41 cm. (21½×16¼ in.)   Blatt IV, erste Fassung. 55×41 cm.

Carceri

Plate VI, first state. 55×41 cm. (21½×16¼ in.)   Blatt VI, erste Fassung. 55×41 cm.   47

Carceri

Plate VII, first state. 55×41 cm. (21½×16¼ in.)   Blatt VII, erste Fassung. 55×41 cm.

Carceri

Plate VII, second state. 55 × 41 cm.
(23¼ × 16¼ in.)

Blatt VII, zweite Fassung. 55 × 41 cm.

49

Carceri

Plate IX, first state. 55×40 cm. (21½×15¾ in.)   Blatt IX, erste Fassung. 55×40 cm.

Carceri

Plate IX, second state. 55 × 40 cm.
(21½ × 15¾ in.)

Blatt IX, zweite Fassung. 55 × 40 cm.

Prison study for the plate opposite,
pen and brown ink, over outlines in
sanguine, signed bottom right
'Piranesi'. 18×13 cm. (7×5 in.)

Skizze zum folgenden Blatt der
Carceri. Federzeichnung, braun
getuscht, mit Rötel.
Signiert rechts unten. 18×13 cm.

Carceri

Plate VIII, first state. 54× 40 cm.
(21¼ × 15¾ in.)

Blatt VIII, erste Fassung. 54× 40 cm.

53

54   Detail of plate opposite.   Ausschnitt des folgenden Blattes.

Carceri

Plate X, first state. 41×55 cm. (16¼×21½ in.)

Blatt X, erste Fassung. 41×55 cm.

Carceri

56   Plate XI, first state. 40×54 cm. (15¾×21¼ in.)   Blatt XI, erste Fassung. 40×54 cm.

Carceri

Plate XII, first state. 41 × 56 cm. (16¼ × 22 in.)   Blatt XII, erste Fassung. 41 × 56 cm.   57

Carceri

Plate XIII, first state. 40× 54 cm. (15¾× 21¼ in.) Blatt XIII, erste Fassung. 40× 54 cm.

Carceri

Plate XV, first state. 40×55 cm. ($15\frac{3}{4}$×$21\frac{1}{2}$ in.)   Blatt XV, erste Fassung. 40×55 cm.   59

Prison Interior, pen and brown ink, brown wash, over a
sketch in sanguine, signed bottom right 'Piranesi'. 17 × 23 cm.
(6¾ × 9 in.)

Innenansicht eines Gefängnisses. Federzeichnung, braun getuscht
und laviert, mit Rötel. Signiert rechts unten. 17 × 23 cm.

Carceri

Plate XIV. 41×53 cm. (16¼×20¾ in.)   Blatt XIV, zweite Fassung. 41×53 cm.   61

Palace Courtyard, pen and brown ink, brown wash. 12×16 cm. (4¾×6¼ in.)

Hof eines Palastes. Federzeichnung, braun getuscht und laviert. 12×16 cm.

Carceri

Plate II. 55×42 cm. (21½×16½ in.)   Blatt II. 55×42 cm.   63

Architecture with Arches and Domes, pen and brown ink, brown wash, over a sketch in sanguine, signed bottom right 'Piranesi'. 18×25 cm. (7×9¾ in.)

Architekturskizze mit Bogen und Kuppeln. Federzeichnung, braun getuscht und laviert, mit Rötel. Signiert rechts unten. 18×25 cm.

Prison Interior, pen and brown ink, brown wash, over a
sketch in sanguine. 17×23 cm. (6¾×9 in.)

Innenansicht eines Gefängnisses. Federzeichnung, braun getuscht
und laviert, mit Rötel. 17×23 cm.

Architecture with Arches and Stairways, pen and brown ink, brown wash. 25× 33 cm. (9¾× 13 in.)

Architekturskizze mit Bogen und Treppenaufgängen. Federzeichnung, braun getuscht und laviert. 25× 33 cm.

Vaulted Galleries, pen and brown ink, grey and brown washes, over a black chalk sketch. 18×24 cm. (7×9½ in.)

Gewölbegänge. Federzeichnung, braun getuscht, grau und braun laviert, sowie Schwarzstift. 18×24 cm.

Varie Vedute di Roma antica e moderna disegnate e intagliate da celebri autori . . ., 1745

Amphitheatrum Castrense near the church of
S. Croce in Gerusalemme. 12 × 18 cm. (4¾ × 7 in.)

Amphitheatrum Castrense bei S. Croce in
Gerusalemme. 12 × 18 cm.

Antichità romane de' tempi della Repubblica e de' primi imperatori, disegnate ed incise da Giambattista Piranesi architetto veneziano, 1748

Plate 6, The Arch of Titus. 13×26 cm. (5×10¼ in.)   Blatt 6, Der Titusbogen. 13×26 cm.   69

Antichità romane de' tempi della Repubblica e de' primi imperatori . . ., 1748

Plate 9, The Arch of Constantine. 13×26 cm. (5×10¼ in.)   Blatt 9, Der Konstantinsbogen. 13×26 cm.

Antichità romane de' tempi della Repubblica e de' primi imperatori . . ., 1748

Plate 17, The Arch in Rimini built by Augustus. 13×26 cm. (5×10¼ in.)

Blatt 17, Der Triumphbogen des Augustus in Rimini. 13×26 cm.

71

Trofei di Ottaviano Augusto . . ., 1753

Plate 3, Memorial to the Victory at
Actium. 60× 40 cm. (23½× 15¾ in.)

Blatt 3, Denkmal für den Sieg bei
Actium. 60× 40 cm.

Le Antichità romane, *opera di Giambattista Piranesi architetto veneziano*
divisa in quattro tomi . . ., 1756

Vol. II, frontispiece. 40×25 cm.
(15¾×9¾ in.)

Band II, Frontispiz. 40×25 cm.

74   Detail of plate opposite.   Ausschnitt des folgenden Blattes.

Band II, Blatt X, Teil des Grabgewölbes des L. Arrunzio.
39×60 cm.

Vol. II, plate X, Part of the Burial Vault of L. Arrunzio.
39×60 cm. (15⅛×23¾ in.)

Le Antichità romane . . ., 1756

Veduta interna di una delle tre Sale sepolcrali credute della Famiglia di Augusto.

Questa Sala sepolcrale spogliata non solo di tutti i suoi ornamenti più riguardevoli, ma ancora d'ogni pezzo di marmo, e della stessa intonacatura, resta per la maggᵒʳ parte sepolta sotto il terreno, come lo dimostrano i due nicchioni, che si scorgono da un lato. Veggonsi girar intorno le pareti con ordine distribuiti i Colombaj senza veruna iscrizione; anzi nemmeno vi apparisce alcun segno d'esservene stata giammai. La ragione di questo però è facile a congetturarsi, essendo caduta affatto da muri l'intonacatura, dentro la quale sol tanto incassate erano le tavole delle Iscrizioni; nè si permetteva lo scavare il muro in conto alcuno, per non indebolirlo, sull'idea, che quegli antichi avevano di perpetuare le loro Fabbriche, e particolarmente quelle de'Sepolcri, a bello studio fatte per custodire in perpetuo le ceneri ivi riposte. Con che essi credevano non solamēte di tramandare a posteri per tutte l'etadi avvenire la memoria de'loro defonti, ma ancora di mantenere all'Ombre di quelli ne'Campi Elisii un più sicuro riposo. Ora serve questa Sala per uso di Tinello.

Le Antichità romane . . ., 1756

Vol. II, plate XLII, Interior of Burial Vault. . . . 37×51 cm. (14½×20 in.)

Band II, Blatt XLII, Innenansicht eines der drei Grabgewölbe der Familie des Augustus. 37×51 cm.

Le Antichità romane . . ., 1756

Vol. II, plate LVI, Interior of Burial Vault. . . . 35×50 cm.
(13¾×19¾ in.)

Band II, Blatt LVI, Innenansicht des Grabgewölbes in der
Vigna Casali bei Porta S. Sebastiano. 35×50 cm.

Le Antichità romane . . . , 1756

Vol. II, plate XIII, Inscriptions and Fragments from Burial Vaults. . . . 39×47 cm. (15½×18½ in.)

Band II, Blatt XIII, Inschriften und Fragmente aus den Grabkammern der Familie Arrunzio. 39×47 cm.

78

Le Antichità romane . . ., 1756

Vol. II, plate XLVI, Fragments of Burial Vault opposite the
Church of S. Sebastiano. . . . 39×47 cm. (15½×18½ in.)

Band II, Blatt XLVI, Fragmente aus der Grabkammer
gegenüber der Kirche S. Sebastiano. 39×47 cm.

79

DI MANES MANES SITIS IAM MORTE MISELLIS
PRAE PROPERA SENIBVS SERO DATVM RAPITIS
HIC ETENIM PVE REST VMBRI DE SANGVINE CRETVS
INVIDA QVEM TENERVM PARCA TENAX RAPVIT
QVO MATRI MVLTOS SCRIBSIT MVLTOS QVOQ PATRI
INGRATIS ANNOS VOTA SATIS MISERA
NAM SOLOS SEPTEM PROLES QVOS DVXERIT ORBES
SEPTVAGINTA FORENT · NI MISEROS CVPERET
QVI PRO VINE TIS FVNDIS TERRAQ · MARIQ ·
HOC SOLVM PROLI · HOC PEPERE RE SOLVM
IVLIANO FILIO
L · VMBRIVS SATVRNINVS

Iscrizione, e Frammenti delle Camere sepolcrali della Villa de' Cinque.

A *Aghi di Avorio per le acconciature di capo delle Donne.* B *Stili di metallo per iscrivere sopra le Tavolette incerate, e per iscancellare occorrendo quello, che scritto vi era.* C *Spatola od altro consimile stromento, con cui levavansi da Vasi gli unguenti odorosi.* D *Scure di metallo di quelle, forse, che ponevansi nell'insegne consolari.* E *Vasi cenerarj di terra cotta.* F *Coperchio de' medesimi.* G *Vasi di vetro per li Balsami, disformati dal fuoco degl' incendj.* H *Bottoni di metallo simili all'uso d'oggidi.* I *Vaso cenerario col suo coperchio, striato, di Alabastro orientale, fiorito, ed agatato di gran preggio, alto palmi due, e mezzo in circa. Ora si conserva presso degl' Illus. SS.ri de Cinque posseßori della Villa.* K *Parte di una Volta delle Camere, segnate A. Ella era di forma angolare, distribuita in varj scompartim. ornati di pitture, e stucchi. Il centro della Volta era abbellito di una Cornice circolare* L, *composta, come appare nella Modinatura* M. N *Tubi, e Tegole di cotto maßiccie, quali congiungevansi l'uno all'altro per mezzo dell'incastro.* O *Bocca, e Coperchio del Pozzo mentovato nella Pianta.* E *della Tavola antecedente.*

Piranesi Architetto dis el inc.

Le Antichità romane . . ., 1756

Vol. II, plate XLIX, Inscriptions and Fragments from the
Burial Vaults of the Villa de' Cinque. 37×50 cm.
(14½×19½ in.)

Band II, Blatt XLIX, Inschriften und Fragmente aus den
Grabkammern der Villa de' Cinque. 37×50 cm.

81

36×51 cm. (14¼×20 in.)

Band III, Blatt XLVIII. Eine der vier Victoria-Figuren mit Lorbeerkranz und andere Fragmente. 36×51 cm.

Vol. III, plate XLVIII. One of four Figures of Victory . . .

Le Antichità romane . . ., 1756

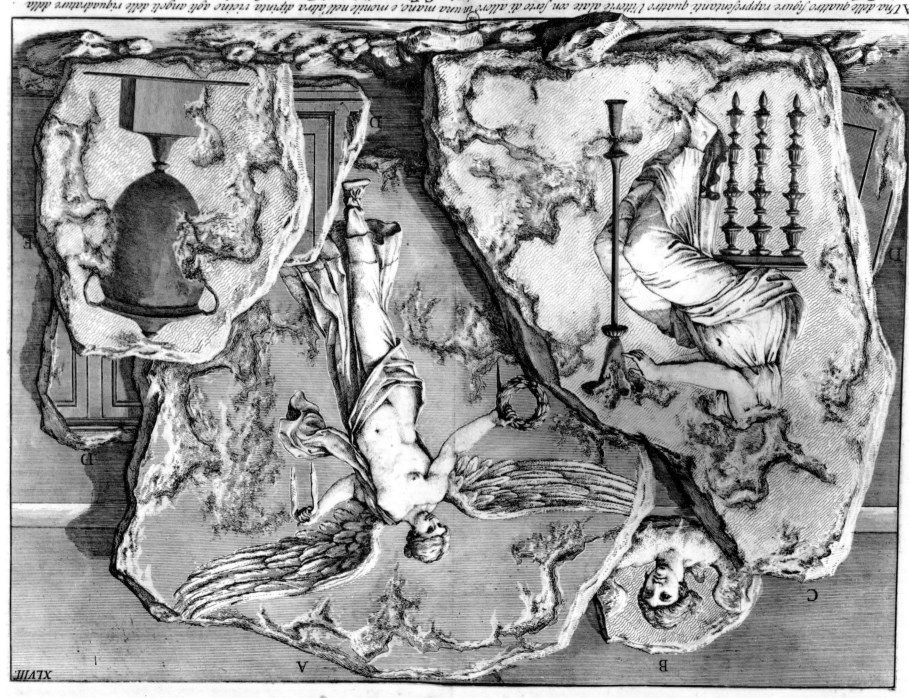

Le Antichità romane . . ., 1756

Vol. III, plate XXX, Inscriptions of Freed Slaves and
Servants. . . . 37×48 cm. (14½×18¾ in.)

Band III, Blatt XXX, Inschriften der Freigelassenen und
Diener der Familie des Augustus. 34×48 cm.

Modo, col quale furono alzati i grossi Travertini, e gli altri Marmi nel fabbricare il gran Sepolcro di Cecilia Metella, oggi detto Capo di Bove.

Piranesi Archit. dis. et inc.

Le Antichità romane . . ., 1756

Vol. III, plate LIII, Methods of raising Travertine Blocks . . . for the Tomb of Caecilia Metella. . . . 35 × 52 cm. (13¾ × 20½ in.)

Band III, Blatt LIII, Technik, mit der die Travertin-Quadern beim Bau des Grabes der Cecilia Metella gehoben wurden. 35 × 52 cm.

84   Detail of plate opposite.

Ausschnitt des folgenden Blattes.

Sepolcro de tre fratelli Curiazj in Albano

Le Antichità romane . . ., 1756

Vol. III, plate X, Tomb of the Curiaci Brothers at Albano.
38 × 59 cm. (15 × 23¼ in.)

Band III, Blatt X, Grabmal der Curiatier in Albano.
38 × 59 cm.

VEDUTA del SEPOLCRO della Famiglia PLAUZIA per la strada che Conduce da Roma à Tivoli vicino a Ponte Lugano.

Piranesi Architetto dis.e scolp.

Le Antichità romane . . ., 1756

Vol. III, plate XII, View of the Tomb of the Plaucia   Band III, Blatt XII, Grabmal der Familie Plauzia. 38 × 60 cm.
Family. . . . 38× 60 cm. (15× 23½ in.)

Le Antichità romane . . ., 1756

Vol. IV, plate XVI, The Pons Fabricius. . . . 36×59 cm.
(14¼×23¼ in.)

Band IV, Blatt XVI, Die Brücke des Fabricius. 36×59 cm.

88   Detail of plate opposite.

Ausschnitt des folgenden Blattes.

Veduta degli Avanzi delle Camere sepolcrali de'Liberti, e Servi, ec. della Famiglia di Augusto.

Piranesi Architetto def. ed inc.

Le Antichità romane . . ., 1756

Vol. III, plate XXII, Ruins of the Burial Vaults of Freed
Slaves and Servants. . . . 38×60 cm. (15×23½ in.)

Band III, Blatt XXII, Ruinen der Grabkammern der
Freigelassenen und Diener des Augustus. 38×60 cm.

Le Antichità romane . . ., 1756

Vol. III, plate VII, The Appian Way. . . .
31 × 23 cm. (12 × 9 in.)

Band III, Blatt VII, Die Via Appia antica.
31 × 23 cm.

VEDUTA del sotterraneo Fondamente del Mausoleo, che fu eretto da Elio ... Adriano Imp.° In questa parte, la qual è opposta alla Facciata, gli Speroni sono tutti co-
struiti di grossi Travertini.   A Parte di Ricopitura, ovvero sia di ... Opera incerta a corpi, la quale veste d'ogni intorno il Fondali. B Palizzate. C Parte del Mausoleo.

Piranesi Archit. dis. et inc.

Le Antichità romane . . ., 1756

Vol. IV, plate VI, Foundations of the
Mausoleum of Hadrian. 87 × 45 cm.
(34¼ × 17¾ in.)

Band IV, Blatt VI, Die Grundmauern
des Hadrian-Mausoleums. 87 × 45 cm.

91

Veduta dell'avanzo di una delle Pile del Ponte Trionfale composta di travertini, peperini, e tufi, i quali rinchiudono, e maravigliosamente legano l'interno lavoro de corsi d'opera incerta. Questa Pila oggi serve di fondamento al moderno Teatro di Tordinona. A. Corso composto di grossi pezzi di travertino co' denti, i quali legavano gli altri corsi, che erano ad essi soprapposti, e formavano il peduccio del Arco B. Altri corsi de travertini nell'esterno, e nell'interno C. di tufi, e peperini. D. Corsi d'opera incerta tra i corsi delle pietre. E. In questo sito la Pila molto più s'estende, ed i corsi de travertini soprapposti formano il gran contraforte al sudetto Teatro moderno. Per lo più parte di questo sperone vedesi scoperto dall'acque ne mesi di Giugno, Luglio Agosto, e Settembre. F. Letto del Fiume moderno G. Lato della Pila, verso la corrente del Tevere.

Piranesi Archit. dif. inc.

Le Antichità romane . . . , 1756

Vol. IV, plate XIII, Remains of one of
the Piers of the Ponte Trionfale.
29×23 cm. (11½×9 in.)

Band IV, Blatt XIII, Reste eines Pfeilers
des Ponte Trionfale. 29×23 cm.

Della Magnificenza ed Architettura de' Romani, opera di Gio. Battista Piranesi . . ., 1761

Plate II, Outlet of the Cloaca
Maxima into the Tiber. 30×23 cm.
(15½×9 in.)

Blatt II, Architektonische
Darstellung der Cloaca Maxima.
39×23 cm.

93

Veterum [Aquae] Marciae ductuum, muris Urbis ab Aureliano constructis intersec [...] ruinae, à Porta Majori ad Portam S. Laurentii; prout habetur in Tom. I. Antiqu. Rom: num. 119, 120, 121 Indic. gener. vestig. Romae veteris.

Della Magnificenza ed Architettura de' Romani . . ., 1761

Tail-piece to page XXVI, the Aqua Marcia Aqueduct.
19×29 cm. (7½×11½ in.)

Teil des Blattes XXVI mit der Darstellung des Aquädukts
der Aqua Marcia. 19×29 cm.

Antichità di Cora, 1764

Vignette on page 1. 20×23 cm. (7¾×9 in.)   Vignette auf Blatt I. 20×23 cm.   95

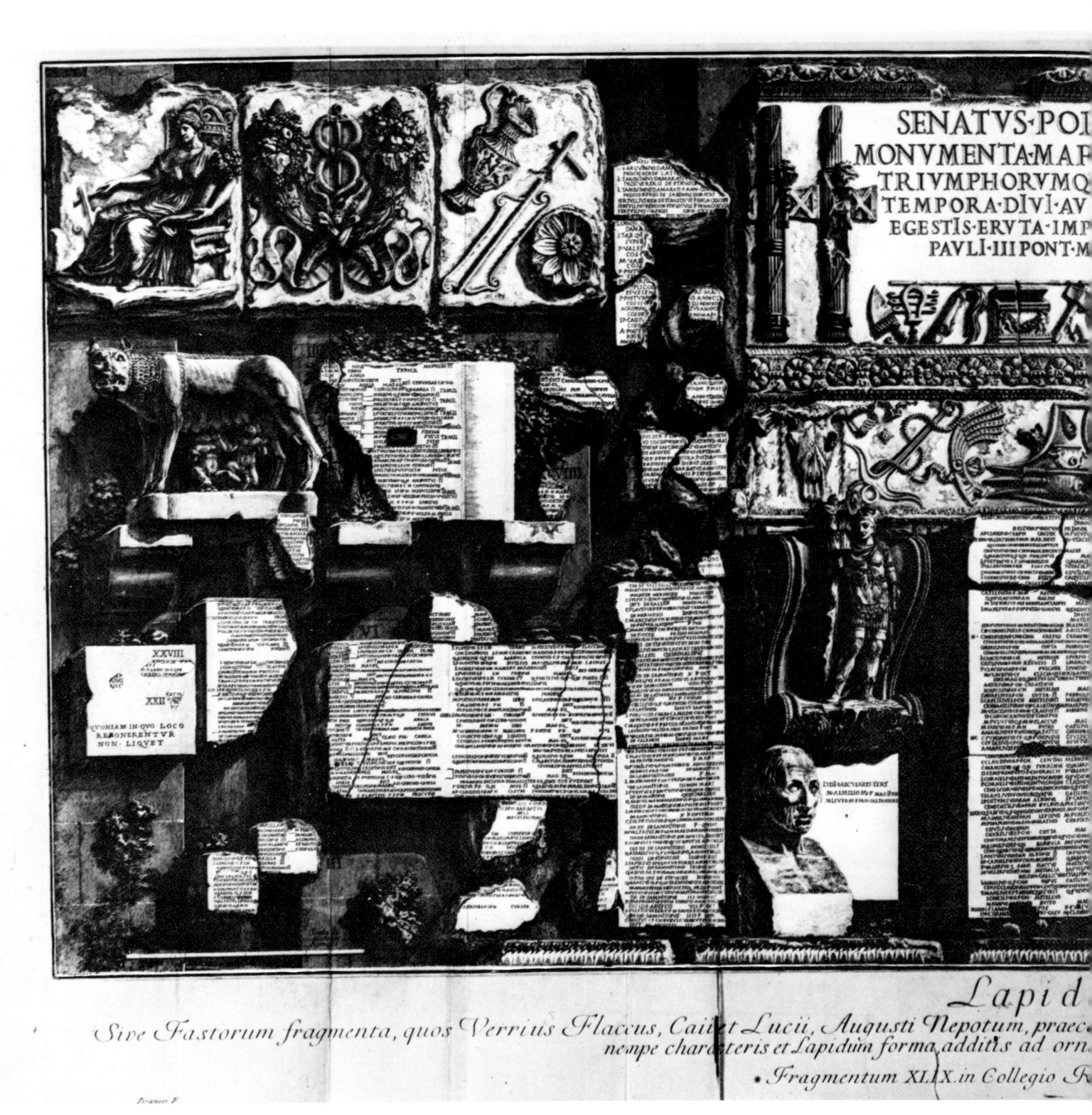

Sive Fastorum fragmenta, quos Verrius Flaccus, Caii et Lucii, Augusti Nepotum, praec... nempe characteris et Lapidum forma, additis ad orn...

*Fragmentum XLIX.in Collegio R...

96   *Lapides Capitolini*, 1762. 50×24 cm. (19½×9½ in.)

Lapides Capitolini, 1762. 50×24 cm.

Plate II, Scenographia Campo Martii. . . . 49×73 cm.
(19¼×28¾ in.)

Blatt II, Scenographia Campi Martii. 49×73 cm.

Il Campo Marzio dell'antica Roma, 1762

1. Reliquiae Templi pseudodipteri Antonini Pij. 2. Novae intercisiones antiquae basis perpetuae, ad totidem pro columnarum numero redactae. 3. Pantheum Agrippae. 4. Columnæ residuæ Aedis Iuturnae. 5. Columnae residua castri aqua virginis. Vide indic. ruinar. n. 46, 47, 48.

Piranesi F.

Il Campo Marzio dell'antica Roma, 1762

Plate XXXIV, Remains of the Temple of Antoninus Pius. . . .
21×34 cm. (8¼×13¼ in.)

Blatt XXXIV, Ruinen des Tempels des Antoninus Pius.
21×34 cm.

99

Tab. XXXVIII.

1. *Rudera viae Flaminiae.* 2. *Solum viae ab imbribus praeruptum.* 3. *Silices, et:* 4. *glarea, quibus via antiquitus muniebatur.* 5. *Iter novum.*
Vide indicem ruinar. num. 6. 7.   *Piranesi F.*

Il Campo Marzio dell'antica Roma, 1762

Plate XXXVIII, The Via Flaminia. . . . 22×35 cm.   Blatt XXXVIII, Geröll auf der Via Flaminia. 22×35 cm.
(8½×13¾ in.)

Il Campo Marzio dell'antica Roma, 1762

Plate XLI, Remains of Foundations. . . . 20×40 cm.
(7¾ × 15¾ in.)

Blatt XLI, Ruinen der antiken Stadtmauern. 20×40 cm.

Il Campo Marzio dell'antica Roma, 1762

Detail of plate XXVI. Size overall 39×28 cm. (15½×11 in.) Ausschnitt des Blattes XXVI. 39×28 cm.

Il Campo Marzio dell'antica Roma, 1762

Detail of plate XLV. Size overall 33×25 cm. (13×9¾ in.)

Plate XV. 38×21 cm.
(15×8¼ in.)

Studies of Architectural Subjects, pen and brown ink, brown wash, over outlines in sanguine. 50 × 30 cm. (19½ × 11¾ in.)

Architekturstudien, Federzeichnung, braun getuscht und laviert, mit Rötel. 50 × 30 cm.

Parere sull architettura

Plate V. 62× 39 cm. (24¼× 15½ in.)   Ansichten über die Architektur.
Blatt V. 62 × 39 cm.

Study for plate VI of *Parere sull'architettura*, pen and brown ink, over a sketch in sanguine. 58×38 cm. (22¾×15 in.)

Skizze zum Blatt VI der „Ansichten über die Architektur". Federzeichnung, braun getuscht, mit Rötel. 58×38 cm.

Parere sull'architettura

Plate VIII. 54 × 39 cm. (21¼ × 15½ in.)   Blatt VIII. 54 × 39 cm.

Funerary Monument, pen and brown ink.
62×43 cm. (24¼×17 in.)

Grabdenkmal. Federzeichnung, braun
getuscht. 62×43 cm.

Antichità di Cora, 1764

Plate II, Ruins of the Temple of Castor and Pollux.
41×57 cm. (16¼×22½ in.)

Blatt II, Ruinen des Tempels des Kastor und Pollux in Cora.
41×57 cm.

Descrizione e disegno dell'Emissario del Lago Albano, 1762

Plate VII, Method of Drainage of Lake Albano.
41 × 63 cm. (16¼ × 24¾ in.)

Blatt VII, Beschreibung und Zeichnung für den Abfluss des
Albaner Sees. 41 × 63 cm.

Prospettiva dello stesso
Delubro
A Residuo di Cornice gia accen-
nato nella Tav. V presso la
lett A
B Muro ed arco fattivi dai
C Moderni

Detail of plate opposite.

Ausschnitt des folgenden Blattes.

Descrizione e disegno dell' Emissario del Lago Albano, 1762

Appendix, Plate VIII, View of Shrine. 60×91 cm.
(23½×35½ in.)

Anhang, Blatt VIII, Ansicht des Gewölbes. 60×91 cm.

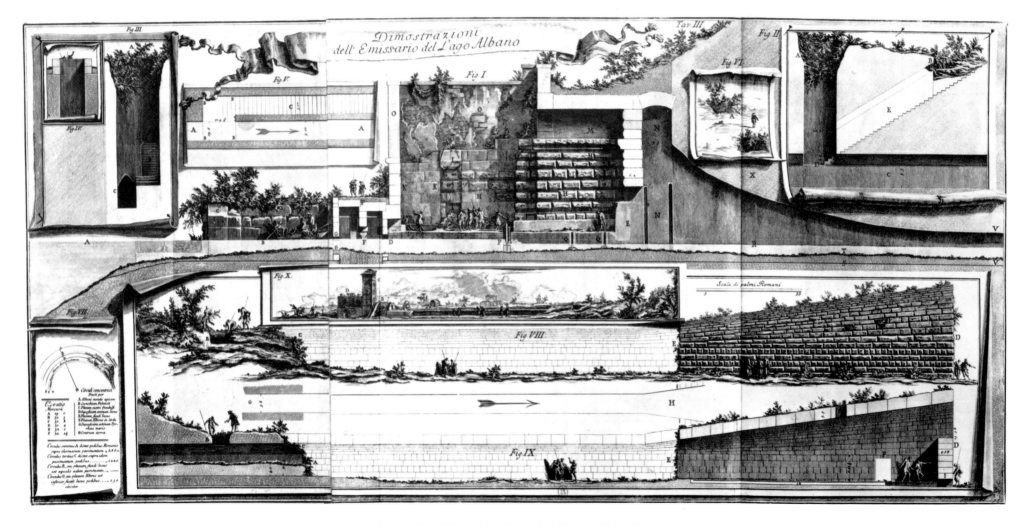

Descrizione e disegno dell'Emissario del Lago Albano, 1762

Plate III, Method of Drainage of Lake Albano.
39 × 63 cm. (15½ × 24¾ in.)

Blatt III, Beschreibung und Zeichnung für den Abfluss des
Albaner Sees. 39 × 63 cm.

Antichità d' Albano e di Castel Gandolfo, 1764

Plate III, Royal or Consular Tomb. . . . 55×64 cm.
(21½× 25 in.)

Blatt III, Grabmal der Könige oder Konsuln in den Felsen
des Monte Albano. 55×64 cm.

115

Antichità d' Albano e di Castel Gandolfo, 1764

Plate V, The so-called 'Tomba degli Orazi'. . . . 39×55 cm.
(15½×21½ in.)

Blatt V, Das sogenannte Grabmal der Horazier und Curiazier.
39×55 cm.

Antichità d' Albano e di Castel Gandolfo, 1764

Plate XXII, Elevation and View of . . . Pool at Castel
Gandolfo. 40× 61 cm. (15¾× 24 in.)

Blatt XXII, Ansicht eines weiteren Bades . . . in
Castelgandolfo. 40× 61 cm.

117

Antichità d' Albano e di Castel Gandolfo, 1764

Plate XIV, View of the Staircase to the
Cistern. 39×28 cm. (15½×11 in.)

Blatt XIV, Ansicht der Treppe zur Zisterne.
39×28 cm.

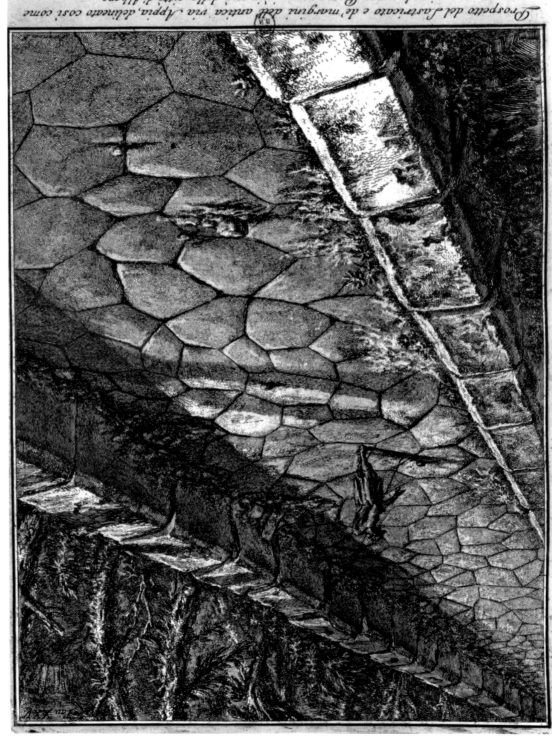

Prospetto del lastricato e de' margini dell'antica via Appia, delineato così come
si vede verso Roma poco più in qua della città d'Albano.

Antichità d'Albano e di Castel Gandolfo, 1764

Plate XXV, Pavement and Sides of the
Appian Way, 30×23 cm. (11¾ × 9 in.)

Blatt XXV, Pflaster und Begrenzung der
Via Appia, 30×23 cm.

Antichità d' Albano e di Castel Gandolfo, 1764

Plate XVII, View of the Pool. . . .
46 × 27 cm. (18 × 10½ in.)

Blatt XVII, Ansicht der Zisterne.
46 × 27 cm.

Antichità d' Albano e di Castel Gandolfo, 1764

Plate XXIV, Ruins of Ancient Buildings in the Villa
Barberina. 38× 54 cm. (15× 21¼ in.)

Blatt XXIV, Ruinen eines antiken Gebäudes in der Villa
Barberina bei Castelgandolfo. 38 × 54 cm.

Antichità d' Albano e di Castel Gandolfo, 1764

Project for repairs to the church of St John Lateran in Rome: longitudinal section of choir, and west transept, pen and brown ink, brown wash, over outlines in black chalk. 32×54 cm. (12½×21¼ in.)

Entwurf zum Umbau der Kirche S. Giovanni in Laterano. Längsschnitt der Apsis, des Chors und des westlichen Querschiffs. Federzeichnung, braun getuscht und laviert, mit Schwarzstift. 32×54 cm.

124

Project for repairs to the church of St John Lateran in Rome: study for the west wall of the transept and the baldacchino, pen and grey ink, with brown ink on the baldacchino. Inscribed top left 'Tavola Duodecima', and bottom right 'Cav. G. B. Piranesi fece.'. 56·7 × 88·5 cm. (22¼ × 35 in.)

Entwurf zum Umbau der Kirche S. Giovanni in Laterano. Skizze für die Westmauern des Querschiffs und den Baldachin. Federzeichnung in grauer Tusche mit brauner Tusche am Baldachin. Links oben der Hinweis: Blatt zwölf. 56,7 × 88,5 cm.

Page 21, illustrations of vases and shells. 38×25 cm. (15×9¾ in.)

Seite 21 (Tafel II), Vasen und Muscheln. 38×25 cm.

Diverse maniere d'adornare i cammini, 1769

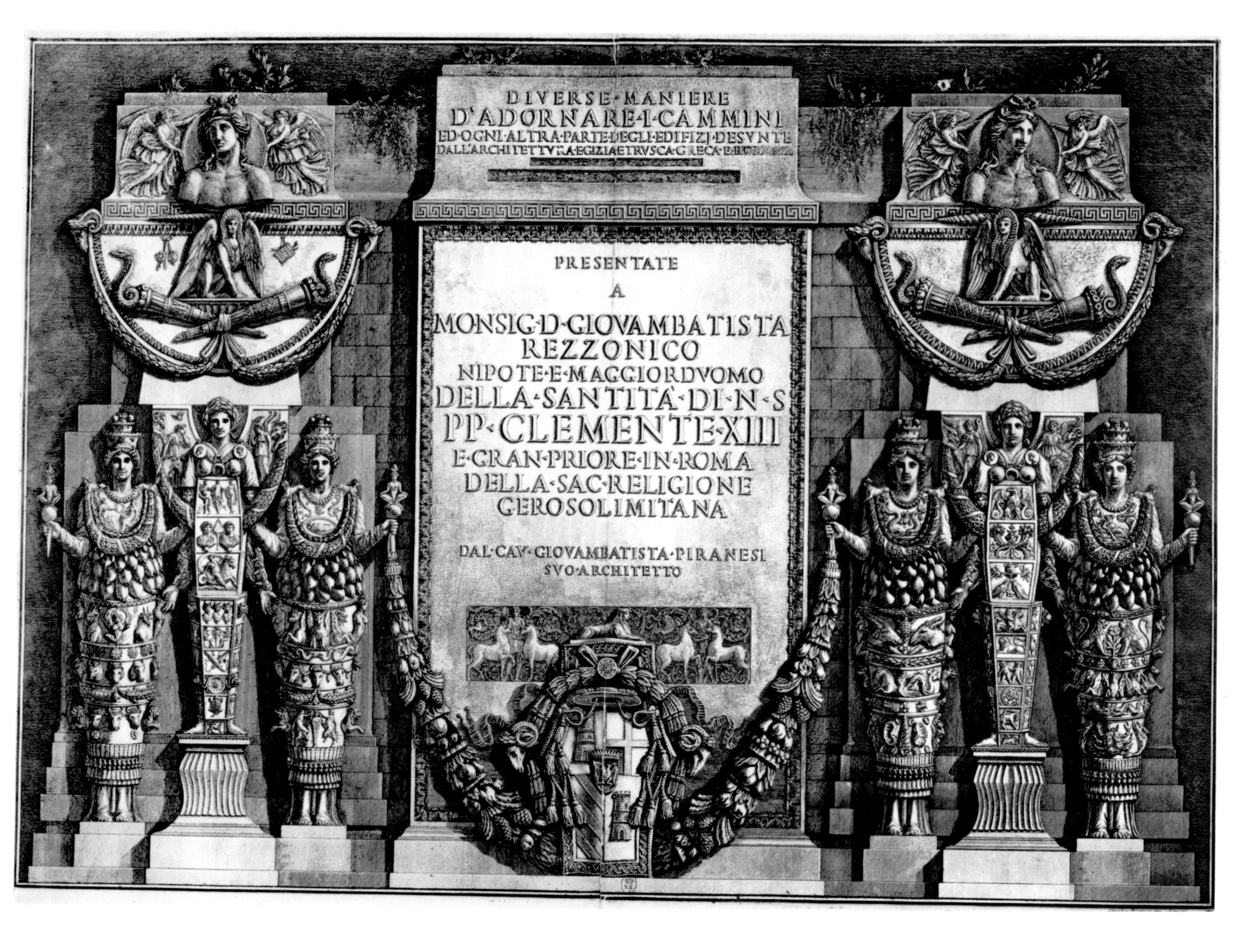

Diverse maniere d'adornare i cammini, 1769

Frontispiece. 48×71 cm. (18¾×27¾ in.)

Frontispiz. 48×71 cm.

Camino architettato alla maniera Egiziana, con istromenti e simboli allusivi alla Religione, e à costumi di questa nazione: come anche si vede adornato con la stessa Architettura il suo Focolare di ferro. Questo focolare, e tutti gl'altri che si vedono nell'altre tavole di quest'opera alla maniera o Egiziana, o Greca, o Toscana, sono in grand'uso presso gl'Inglesi, e vengono travagliati da detta Nazione con grande attenzione e fatica, e con gran bizzarria di trafori ne'loro intagli. Nel sito A B essi mettono il carbone per iscaldarsi.

Diverse maniere d'adornare i cammini, 1769

Plate 18, Chimney-piece in the Egyptian style. . . . 24×38 cm. (9½×15 in.)

Seite 18, Kaminentwurf in ägyptischer Manier. 24×38 cm.

Spaccato della bottega ad uso di caffè detta degl'Inglesi situata in piazza di Spagna. Le pareti dipinte di questa bottega rap=
presentano un Vestibulo adornato di Simboli Geroglifici, e di altre cose allusive alla Religione e politica degli antichi Egiziani.
In lontananza vi si vedono le fertili campagne, il Nilo e quelli maestosi sepoleri della medesima nazione.

Disegno ed invenzione del Cavalier Piranesi

Piranesi inc. 46

Diverse maniere d'adornare i cammini, 1769

Plate 45, Design for . . . the Caffè degl'Inglesi in the Piazza di
Spagna. 21 × 27 cm. (8¼ × 10½ in.)

Seite 45, Entwurf für eine Wanddekoration des sogenannten
Englischen Kaffees an der Piazza di Spagna. 21 × 27 cm.

Design for a chimney-piece, pen and
brown ink. 71 × 53 cm.
(27¾ × 20¾ in.)

Kaminentwurf. Federzeichnung,
braun getuscht. 71 × 53 cm.

Diverse maniere d'adornare i cammini, 1769

Plate 10. 37×24 cm. (14½×9½ in.)   Blatt 10. 37×24 cm.

Designs for wall-brackets (the study lower right was used for
plate 63 of *Diverse maniere d'adornare i cammini*, 1769),
sanguine and black chalk. 23×13 cm. (9×5 in.)

Leuchterstudien. 1769, 23×13 cm., die Skizze rechts unten
wurde in Blatt 63 der *Diverse maniere* . . . verwendet.
Rötel und Schwarzstift.

132

Diverse maniere d'adornare i cammini, 1769

Plate 55. 38× 25 cm. (15× 9¾ in.)   Blatt 55. 38× 25 cm.

Vasi . . ., 1778

Plate 30, with dedication to John Corbet.
53×38 cm. (20¾×15 in.)

Blatt 30, mit Widmung für John Corbet.
53×38 cm.

134

Vasi . . ., 1778

Plate 49, with dedication to John Taylor.
53 × 38 cm. (20¾ × 15 in.)

Blatt 49, mit Widmung für John Taylor.
53 × 38 cm.

135

136   Detail of plate opposite.   Ausschnitt des folgenden Blattes.

Peterskirche und Petersplatz im Vatikan, 1748, 38×54 cm.

View of St Peter's Basilica and Square in the Vatican, 1748.
38×54 cm. (15×21¼ in.)

Veduta della Basilica di S. Lorenzo fuor delle mura

1. Via Tiburtina. Presso l'Autore. Piranesi F.

View of the Basilica S. Lorenzo fuori le Mura, 1750. 37×66 cm.
(14½×26 in.)

Die Kirche S. Lorenzo fuori le mura. 1750, 37×66 cm.

View of the Basilica S. Sebastiano fuori le mura, 1750. 46×65 cm.
(18×25¼ in.)

Kirche S. Sebastiano fuori le mura an der Via Appia. 1750,
46×65 cm.

1. *Palazzo Pontificio*
2. *Palazzo della Famiglia Pontificia*
3. *Statue Colossali rappresentanti Alessandro, che doma il Bucefalo*

opere di Prassitelle, e Fidia Scultori Greci
4. *Quartiere de' Soldati, e Scuderia Pontificia*
5. *Palazzo Rospigliosi Posto l'Autore a Strada Felice vicino alle Torbi di monti*

Piranesi del. et sculp.

Veduta della Piazza di Monte Cavallo

The Palazzo del Quirinale and the Piazza with the Statues of the Horse Tamers, 1750. 36× 54 cm. (14¼× 21¼ in.)

Monte Cavallo, heute Piazza del Quirinale. 1750. 36× 54 cm.

VEDUTA, nella Via del Corso, DEL PALAZZO DELL' ACCADEMIA istituita da LUIGI XIV. RE DI FRANCIA per i Nazionali Francesi studiosi della Pittura, Scultura, e Architettura; colla liberal permissione al Pubblico di esercitarvisi in tali arti per il comodo della esposizione quotidiana del Nudo, e dei Modelli delle piu rare Statue ed altri Segni della Romana Magnificenza, si antichi, che moderni . 1. Stanze ove sono esposti i modelli della Colonna Trajana, Statue Equestri e Pedestri, Busti, e Bassirilievi . 2. Stanze per l'esposizione del Nudo. 3. Appartamento Regio ornato parimente di Modelli. 4. Appartamento del Signor Direttore. 5. Palazzo Panfilj. 6. Via del Corso. 7. Porta del Popolo.

Presso l'Autore a Strada Felice nel Palazzo Tomati vicino alla Trinità de' monti   Gio. Batta. Piranesi Architetto dis. e inc.

The French Academy of Fine Arts . . . founded in the reign of   Via del Corso mit der von Ludwig XIV. gegründeten Académie.
Louis XIV, 1752. 38× 61 cm. (15× 24 in.)   1752, 38× 61 cm.   141

1. *Dogana grande.* 2. *Dogana del passo.* 3. *Arsenale.* 4. *Granari dell'Annona.* ... *Veduta del Porto di Ripa Grande* ... 6. *Avanzi di una delle pile dell'antico Ponte Sublicio, già di Legno, e rifatto po-*
5. *Ospizio Apostolico di S. Michele, e Casa degl'Invalidi, e di educazione nelle arti* ... *scia di pietra da Emilio, e ristorato dai Cesari.* 7. *Avanzi delle Saline antiche*
e correzione de'Fanciulli, e di condanna delle Donne dolinquenti. ... *Presso l'autore a Strada Felice nel palazzo Tomati vicino alla Trinità de'monti* ... 8. *Avanzi di muri de'tempi bassi, falsamente supposti del detto Ponte Sublicio.*

G.B. Piranesi Architetto fec.

The Ripa Grande, 1753. 38×61 cm. (15×24 in.)   *Hafen der Ripa Grande*. 1752, 38×61 cm.

1. *S. Girolamo de' Schiavoni.* 2. *Dogana di Ripetta.* 3. *Colonne, o* mete, nelle quali sono segnate le maggiori escrescenze del Tevere. 4. *Palazzo del Principe Borghese.* 5. *Stalle dello stesso Principe.* 6. *Palazzo della* sua Famiglia. 7. *Colleggio Clementino.*

Piranesi Architetto fec.

Veduta del Porto di Ripetta.

Presso l'Autore a Strada Felice nel Palazzo Tomati vicino alla Trinità de' monti.

50

The Porto di Ripetta, 1753. 37×59 cm. (14½×23¼ in.)   *Der Hafen der Ripetta.* 1753, 37×59 cm.   143

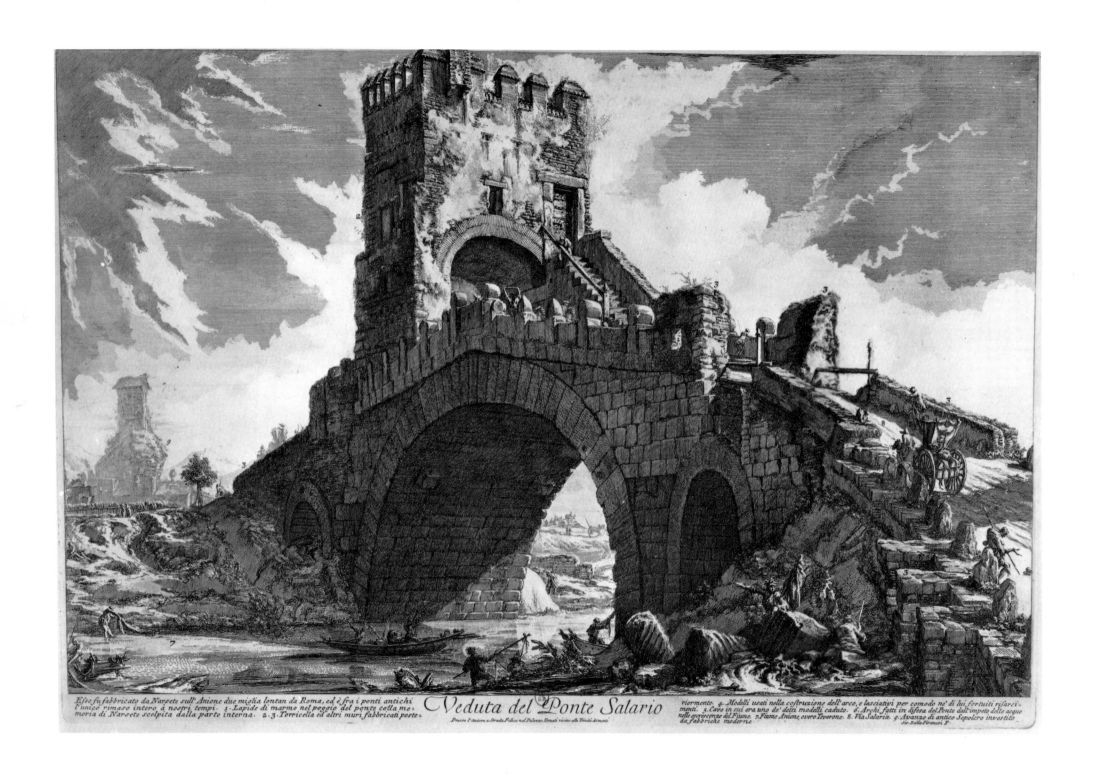

Veduta del Ponte Salario

Esso fu fabbricato da Narsete sull'Anione due miglia lontan da Roma, ed è fra i ponti antichi l'unico rimaso intero à nostri tempi. 1. Lapide di marmo nel poggio del ponte colla memoria di Narsete scolpita dalla parte interna. 2.3. Torricella ed altri muri fabbricati poste riormente. 4. Modelli usati nella costruzione dell'arco, e lasciativi per comodo ne' di lui fortuiti risarcimenti. 5. Cavo in cui era uno de' detti modelli caduto. 6. Archi fatti in difesa del Ponte dall'impeto delle acque nelle escrescenze del Fiume. 7. Fiume Anione, ovvero Teverone. 8. Via Salaria. 9. Avanzo di antico Sepolcro investito da fabbriche moderne.

Presso l'Autore a Strada Felice nel Palazzo Tomati vicino alla Trinità de'monti

Gio. Batta Piranesi F.

144   *The Ponte Salario*, 1754. 38×62 cm. (15×24¼ in.)   *Ponte Salario.* 1754, 38×62 cm.

Veduta del Ponte Lugano su l'Anione
nella via Tiburtina risarcito ne' tempi bassi
A Sepolcro della famiglia Plauzia

The Ponte Lugano, 1763. 45×65 cm. (17¾×25¼ in.)   *Ponte Lugano über den Aniene.* 1763, 45×65 cm.   145

146   Detail of plate opposite.   Ausschnitt des folgenden Blattes.

Veduta del Tempio di Giove Tonante

Il Tempio di Giove Tonante, alle radici del Monte Capitolino, fu da Ottaviano Augusto fabbricato per voto, e ve già lungo aver sofferto incendio con altre Fabbriche del vicino Campo. ...

rara tra i più cospicui ornati edificj, che sono stati innalzati in quel secolo felice. 1 *Colonne di marmo greco, di gran mole, e di un solo pezzo, in gran parte sepolte nel terreno.* 2 *Fianco del moderno Campidoglio, piantato sopra l'antico Tabulario, segnato* 3.

The Temple of Vespasian, 1756. 38×60 cm. (15×23½ in.)

Tempel des Vespasian. 1756, 38×60 cm.

148   Detail of plate opposite.   Ausschnitt des folgenden Blattes.

View of the Capitol, 1757. 40×69 cm. (15¾×27 in.)   *Ansicht des Kapitols*. 1757, 40×69 cm.   149

Piramide di C. Cestio

1 Terreno sgombrato d'in torno alla Piramide sotto il Pontificato d' Alessandro VII. 2 Porta aperta di quel tempo nella Piramide. 3 Colonne ritrovate nella e riposte nell'antica positura. 4 Mura di Roma. 5 Torri della Porta di S. Paolo.

150 *The Pyramid of Cestius*, 1755. 38×53 cm. (15×20¾ in.)   *Die Pyramide des Cestius*. 1755, 38×35 cm.

A *Veduta del Sepolcro di Pisone Liciniano su l'antica via Appia, oltre gli acquidotti di Terre di mezza via d'Albano: il cui lavoro è tutto di terra cotta. B. Sepolcro della famiglia Cornelia, spogliato de'suoi ornamenti. C. Rovine di altri antichi Sepolcri.*

The Tomb of Piso Licinianus on the Appian Way, 1764.
40×50 cm. (15¾×19½ in.)

Das Grabmal des Piso Liciniānus an der Via Appia antica. 1764,
40×50 cm.

The Baths of Caracalla (Thermae Antoniniae), 1765.
42×65 cm. (16½×25¼ in.)

Die Thermen des Caracalla (Ruinen des Sixtus oder Thermen
des Antoninus). 1765, 42×69 cm.

Rovine delle Terme Antoniniane

Consistenti nella cella soleare delle medesime, sotto cui vi rimane ciò che si apparteneva ai bagni, i quali stendevansi nella grand'aja segnata con l'A, ed erano illuminati da tante finestre perpendicolari, alcune delle quali erano scoperte cinque anni sono. B Archi che coprivano il sisto o sia la gran sala della stessa cella. C Atrj della medesima. D Porte di essi chiuse con cancelli di bronzo come tutte le altre interiori della cella. E Rovine dell'Esedre. F Rovine del teatro delle stesse terme. G Rovine d'una delle accademie.

The Baths of Caracalla, 1765. 42 × 69 cm. (16½ × 27 in.)   *Ruinen der Thermen des Caracalla* (Thermen des Antoninus).
1765, 42 × 69 cm.

153

Remains of a . . . Cryptoporticus of a Villa ('Sette Bassi'), 1766.
42×60 cm. (16½×23½ in.)

Ruine eines Kryptoporticus der Villa des Domitian
(Villa Sette Bassi). 1766, 42 × 60 cm.

154

Quelle und Grotte von Egeria, 1766, 39×60 cm.

Fountain and Grotto of Egeria, 1766, 39×60 cm. (15¼×23⅜ in.)

Study in sanguine for the plate opposite.
55 × 48 cm. (21½ × 18¾ in.)

Vorzeichnung zum folgenden Blatt, Rötel.
55 × 48 cm.

156

The Temple of the Sibyl, Tivoli, 1761.
45×54 cm. (17⅞×21¼ in.)

Ansicht des Tempels der Sybille in Tivoli.
1761, 45×54 cm.

157

ALTRA VEDVTA DEL TEMPIO DELLA SIBILLA IN TIVOLI
1 Cella del Tempio. 2 Vestigj del tribunale e della salita. 3 Muro della cella di opera incerta. 4 Emplecton, e sia riempitura del muro della cella. Le colonne, gli architravi, e le altre parti solide di questo tempio, sono di Tevertino. Esso era tutto coperto di stucco, come si riconosce dagli avanzi sparsi quà e là, tanto su l'opera di pietra, che cementata.

Piranesi F.

The Temple of the Sibyl, Tivoli, 1761. 45× 62 cm. (17¾× 24¼ in.)

Weitere Ansicht des Tempels der Sybille in Tivoli. 1761,
45× 62 cm.

The *Villa of Maecenas, Tivoli*, 1763. 44×66 cm. (17¼×22 in.)   *Reste der Villa des Maecenas in Tivoli*. 1763, 44×66 cm.   159

The Temple at Hadrian's Villa, Tivoli, black chalk over a
sketch in sanguine. 48×63 cm. (18¾×24¾ in.)

Tempel der Hadriansvilla in Tivoli. Schwarzstift und Rötel.
48×63 cm.

The (*Temple of*) *Canopus at Hadrian's Villa, Tivoli*, 1769.
44×58 cm. (17¼×22¾ in.)

Ruinen des Canopustempels der Hadriansvilla. 1769, 44×58 cm.

162   Detail of plate opposite.   Ausschnitt des folgenden Blattes.

Ruins . . . of Hadrian's Villa, Tivoli, 1770. 45×58 cm.
(17¾×22¾ in.)

Ruine eines Skulpturensaals in der Hadriansvilla. 1770,
45×58 cm.

Remains of the so-called Temple of Apollo at Hadrian's Villa,
Tivoli, 1768. 47×62 cm. (18½×24¼ in.)

Ruine des sogenannten Apollo-Tempels der Hadriansvilla. 1768,
47×62 cm.

Hadrian's Villa, Tivoli. 43× 57 cm. (17× 22½ in.)   *Halle der Hadriansvilla.* 43× 57 cm.   165

166

The Teatro Marittimo at Hadrian's Villa, Tivoli, sanguine, over a sketch in black chalk. 39×61 cm. (15½×24 in.)

Das Teatro marittimo der Hadriansvilla. Rötel und Schwarzstift, 39×61 cm.

Ruins at Hadrian's Villa, Tivoli, sanguine. 43×57 cm. (17×22½ in.)

Ruinen in der Hadriansvilla. Rötel, 43×57 cm.

167

Study in sanguine for the plate opposite.
41×34 cm. (16¼×13¼ in.)

Rötelstudie für des folgende Blatt. 41×34 cm.

Veduta degli avanzi del Castro Pretorio nella Villa Adriana a Tivoli

The Poikile ('Percile') at Hadrian's Villa, Tivoli, 1770.
36×65 cm. (14¼ × 25¼ in.)

Die Poikile und das Castrum Pretorii in der Hadriansvilla. 1770,
36×65 cm.

Study in sanguine for the plate opposite. 40×54 cm.
(15¾×21¼ in.)

Rötelskizze für das folgende Blatt. 40×54 cm.

170

Ruins of . . . Hadrian's Villa, Tivoli, 1776. 47×62 cm.
(18½×24¼ in.)

Ruinen in der Hadriansvilla. 1776, 47×62 cm.

172   *The Waterfalls at Tivoli*, 1765. 47×70 cm. (18½×27½ in.)   *Die Wasserfälle von Tivoli*. 1765, 47×70 cm.

The Villa d'Este, Tivoli, 1773. 46×70 cm. (18×27½ in.)   *Die Villa d'Este in Tivoli.* 1773, 46×70 cm.

Study in black chalk for the plate opposite.
50×71 cm. (19½×27¾ in.)

Skizze in schwarzer Kreide zum folgenden Blatt.
50×71 cm.

Villa Panfili
fuori di Porta S.Pancrazio.
1.2. Villa Corsini.
3. Villa Ferroni.
Cav. Piranesi F.

The Villa Panfili, 1776. 49 × 70 cm. ($19\frac{1}{4} \times 27\frac{1}{4}$ in.)

Die Villa Panfili. 1776, 49 × 70 cm.

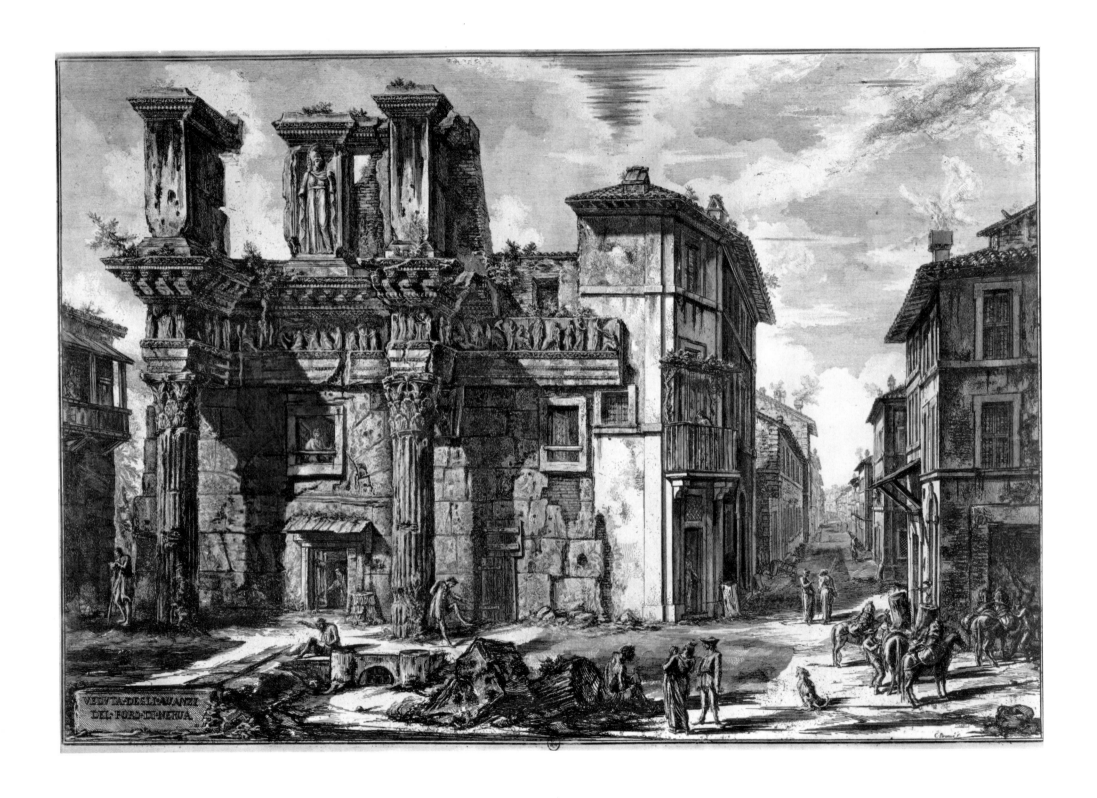

VEDVTA·DEGLI·AVANZI
DEL·FORO·DI·NERVA

176 *The Forum of Nerva*, 1770. 47 × 70 cm. (18½ × 27¼ in.)   *Ruinen des Forum des Nerva*. 1770, 47 × 70 cm.

The Arch . . . of Janus (Ianus Quadrifrons), 1771. 46 × 70 cm.   *Der Janusbogen* (Janus Quadrifrons). 1771, 46 × 70 cm.
(18 × 27¼ in.)

The *Temple of Saturn and Arch of Septimius Severus in the Forum*, 1774. 46 × 69 cm. (18 × 27 in.)

Der Saturntempel und der Triumphbogen des Septimius Severus auf dem Forum Romanum. 1774, 46 × 69 cm.

178

Esso fu eretto a questo Imperadore dopo la di lui morte in memoria della distruzione di Gerosolima, e in oggi è spogliato della maggior parte de'suoi ornamenti. A. Bassirilievi indicanti il di lui trionfo, adornato colle spoglie del Tempio di Salomone. B. Apoteosi dello

Veduta dell' Arco di Tito

Presso l'autore a Strada Felice vicino alla Trinità de' Monti

stesso Cesare, espressa in un'Aquila che lo solleva al Cielo. C. Orti Farnesiani. D. Chiesa di S. Sebastiano. E. Polveriere. F. Rovine della Casa Augustana sul Palatino. G. Strada che conduce a S. Bonaventura.

Gio. Batta. Piranesi Architetto diseg. e incise

The Arch of Titus, 1771. 47×71 cm. (18½×27¾ in.)

Der Titusbogen. 1771, 47×71 cm.

The Isola Tiberina, 1775. 47×71 cm. (18½×27¾ in.)

Die Tiberinsel. 1775, 47×71 cm.

The *Forum Romanum* (formerly called the Campo Vaccino),
1775. 45×70 cm. (17¾×27¼ in.)

Das Forum Romanum (ehemals Campo Vaccino genannt).
1775, 45×70 cm.

181

1. Meta sudante
2. Radice del Palatino

Veduta dell'Arco di Coſtantino, e dell'Anfiteatro Flavio detto il Coloſſeo

3. Veſtigie delle Terme di Tito
4. Radice dell'Esquilino

Preſſo l'Autore a Strada Felice vicino alla Trinità de' monti

Piranesi del. ſculp.

The Arch of Constantine and . . . the Colosseum, 1760. 38×54 cm.
(15×21¼ in.)

Der Konstantinsbogen mit dem Kolosseum. 1760, 38×54 cm.

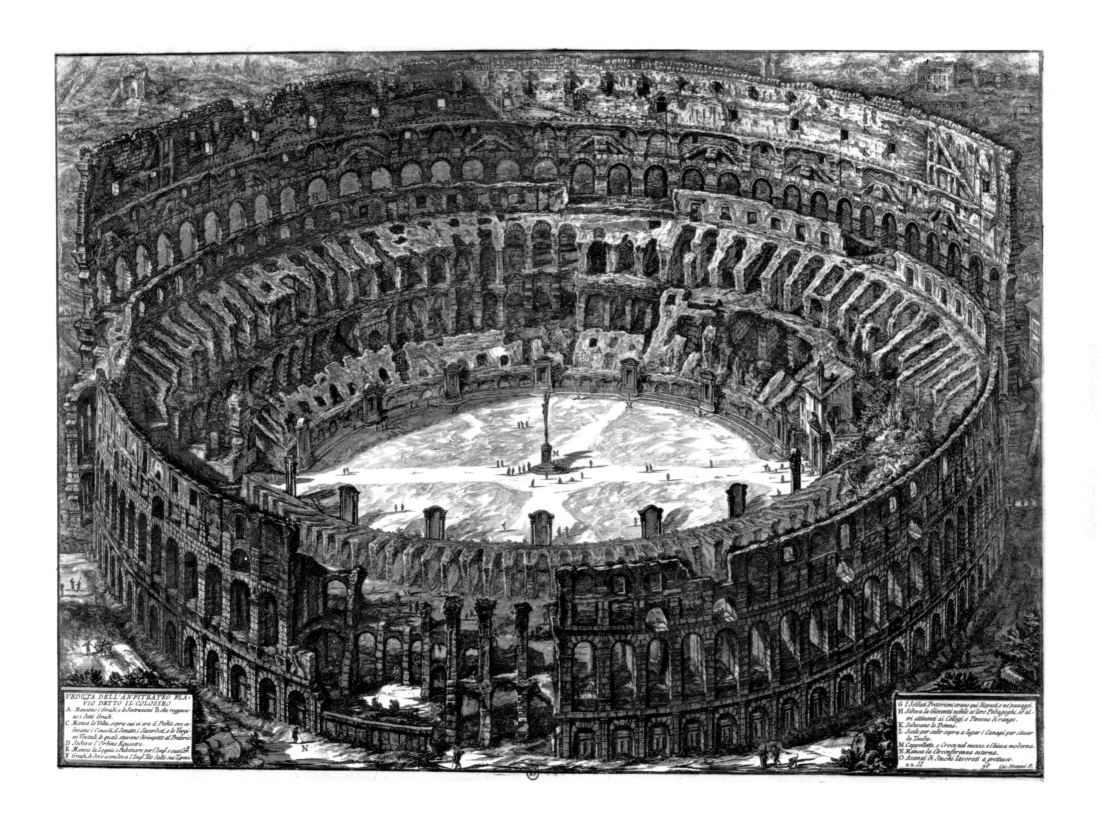

VEDUTA DELL'ANFITEATRO FLA-
VIO DETTO IL COLOSSEO
A Mancano i Gradi, e le Sostruzioni B. che reggevo-
no i detti Gradi.
C Mancava la Volta, sopra cui vi era il Podio, ove se-
devano i Consoli, il Senato, i Sacerdoti, e le Vergi-
ni Vestali, le quali stavano dirimpetto al Pretorio.
D Sedeva l'Ordine Equestre.
E Mancava la Loggia, o Pulvinare per l'Impf. e sua Corte.
F Gradi, di dove scendeva l'Impf. Tito dalle sue Terme.

G I Soldati Pretoriani erano qui disposti, e ne' passaggi.
H Sedeva la Gioventù nobile coi loro Pedagoghi, ed al-
tri attinenti ai Collegi, e Persone di rango.
K Sedevano le Donne.
L Scale per salir sopra a legar i Canapi, per situar
la Tenda.
M Cappellette, e Croce nel mezzo, e Chiesa moderna.
N Mancava la Circonferenza esterna.
O Avanzi di Stucchi lavorati a grottesco.

The Colosseum, 1776. 49×71 cm. (19¼×27¾ in.)   *Das Kolosseum*. 1776, 49×71 cm.   183

The Circus of Maxentius and the Tomb of Caecilia Metella,
sanguine over a sketch in black chalk. 48×70 cm.
(18¾×27¼ in.)

Der Circus Maxentii und das Grabmal der Cecilia Metella.
Rötel und Schwarzstift. 48×70 cm.

The Aqueduct of Nero, 1775. 48×70 cm. (18¾×27¼ in.)   *Ruinen des Aquädukts des Nero*. 1775, 48×70 cm.

The Baths of Trajan (formerly called Baths of Titus), 1776.
48×69 cm. (18¾×27 in.)

Die Thermen des Trajan (ehemals Thermen des Titus genannt).
1776, 48×69 cm.

VEDUTA DELLE TERME DI TITO
Veduta degl'Avanzi del Piano superiore A, ed infe=
riore B delle Terme di Tito. C Avanzi del Teatro

The Baths of Trajan, 1775. 48×70 cm. (18¾×27¼ in.)   *Die Thermen de Trajan*. 1775, 48×70 cm.

Studies of Men, black chalk and sanguine. 21×21 cm. (8¼×8¼ in.)

Bewegungsstudien. Schwarzstift und Rötel. 21×21 cm.

Three Men, pen and brown ink. 19×39 cm. (7½×15½ in.)   *Drei Männer*. Feder und braune Tusche, 19×39 cm.   189

Two Men and Heads, pen and brown ink, sanguine. 21×24 cm. (8¼×9½ in.)

Zwei Männer und Kopfstudien.
Federzeichnung, braune Tusche, Rötel. 21×24 cm.

Two Trees, pen and brown ink, brown wash.
48×44 cm. (18¾×17¼ in.)

Zwei Bäume. Federzeichnung,
braun getuscht und laviert. 48 × 44 cm.

191

Study for the plate opposite, pen and brown and grey ink, brown wash. 48×69 cm. (18¾×27 in.)

Studie zum folgenden Blatt. Federzeichnung, braune und graue Tusche, braun laviert. 48×69 cm.

Plate I, View of Remains of Walls and Temples. 44 × 67 cm.
($17\frac{1}{4}$ × $26\frac{1}{4}$ in.)

Blatt I, Ruinen im antiken Paestum.
44 × 67 cm.

193

The Tomb of the Istadici, Pompeii, pen and brown ink.
51×77 cm. (20×30 in.)

194

Das Grabmal der Istadici in Pompeji.
Federzeichnung, braun getuscht. 51×77 cm.

SOURCES OF ILLUSTRATIONS

All the prints included in this book are reproduced from examples in the Cabinet des Estampes of the Bibliothèque Nationale, Paris, where two of the drawings – reproduced on p. 156 (accession no. B 11, fol. 8 r.) and p. 192 (accession no. B 11, fol. 9) – are also preserved. The other works illustrated, with accession or inventory numbers in brackets where appropriate, are reproduced by permission of the owners as listed below, all the references being to page numbers in the present book:

BAYONNE: Musée Bonnat 105 (1386)

BERLIN: Kunstbibliothek 107 (135–3940), 109 (134–3940), 130 (6301–30015)

COPENHAGEN: Royal Museum of Fine Arts 40, 194

FLORENCE: Uffizi Galleries 160 (96008), 167 (96006), 170 (96012), 174 (96009), 184 (96011)

HAMBURG: Kunsthalle 37 (1915–638), 38 (1915–653), 52 (1915–644), 60 (1915–648), 64 (1915–649)

LONDON: British Museum 39 (1908–6–16–11), 42 (1908–6–16–20), 62 (1908–6–16–8), 66 (1908–6–16–40)

NEW YORK: Columbia University 125; Pierpont Morgan Library 30, 67, 124, 132

OXFORD: Ashmolean Museum 166

PARIS: Ecole nationale supérieure des Beaux-Arts 168 (264 v.), 189 (267 r.), 190 (270), 191 (263); Louvre 188 (RF 29003); Private Collection 14, 15, 36; Société des Architectes D.P.L.G. 43

CONCORDANCE
OF WORKS
ILLUSTRATED

Those works reproduced here which are also listed in Henri Focillon's catalogue raisonné (1918), the catalogue by F. Stampfle of the exhibition at the Pierpont Morgan Library, New York (1949), and in *The Drawings of . . . Piranesi* by H. Thomas (1954) are shown below (references are to page numbers in the present book).

Bacou	Focillon	Stampfle	Thomas
25	2		
26	5		
27	6		
28	4		
29	17		
30		7	14
31	23		
32	20		
33	22		
34	21		
35	786		
38			10
39			19
41	122		
42			18
44	24		

Bacou	Focillon	Stampfle	Thomas
45	26		
46	27		
47	29		
48	30		
49	30		
50	32		
51	32		
52			4
53	31		
55	33		
56	34		
57	35		
58	36		
59	38		
61	37		
63	25		
65			9
67		16	
68	81		
69	47		
70	50		
71	59		
72	136		
73	224		
75	232		
76	264		
77	278		

Bacou	Focillon	Stampfle	Thomas
78	235		
79	268		
80	271		
81	330		
82	312		
83	335		
85	295		
86	297		
87	351		
89	307		
90	292		
91	341		
92	348		
93	934		
94	932		
95	538		
96–7	427		
98	437		
99	464		
100	468		
101	471		
102	457		
103	475		
104	416		
106	978		
108	981		
110	541		

Bacou	Focillon	Stampfle	Thomas
111	489		
113	500		
114	485		
115	511		
116	513		
117	531		
118	523		
119	534		
121	526		
122	533		
123	536 *bis*		
124		56	
126	859		
127	854		
128	878		
129	907		
131	870		
132		106	49
133	915		
134	628		
135	647		
137	787		
138	730		
139	731		
140	808		
141	739		
142	742		

Bacou	Focillon	Stampfle	Thomas	Bacou	Focillon	Stampfle	Thomas
143	814			177	825		
144	744			178	830		
145	773			179	755		
147	819			180	836		
149	747			181	748		
150	745			182	805		
151	777			183	759		
152	851			184			57
153	852			185	850		
154	781			186	838		
155	782			187	837		
157	765			189			74
158	766			191			51
159	768			192			58
160			53	193	583		
161	844			194			63
163	785						
164	771						
165	848						
166			56				
169	824						
171	846						
172	779						
173	826						
174			54				
175	840						
176	750						

SELECT BIBLIOGRAPHY

1779 G. L. Bianconi 'Elogio Storico el Cavaliere Giambattista Piranesi celebre antiquario ed incisore di Roma', in *Antologia Romana*, XXXIV–XXXVI (February–March).

1799 J. G. Legrand 'Notice historique sur la vie et les ouvrages de J.-B. Piranesi . . . rédigée sur les notes et les pièces communiquées par ses fils, les compagnons et les continuateurs de ses nombreux travaux', manuscript in the Département des Manuscrits, Bibliothèque Nationale, Paris (Nouv. Acq. fr. 5968); published by G. Morrazone in *Giovanni Battista Piranesi*, Rome-Milan, n. d. [1959]

1911 A. Giesecke *Giovanni Battista Piranesi*, in the series 'Meister der Graphik', VI, Leipzig, n. d.

1918 H. Focillon *Giovanni Battista Piranesi (1720-1778)*, Paris

1918 H. Focillon *Giovanni Battista Piranesi, essai de catalogue raisonné de son œuvre*, Paris

1922 A. M. Hind *Giovanni Battista Piranesi. A critical Study of his published Works and detailed Catalogue of the Prisons and the Views of Rome*, London

1922 F. Hermanin *Giambattista Piranesi*, Rome

1927 C. Sokol *Giovanni Battista Piranesi*, Paris

1933 W. Körte 'Giovanni Battista Piranesi als praktischer Architekt', in *Zeitschrift für Kunstgeschichte*

1938 R. Pane *L'Acquaforte di G. B. Piranesi*, Naples

1949 A. Huxley and J. Adhémar *Prisons, with the Carceri Etchings by G. B. Piranesi*, London

1949 F. Stampfle *Drawings by Giovanni Battista Piranesi*, illustrated catalogue of an exhibition, New York, Pierpont Morgan Library

1951 H. O. Corfiato *Piranesi Compositions*, London

1952 A. Hyatt Mayor *Giovanni Battista Piranesi*, New York

1954 H. Thomas *The Drawings of Giovanni Battista Piranesi*, London

1958 O. Vogt-Goknil *G. B. Piranesi Carceri*, Zurich

1962 M. Yourcenar 'Le Cerveau noir de Piranèse', preface to *Carceri d'invenzione. Les Prisons imaginaires de G. B. Piranesi*, Monaco

1966 L. Keller *Piranèse et les romantiques français. Le Mythe des escaliers en spirale*, Paris

1970 M.-P. Fouchet *Jean-Baptiste Piranesi. Les Prisons imaginaires*, Paris

1971 P. Murray *Piranesi and the Grandeur of Ancient Rome*, London

INDEX